D1756341

Signage Design Manual

Edo Smitshuijzen

Signage Design Manual

Lars Müller Publishers

This edition first published 2007

Lars Müller Publishers
5400 Baden
Switzerland
www.lars-muller-publishers.com

Typographic design and editing: Huda Smitshuijzen AbiFarès
Illustrations and cover design: Edo Smitshuijzen
Text output: Trinité designed by Bram de Does
Printed by Atlas, Soest, the Netherlands
Bound by van Waarden, Zaandam, the Netherlands

ISBN 978-3-03778-096-1

To Huda Smitshuijzen AbiFarès for her support, advice and cooperation.

Contents

1. INTRODUCTION

1.1. *How is this book set up?* 18

1.2. *The professional field of signage* 19

2. SETTING OUT THE SCOPE OF WORK AND ORGANISING THE PEOPLE INVOLVED

2.1. *Introduction* 25

2.2. *Who will be responsible for the signage?* 26

2.3. *Selecting a signage consultant/designer* 33

2.4. *Who is the signage for?* 35

2.5. *What are the legal requirements?* 42

2.6. *Are there special security requirements?* 45

2.7. *Should a certain style be incorporated?* 46

2.8. *How about the budget?* 47

2.9. *What is the proposed time schedule for completion?* 49

2.10. *Making the work plan or signage program* 50

3. DESIGNING THE SIGNAGE SYSTEM

3.1. *Introduction* 57

3.2. *Spatial planning and architectural design* 59

3.3. *Signage methodology* 67

3.4. *Signage technology* 69

3.5. *Positioning the signs* 78

3.6. *Stating the message and conveying the information* 85

3.7. *Signage plans and traffic flows* 110

3.8. *Database of signs & text lists* 114

3.9. *List of sign types* 115

3.10. *Types of buildings* 117

3.11. *Imaginary walk through a site* 120

3.12. *Library of sign types* 132

4. CREATING THE VISUAL DESIGN

4.1. Introduction 155

4.2. The basic aspects of visual design 156

4.3. Competitions, review and approval procedures 164

4.4. Intellectual Property [IP] issues 169

4.5. Designing in a team 185

4.6. Developing the work plan 187

4.7. Visual design concept 193

4.8. Basic products, materials and techniques 247

4.9. Typography & typefaces 279

4.10. Pictograms & symbols 322

4.11. Illustrations & maps 351

4.12. Systems of measurement; the grid 365

4.13. Colour 386

4.14. Interactive design 392

5. SPECIFYING AND SUPERVISING MANUFACTURE AND INSTALLATION

5.1. Documentation and bidding 403
5.2. Supervising manufacture 413
5.3. Supervising installation 416
5.4. Completion 417
5.5. Evaluation 418

6. ORGANISING THE MAINTENANCE

6.1. Signage Officer 423
6.2. Signage Manual and database 424
6.3. Signage reorder forms 424
6.4. Website reordering 425
6.5. Updating websites and touch screens 425
6.6. Updates for impaired users 426
6.7. Updating strategies 426

Epilogue: Signage in the world to come 429
Appendix I: Diagram signage program summary 431
Appendix II: ADA sign requirements 434
Selected Bibliography 441
Index 442

Foreword & acknowledgments

A design career builds, as well as being built upon, a design culture. After finishing a few large signage projects at the beginning of the eighties, I felt I should express and document my professional experiences in an organised way. I wrote a manuscript about the many organisational aspects of designing a signage project. I proposed to my fellow partners in our design partnership at the time to publish the manuscript as a company endeavour. They refused on the basis that publication could possibly harm our business by 'giving away' specialised knowledge. I did not share their view; the dissemination of professional knowledge is vital to the development of any profession. And a more sophisticated profession attracts more business for all professionals working in one field. The manuscript stayed in the closet, but I did not mind much because the author learns the most from writing a book.

At the beginning of 2000, my wife asked me to work closely with her on a book project on Arabic Typography, a first of its kind. For about half a year we collaborated almost day and night to get the job done. I really enjoyed the book making process and strongly believed that the result would contribute to the emancipation of Arabic graphic design.

The experience made me take my old signage manuscript out of the closet again. The world had changed dramatically since it was written and I had gained a lot more professional experience as well. I had to start more or less from scratch if I wanted to make a book about the subject. I also had to decide what audience I would imagine writing for and which language to write in. I decided to aim for the widest possible audience and to write in the English language. I am very grateful to my close friend and colleague Sarah Rosenbaum for encouraging me to write, as well as to write in English. Special thanks to Elizabeth Burney-Jones for applying her extensive knowledge as a signing practitioner in proof-reading this book.
I also decided not to make a portfolio book. Most design books are portfolio books. I consider them useful, but only for revealing a small part of what designing is all about. It is a bit like telling a life story by showing only the wedding pictures. Or only reading the back cover of books. Moreover, most design projects cannot be captured in one or a few images. All these decisions forced me to do a lot of research work and draw most of the illustrations myself, because available pictures only show the end result and not the process. Signage design touches on a lot of different design disciplines. Ambitious optimists hardly ever think too long about the consequences of their initiatives. Well, in my case, it has kept me busy—on and off—for almost six years. It was a rather lonely journey that seemed to have at times an elusive final destination.

The help I received from my wife, Huda Smitshuijzen AbiFarès, during this long haul was indispensable. She was my sounding board on this project; she commented on all the illustrations I made and edited all the text in the first instance. She made an invaluable contribution. For the rest, I have to thank the many, many sources I used to produce the text and make the illustrations, taken from books, or sent to me on request, using articles and sometimes anonymous internet sources. I am especially grateful for the contributions of my fellow signage designers. Making books is for the most part collecting available data and opinions and putting these together in an organised way. I used only a few illustrations showing signage projects done by design colleagues. Again, this book is in no way a showcase of remarkable signage design. The only exception is the rather complete overview of pictograms for the Olympic Games, which I thought were the perfect way to show changing design preferences over time. I thank the Olympic Museum in Lausanne for providing me with most of this information.

Designers are professional amateurs. Designers have a tendency to redefine the aims of their profession to meet their personal talents and inhibitions. Each designer is more or less a specific branch on a rather wide and nebulous design tree. Designers need to have a wide scope of interests to interact successfully with a large variety of businesses and other disciplines, and to combine this with a strong passion to prevent them from making too many compromises along the way. The design profession cannot build a rigorous knowledge framework with verifiable, scientific facts. This book has no intellectual pretensions whatsoever. However, design should not be a lightweight kite nervously moving along with the changing winds of fashion. Visual style is a strong mind bender, but it can easily become an intoxicating drug. Designers may be tempted to look for a quick fix, constituting a flimsy professional field. Only by laying a solid foundation for sound professional practices, can we prevent this from happening. It will help to create a richer design culture, where clients and designers have a better mutual understanding and can collaborate more effectively resulting in a higher overall quality. This book aims to contribute to that end.

1. Introduction

Being lost is a fundamental human fear. We need to grasp our environment to a minimum level in order to feel secure. After going out, we should at least be able to find our way back home. Pigeons don't need signage to do that, but unlike pigeons, we need signage, in most instances, to help us find our way around. My guess is that we always did, and that man-made signs for navigational purposes may very well have preceded the development of signs for written language.

Our need for signs can drop fast; we only need signage to get around in the initial phase of our explorations into a new environment. After a while, we learn to know the environment and have no need for the signage any more; we even forget the underlying structure of the signage system altogether. The way we familiarise ourselves with our environment is very individualistic; we each 'read' our environment differently and create our own private 'mental map'.

So signage would seem to be useful only for strangers; people unfamiliar with the environment. In principle, this statement is correct, but the snag is that most of us have become more and more like strangers in our own increasingly complex environments. Besides, most of us now live in big metropolitan areas and work in huge buildings, both far too complex to get completely familiar with. We only know a small part of it and simply need signage to be able to use the rest. We have become extremely mobile in our daily life and therefore rely on signage on a daily basis. Navigating through our environment with all signs stripped away would become like watching the TV news with the sound off.

Signage is not only about wayfinding (navigation in the built environment)—which by itself does not involve only signs—though wayfinding constitutes its essential core. Signage also supplies general information about organisations and structures and about security and safety regulations, as well as instructions on how to use machines and facilities. It is clear that we cannot possibly do without signage. Nevertheless, signage is often treated like an orphan. It is not generally associated with being a lot of fun to design or to use, but is more often regarded as an unavoidable nuisance. First, most users prefer to ask someone in person for directions rather than try to decipher the available signage, before consequently making up their own minds.

Second, the major professional creators of our environment, the architects, do not often have a particularly keen eye for signage, to put it kindly. They perceive signage as an assault on the aesthetics of their creation and as an insult to the self-evidence of their spatial design. A lot of them still carry an almost sacred but entirely unfounded belief in the functionality of 'wordless' buildings. They only make things worse for themselves and for others by also following a strategy of postponing the input of a signage designer until the very last moment.

Third, the building tenant, occupant, or investor should make sure they are getting the most suitable building possible for their invested money. This requires giving proper attention at an early stage to all communication aspects—wayfinding, information and instruction—of the built environment. Regrettably, this important aspect is still often neglected. Last minute decisions about signage—sometimes even taken half in panic—are not uncommon. Clearly not the ideal condition for creating the most comfortable accessibility of spaces. Occupants and investors can cut themselves seriously short because of their own negligence. It is unwise to underestimate the contribution that easy way finding (or comfortable way showing) can add to the appreciation of all the users of a building. These users should deserve full attention since they represent the major asset in most organisations nowadays. Good and effective communication is appreciated by everyone, not only in TV commercials or company brochures. The only way to achieve this is to consider signage as an integral and important part in every phase of the design of the built environment.

'Early stage' and 'integral part of the environmental design' are the key words in the proper development of a signage system. Suppressing these two conditions, means reducing signage activities to 'putting up signs'. That limitation may create serious handicaps for the signage designer. Signs work best when the amount of signs needed is reduced to the bare minimum. Putting up too many signs results in none being read. The required minimal amount of signs can only be achieved in an environment with the highest possible level of self-evidence in its spatial infrastructure. Moreover, signs have limited possibilities. Travellers will always be led in the first instance by what seems to be evident in the spatial infrastructure and not by what the signs may say. It has been tried many times to prove the contrary, but it never works. Signs cannot 'heal' or 'repair' mistakes in a spatial infrastructure. Signs cannot make a complex situation simpler. Signs have a supportive function where the spatial environmental design is by definition incapable of supplying the required level of detailed information. Signs can only work as accommodating carriers of information, having the advantageous potential of carrying a far larger vocabulary than the information provided by the spatial infrastructure alone.

The need for signage will only increase over time, as we get more and more mobile, and thus need to use unfamiliar environments more often. Even our work space is no longer stable, with offices becoming laptop dock-in places for a nomad work force. In addition, the amount of (public) facilities that we use daily is ever-increasing. Facilities and machines that need instructional signs will keep on replacing people. The speed at which we live and work tends to shift constantly into a higher gear, giving us less time to orientate ourselves.

New technological developments are of some help in dealing with this situation, but traditional means are likely to remain important tools in signage projects. This might change in the future where technology will provide us with universally used hand-held devices that instruct us in a direct and simple way, like: 'go left...straight on...insert your identity card...lift handle...press yellow button...say your name...' and so forth.
Such devices could certainly simplify the often complex signage systems of today. We would become almost like pigeons, able to find our way automatically without the help of any signage. However, this development would make us humans entirely dependent on complex technology. But perhaps worse still, it might eventually obliterate the need for spending time on creating the most comfortable and civilised of all man-made environments, an environment that needs as little additional instructions as possible for it to be used properly.

Dominance of signage

In some instances, signs dominate the environment entirely, for instance, in places of worship or adoration, like temples, monuments or shrines. The ancient Egyptians covered their holy structures for thousands of years with scriptural narratives. Also the Maya, Buddhist and Muslim constructions make use of text in abundance; only Christianity has preferred imagery over text.
Graffiti has made narratives and imaging.-unsolicited-part of the public environment. Commercial signs may in some places dominate the environment totally. Organising an efficient and safe traffic flow seems to be a daunting task at times, judged by the overwhelming amount of signs sometimes needed.

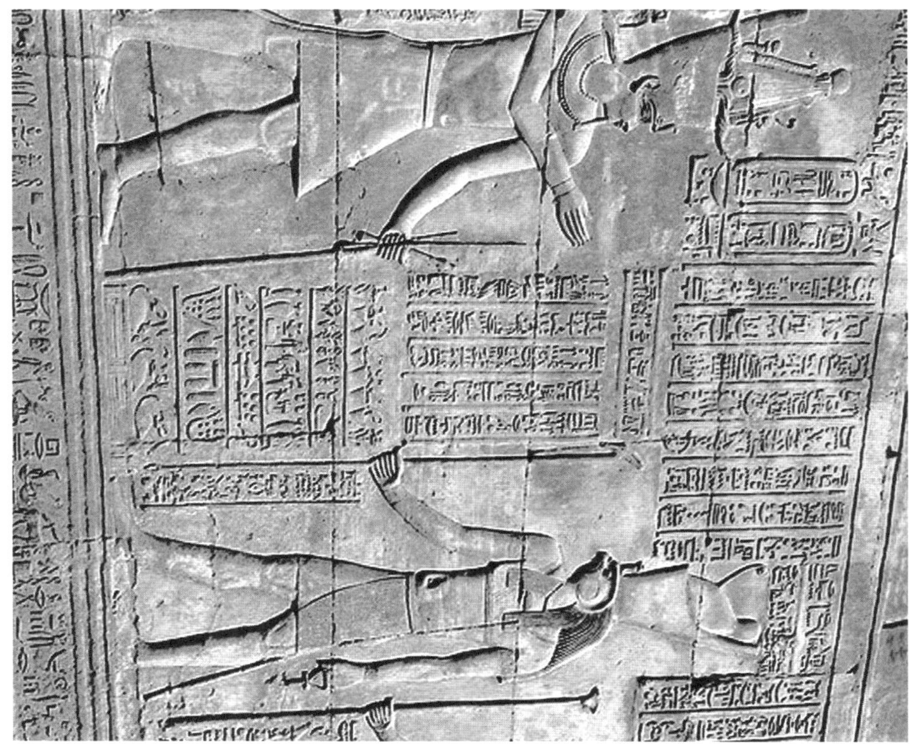

1.1. How is this book set up?

This book is written, illustrated and designed by a graphic designer who has experience in various architectural signage projects. The purpose of the book is to serve as a guide for signage designers involved in average signage projects. The chapters in the book follow the chronological steps of development in most signage projects.

Signage projects can vary enormously in size and complexity. It is impossible to cover all possible situations in one book. Really big projects, or very specialised ones, like highway or airport signage, have their own logistics, specialised knowledge and working methodology. These are beyond the scope of this publication.

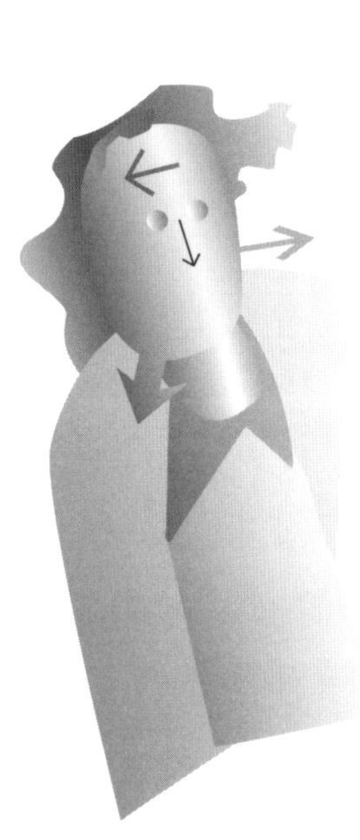

The book attempts to provide a comprehensive overview of the many aspects of a signage project. The illustrations used are thereby created to be an entertaining and effective way to get the message across. The content may be 'consumed' on various levels: as a sourcebook for help in the different stages of a project, as a source of inspiration, and as a way of looking at a signage project from different design perspectives. Sometimes designers need to step away from preconceived ideas or solutions and consider an entirely different approach.
The book is not written to be read from cover to cover, but rather as a reference book.Therefore, overlaps in content do occur.

Signage projects are partly governed by national and local rules and regulations. This book does not provide specific detail about local conditions, since it is intended to reach a wide international audience.

The author of this book did not grow up in an English speaking country. Nevertheless, it is written in English to reach the widest possible audience. Nowadays, the English language comes in variations that one can choose from: American, British and International. The book follows basically the British spelling, though American words are incorporated in the text to serve the American readers.
Another noticeable fact is that the two most used words in this publication are not 'officially accepted'.The word wayfinding is often used in signage publications, although it didn't make it to the dictionaries yet. The same counts for the word signage. Occasionally the word navigation is used as a synonym for wayfinding.

1.2. The professional field of signage

Signage is directly concerned with fundamental existential human needs, like being able to travel effectively, avoid hazards, find one's way back home, let others know where one can be found, or get away safely when one is in a dangerous situation. Everyone is involved in or creates signage in some way or other. For instance, we all put our names on—or next to—our doors, and we all have experienced explaining to others how to get to certain places. Signage is everywhere and is done by everyone, sometimes to quite an overwhelming level.

The professional field is a reflection of this universal use of signage. The field is not concentrated in specialised centres of activity, but is rather widely spread out. The whole field can be divided into three major types of activities:
—commercial signage
—signage for traffic and transportation
—architectural signage.

The research, consultancy, design and production of signage can involve five types of professionals:
—scientists
—specialised engineers
—management consultants
—designers and architects
—signage manufacturers.

Signage is also subject to standardisation, regulation and legislation. This work is done by governmental bodies, international organisations, producers and user groups, national or supranational organisations.

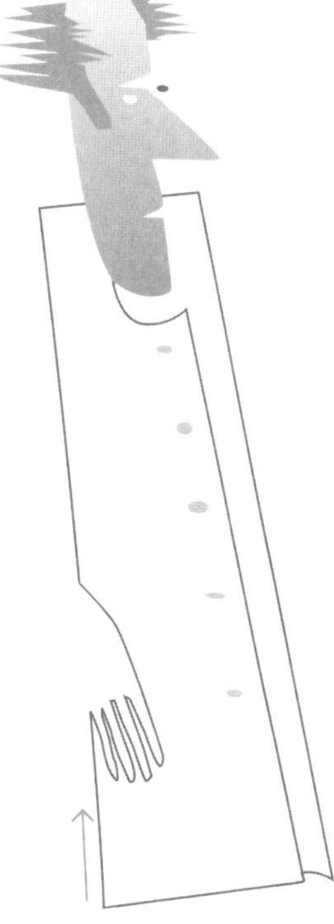

1.2.1. SCIENTIFIC RESEARCH

Most activity in signage research and publication on the scientific level is linked to traffic and transportation—specifically to safety on the roads, in the air and on water. Many universities have a specialised section for transport as part of the faculty of engineering, and some offer doctoral degrees in transport engineering.
In addition, the faculties of physiology and psychology, which have specialised studies on human perception, often concentrate on visual perception in relation to traffic and safety issues. Most written knowledge that exists in the field of signage studies is the result of these types of scientific research.

1.2.2. SPECIALISED ENGINEERS

There are engineering practices that are specialised in traffic engineering, covering national, regional and urban traffic planning and design. Other engineering practices may include expertise in waterways engineering, airport design or air traffic control.

1.2.3. MANAGEMENT CONSULTANTS

Many companies of management consultants have a section dedicated to building management. These type of consultants can be given the function of executive management over the complete building site. A few management consultants further specialise in developing and implementing signage projects.

1.2.4. DESIGNERS AND ARCHITECTS

Architects are renowned for their ambivalent attitude toward signage. Nevertheless, some study programs for architects have involved special studies for the wayfinding aspects in the built environment. All architects have to deal with signage in their own designs whether they like it or not.

Graphic designers often participate, in some way or other, in signage projects. They are educated and trained to deal with communication and graphic signs, the major ingredient of all signage projects. Some study programs for graphic design involve special courses in architectural signage. A lot of graphic designers will get involved in the course of their career in small- to medium-sized signage projects.
Some industrial designers also participate in the development of signage systems. The development of a system for sign panels is industrial design work. Some industrial designers are also trained to design so-called 'human interfaces'—this is the part of design that is concerned with how we use a tool efficiently or operate a machine. Nowadays we all depend heavily on machines, where most human interfaces have in fact become either small or large screens showing sequences of graphic layouts, thus bringing the whole issue of human interfaces closer to the field of graphic design. That, however, has not stopped some industrial designers from getting deeply involved in this particular field.
Communication with the help of screens has exploded over the past decade, including the development of screen applications specifically designed for use in signage projects.

In the future, an exclusively specialised type of designer might evolve from the field of signage design. Already the word 'accessibility' is used in combination with the qualifications 'designer', 'expert', 'auditor', or 'surveyor'. Perhaps future signage specialists will acquire a more distinct professional name.

1.2.5. SIGNAGE MANUFACTURERS

Manufacturers of signage vary considerably in size and in level of specialisation. Many individual craftspeople or small businesses exist that are mostly involved in small commercial and architectural signage. Middle-sized manufacturers often combine signage with other activities, such as commercial interior and exhibition contracting. Larger manufacturers specialise in traffic signage or large commercial projects. Some companies also offer signage design services in addition to their manufacturing activity.

There are also manufacturers that specialise in producing only certain parts of a signage project, such as safety and emergency signs, laser or water jet cutting of loose letters or illustrations, big illuminated signs, murals, electronically changeable signs, or GPS navigation systems. A few manufacturers exclusively deliver basic materials for other sign manufacturers, consisting in most cases of parts of (modular) panel systems, for interior and/or exterior use in signage. There are also a few worldwide operating organisations selling under one brand name that work with franchisees or agents.

1.2.6. GOVERNMENTAL BODIES

A plethora of governmental organisations is concerned with our well-being. Some of these are also involved in and have an effect on the field of signage. Below is a concise overview.

—On the governmental level, many countries have legal requirements concerning the safety and accessibility of the built environment. There are various building regulations and codes of practice where signage is directly affected, for example, signs related to safety at work, or traffic signs.

—Some countries have treaties with each other resulting in supranational bodies, for instance the EEC (European Economic Community). The EEC has also developed streamlining regulations to be adopted by all member states. The EEC has issued directives for emergency and safety signage.

—Most countries have their own standards institutes that develop and issue standards, which are sometimes linked to legislation. There are standards for certain aspects of signage, mostly dealing with safety and mandatory signs.

—An international body, the International Standards Organisation, exists that deals with worldwide standardisation. Member states may or may not either ratify and/or implement these standards after establishment. These standards are called ISO standards (or norms).

—Most countries have organisations with mixed governmental and entrepreneurial participation, for instance, in the fields of transport and aviation. These bodies also develop and issue signage requirements and standards.

1.2.7. PROFESSIONAL ORGANISATIONS

In some countries professional organisations are founded that exclusively deal with signage in the built environment. These organisations are a source of information about the professional field. They arrange meetings and conferences and produce publications. Such an organisation in the US, called the SEGD (Society for Environmental Graphic Design) is by far the largest and oldest organisation around, and was founded in 1973.

2. Setting out the scope of work and organising the people involved

2.1. Introduction

Many different names are used to describe the activities needed in the first phase of a signage project. To name a few: 'making a sign audit', 'developing a strategic signage plan', or simply 'making the initial appraisal of a site'. Whatever the name given, the purpose of this phase is to agree with the client on the scope of the project to be undertaken and who is to be involved to carry out the work.

A signage project may involve many aspects, or may—by contrast—be strictly limited in scope. One project might be strictly concerned with the implementation of the signage 'hardware' needed in and around a building site. Another one can be confined to a general survey in the wayfinding aspects of a building design at an early stage of a project. A commission may also focus entirely on one small aspect of the signage, for instance the signs for a special exhibition in a museum. By contrast, the scope may be extended to the public relations and identity aspects of the (future) occupant of a building, or the building itself. Signage's navigational concerns may begin even before a user starts to approach the site by sending relevant information to visitors in advance, or making relevant information available through web sites. The spectrum of modern communication media and technology is very wide. A selection must be made as to which media to include and which to exclude from the signage project.
The overall purpose of a signage project cannot be other than preventing visitors and/or staff from getting confused or even lost. Being confused about where one should go, generally generates irritation, and consequently the irritation enhances the chances for further mistakes to occur. When that happens, one might feel like an unwelcome guest. Development of such feelings in visitors can hardly be seen as desirable or effective, regardless of what intention the visitor may have had for making the visit.

2.2. Who will be responsible for the signage?

1. The client
2. Financial administrator
3. Operation, maintenance, and housekeeping
4. Safety and security
5. Public relations
6. Architect
7. Interior designer
8. Landscape architect
9. Heritage architect
10. Environmental artist
11. Traffic engineer
12. Electric system engineer
13. Specialised physiologist, psychologist or communications expert
14. Building management
15. Building contractor
16. Signage manufacturer
17. Fire brigade
18. Signage designer

Setting up and realising a signage project involves many people, each with their distinct responsibilities. The organisational structure needed to make it all work smoothly mirrors the complexity of creating the entire building. Interdisciplinary teamwork is the basis of practically all successful efforts to create effective signage projects—with the exception of very small ones.

Establishing the scope of work, together with gathering the team of people that will participate in the realisation of the signage project, is the first and quiet essential step in the process. The number of people involved depends almost entirely on the size of the project. Do pay sufficient attention to this first part of the project; mistakes or errors forthcoming out of negligence during this stage will create painful and increasingly sore spots throughout the duration of the project . The scope of the project and the team of people participating in its realisation are best seen as one entity where one cannot exist without the other.

Modern buildings have become more complex, in both amount of facilities and scale. This development is ever growing. Ownership has also often changed from private to publicly listed companies, which results in a more complex management structure and the involvement of ever more specialist consultants in the building process. Put in general terms, one can say that responsibilities have been split up into four major clusters: management, aesthetic design, technical engineering and marketing/communication. The more specialised input in today's building process has certainly created better quality buildings, in certain aspects, for lower costs. The downside of this new method of production is that the development of an overall building concept is often lacking, where it used to be the prerogative of the client in collaboration with the architect. This nucleus no longer exists in big projects. Investors like to work with standardised budgets that are closely related to expected returns on investment. The architect's role is to provide breathtaking aesthetics within that context. Designers and architects are nowadays more and more forced to limit their involvement to the 'skin' of the building. In the long run this might not be a favourable development. It can easily lead to a certain level of superficiality and uniformity. Design and architecture need richer sources than just aesthetics in order to remain fully alive.

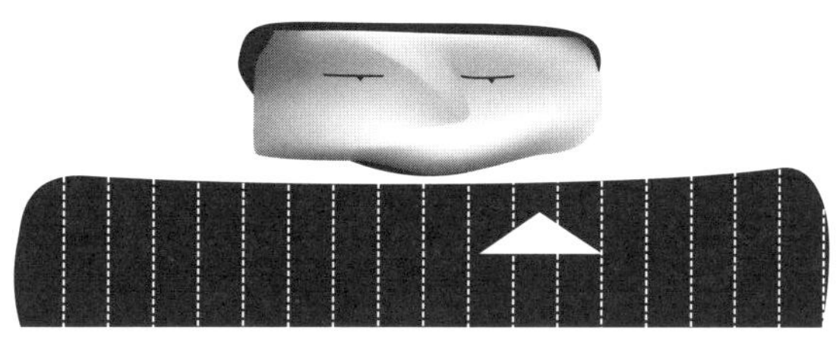

2.2.1. THE CLIENT

By far the most important player in any signage project is the client. The client decides on the scope of the project, on the overall budget allocated for design and realisation, and makes the final decisions in all crucial stages of the project. Being a good client is therefore the most difficult position in any project. Clients are not always individuals, but can also be large organisations. Sometimes this leads to nebulous responsibilities divided among the various client representatives involved in the project. It may happen that the person present at meetings does not have the final say on decisions. The quality of the whole project is best served when a client is represented during important meetings by a person who can really make decisions on the spot. 'Messenger-managers' are often extremely frustrating for all involved in the decision-making process. Moreover, the project tends to generate less 'bang for the buck' under these circumstances.
Quality suffers and costs rise when the decision-making process is complicated.

Clients for signage designers (or signage contractors) may differ substantially in their relationships to the project. The (future) occupant of the building or the investor (owner) may be the client. General practices in signage contracting differ considerably from one country to another. In many countries the building contractor can also act as a client. Sometimes, the real estate agency responsible for finding occupants for the building is the client. In some cases, the architects themselves may be the client. In general, it is most rewarding when the signage design is based on the demands and constraints given by the (future) occupant of the building. The occupant tends to provide the most relevant information for the way the built environment will be used and is thereby likely to result in the most adequate signage.
Occupants over a certain size may decide to involve more than one person employed by that organisation in the signage project. The number of staff involved depends on size and complexity of the organisation. Staff coordination can be best done inside the client's organisation. Ideally there should be only one liaison officer working with the signage designer.

2.2.2. THE FINANCIAL ADMINISTRATOR

Clear financial responsibilities should be the basis of all assignments. It is therefore advisable that the person responsible for the financial administration be involved in the final establishment (issuing) of all contracts relevant to the signage project. Often frustration and aggravation can be avoided by considering the 'money-track' as a separate issue. After the contracts are signed, it is often better to deal with money related matters directly through the responsible administrator.

2.2.3. OPERATION, MAINTENANCE & HOUSEKEEPING

Maintaining the signage after completion is often a task for housekeeping. It is therefore important that the responsible staff have some involvement in the design development of the project. Signage maintenance is the well-known Achilles Heel of all signage projects. The importance of creating commitment at an early stage from the people who must take care of it all after the initial installation should not be underestimated.

2.2.4. SAFETY & SECURITY

Some organisations have secured sections in their buildings. Signage can help to make security procedures clear to everyone. Involvement of security staff in the signage project might be useful, depending on the complexity of the security procedures. Tenants of big buildings often have specific safety procedures to use in case of emergency. A part of these procedures often relates to emergency evacuation of the building. Some members of staff play key roles in the execution of these procedures. Occasionally the need may arise to add a few extra signs to facilitate their task.

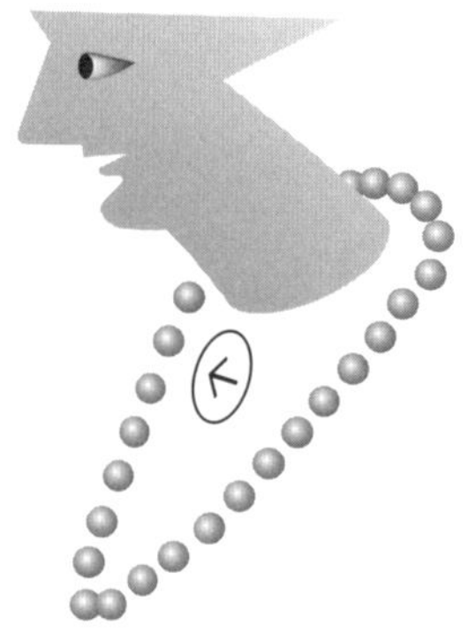

2.2.5. PUBLIC RELATIONS

Signage is often regarded as a part of the corporate identity of an organisation. That view is correct. Signage consists mainly of letters, colours and illustrations. It only makes sense to match these visual elements with all the other expressions of the client's visual identity. Besides, some signage elements, like maps and/or logos, will also be used in print or on websites.
The match between signage and all other visual material is not the only important factor; the PR values related to the organisation are also at stake. An organisation can express effectively how it wants to communicate with its users, and how it wishes to be perceived, by the particular way attention is given to the signage of its building(s). This attitude can be, for instance, friendly, open, restrained, or reserved. Signage can be an effective public relations, or even branding, tool.
That is the reason why a member of the public relations staff may be part of the signage team.

2.2.6. ARCHITECT

Obviously, the architect of the building—and its environment—plays an important role in the process of the decision making. The architectural designs are based on a visual concept. The signage has to be an integrated part of that concept. The authorship of the architect often dictates that his/her creation may not be altered or damaged without his/her consent. This position sometimes puts the right of veto about all visual aspects of the signage into the architect's hands.

Within the visual context of the design, the signage designer has to face two major constraints: on one hand the corporate identity of the occupant of the building and on the other hand the visual identity of the building itself. It is the designer's task to create a happy marriage between the two.
In big projects architects are not individually responsible for all aspects of the architectural design. The responsibilities may be divided into three separate ones: one for the exterior of the building, one for its interior and one for its surroundings. The interior architect and/or the landscape architect may be part of one large architectural practice or may be commissioned on a project basis as separate individuals/companies.
A growing number of architectural practices nowadays also employ graphic designers. In that case, the architect's commission could also include the signage for the building.

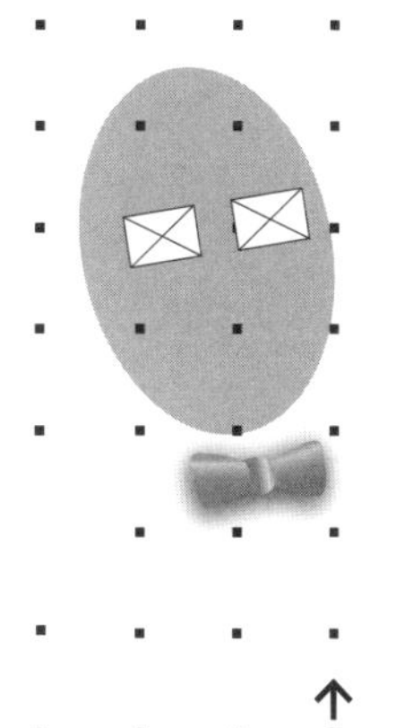

Not only does the architect have a large influence on the signage design, but also the architectural design itself is in many respects an essential constraint for the signage design.
Wayfinding is initially entirely determined by the design of the spatial architectural structure and by the visual designs of key wayfinding facilities in the building. The architectural design can have an easily perceived spatial structure or a very complicated one. Entrances, paths and transport facilities (stairs, elevators) can be obviously present or can be more or less concealed.
A building site does not start to communicate with its users through the signage, but rather through the actual physical spatial structure itself. Therefore, the communication process begins initially with the first sketches of the architectural design.

2.2.7. INTERIOR DESIGNER

Most signage is likely to be done inside a building. The interior architecture is another important constraint for the signage designer. Early involvement of the signage aspect in the interior design process may very well help in avoiding visual disasters in the end result and professional embarrassment along the way.
The interior design creates the type of essential constraints for signage such as the selection of materials for walls, ceilings and floors; the selection of furniture, furnishings and other fittings; the choice of colour scheme and lighting conditions. The last being of extreme importance for the signage design. Ideally, signage should be an integrated part of the interior design. It is not always simple to realise this, but any attempt to bring the two closer will create a more effective end result.

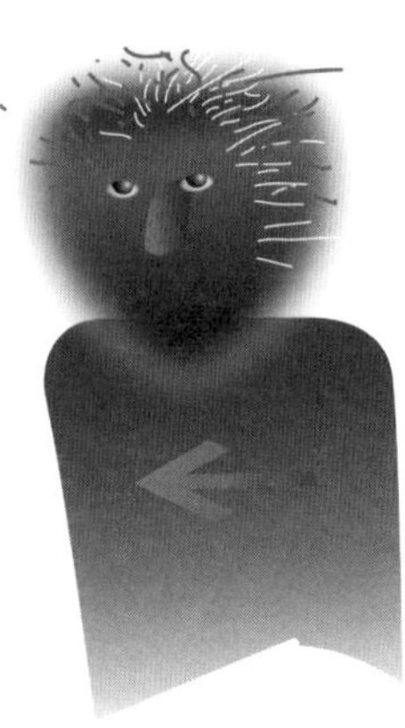

2.2.8. LANDSCAPE ARCHITECT

The landscape architect is vital in creating easy and visually self-evident access to the entrances of a building. However, some signs in the exterior environment of the building might still be unavoidable to reassure users about finding their way around. The amount of external signage needed fully depends on the set priorities of the landscape design.

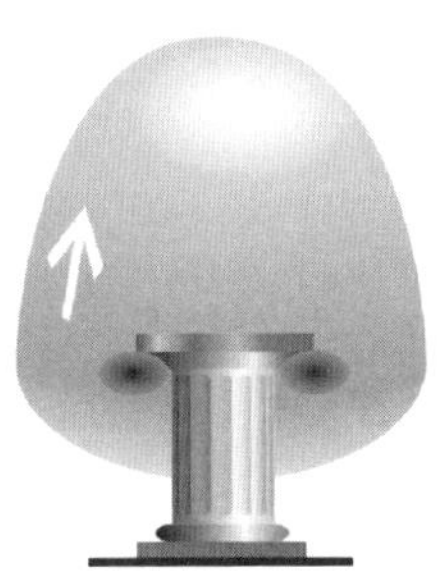

2.2.9. HERITAGE ARCHITECT

The project may be a site with specific historical and/or cultural value. In these cases, the cultural heritage must be protected. The level of protection may vary from pure conservation to restoration or refurbishing. Conservation means basically creating conditions that would avoid further decay; restoration may allow bringing the site as much as possible back to its original state, which is not easy to determine in some cases. Some architects have specialised in this kind of work, either as conservation specialists or as having profound knowledge of architectural style periods. The signage style may also be affected by heritage constraints.

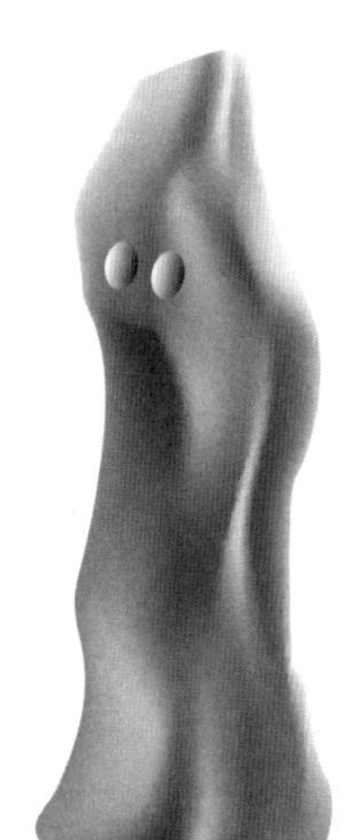

2.2.10. ENVIRONMENTAL ARTIST

One or more artists may be invited to create special art pieces for the interior or exterior of a building. In some countries it is customary to invite artists to participate in building projects over a certain size. This artistic participation often enhances the overall quality of the site. It is extremely valuable to maintain and nourish this long-standing traditional 'marriage' between fine arts and architectural design. The two are natural-born companions. Environmental artists can create eye-catching landmarks with their art pieces, landmarks that might become useful to the wayfinding process.

2.2.11. TRAFFIC ENGINEER

Large and specialised projects, like airports, use traffic engineers to design routing plans. In other projects their work can be limited to the parking garage part of the building. In specialised projects a close collaboration must be established with the traffic engineers. Some engineering practices are specialised in designing certain types of buildings.

The signage designer has to collate the maps taken from the architects with those of the traffic engineers (when they are involved in the project) to create a concise overview of every level of the whole site.

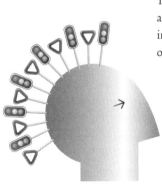

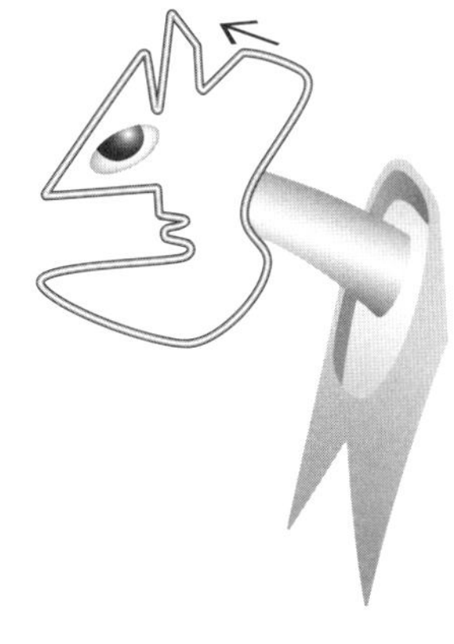

2.2.12. ELECTRICAL ENGINEER

The electrical engineers —as a separate firm or as part of the general contractor— design the complete electrical infrastructure of a building site. Often the signage designer needs to know where specific facilities are located and how they function precisely. Getting hold of some of the drawings made by these engineers together with some personal explanation can be of great value for the signage designer.

2.2.13. SPECIALISED PHYSIOLOGIST, PSYCHOLOGIST OR COMMUNICATIONS EXPERT

In some cases specialised scholars on the field of signage are invited to participate in the project. Their role in the project and the extent of their commission is not traditionally defined. The result of their work may or may not be relevant or even important to the signage design.

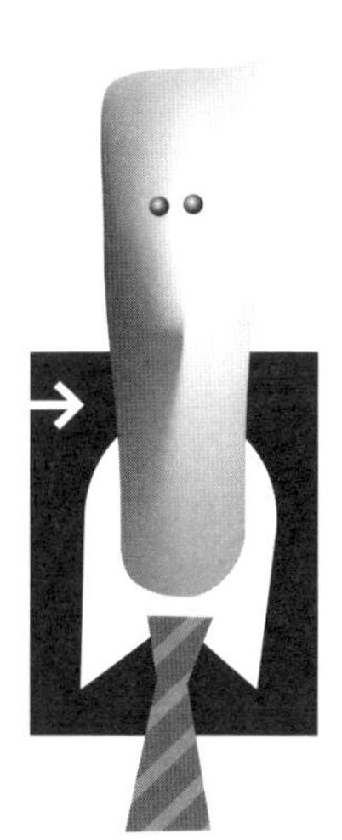

2.2.14. BUILDING MANAGEMENT

The task of managing the building process and all that it involves has become a complicated and extensive task. The traditional role of the architect in building management has been reduced significantly over the years. Buildings have become like complex machines, with a lot of specialists involved in creating the whole structure. The owner of the building often leaves the management of the building process to specialised management consultancy firms.
Building budgets, once agreed upon, are often left entirely under the responsibility of the management for execution and project coordination. The building management will therefore allocate all resources, coordinate all activities, inspect the work, and chair all important meetings.

Signage design will flourish and deliver better final results when the signage of the building is also a specific topic in a number of the coordination meetings—preferably on the agenda at an early stage in the building process.

2.2.15. BUILDING CONTRACTOR

The general building contractor is responsible for the building up until completion. Practically all contractors make use of sub-contractors for specific parts of the building. However, the general contractor holds the general responsibility for the building. For instance, the permission of the general contractor is often needed to access the site.
The signage could be part of the general contractor's contract. It could also be done under a separate contract with a specialised manufacturer and installer of the signs. In any case, work coordination is essential since work on the signage has to start before the completion of the general contractor's work.

2.2.16. SIGNAGE MANUFACTURER

The signage manufacturer is responsible for the fabrication and installation of the signs. Special signs (eg. illuminated signs or fire exit signs) can be produced under sub-contract by the signage manufacturer.

The signage manufacturer may be formally commissioned by the general building contractor to avoid complications about responsibilities during the building process.

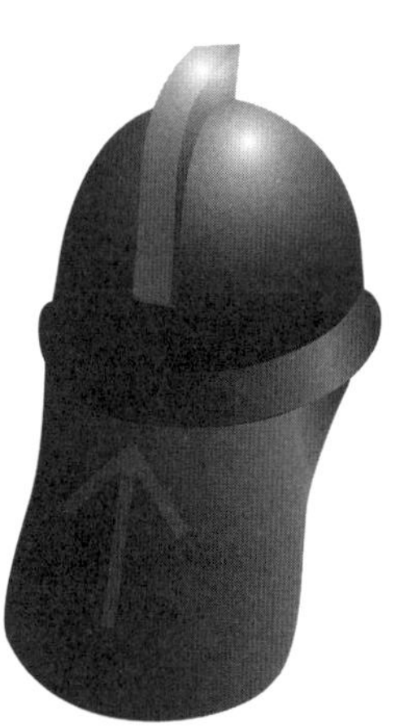

2.2.17. FIRE BRIGADE

Some governmental and statuary bodies have specific responsibilities in relation to all types of construction. These responsibilities as well as the way they are carried out may vary considerably between countries.
As far as signage is concerned, the most important governmental interference is that of the fire brigade or fire department. The emergency exit and fire signs have to be approved by the local fire inspector before the building can be occupied; this can sometimes even be required during the building process. Some legislation (and some inspectors) are very rigid about the way rules have to be obeyed and the way the inspection must be carried out. So, proposed signage designs can be judged quite differently, depending on local circumstances or the individual responsible for the approval. In some cases all designs have to follow the standards to the letter. In other instances the only matter that counts is that the proposed emergency signs are clearly visible, understandable and follow an efficient routing.

2.3. Selecting a signage consultant/designer

As previously stated, the role of the client/commissioner is the most difficult one of all. A good preparation for a potential commission is important in order to avoid disappointment. Regrettably, in most projects preparation for the signage is postponed for far too long and done too hastily. Early preparation and some brief initial personal interviews with a few signage consultants will, however, prove to be a quite good investment in retrospect.

Who should be asked to do the signage job ?
For large and/or specialised signage projects, there are only a few very specialised practices around that are experienced in comparable projects. The choice in this league is fairly limited. For all other projects, the choice is much wider. The work can be done by either an in-house graphic designer in an architectural practice, or an independent signage (often graphic) designer, or a signage manufacturer. The advantage of involving the in-house designer is the familiarity with the project and the expectation of a flowing integration with the architectural design. However, the disadvantage is the lack of an unbiased view on the wayfinding qualities of the project. Most architects have a very particular view on signage and generally overestimate the amount of self-evidence of the environment that they themselves have created. Architects know their projects inside out, often having worked on them for years. It seems that too much familiarity with the site can become a barrier for creating effective signage. Thus the choice of an independent signage designer may overcome this disadvantage.

On the other hand, the signage manufacturer has lots of experience in various projects and an excellent understanding of his own production capabilities. Understandably—but nevertheless regrettably—the manufacturer's own production capabilities are often his major concern. This circumstance is a major handicap in creating the best quality for the signage design. It is therefore unadvisable to give the manufacturer the entire responsibility for signage production as well as the design, unless the project is very small or the client is willing to do all the preliminary research himself and has prepared very clear instructions for the manufacturer to follow.

In some cases, signage design instructions are already available. Many corporate identity manuals include instructions for signage. In these cases a part of the design work is already done. However, adaptations of the existing standard designs will be needed in most cases and, moreover, each building will be different in size, design and structure and will therefore need its own customised signage.

Still, a lot of the work involved in a comprehensive signage project can be done without the help of external consultants. The necessary preparation work for any signage project can be done by someone who roughly follows the procedures as laid out in this book. The client and a member of his/her staff can do a lot of this necessary preparation themselves. Experience, of course, may improve quality and speed up the process. But experience is more important in some phases of the project than in others.

Experience is crucial in the initial phase and in the phase of preparing for production and procurement. In cases where an independent signage designer is sought for the job, it is advisable to involve a (graphic) designer who is experienced in projects comparable to the project in hand. The precise content of the signage assignment depends for the most part on the circumstances of the project, such as the existence of a signage manual as part of the corporate identity, or the availability of in-house staff who can work on the project, or the required level of depth or sophistication for the signage. Some clients feel that all the signage that is needed is to put up one logo on the facade and another near the entrance of the building. Others may wish to include the fire exit signs or a complete identification system for all maintenance personnel in the signage project. Comprehensive signage is still a rather elastic entity, and the content of the assignment can vary from one assignment to another.

During an initial interview with potential signage consultants, possibly the most important question to ask is about the consultant's own vision for the best content for the assignment. The answer given could be quite helpful to the client in deciding who would best serve the client's own needs.

Signage relies heavily on visual perception. The quality of our visual perception deteriorates with age. From top to bottom: our ability to focus gets reduced, our ability to see details gets less and in the second half of our life we need up to 4 times more light to perceive the same contrast.

2.4. Who is the signage for?

At an early stage, the target group for the signage project has to be taken into consideration. The specific needs of the expected audience can be separated into two categories based on the two distinct aspects. First, the needs related to the general physical and mental condition of the expected users. Second, the needs related specifically to their background, profession and/or function.

2.4.1. GENERAL PHYSICAL OR MENTAL CONDITION OF USERS

Obviously, well-designed signage should be useful for as many people as possible. This includes those users who might be considered handicapped, impaired or in any other way exceptional. Please be aware that to be in the state of being deviant from 'normal' can be applicable to all of us under certain conditions. The task of extending the proper use of all signage to as many potential users as possible must have reasonable limitations, for instance, when costs are becoming disproportionate to accommodate only a few extra users, or when specific provisions start to hinder the effectiveness for the average user.

The major problem for the signage designer when making such judgments, is that there are no reliable —if any— data available that could be of help in setting out reasonable requirements for a design that would extend usefulness for specific groups of users. Some requirements for specific groups of impaired people have become a political issue in some countries, resulting in legislation. These requirements will be discussed in further detail in section 2.5.6 of this chapter.

The type of user who is often —unconsciously— taken as the 'norm' for designers, can be described as physically and mentally in good shape. Nowadays classified in terms like an 'unimpaired' or 'non-disabled' user. Of course this is only a theoretical norm. People vary individually within the boundaries of this classification, which in itself is already rather vague. Besides, people's conditions are always in a dynamic statc and are not static. People's abilities do change over the years, and can sometimes change in the short term or even instantaneously, depending on their emotional state. Angry or confused people tend to make unexpected decisions and perceive their environment quite differently than they would when calm.

Despite the many uncertainties about adequate remedies, it is useful for designers to be informed about the types of impaired users and their need to use signage effectively.

2.4.1.1. *Visually impaired users*

Signage is for the most part a coherent set of visual instructions. Therefore, it relies heavily on the quality of our visual perception. The quality of our visual perception deteriorates with age. Our ability to focus and to see details (our visus) will be reduced. In fact, our visual environment gets more and more blurred over time. Perhaps this is not a problem in every aspect of daily life, but it is certainly a handicap when reading signs.
An effective remedy for the reduced ability to focus is wearing glasses. The loss of seeing detail can only be remedied with the use of bigger letters on a surface with a colour that strongly contrasts with the lettering colour. More ambient light also helps to enhance contrast. We need more and more light as we get older. We might start off by choosing our life's partner in candlelight or less, and we end up needing a flashlight to read the menu in a restaurant—or someone friendly to read it for us. The percentage of people over retirement age in relation to the total population is rising in all western societies. It makes this group of users relatively more relevant, simply because of its sheer size.

Visually impaired people suffer from a variety of types of reduced visual abilities. Some can only see the centre of a normal view (a so- called tunnel vision), as opposed to others who can't see the centre, but only the periphery of an image. Some suffer from a mix of both and some see everything only in reduced contrast. Remedies for this category are basically the same as for reduced eyesight caused by age.

Types of visual impairment from top to bottom: Some cannot see the centre of an image, some can only see the centre (a so-called 'tunnel vision'), some see everything in reduced contrast and the 'legally blind' need to be up to 10 times closer to an image to be able to read its information.

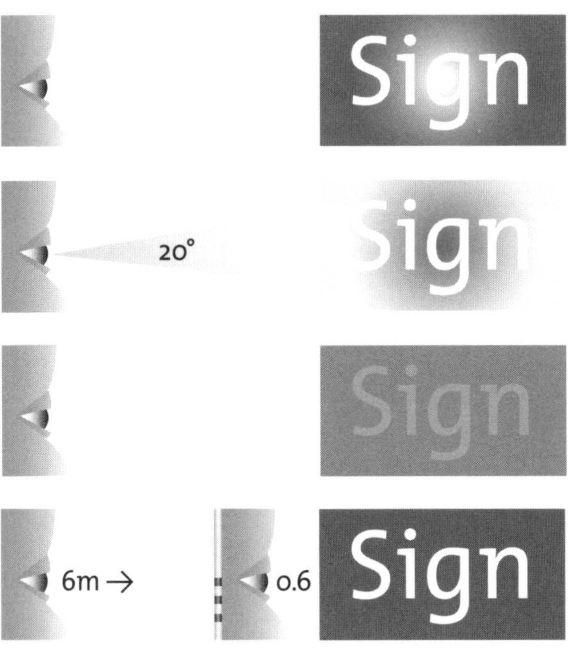

The 'legally blind' can have severely reduced eyesight, or might not be able to see at all. This category of users needs other (mostly tactile or auditory) stimuli to get an important—but smaller—part of the same information about the environment as visually fit users. Audible information is likely to replace, at least partially, the information that is still offered in a tactile form today.

Statistical information about the size of the blind and visually impaired part of a population is not available. It is assumed to be between 0.5–1%.

There are a few other specific types of reduced visual abilities. Some, especially men, have problems distinguishing certain colours from each other—often red from green. This so-called colour-blindness seems to apply to about 5–10% of an average population.

Some people have problems seeing under greatly reduced light conditions. The eye uses a different part of its retina under these low light conditions. That part might not function properly with some people. This condition is called 'night-blindness'. On the other hand too much or extremely strong light will reduce visibility for all of us.

2.4.1.2. Hearing impaired users

People with hearing difficulties add up to about 1% of a population. In certain particular situations, sound can be an essential part of a signage system. Access to buildings, or parts of a building, for instance a parking garage, is sometimes only possible using verbal communication through an 'intercom' device. Sound effects are also sometimes used as an 'alert' or alarm signal to indicate a changing situation or a state of emergency. Sound is also used in interactive situations, for example, when pushing a button either on a screen or in real life. Pedestrian crossings often have both visual and audial alerts.
Hearing-impaired users are best accommodated by shielding the environmental noise away from facilities that need speaking and/or listening to.

2.4.1.3. Cognitively impaired users

Signage does not solely need to be perceived, it must also be properly understood to be really functional. That can be a daunting task in some cases.

Cognitive impairment includes a mix of more or less severe inabilities. It should be noted that these inabilities can be definitive—caused by illness, genetics, accident, or age—but can very well be temporary. People in severe stress, anger or anxiety lose their normal capabilities to comprehend and to take appropriate navigational decisions. Some types of buildings may expect to receive more people in the latter category than others, such as

hospitals, airports and certain public buildings related to tax collection, welfare, or unemployment.
Clearly, the part of the signage system that deals with the emergency routing must be understandable to people under stress.

The biggest group of users with some kind of permanent cognitive impairment are some elderly users. Some form of dementia, an irreparable degeneration of the brain functions, is suffered by an estimated 1% of a population.
There are no special means by which cognitive impairment can be countered in signage design, other than by making the system as simple and as self-evident as possible.

2.4.1.4. *Illiterate or foreign users*

Language is the cornerstone of every signage system. Architects often claim that the facilities they have designed will speak for themselves. That might very well have been the intention; however, in most cases, there will be a huge language problem. Architects tend to forget that the 'design language' they use is only comprehensible to their closest colleagues. Nobody else really understands it. Ultimately the building will have an entirely differently skilled audience than the architecturally skilled so abundantly present in the design and construction phase of the project. The type of audience that will ultimately use the building, however, will definitely need written text to find their way around.

Illiterate or foreign users might not completely understand the language used on signs. Research has revealed that this group of users do still use, in some way or other, the written information on signs. A simple written coding system can be understood by most, despite illiteracy or unfamiliarity with a certain language. Pictograms try to overcome the limitations of literacy and language. This claim is only true for pictograms that users have become familiar with, like men's and ladies toilets, phones, wheel chair entrances, cloakrooms and information counters.

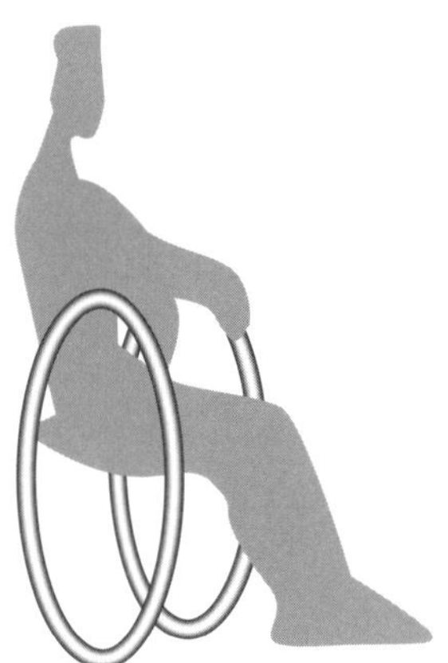

2.4.1.5. *Mobility disabled users*

It is not precisely known how many people of a total population cannot use their legs to move around freely. For some this might be a temporary situation, and for others it is a permanent handicap. Accessibility of buildings for wheelchair users has been a governmental concern for most countries for many years. Some countries have established legal requirements for accessibility for this group of users.

It is common nowadays to see ramps or small elevators next to the entrance stairs of buildings. Also control panels of essential facilities in buildings, such as lifts/elevators, are brought within the reach of wheelchair users.
Most mobility impaired or disabled users share a lower than aver-

age level of vision. That fact should be taken into account when positioning the signs.

2.4.2. PROFESSION, FUNCTION OR BACKGROUND OF USERS

A fundamental difficulty when designing for a signage project is the difference in needs between so-called first-time users of a built environment and the regular staff of the building occupant. People experience and perceive an unfamiliar environment in an entirely different way than a familiar one. The difference between the two experiences is enormous. This fact makes some provisions redundant for a majority of the users of the signage. The problem is not only having to deal with such different user groups. The professional pitfall is also the familiarity with the environment that the designers themselves develop over time. What they consider as being crystal clear to everyone might not be as clear in the eyes of a first-time user. Signage designers should be aware of this phenomenon and try to avoid becoming a victim of this typical 'architect's disease'.

Moreover, there is not always a complete awareness during the signage design that the modern built environment has become a complex structure with a lot of different users, including visitors, staff, maintenance, security, couriers, emergency services, and so on.

2.4.2.1. Visitors

Visitors, especially first-time visitors, generally have little knowledge about the environment. They are for the most part entirely relying on the signage to find their way around. In some corporate or governmental buildings visitors are sometimes accompanied, but in most cases they have to rely on what can be found on signs. Receptionists are occasionally available to provide extra help. Often sufficient attention is given to directing visitors to their destination, while directing the way back out of the building is somewhat neglected. General facilities, such as toilets, washrooms, phones and cloakrooms, should also be made easy to find for visitors.

The number and variety of visitors to be expected is of course essential in determining adequate signage. A hospital is expected to receive far more emotionally distressed visitors than a library would. Some governmental buildings, like city halls or offices that deal with taxation or welfare, are expected to receive more foreigners than the average office building.

Analysing the kind of visitors to expect is an important part of establishing design requirements.

2.4.2.2. Staff

There is a tendency to underestimate the need of the in-house staff for signage. That is based on a misjudgment that assumes that staff are familiar with their surroundings and therefore have little need for signage. This is basically true, if staff was still a steady population like it used to be. That is hardly the case any more. Turnover of staff has become considerably higher. Some companies see half their staff change every year. Temporary and free-lance staffing have become an essential part of all governmental and business activities.

Not only do staff change position faster, so do the work spaces in a building. Relocation of work spaces within occupied buildings has become an almost permanent state of being for most organisations. A growing number of organisations are abandoning office spaces with steady occupants altogether and are adopting some form of daily rotating—'hoteling'—of office spaces.
In any case, well-designed signage can contribute to the staff's efficiency.

2.4.2.3. Maintenance personnel

Building maintenance is often carried out by external agencies. This work includes not only the daily cleaning of a building but also regular technical maintenance of the many devices that have become part of a modern building. The locations of lift/elevator control rooms, risers, service ducts, air conditioning machine rooms, alarm systems, computer and telephone network servers, need to be found easily.

2.4.2.4. Couriers

Electronic media have taken over a lot of the physical paperwork transport. Still couriers, deliveries and internal mail are important parts of the organisation's infrastructure. Supplies of all kinds need to be delivered to their destination efficiently.

2.4.2.5. Internal emergency

Buildings over a certain size have developed internal emergency procedures. Some members of the staff play a key role in the execution of these procedures. Efficient emergency evacuation of a building in particular will need dedicated signage.

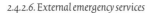

2.4.2.6. External emergency services

Members of the fire brigade/department must be able to orient themselves quickly both inside and around the building. Special provisions, such as indicator panels, fire hose reels and fire extinguishers, must be clearly marked.

2.4.2.7. Safety and security services

Many organisations use external agencies to provide safety and security during and/or outside working hours. Additional signage might be needed to make this work more efficiently.

2.5. What are the legal requirements?

The legal requirements for signage in buildings are growing in some countries. A listing of the various governmental bodies involved in legislation that includes signage in some way has already been given in chapter 1. Before going into the matter in further detail, let's take a look at the legal background.

2.5.1. BACKGROUND OF SOME LEGISLATION

Building activities have always been subject to regulations and legislation. That also applies to transportation. Over time, legislation has become more complex following the growth in complexity of the built environment itself. Securing the safety of the users of facilities has been the core of most of these laws and regulations. More recently, additional legislation concerning healthy and safe working conditions has been established.
The political interest resulting in legislation for the accessibility of buildings is relatively new. This legislation was made exclusively for disabled or impaired users. It sprang out of the many 'equal rights' movements that were particularly popular in the second half of the last century.

2.5.2. US AND UK IN THE FOREFRONT

Some countries, notably the US and the UK, have far more detailed and extensive legislation on these matters than other countries. Nevertheless, extensive legislation on these matters is in no way an expression of a more general concern for the underprivileged or deprived parts of society. These two matters are entirely unrelated.
The impact of this legislation on the professional field of signage is in some respects remarkable, if not rather peculiar. For instance, some type of signage in buildings is now a legal requirement for the impaired users, where that is not the case for the unimpaired, though they are still the vast majority of all users. 'Rights' do not seem to be equal in this respect.
The parts of signage that must be legally present for everybody to use are the fire exit and emergency signs. These types of signs are considered to be of extreme importance, even up to a level of being potentially a crucial matter of life or death. Ironically, these signs (and all other accommodations serving this purpose, like emergency staircases) are not of any use at all to the impaired users. This all leads to the somewhat bizarre situation that only the impaired must be accommodated legally to have easy access to a building. But once being comfortably inside and confronted with an emergency, this group of people is suddenly legally considered to be the same as the rest of the users. One would expect that the law would provide extra protection for those that need it the most in a potentially critical situation. Unfortunately, that is not the case.
The law may require that certain provisions need to be present to

enhance comfort of access, but that requirement concerns exclusively the impaired group of users. In the case that leaving the premises as fast as possible is crucial, legal requirements are made that are exclusively useful for users that are completely fit and must certainly not be impaired.

Furthermore, the legally required additional provisions for the impaired users of a building have in some cases a somewhat nebulous statistical funding to prove their usefulness, though not in all cases. It is clear that a ramp is a useful replacement for users who are unable to climb the entrance stairs, and so is making the control panels of elevators within reach of a wheelchair user. However, as already mentioned, all these provisions are of no use at all in cases of emergency.

When judging the usefulness of all the provisions required for visually impaired users, then matters become less obvious, to say the least. There is no statistical solid data available that provides essential information about the number of visually impaired people around, let alone in relation to the precise character of their impairment. Extensive tactile provisions for signage purposes in all buildings are now mandatory under the laws of some countries, while no one knows how many people are actually capable of using or do actually use these provisions properly. The number of braille users is also unknown, and seems to be diminishing. This is due to new technology that is replacing tactile provisions with more effective auditory ones.
Not only information about general use is lacking, there is also no estimation about the costs incurred by society with the installation of these provisions in all buildings. The only thing we know for sure is that the signage industry seems to be pretty content with this legislation, as if they were the lobbyists that made it all happen.

Not only is the content of the laws somewhat haphazard, the procedure by which the legislation was created also seems to be remarkable in some cases. It appears that in the US one signage designer took out, single-handed, the most striking idiocies that were present in the preliminary proposals for the US legislation on these matters, before it took its final form. An action he undertook entirely on his own initiative and on his own account.

2.5.3. FUTURE DEVELOPMENTS

It is clear that legal interference with signage in the built environment can be considered as having somewhat unbalanced aspects. Associations of signage designers might feel a responsibility to try and bring more balance in existing legislation that can be beneficial for the whole professional field.

The effect of more extensive legislation will make complying with the law a complex matter. And 'experts' will be needed for advice on signage installation and control of building sites. Already expressions like 'sign audits' are popping up. Using the same wording as the legally required financial audits for companies, this may ultimately lead to 'chartered' signage experts.

We should be aware that this development is no guarantee whatsoever that signage would receive better attention in the future, or that the profession would grow more mature and reach a higher professional level. Such a result is even less likely to happen in circumstances where the legislation appears to be, in some ways, slightly eccentric.

2.5.4. EMERGENCY EXIT AND FIRE SIGNS

The shape, colour and size of fire and emergency exit signs are standardised in most countries. There are publications available about these standards on various levels:
—on the supranational governmental level, the EEC has issued standards on this matter
—on the national governmental level, publications about safety regulations are available through the public bodies that produce and distribute information about legislation
—on the local governmental level, some fire brigades/departments of big cities issue publications about standards. In most cases the local fire officer must approve all provisions for cases of emergency and fire fighting equipment
—on the international level,the international body for standardisation (ISO) issues their standards
—on the national level, some national bodies for standardisation issue standards
—some commercial publishers also issue standards.
—some specialised commercial sign manufacturers issue catalogues containing signs in compliance with various standards

2.5.5. SAFETY AND MANDATORY SIGNS

The difference between this type of sign and the emergency signs, is that the fire brigade has no special responsibility in this matter. Except for the signs that indicate the location of fire equipment, or those that need to be present to accommodate the fire brigade. Responsibility for approval and inspection of these types of signs is in the hands of the local building and/or health authorities. Producers and issuers of publications on this matter are globally the same as for the emergency signs

2.5.6. SIGNS FOR DISABLED USERS

Legislation on this matter may vary quite substantially from one country to another. The USA has quite extensive regulations under the so-called ADA (Americans with Disabilities Act). Britain has the DDA (Disability Discrimination Act) which will be coming into force gradually.

Publications are available on these matters through governmental publication houses. Organisations for disabled people and professional organisations related to the built environment have published information on this topic as well.

2.6. Are there special security requirements?

Some types of organisations, for instance banks or certain governmental institutions, need special security measures in some parts of their buildings. If that is the case, these areas should be clearly indicated. To serve security, sometimes a strategy is pursued for withholding general information about the exact layout of the building. This kind of secrecy about the exact structure of the building and its organisation can also easily lead to confusion.

Security procedures and their related technical facilities tend to become rather complicated. Comfortable access to the building as a whole, and even security itself, might be served best by providing clear and simple information about secured sections of a building and related procedures for access.

Regrettably, more and more public buildings are adopting security portals for general access. Public transportation areas like airports are getting more and more facilities that resemble prison security systems, ironically leading to a situation where free and open societies are locking themselves in to secure their openness and freedom.

2.7. Should a certain style be incorporated?

The architectural style is a given constraint for practically all signage design. Most occupants have a corporate graphic style. Some of these corporate styles are very extensive and include signage of buildings as well. Corporate design manuals may be available that provide detailed information or even signage design guidelines.

Extensive printed corporate or governmental design manuals have fallen somewhat out of grace these days, since the years around the turn of the century were filled with mergers and acquisitions. The shelf-life of the average corporate manual became a bit short under these conditions. Still it is sensible to integrate the corporate style of the occupant in the signage design, unless of course it is not consistently used by the occupant of the building. In that case, it would be senseless to pursue that style only for the signage.
The argument that following a corporate style would include a potential financial risk in case of a change in corporate style does not hold water. The cost incurred with the signage is irrelevant in comparison with the cost involved in mergers or acquisitions. The commercial advantage of supporting the corporate image while it lasts will certainly outweigh the possible costs of adaptation of a new future style.

The need to express a corporate style in the signage may vary considerably from one organisation to the other. Retail chains, for instance, cannot live without a very strong visual identity, also expressed through their buildings and signage.

Some types of buildings may need their own identity or even branding. Buildings or complexes that have multiple tenants, like shopping malls or certain office buildings, are in need of a strong identity themselves. The building itself has in fact become a product on the market. Also museums or buildings that are part of the 'national heritage' may need an identity closely related to the building itself.

2.8. How about the budget?

Practically all types of buildings, in close relation to their respective location, have global construction prices per square meter or foot. Investors and developers work with these benchmarks and so does the building management. Budgets for signage are in many cases still somewhat vague, if existing at all. Signage is not a standard part in all building budgets. Also the precise content of a signage project still varies a lot. Both situations should be changed. The professional field should provide clear indications about the extent of a general signage project, in such a way that it could be adopted as a standard part of building budgets. In some countries the situation is somewhat better than in others. There might be some favourable change in the future. There is a growing tendency to incorporate signage as a standard separate issue in general building budgets. So things are moving in the right direction, though a bit too slow. There remains plenty of room for improvement.

The following are some aspects that may influence the budget.

2.8.1. SIZE OF PROJECT AND LEVEL OF COMPLEXITY

Obviously, the size of the project and its complexity are the determining factors for the size of the budget. A library or a hospital are complex buildings with lots of daily visitors, as opposed to an industrial office building that has far fewer visitors and therefore requires much simpler signage.

2.8.2. LEVEL OF INNOVATION

Producing a reliable budget for signage is only possible after the scope is determined and the list of needed sign types is completed. Even at that time, the reliability of a budget may depend on the amount of ambitious innovation needed or put into the project. Innovative solutions are by nature much more difficult to estimate, in terms of time and costs incurred, than the conventional ones.

2.8.3. RULES OF THUMB FIGURES

Again, reliable budgeting is best done after reliable data have been gathered. The budget for gathering these data will be around 15% of the overall signage budget. Any estimate before this phase is based purely on rule of thumb figures.
Here are some of these sorts of figures:

2.8.3.1. Overall budget

The signage budget will be about 0.5% – 0.3% of the overall building budget.

Breakdown signage budget

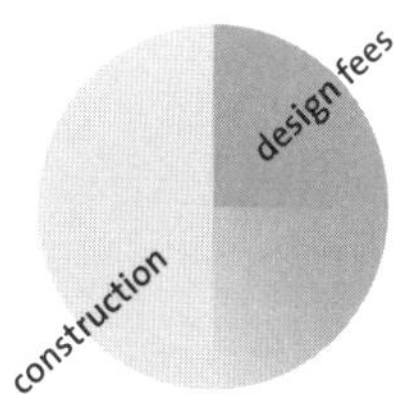

2.8.3.2. Designer's fees

The part of the signage budget spent on the consultant or designer's fees depends mostly on the distribution of work between the client, the designer and the manufacturer. Gathering of data is an important part of any signage project. This part can be done by the client as well as by the designer or even by the manufacturer. Preparation for production involves extensive work on a computer. In general, there is no special software needed for this type of work. In fact, suitable computers for carrying out this work can be found on the client's desk, the designer's or the manufacturer's alike. Preparing art work and type is a big chunk of the work of any signage project.

In most cases the percentage of the signage designer's fees in relation to the total budget for the signage is considerably higher than that of the architect's in relation to the overall building cost. It will be at least 2 to 4 times higher. Depending on the circumstances, the signage designer's fees might be between 25% and 50% of the total budget.

Breakdown design fees

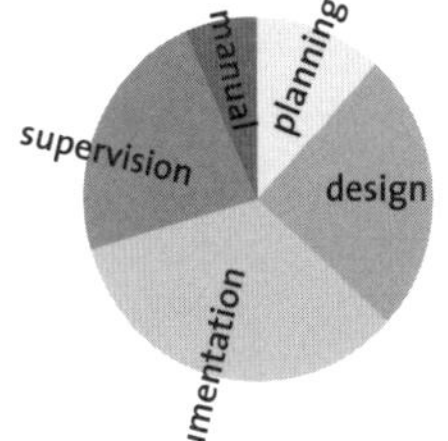

The breakdown of the overall designer's fees will be: scope and planning 10% – 15%, design 25% – 30%, documentation and bidding 30% – 40%, supervision and manufacturing specifications 20% – 30%, maintenance manual 5% – 10%.

2.8.3.3. Manufacturing & installation costs

Door signs have a special and peculiar position in the signage projects of office buildings. Price competition between manufacturers is often reduced to the competition on price (and quality) of the door signs. The number of doors used in a project may be relevant to the overall cost of signage. However, the focus on this one item is rather odd, considering that the amount of the signage budget spent on door signs will not exceed 20% of the total manufacturing costs.
Signage outside the building is considerably more expensive than inside. Comparable items will be 5 to 10 times more expensive when placed outdoors.

Internally illuminated items are also far more expensive that non-illuminated ones. The price difference will be 3 to 5 times as much. In addition to that, the unavoidable maintenance costs of illuminated signs should also be taken into consideration.

Installing the signs on site will take about 20% of the manufacturing budget.

2.9. What is the proposed time schedule for completion?

Signage projects start notoriously late. Ideally, a limited study assignment about the signage aspects of a site should be made when a new building or complex is still in its master plan phase. This seldom happens, if ever. In many cases, signage comes into view about six months before the opening of a new or refurbished building is planned. That is really far too late for bigger projects to have signage fully implemented by completion. In cases where time for final production is too short, producing temporary signage should be a part of the signage project. This might also be the case for projects where signage is needed during the construction phase. Final signage facilities can also be implemented in stages. Sometimes completely installed fire exit signs are required by law even before the building is completed.

Avoiding the costs of producing temporary signage might be an incentive for clients to start the signage project at an earlier stage. However, starting too late may have one merit. There is a design advantage in making temporary signs, that is, if it opens up the possibility for the designer to reconsider the designs after temporary installation and before final production starts. Models of signs in actual size, placed in the real environment, are very valuable aids for making final design decisions. It is very difficult to foresee the precise visual impact of a sign in its final surroundings. Signs are designed to draw the maximum visual attention by means of minimal visual impact. That is a daring task and a delicate exercise. It is in fact a very subtle balancing act that is best carried out right on the spot where it has to do its job. A mock-up, or the installation of temporary signs, can be of great help in making final design decisions.

2.10. Making the work plan or signage program

Signage projects follow in principle the same stages in development as all other design projects. Each stage ends with a review and approval session with the client and all others involved. The number of stages that must be included in the proposed work plan depends on the personal preferences of the designer as well as the size of the project.

The major project phases are: 1. analysis and planning, 2. designing, 3. documentation and bidding, 4. supervision and manufacturing specifications, 5. evaluation and maintenance instructions. For bigger projects, the first two phases can be broken up into two or more parts. Design proposals often have a preliminary stage and a final one. For signage design, the design phase should be split into two: the first part concentrates on the design of the signage system, leaving the visual aspect for the most part out of the proposals. The second part focuses on the design of the visual appearance of all elements of the signage system.

It is in the hands of the client to decide at what stage a designer will be selected. A lot of the analysis and data gathering can be done internally by the client. Also a lot of the production preparation of the designs can be carried out by the client. In any case, the nomination of a signage coordinator or a liaison person on behalf of the client is imperative. It will certainly enhance the quality of the project.

Sometimes the designer will only be asked to do the 'visual styling' of the signs while another practice will be asked to do all the other work. At first glance, it appears to be sensible to limit the involvement of the designer to what is often seen as the core of the business. There is a danger in this approach, though. It can easily lead to very superficial and unsatisfactory design solutions, more likely to contribute to the visual impact of the designer's own portfolio than to the comfort of the users of the signage. Design is not solely an exercise or experiment in visual style, it is also about the development of ideas for finding new and appropriate solutions within the boundaries of given constraints. This kind of design development can only be based on a profound understanding of the project in every aspect.

2.10.1. PHASE 1: PLANNING

The purpose of this phase is to create a 'human platform' for the whole project and to make all the necessary preparations for the first design phase. This phase consists of the following:

—initial meeting with the client about the outlines of the project, such as 'tone of voice', budget, scope, and time schedule

—establishing and signing a written signage design contract with the client

—nomination of the signage project manager, or client liaison, by the client
—nomination of other representatives of the client who will be involved in the project
—meeting(s) with the client's representatives, project coordinator, and project's architect about the functional aspects of the building and occupant
—incorporation of the topic 'signage' on the agenda of the regular building meetings (preview of meetings with architects and other key people for the signage project might be advisable at certain stages)
—gathering of data about the type of users and code, or legal requirements
—gathering of data about security and corporate identity requirements
—making the report about findings and vision on scope of the project
—review meeting with the client.

2.10.2. PHASE 2: DESIGN OF THE SIGNAGE SYSTEM

The purpose of the second phase is to design a system of individual signs that will fulfil all the navigational and instructional needs of the project. This phase will result in providing all data and requirements for the design of the visual aspects of all the signs. This phase consists of the following:
—making special site and floor plans
—marking major traffic flows on the plans
—making the first imaginary, and later real walks (if possible) through the building and the site, and visiting all the areas
—marking the four basic sign types on plans, emphasising the wayfinding aspect
—making a card system and/or a database on the computer for the preliminary messages that will appear on each sign
—starting to make the list of sign types
—reviewing the list and plans with the help of the library of sign types
—reviewing existing numbering systems
—developing a coding system for all signage
—finalising the plans and indicating global locations of all signs
—finalising the list of sign types
—refining the budget and time schedules
—review and approval by the client.

2.10.3. PHASE 3: VISUAL DESIGN

The visual design phase consists of the following:
—making the typeface chart, including the standard sizes to be used
—making the chart of all other graphic elements, like symbols, pictograms, or illustrations
—making the basic materials chart (if applicable)
—making the colour chart

—making the standardised panel sizes chart, including standard layouts
—making the elevation placement chart
—making a design for each individual sign type in elevation drawings, 3D models, and/or real-size mockups
—review and approval by the client.

2.10.4. PHASE 4: DOCUMENTATION AND BIDDING

The documentation and bidding phase consists of the following:
—setting the general conditions and regulations related to the production work
—making a working drawing for each sign type
—making a quantity list of each sign type
—making the specifications for all materials, construction details, fasteners, type of finishings and colours
—making the complete and final text files corresponding to each sign type
—making all artwork
—review and approval by the client
—assisting the client in manufacturer selection and bidding process.

2.10.5. PHASE 5: SUPERVISION

The supervision phase consists of the following:
—making detailed signage location plans
—making detailed signage placement elevation drawings
—ordering and checking samples and prototypes
—checking, together with the manufacturer, all signs on site upon completion
—making the completion report for the client's perusal
—checking, together with the manufacturer, the second stage (or further) completion.

2.10.6. PHASE 6: EVALUATION AND MANUAL

This phase consists of the following:
—evaluating the signage about two months after completion
—producing the documentation necessary for producing future alterations or additions
—making the signage manual for the production of updates.

See also Appendix I: Diagram signage program summary.

3. Designing the signage system

3.1. Introduction

Signage design is in most cases the type of design job where the visual design is a relatively small part of the whole commission. Graphic designers are regularly involved in signage jobs, but are generally not used to dealing with such extensive phases of planning and 'content making', which are preliminary to the visual design part. Also the extensive work to prepare for production and the maintenance after initial installation is unusual in the practice of most graphic designers. Graphic design is the exception, because in most other design fields related to the built environment, like industrial design and architecture, designers are more used to dealing with extensive phases of research and production.

The design of an extensive signage commission has two major parts. First, the design of the signage system and second the design of the visual appearance of each sign (or provision). The completion of the first phase is indispensable before any useful work can start on the second phase. The design of the signage system is preliminary, because it creates a list of important requirements for the visual design.
Ultimately, the signage design phase has to provide the answers to all the questions about the signage project, which are needed for the final execution, such as:
—How many and what type of signs (or provisions) do we need to do the job?
—Where should these signs be placed approximately?
—What should each sign say and how would that information be best conveyed?
Clearly, these questions have to be answered in relation to each other. The type of sign selected will indicate its content, and the sign location will be an indication for the type of sign to be used. All items in a signage project are more or less related to each other. That's why this first phase is called the 'designing of a signage system'.

The three questions above seem to be simple to answer. However, there are quite a few different considerations to be taken into account before complete, adequate and consistent answers can be provided. Not only the target audience is important, but also the type of building site, as well as the signage technologies that will be chosen for the project, and even the signage methodology that will be applied. These aspects and more will be discussed in detail in this chapter. There is not a precise chronological order in which the different considerations become important in corresponding design stages. A number of decisions on some aspects of the signage design will also have influence on other aspects. In the end, a concept that will function as one coherent system of individual signs and provisions has to be developed.

There is no hierarchy in the various considerations while making the signage design. But, there is a set order in the way we structure the execution of the system design. The standard way to collect and organise the answers to the basic questions in the signage project are as follows:
—A list of sign types to be used in the project
—A set of plans of the site with approximate locations of each sign marked.
—A database or text list with all the messages on each sign.
These lists will be filled in and updated gradually, first concentrating on the major wayfinding aspects, and then afterwards getting into the more detailed aspects.

An overview is given below of the various aspects of the signage design phase. It can also be used, in moderation, as a hierarchical list.

3.1.1. DESIGN OBJECTIVE

The purpose of the signage system design is to create the best possible navigational capabilities for the site, to provide all the mandatory and complementary instructions for safety and security purposes, and to create opportunities to convey PR, branding or general information about the building and/or its occupants.

3.1.2. CONSIDERATIONS

There are various types of considerations that influence the final design.
—The previous design stages of spatial and architectural design have a huge impact on the navigational qualities of the site.
—The signage methodology divides the design objective into separate aspects that have to be addressed.
—The signage technology provides an overview of the various technologies that can be applied in the signage system.
—Positioning the signs in space gives an overview of the design aspects related to the positioning of the signs.
—Stating the message and conveying the information deals with the establishment of the final information on the signs and the way it can be conveyed.

3.1.3. DESIGN EXECUTION AIDS

The design is best made using the following type of documents:
—Signage plans showing traffic flows and approximate locations of the various sign types
—A database containing all information that appears on each sign, per sign type. Sometimes separate text lists will be useful for specific sign types
—A list of sign types, giving the overview of all different types of signs that will be used in the project.

3.1.4. HELPFUL INFORMATION

—Type of building(s).
—Imaginary walk through a building site.
—Library of sign types.

3.2. Spatial planning and architectural design

3.2.1. INTRODUCTION

The most important navigational qualities of a site are created in the first design phases, long before one starts to think about signage. Urban planners/designers, architects, landscape architects, governmental bodies and investors make the most important signage decisions way before a signage designer is invited to the scene. An extremely unwise practice, but still a reality.

The phases preliminary to a comprehensive signage design phase should at least include a short 'signage audit' or 'signage check-up' before final approval of the architectural designs. No matter who is asked to do the task of making a report on the navigational qualities of a site; it has to be done. If the first signage concerns are only initiated after the contractors are already commissioned and under way with their work, then that is way too late.

As said already, a spatial or architectural design can never be self-explanatory up to the detailed level required for effective wayfinding. Moreover, the signage designer cannot improve or repair what is complicated or obscure in the spatial planning or the architectural design. Just don't even try. A signage designer is only capable of reinforcing architectural and spatial information and making it more explicit. Forget about the rest. Those are dreams that will never come true. The only realistic option to repair bad navigational qualities of a site is partial demolition and rebuilding.

This publication emphasises the signage design part of wayfinding (navigation), instruction and information. All other wayfinding matters related to the spatial and architectural design will only be relatively briefly discussed here, although they do deserve full attention in the design process. There are existing publications that deal with these matters more extensively.

3.2.2. URBAN PLANNING

Urban planning and design is a business involving many different parties, who mostly have huge interests invested in a project. This makes it an extremely difficult business, prone to failure. To reduce the risk of failure, governments should have influence in the matter by means of legislation and active participation in the planning. Urban design cannot be left to the 'invisible hand' of the free market place to find its final shape. A proof of this argument is not difficult to find. Just visit the many cities on this globe that were left entirely to private builders and investors. These cities are all, without exception, a pitiful mess. When everybody is allowed to build their own private dream without the guidance of a bigger and mutual scheme, the result will inevitably be a nightmare for everyone.

The state of affairs in the more organised societies is better, but not much. Some professionals in the field even believe that the level of urban and environmental planning that was reached during the middle of the previous century will never return. For instance, Tokyo, or worse, Mexico City, are more likely examples of the future of city planning, than the centre of Paris, Manhattan or Amsterdam. That development could hardly be seen as a sign of progress of human civilisation.

Travel speed and infrastructure are related. Pedestrians only need a 'human-scaled' environment. The faster we want to travel the more we need a big 'vehicle-scaled' environment. A satisfactory blend of the two types of infrastructure is realised practically nowhere.

Somewhere in the sixties all large scale, detailed urban and environmental planning came to a grinding halt in all western countries. There were various causes for this happening. City councils and governments became more decentralised in order to make management of the fast growing cities more efficient. The internationalisation of companies and the massive migration of people provided more influence for the free market on city planning. Urban planners and architects also had a few dramatic misconceptions about how and where people would want to be housed. As a result of these misconceptions, the comprehensive and compelling design philosophy of Modernism dramatically died, and has not been succeeded, so far, by another convincing design vision on that level. The major culprit in the current and rather sorry state of affairs is, without a doubt, the widespread private ownership of motorised vehicles. Though essential devices to encourage economic growth, vehicles have reduced the amount of 'human-scaled' spaces dramatically in favour of the 'machine scaled' ones. We still have not found a proper solution to deal with motorised traffic while claiming back the dominance of human-scaled environments. Machines still dominate—embarrassingly in literally every sense—the quality of our environment.

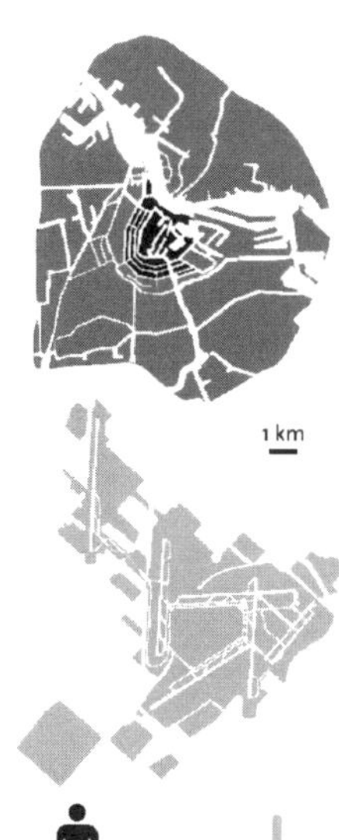

The city of Amsterdam and its nearby airport 'Schiphol'. The human-scaled old city centre took centuries to build, the vehicle-scaled part about 150 years, and the airport about 25 years.

To give one example: France is a country that attracts the most tourists every year. There are a lot of beautiful cities, towns and countryside to be seen there—so far. However, the quality of the environment is changing fast, and in the wrong direction, everywhere around the country. Many small towns in France all still have beautifully structured town centres. Nonetheless, it is getting more and more difficult to get to that beauty. An ever thickening peel of mind-boggling highways, mixed with gigantic supermarkets and depressing concrete housing blocks, is surrounding them. France is wrapping a lot of its beauty in disgusting ugliness. France is only one example of what is happening in most other places around the globe.

The current tourist industry is the ultimate example of the absurd level of modern mobility. Gigantic machine-scaled environments are created to allow millions to efficiently flock into ancient human-scaled environments, leaving the latter at times in an almost terminal state of exhaustion.

Urban planning is extremely important for the quality of our environment, far more important than the architectural quality of individual buildings. A beautifully designed street or area can't be ruined by some ugly, badly designed buildings. By contrast, exquisite architecture can never save or raise the quality of bad urban planning; its individual beauty and quality will simply evaporate when located in poorly designed environments.

The most satisfactory blend of the different infrastructures related to travel speed is by making a separate level for each. The pedestrian level best remains always on top. It can either be elevated from the rest, or the motorised level be put underground. The alternative of elevating the motorised level is much practiced, but often creates a grim environment. The film 'Blade Runner' portrays this method in its ultimate consequences. Airports are best put in an uninhabited area, like on a floating platform at sea.

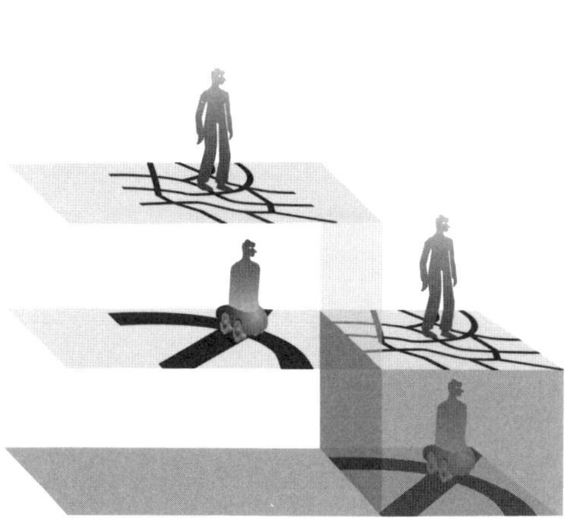

3.2.3. ARCHITECTURAL DESIGN

Both urban planners and architects, on different scales, allocate spaces to required functions and create a circulation system between these spaces. In both cases, this almost entirely establishes the navigational quality of their work. The work of the architect has one more ingredient, and that is creating a visual style. Increasingly, that part of the job has become the most important part of the architect's work. Architects, like all other designers, are more and more selected on the basis of the impact of the visual presentation of their work. Visual style has a tremendous influence on any decision-making process, not only on the selection of an architect. Most clients find it extremely difficult to reasonably weigh their personal aesthetic taste against all the other aspects of a design proposal.

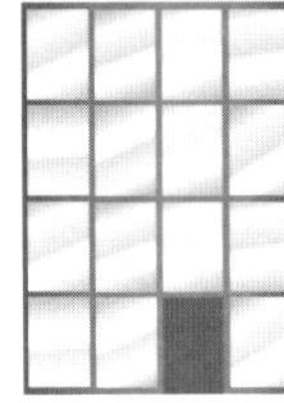

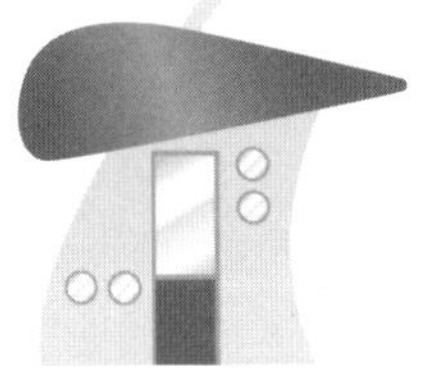

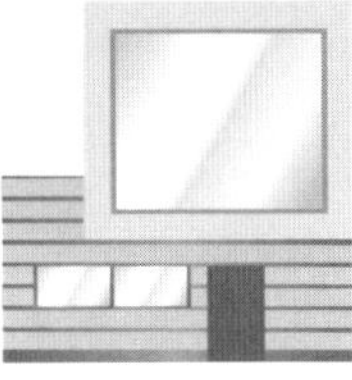

The visual appearance or style of buildings plays an ever-increasing role in the appreciation of architects' work.

Modern technologies have aggravated the situation even further. Books about architecture have become common coffee table literature. Architects are more and more selected on the representations of their designs in print rather than in reality. Visual presentation techniques to show architectural design proposals can be extremely impressive and persuasive nowadays. Other than what one might expect, these techniques do not stimulate the decision-making process to be more focused on the expected end result. On the contrary, visual presentation has become more a quality to its own end. The relation between the design presentation and the final outcome is not getting closer, but instead growing further apart. One can make a smashing visual presentation for an horrendous design proposal.

Creating visual style was always an important part of the architect's work. Times have changed though; there is a distinction now between the former design credo of 'form follows function' and the current one of 'form follows marketing appeal'.

The emphasis in architectural design on creating remarkable visual appearance or style of individual buildings can be useful in creating landmarks within the environment. Wayfinding needs landmarks. Creating an overall visual style for a whole neighbourhood or district is also a very helpful navigational quality. A quality that can only be achieved by designing buildings in consideration of the context of their environment. More and more buildings appear around us that seem to have no relation whatsoever to the environment they are supposed to be part of. These constructions are like aliens, dropped and parachuted from outer space to their final destination and making any sense of a place a total impossibility.

3.2.4. THE 'NON VERBAL' WAYFINDING PROCESS

Urban planning, landscaping and architectural design provide the essential 'non verbal' information in the wayfinding process. The design 'vocabulary' used—if translated into verbal instructions—is pretty limited, but that does not make the message less important. Environments can be designed in an easy and comprehensible way, because they 'speak' a simple and clear language, or they can be extremely confusing or even 'mute'. Though these metaphors generally refer to our aural sense—which is certainly not the most important communication channel in spatial design—purely visual means remain by far the most important way to convey information.

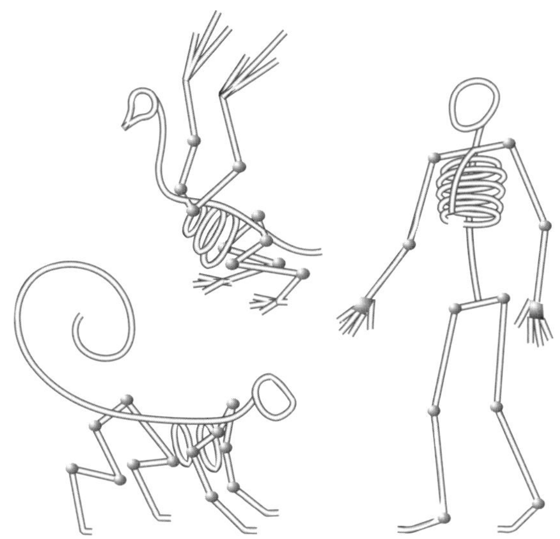

Nature is sometimes used as a model for creating a logical skeleton structure for spatial design.

What are the basic kinds of non verbal information that we need to find our way around, and that we must therefore be able to extract from our environment? We need two basic kinds of information. First, we need to be able to create some sort of 'mental map' in our head about the environment we are in. A mental map is a rudimentary image, somewhat comparable to a real map, containing the structure of roads, the position of areas and the position of landmarks in relation to each other. Second, we need feed-back on our mental map during our trip. We need visual clues or reference points in the environment to guide us in the right direction. These are the two basic ingredients we need as non verbal information to get to where we want to be. The key aspect by which to judge the wayfinding quality of an environment is the ease with which we can make our own mental map. Put in contemporary jargon, the level of intuitive wayfinding determines the quality of our environment.

All wayfinding is based on a hierarchical method of searching. First we get to major destinations and consecutively move on to smaller ones, inevitably ending in front of one single door. First we go to a city, then to a city district, then to a neighbourhood, then to a street and finally to a house number. Translated into more real-life instructions like: 'take road number Y10 to city X, take the belt road to district Z, take a right at the big church, you're on street Q, take the left street at the third traffic light, you're in a street with trees on both sides, take another right at the first corner and look for number 567 on your right hand side'.

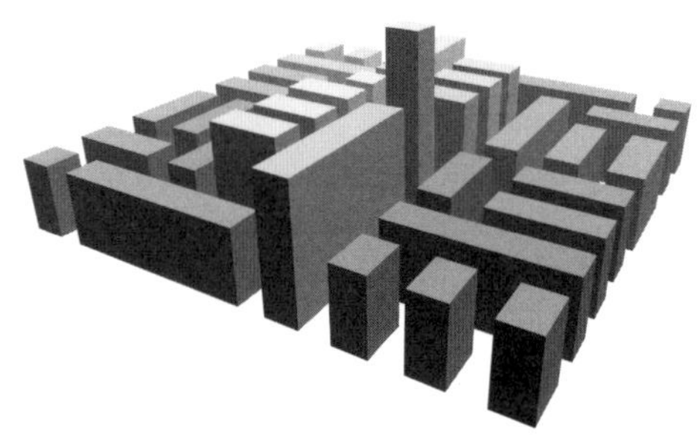

Strict uniformity is the basic requirement for designing labyrinths. A few changes in such a design will inevitably create visual hierarchy, an essential ingredient for good spatial design.

3.2.4.1. A labyrinth or maze

What are the rules for creating good navigational qualities in urban and architectural design? There are no strict rules other than a rather global one, which is that a spatial structure must be easy to explain to anyone and must have an 'intuitive' circulation system. It is easier to give an example of the opposite of an ideal situation. A labyrinth or a maze is designed to disorient a person. The ingredients for constructing a labyrinth are to design a path structure with no hierarchy or simple pattern, also with no 'clues' (like landmarks) in the environment. All possible positions in a labyrinth look more or less the same. Everything must look identical in a labyrinth so that a mental map cannot be formed.

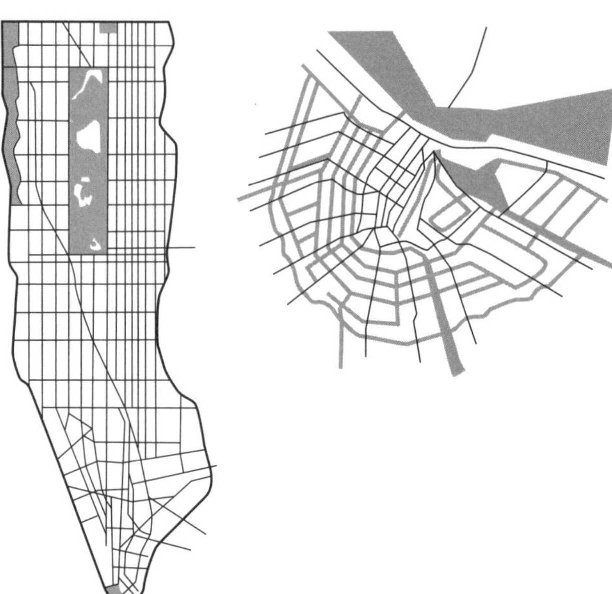

The urban structures of Manhattan and Amsterdam are examples of good city planning. Such recent large-scale good examples are hard to find.

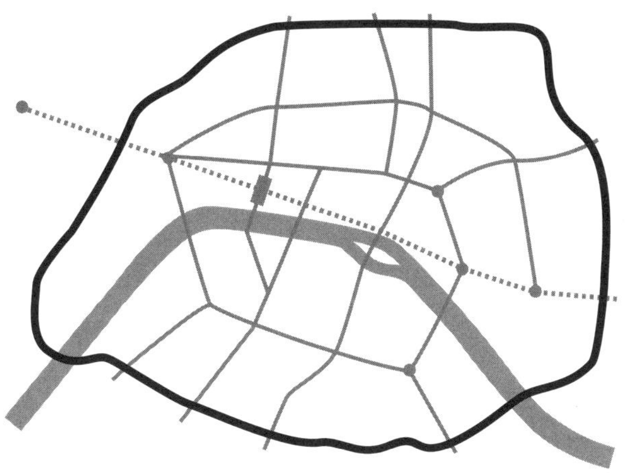

The belt road or ring road and the linking radial roads of Paris are an example of a much-used combination. A river through a city always helps orientation, as do axis roads, like the very long one in Paris from 'La Defense' to 'Le Palais Royal'.

3.2.4.2. The circulation pattern

The structure or 'pattern' of roads (or corridors) can be made almost randomly or in an easily recognisable way. A tree structure may seem complex but it is a simple principle. A strictly grid structure (like Manhattan) is the opposite extreme for creating a simple structure. The centre of Amsterdam has a concentric circulation structure that is easy to understand. Paris has straight axis roads, like the Champs Elysées. Many large cities nowadays have belt roads in combination with a structure of radial roads. All are examples of clear structures that are easy to comprehend.

3.2.4.3. Hierarchy and landmarks

Many cities have a river running through them. Often the river divides the city into two clear sections. The 'river' can also be a special road like Broadway in Manhattan. Other structural elements are parks, squares, special buildings, bridges or other eye-catching (art) structures. Neighbourhoods with a special architectural style or atmosphere also surely help to create a 'sense of place'. One has to be able to create a simple mental map of the location of large elements.

A sequence of traditional transition points from the outside to the inside of a building: a main gate as entrance marker of the terrain, then a canopy as transition to the entrance of the building, then an entrance hall that gradually leads to the smaller spaces inside the building.

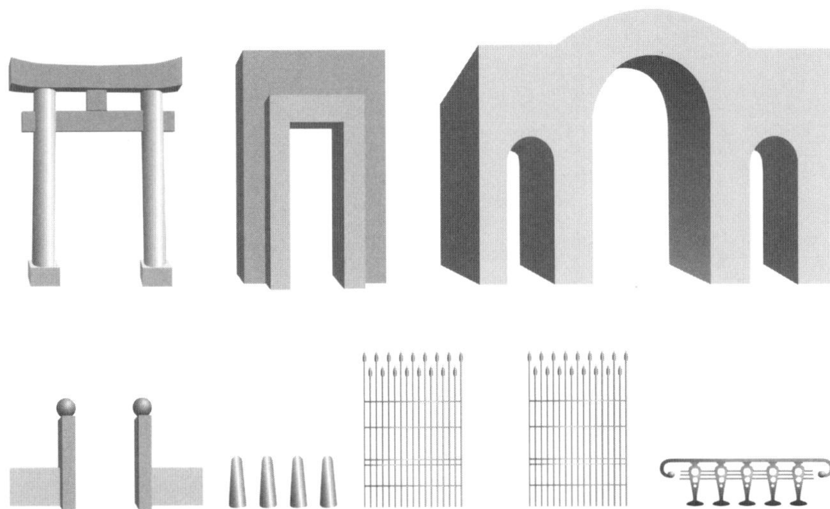

Samples of the wide variety of transition point markers, such as arches, gates, and railings.

3.2.4.4. Distribution nodes and transition points

Organising motorised traffic often needs complex distribution facilities. Intersections, seen from the driver's point of view, are often no longer perceivable as part of a larger structure. A mental map cannot be made; one simply has to follow the signs. Keeping distribution nodes as simple as possible surely helps the ease of navigation. The same can be said for clear transition points. Transition points are the spots where one goes from one area into another. Gates or arches traditionally had this function. Old cities, large estates, and Buddhist temples all have gates. In eastern countries, certain entrances to a city are still marked with gates. Moreover, there is a revival of their use on a small scale in modern architecture. Clearly marked transitions from one area to another are valuable guides for orientation.

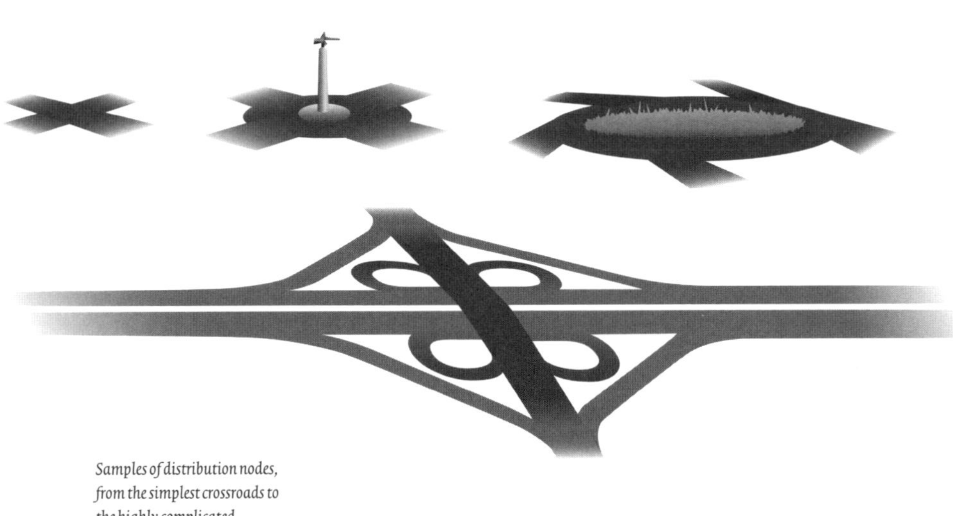

Samples of distribution nodes, from the simplest crossroads to the highly complicated cloverleaf intersection.

3.3. Signage methodology

The basic methodology for creating a signage system is not complicated. It follows in principle the same method as that applied to the navigational aspects of spatial and architectural design. However, signage instructions are far more specific and detailed. The range of different, yet related, items in a signage project can make the job exceedingly complex, but not the underlying method. Many different data have to be incorporated on many different signs. Individual signs are hardly ever identical; every sign is more or less different from the others and all need individual specification to produce and to install. The application of many different types of signage technology within one signage system may complicate matters even further.

There is a work hierarchy in addressing the various aspects of a signage project. All signage design projects will start by covering the wayfinding needs of the site, followed by covering the needs for mandatory safety and security instructions in addition to other kinds of information.

3.3.1. BASIC SIGNAGE FUNCTIONS

The basic function of every element in a signage system is pretty simple. First, information must be provided to enable orientation and preparation of a 'travel plan'. Second, facilities must be provided to guide along the way. Third, the final destination must be clearly marked. And finally, instructions must be given to make the journey as easy (and perhaps as entertaining) and as safe as possible. These are all the basic aids we can provide to assist people to get comfortably from A to B.

Wayfinding is by far the most important, but not the only purpose for a signage system. The other goals are providing mandatory and general information about the occupant or the building, creating aids for internal communication and creating items that can be best considered as PR or branding tools.

3.3.2. A HIERARCHICAL SYSTEM OF DESTINATIONS

All navigation is about finding specific destinations. Therefore, all relevant destinations have to be given a unique identity. That identity also has to fit into an overall system that is easy to understand. Individual destinations must be able to be grouped together. Efficient navigation requires the possibility of creating clusters of destinations. To get where we want to go, we need a simple hierarchy of steps from large and general destinations to smaller and more detailed ones. There are various ways to set up a system of destinations, which will be further discussed in section 3.11.

There are two types of destinations. First, parts of the architectural structure and certain facilities within it must be named as destinations. Second, names of parts of the occupant's organisa-

tion will be used as destinations. That part is often a bit problematic. Organisational structures tend to be complex. Names of departments are likely to be rather long. Signage requires simple and short names because long text on signs will simply remain unread. A translation of the 'official' names to a more concise version is a must to make these useful for signage.
Once the inventory of all possible destinations has been clearly defined, then guides will be created in order to efficiently lead users to their final destination.

3.3.3. CONSISTENCY AND REPETITION IN DIRECTIONAL INFORMATION

When people travel and use signs, they are often not absolutely certain that they have understood the signage completely or are afraid that they might have missed one sign. Never underestimate the many different ways signs might be understood. Consistency of names or other indications of destinations is essential to make the system work. Also travellers need regular reconfirmation of still being on the right track. Repetition of signs at regular intervals is important and conformity is vital. A signage system creates expectations about how and how often one will be informed along the way. The manner in which this is done must also be uniform throughout the whole project.

3.3.4. SURPLUS INFORMATION

Surplus information in a signage system is very helpful in countering the general feeling of uncertainty and the various ways people tend to interpret signs. Two clues are simply better than one for reassurance that one is on the right track. For example, a code for a room that includes not only the room number but also an indication of the floor level and the section of the building where the room is located, is better than one without these extra clues. Colour coding is helpful, but only as surplus information. Making illustrations next to names can aid in remembering destinations.

3.3.5. CRITERIA FOR SYSTEM EVALUATION

There are six detailed steps that are generally used to describe the various aspects of information processing of signs during navigation. These steps may also be used as criteria for evaluating the signage system.
—The signs have to be detectable and clearly visible within their surroundings.
—The content should be legible, or otherwise accessible.
—The content should be comprehensible.
—The content should be be consistent with the information already provided.
—The signs should ease the travel decision process.
—The information provided on the signs should be as easy to execute as possible.

3.4. Signage technology

Since ancient times, signage has always been present in the form of more or less constant physical marks in the environment. That basic signage method may change in the future. Technological developments have created alternative solutions to wayfinding with the help of virtual 'signs'. Potentially, signage could be done in the future with entirely different means than the ones in use today. High-tech signage solutions could reduce the number of signs dramatically to almost none. The different production methods by which signs can be manufactured are extremely wide—signage has been around at all periods in history. These various possibilities will be discussed more extensively in the design chapter. The principles of signage technology that focus on updating information are discussed here because of their integral role in the design process of a signage system.

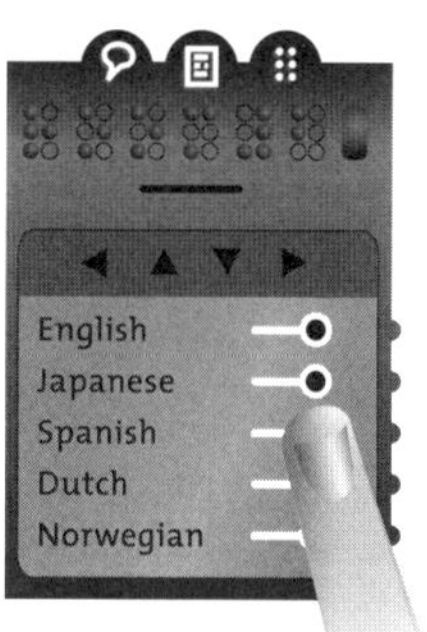

Four 'generations' in the development of signage technology: The first generation uses mechanical means to update signs, the second electronic grid boards or screens. The third generation of signs has become interactive; one can communicate with the sign through a touch-screen to retrieve relevant information. The latest generation no longer needs steady signage; a personal navigation guide will provide all information in a personalised way.

Most signage information will still be put on sign panels. The way these panels are designed and manufactured has been—and will remain as long as sign panels are around—the subject of constant innovation. Apart from the inevitable variations in visual style, most of the innovation for sign panel systems has been focused on the changeability of an individual sign. Effective signs have to be fully adapted to the infrastructure of an organisation at any given moment. That infrastructure is always a dynamic one and getting more and more so all the time. Office tenants, staff, and visitors tend to migrate almost constantly these days. So signs must be as easy to update as possible in order to accurately convey, at all times, the latest organisational changes (ie. staff, functions, locations, names of departments, etc). All information on signs must be actual and relevant information, or it should simply be removed. It is better to give no information than false information.

'Updatability' is—and has been for a while—the buzzword for many technological developments in signage. Updates must be carried out in a simple and fast way, preferably in-house. The digital revolution has generated ever more products that ease updating of individual signs, and that can become part of complete electronic networks.

Moreover, the 'digitisation' of our lives is continuously changing the way we communicate with each other, and hence the way we convey information (on signage). Powerful devices that will change signage systems dramatically are already on the market, and will undoubtedly be further developed. Individual signs will no longer carry only static information, but also dynamic information, which will be available in various media, in visual, audible or tactile forms. Signs will no longer be autonomous and static, but might contain information that can be retrieved through personal interaction with the signs. 'Intelligent' signs will change information automatically to suit particular circumstances, such as the type of audience or the conditions in the environment.

The most drastic change will be when the 'personal electronic travel guide' becomes widely available. Such devices will effectively make all individual signs obsolete. We will be obliged to carry our personal guide with us at all times.
It will be a guide that speaks our language, knows our physical condition, is familiar with any surrounding, and that will lead us along the way, safely and efficiently. In other words, it will be our ideal travel companion.

For the time being, signage systems still consist of a mixture of traditional and technologically advanced devices.

3.4.1. PHYSICAL CHANGEABILITY

The most straightforward method for changing a sign is either to remove it completely, or to replace the whole or a part of the sign with something new.

3.4.1.1. Mechanical alteration

Signs can be produced with parts that change position, revealing one message while hiding another one. 'Free/occupied' or 'open/closed' signs are traditionally made that way.

3.4.1.2. Inserts

Technical solutions to update individual signs were invented to make signs partially changeable using inserts. The parts of the sign that need to be updated were put on easily produced inserts that could be replaced by new ones, leaving the rest untouched.

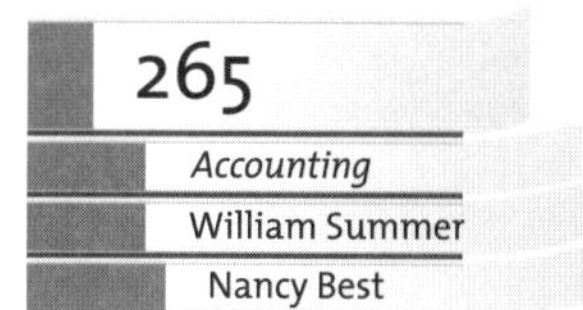

3.4.1.3. Modular components

Later, systems were developed by which the entire sign was assembled out of standard components. A lot of these so-called modular sign systems are still around on the market. Updating an individual sign was limited to producing only one new component. In some cases no new parts had to be produced. Certain parts of relevant signs could simply change position to convey the updated information.
Owing to the nature of their production method, modular sign systems also helped in creating a 'family look' for all the different signs within a system.

3.4.1.4. Magnetic components

Thick magnetic foil cut into panels, strips or even loose letters are also used to assemble signs. This type of sign needs a metal base and a transparent cover for protection against unauthorised modifications.

3.4.1.5. Loose letter systems

An offshoot was the development of sign systems where individual letters could be used to compose messages on a specially designed board that could hold the loose letters in their place. This type of system has disappeared except in its smaller versions; it is mostly used for price tags placed next to products in shop windows.

3.4.1.6. Laserprint cassette systems

Further technological developments made it possible to produce quality type on every desktop. It provided the possibility of separating the production of the message from the production of the rest of the sign. This resulted in a modular system of cassettes that can hold laser printed messages on paper or film of various sizes.

3.4.1.7. Electronic paper

The most extreme version in the category of in-house printing is still under development. It is a system by which the sign panels themselves can be changed electronically without the need for an electrical current to sustain the message on the panel. This development is known as the creation of 'electronic paper'. The arrival on the market of this product is often announced, but just as often postponed, or offered in a modified version.

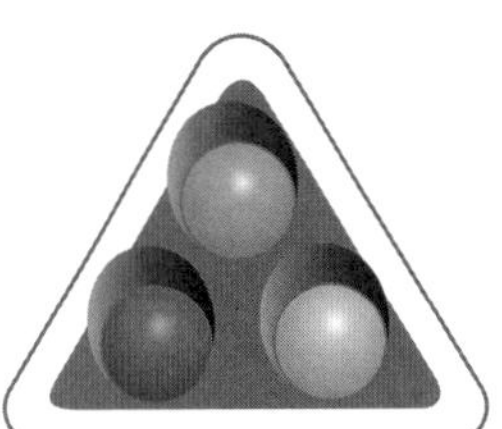

3.4.2. ELECTRICAL CHANGEABLE SIGN PANELS

Numerous sign panel products or electronic message boards are on the market where messages can be changed with the help of electrical power.

3.4.2.1. Traffic lights

Standard traffic lights are the example of an omnipresent type of sign that provides simple and straightforward changeable information.

3.4.2.2. Neon signs

Neon signs are another wide category of sign types that can change their message or show a dynamic 'moving' one. Most neon signs are used for advertising purposes.

3.4.2.3. Split-flap message boards

The earliest electric products that were used to update complex lists of information were panels with text on thin metal blades that could flip over each other, thus the name: split-flap message boards. Originally, directory boards at transit terminals, like airports and train stations, employed this type of technology.

3.4.2.4. Projection

Slides or video projectors can be installed to illuminate translucent screens from the back, or to project directly on the wall.

3.4.2.5. Laser beams

Laser beam projection can be used for advertising and signage purposes. Laser light is extremely strong and projects over very large distances.

3.4.2.6. Grid boards

Changeability of messages is dramatically enhanced by composing letters out of units on a grid pattern. Complete messages can be composed and modified using one changeable grid board. The grid size of the units is the practical limit for its use in signage.

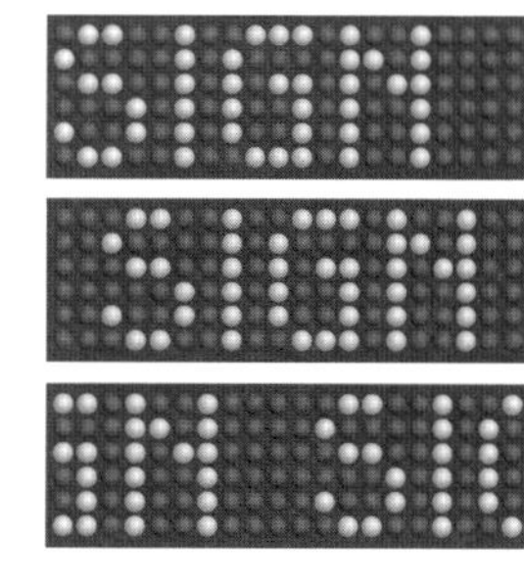

Letters in the Latin script (upper and lowercase) need to be at least 8 units high to be constructed as legible letterforms—whereas Chinese characters would need more units. Therefore, the type size is limited by the coarseness of the grid. The efficiency of changing the pattern of the grid sets the limits for the dynamic use of messages.

The grid could be made of small light bulbs. By switching some off and some on, letters can be formed. The first electronic switch boards could make text 'move' on a board by rapid light switches. It produced endless lines of literally 'running text'. News headlines could be displayed directly in public places. One of the first so-called 'light journals' was placed on Times Square in New York and was a sensation in its time. The first electronic light boards were made out of traditional light bulbs.

3.4.2.7. LED display boards

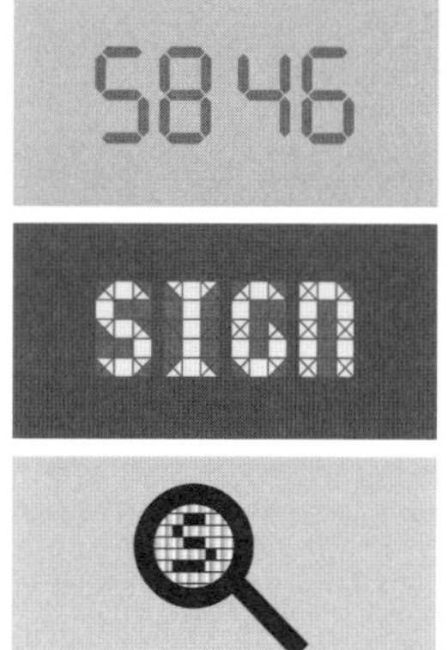

Further development in electronics created miniaturised low energy light sources like light emitting diodes (LED). These devices are still in use for medium to small grid-based text panels, in red or yellow coloured lights on a dark background. Recent developments in LED technology have dramatically widened its application range to include large billboards and traffic lights.

3.4.2.8. Liquid Crystal Display (LCD)

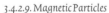

Crystal can change opacity under the influence of small changes in electrical current. The first LCD screens could produce dark letters on a light grey background using a simple grid pattern. The technology has dramatically advanced since. Nowadays there are many LCD applications on the market. For instance, all laptop computers use the LCD technology for their displays.

3.4.2.9. Magnetic Particles

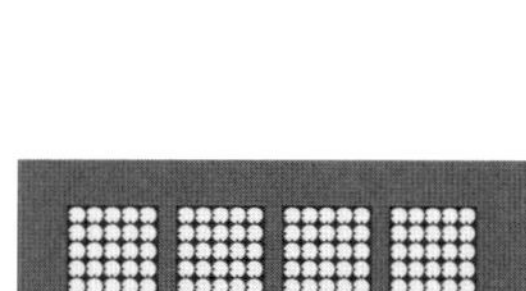

Sign panels are produced for billboards and public transportation using disc-shaped particles, with a dark and a light side, that can change position.

3.4.2.10. Optical Fibre Display

Optical fibre can conduct light without losing much of its intensity. Only one light source is needed to create many light spots at the end of each fibre. A shutter system can cover or expose each fibre individually. The technique is much applied in the automotive industry, to light up instruments in cars. There are also such applications for signage.

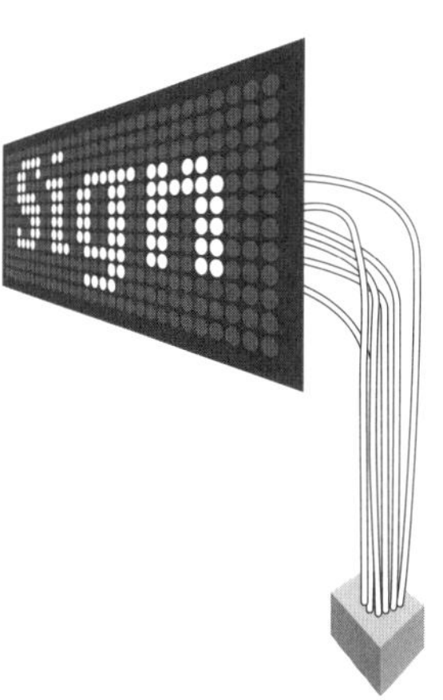

3.4.3. TV OR COMPUTER SCREENS

TV or computer screens are also used for signage purposes. Application of this technology is likely to expand still further. The possibilities for these devices are in principle unlimited. Computer screens have the potential for showing all graphic signs in all sizes. The 'grid size' or resolution of the image is high enough for all possible signage applications. The application of colour and dynamics is numerous and open-ended.

3.4.3.1. Interactive screens

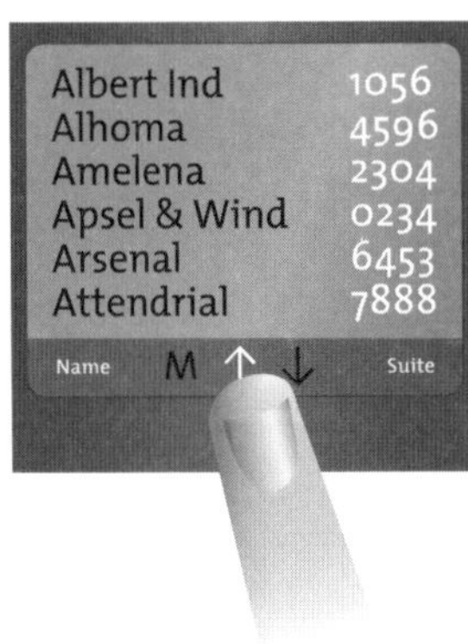

Computer screens have also created a complete new type of signage aid. Signs are made interactive by providing touch screens, thus creating a completely new category of signs. Users can 'communicate' with one sign the way they do with a computer. This means that not all useful information has to be displayed completely on one screen panel, as is the case with all other signs. The users can interact with the screen panel to extract the information that is relevant to them. Interactive signs can provide access to a complete built-in database of information. Directories in large office buildings often make use of this technology. A lot of information can be put into a relatively small device.
Applying computer technology to one sign makes its possibilities—as previously mentioned—in principle limitless. Individual signs can contain huge amounts of information, including fully-fledged software to manipulate the information. The information is stored inside the sign in a digital format. That implies that there are no longer constraints in size of content or forms of output. The sign can show visible and/or audible information in as many languages as needed.

3.4.3.2. Types of screens

Computer (TV) screens are in the process of changing from the original and rather bulky glass CRT (Cathode Ray Tube) screen into flatter, bigger and lighter screens. Plasma displays make bigger and flatter screens possible. LCD screens can be far lighter and need less energy. Further development is likely to bring even thinner screens that use even less energy.

3.4.3.3. Screen networks

The latest development in computer screen signs is using screens with different functions connected to one single network. A directory is linked to directional signs as well as to door/destination signs. An update of the information can then be applied to all signs within the network at the same time. Planning software for scheduling meetings can be directly applied to a signage system. The scheduled meetings will appear on all relevant signs at the planned date. Networks are useful for conference centres and highly frequented conference rooms.

Further technological development will without a doubt result in wireless connected screen networks. The internet is likely to get a more central position in networks.

3.4.4. AUTOMATED SIGNS

Devices can have built-in technology that reacts to various circumstances. A light bulb doesn't have to be switched on by hand alone anymore. Built-in sensors or detectors can activate the switch. Sensors can be made sensitive to all kinds of stimuli. A movement sensor can switch on the light bulb when something moves in its vicinity. A light sensor can do the same when the surroundings get dark.

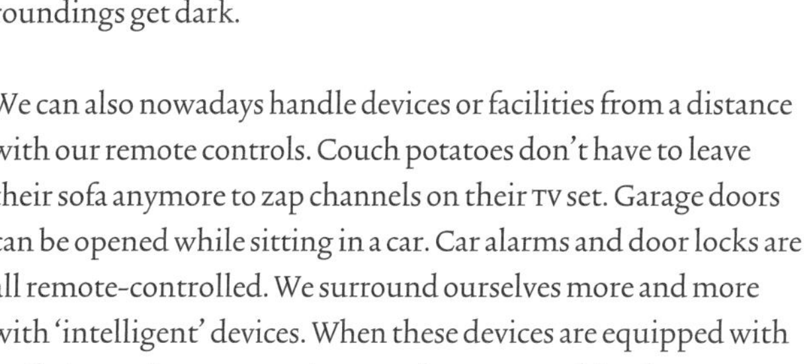

We can also nowadays handle devices or facilities from a distance with our remote controls. Couch potatoes don't have to leave their sofa anymore to zap channels on their TV set. Garage doors can be opened while sitting in a car. Car alarms and door locks are all remote-controlled. We surround ourselves more and more with 'intelligent' devices. When these devices are equipped with built-in receivers, transmitters and a memory chip, then we can communicate with them.
Some of the above technology can also be applied to signs or guiding systems.

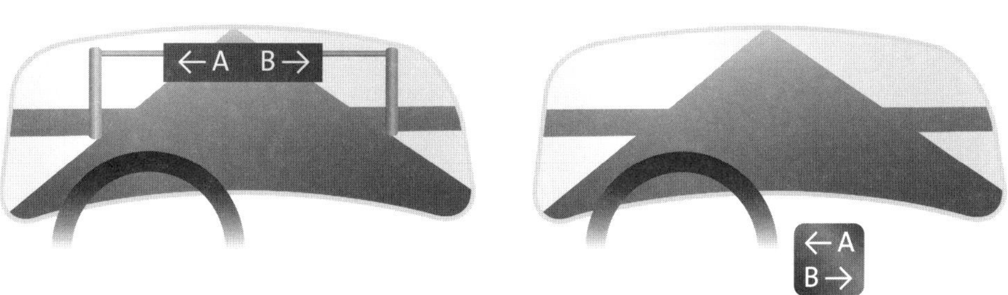

3.4.5. PERSONAL NAVIGATION SYSTEMS

The wayfinding aspect of signage might take a dramatic turn with the general introduction of personal navigation systems. All signs put up on a site might become entirely obsolete, or at least redundant, when these systems are widely implemented.

Today, many navigation devices make use of GPS (Global Positioning System) technology. GPS allows for navigating accurately in signless environments, like at sea or in the air. Soon, navigation screens will be standard equipment in all cars. Road signs may become obsolete.

A Global Positioning System (GPS) was originally developed for military purposes to obtain exact positioning data for aircraft and ships. The system has been introduced for use in vehicles, for cyclists or pedestrians. GPS will become standard equipment in cars. Soon it will be available for everybody carrying a mobile phone. More and more people carry a mobile phone on them all the time and/or a personal organiser. These two pieces of equipment will become integrated into one single device. Information can be sent wirelessly and displayed on personal screens. There are many alternative options; signs on highways can be replaced by small senders that will project the image of the sign message on a screen inside the car. Physical signs are no longer needed in such a system. Updating signs will become very simple and thus could become very dynamic. Hand-held wireless navigational systems can direct people to their destination without the need to place any physical signs in the environment.

3.4.6. TELECOMMUNICATION SYSTEMS

Personal navigation does not have to be based on the GPS system alone. There are various ways around today to obtain and convey information or instruction. Most organisations already use various media to convey information about themselves, including wayfinding information. More extensive possibilities for conveying accessibility instructions will only grow over time. Telecommunication plays the key role in these developments. It is unclear at this stage which kind of technology will prevail and be used specifically for signage.

3.4.6.1. The internet

A stand-alone kiosk, an integrated console or a mobile hand-held device can easily make a connection to an internet site. These sites can have special pages for signage purposes. A building directory, for instance, can be almost the same on the internet site as it appears on a kiosk in a building. Maybe it will be easier to update an internet site (or Intranet site) than other computer-based signage systems in the building. Using this technology for signage is still in its infancy.

A combination of state-of-the-art telecommunication and computer technology can turn kiosks into complete information centres. It can consist of a video camera, a touch screen, a microphone, a loudspeaker, a printer and a mobile handset.

3.4.6.2. Wireless technologies, I-mode, Wi-fi, Bluetooth

The internet has created the possibility of making public —worldwide—practically everything that can be produced by anyone owning a computer. Worldwide dissemination of any type of content no longer has barriers. The limitation is the amount of data that can be transferred from one computer (the server of the information provider) to the computer of the receiver within a reasonable time. Put in technical terms, this limitation is determined by the available bandwidth (or speed) of the connection.

The efficiency of connections has improved dramatically. Telecommunication changed totally when switching from analogue to digital data transport. Analogue connections did have a rather generous nature. A connection once 'opened' is occupied entirely, but effectively used to exchange information only for a fraction of its capacity. Like making a phone call; even if you don't exchange any useful information with the one you're talking to—because you need to think about what is said—you still use the line and have to pay for it. The content of a complete telephone conversation can be compressed and electronically exchanged in fractions of a second. Only computers can 'talk' to each other at this incredible speed. We cannot; we need far more time to exchange information when in direct contact. A direct and active link with a human in a computer-based network is a disaster for the speed of the whole system. It is also quite inappropriate for linking the most suitable parts in a chain. Humans are still completely different animals from computers.

Technological development attempts to find ways around the inefficient way humans communicate. Most mobile phones can already exchange short messages and receive text. The cost of this type of transmission is only a fraction of the cost of an oral transmission. A whole new language of abbreviations was created to avoid the composition of lengthy words, when using the limited amount of keys on a phone. Ultimately, phone costs that are traditionally calculated according to time and distance will be replaced by a calculation of costs based on the amount of bytes

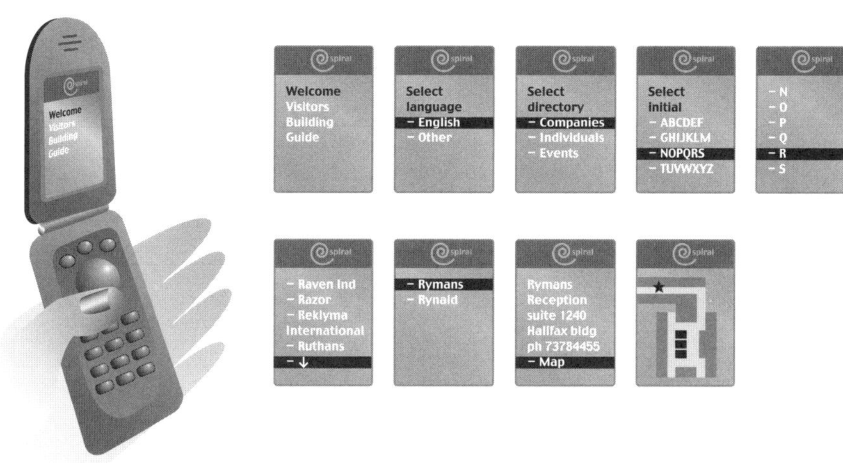

I-mode are simple and low cost telecom connections. With the help of easy-to-use menus, I-mode sites provide all information normally found on signs in reception areas. Information updates can be made instantaneously.

exchanged.Other ways of exchanging information are already on the market and will certainly be further developed in the future. More efficient systems will be based on the principle that the human participation in the process is limited to making simple choices from menus put on offer. The connection will be used exclusively to exchange this kind of multiple-choice information. This method will dramatically reduce both connection time and costs for the user. The result will be that connection costs will lose importance to the user of certain personal mobile telecommunication devices. It will be like having a miniature public telephone directory on you all the time that contains a lot of easily accessible information. At the time of the writing of this book, I-mode, Wi-fi and Bluetooth are all names for network technologies that will make equipment, mobile phones, or computers less dependent on wired proprietary networks. General use of wireless networks will—again—change the way we work and live.

The design process described in this book will address the need for signage with the assumption that personal navigation systems have not completely taken over the role of traditional signage.

3.5. Positioning the signs

The effectiveness of individual signs depends in large part on where these signs are placed in the environment. Signs have to be easily detectable in order to function properly. The appropriate spot to position each sign has to be carefully selected.

Careful and sensitive design can have an unexpected downside for signage design. Meticulous design creates a harmonious environment where individual elements are well-balanced in relation to each other. The visual result will be that everything blends together into one visually quiet setting. However, signs have to be noticeable right away, and therefore, will have to stand out a bit. It is frustrating for the signage designer to see that bluntly placed pieces of paper with scribbles on them tend to work well enough as signs. Disharmonious elements that are positioned 'right in your face' apparently function well, but only because they are placed in a carefully designed environment. In the 'wild west' chaos of sticker and graffiti-covered walls of some public spaces, this quality would disappear completely and thus become worthless. Still, some form of straightforwardness in the positioning of signs is highly recommended.

There are two spatial aspects to consider when selecting the right spots for placing signs. A position is required both in plane and in elevation. Some call the first the location of a sign and the second its placement.

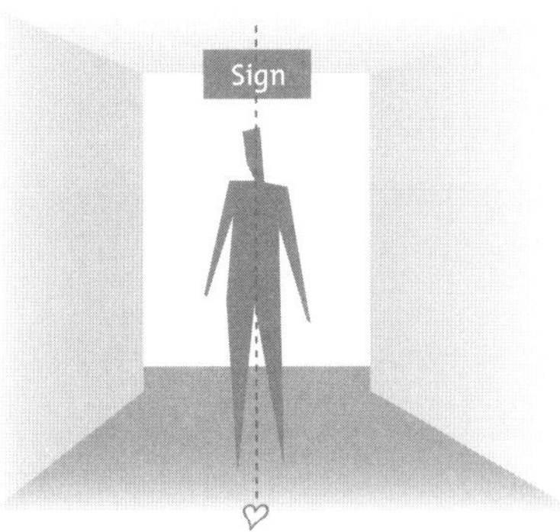

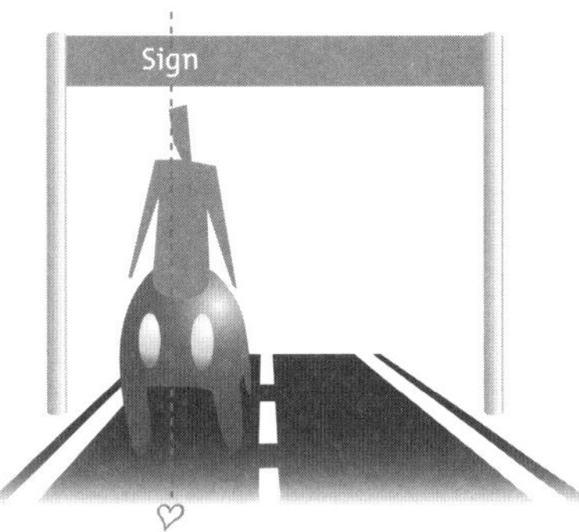

3.5.1. POSITIONING IN PLANE

While travelling, most people will position themselves instinctively in the middle of pathways. Therefore signs are also best positioned in the middle.

Going to our destination, we all tend to position ourselves in the middle or the axis of traffic facilities, unless these facilities are very big. We take the middle of a doorway or a hall and walk in the middle of a corridor or in the middle between the indications of any other walking area. Our behaviour when driving a car is not any different. That is why there are so many lines on the road, just to keep us in the middle of a lane that is designed to avoid collisions, thus making travel decisions as simple as possible. Accordingly, the positioning of signs is also best put on the axis of a traffic flow. In cases where that is impossible or impractical, a position just next to the flow is the second best option. In fact, these two positions are precisely the way signage is placed on most highways.

3.5.1.1. Intersections, forks, branches

An intersection with a different traffic flow, or a division into two or more flows out of one flow, are the typical 'travel decision points'. Signage is unavoidable in these spots. It is difficult to reduce the number of signs needed to a bare minimum. Ideally, each flow should have an indication over its 'entrance portal'. That means that a 'crossroad' should have 4 signs over each possible direction, or—next best—4 signs on each corner. One-way roads do not exist in buildings, so directional signs need to be positioned to be useful for people coming from all directions.

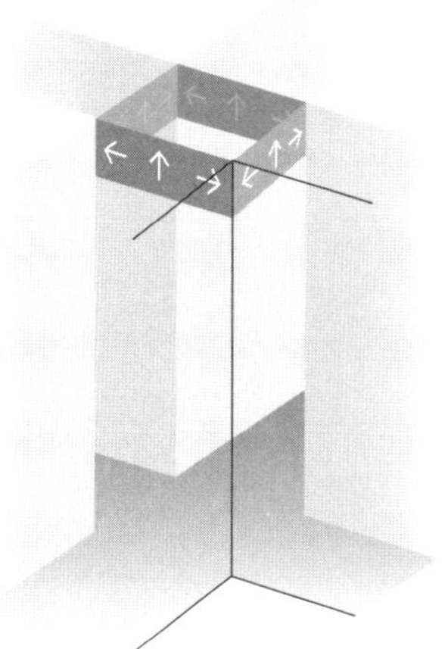
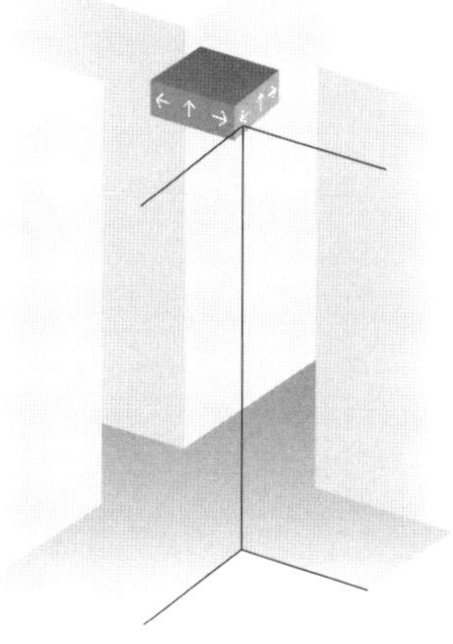
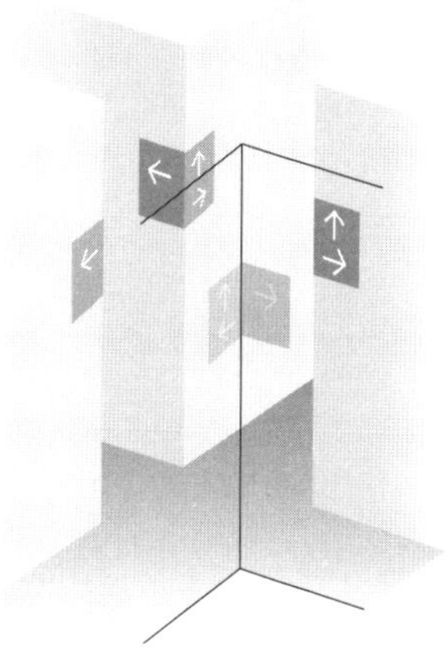

Three basic ways to position signs at intersections: as portals, as one centrepiece, or on all four corners.

The signs on intersections can be placed in three different ways:
—as portals over each direction of the intersection
—as a sign bloc in the centre of the intersection with sides facing all directions (a chandelier-type of sign)
—on all corners of the intersection.

Outside buildings all directional signs have to be placed before the point where a decision to change route can be carried out, not after this point.

3.5.1.2. Entrances and reception

All relevant signs, as for instance a directory, are best placed straight in the axis of all important entrances. After entering a building the directory can be seen as the 'welcome' sign of the building. That role can also be fulfilled by a traditionally staffed reception. There will often be a combination of both reception and directory. Depending on the way the reception of visitors is arranged, it should be decided which of the two facilities is given visual priority for visitors entering the building. Both facilities should be carefully positioned in relation to each other.

3.5.1.3. Lift/elevator lobbies

A floor level sign in addition to directional signs is needed after stepping out of an elevator. These signs should preferably be positioned on the axis adjacent to the lift door, but in most cases this is not possible. A typical lift lobby has lifts on both sides or has a landing in a relatively big hall. Suspending signs might be a consideration to overcome these obstacles.

3.5.2. POSITION IN ELEVATION

The area of our cone of vision that gets most of our attention is probably the central part of that cone. This implies that signs should be best positioned within this zone. This zone is not within the same fixed area for all visitors. Our individual eye levels are different, depending on our height. Also people in wheelchairs have a considerably lower eye level than average.

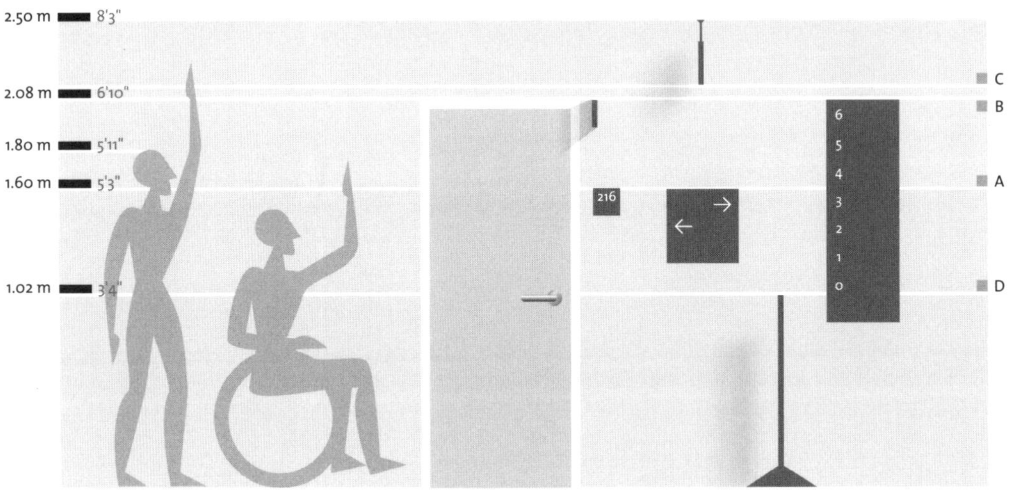

Placement of signs should be related to the standard heights in buildings:
A-top level of small- and medium-sized signs, matching average eye-level.
B-top level of large signs, aligned with door frames.
C-bottom level of suspended signs.
D-top level of freestanding signs, matching level of doorhandles and railings.

Nevertheless, good signage needs uniformity in the position (and shape) of all signs. Our mind doesn't scrutinise in every detail all images in a dynamic field of vision. It scans efficiently for what interests us, leaving the rest literally unseen. Ultimately we see with our brains; our eyes are merely the instruments. Familiarity in shape or position in space helps in the process of recognition. To achieve this familiarity when placing signs in elevation, normally two major standard virtual bands are created. All (or most) signs will be positioned within the limits of these imaginary bands. One band will be around the eye level of an average visitor and the other will start just above the standard door height. This way we know where to expect to see signs within our field of vision.

3.5.2.1. Basic heights in buildings

The standard heights of all elements used in a building design create an important sense of visual order throughout the whole building. Ceiling heights are quite important for our sense of space. A lot of facilities or types of equipment have standard heights; some are even subject to legislation. There are minimum sizes for doors, depending on their function. Door handles are mounted at a fixed height. Parapets must have a minimum height, (stair) railings are made at standard heights.
Light switches are put at a fixed height throughout a building.

In fact, most of the standard heights are related to our movements within spaces, like opening doors with handles, holding on to railings while climbing the stairs, pushing on switches or buttons, and going comfortably through openings from one enclosed space to another. Signage is another necessary facility for efficient travelling that also needs a standardised installation height.

3.5.2.2. Eye level and cone of vision

The average eye level while standing up is about 1.60 meters (5'3"). While sitting or in a wheelchair it is about 1.25 meters (4'1"). Sitting in a car, the eye level can be a bit lower, depending on the type of vehicle used. The cone of vision of a normal eyesight is 55 degrees.

The average eye level heights of a pedestrian, a wheelchair-user and a driver. The position of the last depends heavily on the type of vehicle used.

3.5.3. LIGHTING CONDITIONS

Careful sign positioning in plane as well as in elevation is important to create an efficient signage system. Lighting conditions at selected spots might literally put all careful positioning under a totally different light. Lighting conditions are extremely important, therefore, and reconsidering positioning might sometimes be necessary. All signs need to be sufficiently lit (internally or externally) to be properly functional. This aspect must never be underestimated in signage.

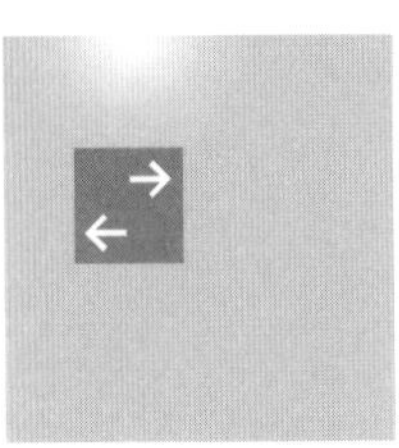

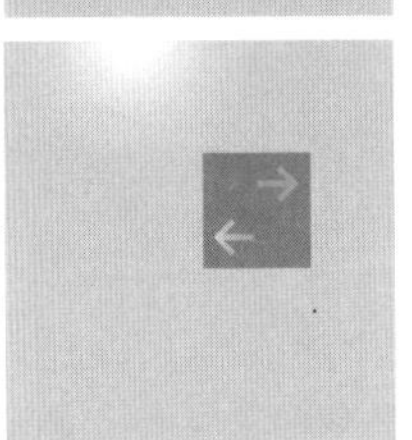

The functionality of a sign is heavily dependent on its position in relation to that of a light source.

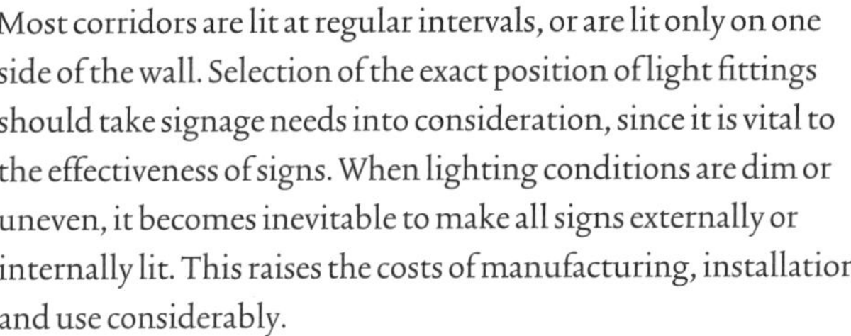

Most corridors are lit at regular intervals, or are lit only on one side of the wall. Selection of the exact position of light fittings should take signage needs into consideration, since it is vital to the effectiveness of signs. When lighting conditions are dim or uneven, it becomes inevitable to make all signs externally or internally lit. This raises the costs of manufacturing, installation and use considerably.

3.5.3.1. *Natural or diffuse light*

Diffuse or natural light is often ideal for signs. Overviews, directories and maps work best under these lighting conditions. Natural light can vary dramatically in intensity during the day. This fact needs to be taken into account.

Outdoor signs often practically disappear after dark. Many buildings nowadays are used until far into the hours of darkness. It is therefore advisable to investigate the importance of all outdoor signage when it gets dark.
The same counts for indoor as for outdoor lighting : positioning of all light fittings should accommodate the signage needs.

3.5.3.2. *Spotlights and glare*

Spotlights can be of help in enhancing the functionality of signs, especially when used outdoors. The disadvantage of spotlights is the likely occurrence of glare, either as light reflection on the surface of the sign or as direct projection into the viewer's eyes. Positioning signs against a bright background or using glossy reflective surfaces for sign panels must be avoided.

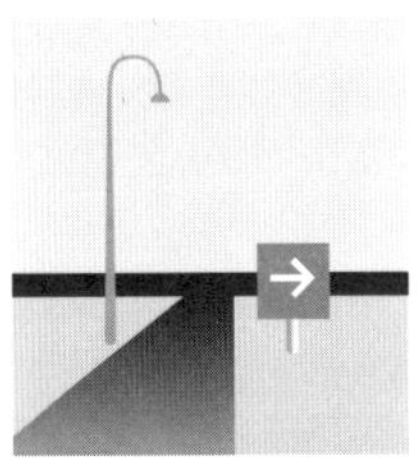

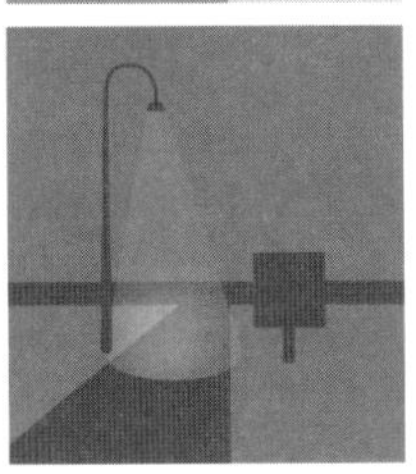

Lighting conditions for outdoor signs may change dramatically during the course of the day. At night, signs may completely lose their functionality.

3.5.3.3. *Colour and light*

Anyone who has taken photographs inside a building knows how different light sources can affect colours.
Colour schemes for signage and special colour coding systems should be tested under the lighting conditions in the building. Some colours change dramatically when lit by certain light sources. Especially the type of light that can be used for outdoor illumination.

3.5.3.4. *Light fitting & sign combination*

It is surprising that manufacturers of light fittings still do not bring products onto the market where a sign can be easily added to a light fitting. There must be a need for such a product in the market; the type of light fittings that can be integrated in ceiling systems especially seem to be ideal products for such a combination. Integrating signs into these systems that already combine lighting and ceiling covering would work nicely.

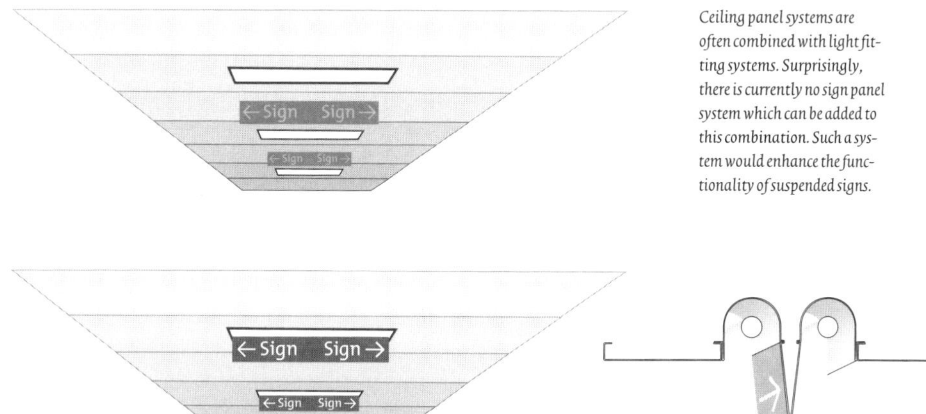

Ceiling panel systems are often combined with light fitting systems. Surprisingly, there is currently no sign panel system which can be added to this combination. Such a system would enhance the functionality of suspended signs.

3.5.4. BASIC SIGN MOUNTINGS

There are in principle 5 ways for signs to be mounted inside and outside buildings. The type of mounting is selected on the basis of finding the most efficient position for each sign in relation to the traffic flow.

3.5.4.1. Wall-mounted sign

The vast majority of all signs in a building are wall-mounted and placed in the direct vicinity of wall openings and/or doors.

3.5.4.2. Projecting sign

Projecting signs are fixed not flat to the wall, but at a right angle. This position makes this type of wall-mounted sign more visually prominent in a corridor that has many doors and other wall signs. Moreover, projecting signs can be viewed from both sides.

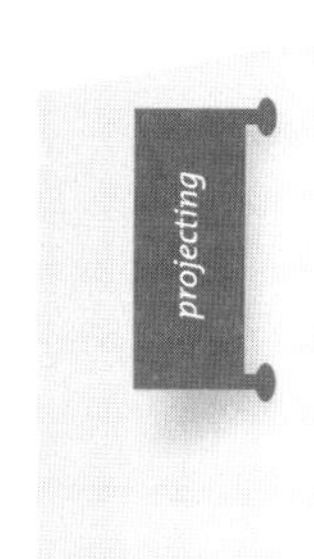

3.5.4.3. Suspended sign

Suspended signs are fixed to the ceiling. It often makes positioning at the best visible spot easier than for wall-mounted signs. Suspended signs can be read from a further distance, thus need bigger lettering. The length of messages on these signs needs to be very compact and as short as possible.

Suspended signs have an eye-catching appearance in space and deserve special attention to visually match harmoniously with the existing architecture.
Suspended signs can also be viewed from both sides.

3.5.4.4. *Free-standing sign*

Free-standing signs can be positioned in such a way as to be impossible to miss or to overlook. This quality implies that free-standing signs can sometimes also be literally in the way.

Free-standing signs can either be fixed in one spot— most of the time fixed to the ground—or be moveable signs. Moveable free-standing signs are limited in size. They are mostly used to inform about special events or circumstances. Moveable signs need special maintenance attention because they might easily end up in a corner somewhere and become entirely useless. Most moveable items on a floor will be put temporarily in a corner during the regular cleaning sessions in a building. The fate of a lot of moveable signs appears to be that they tend to get forgotten and are not returned to their initial place.

Fixed free-standing signs are mostly used outdoors, or in big covered spaces like public halls. There are three basic varieties in visual appearance of this type of sign:
—finger-post sign; a directional sign on one pole with small panels pointing in the relevant directions
—monolith sign; a fixed free-standing sign with no visible frame. It appears as one thick panel standing protruding from the ground
—normal free-standing signs (post/panel signs); a free-standing sign with a visible frame, in most cases a 'two-legged' structure that holds the sign panel.

Free-standing signs can be used double-sided, though often only one side is needed.

3.5.4.5. *Desktop or work-station sign*

Desktop or work-station signs can be clipped onto furniture elements (or partitions), or can simply be put on a counter or a desktop. These signs are small in size and are used to identify the name of employees or give information about procedures in reception areas.

3.6. Stating the message and conveying the information

At this point, a foundation has been made for the signage system design; it has been decided who will be responsible for the signage, how the development and implementation will be organised, for whom it will be made, and on a preliminary level, what type of signs will be needed and where they should be placed. Now it must be decided how the information can best be communicated to the audience. Here signage design can become rather complicated, or as some would see it,challenging and interesting.

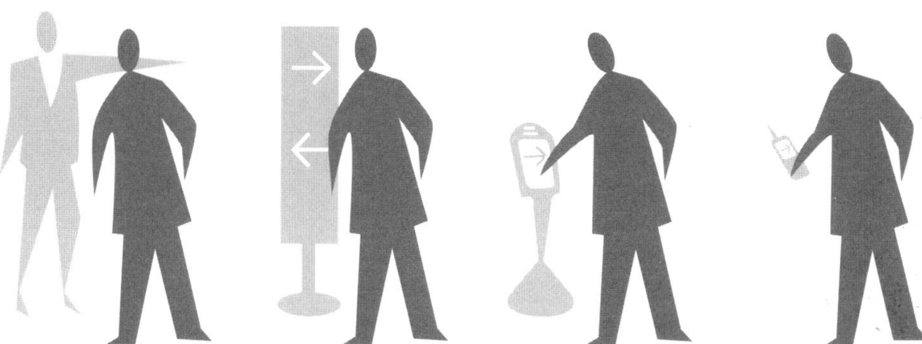

Wayfinding information is provided in a growing number of ways: given in person, on autonomous signs, on interactive signs and on wireless hand-held devices.

In fact, the implicit goal of signage is quite implausible. Ideally, it would encompass the design of a system of communication that would be understood by practically everyone, and under any circumstances. Of itself, this already looks, by definition, like an invitation to failure. What makes it into an effort of real universal dimensions is the fact that all possible media are considered fit to be used for conveying the information. This unbounded approach to signage design can risk obstructing true professionalism, especially when there is often so little feedback about the effectiveness of executed signage systems. The best result a signage designer can hope to achieve is that nobody will talk about the design qualities when the job is completed. Good signage always looks self-evident and simple. It is taken for granted. In the worst case, people start complaining and putting up paper notes with additional information. But even this act is often not taken seriously because people will always complain and have an irresistible urge to post paper notes.

A well functioning signage system must encompass a range of various aspects. However, it can only create outstanding quality by defining its limitations sensibly. Only in this way can the wide variety of means of communication be included in the signage system. There are three major aspects to be taken into consideration when deciding on how the message could best be stated and conveyed: first, the capabilities and limitations of our senses; second, the appropriate information methods; and third, the technological developments that will profoundly influence the way we deal with signage.

3.6.1. OUR SENSES

The 'tentacles' we possess for scanning our environment for information are our senses. We have five different senses that allow us to see, hear, smell, touch and taste. Seeing, hearing and touching can be relevant for signage design. These senses have overlapping possibilities in their ability to process verbal information. Smelling and tasting are both undoubtedly related senses, but do not have much potential for signage design.

3.6.1.1. Our senses and technology

Most communication is verbal communication, or at least a message can also be expressed and conveyed in a verbal alternative. Our eyes and our ears are the major receivers of verbal information. Deaf people can learn to 'read' our lips, the visually impaired can learn to read with the tips of their fingers. The visual sense can be partially replaced by the tactile sense.

Practically all communication is digitised before transmission. The digital format creates almost endless possibilities at the receiver's and at the sender's end. Input can be spoken, typed, scanned, photographed or taken directly from digital storage devices. The output can be 'humanised' to accommodate our senses in almost any conceivable way and adapt itself to specific individual conditions. Incredible amounts of information are accessible at all times from an exponentially growing worldwide network.

Most modern verbal communication is no longer done face to face, or by using solely material means like a letter. Practically all

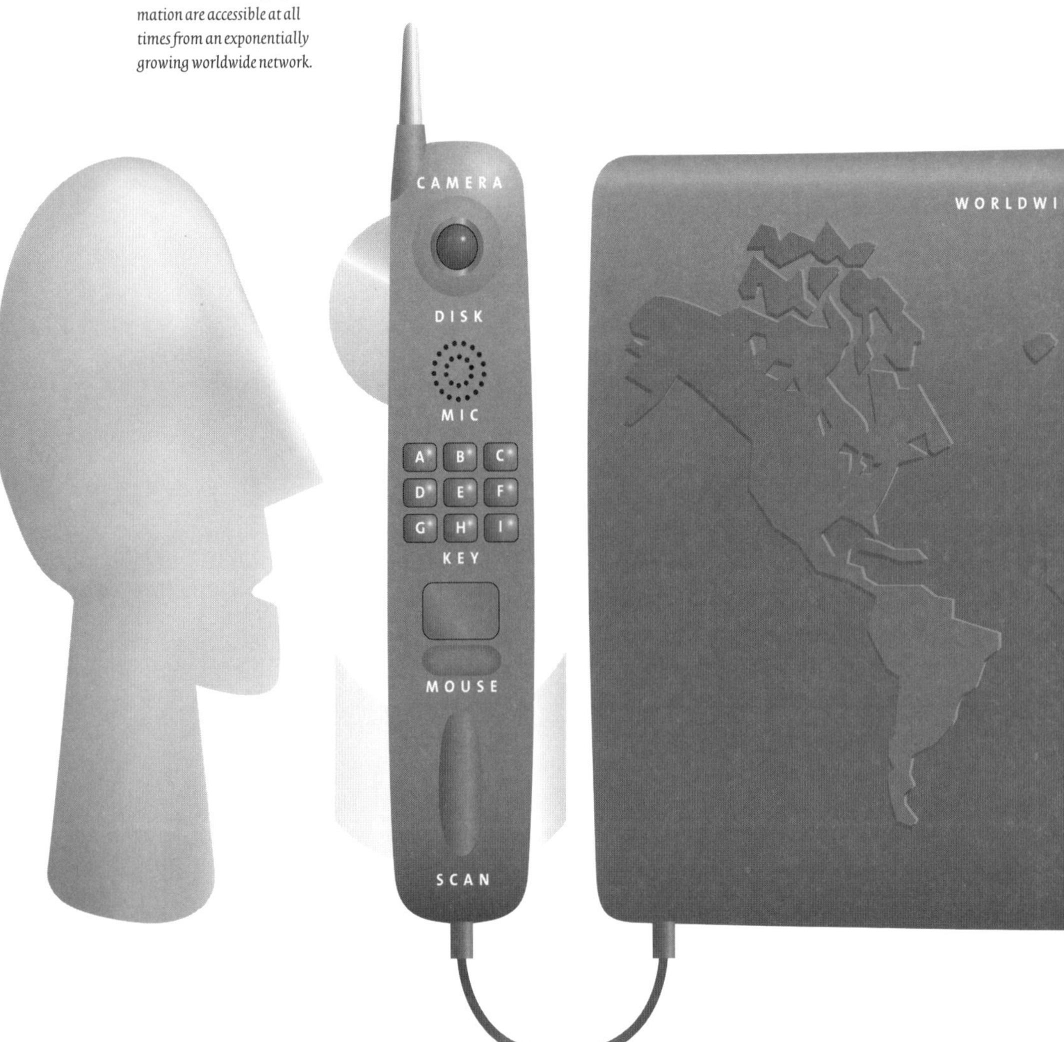

communication nowadays that bridges a certain distance is digitised before it is conveyed. This stage of digitisation has created enormous possibilities. Digitised information can be stored easily and software can instantly translate its content, 'on-the-fly'. Hereafter, it can be distributed and reproduced when needed, with a plethora of different devices in whatever form required. Distribution by wireless transmission will create some quite impressive possibilities. For instance, when we speak in the presence of an electronic speech receiver, the spoken words will be digitised. These words can be stored and be reproduced at any time in whatever format, language or script. Available software determines the limits of possible transitions. The words can be reproduced through loudspeakers, made visible as written text on screens or paper, or materialised in practically any other way, for example, being cut out of a slab of marble or a sheet of stainless steel. Most production machines nowadays also work with digital information. Dedicated software will become the universal interpreter into whatever format and end-result.

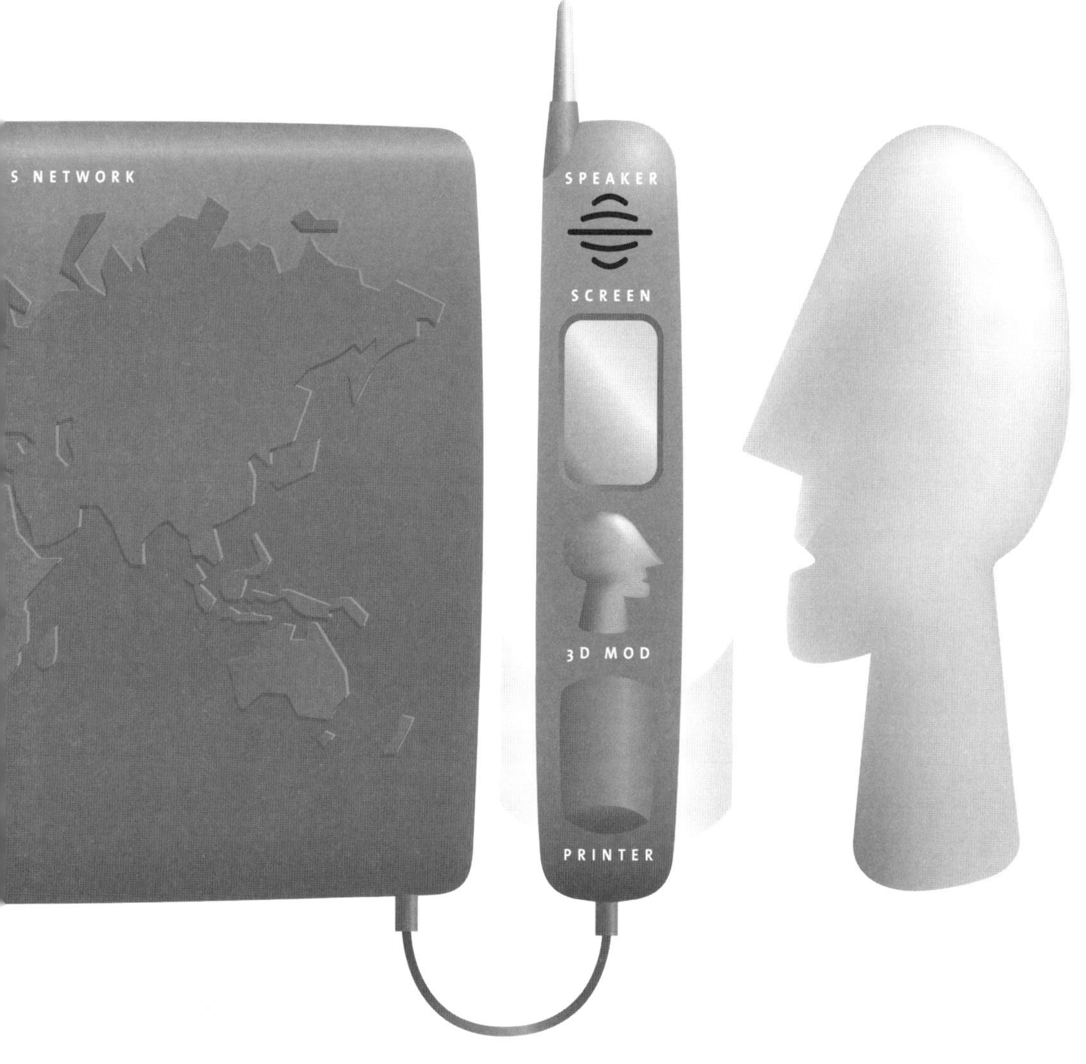

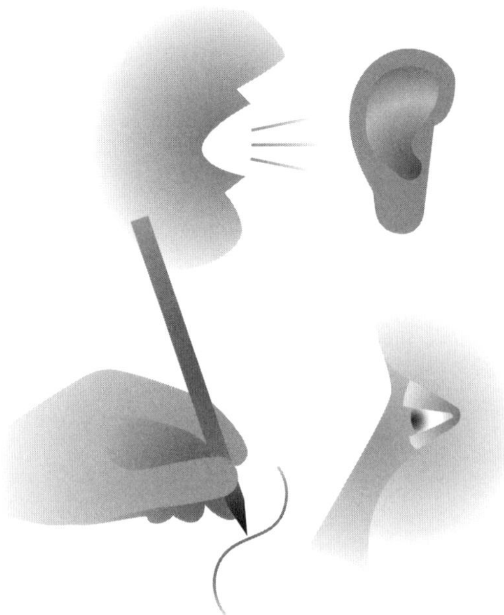

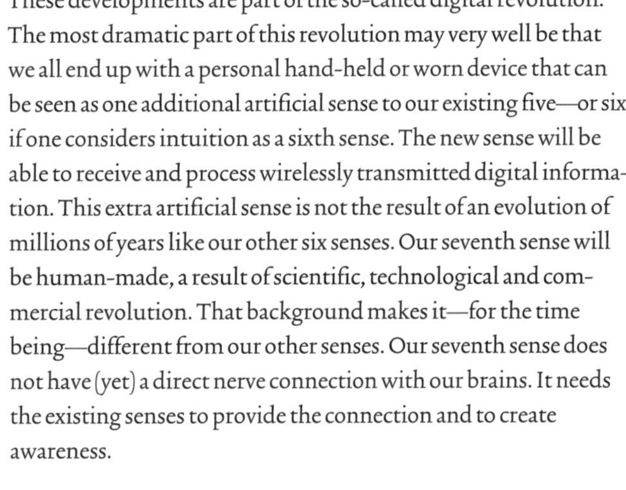

These developments are part of the so-called digital revolution. The most dramatic part of this revolution may very well be that we all end up with a personal hand-held or worn device that can be seen as one additional artificial sense to our existing five—or six if one considers intuition as a sixth sense. The new sense will be able to receive and process wirelessly transmitted digital information. This extra artificial sense is not the result of an evolution of millions of years like our other six senses. Our seventh sense will be human-made, a result of scientific, technological and commercial revolution. That background makes it—for the time being—different from our other senses. Our seventh sense does not have (yet) a direct nerve connection with our brains. It needs the existing senses to provide the connection and to create awareness.

Wireless Personal Digital Assistants will become our human-made seventh sense. These will be crucial tools to detect and interpret information that will increasingly be made available only in a digital format. These devices can be customised to meet our personal needs and physical abilities.

Still, the impact of our new artificial sense should not be underestimated. Its capabilities outperform our existing senses in many ways. Though not able to reach our consciousness directly, it is

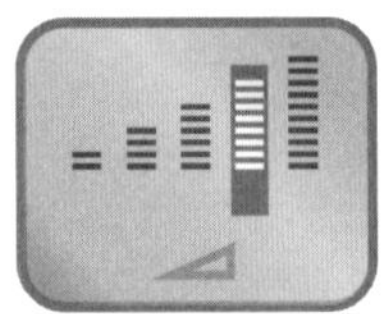

capable of translating digital information in such a way that it can be processed by any of our natural senses. This means that, for instance, visually impaired people can carry a personal digital receiver and processor that will be able to make digital information available in Braille, embossed text, or spoken words. Information does not have to be supplied in Braille anymore, and the visually impaired can make the kind of translation that is

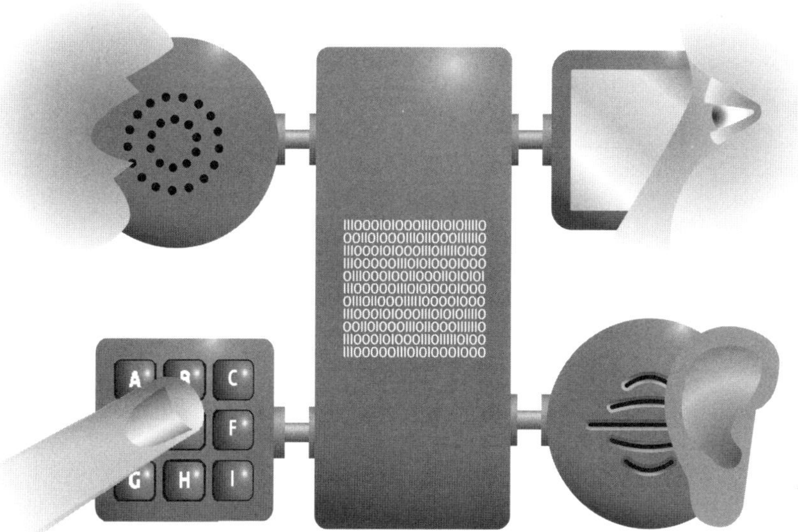

most suitable for them. This could be done with a device that could first scan the available visual information—like text—then make a translation into Braille or, most likely, into speech. In the future, information would be provided directly in a digital format. Miniaturised transmitters will take care of that part. Transmitters used to be clunky machines, but now they are miniature chips that can be activated by distorting infra-red beams or by customised electronic cards. All information would in fact be made available in an invisible, noiseless and wirelessly transmitted signal in a digital format. All individuals will carry their own personalised/customised seventh sense that will make the information available in a way that would best fit their own abilities to comprehend (familiar language) and to process (according to the fitness of their senses) the information. It would be a bizarre world where all information is made available in a manner that cannot be detected by any of our natural senses. It cannot be seen, heard, touched, smelled or tasted. Only our seventh sense can receive it and make it available in a way that suits us best. Limitations of individual physical possibilities and languages would completely disappear. Digital information would be the universal language understood by all holding their own portable seventh sense. This situation would simplify all signage efforts tremendously. It sounds like science fiction. Not entirely. The principle of conveying information in a digital format is already daily routine nowadays. That process will continue to spread exponentially. The world will ultimately be exclusively accessible through our personal digital assistants. It will become our most important sense; our essential portal to the human-made world.

Traditionally, all verbal information could be communicated in only two ways: listening to spoken text or reading a written version. Digital media changed it all in a fundamental way; once input is digitised, it can be stored, transmitted over any distance, and made available in every possible way.

Until that stage arrives, we will still have to use only our traditional biological senses. For signage purposes, some of these senses are more useful than others.

3.6.1.2. Visual sense

Signage relies almost 100 percent on visual signs. Our visual sense is by far the most suitable 'tentacle' we have to find our way around and to use facilities and machines. With our eyes we can 'browse' the environment to find clues that would help to lead us in the right direction. With our eyes, we can concentrate on the scenery as a whole and we can focus thereafter on details. This browsing facility is essential for the design of any signage project.

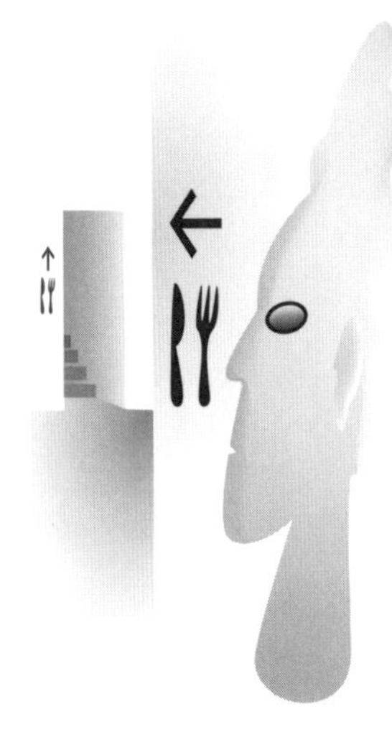

Impaired or reduced eyesight limits our ability to visually browse our environment. Such a condition makes adequate signage rather complicated and only possible by reducing our signage goals.

There is another, rather basic, behaviour that is related to our visual sense. We are—like most other living creatures— attracted to light. Like insects, we instinctively tend to move in the direction with the most light. Light can create a natural path in an environment. Light can also attract our attention to specific objects around us, especially when it is used dynamically. Some companies spend fortunes to make us gaze at public light shows, most of the time featuring a company's logo or a product's brand.

3.6.1.3. Aural sense

When visual signs are absent, or incomprehensible to us, we often ask somebody which way to go, or what to do. Hearing is on some occasions important in signage projects. Information delivered in person is often available as a last resort, or for security purposes. Not all spoken messages in signage projects are given by flesh-and-blood humans. More and more facilities mechanically 'speak' to us. Their ability to 'listen' is also progressing. Elevators tell you which floor you're on and when the doors will be closing. Artificial speech will also be used more frequently, specifically for accommodating people with impaired eyesight. It is far easier to absorb spoken information than to read Braille or embossed letters. Text on computer screens can already be converted to artificially spoken text. Some machines can understand simple human speech. All of us will eventually get more used to communicating with speaking, listening, or otherwise interactive machines. The field of exclusively visual communication will shift partially to audible communication. One of the results of this development is that the number of people capable of using Braille is dropping fast.

It is interesting to note that visual information often replaces the once spoken information given by reception staff. Now artificially spoken information is replacing—or provided in addition to— visual information.

In a few specific instances, audible signals are traditionally used for general signage purposes. For example, they are used as warning signals or as an indication of an emergency situation. Interactive screens also use sound signals to confirm instructions.

Sound appears to work well in creating a certain mood or atmosphere. Music can bring us almost instantly to a certain state of mind. Therefore, stores use music to attract clients and to strengthen the style of their business, using sound as an effective branding tool. Corporate buildings also sometimes use music in corridors and elevators. This used to be more in fashion and was called 'Muzak' after the name of the company that sells this kind of product. Nowadays, 'silence' is what seems to touch the appropriate mood button in corporate buildings.

There have been experiments to use different music to differentiate floors from one another. Translating simple standard visual codes into other equivalents can result in the witty brainwaves of designers, but originality often gets in the way of the simple directness that signage requires to be understood.

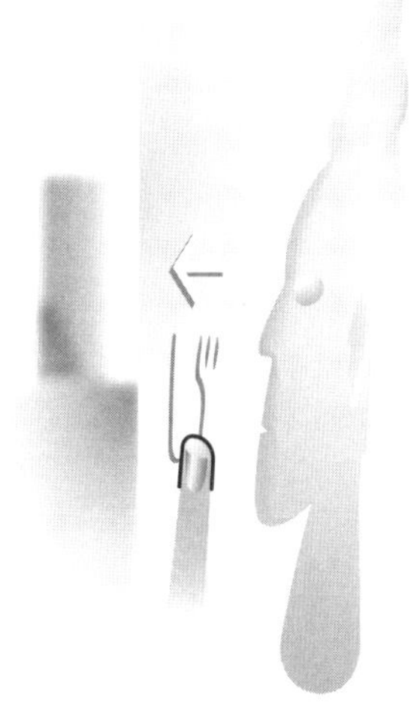

3.6.1.4. Tactile sense

Accessible tactile information is still often applied as the best replacement for people who cannot use visual information well. Legislation made to accommodate visually impaired people still relies almost completely on offering alternative information that can also be 'read' using our fingers, or made clear using our feet or a handheld stick to 'read' the pavement or the floor. Embossed alphabetic letters or Braille can provide the same information as visual text and symbols. Provisions like tactile underfoot tiles can lead the visually impaired along the way. Clearly, these facilities have considerably reduced practical use when compared with the possibilities of visual signage. Legislation and effective application of accessible tactile information varies greatly between countries. The USA has probably the most extensive legislation for signage in buildings. In Japan tactile underfoot tiles are widely used in important public places.

It is to be expected that audible information will more or less gradually replace tactile information in the future. Existing legislation might become partially outdated over time.

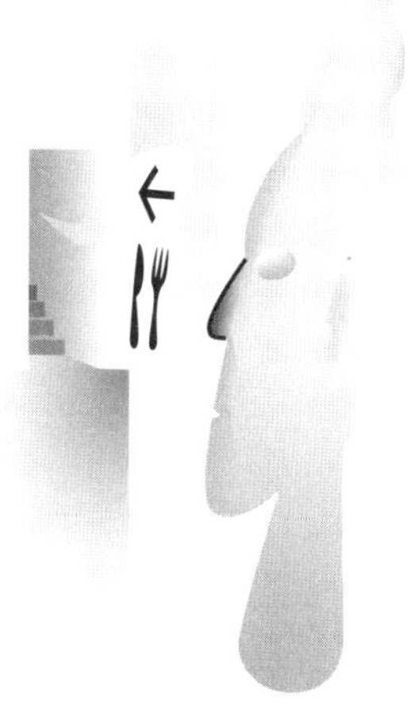

Visually impaired people often develop an enhanced sensitivity of their other senses. Sounds, air flows and smells can provide useful navigational information for the visually impaired, though they might remain unnoticed by the visually unimpaired.

3.6.1.5. Taste and olfactory senses

The senses that enable us to taste and to smell can contribute considerably to the enjoyment of life and so are quite important. It seems that they even play a crucial role in the process of 'natural selection'.

Some people have the ability to distinguish hundreds of different smells and tastes. These people are rare and most in demand in research laboratories by manufacturers of fragrances or food products. The blind leading actor in the movie 'Scent of a Woman' showed remarkable ability in analysing people by using only his nose. Still, these qualities are exceptional and of little use in wayfinding. Although washrooms, dining and coffee areas do produce recognisable smells, this can hardly function as a sensible strategy for navigation.

3.6.2. INFORMATION METHODS

There are a lot of different ways to convey information, other than those based on the differences in our senses. Most signage systems will use more than one method to inform. Let's first start with a theoretical overview of the various possibilities, followed by a more extensive description of the way the different aspects are commonly applied in a signage system.

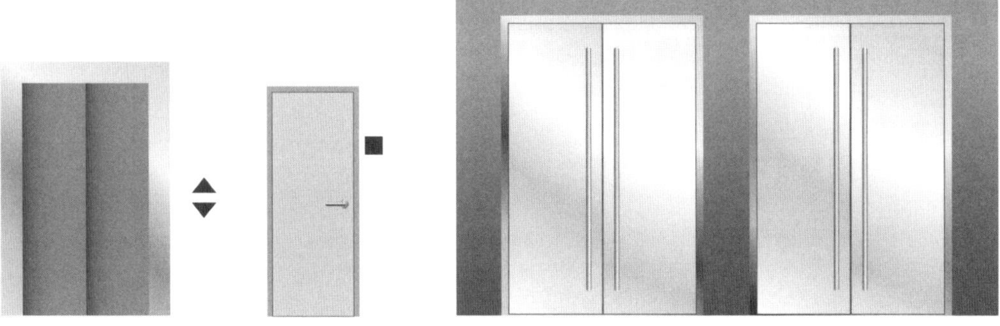

The characteristic shape of a door informs us about its function: an elevator door, a generic office door, and main entrance doors.

3.6.2.1. Characteristic marks

The most basic form of visual (or tactile) language is the shape of an object itself. Most people will recognise a door, a door handle, a gate, a tunnel or a bridge immediately by its generic shape. No extra indications are needed to explain their basic function, unless these objects are unusually shaped. Characteristic marks or shapes have their informational value based in convention. Making use of conventions is very important in any form of communication. One must use the familiar to explain the unknown. There is no other way.

Not only can the key facilities in wayfinding be made self-explanatory through their shape, but also through the way the signage itself is presented. Nowadays, people expect most places to carry signs, so they automatically look for them, thus reducing the chance of unnoticed signage. That is helpful, especially when signs are positioned in spots where they are most expected.

3.6.2.2. Graphic signs

The core of our information/communication system is based on the use of (graphic) signs. Semiotics is the name of the science that

describes the functions of signs and symbols. It divides signs in three major groups:
—Signs that use a representation of a real object as a direct reference to that object. Pictograms and icons belong to this category.
—Signs that use a representation of a real object as an indication for a meaning related to that object. Signs falling under this category are pictograms, icons, crests and logos. Chinese characters also have their source in this category, but became abstract over time.

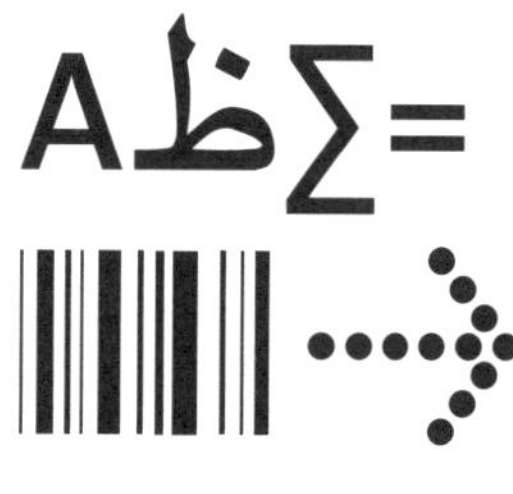

The three major groups of graphic signs: illustrative with a direct reference to the real object, illustrative with an indirect reference to the meaning of the sign, and totally abstract with an arbitrarily assigned meaning.

The difference between the first two categories is that, for instance, a graphic representation of a human heart that can refer to the real object and be used to show its location in the human body. It can also refer to a state of emotion called love, or to the location of heart surgery in a hospital, or it could be used as a logo for a humanitarian organisation.
—Signs that are visually abstract. An arbitrary visual form is used as a reference to its meaning. Letters, symbols and marks fall under this category. Letters are a special case of abstract shapes. Letters, along with other marks, form a complex system of signs that we use to visually represent language. This system is also closely related to spoken language.

Many graphic signs that surround us cannot be classified exclusively under one of the above mentioned categories. Often signs will fit under a combination of more than one category.

3.6.2.3. Signals

Signals do not need a direct graphic representation to function. In signage, signals are often used as a warning or to indicate an emergency situation. Various types of simple light and sound signals are used for this function. A red light is also used as an occupancy signal. Code signals that represent verbal messages (like Morse Codes or light signals) also exist, but do not play a role in wayfinding.

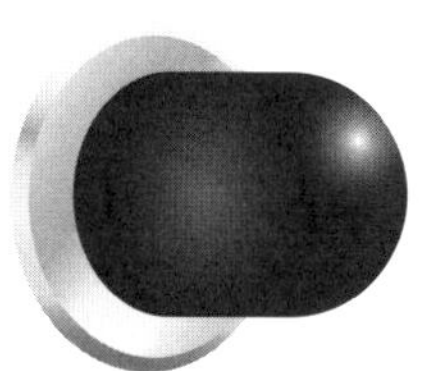

3.6.2.4. Illustrations

Photographs, drawings, paintings and sculptures can be used in a signage system. Illustrations can replace pictograms. Maps can be made as very schematic drawings but can also be very illustrative representations. Overviews of a site can be built as three dimensional facsimile models of the real environment.

3.6.3. DESTINATION IDENTIFICATION

An important part of the design of the signage is setting up a coherent identification system for all the possible destinations in the project. Destinations will fall into different categories; they vary in type, size and function. This variety requires different kinds of description. Besides, there are arbitrary ways to identify a destination. Consistency and coherence are the most important factors in deciding on the way the identification is best achieved.

3.6.3.1. Verbal description

Words will be the most common way to identify a destination. The verbal description can refer to different aspects of the destination, as described below.

—Visual appearance

In some instances, it might be practical to use for a verbal description the actual visual appearance of a building feature or of a certain space; for example, the 'Blue Suite', 'Palm Alley' or 'Fountain Square'. Remembering the destination is easier when a given name refers to the real visual appearance of the space.

—Arbitrary

Main spaces or gathering places are sometimes given the names of important people or benefactors, such as 'Lord Nelson Hall', or 'Kennedy Suite'. This method is also used to group destinations together without using codes. All names of destinations within one area can be grouped together by giving them names from the same classification, like names of plants, or names of big cities, or names of precious stones.

—Function of a facility

The formal function of a room or a facility will also be used for its description, like reception, toilet, meeting room, or coffee corner.

—Organisation occupants

Departments, or divisions of the organisation that is occupying the building are also used as names for destinations in a building. This often turns out to be not an easy task. The names that organisations generally use to describe their divisions are often lengthy but need to be squeezed into a format that is concise and memorable enough to be usable in a signage system.

—Basic requirements for verbal information

The verbal information used in a signage system should follow quite strict demands.

—Text should be simple and clear. Text must be understandable for the average user. Technical, formal, or complicated wording should be avoided completely. Abbreviations will not be allowed.

—Text should be consistent. Names for destinations should be identical everywhere: on a directory, on a directional sign and on the final destination.

—The amount of information given on each sign should be limited to the bare minimum. Being concise is elementary in signage. Too much information will either be ignored or poorly remembered. Chopping up all the information needed into easily digestible snacks at each decision point is the secret behind offering good wayfinding information.

3.6.3.2. Coding

Some coding methods will be used in all signage systems. The number of rooms and/or spaces that have to be identified needs to follow a simple coding system in order for them to be easily found.

—Letter/number coding

Everybody is familiar with a room numbering system that is based on a letter and/or number combination. The first (optional letter) might be used to indicate a part of a building, the second (number) is an indication for the floor level, and the final number(s) are like the house numbers in a street. See the more extensive paragraph about room numbering systems (section 3.6.5).

—Colour coding

Colour coding is a coding method favoured by architects as well as by clients. There is little reason for this preference judged from the functional aspect. Colour codes can be visually attractive but have quite a number of drawbacks as instruments for identification. First, one has to learn what each colour stands for, which is never obvious. Second, the number of colours to be used is very limited; a maximum of six to eight different colours can be applied, otherwise people get mixed up. Third, colours are unstable because they depend on lighting conditions. Colours may look very different when lit by different light sources. Fourth, each individual sees colours differently. These differences may be large when a person is so called colour blind (about 10 % of all males), but minor differences in colour judgment are quite common. Five, colours change over time.

Colour coding is best used, exclusively as surplus information and in limited amounts. It can certainly be helpful in wayfinding when certain parts of a building complex can be identified easily and directly by specific colours. It is comparable with creating a different visual atmosphere in parts of a building. It supports the experience of transition. (For more about colour coding, see section 4.13.)

—Barcodes

Barcodes (some call these Zebra codes) have all kinds of applications. The application we are most familiar with is the barcodes on products we buy in a supermarket. Product type and name are put in barcodes on each product so that the cashier only has to scan the code for the information to be matched with the most recent product price, and be kept in memory in order to appear on our receipt. There are barcode applications for signage as well. Barcodes can be added to signs, and can contain information regarding the inventory of rooms. 'Radio Tag' technology may replace barcodes completely in the future.

3.6.3.3. Illustrations or sculptures

Verbal descriptions will be the basis for describing most destinations in a building or complex. An additional alphanumeric coding system is essential for the overall room numbering. Colour coding can make the whole system visually more attractive and can create overall atmospheres in different parts.

Figurative illustrations have empathetic qualities. Therefore, they may easily get into our memory and stay there longer than alphanumeric codes.

Illustrations or sculptures have empathetic qualities for creating an atmosphere or mood. Figurative images will stick more easily in our memory. Applications of illustrations for wayfinding purposes may vary from a big mural that merely functions as a landmark to a supporting illustration next to a verbal description. For example, parking lots and garages often use an alphanumeric coding as location system. Parking facilities around airports are huge nowadays, so people tend to forget the code of their parking space when returning, often days later. Illustrations are used to replace the alphanumeric coding system in order to make locations easier to remember.

The fact that illustrative additions will enhance recollection of verbal information has long been known in advertising. Brands and advertisements use the eternal twins of 'art and copy' practically without exception to get the most memory adhesive message across. The same principle that works so well in conveying commercial messages can also be applied to signage.

Pictograms are a special kind of illustration. They play a role in all signage projects. Not only are they used to describe a destination, but they are also frequently applied to mandatory signs. Pictograms will be discussed in further detail below.

3.6.4. PICTOGRAMS

A pictogram is a type of illustration that also falls into the category of signs. Both the content of the image and its graphical representation are kept very simple. Pictograms are sometimes described as being part of a picture language, in other words a language consisting of pictorial symbols. Such a language may perhaps not be as precise in expressing our verbal language as alphabetic signs, but it has potential advantages such as being very concise and capable of crossing the boundaries of all existing languages. Pictograms strive to be universally applicable.

Over the years many attempts have been made to create more or less complete sets of pictograms that could be used for general purposes as a replacement for alphabetic signs. To create a universal pictorial language has become a life-long challenge to some. It is very difficult to create a set of concise images that everybody will understand immediately. We needed to discover the Rosetta Stone to decipher the old Egyptian hieroglyphs. Even when the set is limited to simple realistic pictures, there is no guarantee for accurate comprehension. Images are likely to be ambiguous in expressing their meaning, or possibly misleading. A pictorial language that is universally understood is still not around. However, simple pictorial images have found a secure place next to written verbal language. Everyone using a computer these days has small pictures all over the screen. In fact, the universal use of the graphical user interface for all personal computers has created something like a universal picture language for all the standard elements we find on our virtual desktop (ie. folders, documents, a pointing or grabbing hand and a trash can). Even the worldwide use of email generated a new form of small icons made with punctuation marks, called 'emoticons', that are used to add an expressive tone of voice to the written information. Pictorial information in whatever format—whether called icons, pictograms, or whatever—has become a standard part of visual communication, in addition to written language.

Human cultural progress may have surprising results. Both illustrations portray a running man. The first was painted on an ancient Greek vase, the second was conceived by an EEC *committee for standardising emergency exit signs. Apparently the latter had peculiar views on the human anatomy despite many existing excellent examples from the past.*

Signage design was one of the first professional activities to be attracted to developing sets of pictograms. The advantages of being both concise and unrestricted by language seemed very tempting. Soon the limits of this pictorial language became clear. First, not everybody has the same talent for linking a graphical representation to a real life object; many viewers simply do not see what the pictogram represents. Second, the meaning of the picture is often not straightforward; for instance, there is no picture that could unquestionably express the word 'exit'. In reality there is no specific type of door that could be used in such a pictogram; an 'exit' door looks just like all other doors.

In short, one simply has to learn the language of pictograms to be able to understand it. To avoid the pitfall of being entirely misunderstood it is often recommended not to use pictograms without adding (at least in one language) text explaining its meaning.

Some pictograms have become familiar to most of us. These can be used without restriction. Only when designers get too pictogram happy, is it likely that users will end up missing or misinterpreting some lines in the pictorial story.

The creation of a set of graphical symbols has always been—and will always be—linked to professional activity. Professionals have an unstoppable need to create abbreviations for terminology that they often use, thus creating some distance between the informed and the laymen. Hereafter, some abbreviations will be replaced at some stage by a symbol.
There is a universe of graphical symbols around, and like our real universe, it keeps on expanding. Attempts have been made to produce encyclopedias of all the symbols we use. One of the first was made by Henry Dreyfuss, entitled 'Symbol Source Book'.

The various professionals involved in traffic and safety have created quite a few graphic symbols that have also found their way into the signage that surrounds us. A lot of the signs used for signage projects have become subject to standardisation and legislation. Practically all signs related to traffic and safety are standardised. The same goes for signs related to fire fighting and emergency escape routes. Signs to accommodate accessibility for the impaired form the latest addition to standardised signs. All legislation and standardisation is still done for a most part at the national level, and every country has its own rules. A few international operating bodies are issuing recommendations and rules for international use. National/local governments can adopt and implement these rules and recommendations by ratifying them. There is the International Standard Organisation (ISO) based in Switzerland that creates international norms and procedures for updating and changing the existing ones. Many western countries support their recommendations. The European Union also has various bodies and committees that try to deal with the matter. Standardisation doesn't appear to be a simple matter. Technological developments are fast and widespread these days; also political views on the subject of standardisation vary.

There are a few other organisations that have a long-standing interest in creating sets of pictograms. First, facilities all over the world involved in public transportation, like tramways, railways, and airports, have designed sets of pictograms over the years. One of the first attempts to create a consistent set was done by the US Department of Transportation (DOT) in 1974. The DOT commissioned the American Institute of Graphic Arts (AIGA) to design a comprehensive and consistent set of pictograms to be used for all transportation facilities. The set got the name of DOT74. This set had quite a lot of influence on further development by others. Second, each city that hosts the Olympic Games makes a new set of pictograms for the event. Some sets are very well designed. Third, public institutions like national recreation parks create pictogram sets to use on their signage systems. More and more countries create a set of standard pictograms to be used in all public places.

The standardisation of sets of pictograms has the obvious advantages that people get used to the images and will gradually learn their precise meaning. There is also a downside. Standard sets have a specific appearance or style. It is never wise to standardise a style when the applications will be very wide. Pictograms are signs like the signs in an alphabet, and nobody would sensibly suggest standardising type designs. This serves no purpose; on the contrary, different styles will enrich and enhance our environment, creating the different atmospheres we need to move around comfortably.

Designing pictograms is best not left to committees. Standardisation of pictograms is useful but should be limited to a verbal description of the required visual representation.

Standardisation is best limited to the 'content' of an image (eg. the image of a fork and a knife which stands for a restaurant). The final design can be best left to individual designers to create sets that either become popular or not—just as is the case with type design. This way, the ultimate choice will be the user's. Standardisation is always a decision-making process done in big committees. That is certainly not the ideal setting for making the best designs, and as the expression goes, 'a camel is a horse designed by a committee'. There must be some truth in that saying. Just take a look at the standard fire exit sign that came out of the European standardisation committee; you'll see that it resulted in one of the most awkward pictorial representations of a running human being. (More about pictograms in section 4.10.)

3.6.5. ROOM NUMBERING SYSTEM

Room (or space) numbering starts on the detailed drawings produced by the architect. All possible spaces on these drawings, including halls, stairways and corridors, get a number to facilitate the building process. In most cases, this numbering system is also used for the signage, often not leading to an ideal wayfinding situation. Constructing a building is quite a different process from using that building after it has been completely built.

3.6.5.1. The unit system

From a wayfinding point of view there are two important aspects to creating an efficient numbering system. First, the point(s) of access to the floor(s) are a logical starting point. Second, the flexibility of the numbering system will allow refurbishment, including restructuring rooms into smaller or bigger units.

Flexibility in room numbering is best achieved by making a grid of the smallest possible units on each floor. These units often follow a grid already used in the building itself. The positions of the windows are often an indication of the positions of these units. Each unit gets a number. The numbers start on the right-hand side from the major point of access (lift, staircase) and continue to increase in that direction. It is not important that even numbers are on one side of a corridor and odd numbers on the other, as in most street numbering. It is far more important that numbers left and right increase gradually and equally on both sides. The number of the room will be the number of the unit where the entrance door of that room is.

A room numbering system that is based on the smallest room unit limits the updating of the signage system to the minimum.

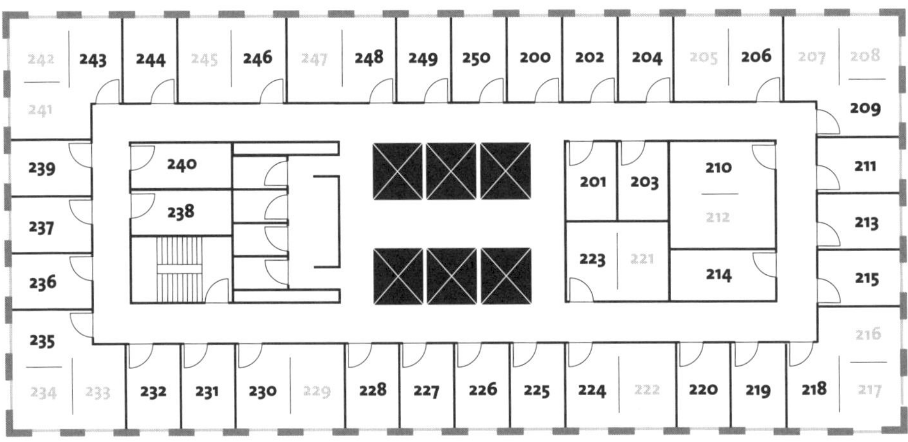

This system only has the disadvantage that numbers will 'jump' in a corridor, because not all available numbers will be used. However, the advantages far outweigh this disadvantage. First, hardly anybody ever looks for a room number that does not exist. Second, all other signage related to this numbering system will never have to be updated again.

3.6.5.2. Service rooms and keys

In many cases it is advisable to link the numbering of small service rooms or closets to this system. These are small storage spaces that can also contain all kinds of technical or cleaning equipment. An extra number can be added to the unit number. Even the key numbering system can be linked to this system, although some consider this not secure enough since it would be too easy to locate the corresponding room if its key carrying the number falls into unauthorised hands.

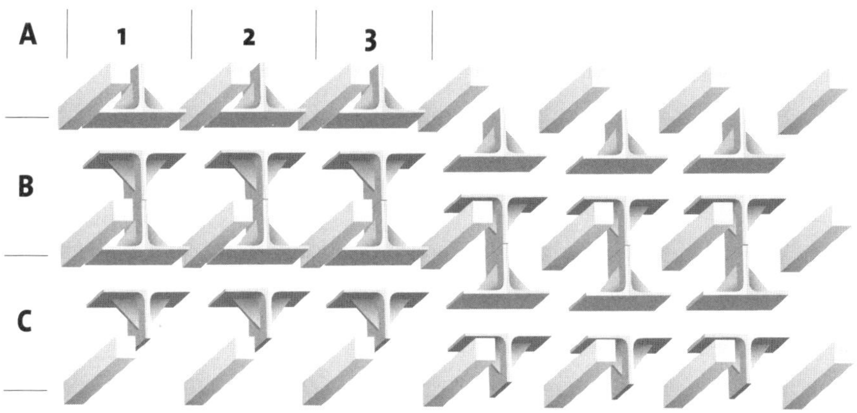

3.6.5.3. Open office spaces

Many offices do not have separation walls and doors between traffic areas and the work spaces. Work stations surrounded by low dividers, or landscape offices, still need some system of numbering. It is often best to use the grid of the columns as starting points for the units. In this case the numbering system has to be alphanumeric, as used on most maps, where the columns of units are assigned a letter and the rows a number.

Usually, open-plan office spaces do not have a clear circulation pattern like corridors have in more traditional offices. Unit numbering is best done using a grid with horizontal and vertical rows.

3.6.5.4. The information in the number

A room number should include as many clues as possible about its position in the building. The first digit or letter is the indication of the building in a complex of many buildings, or a part in a huge building. The second is the number of the floor level. The third (possibly fourth) is the number of the room on that floor. For the service rooms, closets, and technical ducts, eventually more numbers can be added. It is advisable for the sake of clarity to separate each type of number by a point.

205
205.1
B 205
BI 205

In very complicated cases, where the combination of letters and numbers is not sufficient for creating essential variations, a distinction can be made between our normal Arabic numerals and the old style Roman numerals.

3.6.5.5 Mystical properties in numbers

Numbering spaces and floors may not be a completely straightforward task, as certain numbers have a mystical property for some people. Certain numbers are considered lucky numbers or are just the opposite. For Westerners, 7 is a lucky number and 13 an unlucky one. For many Asians the number 4 signifies death. Signage designers and their clients may decide to avoid the use of unlucky numbers altogether, especially in 'sensitive' buildings, like hospitals.

4	4	5
3	3	4
2	2	3
1	1	2
0	G	1
-1	B1	
-2	B2	
-3	B3	

The US system of floor numbering is also used in Russia, some Eastern European countries, most Eastern Asian countries (Japan, China) and Canada.

3.6.6. FLOOR NUMBERING

Giving numbers to floors is in principle a rather straightforward activity. There are, however, a few complications, the first being the number given to the ground floor. In most countries, this floor will be given a letter, like the letter G (for ground floor), or R (for rez-de-chaussée), or the number 0. The exception is for countries following the US system where this floor is called the first floor, whereas elsewhere the first floor is the one above ground level.

The second complication is the numbers given to the floors below ground level. One method is putting a minus symbol before each number, so -1 will mean one level under ground level. Other methods will use an alphanumeric code instead, such as B1 for the first level below ground level (B standing for 'basement').

The third complication might be the number given to mezzanines. The solution is often also an alphanumeric code; M1 is the mezzanine between the ground and the first floors. The use of fractions, like 1/2, for this purpose is probably a more logical solution but is practically never used. In some instances letters will be used to indicate specific functions of floors, such as a P for parking levels.

The last complication may arise in situations where the ground floor level is not obvious. This happens in mountainous or large-scaled urban areas. People tend to consider as ground floor whichever floor they enter a building on, regardless of whether or not it is physically the ground floor.

3.6.7. ROUTE GUIDING INFORMATION

When all destinations have been given a unique identity, these indicators will also be used in some way to point the travellers in the right direction, along the way to their final destination.

There are a lot of potential high-tech solutions to do this job. Personal navigators are a booming business at the moment of writing. For the time being they are mostly used for outdoor use and in cars, but this might change. One can fantasise about all kinds of new wayfinding applications with micro-senders and transmitters that could be used for guidance along the way. Exact positioning and finding a 'target' with the help of all kinds of sensors and transmitters have quite a lot of scientific and technological interest. Some day this will have its influence on navigating in buildings.
For instance, you might find a person by dialing the number of the person one is looking for on your own mobile phone. This signal would activate a system of changeable arrow signs that would guide you along the way. Or even consider the possibility of a small robot that would guide you personally to your destination.
The traditional methods of guiding or directing are basically done by grouping and repeating the destinations and adding an arrow to show the right way for all destinations. This method is still by far the most used. Another (slightly archaic) method is making a more or less continuous line on the floor, the wall, or the ceiling that leads from the starting point to the final destination. Different colours (or type of lines) can be used for different destinations. This method has been applied in a few signage projects for buildings (notably a hospital), but it has far too many limitations to be seriously considered in most cases.

Technological developments allow for much fantasy in designing possible route guiding systems. From left (opposite page) to right: a 'transmitter-card', automatic sensors, simple line-tracking, traditional signage and personal wireless navigation.

Comparable with the continuous lines method is the way tracks for footpaths in the countryside or in parks are indicated. Simple

colour coding (sometimes with numbers) is used at regular intervals, and at crossings or forks in the road. This rudimentary basic need to follow a track of marks, as well as repetition and constant confirmation, are all important elements for signage systems.

3.6.8. ORIENTATION INFORMATION

Orientation information is needed for everyone who wants to know precisely where the destination is to be found and the best way to get there, thus which destination signs will be relevant to follow during the journey. Basically there are two ways to provide this kind of information: with a map or with a list (or directory) of all destinations. Both are used either as separate items or in conjunction.

In office buildings, orientation information is also used to inform users about the organisation that occupies the building. There is not always a strict correlation between the information that is found on orientation boards and the rest of the signage.

3.6.8.1. Maps

Maps are stylised and simplified representations of the realistic situation. Maps and navigating seem to be inseparable. The first explorers used them and today practically all organisations have a map somewhere on their website showing where they can be found. Maps are still very useful aids in wayfinding, though perhaps not equally useful in all occasions. Scale matters; a small- or medium-sized building does not really need a map to accommodate wayfinding. But maps are also used to impress visitors, to give the impression of importance and scale.
Graphic designers might find maps an ideal opportunity to create visually breathtaking graphics. Entrance halls may have panels with eye-catching overviews of all floors of the building brought together in one impressive illustration. Artistic pleasure often outweighs pragmatic functionality.

Maps attached to the wall must have exactly the same compass orientation as the floor they represent.

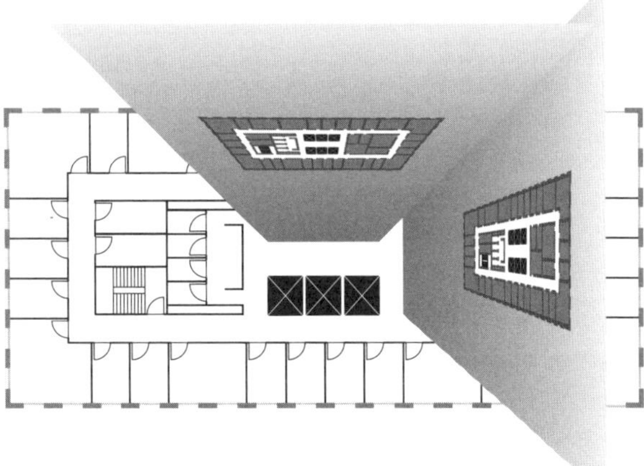

There is a rather unpleasant complication with using maps, although some suffer considerably more from this complication than others. The difficult part is to understand how the situation shown on the map relates to the real situation one is in. That is not always easy or straightforward.

Every effort has to be made to make the gap between the real situation and the one on the map as small as possible. The most important part is the position of the map in space.The handiest map is one that is put in a horizontal position, because it relates as much as possible to the real situation. Of course, the compass directions on the map must be the same as in reality. Orienting a map in this ideal situation is what we do automatically when we consult a map that we carry with us.

Maps and navigation are inseparable and are produced in endless variations. Three variations are shown above: a traditional flat representation; a 'bird's-eye' view; and one that can be consulted during the journey, the latter being the most practical.

However, horizontal maps are not very practical things when used in buildings. Most maps will be mounted on the wall. It makes the translation of the information on the map a bit more difficult. Still, the most important rule is that the the compass directions on the map on the wall are precisely the same as the ones of the viewer looking at the map. This basic rule is very often violated and reduces the functionality of a map dramatically. Also bear in mind that a lot of visitors will never use a map. Any unnecessary complication will only reduce the practical use even further.

—Portable maps

The best and most used maps are often the ones that you can take with you. The information on fixed maps has to be remembered; a portable map can be consulted when in need. Maps don't have to be detailed. Very simple graphical representations, even on a small scale, can be sufficiently helpful. A lot of museums print a small map of their premises on the entrance ticket. These are handy aids. Simple print-out maps can also be useful as simple handouts at reception counters.

—Exploded views

Maps show only the reality in a two-dimensional aspect: as a flat plan. Visual references are exclusively the proportions and spatial relations shown in planar format. It is still a rather abstract representation of reality. An 'exploded' or 'birds eye' view provides far more visual information. Heights and shapes of constructions also become visual references on the map. It can enhance the functionality of a map considerably. Giving more visual clues will make the relation with the real situation easier to comprehend. The design problem is to still keep the total overview image quite simple.

3.6.8.2. Directories

Directories consist of listings of all destinations in a building. They can also be an overview that shows the link of destinations with additional information needed to find the final destination. For instance, in multi-occupancy buildings most destinations are only (or mostly) indicated by room numbers. The directory will list the names of the tenants with their corresponding room numbers.

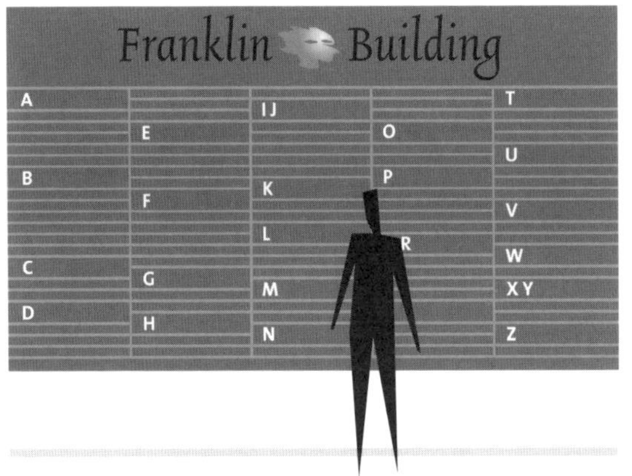

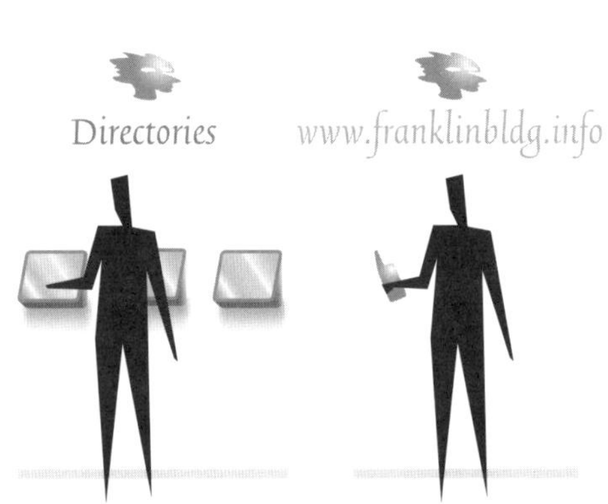

Traditional directories in large buildings can become huge signs. Interactive electronic directories have replaced those impressive overviews. Eventually, directories may disappear altogether from the site and will only be retrievable through a website, for instance with a mobile phone.

—Electronic directories

Large buildings nowadays often make use of electronic directories. The listing is no longer completely visible in one big overview. All relevant information is put in a computer. This information can be retrieved through a relatively small, interactive touchscreen. It can provide all the information needed, even for the largest buildings. The screen works like any computer database; one can retrieve all kinds of information, the limits being the budget available to build the interface and databases.

Electronic directories can be expanded with all kinds of additional features, like a printer, a camera, a card reader and a phone handset.

—Building directories

Building directories provide an overview of the whole building or even the whole site. These directories are often located near the main entrances. Retail buildings use directories in far more locations and in various sizes, depending on reading distances.

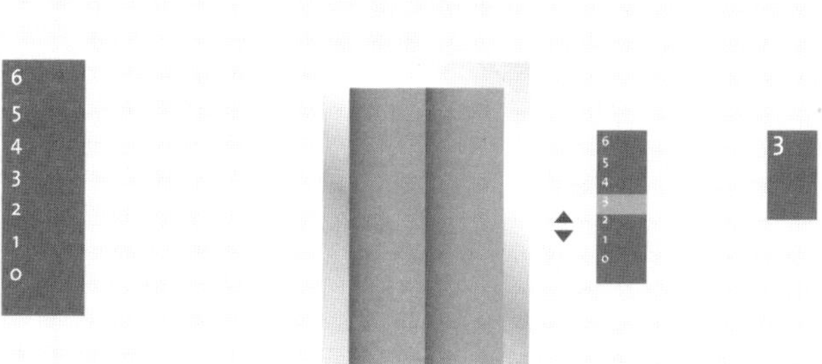

Three basic types of directories: a building directory, an elevator directory and a floor directory.

—Floor directories

Floor directories are typically located near all floor entrance points, like stairs, lifts and escalators. The listing on the directory is restricted to the the information relevant to one floor and is often combined with a big floor identification number.

—Elevator/lift directories

Elevators are important transportation channels in most buildings over a certain size. A directory is needed near call buttons on the outside of the lifts. This directory will also highlight the specific floor one is standing on, in addition to relevant information for selecting the 'car up' or the 'car down' button.

Directories inside lifts are not necessary. Nevertheless, they can be quite handy and are therefore sometimes used. The floor selector and indicator panel are of course the most important facilities inside an elevator.

One will find inside lifts all kinds of different designs using combinations of directory information and the floor indicator and/or floor selector. Dynamic electronic displays have also found their way into elevators.

3.6.9. INSTRUCTIONS

Not all signs are directly related to the wayfinding process. Quite a number of them will support the safety of procedures and working conditions in the building. A few others will serve more general informational or PR functions.

3.6.9.1. Operating instructions

We surround ourselves with an ever-growing army of machines. Working or travelling can only be done with the help of devices of all kinds. Our buildings are becoming packed with machines that serve the best and safest living and working conditions. All these machines need some kind of operating instructions. Often machines will be delivered with operating instructions produced by the manufacturer directly written on the surface of the equipment. It may be advisable to consider removing these instructions and producing new ones that are completely integrated with the rest of the signage system.

The plethora of machines will include devices for:
—communal services: such as copiers, faxes, and vending machines.
—access and transport: such as intercoms, special doors, escalators, and lifts.
—light, air control, and heating: such as light switches, thermostats, and air conditioners.
—potentially hazardous facilities or devices: such as radiation and production machines.

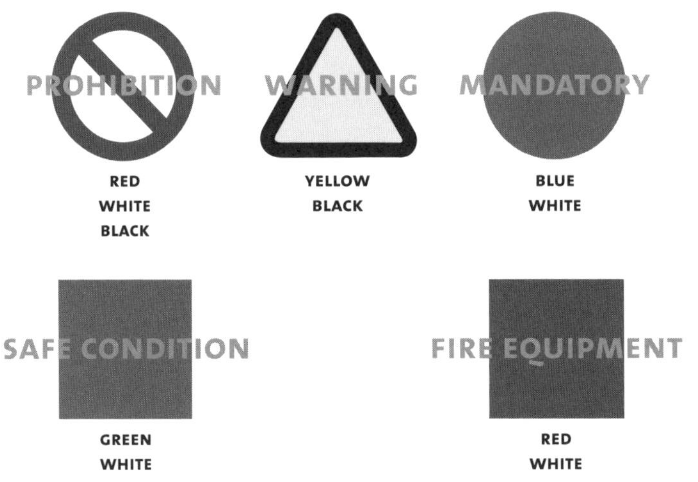

3.6.9.2. Safety & mandatory instructions

A large number of signs will be mandatory signs. The number of signs required in a building may vary considerably from one country to another. Practically all signs in this category are standardised in content and appearance. Some organisations might add a few extra signs on their own account.

3.6.9.3. Security instructions

Security measures are becoming a greater consideration in most buildings. Unfortunately, this development does not make our environment a friendlier one. Still, there are various ways to deal with the necessity of security. A prison, for example, must not only be a strictly secure building, but must also look like one. However, it is best for other types of buildings to avoid any visual or procedural reference to traditionally secured buildings. Security procedures can easily generate irritation in visitors. To avoid negative feelings, procedures and signs should therefore be clear, easily understood, and simple. Architectural facilities and security devices should be made as user-friendly as possible and should avoid using grim-looking elements like steel bars and heavily constructed metal gates.

3.6.9.4. Emergency & fire fighting instructions

Fire is historically the most devastating hazard in buildings, although prevention and modern building techniques have tremendously reduced that risk. Nonetheless, indications of escape routes, emergency exits and fire fighting equipment, are important parts of all signage systems. Some manufacturing plants or laboratories need additional emergency instructions. Some organisations develop in-house procedures for evacuation or first aid that might need specific signage.

Most signs in this category are standardised in both content and visual appearance. Legal requirements vary considerably between one country and another.

3.6.10. GENERAL INFORMATION

Some information on signs is related to neither instructions nor to wayfinding. The purpose of such signs is to provide general information about the building or its occupant: for example, the history of the building, or the occupying organisation, or its relationship to other organisations.
Noticeboards and bulletin boards also fall into this category. These items serve the internal communications of an organisation. Some signs in this category can be combined with the type of signs that serve a pure PR function.

3.6.11. WELCOME & BRANDING

All signage has a public relations and visual identity aspect. The level of attention given to the functional and aesthetic qualities of a signage system are indicative of the way an organisation wishes to be perceived.
A few signs can be added to stress the image an organisation wants to convey. For example, some signs are only there to show the organisation's logo, display slogans, or simply say 'welcome'. Translated into advertising terms, this activity is called PR or 'branding'.
Very few buildings have a 'star' quality. The silhouette of the building or specific architectural details are widely known, like the Empire State Building in New York, the Eiffel Tower in Paris or the Tower of London. Cities or other organisations may adopt star buildings as a logo for their organisation. In these cases, buildings may become brands themselves.

3.7. Signage plans and traffic flows

Making special signage plans and studying the traffic flows is the first step in designing the signage system. The accessibility and wayfinding qualities are for the most part determined by the way traffic flows are organised. The flows can best be made visible on paper for better understanding and analysis. Only small signage projects might be excluded from this task.

In order to make these flows visible, a special set of plans of the built environment is needed. Often these plans are not available and have to be drawn specifically for this purpose, based on other existing plans.

3.7.1. SIGNAGE PLANS

The signage plans consist of one ground level plan of the whole site and floor plans of each level of the building(s) involved. Architects and landscape designers often produce small overall plans in the 'master plan' phase of their commission. These plans might still be useful for signage purposes, though often they are no longer accurate or may miss essential details. In most cases it is best to assemble the section plans that architects use at a later phase of realisation.

Sometimes architectural computer drawings can be used directly as input for the drawing software that's best applicable for signage purposes. However, compatibility problems may arise between the different software used by each professional. In these cases photographic collages can be made that can be traced and/or scanned to serve as plans for the signage project.

It is essential for design and presentation that a set of plans is produced showing on only one sheet, all entrances, lifts, staircases, corridors and other connections between each level of the building and its immediate environment. Providing a clearly comprehensible overview is important.

This set can be used to show the traffic flows, or to mark the global locations of the different type of signs needed in the project. It can also serve at a later stage for the location overview of the various signs. Obviously, these plans are easier to use and update when produced in a digital format.

3.7.2. DIFFERENT TYPES OF TRAFFIC

Visualising traffic flows on maps can easily result in visually complicated drawings. To reduce visual clutter it is best to make the flow lines as simple as possible. A minor indication within each line indicating the flow direction is helpful. These types of lines can be easily produced on illustration software.

It is best not to put all the different types of traffic flow charts onto one single map, but onto separate sets of maps. A building site is best divided into functional areas: for instance, all traffic related to parking and main entrance, or to parking and deliveries. Within the building, traffic flows around heavily frequented meeting areas can be put on separate drawings. Big projects like sports arenas, shopping malls, airports, bus or train terminals, need separated flow drawings since they often involve different types of specialised experts.

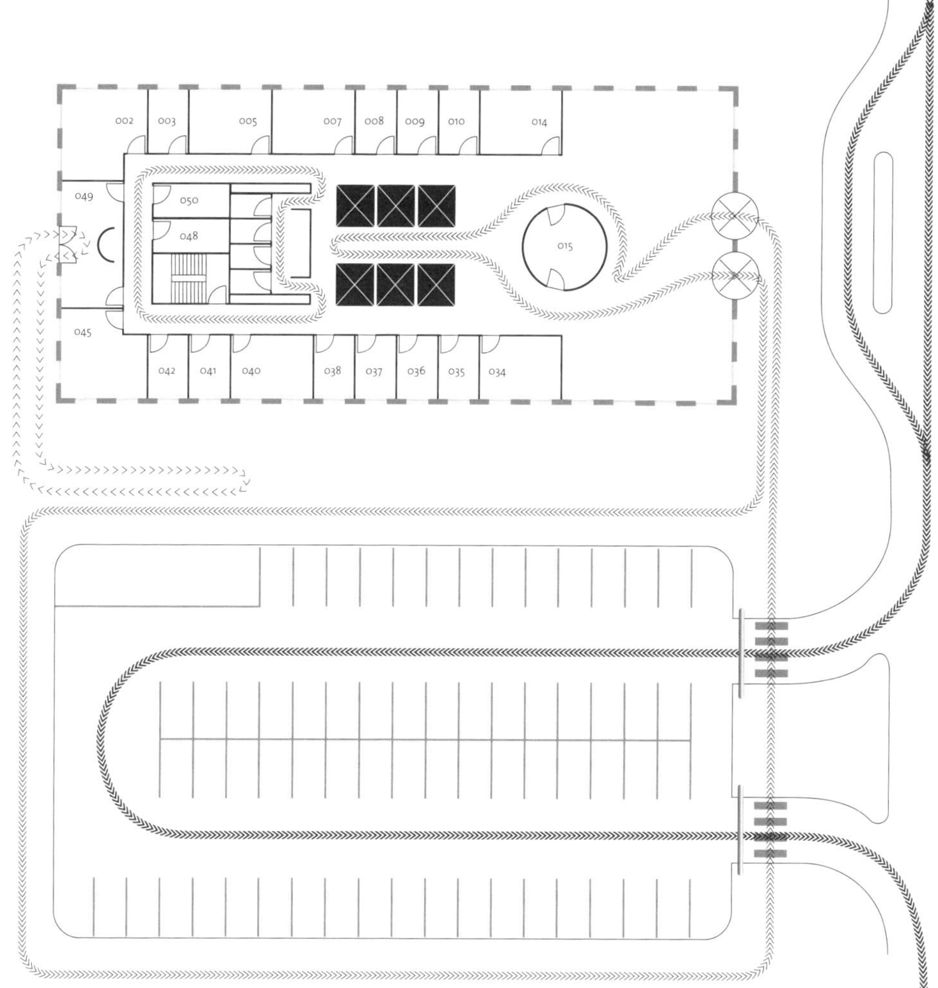

The first step in designing a signage system is making a map that shows all important traffic flows.

3.7.3. BASIC FUNCTIONS OF SIGNS

After traffic flows are clearly charted on the maps, the need for signage becomes visually evident. Some flows will be impossible to guide users through without the help of signs. It is best to start by putting small stickers on the signage maps using four distinct colours, each colour representing a basic type of sign that is needed either to control the flow or for instructional purposes. At a later stage, each basic group will be divided into subgroups of more detailed sign types.

3.7.3.1. Orientation

As already said, for wayfinding purposes, three basic sign types are needed. The first type is the one that allows the traveller to get oriented. Orientation is the phase in the wayfinding process where one needs to make up one's mind on where to go and how best to get there. In other words, it is the phase where ones needs to make a 'travel plan'. Sign types like maps and directories serve this need. These kinds of signs inform you, for instance, that you have to go to the third floor to find your intended destination, or that the restaurant is located in building E, etc.

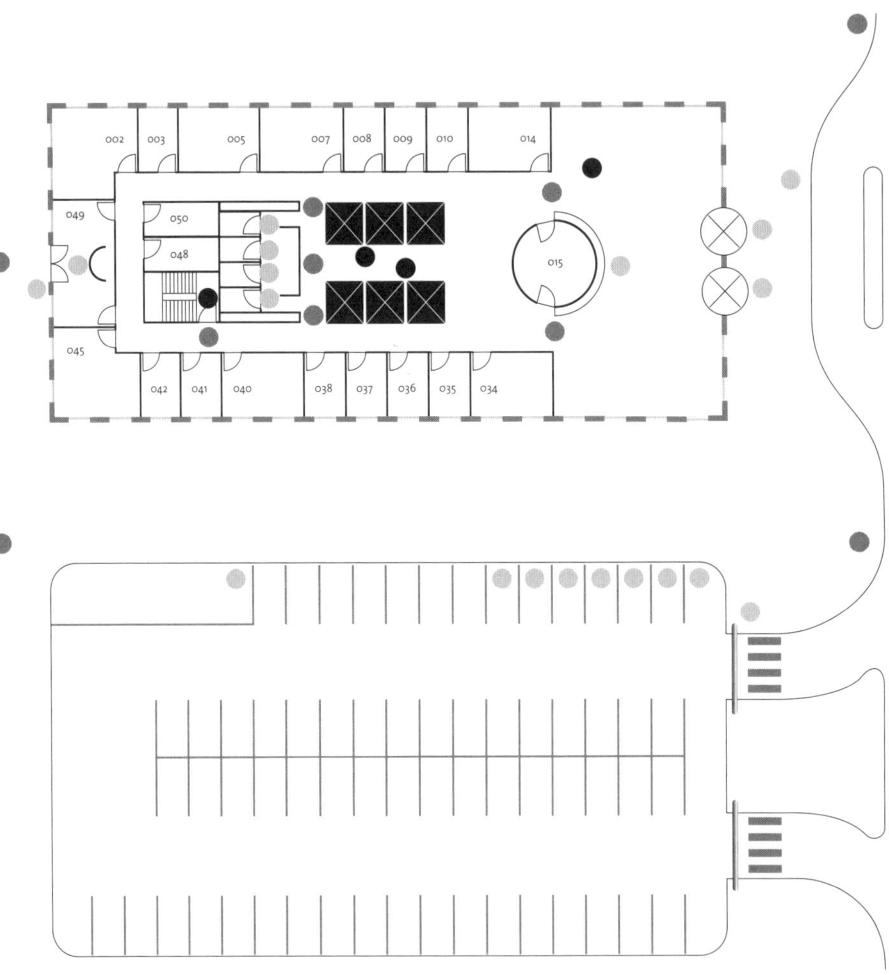

The second step in designing a signage system is making a map that shows the global positions of all four elementary sign types. Small coloured stickers mark the different sign types in their position.

3.7.3.2. Direction

The second sign type directs the traveller along the way. It is the most archaic of all sign types. This type of sign can be found everywhere, even in fairy tales—like the bread crumbs that 'Hansel and Gretel' used to be able to find their way back out of the forest. In the countryside, we also find such directional marks along footpaths. Arrows are found on practically all signs we use in the environment that fall into this category. Sometimes, arrow-shaped signs are used instead.

3.7.3.3. Destination

The third sign type is the one that marks the destination. It indicates the final goal of travel. It also indicates all the other destinations in between that we use as stepping stones before reaching our final destination. This sign type is also called a location sign or identification sign.

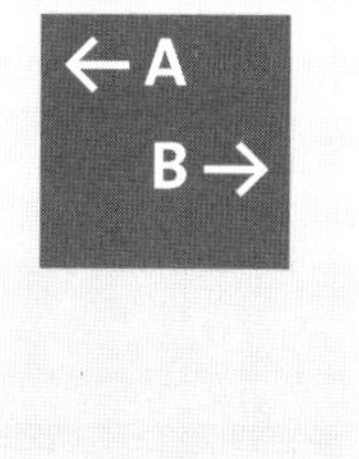

The three basic sign types used for wayfinding: a directory, a directional sign and a destination sign (or location sign).

3.7.3.4. Instruction & information

The fourth sign type is not directly related to the wayfinding process. This category is a sort of 'trifle' category; a mishmash of all the other kinds of signs found in and around the built environment. They include signs for general safety, security, fire safety, mandatory information, instructional signs, or signs for general information. The major part of these signs have to be legally present in the building. They indicate the location of fire fighting equipment and might give instructions for their use, they give warning messages against hazards, or they direct people towards emergency exits.

Other instructional signs might simply say 'push' or 'pull'—simple but rather useful instructions. Not only instructional signs fall into this category, but also general information signs. For instance, they might include signs that inform visitors about the occupant(s) of the building, or opening hours, or a brief history of the organisation(s) housed in the building, or a list of benefactors, etc. A special type in this category is emerging and being frequently referred to as 'branding' signs. These are signs that are specially produced to support the corporate image of an organisation. The 'welcome' signs usually fall into this latter category of sign types.
It is advisable to make a separate set of plans with only the emergency/fire exit signs in case this is a part of the signage commission. In fact, these signs should not be in this category of instructions, but instead in a special category of wayfinding signs, since they represent a particularly crucial type of wayfinding under extreme circumstances.

3.8. Database of signs & text lists

A signage project can easily consist of hundreds of individual signs. Each sign must be specified in three ways; its exact physical manufacturing specs, the precise message it will carry, and its accurate mounting location. Providing all these data for each sign and keeping track of all of them during the design and approval

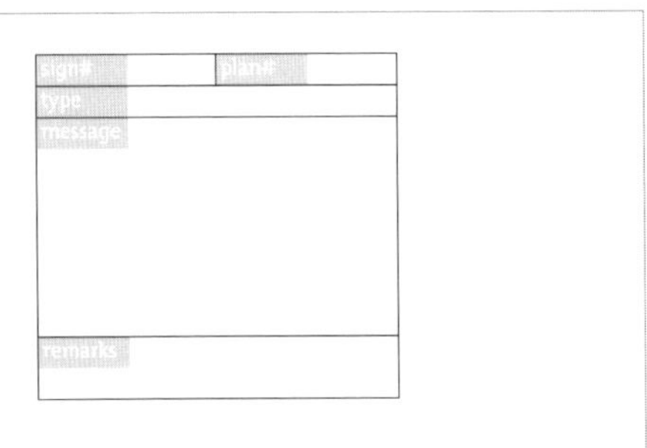

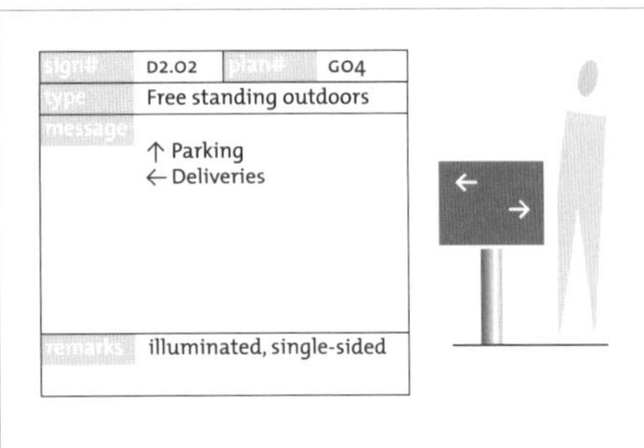

The final step in designing the signage system is to make a database of all signs. Accompanying maps will show references to each sign in the database.

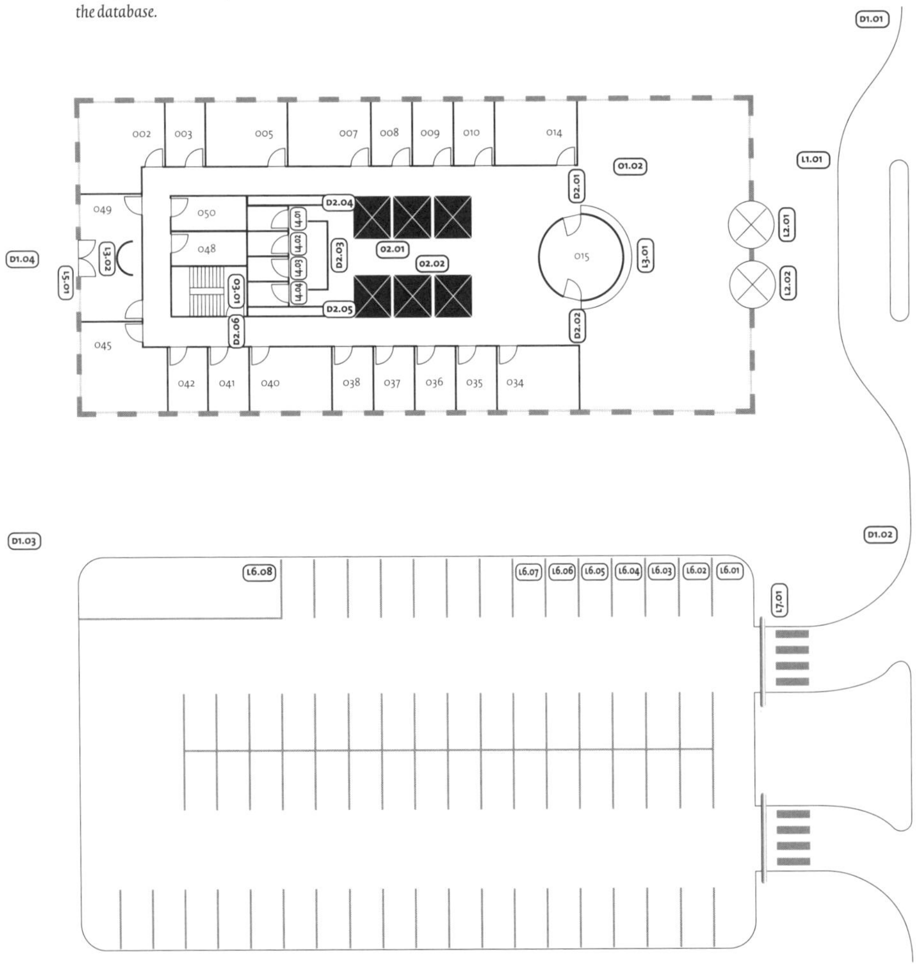

phases makes signage design often a rather tedious job. This task is best dealt with by setting up a solid system of file cards or an electronic database. Each sign must get a unique number in the database, and all the signs must be grouped according to their sign type and specific location in the building or site.

The first suggestions for the messages that will appear on the individual signs start with placing the basic sign type stickers on the traffic flow plans. Afterwards, the database will be extended and updated regularly. It is important for the client to be able to use the database as well. Some data for specific sign types are best entered directly by the client at a certain stage of the project.

3.9. List of sign types

The first four basic sign types are useful to make a first outline of the overall signage needs of a site. The basic sign types will need more refinement in detail during the design process. Making a final list of all the different sign types needed in the project is an important part of the development of the signage system. This list determines in fact the amount of work that has to be done in the next phase of the visual design.

All signs proposed for the building must be divided and grouped into sign types. Different signs within each sign type group can only vary in content (text and/or image). In all other aspects, all signs within one sign type group are identical . The visual design —done in the next stage—is limited to one design for each individual sign type. To provide production instructions for each individual sign, the visual design will also include a 'layout grid' and related instructions that will facilitate applying different content or messages on each sign within the same group. In this way, only one design is needed per sign type, and will be applied to all signs belonging to each particular sign type group.

The establishment of a final list of sign types is a process of ongoing evaluation. One starts by making a basic list of only the very global function of each sign type. Next, this list will be repeatedly scanned for further aspects of functionality of each sign within one group. For instance, the desired level of changeability or dynamic features of a specific sign, or the desired position in space (mounted on the wall or free-standing). Furthermore, there is the functional aspect of size often related to the reading distance, or the need for internal illumination of the sign, or specific vandal-proof qualities (especially for external signs). Also requirements for impaired users may need to be incorporated into some types of signs. Proceeding in this way with ongoing evaluation will make the list of sign types longer, since some signs will need more special functionalities than others within the same category.

Next to the evaluation of purely functional aspects, there are different ways to meet a certain functionality of a sign. For instance, the use of a banner instead of a solid panel. To specifically accommodate this functional aspect, a library of sign types is created for browsing and selection. Please note that not only strictly functional aspects dictate the choices in sign type selection, since this activity is situated between signage system design and visual design. These two features of the conceptual design work must be separated in the phases of development of the signage project. However, the two aspects are sometimes closely related and a total separation of the two aspects is neither possible nor entirely desirable.

Eventually a complete list will be established on which each sign will be listed as an individual sign type when it differs from another sign in any other way than a strict difference in message. Obviously, economy in design and production requires that the number of different sign types proposed for the whole project is kept to the absolute minimum.

For further reference during the project, it is useful to give the different sign types not only a short code, but also a name, such as wall-mounted elevator/lift directory, or door sign with laserprint pocket.

3.9.1. CHECK-LIST FOR SIGN TYPE SELECTION

Underneath is a check-list of most aspects that may influence the creation of a separate sign type.
—Basic function of the sign.
—Signage technology applied.
—Position in space, method of fixing.
—Size in relation to reading distance.
—Illumination.
—Requirements for impaired users.
—Level of vandal resistance.

3.9.2. WORK STRATEGY FOR PRODUCING THE LIST OF SIGN TYPES

Research is the first phase in establishing a list of sign types. The difficult part will be to decide which kind of technologies to adopt for the project. Following this, making sign plans with traffic flows will reveal the first (basic) needs for different types of signs. Next, there will be a list of requirements that have to be applied, established in the first phase of the project. Finally, it is best to make real walks through the building site in order to make decisions concerning the positioning and fixings of signs. These decisions are best taken after experiencing in reality what the users of the building will go through when they start using the facilities.

3.10. Types of buildings

Showing traffic flows and applying basic sign type stickers helps in the creation of a rough image of the signage needed in a built environment. A basic understanding of the type of building and the way it functions is of course equally important in weighing the behaviour of traffic flows. A sports stadium attracts a lot of visitors and so does a public library, but there is a big difference in signage needs between the two. For example, a sports stadium has to bring thousands of people to their seats within an hour, whereas a library has to accommodate a far more sophisticated search process between within 8- to 12-hour periods (or more) on a daily basis. Below the different needs for a wide range of types of buildings will be briefly discussed.

3.10.1. MANUFACTURING PLANTS, LABORATORIES

Signage is closely related to the production process and can be very specific for certain industries. The emphasis for the signage design will be on safety and security aspects. Office buildings are often a separate part of the complex.

3.10.2. OFFICE BUILDINGS

Office buildings are by far the majority of all non-dwelling types of buildings. Office buildings are the homes of the ever-growing service industry, and can house huge organisations or very small ones. Many are multi-occupancy buildings with different tenants.

More and more office buildings are introducing a 'hotel occupancy system'. In such systems, staff do not have their own workstation anymore; each staff member is booked in instead, for a certain space (depending on the need) and a certain period of time. Government buildings on all levels occupy an important place in societies around the world, and generally attract a large number of visitors. Most buildings are in fact partially public places and must be able to accommodate a diverse audience. Carefully planned signage can be very helpful in fulfilling this task.

3.10.3. EXHIBITION SPACES, CONFERENCE CENTRES, MUSEUMS, NATIONAL PUBLIC MONUMENTS, THEATRES AND CINEMAS

Nowadays, buildings made for both commercial and recreational (or in some cases scientific) purposes attract a lot of visitors from all over the world. The building itself can be, or become, an important identity (or even brand) for the organisation it houses. The announcement of changing events needs special design attention. Electronic and computer-aided systems might be applicable in this case.

3.10.4. RECREATION BUILDINGS AND ARENAS

Sports arenas, stadiums, zoos, and parks also have a very wide range of users. One would expect visitors to be relaxed in these surroundings, but surprisingly enough these environments are also often subject to vandalism. Signage design should take this aspect into consideration.

3.10.5. SHOPPING MALLS, RETAIL STORES, SUPERMARKETS

The signage in these environments is in an atmosphere closely related to commercial signage. Signage is not only considered as being important for wayfinding, but also for drawing attention and encouraging sales. Some argue that the wayfinding aspect of the signage is in fact irrelevant in these kinds of surroundings, and that it would be best for business when visitors get lost in these places. 'Welcome in... and get lost'. This concept of making shopping an adventurous experience is—when pushed a bit too far—detrimental. Research reveals that shopping malls where people often felt lost were doing commercially pretty badly. Retail chains need a strong visual identity for all their outlets to be easily recognised. Signage becomes an important part of their corporate branding.

3.10.6. HOSPITALS, HEALTH CARE FACILITIES

These places can be moderate in size or enormous building complexes. Careful signage design is very important for these types of buildings. Visitors and patients in hospitals can be easily upset and anxious. Building complexes for health care have often grown over the years and have therefore become hopelessly complicated in structure. Moreover, the health care profession still has a tendency to focus primarily on the fulfilment of their own professional needs, probably with the assumption that this would also be best for serving the patients. That assumption is plainly wrong, however: only take a look at the names that are often given to specific departments in hospitals! For signage purposes, the starting point should be the expected level of understanding of the patient and visitor. Surely staff will also be able to find their way around perfectly well with the help of such signs.

3.10.7. UNIVERSITIES, COLLEGES AND SCHOOLS

Sometimes building complexes in this category can be huge and signage can be quite complicated. Some universities have academic hospitals as part of their campus. These projects are on average relatively straightforward signage jobs. Matters can become more complicated when sites are big, or when institutions offer many extra-curricular courses for which students can register per course on a part-time basis, or when special seminars or business courses are offered that attract a lot of first-time visitors, often arriving in the evening. Moreover, some schools might be vulnerable to acts of vandalism.

3.10.8. HOTELS, MOTELS, RESTAURANTS

Hotels, motels, and restaurants need relatively simple signage jobs with little need for complicated information updates. Sometimes, hotels are part of conference centres or other buildings. Those that are part of a chain or group are comparable with retail chains.

3.10.9. TRANSIT FACILITIES

Airports, railway and subway stations, bus or ferry terminals require complex signage jobs. Clear and simple traffic flows or routing are extremely important. Transit centres can be landmarks in the environment, but breathtaking architecture should not obscure or obstruct the basic functions of transit centres—an obvious constraint that one would expect to see respected and applied everywhere. Regrettably that does not always appear to be the case. The level of signage design in a lot of these places is still far below the minimum professional standard.
The fact that transit hubs are visited by many every day, makes them commercially very attractive. The result is that the signage has to compete with a plethora of commercial signs. A battle that is generally won by the commercial party.

3.11. *Imaginary walk through a site*

The initial appraisal of the site can be done behind the desk. It is best to start with making an imaginary trip to the site, into the building, and then a visit to all areas inside. An example of such an imaginary walk through the site is described below and is based on a tour through an office building. Other types of buildings may have a sequence of different areas and spaces, but as a case study, the office building works well.

The imaginary tour is not limited to the wayfinding aspects. To make the overview of the possible needs for signage complete, some type of signs are added that are not relevant to the wayfinding aspect of the signage.

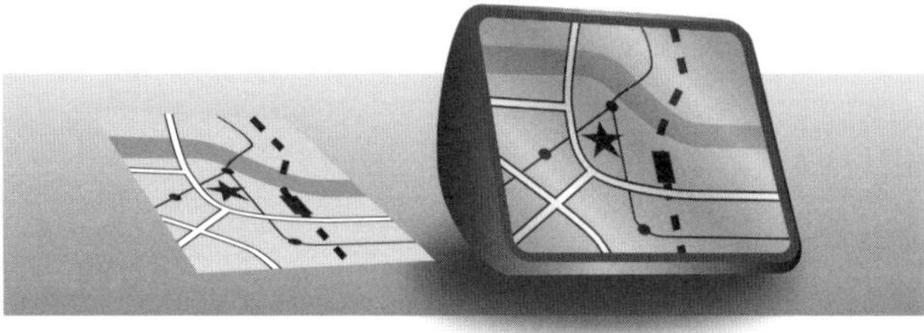

3.11.1. INFORMATION BEFORE STARTING THE JOURNEY

It is always an appreciated gesture when visitors receive in advance by fax or by mail a small map indicating all the different ways to get to a building, by foot, bicycle, car, or public transport. A lot of websites also provide a page with a location map. Maps are considerably more useful when they can be taken along during the journey. So maps must be sent in print or otherwise be easily printable by the visitor.

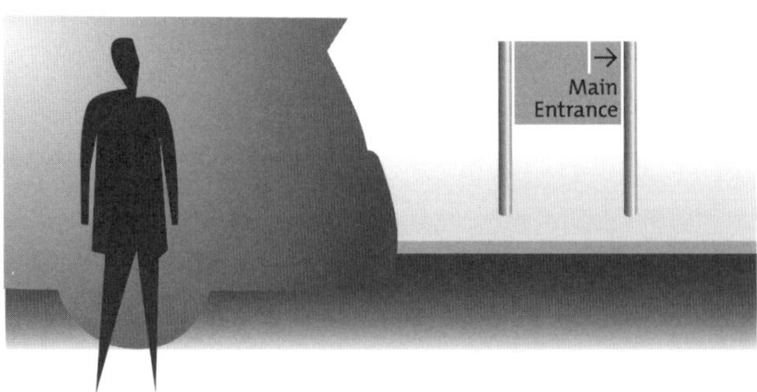

3.11.2. PUBLIC TRANSPORTATION STOPS

Public transportation stops near the building should be examined, and the ways that people will approach the building starting from the different stops should be carefully studied. It could be that the main entrance is not always obviously visible when approached from certain directions. Some buildings have special drop-off and pick-up points for taxis and private cars that might need directional signs.

3.11.3. IDENTIFICATION OF THE BUILDING

Some buildings may become landmarks or even acquire names relating to their original owner or architect. Some owners or occupants want their name and/or their company logo quite prominently displayed high up on the building. The impact of this type of sign might be more effective for commercial than for navigational purposes.

3.11.4. CAR PARK OR GARAGE

Many visitors travel in their own cars. They have to park their vehicle first before continuing their journey on foot inside the building. Car parks or garages are sometimes separate buildings connected to the main building. Signage for these buildings can become a separate issue.

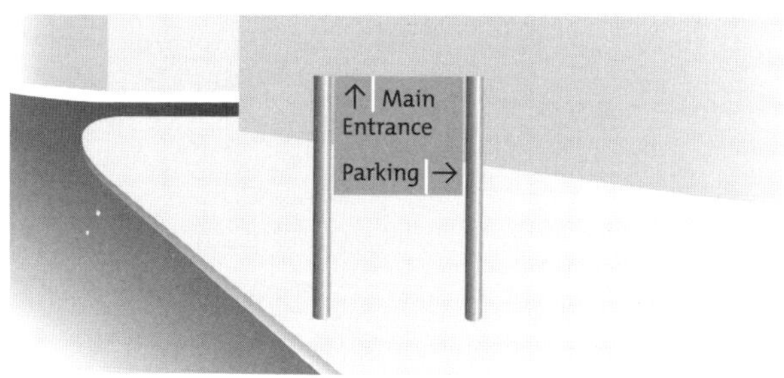

3.11.4.1. Directional signs to parking facilities

It might be necessary to place directional signs for drivers to guide them to parking facilities.

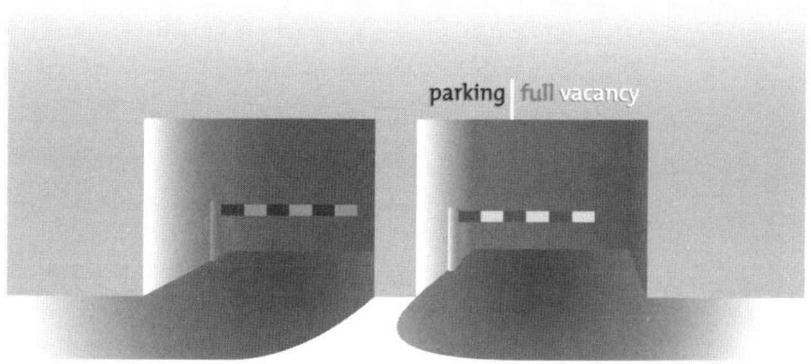

3.11.4.2. Parking entrance

The entrance has to be clearly marked. It might be necessary to make this an illuminated sign. Large public car parks have changeable 'full/vacant' signs near their entrances.

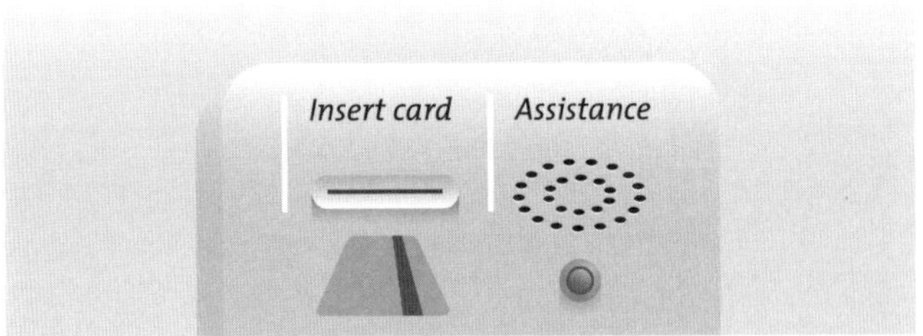

—Entrance procedure
Most parking garages have a barrier of some sort in front of their entrances. In addition, there is a specific procedure to follow in order to gain access. Signage might be needed to inform users properly about the following:
- functions of intercoms or other machines
- parking tariffs
- general rules and regulations.

—Parking space identification
Most car parks have marked spaces for visitors, staff, and disabled persons. Some facilities maintain an easily updatable system using electronic text panels. This type of panels allows the indication of specially reserved parking spots, by using the visitor's own name.

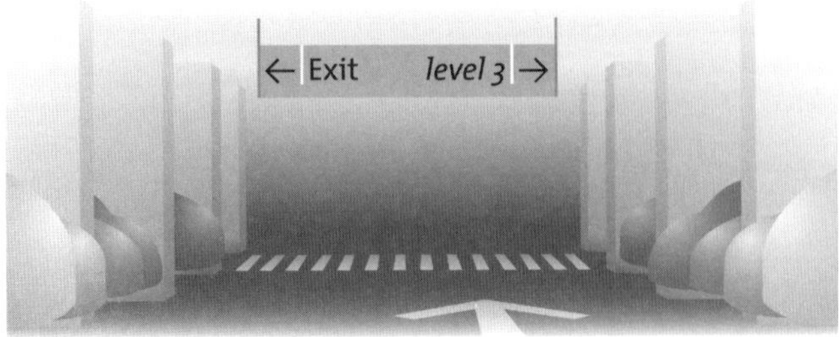

—Directional signs for cars and pedestrians
Parking garages have two main traffic flows. First, vehicles cruising and leaving, and second, visitors looking for their cars or the nearest pedestrian exits. These two flows need clear directional signage throughout the parking facility. Sometimes pedestrian paths and driving circulation are clearly indicated on the ground.

—Floor level indication and/or area indication

In large car parks or garages an indication is needed to help retrieve one's car easily upon return. Clear floor level indicators, different names assigned to different segments of the parking facility, or names related to nearby exit/entrance doors for passengers, can be of great help.

—Stairways or elevators/lifts

Pedestrians are often brought into and out of the car park building with staircases and elevators. Clear signage is needed in these facilities, and special attention must be given to accessibility for impaired users. Sometimes cash machines are also present in these facilities.

3.11.5. MAIN ENTRANCE TO THE BUILDING

The architectural style determines how obvious the main entrance will be. In some cases a clear sign is imperative. The name of the building or the company occupying the building is often used, with or without the addition of the logo. This sign is often an illuminated sign.

3.11.5.1. Main entrance directory

A directory of major departments or tenants can be placed outside the building near the entrance. Building complexes with many entrances might even need a map to point to the different entrances.

3.11.5.2. Street number

A sign with the street number is often required by city regulation. The number can be combined with another type of sign, such as the directory.

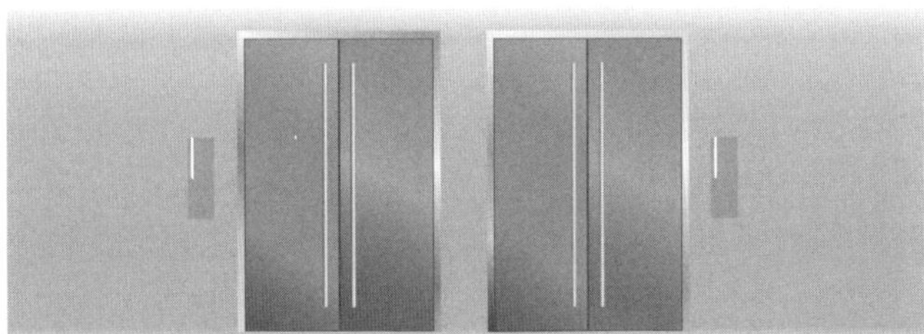

3.11.5.3. Entrance regulations

Regulations for entrances can be simple or complicated depending on security procedures. Providing a sign which shows opening times is advisable.

3.11.5.4. *Entrance for the impaired*
There must be a clear indication for mobility impaired people to guide them to the appropriate entrance.

3.11.6. OTHER ENTRANCES INTO THE BUILDING
Deliveries could be directed to a separate entrance. Hospitals may have various entrances of equal importance. Entrances other than, or next to, the main entrance would need directional signs. Whatever the case, destination signs are required for all entrances.

3.11.7. MAIN LOBBY
The main lobby is the place to orient and inform oneself about the building and its occupant(s), to make inquiries, or to wait for someone. Main lobbies are sometimes partly used as exhibition spaces, and may have other facilities to comfort, entertain, inform, or impress the visitors.

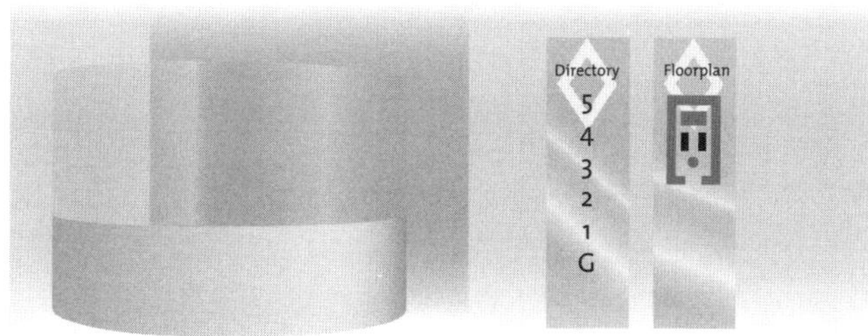

3.11.7.1. *Main lobby directory and map*
The main lobby directory is the central orientation point in the building.This type of sign can be produced in a wide variety of ways, from a simple list of tenants or departments, to interactive screen consoles where the visitor can find the exact locations of all tenants or departments in the building, or even to a detailed listing of people's names and room numbers. Maps are also used when floor levels are complicated. In some cases maps may have a more decorative purpose.

3.11.7.2. *Central information desk*
Organisations may feel the need for a staffed reception. In this case, a clear location sign for the information desk is needed. In addition, opening hours for staffed receptions should be clearly indicated. Sometimes, a visitor has to call on reception to be guided personally to the desired destination. When visitors need

directional information in complicated situations, a simple map of the building with a marked destination may be given as a hand-out. This can be very helpful to the visitor.

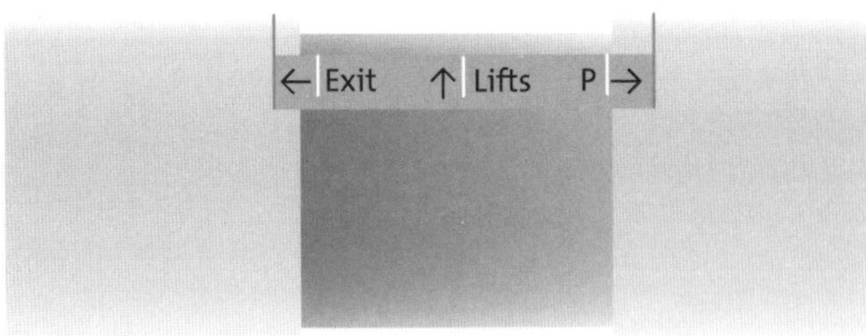

3.11.7.3. Main lobby directions

As part of the main lobby, or not too far away from it, there will be stairs, lifts or escalators for vertical transportation. In most cases one needs these facilities to reach the next step in the journey.

3.11.8. COMMUNAL FACILITIES

Washrooms, toilets and cloakrooms are, in terms of quantity, the most important facilities in this category. Sometimes communal facilities include places where one can buy drinks, snacks, or a whole meal. Libraries, exhibition spaces, or telephone booths are also considered part of communal facilities.

3.11.8.1. Toilets, washrooms

Toilets need clear directional indications throughout the building and a gender identification near the entrances. Special toilets for the mobility impaired need dedicated identification.

3.11.8.2. Cafeteria, coffee corners

Cafeterias need in addition to information about direction and entrance identification, hours of service, a menu with a price list, as well as a smoking area—if there is one allowed.

3.11.8.3. Other communal facilities

All other facilities need a clear entrance identification and hours of service information.

3.11.9. DEPARTMENTS, OFFICES & MEETING ROOMS

This category constitutes the great bulk of all signage in the building.

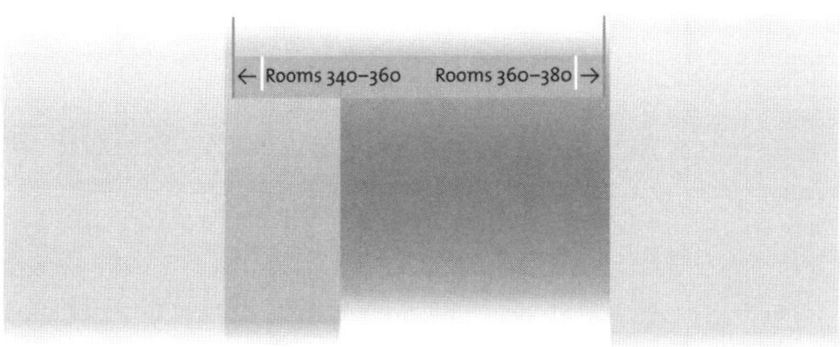

3.11.9.1. Directional signs

A clear coding and/or room numbering system is the basis of all directional signage to offices. Names of departments and meeting rooms may be added to give a better insight about the organisation's, or building's structure.

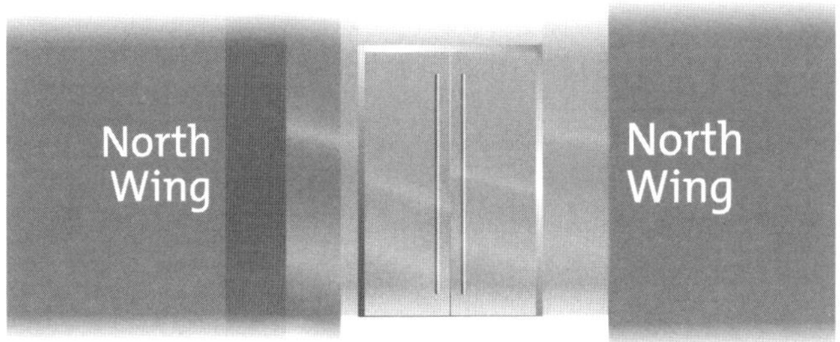

3.11.9.2. Section identification

When the building is divided into sections for wayfinding purposes, these sections need identification upon entering them. Restricted areas should be clearly indicated as such.

3.11.9.3. Department reception

Department receptions need 'hours of service' signs with adequate availability information. In addition, a desk sign with the receptionist's name may be used.

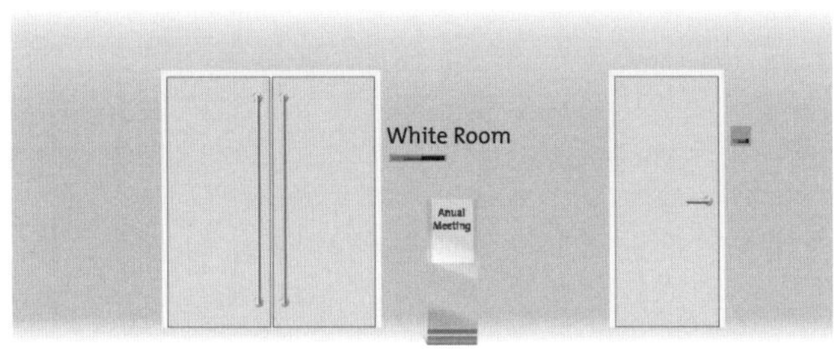

3.11.9.4. Meeting rooms

Meeting rooms come in various sizes; small or sometimes quite large. The small ones will look very much like the standard offices, whereas the large ones may need a more special type of identification. All meeting rooms will need a 'free/occupied' sign. For some meeting rooms it might be useful to have special movable directional signs in case of special events that can attract a lot of visitors. Some organisations use various meeting rooms rather intensely, attracting a lot of first-time visitors. The installation of a centralised and electronically-updatable signage system might be a useful consideration under these circumstances.

3.11.9.5. Office doors

All office doors need a room number and/or an alphanumeric code as identification. The door sign can also bear the name(s), the department, and/or the function of the occupant(s). In open-plan areas these signs will be put on the divider panels between workstations. Some office doors might require an extra message, such as to call on the receptionist first.

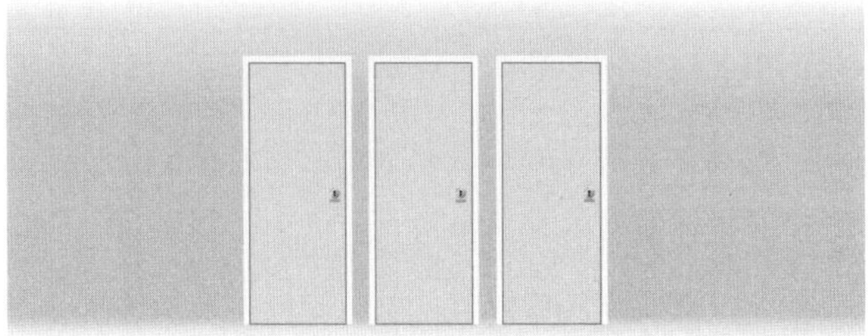

3.11.10. TECHNICAL ROOMS

A considerable number of doors in a building close off spaces or rooms used for technical purposes, like control rooms, risers, service ducts, switch rooms, alarm systems, air conditioning or cleaning equipment. Repair and maintenance personnel need to be able to locate these rooms easily. Proper identification signs are therefore needed for this type of room.

3.11.11. INSTRUCTIONS, NOTICES, DISPLAY UNITS

Some machines or facilities (eg. light switches, movable windows, intercoms, heating and ventilation controls, communal office machines) need specific instructions. These may be complicated instructions or simple push/pull signs. Similarly, bulletin boards are used to inform staff or visitors, and some display signs can also be used as notice boards in addition to serving an often commercial purpose.

3.11.12. SAFETY & MANDATORY SIGNS

Building and working condition regulations require certain signs to be placed in prescribed circumstances. Practically all these signs are more or less standardised.

3.11.13. EMERGENCY, FIRE EXIT AND FIRE EQUIPMENT SIGNS

These signs are legally required to be displayed in all buildings. Fire exit signs need to be illuminated in many cases with special battery facilities. Fire-fighting equipment needs clear location signs and possibly additional usage instructions. Emergency procedures and maps showing fire evacuation or escape routes may be posted at various locations in a building.

3.11.14. ELEVATORS OR ESCALATORS

Elevators/lifts are important signage locations. Vertical transportation is often concentrated around elevators. All control panels inside and outside the elevator cars must be within reach of people sitting in wheelchairs, and are often printed and embossed in order to accommodate the visually impaired.

Inside the elevator cars there will be an electronic floor level indicator and the legally required capacity sign about maximum weight and maximum number of persons. There will also be a telephone or intercom for use in emergency cases which may need usage instructions. Certainly there will be a control panel for buttons with floor and 'open/close door' indicators.

Outside the elevator there are call buttons for going up or down. There may be other indicators for special purpose use, or for elevators that will only reach certain floors. There might be an emergency sign not to use the elevators in case of fire. A technical door number may be added for maintenance purposes. As for escalators, they may need safety and/or emergency instructions.

3.11.14.1. Elevator directory and floor number

A directory inside each elevator is often appreciated by visitors. Outside the elevator a directory is needed on each floor. Escalators often have a floor number sign in combination with a directory of the specific locations that are found on that floor.

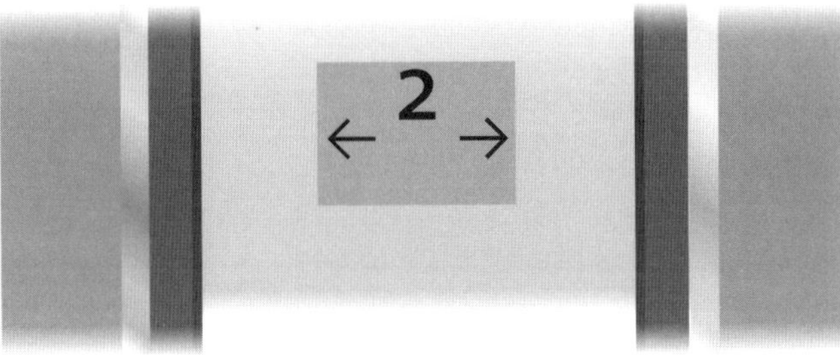

3.11.14.2. Elevator lobby directional signs

When leaving the elevator, directional signs, in addition to a floor number, will be needed. Probably the best place for these signs will be opposite the elevator door.

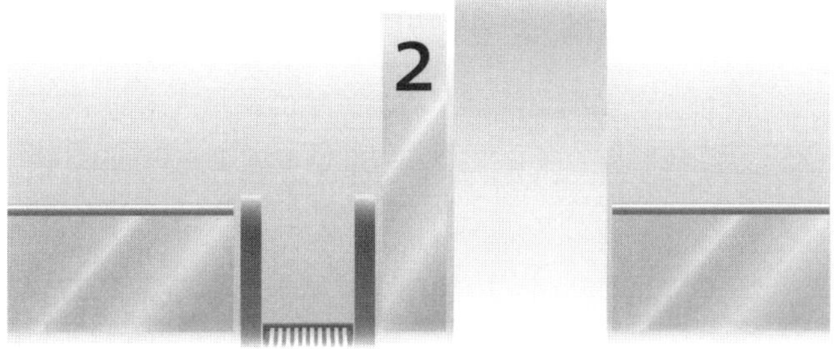

3.11.15. STAIRCASES AND ESCALATORS

Staircases can be exclusively assigned as emergency exits, often taking the shape of an open metal frame constructions outside the building. Many staircases though have a mixed function; they can be used for vertical transportation as well as for emergency exits in cases where lifts are malfunctioning. Some staircases are only used for vertical transportation. Staircases need a floor level identification on each floor, and in some cases a floor directory may be added.
Escalators may be major transportation facilities in large commercial buildings or transportation hubs. In this case, clear floor level indications, directories and directional signs become crucially important.

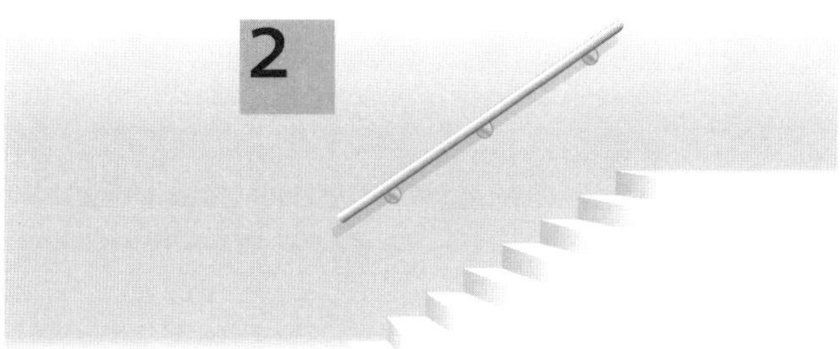

3.11.16. ADDITIONAL FACILITIES

Most standard sign types are covered in this overview. However, some buildings will have special facilities that need additional signs. To name a few: 'welcome' or branding signs, sponsor or donor recognition boards, and signs in exhibition areas.

3.12. Library of sign types

Making a list of all the sign types needed in a project is essential before starting the visual design phase. It would be helpful if there was a generally accepted classification of sign types or a standard sign type library to choose from. Regrettably, that is not the case. Maybe this is not difficult to understand when realising the huge scope given to the signs we put into our environment. Some sign types have a legal status and are specified and classified. This category of sign types alone covers already extended libraries, certainly when all international variations are taken into account. Other sign types have no other purpose than to sell or to entertain. This type is hard to classify since the various ways to sell or to entertain are endless. Furthermore, there is hardly any specific type of human activity that does not use its specific set of sign types. Even if we limit the purpose of the signage projects to what is the major topic of this book, often referred to as 'Architectural signage', the number of different sign types is still pretty wide considering the vast amount of different building functions. Nevertheless, signage designers and sign manufacturers do use different methods to classify sign types. These methods often mix different criteria, sometimes being classified according to the basic function of the sign; sometimes the order is according to the way the signs are manufactured, or related to a specific sign location or position. Sometimes manufacturers create new names of sign types linked to product innovation.

To provide some kind of overview, three different listings are given below, first a hierarchical overview that follows the prime aspects of a sign like basic function, type of content, means of reproduction and type of physical support to keep it in place. This overview is far from complete but the given aspects are often used to describe sign types. Second is an alphabetic directory of names sometimes given to sign types. Third is a illustrative overview of sign types as they occur in specific, archetypical settings.

3.12.1 SIGN TYPE CLASSIFICATION

1. Basic functional aspect

1.1. Sales/advertising
1.2. PR/Branding
1.3. Entertaining/commemorating/art
1.4. Providing wayfinding/navigational information

1.4.1. Orientational, assisting the making of travel plans and creation of intuitive traffic flows by providing maps, directories, simple path structures, enhancing area recognition and transitions , erecting landmarks.

1.4.2. Directional, guiding to destinations by all signs bearing an arrow.

1.4.3. Instructional, providing legal, mandatory, security and other instructions along the way.

1.4.4. Destinational identification, confirming final destinations: area, building, venue, room, device, item or person.

1.5. Giving legal, mandatory, emergency notices and warnings
1.6. Assisting disabled users

2. Type of sign content

2.1. Text one language
2.2. Text multiple languages
2.3. Pictographic
2.4. Illustrative
2.5. Visual
2.6. Tactile
2.7. Audible
2.8. Olfactory
2.9. Electromagnetic signals

3. Fabrication method

3.1. Message or content fabrication
  3.1.1. Hand painted
  3.1.2. Hand carved
  3.1.3. Silk screened
  3.1.4. Inkjet printed
  3.1.5. Vinyl cut
  3.1.6. Panel/slab cut
  3.1.7. 3D channel
  3.1.8. Machine engraved
  3.1.9. Sandblasted/etched
  3.1.10. Moulded, cast, die-cut
  3.1.11. Neon
  3.1.12. Projected light
  3.1.13. Electronic display board
  3.1.14. Digital screen display
3.2. Content carrier fabrication
  3.2.1. No carrier, message directly put onto object
  3.2.2. Flexible: paper, mesh/fabric, thin synthetic sheet
  3.2.3. Rigid transparent: glass, synthetic panel, perforated solid sheet

3.2.4. Rigid solid: steel, wood, stone, synthetic material
3.2.5. Rigid fabricated: various forming techniques
3.3. Method of updating sign content
3.3.1. Inserts
3.3.2. Cassettes, containers
3.3.3. Mechanical
3.3.4. Electronic display boards
3.3.5. Interactive touch-screens
3.3.6. Screen display
3.3.7. Digital signage

4. Method of mounting or positioning in space
4.1. Flat wall-mounted
4.2. Projected, or flag-mounted
4.3. Suspended, or mounted overhead
4.4. Free-standing
4.4.1. Fixed
4.4.1.1. Monolith
4.4.1.2. Panel/pole combination
4.4.2. Portable
4.4.2.1. Floor/sidewalk/pavement
4.4.2.2. Desktop/counter
4.4.2.3. Workstation

5. Detailed functional aspect is often related to a specific location.

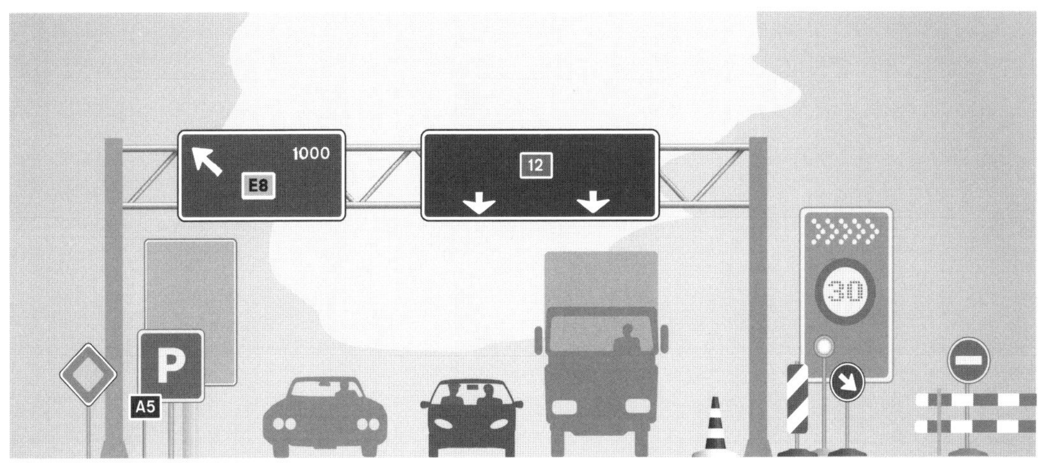

Highway signs are an extensive category of regulated sign types that should enhance ease of circulation and road safety. Sign types include huge portals, road and traffic signs. Constant highway repair and reconstruction requires a large number of temporary sign types. Military vehicles have a small category of dedicated sign types. Accident, weather and road condition warnings or indicators may be part of the signs. Standard on-board navigation systems will make most of the information on signs redundant.

Secondary road sign types include commercial signs next to the regulated signs for traffic circulation and safety. Some countries have a tradition and/or allow a greater liberty for placing big commercial signs in the vicinity of roads. This illustration shows a typical situation in the US where many 'monumental', 'high rise' and 'sculptured pylon' sign types are the custom.

Within cities, street signs include a very large variety of sign types; some dealing with traffic regulation and (parking) regulations, but most have commercial purposes. Huge billboards and murals are particularly popular in some countries.

Offering parking space has become a lucrative business opportunity in most countries. Slowly parking building owners are starting to understand the importance of proper signage and a routing that allows for comfortable traffic circulation. Even sophisticated architectural style has become a consideration for this type of building. Sign types will include machines and instructions for payment, sector indication, vehicle separation, pedestrian and wheelchair direction and identification, signs for dedicated parking spots, and shuttles to and from the parking space.

In all affluent societies the number of public and private transit facilities has increased. As soon as there is money to spare, people start travelling. They begin, transfer and end their journey in a large variety of transportation hubs or transit centres, like train, tram or underground stations, airports, bus, boat, or ferry terminals and taxi stands. All these places use a large variety of sign types. Electronic message boards and screen networks are becoming standard facilities. Transit centres attract a lot of visitors, which make these places attractive commercial locations. Wayfinding information often has to compete visually with commercial messages. Airports start to look like shopping malls and supermarkets are built around transit stations.

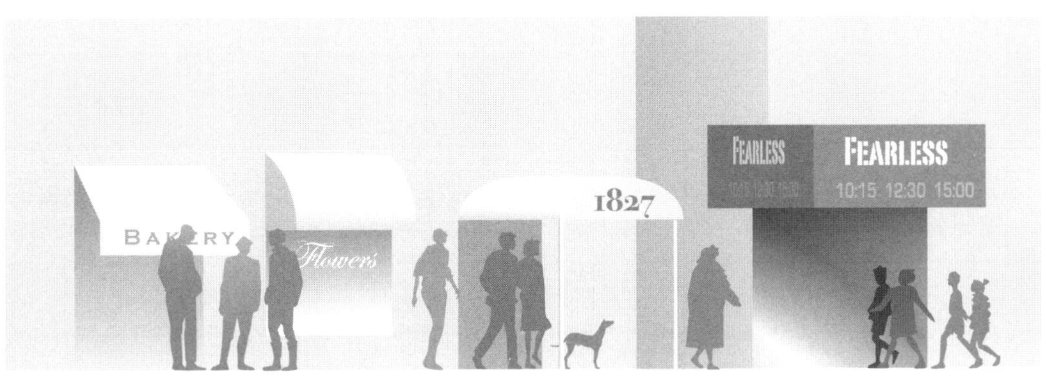

Sign types like marquees, canopies and awnings use light (transparent) synthetic material or fabrics in combination with some type of metal frame to build a simple, light but visually voluptuous construction. They serve many goals, like protection from bad weather or sun , as well as being carriers of identification signs, advertisements or welcome signs.

The often visually slightly messy world of display signs counts an endless variety of sign types. Most are free-standing, temporary, easily changeable and portable signs. The majority of the sign types used will have commercial purposes and carry names like 'pop-up' or 'pop' (point of purchase) signs. Large format printing techniques on all kinds of (weather resistant) material have made pop signs cheap and extremely popular.

Flags and banners are an attractive and joyful category of sign types. They are light, easy to produce, visually spectacular and will only need a simple pole or a pair of tubes to hold them in place. They are lively and pleasant companions of the more sturdy sign types.

Humans have an irresistible urge to leave behind traces of their existence in their environment. Sometimes these signs have a clear purpose, often it is just a mark of presence, maybe similar to the territory markers some animals leave behind. This category of informal (and often illegal) signs or graffiti makes up an immeasurable variety of sign types.

Handcrafted sign types are still popular (although popularity varies largely from one country to another). Handcrafted signs include an endless variety, like hand-carving in wood, metal or stone, hand-painting and hand-forming neon tubes or hand-cut solid or channel letters. Not only extremely elaborate sign types fall under this category, but also simple stencil letters or illustrations.

'Dimensional Letters' is a large category of sign types which comprises all signs that do not make use of a dedicated carrier such as a panel, a board or a screen. Individual letters are directly applied to the building surface, sometimes with the help of a simple frame or tube. Dimensional Letters cover a wide range of methods of fabrication, from simple cutout vinyl foil to elaborate channel-neon letter combinations. In practically all cases Dimensional Letters are superior to the cheaper Light Boxes used for the same purpose.

Some cities have a reputation for the abundant use of the category of sign types sometimes referred to as 'electrical spectacular', notably cities like Tokyo, New York (Times Square) and Las Vegas. Surely Chinese cities will soon challenge existing reputations or have already crushed some. Traditional sign types like huge dynamic neon installations and gigantic light boxes are used together with more recent technologies, like LED screens, and applied in almost limitless dimensions.

Reception areas bring together a large variety of sign types, ranging from very small and simple ones, like desk or counter signs, to advanced and/or big ones, like building identification and directories, interactive kiosks, donor recognition boards. Reception areas can also have facilities like literature racks and special exhibitions.

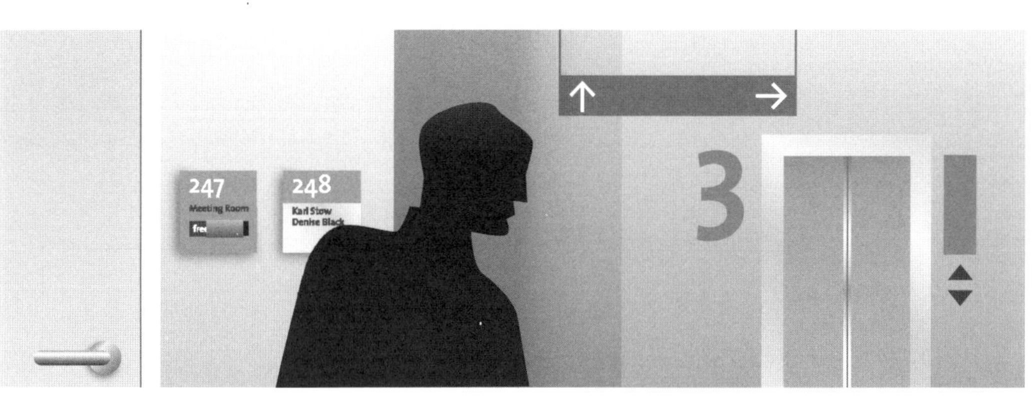

Governmental and commercial office buildings or healthcare facilities make use of a wide range of sign types for comparable purposes. All buildings have a need for a variety of different directories (building, floor, elevator), identification signs (door, stair, department, section, building), regulated, mandatory, security, and emergency exit signs, directional signs to facilitate circulation in the building. Most of these signs are relatively small in size (plaque size) but rather large in number and variety. The category of these sign types is often referred to as 'Architectural Signage'.

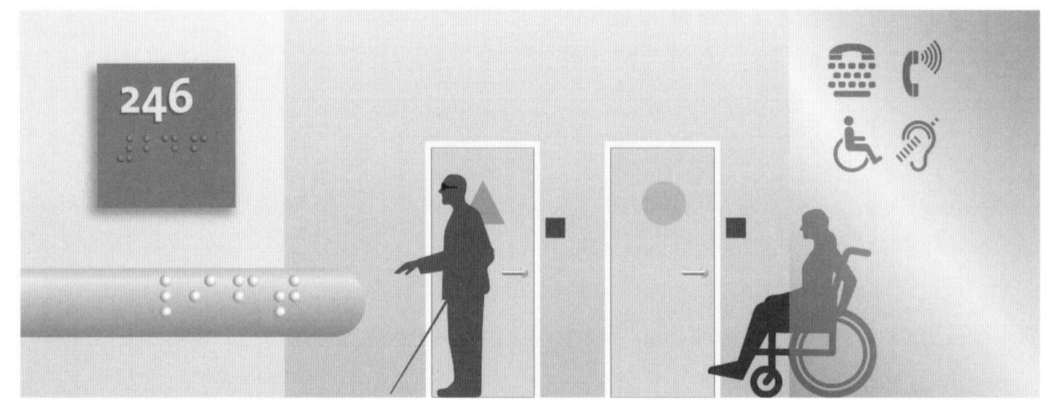

Signage projects that explicitly facilitate the needs of various groups of handicapped, impaired or disabled users are called 'inclusive' signage projects. In certain countries some of this kind of provision is mandatory. Most facilities attempt to accommodate the visually impaired and wheelchair users. The number of sign types involved can be extensive depending on the desired sophistication of the facilities. Constant product innovation is likely to reduce the need for general provisions in favour of customised personal equipment.

The oldest and most basic type of signage is trail marking on a track or a footpath. There are various ways of doing this, from simple brush strokes of coloured paint to more sophisticated icons used to identify different trails. National Parks and other dedicated areas may use a large variety of sign types to accommodate visitors.

The outdoor sign types used on campuses and estates can be quite numerous and may include an arch as monumental entrance identification, followed by a large variety of primary and secondary directories, directionals, and identification signs dedicated for vehicle users and pedestrians. Street names, parking section indicators, event cabinets, disabled access are only a few of the additional sign types that may be employed.

Exhibition spaces make much use of a specific category of sign types: display cabinets, illuminated or non-illuminated. These cabinets can be relatively small and fixed to the wall or robust and big free-standing facilities that need to be secure, vandal-proof and rugged. Of course, all varieties in between these two types are also available.

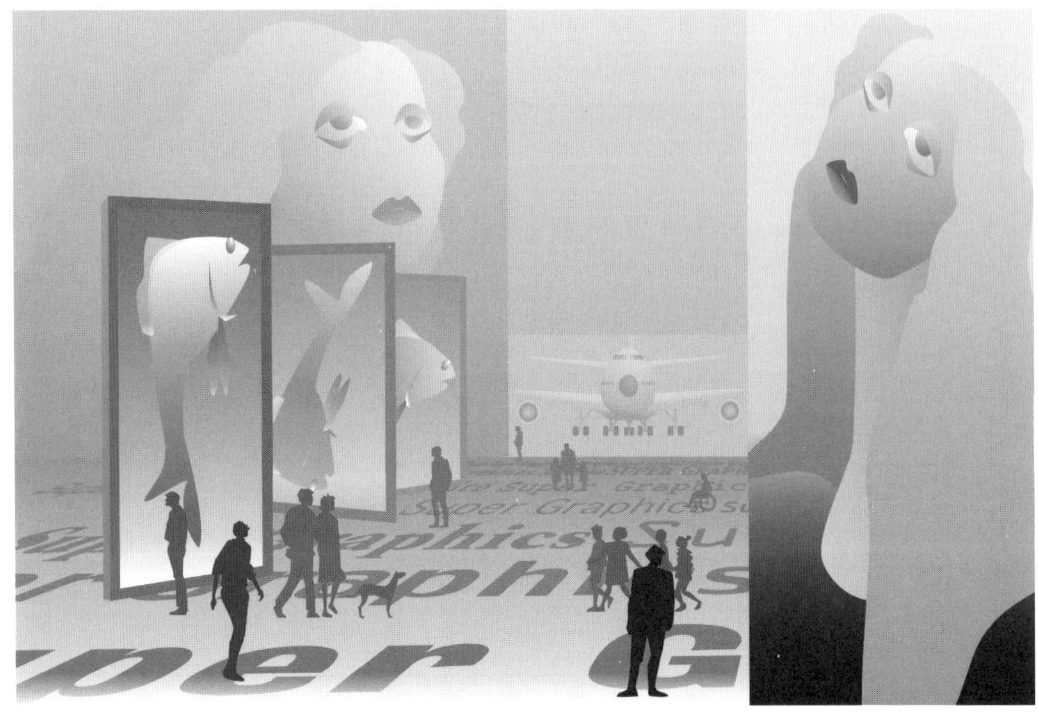

'Super-Graphics' is the name of a category of sign types that have only one quality in common: a huge size. Technological developments have made size an almost irrelevant constraint. Graphics can be produced in almost any size and applied on almost any surface, including the floor and the pavement. These manufacturing possibilities are no longer limited to static images. LED *technology has made fabrication of very large screens possible. Shopping malls, commercial centres and sports stadiums were the first to use these applications.*

Emergency exit signs are a legal (code) requirement in all structures. In some countries they are even required to be present during the construction phase. This category of signs may consist of a lot of different types. To keep their functional quality after a collapse or failure of the main electricity network, emergency exit signs will be connected to a dedicated network, contain batteries or make use of light emitting fluorescent material.

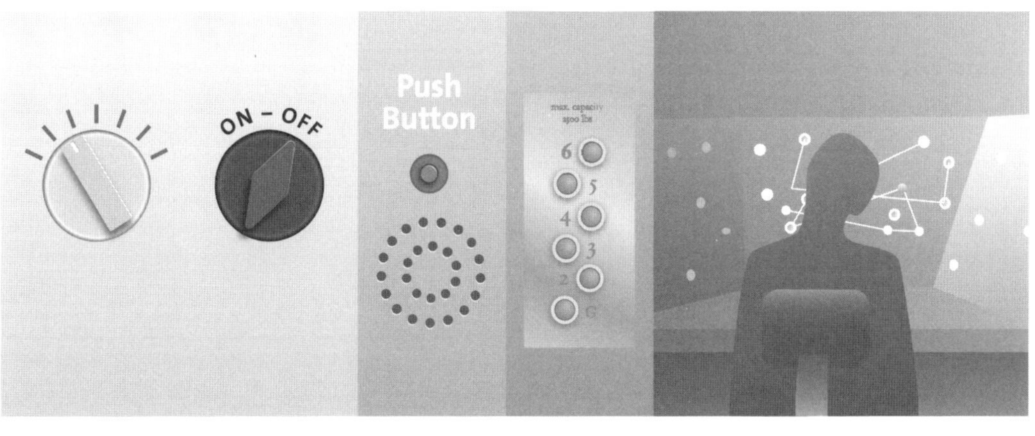

Machines, instruments and equipment use graphic signs to explain their use. These can be very simple on/off indications or more complex instructions on elevator/lift panels. Some types of consoles are designed to make complicated situations or processes clearly visible in a concise format. These types of consoles are often related to evacuation routes, fire protection or key security points. All will have some sort of activity or occurrence detection boards. This category of sign types may also be part of a signage project.

Industrial production plants must use a lot of different sign types. Most of these sign types are internationally standardised. They include identification marks for type of products and instructions for their use. Most are related to work safety and process control.

Eventually, some of the facilities we still use will disappear or will be marginalised. The current changes in the rather complicated process of travelling by air are an indication of the developments to come. There will be less need for human intervention in the process of allowing access or distributing availability. Digital devices will take over most of the communication still done by people today.

3.12.2 ALPHABETICAL LIST OF SIGN TYPES

A

ADA *Signs*, a category of sign types regulated by the ADA (Americans with Disabilities Act) guidelines, for the most part comprising room identification signs and overhead signs.
A-frames, double-sided free-standing signs with two panels hinged at the top and connected near the bottom.
Architectural Signs, a category of signs used in and around buildings for wayfinding/navigational, legal, branding, informational or instructional purposes.
Awning, a sheet of framed fabric to keep the sun or rain off a storefront, often used to carry a sign as well. (see canopy)

B

Balloon Sign, air or gas inflated and sealed sac carrying a message.
Banner, strip of fabric fixed on poles or against the wall on the inside or outside of buildings.
Belt Signs, covering a long strip on an (outdoor) wall.
Billboard, a large outdoor board for displaying advertisements. Also used in combination with specific use, like events.
Building Directory, overview of all tenants, departments or sections in a building.
Bulletin Board, a board for displaying notices.

C

Canopy, a roof-like projection or shelter over the entrance to a building, often used to carry signs as well.
Chalkboard, also called blackboard (but not always black) used with white chalk or water paint. Today often replaced by synthetic boards used with felt-tip pen.
Chandelier Sign, a sign type located in the middle of a crossing holding sign content for each direction.
Channel Letters, hollow letters fabricated from metal, synthetic sheet material or combinations of different materials.
Civic Sign, a sign related to non-profit organisations.
Code Signs, all signs required by law or regulation.
Console Signs, on panel or unit accommodating controls for electronic or mechanical equipment.
Construction Sign, a temporary sign placed on or near the construction site providing data related to the site.
Cornerstone, a ceremonial stone inscribed to commemorate the erection of a building.
Counter sign, a free-standing sign on a counter.
Cut-and-fill letters, are first cut out in a (metal) panel and thereafter filled in seamlessly with contrasting (transparent) material, flush with the panel surface .

D

Desk sign, a free-standing sign on desk or counter.
Digital Graffiti, a technology to use mobile phones for displaying messages in public spaces. Also called Public Texting and Wiffiti.

Digital Ink, a digital display technology on very thin sheet material aiming to replace print on paper.
Digital Signage, the sign content can be remotely and electronically changed, typically with the goal of delivering targeted messages to specific locations at specific times. Also called Dynamic Signage.
Dimensional Letters, individual letters cut out of a sheet, panel or slab.
Directory, a textual overview of the locations of tenants, businesses, activities or departments within a building or a group of buildings. (see Building Directory, Floor directory and Elevator/lift Directory)
Directional Sign, a sign guiding circulation and traffic flow by indicating directions to destinations along the way.
Distraction Strips, lines or dotted lines on glass doors or sidelights to prevent people bumping into glass panels.
Disabled Access, all facilities to accommodate disabled access to and use of a building or a site.
Donor Recognition, information on how donors are recognised for their contributions, gifts or support.
Door Hanger, a sign hanging on a door handle.
Drop-off Sign, identification of a dedicated location to let visitors out of vehicles.
Dynamic Message, sign content that can be updated electronically.

E

Etched Plate, a sign with a chemically etched message.
Electronic Directory, a touch-screen directory.
Elevator Directory, overview of all departments or sections on different floors, placed outside and/or inside of the elevator car, also called lift directory.
Elevator Signs, the various types of signs inside the elevator car and in front of the access doors on each floor.
Environmental Graphics, graphic signs used in the built environment
Event Signs, dynamic or temporary information about events.
Entry Sign, a sign indicating the entrance to a building or a site.
Escape Routes Map, see Fire Evacuation Map.
Exhibit and Display Signs, easily erectable and removable signs .
Exit Sign, a sign indicating the exit doors or directing to these exits. Mostly used for emergency (fire) exits.

F

Face-fitting System, sign panel components that can be replaced from the front. (see side-fitting)
Fingerpost, pole-mounted directional sign with small panels pointing in the direction of one or more destinations.
Fire Evacuation Map, floor map indicating fire exits and instructions for what to do in case of fire.
Flag, a piece of fabric typically attached to a pole, used to display symbols or emblems or for decorative purposes.
Flag Sign, a sign mounted projecting from the wall.

Fleet Marking, signs and (branding) symbols for fleets of vehicles, like trucks, vans, trains or aeroplanes, often made of adhesive vinyl sheet.
Floor Directory, overview of all the different departments, tenants or sections on one floor.
Floor Number, floor indication in stairwells , outside elevators/lifts and escalators.
Frame Holder, a free-standing frame for holding commercial posters.

G
Gateway Arch, a monumental structure over the entrance of an estate.
Grid-locator Identification, letter, numeral , symbol or illustration that identifies a cell in a grid. Used for identification of sections in parking lots or work units in 'office gardens'.
Gray Light Directory, a backlit building directory with versatile name strips. A grey transparent sheet cover makes the individual strips invisible and only shows the illuminated elements.
Ground Signs, all signs other than pole signs in which the entire base is set into the ground.

H
Highway Signs, regulated signs specific for use on highways. (see Road and Traffic Signs)
I
Illuminated Letters, channel letters with neon illumination.
Inclusive Signage, dedicating much attention to the needs of impaired users of a project.

J

K
Kiosk, telephone or information booth. Today often used for interactive free-standing signs.

L
Large Format Digital Printing, Ink Jet printing on large formats of all kinds of flexible material.
Lectern-shaped sign, sign face slightly tilted.
Letter Board, a panel with manually changeable text.
Letter Cutting, engraving letters in stone or wood.
Lift Signs, the various types of signs inside and in front of lift doors on each floor.
Literature Rack, structure to hold printed material, often free-standing.
Logotype or Crest Sign, showing the mark or (brand) name of an organisation. (also called Logo Sign)

M
Machine-cut Letters, individual letters cut out of material using a machine.

Marquee, a roof-like projection over a theatre entrance often used to display the program as well.
Medallion, oval or circular shaped panel or tablet used to decorate or commemorate.
Message Centre, a board or boards with electronically changeable messages, like timetables or advertisements.
Modular Sign System, a system of modular parts for composing different types of versatile sign panels.
Monolith, a large upright sign without a visible frame or poles.
Monument, a statue or structure erected to commemorate, also used for large signs made of concrete or stone as entrance signs or marking a property. Specifically popular in the US.
Moving Copy Sign, an electronically or mechanically changeable text message within the sign frame.
Mural, a large illustration applied directly on a wall.

N

Neon Sign, an illuminated sign made from free-formed glass tubes filled with inert gas and phosphors.
Noticeboards, see Bulletin boards.
Notice Signs, information and instructions about use of buildings, sites or facilities.

O

Orientation Signs, sign types like directories, maps or landmarks to facilitate ease of orientation in a site.
Overhead Sign, mounted suspending from the ceiling, or projecting from the wall.

P

Paperflex, sign holding a paper insert.
Pedestal Sign, plaque or inscription on base or support of statue.
Pedestrian Signs, signs specifically made for pedestrians.
Pennant, a flag denoting a sports championship or other achievement.
Permanent Room Designation Signs, a sign category defined by the ADA (Americans with Disabilities Act) for which raised letters and Grade 2 Braille are required.
Plaque, a small panel sign. Originally only used for small commemorative signs.
Point of Purchase Signs, easily erectable and removable free-standing signs outdoors and indoors.
Point of Interest Marker, providing historical or contextual information about buildings, sites or facilities.
Pop-up Signs, easily erectable and portable free-standing signs.
Portable Signs, signs that can be moved by one person.
Post/Panel Signs, fixed free-standing signs using poles.
Post and Panel System, signs made with a combination of standard poles and panels.
Poster Display, a cabinet to show printed posters, illuminated or non-illuminated.

Primary Signs, category of sign types needed when entering a site. (see Secondary Signs)
Projecting Sign, mounted perpendicular to the wall, also called Flag Sign.
Public Texting, a technology to use mobile phones for displaying messages in public spaces. Also called Digital Graffiti and Wiffiti.
Pylon, a large sign on a pillar-like structure, a tower or a post.

Q

R
Readerboard, a sign containing loose letters or numbers that can be changed manually.
Regulatory Signs, deal with all mandatory and other regulations in a building or a site.
Restrictive Information Signs, 'do-not' instructions and restricted access.
Road Signs, regulated signs for secondary roads. (see Highway and Traffic Signs)
Roof Signs, erected wholly or partially on a roof top.

S

Sandwich Board, two sign panels hinged together on top or with shoulder strap-bands to be carried by a person in front and back.
Sandwich Panel, a composite material panel consisting of a core material and two surface layers. The thin aluminium surface with a synthetic core sandwich is popular for signage panels.
Scoreboard, a board displaying the current score of a sports game.
Side-fitting System, sign panel components replaced by a sliding manipulation. (see Face-fitting)
Sign Administrator, person in charge of controlling regulations concerning signs posted in public areas.
Signage Officer, organisation employee in charge of the maintenance of the signage of a site.
Sign panel, a sign panel over a certain size. (see Plaque)
Site Identification, (monumental) sign that identifies the site.
Slat, small, long piece of material holding one line of text or pictogram, also called bar or plank.
Snipe Sign, sign posted in contravention of local regulations.
Stair Markings, number on individual staircase often combined with floor number.
Stonemasonry, messages made in stone by a letter cutter or stone carver.
Stone Carving, see Stonemasonry.
Super Graphics, inkjet or vinyl-cut graphics in large format.
Suspended Sign, mounted hanging from the ceiling, also called Overhead Sign.

T
Tablet, a small slab of wood, stone or clay with a carved inscription.

Tack Board, a board for displaying notices using thumbtacks or drawing pins. (see Bulletin Board)
Traffic Signs, standardised set of legally enforceable signs regulating circulation of traffic .
Transitional Sign, indication of leaving one section and entering another.

U

V
Vehicle Graphics, signs on vehicles, often made of adhesive vinyl sheet or magnetic rubber sheet (see Fleet Marking).
Video Wall, multi-screen combination to show huge animated images.
Vehicle Signs, signs to direct drivers of vehicles.
Vinyl Graphics, letters, symbols or illustrations cut out of adhesive vinyl sheet material.
Vitreous enamelled, an extremely durable way of fixing the message on a metal sign; enamel is glazed under high temperature, like porcelain.

W
Wiffiti, a technology to use mobile phones for displaying messages in public spaces. Also called Public Texting and Digital Graffiti.
Window Sign, applied or painted on the inside of a window or glass door exposed to public view.

X

Y
'You-are-here' Sign, orientational sign including a map that indicated the spot where one is standing.

Z
Zebra codes, optical readable codes, sometimes used for inventory information on door signs. (also called Bar codes)

4. Creating the visual design

4.1. Introduction

Like any other type of design work, signage design also has two distinct design aspects and two related work phases. First, the content needs to be created and the functional/technical requirements or product concept need to be formulated. The first part of this book is about this work phase. Second, the visual appearance, or the shape, has to be designed. Visual appearance and content always remain separate aspects of the final outcome of all design work. Such a distinction is absent in all other visual art, though there is no sharp borderline between these two aspects. Visual design can establish certain conditions that can also be obtained through the content. The visual design can create, for instance, a sense of order. This effect can also be created by the content of the design. In fact, the two aspects have a strong symbiotic relationship. One influences the other. Ideally, one supports the other to its maximum effect, like the 'yin' and 'yang' combined in the perfect circle. Shape and content are separate design aspects, yet for a major part are inseparable in their specific relationship. Clients often do not fully understand the delicate relationship between function and form when they require minor changes in the final stage of a design work. High quality design is a sophisticated balancing act of all the ingredients involved. The balance can easily be disturbed by minor changes. Well prepared work that reduces the risk of last minute changes usually pays off handsomely in the end.

The priority of visual appearance versus content (or function) is continuously debated in design theory. The credo of the Bauhaus vision on design was: 'form follows function', giving a clear priority to the development of the functional aspects of the design work and trying to avoid all unnecessary decoration. The playful and exuberant years of the eighties and the nineties tried to shy away from what was perceived as being a too rigid, limiting and even boring vision of the general purpose of design. The Bauhaus credo was metamorphosed into: 'Form follows fun'. All emotional aspects of any work of design were also considered to be 'functional aspects', equal to the more obvious functions of a product.

Later, the 'Post Modern' philosophy gained ground. This philosophy is not straightforward in its aims and postulations. Basically, it rejects all fundamental statements about the nature of design (or art). Technological developments have created a world with endless possibilities in which all earlier respected frontiers have been blurred into irrelevance. Citing, copying and sampling others people's work became extremely simple to do. Existing legislation on authorship and copyright had to be reconsidered. Creative productivity and design output can today reach unprecedented levels. This borderless and anti-authoritarian design philosophy has created a kaleidoscopic pandemonium of design styles.

4.2. The basic aspects of visual design

It is important to first highlight the basic aspects that the visual part of a design can bring forward. What are the basic aspects? There are quite fundamental differences between the way the functional part of a design proposal is judged against its visual representation. Where functional aspects are usually debated or argued in reasonable terms, the visual design often leads to confrontations in emotional terms. Regrettably, the dialogue is usually kept very simple and uncompromising. One likes the visual part of a design, or one doesn't. Appreciation can reach extremely high emotional levels at times, designs can be deeply admired or profoundly hated, without too much supporting argument, thus reducing all judgment to a matter of personal taste, which by common wisdom is not debatable. This is an unnecessary and quite unfruitful approach to the appreciation of visual design. Sure enough, one has to acknowledge the fact that visual design is capable of generating very strong emotions, but these are not its only abilities.

4.2.1 THE BEAUTY AND THE BEAST

Beauty or ugliness are major emotional responses to all visual design.

The part of the appreciation for the visual design that generates strong emotions revolves around what we personally perceive as something (or someone) very beautiful—or at the other extreme, very ugly. The first stimulates our appetite, the second our disgust. We do not know precisely what it is that turns us on or off visually, or what we see as attractive or repulsive. Whatever it is, it is something quite individual, very basic and important to our emotional life. Practically everyone has very strong opinions about these matters. A lot of our behaviour can be related to our visual preferences. Personal taste is often presented as the determining factor in the appreciation of visual design. However, my personal experience as a designer has taught me that appreciation of a particular design is not a matter of personal taste alone. Some designs are spontaneously considered to be beautiful (or ugly) by more than the statistically probable number of viewers. To make this phenomenon functional, one only has to limit the choices to no more than two. When given the possibility of choosing between only two options, people's preferences are surprisingly coherent. Of course, there are strictly individual aspects in visual appreciation and there are certainly differences between various cultural groups, but good visual quality is universally recognised.

Creating something that may be perceived as desirable is the strongest power in a designer's hands and mind. There is little point in denying this important tool. However, the pursuit of this power can also become an obstacle in the quest for maximum overall quality. Aesthetic visual qualities can easily become too prominent in the judgment of design work. Detailed discussions about visual appearance are hardly ever fruitful and may lead to confrontations that are best avoided. Compromises between design proposals and the individual visual taste of clients seldom deliver satisfactory results. Discussions about the other aspects of the visual design are likely to be far more fruitful. Wise clients will leave the purely visual aspects entirely to the professional. Some seasoned designers even go as far as putting obvious mistakes in their design proposals in order to 'orchestrate' the focus of attention and avoid disputes about aesthetics.

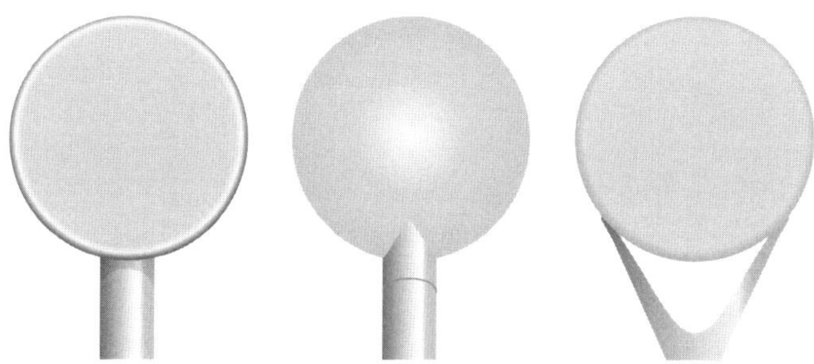

4.2.2. VISUAL PERSONALITY

All objects, designed or not, convey a specific visual identity.

Beauty or ugliness, attractiveness or repulsiveness are simple and conclusive appreciations. The underlying reason that leads to such a consideration is not only based on a personal judgment about aesthetic values, but also on more complex issues. We do not only perceive visual design on purely aesthetic qualities. We might assume we do, but in fact we react to it as we do to all other visual matter that surrounds us. We perceive an object or a scene by its visual appearance, as friendly or reserved; outspoken or introvert; bold or shy; flimsy or durable, sexy or plain, rich or poor, etc. In short, we are used to 'personalising' everything around us, in a first and immediate instance, based only on its visual appearance. This natural reflex is a strong and an influential one.

Objects and environments are not perceived within a one dimensional scale between beautiful and ugly. They have a more complex visual identity. All objects and environments—designed or not—have an identity. Design does not give these items an identity; it can only help to reinforce a desired identity or visual personality. There are limitations in this pursuit. Individuals ascribe different personalities to the same object or environment. Yet, there is sufficient common ground to create a generally accepted image. However, there are major differences between various cultural groups. Emotions connected to specific colours, for instance, to love, sadness or wealth, can vary (or even generate the opposite meaning) from one culture to the other. In addition, our age and era we live in play a determining role in the way we perceive visual personalities.

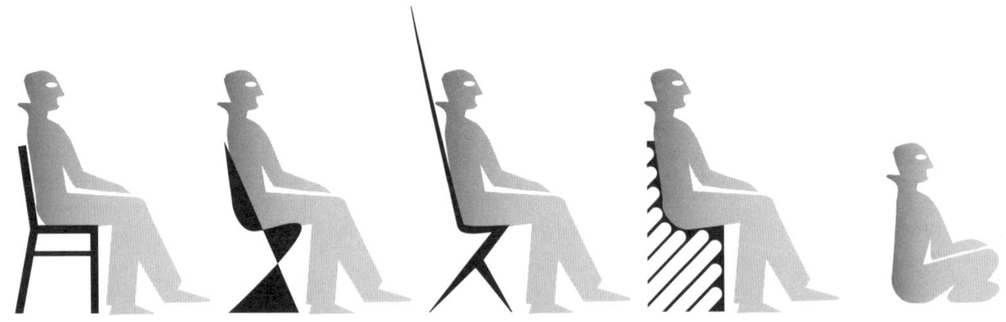

4.2.3. VISUAL SECURITY AND EXCITEMENT

Visual design can generate a wide range of emotions; from the secure feeling provided by conventional design, to the excitement of the novel.

Visual design is capable of creating something familiar, or by contrast, something new. The two will generate opposite types of emotions in the viewer. Creating visual novelty is almost exclusively connected to visual design and art. Presenting something 'not seen before' is very effective in drawing the viewer's attention. Novelty can easily generate excitement and attraction. It is an important initiator for communication, but a lousy tool to use for further effective communication. We need familiar forms to communicate more complex information, because we all share a mutual understanding about their meaning. Design cannot function without the use of familiar visual material, at the risk of being entirely misinterpreted by the viewer.

These are the two essential ingredients for effective visual design: providing security by using familiar forms, and acquiring attention through the excitement and natural attraction often generated by novelty.

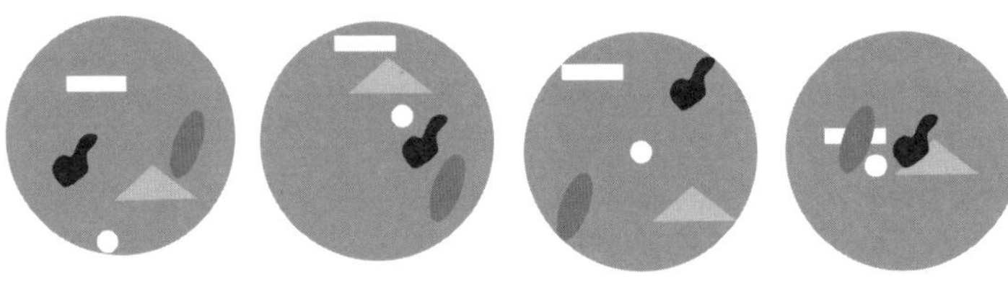

4.2.4. VISUAL ORDER

Creating visual order contributes most effectively to clear visual communication.

Visual design can create order. This ability is related to the one that can generate emotions, but applied on a more rational level. Order enhances the accessibility of information, avoids misinterpretation, and stimulates the learning process by easy recognition of repetitive (whole or parts of) information.

By making use of all the visual properties, like size, colour, shape, alignment and positioning, the visual designer can link or separate individual parts, can create a hierarchy within parts of information, and create a pattern of expectation in the user. The possibilities to create visual order are too often neglected. Exploiting these possibilities will contribute the most to the overall efficiency of the communication process.

4.2.5. DESIGNING AND STYLING

There is often confusion over the difference between 'styling' and 'designing'. Creating a visual style is often used as a synonym for making the visual design. Styling and designing are two different activities, though. The visual design aims to provide a unique design solution to meet a unique set of constraints. Styling aims to apply a specific and a well-known style to a product or an environment. Designing aims to create a unique visual identity, whereas styling creates a conformity with a desired style. Clearly, this makes design and styling two quite distinct activities.

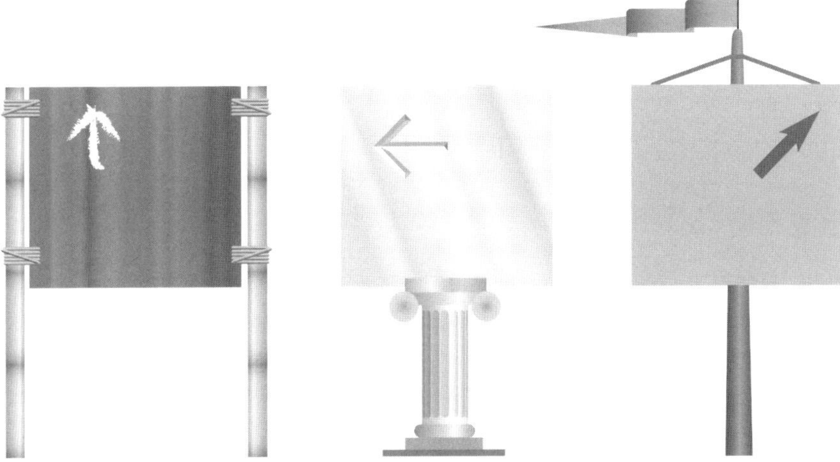

Visual design can apply well-known styles to create a specific atmosphere. This activity is called 'styling'—some may call it kitsch.

However, there are some similarities between the two. Style is linked to design in various instances. First, all designers each have a certain personal style, especially the influential ones. Yet, designers shouldn't cultivate a personal style, though it is often an unavoidable result of the designer's work. We all have a specific handwriting and way of thinking that cannot be switched on or off. For commercial reasons, it is tempting to cultivate a personal style—or signature. All brands thrive on maintaining a consistent style. Similarly, the designer may also benefit from successfully branding him/herself.
Second, designers are often asked to comply with an existing style. Signage designers must match their designs with the existing architectural style. Third, all visual art and design is a product of its time. When put into an historical perspective, all design and art can be grouped into astonishingly coherent style periods. Fourth, marketing and communication techniques nowadays have blurred the differences between designing and styling. Before any design takes place, marketing and communication experts are asked to create strategies and concepts, often based on market research. Design has been given a position in these con-

cepts as a surface embellisher, more like a sort of stylish contribution to give some specific visual flavour to the whole idea. This is far from the more integral and holistic approach of design. Marketeers are trained to think in strict commercial terms that push a design concept to create a specific atmosphere that research revealed as appealing to a certain target group. The influence of marketeers and communication experts on the formulation of the design brief is still increasing. They have secured a position for themselves between executive management and designers in almost all organisations over a certain size. It could very well be that this development has cut off a quite important channel for exchange of information between the major creators of the identity of any organisation—its directors— and the professionals—the designers—who are trying to give that identity a matching visual shape. Making a brief for visual design work and the judgment of the results remains a rather delicate process that cannot be entirely predicted or controlled. Communication experts dramatically overestimate their abilities, tools and professional insight when they believe themselves to be best at controlling this process entirely. Their design briefs and evaluation comments tend to be shockingly uninspiring for designers. It is vital for the quality of design that executive management and designers keep a direct and open dialogue with each other. Marketing and communication experts should move position and sit next to design professionals and not between management and designers, as is more and more the case. There is plenty of room for a justified fear that if this situation remains unchanged, a vital artery will be cut off and will ultimately result in a poor design environment, where design is reduced to a kind of superficial craftsmanship. This will be a huge loss and not an easy one to reverse.

Traditional headgear has a distinct symbolic value.

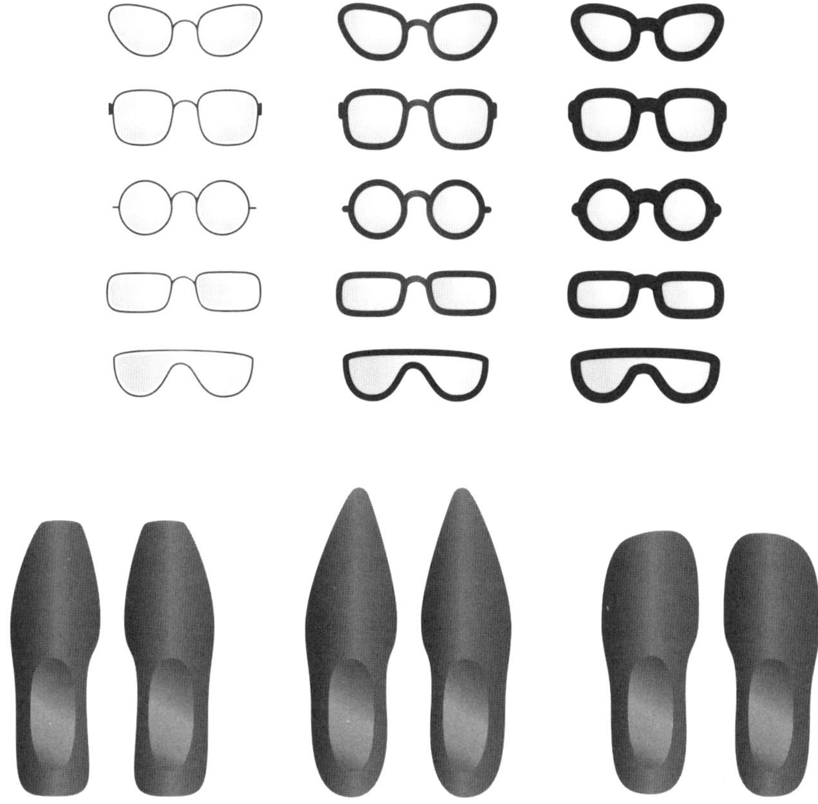

Personal items like shoes and glasses are subject to ever-evolving fashion styles. These items are important to express our 'desired personality'.

Consistent styling requires appropriate combinations of elements—though fashion is unpredictable.

The client's aim for involving marketing and communication experts is to make the results of design work more controllable and more effective. It is in fact an attempt to forecast how the design results will be perceived by target groups. This type of forecasting—even eliminating the involvement of designers altogether—is the business of so-called styling agencies. These agencies' main practice is to forecast style trends and/or advise companies on style aspects of their product and all related visual presentations, without making actual design proposals. In an attempt to reduce their commercial risk with the production of their garment collections, manufacturers in the fashion industry were the first to employ such forecasters. The involvement of one individual designer in creating the collection was seen as too expensive and/or too risky because of the 'too personal and subjective' view of that one particular designer. This fear of taking a commercial risk was justified at the expense of overlooking the potential core asset of a designer.

Three rows that visually express, by combining everyday items, different nationalities. Even the identical newspapers seem to look different within these settings.

Today, there are a number of organisations and private companies around that provide styling advice and forecasts. Clients of these agencies are no longer limited to the garment industry; interior product and even car manufacturers use their services. With all this advice around, it is wise to realise that there are trendsetters and trend followers (and trend outcasts). Trendsetters and trend followers are not necessarily designers; they can be buyers as well as entrepreneurs (in the role of clients). Nobody can forecast what trendsetters are going to do next, not even the trendsetters themselves, so any sensible advice in this matter is at best limited to a smart analysis of what is already going on. It can never reveal what will be the most rewarding commercial initiatives.

4.2.6. CRITERIA FOR DESIGN QUALITY JUDGEMENT

There are a limited number of criteria that are used to judge or express a design's quality or its characteristics. These may overlap since it is not always possible to separate one completely from the other. Individuals will definitely favour one design aspect over the other and will set their priorities accordingly.

4.2.6.1. Functionality

The aspect of functionality refers to the straightforward and practical considerations. Does the design do what it is basically suppose to do? Functionality judged on a very basic level will, for instance, require that all typography should at least be readable, or that a chair must be a device able to bear the weight of a sitting person.

4.2.6.2. Communication

All designs convey a message that may be a simple or a complex one.The design quality of this aspect is determined by the effectiveness with which the intended message is understood by its users.

4.2.6.3. Style

All designs will carry a style or signature, whether intentional or not. The style of a design is the reference to existing and known general or individualistic style elements. Style characteristics can be strong or weak.

4.2.6.4. Novelty

Designers often aim to create something genuinely new or original. Novelty tends to draw the attention, attract, and generate excitement.

4.2.6.5. Aesthetics

The aesthetic quality often invites personal judgement of appreciation or dislike, generally expressed in terms like beautiful or ugly. It is unlikely that we are capable of separating our sensitiveness for aesthetic qualities from other emotions we experience in confronting design. However, aesthetic sensitivity varies tremendously between individuals.

4.2.6.6. Identity

We all have quite a strong empathetic relation with everything that surrounds us. It is not limited—as one might expect—to a selection of fellow human beings, but encompasses all living and even all inanimate objects. We are unable to exclude our emotions from the awareness of everything around us. Objectivity is not an option for humans. We form an 'emotional opinion' almost instantly about everything we experience. The emotional aspect is called the personality or the identity of a design. All designed or non-designed objects will carry one. We may not be able to understand the meaning of everything that surrounds us but we invariably do have a strong (or indifferent) feeling about it.

4.3. Competitions, review and approval procedures

Design proposals need to be approved first before becoming part of the real world. Judgment of design proposals—especially visual design proposals—has its own specific problems. It is wise to be prepared for the various dynamics involved in approval procedures.

4.3.1. REVIEWING MEETINGS

The major goal of reviewing is to make the best use of the differences in knowledge between the reviewer and the reviewed. Communication between the parties involved needs careful attention. The difference in background of the participants can easily lead to misunderstandings, but the major task is to overcome the striking difference in the level of involvement in making the proposals. One party may have spent a long time thinking about the brief and have reached a conclusion after going through a process that involved much consideration and reconsideration. The other party may not have had that same experience, and may have a limited knowledge about the design profession. The most common mistake the designer can make is to be insufficiently aware of the huge discrepancy between the involvement of the creator versus that of the reviewer(s). Designers have to spend time in preparing logical and coherent presentations in which all steps in the design process are clearly and simply explained. This is just as important as the quality of the proposal itself. Good preparation is essential.

Creating an open dialogue is the major achievement in all review meetings.

The next important goal is more difficult to achieve. That is to create an atmosphere of open dialogue between parties; an unbiased exchange of ideas and thoughts. The best design results require the input of more than one party. Designers and reviewers should never forget that. The best results need the best efforts of all involved in the decision-making process. Easier said than done. Good judgment is not easily achieved; it needs mutual respect between all parties involved in a delicate process. Review meetings often follow the dynamics and logic of negotiation and group processes. Reviewers want at least a part of their remarks honoured—never mind their value or relevance. When there are many reviewers around the table, it means that a lot of people would like to put their own 'mark' on the end result as proof of their respected participation in the judgment process. Collecting and applying this kind of marks is a sure path to inappropriate solutions and striking ugliness. Some designers deliberately put parts in their proposals as negotiation ploys to safeguard the integrity of their designs. It is a tricky strategy. It is difficult to avoid the traditional give-and-take dynamics during review meetings, but too much wheeling and dealing leads surely to bad results. Design proposals should not be taken for granted, there is often room for improvement. However, polishing the design proposal can only be done based on the quality of the remarks made and not by accommodating all the remarks equally.

Visual design proposals mimic a situation as if it was real. It visualises an environment and items within it that are yet to be realised. It is essentially a dreamed-up reality, nothing more. It requires fantasy to imagine how proposals will look in real life. That is not easy to foresee, not even for the most experienced designer. Designers are generally generous in taking a leap of faith. Design proposals are also often intentionally ambitious. Designers want to create something new and original, something that is yet unknown. Good designers are curious people and are prepared to take risks to satisfy their curiosity. Clients should weigh these risks but be equally aware that it is impossible to eliminate all risks. Good design is adventurous by nature and good reviewing also takes some courage.

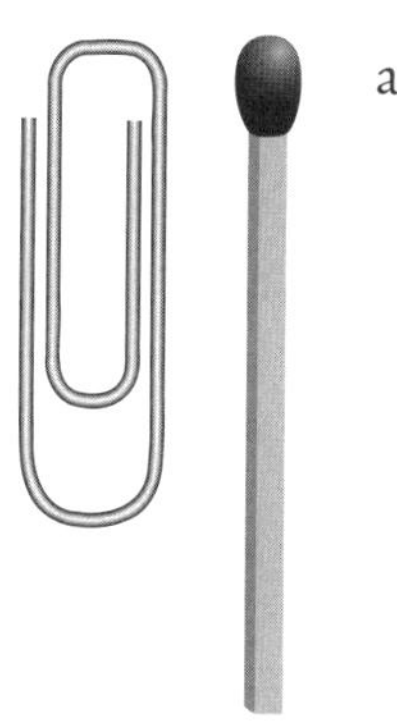

People's perceptions change when put into a position to judge design results. The usual size of a letter used in the daily newspaper suddenly seems too small to read.

As said previously, visual design can generate strong emotions and it is not always easy to explain the essence of the visual quality. A reviewer's talent and experience is helpful in reaching a valuable judgment, particularly when reviewing visual design proposals. The people gathered around the table during review sessions often have one quality in common: the competence to express their point of view in a verbally convincing way . This, and not so much their experience and talent in judging visual matter, is a shared quality. Yet a strong personal visual taste is present in each individual. This combination often leads to a rather bizarre way of arguing. Instead of simply declaring that a proposal is not matching one's personal taste, some feel it is more appropriate to give more substantial remarks to win the argument. The true reason is concealed and often replaced by over-stressing the potential implementation problems of the designs. This strategy is totally wrong; it is an inappropriate approach that is extremely confusing and frustrating. Regrettably, it happens very often in review meetings.

Reviewers and clients should be aware of a phenomenon that can easily obstruct good judgment. People start to behave differently when put in a position as judge. It is a peculiar phenomenon, but a very real one. One starts to look with different eyes when assuming the role of reviewer. One suddenly starts to pay attention to things that under normal circumstances would remain unnoticed. Here is an example that illustrates this effect. Signage design proposals always involve typography and type. Sometimes the size of the type proposed is discussed, when generally nobody pays attention to this aspect. When the designer asks explicitly to review the size of the type used, he/she always gets the same remark: the type is always judged as being a bit small and should preferably be used in a bigger size. There is hardly any exception to this, regardless of the proposed type size. The explanation for this phenomenon must be that nobody realises how small the type is that we read effortlessly in our daily newspapers, for instance. This aspect remains totally unnoticed until you ask people to give their opinion about it. Suddenly we all realise how small these little signs really are. This common pitfall when reviewing visual designs should be avoided.

4.3.2. DESIGN COMPETITIONS

Design competitions have gained popularity. Architects are used to participating in this kind of selection process. Graphic designers are more and more often confronted with competitions, even for smaller commissions. It is in general not a very positive development.

The assumed advantage for a client in holding a competition is to receive a lot of competing proposals based on a given brief. The client just has to select the best proposal amongst comparable ones. It seems like a fun session. Customers have become so used

Design competitions may very well end up being superficial beauty contests.

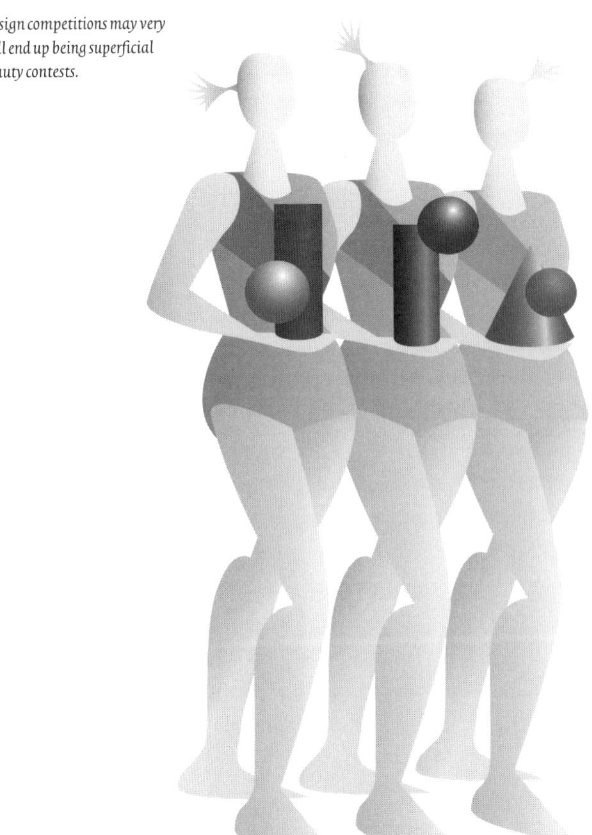

to being offered unlimited choices these days that anything less than having the joy of picking from a mind-boggling abundance feels poor.

It also seems to be a quite efficient method of collecting the best advice. The costs of receiving design proposals is generally low, but may depend on the prestige of the project or on the level of competition in the professional field at a given moment. Some professions have codes of conduct that set rules for competitions. Sometimes competitions are open and participation may involve no design costs at all for potential clients. It is very tempting to receive a lot of different ideas and free advice so it is hard to resist such temptation. Yet, it is worth contemplating other alternatives.

The assumption that a design competition is cost effective and generates the best solutions may only be true in a few cases. And even in these cases, it takes time-consuming and careful preparation on the side of the organisers. The level of preparation of the brief needs to be far higher than what is given in direct commissions. In most cases, competitions are an enormous waste of time for everybody involved. Good design simply needs the active and serious contribution of a lot of parties during a well-organised process. A client's contribution in this process is essential for the overall quality. Clients can only expect to receive the most effective design proposals through their own active participation. There is no nice and easy way around it. The assumption that the designers will come up with the good ideas and the client only has to sit back and do the picking is wrong. Good design is the result of an intense dialogue on a high level within a well-organised setting. Even a brilliant monologue can never replace it. Because of the absence of a dialogue in a competition, designers are forced to do their own guesswork on what is needed in a project. Even a carefully constructed brief cannot entirely avoid this kind of guesswork. Most of the designer's assumptions may be wrong or non-specific. Designers tend to concentrate on the visual appearance of their designs. This matches the way proposals are judged; often based almost entirely on the design's visual impact. All the proposals will effectively be lined up in a simple beauty contest, dramatically limiting the potential of good design. Ultimately, the design profession itself will lose its identity and be transformed into sophisticated visual acrobatics at best, or a make-up service at worst. That process is unfortunately already under way!

Designers will play a 'design solitaire' when the essential contribution or input of the client is absent from the design process.

Most competitions reap what they sow: a giant heap of superficiality—as if we really need more of that. There are no methods that only need hot air as input in order to generate genius. The reality is like the expression used in the field of information technology: 'Garbage In, Garbage Out'. There is just no way of cutting corners or escaping that reality.

A second potential danger lies in the selection process of competing designs itself. When a lot of jury members take part in the selection process of the best design, often a sort of grading system is used to reward the various proposals (as is done in schools). That is a bad method, for it is likely to reward mediocrity. Good design tends to be controversial. It is likely to collect both very high as well as very low scores, resulting in low averages. A winning design can easily be a 'middle-of-the-road' solution collecting the best average. That would be a senseless result for any competition; nevertheless, it happens quite often.

Regrettably, there is no easy way to create or select outstanding design, it needs more than the involvement of an outstanding designer.

4.3.3. PITCHING MANIA

It looks more and more as if commissioning a designer on the basis of reputation or someone's recommendation is considered to be commercial madness these days. All commissions seem to require an initial pitching stage. This pitching mania may easily have the same flaws as all other design competitions. It generates often gigantic superficial results and will eventually degenerate professionalism. The basic flaw of the pitching system becomes apparent when a design team wins the pitch but loses the commission. This happens regularly when client and designer discover to their own embarrassment that real collaboration turned out to be entirely impossible because the mutual appreciation was based on an extremely superficial judgment. Such a result is the worst possible outcome of a pitch. The more likely outcome of pitches is that the entire interest of the pitching team often lies in whether the pitch was successful or not. All commercial interest is understandably focused on winning the competition and not on the follow up of implementing the design.
Pitching is only a sensible strategy when the winners and the losers both walk away after the pitch. One with a successful sale, the others with another learning or character-shaping experience. In all other cases it remains a seriously flawed and exceedingly wasteful method for selecting a design team.

4.4. Intellectual Property [IP] issues

Signage designers, like all other designers, are expected to create something unique and new—at least in some aspects of the end result. Designers are so-called creative professionals. That special badge of creativity may easily lead to false pretensions and expectations, or even inappropriate professional behaviour. Nevertheless, the result of their work is in most cases protected by laws on intellectual property. For this reason, the signage designer needs to have some basic understanding of intellectual property issues.

4.4.1. SHORT HISTORY OF INTELLECTUAL AND INDUSTRIAL PROPERTY RIGHTS

Authors, inventors and entrepreneurs have long had in common, a wish to have the result of their work recognised as original and protected against imitation.
Intellectual property rights did not start with rights granted to authors of intellectual work; instead it started with protection of the owners of the physical work or its disseminators, like publishers. In Ireland, in the fourth century, a dispute arose between a person who had hand-copied and disseminated parts taken out of books and the owner of these books, in this case a librarian. The royal court ruled: 'To every cow its calf, to every book its copy'. This 'right to copy' principle was followed by most religious and royal powers everywhere. It was considered to be in the interest of the ruling powers to control the flow of information by granting a monopoly for the right of copying books or pamphlets and the right for their distribution. From the late fourteenth and into the fifteenth century, printing started replacing hand copying completely. The invention of movable type during this period industrialised the production of printed books. Books became far easier to produce and with it the power of the publishers evolved. In order to keep control of what was printed, the English crown implemented in 1662 the Licensing Act. Only registered books were allowed to be printed and distributed. The Stationers Company was given all powers to oversee this process, including the right to burn unauthorised books, and to search for illegal copies wherever and whenever they pleased, even in private possession, and to seize all found. The Stationers did not always use their power properly; unpopular ideas were censored and authors were underpaid. Intellectual progress became seriously undermined and threatened. In 1709 the British Parliament drafted the 'Statute of Anne'. This law introduced two new important principles; the exclusive (copy)right of the author for a limited period of time, and subsequently, the public right to access and use of information. Copyright became 'private intellectual property' only for a limited period and when this period elapsed the intellectual property became automatically public as it fell into the so-called 'Public Domain'. The law was heavily contested by the publishers who based their perpetual copyright claims on those of

normal property rights, as stated under common law. A UK court ruling in 1774, in the Donaldson case, created a lasting precedent against perpetual copyright.
During the late 19th century, copyright became an international issue. The UK and the USA both shared one language and therefore a mutual interest in comparable legislation for a huge market. It resulted in the Berne (Switzerland) Convention of 1886 in which other countries also participated. Since the twentieth century, copyright has been subject to many revisions and extensions of works covered under copyright law protection. Also an ever-growing number of countries are taking part in conventions and ratifying existing treaties. However, the influence of the USA on international copyright matters has been overwhelming. The UNESCO played a major role in further globalisation of copyright matters, for instance by organising conventions like the Universal Copyright Convention in Paris in 1971. Also the WIPO (World Intellectual Property Organisation) is active in this field, sometimes in collaboration with the UNESCO.

Patents started off in a way comparable to copyright. Royal powers granted rights specified in 'Patent Letters' to certain manufacturers and traders. Originally, these rights did not need any specific requirements nor did they have a fixed duration. Industrial developments changed this situation as it did with copyright. Manufacturers had to describe their inventions, novelty became a requirement for granting a patent, and the duration of the monopoly of the invention's use became limited, falling into the Public Domain after elapsing. This was to serve the general public interest. International trade exhibitions made international regulation necessary. The international exhibition of inventions in Vienna in 1873 was hampered by the fact that many countries were unwilling to participate in the fair because they feared in-sufficient protection. The Paris Convention in 1880 for the protection of Industrial Property was the first step to further inter-nationalisation. At present, the WIPO in Geneva is active in coordinating conventions and treaties in collaboration with other international bodies like the World Trade Organisation (WTO).

Trade Marks also go back to ancient times. The marking of goods to identify its base material, its producer, or its owner has been a fundamental need in human civilisation. The medieval guilds created specific rules and regulations for the use of marks. The first legal registry of Trade Marks was opened in London in 1876. Trade Mark Right has been extended considerably over time. International registration has been simplified for countries within the European Union. The WIPO facilitates worldwide registration.

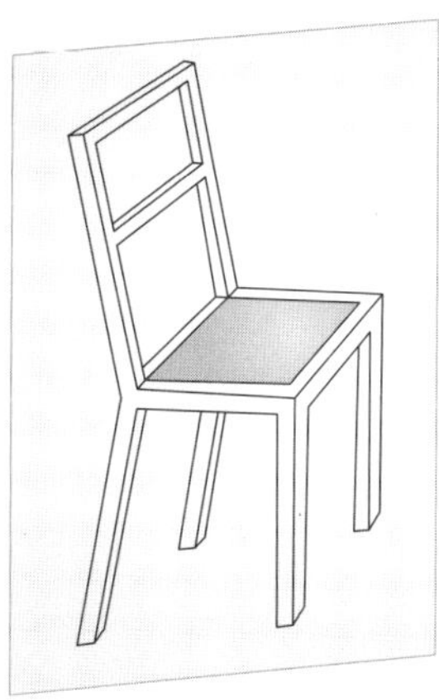

The drawing is copyright protected. However, the actual product in most cases requires registration to obtain time-limited protection.

In most countries, architecture is considered art. Both drawing and actual building are copyright protected.

The design itself is copyright protected. When used for example as a textile print or applied to a vase, the duration of design protection drops dramatically.

(Industrial) Designs are relatively the most recent extension of the various forms of Intellectual Property. It began in the 18th century with a form of protection for the patterns and prints on textiles. Over time, it was extended to all kinds of design work. Effectively, it has been an attempt to fill the gap between patents and copyright. At the moment there are many overlapping parts in design right coverage with the rights protected under copyright, while the level and duration of protection between the patent and copyright vary considerably.

4.4.2. OVERVIEW OF INTELLECTUAL PROPERTY RIGHTS

There are many different ways intellectual property is or can be protected. Relevant legislation and thus extension of protection is a dynamic and ongoing process of development. What all types of protection have in common is that the rights covered under the various sorts of protection have been expanded dramatically over the past 50 years. In fact, today many different types of protection have overlapping coverage.

4.4.2.1. Copyright

Copyright may be the mother of all intellectual property rights. Not all countries call this copyright; a lot call it author's right, a name that describes the type of right in a more complete sense. Copyright is often referred to as the right for creators of literary and artistic work. Today, that may be a rather confusing description. This right covers works like novels, poems, reference works, journalistic work, films, plays, musical compositions and recordings, choreography, paintings, drawings, photographs, sculpture, architecture, advertisements, typography—even maps, technical drawings and computer software. Hardly anyone would consider the latter as necessarily the result of an artistic endeavour. A more comprehensive definition might be that copyright exclusively covers the protection of the 'expression' and not of the underlying concept or idea. Patent right, on the other hand, covers the concept or idea.

Copyright is implicit in the creation of creative works; no formal registration or deposit of originals is required, although some countries demand registration prior to any legal action against infringement. Copyrighted works are often indicated with the character © together with the date of publication or creation. For some countries this marking is a requirement. The duration of protection is extremely generous these days, thanks to Hollywood and other American entertainment and software giants: between 50 and 70 years after the death of its creator or between 50 and 90 years in case the owner is a company. A lot of countries have ratified international copyright treaties, which means that a lot of copyright crosses boundaries effortlessly. Some types of copyright fee collection is in the hands of very powerful copyright management bodies.

The bicycle and IP rights

Patents deal with new concepts. A patent registration grants exclusivity to use the concept within the boundaries of its description. This exclusive right is granted only for a limited period of time.

Designs deal only with a specific shape. Registered design grants exclusive use of a shape (model) for a limited period of time. Registrations have to be renewed to remain valid.

Pictograms, typefaces and graphic designs are copyright protected.

Signs used as trademarks may obtain exclusive right of use that is extendible into perpetuity.

Some signs may become legally enforceable instructions.

4.4.2.2. *Patents*

Patents can provide the right for a temporary monopoly to exploit an invention. An invention is considered something 'not known' at the moment of its invention or registration and also something not obvious and of practical use. Inventions may cover a wide array of phenomena today, from products like new medicines or vacuum cleaners to new methods of construction or doing business, from medical treatments (not necessarily medicines) to plant varieties created by breeding or genetic manipulation. Patents are granted on the basis of a new concept, not on the specific physical shape of executing that concept. However, there are huge differences between various countries around the world on what is considered patentable. It is not surprising that the USA allows by far the widest variety of patents, and not following much of a sensible order. Interestingly, groundbreaking scientific discoveries like Einstein's equation $E=mc^2$ are not patentable on the grounds of being a scientific theory on a natural quality of matter.
Patents can only be granted through national patent offices after registration and assessment of novelty. Some countries grant 'petty' patents that—after registration—are only examined on formal grounds, skipping the far more elaborate novelty examination.
Patents—when granted—routinely give protection for a maximum of 20 years after the date of application. International applications can be made through the WIPO in Geneva. Patent applications have to be made public eventually, and after the monopoly period the concept of the patent falls into the public domain. These conditions are the reason why some companies decide not to register for patent protection, and instead keep their (production or sales) methods secret and opt for the everlasting protection of trade secrets.

4.4.2.3. *Designs*

Designs are the step-children of intellectual property protection. The reason is that design protection and registration protects only works of small businesses and individuals, thus hardly creating any powerful lobby for legislative change. It is supposed to protect the visual appearance of products, nothing more, as opposed to the mechanical/functional product qualities protected under patent law, or the artistic qualities of works protected under copyright. The duration of protection is short, from 3 to a maximum of 25 years. Registration—and renewals— are required to be eligible for the longest duration of protection. Novelty examination of registrations is very limited or completely absent. The most recent development is the creation of 'unregistered' design rights. In the UK unregistered design rights occur automatically after creation. Protection is for a maximum period of 10 years after marketing the design or 15 years after its creation, whichever period is longer. The USA does not have a separate design registration or protection, but has instead the so-called design patent registration and protection.

In practice, there are huge overlaps with copyright protection. It is difficult—if not impossible—to distinguish art from design or design from unique and novel products of craft. Some long accepted forms of design, like architecture, photography, advertisements and typography (in some countries) are already covered by copyright protection. It is hard to see why other fields of design should be excluded from copyright protection. Design organisations should try to abandon design rights altogether and to bring all design under copyright protection.

4.4.2.4. *Trademarks*

Trademarks used to be limited to specific signs or names given to products or services as an aid to distinguish one from the other in the marketplace. The protection of trademarks has been extended dramatically over time. The invention of inclusive 'branding' has made all means to serve this goal potentially part of trademark protection, like colour, sound (music), packaging, retail interiors or even fragrances.

In principle, trademark protection arises by its use in a certain territory. Formally, registration is not required but strongly advised, since it is almost impossible to know if others are using potentially conflicting similar or identical trademarks. Trademark protection used to be geographically limited, but ever-expanding international trade and the advent of the internet have changed all that. (Although the internet still has a separate registration body). Moreover, protection used to be limited to certain product classes, but some well-known international brands are seeking wider protection.

Fragrances try to create the ultimate 'signature' brand identity. All sensual aspects have to match seamlessly into a single coherent impression. The bottle designs reach the status of trademarks. The perfume recipes are usually trade secrets.

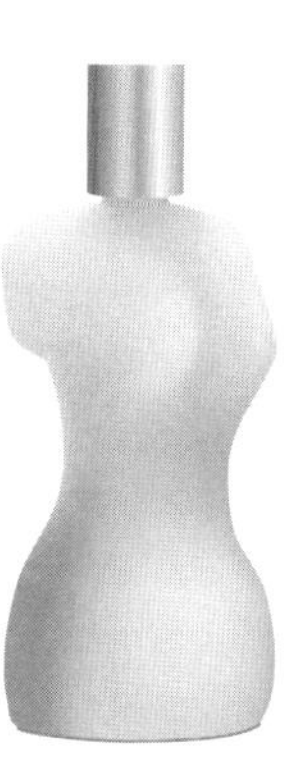

Trademark protection may last for eternity as long as the brand is effectively used in the market and also actively protected against infringement. Trademark registration can be extended without limitation. Not all words or signs can be protected as trademarks. The mark may not be part of common language, for instance. This limitation is the most peculiar reason a successful company may lose its trademark protection. It happens when an original trademark becomes a generic word in everyday language, as happened with 'aspirin' medicine, 'tweed' fabric, 'jeep' vehicles and 'walkman' devices. Some countries have different regulations for company names versus brand names.

4.4.2.5. *Trade Secrets*

Products and services have more aspects than those that can be publicly seen and scrutinised. Unprotected and ongoing research for product development, as well as specific marketing and production methods, both fall under this category. All products and services are the result of rather complicated working relationships between many individuals, involving not only company directors and staff, but also external sales agents and suppliers. To avoid any of these original collaborators suddenly turning into competitors, the law on trade secrets may be of help. Also, some companies follow a strategy of not seeking patent protection because of its limited duration and the need to eventually make the knowledge public from the day of its registration. To make trade secrets protection effective, non-disclosure or confidentiality agreements must be made with all parties directly involved. Additionally, non-competitive agreements can be drafted, although some countries have legal limitations on the content of these kinds of agreements. Trade secrets only protect know-how that is not familiar to the public or to the trade. When the secret is no longer secret, the protection ends. Companies or individuals must take reasonable measures to protect their secrets. Coca-Cola is the most famous example of protecting the recipe of their soda. In written form the recipe is kept in a well-protected vault and never more than two employees in the company know the formula at one given time.

Trade secret protection may vary from one country to another. Violation of trade secrets is a criminal offence in some countries .

4.4.2.6. *Unfair competition or 'passing off'*

Unfair competition is part of the common law that protects companies against all kinds of trade methods that are considered damaging or illegal. Imitation at the level of counterfeiting is a criminal offence in most countries. Both buyer and producer can be prosecuted and may also be subject to damage lawsuits. Also companies creating imitations (even subtle ones) may be forced by court action to stop their activities and pay damages. In principle, unfair competition applies to all methods of trading that are parasitic on the trade success of others. In effect, it covers products or services that are confusingly similar to existing ones and may therefore mislead potential buyers.
Legislation about what kind of commercial activities are considered unfair in a legal sense may vary considerably from one country to another.

4.4.3. LEGAL AND MORAL ASPECTS OF INTELLECTUAL PROPERTY

New legislation and international treaties about intellectual property rights have exploded over the past 50 years. The reason is that the affluent western world has gone through a rapid change in economic activity. Services of all kinds have become the major source of wealth and the biggest value in international trade. Health care and tourism are now the largest industries. Billionsworth of development culminates in products that fit on a single CD, or can be transported over any distance in minutes through wireless connections; a lot of property has become completely intangible.

4.4.3.1. The basic social trade-off

Most of intellectual property protection is based on a basic social trade-off that creates a balance of interest between the community that provides the protection and the individual that reaps the profits of that protection. The State (The People) provide protection only when in return works and knowledge are made public in an explicit way. It only actively supports for a limited period of time a trade monopoly for the creator(s), when in return, and after this period, the work and knowledge will become public property. This basic trade-off was considered in the best interest of all parties involved. It encourages economic development and avoids stagnation.

4.4.3.2. The public interest in the matter

The development in the legislation relating to intellectual property rights during the past decades has distorted the balance between the public interest and the interest of the individual (or company), in favour of the latter. The duration of copyright protection has been extended several times by the American Congress under pressure from powerful interest groups assisted by armies of lawyers. Current levels of protection have very little to do with the original idea of reasonable protection for authors. In fact, the major benefits of the protection have shifted from authors or creators of copyright to the owners of the resulting products. The duration of the right is at the moment outrageously disproportional and is beginning to be protection in perpetuity. Effectively, we're back to the times prior to the Statute of Anne. As a result, and in a similar way, monopolies have developed that misuse their market position.

Furthermore, what can be protected and how it may be protected, plus the overlaps of various types of protection, do not create a consistent or reliable legal foundation. In fact, the current situation is rather confusing. The major culprits for this situation are the politicians who make laws or support legislative proposals and the legal profession. Both groups have either by law, oath, or professional code of conduct, the obligation to serve the public interest and not solely their own power or wealth. It is hard to see what they have done to support the public interest in the matter and they are likely to pay for this with the diminishing of public respect.

4.4.3.3. Copyright and copyleft

The current extremely unbalanced situation in some aspects of intellectual property right protection has instigated the so-called 'Open (or shared) source' movement, like the 'Copyleft' movement. This movement unites creators, lawyers and distributors that support the other extreme of current copyright protection. The group advocates the Public Domain as exclusive owner of all works from the moment of creation. No individual rights whatsoever are accepted; all the rights are 'by the people and for the people'. All material can be freely copied or incorporated in another's own creations. For example, the so-called 'Open Source' software has created a system software under the name of Linux which is downloadable for free. Following the spirit of the time, powerful business players are now forming consortia pursuing open industry standards.

The different copyright marks in use today, from left to right: the traditional 'copyright' mark, the 'copyleft' mark, the 'share alike' mark, and the 'attribution' mark. The last three marks indicate a copyright-free use under certain conditions and the original author must be mentioned. 'New' work that makes use of the last three categories must also be released under the same conditions.

4.4.3.4. Commercial rights and moral rights

Intellectual property rights cover not only the commercial aspect, but also the moral aspect. However, there are differences between countries in the legal emphasis given to each of the two aspects. Countries following a the Anglo-Saxon legal system tend to see rights merely defined in economic terms. Legislation following this system has less constitutional (statutory) legislation and more jurisprudence (court rulings in individual cases), and therefore is more likely to deal with economic disputes.

In a moral sense, the work of an author can be seen almost as an extension of his own physical self and likewise protected against any attempt to violate personal integrity. Under moral right protection, authors have the right to claim authorship and sign their work, give permission to publication or disclosure and to object to any distortion, mutilation or other type of modification. These rights imply a limitation in the rights of physical ownership of work that is protected under copyright. One is not free to do whatever one pleases with something one otherwise completely owns and has paid for. For instance, you may not even be allowed to destroy it. The moral rights have resulted in some bitter fights in cases of architects, sculptors and others who saw their work destroyed or altered in the course of time. Obviously, authors must be reasonable in their claims, and an author's resistance against modification will only be granted if the result may harm the honour or reputation of the author.

Some countries allow a complete transfer of an authors' rights including the moral right (droit moral). In other countries, this right cannot be transferred and will remain with the author (or his successors) for as long as the legal term of copyright protection exists. Trading in moral rights is just as inappropriate as trading in moral or personal legal obligations.

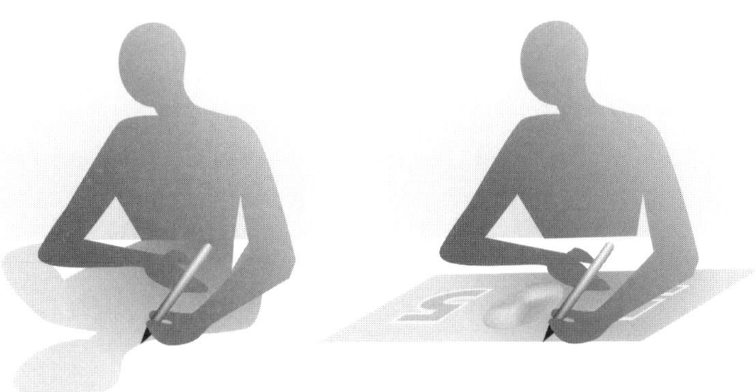

Countries following the 'Roman' legal principles emphasise the integrity of the personal creation. Countries following the American-British legal principles lean strongly toward the economic aspects of IP rights.

4.4.3.5. *Stealing intangible property*

Often we use the same terms for events related to both tangible and intangible property. We say someone 'steals' someone else's design, for instance. Yet, there are obvious differences between tangible and intangible matter, especially in the way we deal with it in general. When I steal something intangible from someone else, the original possession remains unchanged and still in the possession of that other party. That type of stealing would be impossible in the material world. Irrationally, some justify intangible robbery on these grounds. Certainly, stealing of intangible matter in our modern world has become extremely widespread. There is practically no art student who is not using illegal copies of some sort of software; even knowing that while doing so, he/she may be devaluating the very source of their own professional future. In a way, it is sad that illegal possessions have become such a normal part of everyday life. All stealing used to be a criminal offence.

What intellectual and industrial intangible property shares with all other tangible assets is the fact that it represents a certain value. Accountancy rules do not make any distinction between the two, other than that they will be specified separately on the balance sheet. For the rest, the differences could not be greater. We are all in some way or other influenced (or inspired) by other people's intellectual property. Many of us possess illegally obtained intellectual property. The use of someone else's intellectual property is judged on a sliding scale from fully accepted and even encouraged to totally unacceptable, with an extremely wide range of opinions in between. True, intangible property is very ethereal stuff with very peculiar qualities; for example, not having any difference whatsoever between the original and the copy, and having the possibility to make unlimited multiples and transporting these over any distance at practically no cost or effort. Some find it hard to see the value of something that is so easy to multiply and to obtain. Nevertheless, in economic terms there is in principle no difference between stealing intangible or tangible property; both will affect the value of the property of the original owner. Economics does not recognise the concept of free lunches: taking something and giving nothing in return. The same concept is also the standard in any ethical judgment. Of course, one should accept that most of what we deal with has become increasingly intangible and this fact has affected our behaviour; 'sampling' (copying a part of somebody's work) has become an accepted part of contemporary creative activities. But the same notion of creative creation will remain the ultimate benchmark for all authentic work. 'Stealing' is allowed as long as sufficient novelty is given back in return, and in a comparable way. Without that condition, it will remain plain theft that should be punished, never mind whether the property is tangible or not.

4.4.3.6. Involvement of the legal profession

Claims about violation of rights concerning intangible property are hardly ever obvious. Even when we have done everything possible to register our rights, the courts still have the final say in the matter. Only the courts can decide whether our claims for protection against violation of our (registered or not) intellectual property are valid. Never assume that registering intellectual property is something like registering ownership of a piece of land or a house. It is not, even though well examined patents may offer a degree of certainty after issuing.

Obviously, in a complicated matter as Intellectual Property Rights specialised lawyers of all kinds play an important role. In general, designers need a lawyer in most cases for help to make complicated registrations, drafting contracts, and making claims against infringes. Be aware that IP lawyers are amongst the best paid in the business.

Different types of IP violations. The left-hand bottle in each pair is the original design. The first pair shows an identical copy; this is called forgery or counterfeiting and is a criminal offence. The second pair shows a possible design right violation, or a trademark violation in case the bottle is registered as a trademark. It may also be judged as unfair competition. The third pair shows a trademark violation.

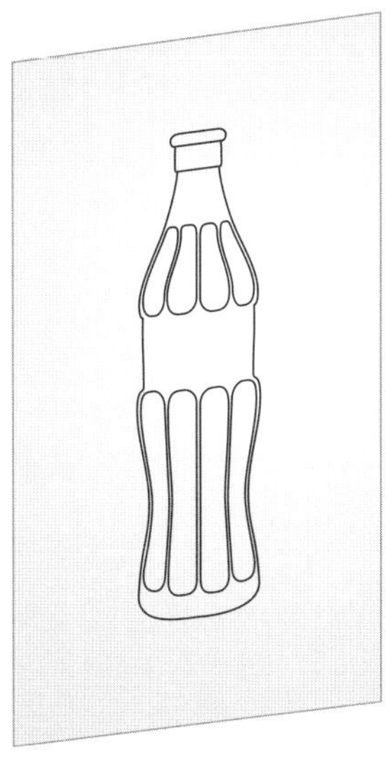

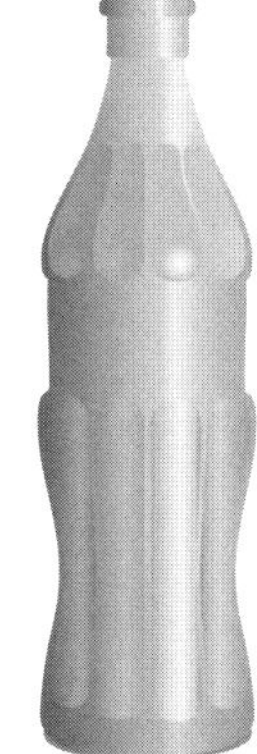

The design drawing is copyright protected, the bottle may have a time-limited design protection, and the complete product may be protected as a trademark which can be perpetually protected.

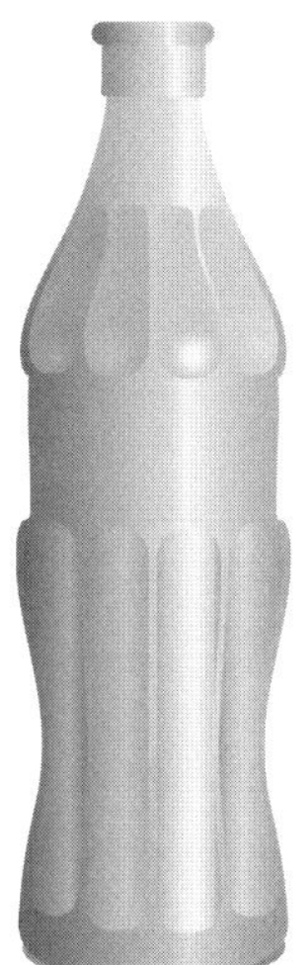

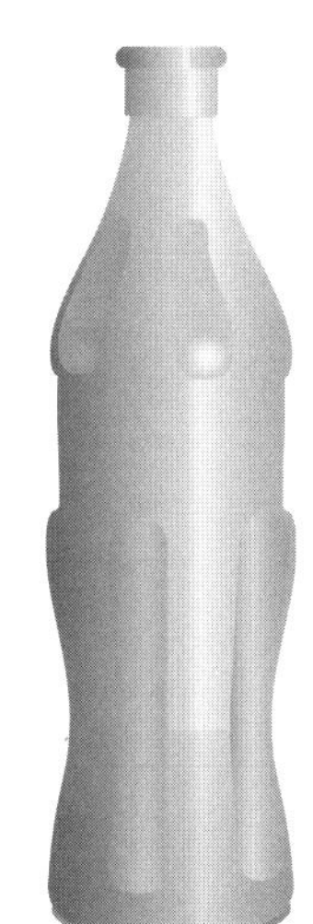

Minor differences in design may be judged as design right violation. In some countries most designs are considered copyrighted works.

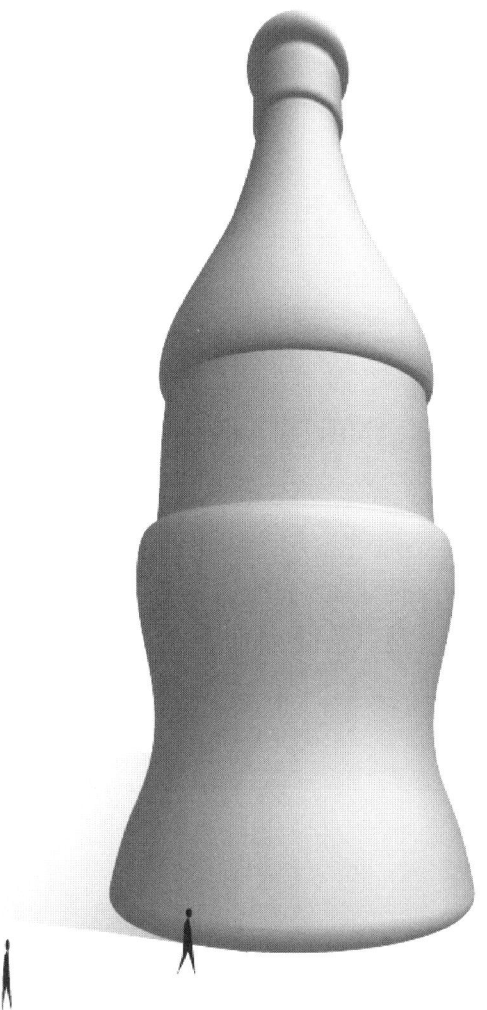

Buildings and architecture are widely considered art and are therefore copyright protected.

4.4.4. PRACTICAL IP ADVICE FOR SIGNAGE DESIGN PROJECTS

A signage project design may touch on a lot of different aspects of IP protection, because signage design has so many multi-disciplinary aspects.

4.4.4.1. Overview of possible IP rights in a signage project

—The development of a signage panel system may be protected under unregistered design rights, or—after registration—protected under registered design rights. In very rare cases, it may be sensible to contemplate a patent registration, but that will only be a consideration if the system is likely to have an extensive use that needs protection. In some countries signage panel system designs may be protected under copyright law protection.
—When the signage panel system is given a product name, that name will be protected under trademark law. In some countries registration of the name is required; in most cases it is not.
—All technical drawings related to the signage projects are protected under copyright law.
—All illustrations, pictograms and typography may be protected under copyright law. It may vary from one country to the other.
—All map designs are protected by copyright law.
—New software developments, for instance for interactive signage applications, will be protected under copyright law.
—All typography and layout may be protected under copyright law, depending on the country.
—All three-dimensional objects, super-graphics or murals may be protected under copyright law, depending on the country.
—All aspects of the design may be protected under the author's moral right. The level of protection varies between countries.
—All unusual production methods, design and installation know-how, are protected under trade secrecy protection as long as appropriate measures have been taken to protect these production methods, for instance, by demanding written confidentiality statements from all parties directly involved in the project.

4.4.4.2. Protection of IP rights

Designers often fear that the world is out there just waiting to steal their designs. That is a bit of an over-sensitive concern. True, most businesses are not particularly creative in their ways but to insinuate that most products or services are the result of design robbery is a bit far-fetched. A not particularly inspiring collection of existing material and ideas would be a better description of the average core business. Humans tend to be a bit like ants. Moreover, designers themselves are also heavily influenced by each other, including the leading ones. A look at design work from the past reveals how style waves come and go, as if they were seasonal weather changes. Nevertheless, arranging maximal design protection is a sensible action. The most important and basic protection is to organise your own work meticulously by keeping records of design advancements, and by making in advance (!) proper written agreements with all involved. The assumption that violation of a designer's IP rights is more likely to come from a remote party is entirely wrong. Problems with IP infringements are more likely to happen in the immediate environment of the creator; therefore, these kinds of infringements are best prevented by making agreements with all directly involved, such as non-disclosure or non-competitive or confidentiality agreements.

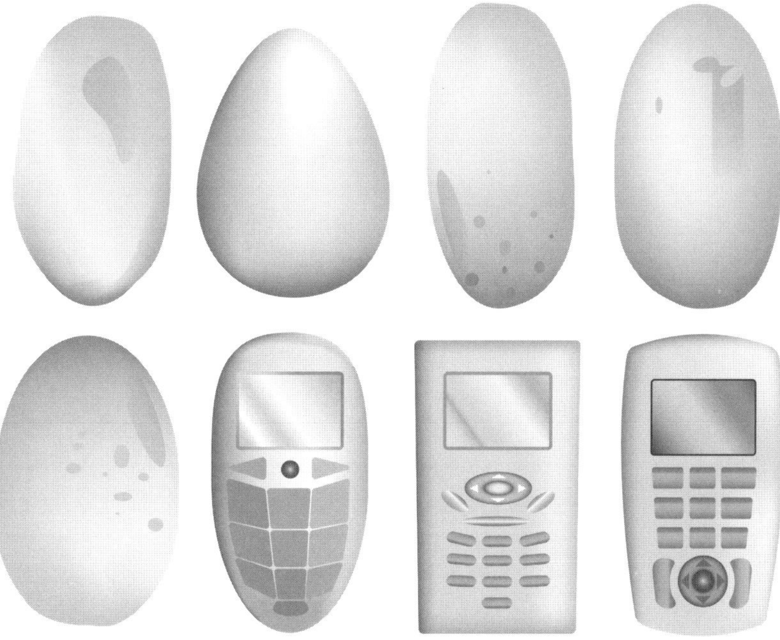

IP rights violation is judged on the amount of similarity to the original. That is seldom obvious. For instance, pebbles, eggs and potatoes may look similar but are quite different objects. Mobile phones come in endless varieties. To most of us they all look similar, only experts (and owners) can tell them apart.

Any designer who makes a commercially successful new design is likely to have followers. As said already, most businesses earn their money in the 'me-too' line-up. But the degree of copying of existing designs in this category constitutes in most cases no violation of IP rights. Infringements must be really obvious to consider proceedings. Is design registration a sensible action to enhance protection? It depends on the type and the importance of the design. Manufacturers and other businesses that depend heavily on design follow different strategies. Some find that registration and instigating proceedings against infringement is more financially interesting for law firms than for the business trying to protect their IP right. Others find that design registration works as an effective deterrent against potential infringement. Expected turnover of new models in a particular business may also be a consideration. In the fashion industry, turnover of models is so fast that registered design protection is generally not seen as sensible. A lot of design work is rapidly moving into the fast track lane of fashion design. For products—or services—that are likely to stay long on the market, registration is in general advisable. Design classics should seek all possible means for protection; the problem is that nobody knows in advance which design will become a classic, and once you do know, it is far too late for registration.

4.4.4.3. *Novelty and 'prior art'*

Novelty is the essential prerequisite to obtain and protect IP rights. Practically all disputes about IP rights claims come down to disputes about the level of novelty of a product or a service. Challenged parties will always claim the existence of so-called 'prior art', which means there was already something similar on the market prior to the arrival of the supposedly infringed design. Obviously, similarity is not a very precise notion and nothing is ever 100% new, so there is always room for argument. Lawyers may spend fortunes disputing novelty. There is little designers can do to avoid these kind of disputes other than staying away from any confrontation altogether. However, there is one thing designers can do to improve their position and that is to have proof of what was designed and when it was completed. There are a number of ways of doing this. First, registering the design is a possibility; second, many countries have offices that will give official date stamps on drawings and other papers provided; third, you can make a deposit at a public notary; and fourth, there are a number of websites where you can make an electronic deposit.

4.4.4.4. *IP rights in agreements*

All design commissions should have clauses dealing with the IP rights of the designer (see section 5.1.4.2). Special agreements, like licence agreements, need the involvement of a specialised lawyer. For the designer it is important to realise that these agreements are often between two parties that are very disproportional in size. Therefore, the designer's liability must be very limited and remedies for breaches of contract by the other (far more powerful) party must be very straightforward and easily enforceable. Regrettably, and on average, holders of financial power are better served by the judiciary system. Never sign an agreement that you do not fully and completely understand. Listen carefully, but do not be impressed by lawyer-speak; ask for explanations. Make your wishes for the precise wording in the contract explicit and do not assume that proposed wording will necessarily cover the specific meaning you wish to express.

4.4.4.5. *Employees and design commissions*

On a few occasions IP rights will—in the first instance—not be given to the creators of the intellectual property.

—Employees do not have IP rights, even in the case where they contributed substantially to the intellectual property. All IP rights fall automatically to the employer. The same happens if someone is working under the guidance of a tutor or a teacher.

—In some cases, and in some countries, IP rights may be (partially) transferred automatically to the client in a design commission, if no specific arrangement is made between the parties. It is strongly advisable to incorporate IP issues in all design commissions and contracts.

4.5. Designing in a team

A lot of design commissions have become too complex to be carried out by a single designer. A practice of one can only deal with relatively small commissions. Clients are often worried about the risks involved in dealing with single head practices. In more extended design practices, the collaboration between senior designers and their assistants—being either juniors or apprentices—becomes essential for the quality of the designs. Extensive commissions commonly involve various designers, with different professional backgrounds and specialisations, each with their own design team. In most signage commissions, collaboration is required with at least the architect(s) of the project. Designing in a team has special dynamics and peculiarities.

A 'conductor' is needed for successfully executing complex design projects involving many players.

First there is a need for a 'conductor' who orchestrates the design team, not only for logistical purposes but also in order to control and ensure the consistency of the creative output. Every design team needs its own conductor and the architect is generally the 'president of conductors' of all teams involved in signage projects. Designers tend to be uneasy working in a team, especially when it comes to the visual design part. The creative process for visual design is not entirely rational. Instinctively following one's own path towards an unknown destination is a strategy that cannot be avoided in visual design. Visual designers love 'to do their own thing'. Of course, this applies not only to the team members, but also to the creative conductors themselves.

Second, a good design team needs a steady and firm leading mind. It is very difficult to make compromises in visual design. Visual design can only impress when it delivers a thorough and consistent image. Every detail has to fit in neatly and has to contribute to one single overall look. Creating the impression that 'nothing is missing and nothing can be missed' can make visual design an overwhelming experience. Clearly, this delicate result can only be achieved by an uncompromising attitude.

Third, the assumption that good visual design can only be accomplished by overly self-confident despots is entirely wrong. There is a tendency in designers' attitude to pump up their egos to slightly preposterous dimensions, but that's more of a handicap than a virtue. In fact, excellent fellow designers are the gold mine of every successful design practice. Successful designers combine a fluent tongue, to win arguments, with a fine nose for talent. The work of colleagues is the major source of inspiration in all creative work, and even more so within a design team.

Creativity depends on a 'fresh look' at often comparable clients' briefs. Most companies wish to radiate a young and dynamic image, for instance. Visual design work is a constant series of considerations and reconsiderations, a sequence of hits and misses, trials and errors. Often there are moments when one is stuck, the result is not there yet, the ideas for making improvement have suddenly stopped flowing. The infamous 'writers block' has set in. Visual designers have all kind of tricks to create a fresh look. A good night's sleep can do wonders, or looking at the design in a mirror, for instance (leaving out the use of more aggressive and potentially addictive substances to find fresh 'inspiration'). One of the most surprising aspects of the human mind is that the best ideas appear while not sitting behind the desk or while not even contemplating design problems. The mind needs relaxation and a different focus to come up spontaneously with fresh solutions. Problem solving doesn't seem to work only by better focusing or thinking harder, quite the contrary: an 'empty' head and looking sideways seems to be more efficient. The conductor of the design team has an unfair advantage over the designers in the team that deal with the projects on a daily basis. Not being involved in a design project on a daily basis like the other designers in the team makes for the right conditions of an empty head and a fresh view. Being personally unattached to any of the design proposals put forward by the members of the team makes it easier to see good combinations and new directions. The creative leader could never have had such a fresh approach had all the design work been done by him or herself alone. This reality is unavoidable and often quite frustrating for the other members of the team. It is helpful for everybody to realise the importance of this mechanism.

4.6. Developing the work plan

All signage projects over a certain size involve the design of many different items, combining various techniques, types of messages, and different professional skills to produce the final designs. It is essential to develop a work plan that deals efficiently with all these different aspects. The workplan must have a sequential order that connects the work phases in a logical manner. Items should not be designed individually, piece by piece. One of the major problems with designing a signage project is to create visual cohesion between all the signs needed for the project. This goal is best achieved with the development of a set of visual instructions with which a large, coherent set of various signs can then be specified easily for manufacturing and installation.

4.6.1. CONNECTION BETWEEN SYSTEM DESIGN AND VISUAL DESIGN

In the system design phase, the foundations for the visual design are laid. To repeat the activities in shorthand during the system design phase, first, an overview of all requirements or constraints is produced covering all the relevant aspects of the project: user profiles, requirements for technical, legal, security, house-style, PR, budget or time-planning. Second, a system of related items is developed that serves all the communication needs for easy wayfinding and essential instruction for the site. The content of each item and its global position in space is set. All this is essential in some way or other to the visual design.
The most important part for the visual design is the list of sign types developed during the initial system design phase. This list consists of an overview of all standard items that have to be designed individually. The content of this list might be amended during the phase of the visual design because design solutions may combine certain functions in a different way from that originally proposed.

4.6.2. VARIOUS PROFESSIONAL FIELDS INVOLVED

Most professional activities have become rather complicated. Nowadays technology is a part of practically everything we do. The professional field of design is by no means an exception to this rule. Moreover, signage design is an inter-disciplinary activity. Most projects over a certain size can no longer be carried out with only one person's skill. Most knowledge needs a continuous update, and professionals have to specialise to be able to stay on top of their field.

Signage is particularly sensitive to this development. The overview of people given in chapter 2.2 shows the different professions involved in signage design. For the visual design part, the following professional fields are relevant:

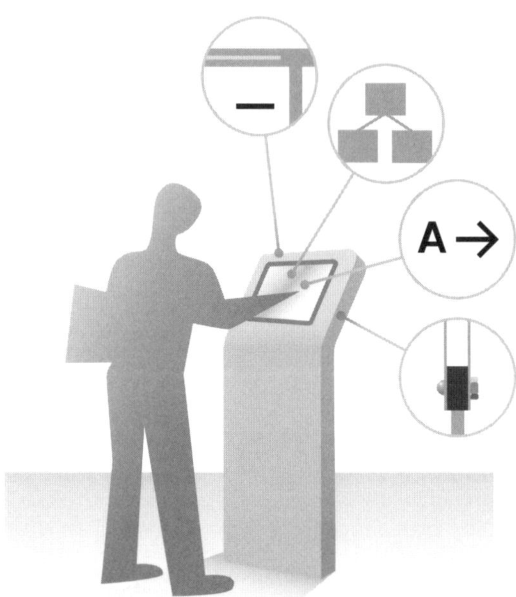

Signage design combines various design disciplines: architectural, interactive, graphic and product design.

4.6.2.1. Architectural design

All signs correlate in various ways to the architectural design. Accessibility of a site, or the 'routing' is a part of every architectural plan. It is also the foundation of every signage design. Most architecture is based on measurement grids that have to be respected in the spatial positioning scheme for all signs. The existing colour scheme and design (style) details of the architectural design are the basis for the colour scheme and design details for the signage design. Some types of signs can be an integral part of, or closely related to, interior or furniture designs.

4.6.2.2. Product design

Product design can be an important part of the signage design when specific functional aspects need to be integrated in different sign types. For instance, when interchangeability of messages has to be possible between various sign types. Only large projects may have a need for customised product design. In most cases, existing signage panel systems will be used to cover this need.

4.6.2.3. Interactive design

Digital media are playing a growing role in signage projects. Some of these media are interactive. This means that the user needs to actively interact with the signage facility to retrieve the necessary information from it. This interaction usually involves a (touch)screen; sometimes a mouse and a keyboard are added. The way these devices will be used, together with the design of the various screen images involved in the process, is called the Graphical User's Interface (GUI). The use of the internet is based on the same principle. Exploding internet use created a huge demand and has generated a whole new specialised field in design: the multi media designer, or web designer, or user experience designer (or whatever the latest invented name is for this professional field).

4.6.2.4. Graphic design

Graphic design remains the key skill for signage designs. The major ingredients of signage are type, pictograms, lay-out, illustrations and maps. These visual components are within the realm of the profession of graphic design.

Signage design has gradually become a specialised field on its own. Developing a signage system and combining a visual appearance that integrates all (design) aspects sensibly requires quite specific knowledge and experience.

Keeping some visual traits identical is an easy way to create a family look.

4.6.3. CREATING A FAMILY STYLE FOR ALL ITEMS

Effective visual communication between ourselves and the built environment that surrounds us is only possible because we have a basic familiarity with our visual surroundings. We have an amazing ability to constantly scan our environment and decide instantly what's familiar and what is new. We can only do this because we all have a large set of expectations about how certain things will look. All cars look like cars, bridges look like bridges, and cash registers must look like cash registers in order for them to be recognised and consequently used as such. Products must first have a 'visual family trait' that shows their basic functionality for them to be recognised.

Therefore, signs must—first of all—look like signs. But that's not enough. A signage project basically comprises a rather extended set of quite different types of signs spread over a wide area. A lot of these only function properly in relation to each other. So the essential requirement for the visual design of all signs within one project should not be missed. All signs should be easily recognised as parts of one coherent system of individual signs. The stronger the visual family trait between each individual sign, the more efficient the system will be.

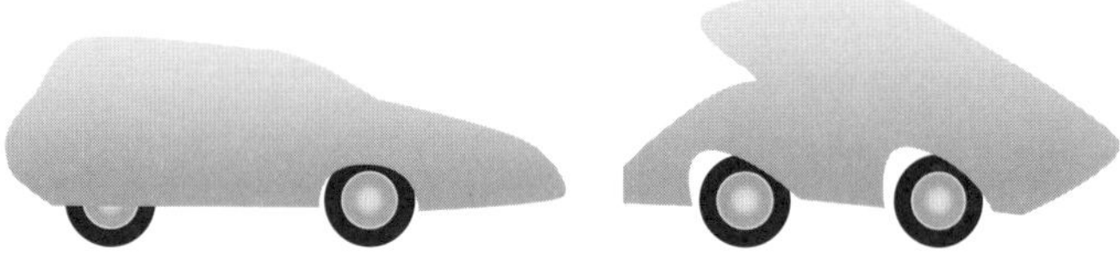

Some products have a very strong visual identity. Practically all shapes on four wheels will look like cars.

4.6.3.1. Creating a visual identity

A visual family trait consists of two related elements: identical details in visual appearance and an identical 'character'. In other words, all the items within one system must have an identical 'look and feel'. Just as is the case with human families, all members have similar physical features and character traits.
A family style of a series of products is also described as its visual identity. The development of a visual identity has two stages. First a decision has to be made about the desired character that the visual design has to express. This can be done by formulating catchwords taken from the same category as we would do to describe a person's character or specific quality. For instance, using words like innovative, or energetic, or friendly, or

The archetypical visual impression of signs in a building. This is the way everybody expects signs to look.

trustworthy. Another possibility is describing a desired style or 'atmosphere', like classic, or advanced, or vernacular, or Italian, or tropical. All these descriptions are rather global and subjective criteria for creating visual identity. Nevertheless, they are important and we all immediately and unconsciously give such subjective characteristics to all visual design.
The second stage in the development of a visual identity is to collect visual material that expresses the desired character in the most effective way. It is in fact an attempt to bridge the gap between what can be described verbally and what can be shown in matching images. These images can be used in the later stages for the development of the so-called basic design elements. Not in all cases, but sometimes, signage projects have to deal with implementing existing visual identity programs.

4.6.3.2. Basic design elements

Once the delicate transition of verbal descriptions into visual ones is done, the further development of a family style is more straightforward. It basically comes down to creating detailed design specifications that can be applied to all (or most) items. This is a very effective way to create a visually consistent set. To this end a series of charts or diagrams are produced that specify all the different fundamental aspects of the visual appearance of the signs, like for instance colour, typography and use of material. Before making the design specifications for each design aspect separately, there may be a need to specify first a sort of general visual 'theme' that holds all the different formal aspects together. This theme gives an overview of the key design features in its most concise format. It is best compared with a theme in musical terms, where a whole musical piece is often based on all kinds of variations on a central theme. Basically the same can be done with visual material, where a number of simple visual characteristic can be created that allow for variation in various visual aspects. It is an interesting and playful way to create a visual family style. In musical terms, the basic design elements become the prelude to the rest of the complete piece.

4.6.3.3. Detailed charts or diagrams

After the theme is visualised, each aspect of the visual appearance needs to be specified. Each aspect will be discussed in more detail later. An overview is given below:

—Type and typography
A chart with the selection of typefaces to be used, together with all their typographic specifications, like standard sizes, word- and letter spacing, leading and other typographic details.

—Other graphic elements, like symbols, pictograms and illustrations
A chart with an overview of all the artwork (or graphic principles) of other graphic elements, with specifications comparable to those made for the typography.

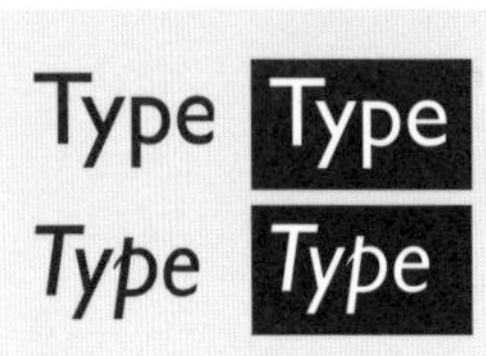

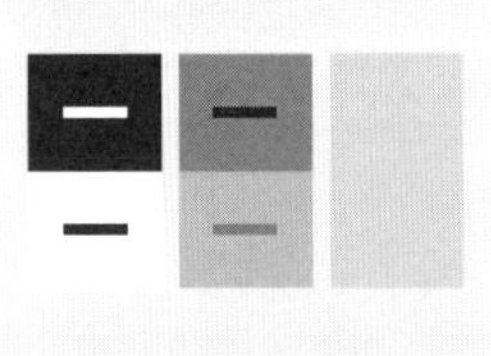

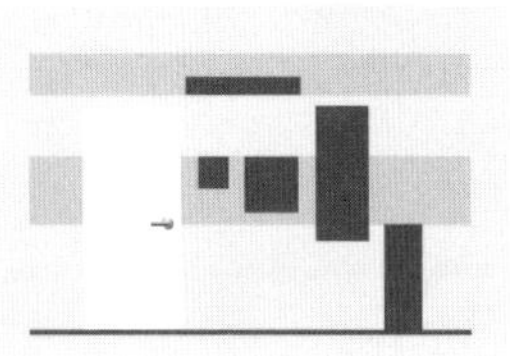

The set of master charts that cover all design aspects for a project. From top to bottom:
- typeface and typography
- other graphic elements
- use of materials
- use of colours
- layout and panel sizes
- standard sign positioning in elevation

—Materials to be used
A chart with samples of all the basic materials to be used. The concept behind a material selection can be shown best with a chart where small pieces of the material are shown next to each other. In most cases, it is advisable to make this chart in combination with the colour selection chart.

—Selection of colours
A chart with all the colours to be used in the project.

—Standard panel sizes with standard layouts
A chart with an overview of all the sizes of the sign panels to be used in the project. The standard layout of the messages (text and graphics) on these panels will also be shown.

—Positioning of signs in elevation
A chart with an overview of the positioning of all the signs in elevation in relation to the standard heights of all the architectural elements within the building and/or site.

The above charts can be made separately or in combination with each other. It all depends on the type of project and on personal preferences. It is advisable to show the charts for colour and materials for signage and interior design together.

4.6.4. MAKING DESIGNS FOR EACH SIGN TYPE

All the design principles described so far have to be applied to the designs of each individual item on the list of sign types that is established in the system design phase. All final designs are best presented and shown as 3D models, preferably at real size or otherwise in a relative scale to each other. Elevation drawings with a reference to human size can provide additional useful information for each design. Sophisticated software can produce all kinds of impressive 3D or even animated artwork presentations of signage designs shown in their environment. These tools can be very helpful in imitating reality. The same quality is also the danger when using these sophisticated tools; it can create a pretty convincing reality of its own which hardly matches the real situation. An accurate visual representation of a site does not need photo-realistic imagery. When images that look like photos are used, representation will often be misleading because it all looks so real, while the real situation may look substantially different. Making the final design for each sign type used in the project is the essence of the visual design phase of the signage program. This doesn't mean that the development and presentation of the underlying design principles should be forgotten or neglected. That would be extremely unwise. The designer benefits greatly from making the visual foundation very clear to him/herself, and this will certainly help the client to understand the design proposals. Review and approval meetings of all the individual sign type designs is better done along with introducing the design principles responsible for the visual coherence of every item.

4.7. Visual design concept

Good preparation and a sensible design methodology can be explained and are very helpful in the design process, but not everything can be done by the book. There is one critical phase where a straightforward method is not available. That is the phase of making a visual design concept. Design cannot be of high quality without intelligent analysis and organisation of the specific project at hand. Moreover, it cannot live without an inspiring concept for that design project. Concepts do not totally come out of the blue , but there is some mystery about how they do precisely come about. Methods have been developed to 'organise' the creation of interesting concepts, for instance brain storming or 'thought-showering' sessions. There is even software on the market that tries to enhance the brain function and the development of ideas, called 'brain mapping' software.
Whatever the value of these methods, it is certain that serendipity (coincidental discovery) plays an important role in developing concepts. Allowing for a phase where the only purpose is to generate a free and uncritical flow of ideas is often very useful. The basic problem with making concepts is that one doesn't have much of a clue what one's looking for until it's found. It is the basic oxymoron of all creation. A period of unrestricted trial and error, keeping the mind as open—and at times as empty—as possible, is probably the surest way to discovery.

A few conventional methods are used as sources of inspiration. The first thing designers often do is to refer to illustrated design books and look at what other designers have done. Checking out the work of colleagues is a traditional source of inspiration. Second, it is good to have some knowledge about the basic style development that has taken place in signage design. Third, a theme, or a metaphor, can be established to be used as a visual link between all the designs. Fourth, existing products, or architectural elements, can be a starting point for the designs. In the sketching phase, it is useful to test ideas by applying these to the basic elements of all signage design. At a later phase concepts can be tested on the elementary set of sign types.

Really big signage projects may lead to product development for a signage panel system. The product development of sign systems —the name still often used for signage panel systems—is also done by a few companies that sell off-the-shelf signage systems. A growing amount of product development is not done exclusively for architectural signage. These products may have a wider commercial application, such as products based on electronic media, like interactive kiosks, electronic display boards and network display systems.

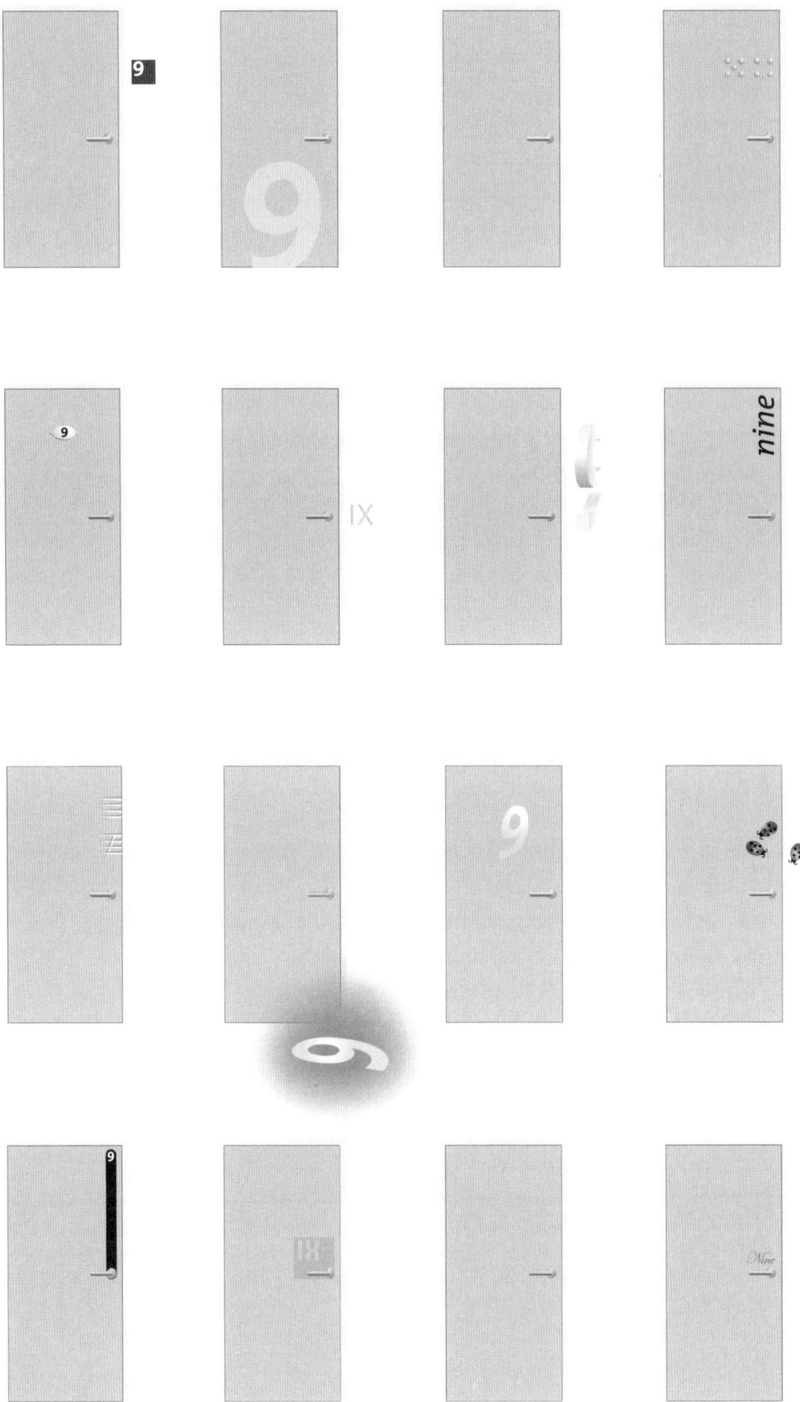

Potential design solutions for the archetypical door number are endless.

The design possibilities increase even further when the design of the doors becomes part of the signage design.

4.7.1. RESEARCH OF EXISTING SIGN PROJECTS

A traditional source of inspiration is to look at what other designers have done for comparable signage projects. There are quite a number of books available on the market today. Most of them in the English language.

It is difficult to make a good visual documentation of a signage project. A signage project excels by its coherent structure of signs, spread over a wide area, not by the visual quality of one single item. It's almost impossible to visualise a structure of related signs; that's why the emphasis in illustrated signage books is often on one (or two) eye-catching item of a signage project.

4.7.2. HISTORIC STYLE DEVELOPMENTS

The design profession is a relatively young one, so signage design is an activity certainly not more than 100 years old. All design work started with the Industrial Revolution. Craftsmen who were individually responsible for the functional as well as for the aesthetic quality of their work (and for the production as well), were slowly replaced by machines that not only needed a lot of clever engineering in order to function but also needed the skill of people capable of understanding the possibilities of these new and complicated tools in order to produce not only functional, but also visually attractive things. The latter became designers. They did not have to use these machines/tools themselves, like the traditional craftsmen, but they had to 'design' products that could be produced by using these machines. The first design professionals were what we would now call functionalists. Their emphasis was on the functional aspect of a design. Decoration or

A sketchy overview of historic style developments. From left to right:
- round corners and streamlined shapes (early TV)
- simple grid shapes (early digital)
- curved and sloped shapes (advanced digital)
- glass and stainless steel (high-tech)
- hybrid shapes (postmodern)

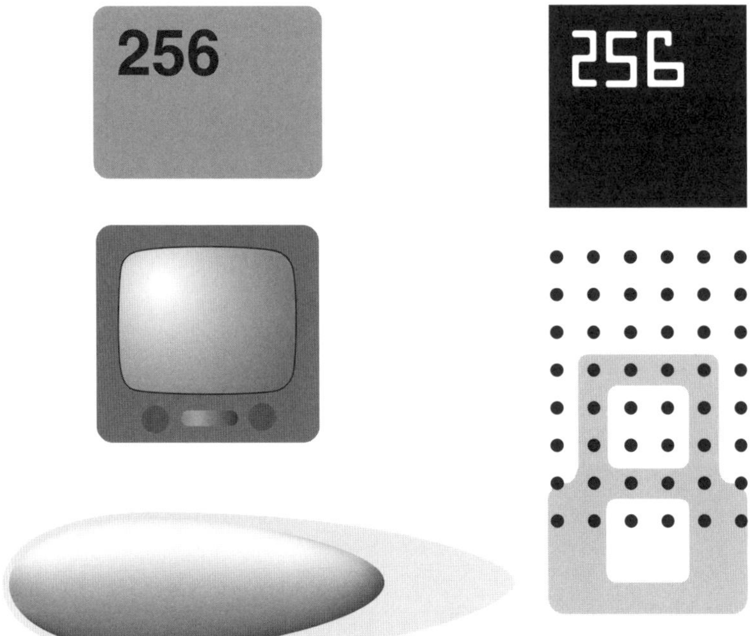

other visual thrills were not allowed. Products had to show nothing but their naked functionality. Beauty would appear almost automatically just by following this route. The results were minimalistic and often somewhat plain-looking products.

For signage design, the first style results were square panels and the design concept was making the signage facilities completely autonomous and not visually related to the architectural design. The square shape was considered a 'neutral' shape that could match the visual style of any existing surrounding. Basic shapes were a popular style feature at the time: a square, a circle and a triangle. The typefaces used were simple and geometric. Sans serif faces were considered especially appropriate for signage.
Signage panels also became subject to product development. Panels were designed to be built up with modular elements. These elements could be interchanged between individual sign panels, creating a sign system that could closely follow the dynamics of an organisation. The signage panels were designed in one colour that was strongly contrasting with its surroundings. Primary colours were 'en vogue'.

The separation of the signage design from the rest of the architectural design was a sensible development when dealing with bigger and more complex built environments. Still, to this day we suffer a bit from the negative aspects of this separation. Signage must be organised and designed as an autonomous entity, but it also has to be calculated for in the architectural design concept, just as is the case with the light fittings in a building. If not, signage will remain a rather clumsy visual intrusion into any

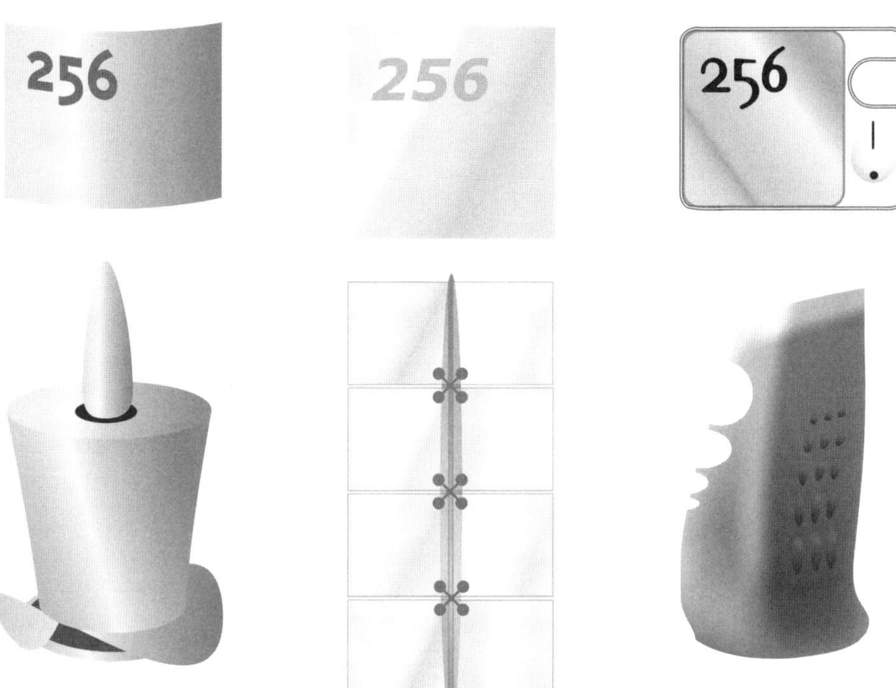

building. Oddly enough, the samples of exquisitely integrated lettering in the architectural design from the periods preceding industrialisation are abundant. The Art Nouveau and Art Deco style periods just before industrialisation have produced magnificent examples of text on buildings. Going further back, the Romans integrated text on building designs in a superb way for hundreds of years. Going really far back in time, the Egyptian architecture of temples and tombs is a showcase of the ultimate blend between script, illustrations and architecture, often with breathtaking results.

The modern world of industrialisation exploded in a plethora of different style periods, and signage design was inevitably influenced by some of these. With the advent of the massive introduction of television, the shape of the TV screen itself became popular; consequently all signage panels got rounded corners. Rounded,'natural' shapes became the favourite, especially in the USA where the style that created flowing and soft shapes was called 'streamlining', a term that referred to the design results of wind tunnel testing for modern transport vehicles.

After mechanical machines became an inseparable part of daily life, electronic devices completely took over, or at least became the crucial part of all machines. The computer was the tool we all had to learn how to use, not only to be able to earn our daily living, but also to live our daily lives. Of course, this too had an effect on signage design. Text to be used on sign panels can today be produced in-house , easily, and on widely available laserprinters.

The computer also became a design instrument. Shapes that before were difficult to specify for production purposes, became

Two style developments in typography that were specifically useful for signage design: putting type in boxes, and positioning letters on the baseline.

Baseline *positioning*

exactly measurable using computer software. CAD (computer aided design) was born. Buildings got complicated shapes, curved silhouettes and walls with sloped angles. All flat surfaces became more or less curved, and signage panels were no exception. Industrialisation transformed itself into a high-tech activity. Architects were designing impressive eye-catching glass and steel constructions that almost seem to deny gravity and float in space rather than being firmly grounded on earth. The amount of typefaces available started to be part of an exponential growth curve. Graphic designers were more and more capable of doing a part of pre-press production on their own machines and could design immensely complicated designs and illustrations themselves. Typography saw its terrain invaded by a wide array of extra elements, like 'boxes' and lines. The influence of Graphical User Interfaces for screens or screen typography was evident on all typographic design that was also for print. Icons started to replace words. Specifically interesting for signage was the style development of connecting the baseline of a line of text, or words, with another element. Words could literally 'sit' on building elements. Text often has to be squeezed in on buildings, since most buildings are designed as illiterate structures. There is little room for words, let alone spacing around words. Making a direct connection between the letters and building elements is a very efficient as well as a visually satisfying solution.

Now, we have entered the so-called post-modern era. The world of real objects develops its 'shadow' version more and more in digital format. Our communication with machines, facilities and with each other takes place through digital data transmission. The implications of this phenomenon is hard to overestimate. The way we communicate and manufacture things will undergo

further profound changes. Signage will certainly start to make use of personal digital assistants in some way or other. Digital guides will lead us more and more the right way, as a complete replacement or as addition to traditional signage.
The post-modern visual style reflects the borderless possibilities of a digitised world. Production constraints seem to disappear, transitions between media are easy, traditional professional frontiers get blurred. Everything that can be shown on a screen can also be produced in reality and digital representation will become a growing part of our everyday reality. Our familiar environment will become less static and more fluid and dynamic. Only the latest updated version of our environment will count as the real one.

The certainty of traditional order in almost every aspect of our society will be challenged further. The traditional boundaries of the different arts have already become vague or disappeared altogether. Even fundamentals, such as authenticy and authorship, are redefined. A museum, for instance, no longer has to refer to an impressive building, constructed expressly to expose original art; now it can also be a virtual electronic site, or a cluster of widespread small public display boxes containing reproductions or videos. The built environment will be more and more dynamic, holding ingredients that resemble a theatrical stage set rather than the solid steadiness of concrete, steel, bricks and stone.
Visual style is no longer an expression of an advancing world, but more of a specific type of entertainment, a marketing tool, a gimmick, or marks of individual existence. Consistency and authenticy are no longer virtues. 'Hybrid' style combinations and 'citation' of existing art are accepted or even celebrated forms of expression. Style appreciation has become ever more short-term. Modern times allow little time to reflect. Attention spans are short and any attempt to attract attention by conveying subtleties no longer works; on the contrary, it requires a firm shock to a basic level of emotions in order to function. Sound has to be physically felt in order to be heard. Designers and clients alike can easily get addicted to their daily doses of 'eye-candy'. Maybe it's time for an Atkin's diet to get us back in shape.Young designers are already turning to the meagre years of the fifties for inspiration. But certainly not for long...

4.7.3. THEME OR METAPHOR

Visual design communicates in principle by speechless confrontation. Understanding images requires a different hemisphere of our brain from understanding language. The impact of visuals can be very strong (one picture can tell more than a thousand words), but we can discuss the matter only by using words. Words are indispensable as a reference to a visual style or atmosphere. We need language to describe visuals. Eloquent use of language is particularly important during the presentation of visual design proposals. Meetings are ruled by verbal arguments and designers with a verbal talent have an easier time getting their

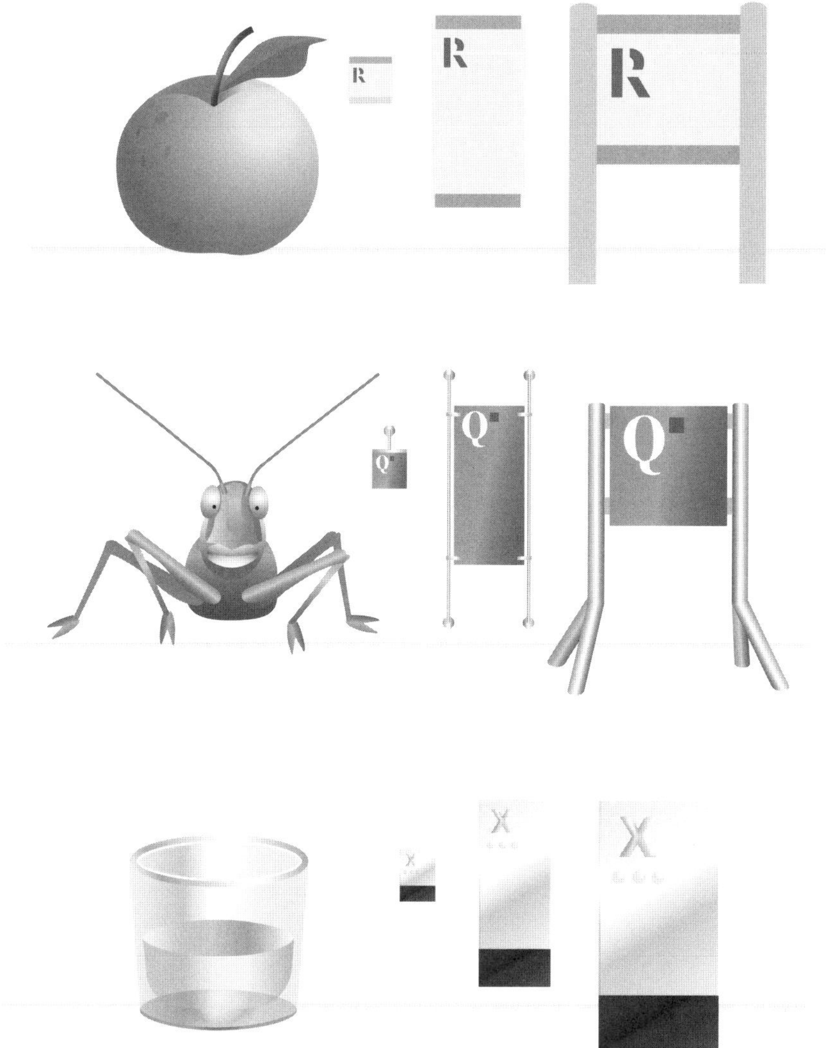

proposals accepted. Language can also be the source for visual design. An ideal, character or spirit can be expressed in words to be used as a starting point for the visual design. Words can be helpful in the concept phase. Catch words are the starting point of all identity programs. Images almost automatically pop up when reading certain word combinations: for instance, fresh/natural, or synthetic/advanced, or friendly/client-oriented, or dynamic/innovative, or refined/sophisticated/upmarket, or gay/sunny/leisure. Each word combination creates a specific atmosphere that can be matched visually. So called 'Mood Boards' are much-used tools to make the translation between the verbal and the visual realms. The possibilities for visualising words are limited, though. Visual design can only express simple and straightforward connotations. A theme must be kept very simple for it to work as a source of inspiration for visual design.

A visual theme or metaphor may be helpful in developing the visual design of a set of sign types.

A metaphor is the ultimate transition of language into a visual.

Here, a real object is taken to symbolise an entity. For instance, the long-haired and blindfolded virgin with her scale and sword, stands for Justice. Real objects are often taken as carriers of ideas. One might even say that all visual design has metaphorical aspects. The abstract, metaphysical world of thoughts and emotions always seeks materialisation in some way. In turn, the material world cannot exist without mystification of some sort.
For visually talented people, real objects can also be a source of inspiration. Looking for simple objects, or a combination of objects, may be useful. For instance a butterfly, or another insect, expresses a certain visual language. The intriguing structure, colours and surfaces of insects, rocks, fire, running water or trees, or the skin and shape of fresh fruits and flowers—each may be inspiring for the creation of a family of related objects.

4.7.4. RELATED PRODUCTS

Individual signs within one signage project are often made by using different materials or applying different sorts of technology, such as a touch-screen, a laser printed door sign or an illuminated exit sign. Moreover, signs are put literally all over the building: on doors, floors, walls, ceilings and counters. It is almost impossible to make one visually coherent signage design that matches all these different conditions and situations.

Full integration of the signage design into the architecture may deliver the most satisfying results.

This problem is not a unique signage problem. All architects struggle to keep the startling amount of different items needed in a modern building within the boundaries of one visual concept. The first thing they do when the budget allows it, is to refrain from using existing products but instead design all the facilities needed themselves, to make visual matching between all the elements easier. There are many famous examples of buildings with a lot of integrated design. Belgian architect Henri van der Velde designed practically everything in his own house, even the cutlery. Others, like Charles Rennie Mackintosh or Frank Lloyd Wright, did comparable projects. The Dutch HP Berlage designed both building and graphic identity for a Dutch insurer.

Damien Hirst started a completely self-designed pub. Physically integrating signage into existing architectural elements is definitely a good way to avoid visual clutter. There are a number of products or facilities in each building where integration is worth contemplating.

4.7.4.1. *Facade and main entrance*

The name of the building, the name of the company that occupies it, or the street number are a part of the signage that can become an integral part of the architectural design. During the twenties and thirties of the last century, many examples were created where typography was cast into concrete walls or made with bricks and mortar. Decorative stone fitted into facades of buildings was also used for signage purposes.

Integration of interactive signs in the reception area.

4.7.4.2. *Reception furniture*

Special furniture is often designed for reception areas. The reception area is also the location of many different types of signs. For instance, building directories can be an integrated part of the interior design and interactive screen directories may be built into reception area counters.

Integration of signs in system separation walls.

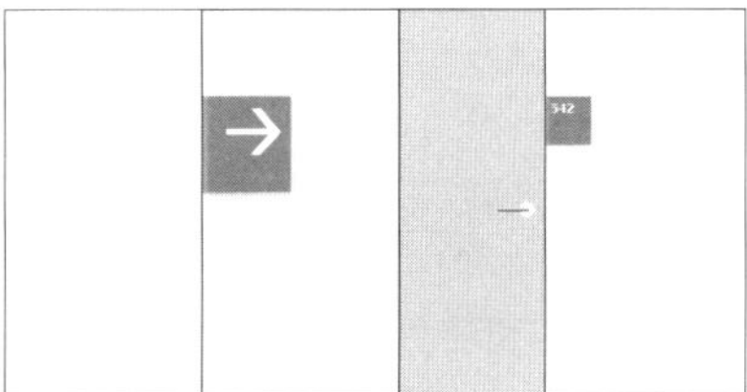

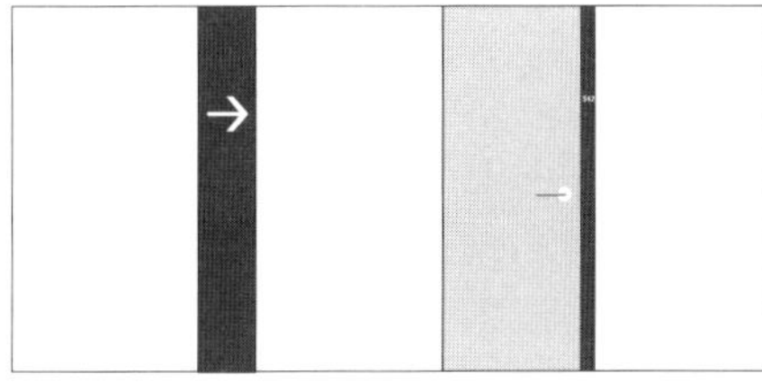

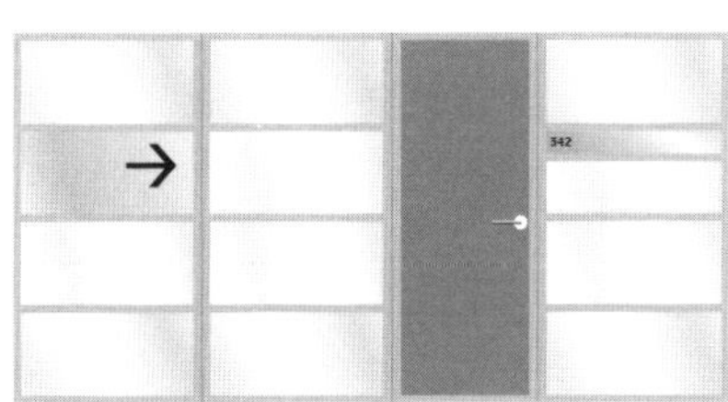

4.7.4.3. System walls and ceilings

Modular systems for separation walls and ceilings are found in every public or commercial building. Walls and ceilings are also indispensable carriers of signs. Yet no manufacturer of these kind of systems has offered a matching system of signage panels that can be integrated with them although it seems an obvious opportunity for integration.

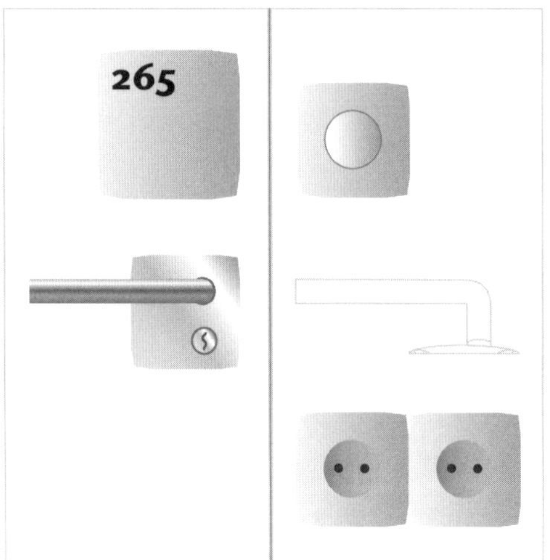

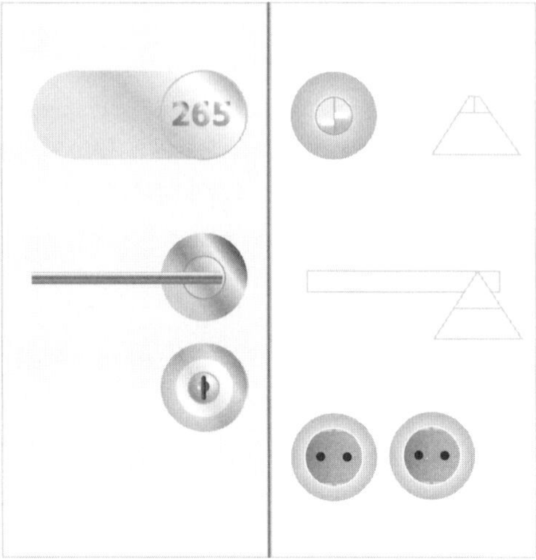

Integration of door and electrical fittings within the signage design.

4.7.4.4. Door fittings

Doors separate as well as create accessibility between spaces. Architects typically select a limited number of door models taken from the collection of one or two manufacturers.The same counts for the models and suppliers of door handles, hinges and locks needed for these doors. Doors are also typical sign locations. Integration of door fittings and signage is a design option.

4.7.4.5. Electrical fittings (fixtures)

Light switches, buttons and plugs are subject to the same selection process as doors (4.7.4.4 above). A building will have one (or a few) model(s) of these appliances. Integration can be a design option here as well.

4.7.4.6. Light fitting (fixture) systems

Ceiling (cladding) systems are applied in almost all buildings. A lot of these systems allow for an integration with (fluorescent tubes) light fitting systems. Lights and ceilings are also quintessential in most signage projects. Surprisingly, no products are available that can integrate signage within these systems.

4.7.4.7. Illuminated emergency signs

Illuminated emergency signs are mostly delivered by specialised manufacturers. The signs can be part of a complicated electronic detection system. Emergency signs may need individual batteries in case the major electricity supply fails or stops. The technology involved in these signs can be quite complicated. A large number of products are available on the market. However, very few, if any, products are satisfactory in every respect. Judged by aesthetic standards, most products available on the market under-perform. Practically no product allows for customising or adaptation to an existing signage design.

4.7.4.8. Lecture room equipment

Perhaps this is a bit far-fetched, but lecture room equipment can be seen as devices for temporary signage. Blackboards, flip charts, and all kinds of projection equipment, have some similarity with certain other sign types in a building.

4.7.4.9. Screen network systems

Electronic screens have become the common carriers of messages. More and more appliances have screens that interface with the user. Some types of sign panels are also replaced by screens. These screens function in a network that allows constant and centralised updating.

4.7.4.10. Telecom systems

Wireless telecommunication opens up an almost magical world for exchanging information. Obviously, many telecom enterprises got carried away with this potential and suffered serious commercial setbacks as a result. Yet these systems will, no doubt, sooner or later play a role in signage design and must be integrated.

4.7.4.11. Street furniture

A benchmark for a civilised society may be found in the quality of its public spaces. Cities and villages are discovering the PR value

Street furniture is often a haphazard collection of items. Integrated design may create a more pleasing environment.

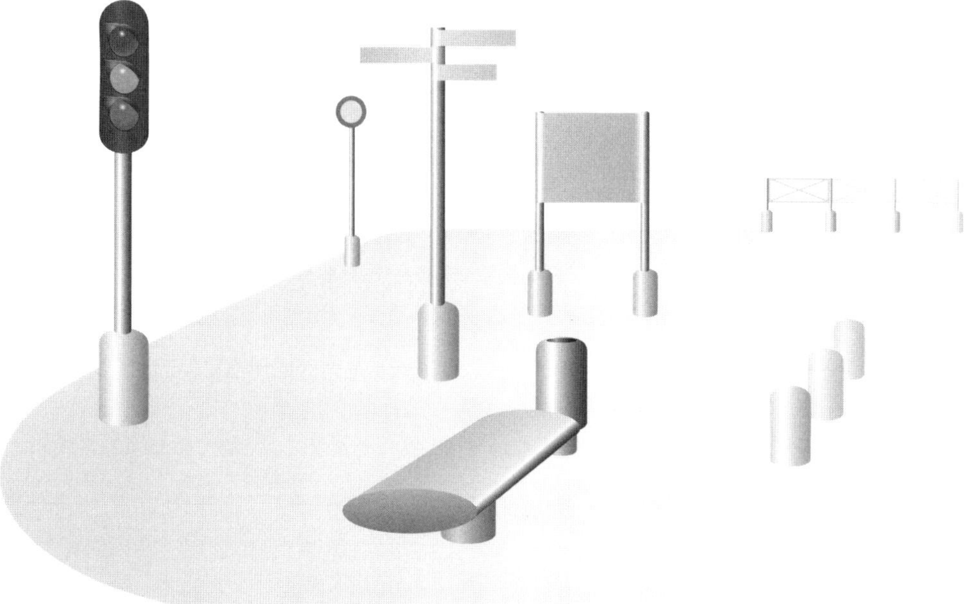

A sketch for integrated traffic signage.

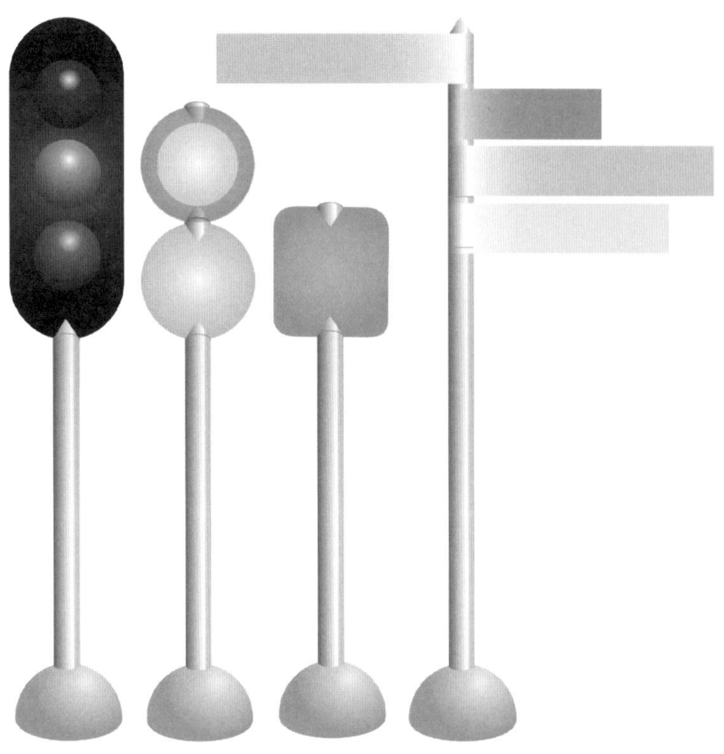

A sketch for pavement elements to be integrated with the street furniture.

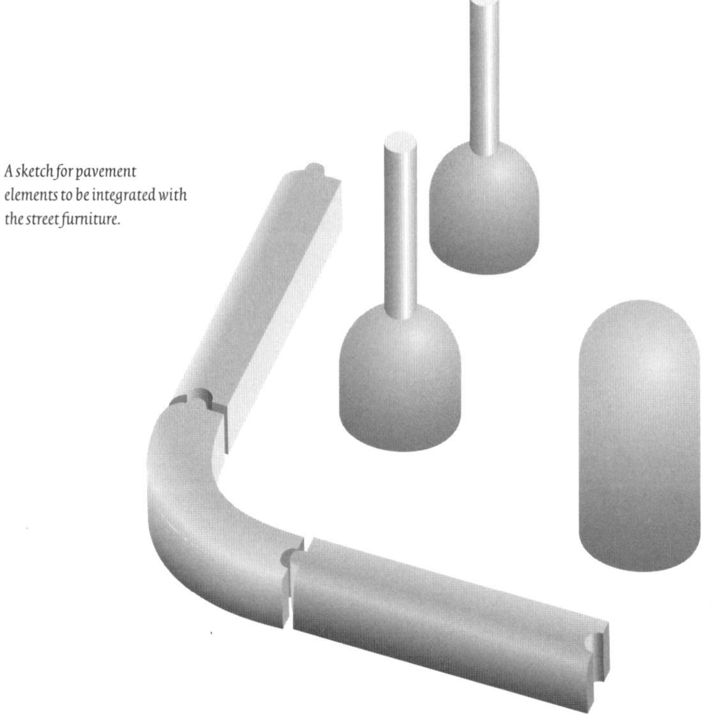

A sketch for integrated street furniture: a bench, a sign and a shelter.

of their public domain. Regrettably, this is often limited to the more touristic city centres and areas. Equipment and facilities in public spaces are called street furniture, like benches, railings, traffic lights, underfoot facilities for the visually disabled pedestrian, public toilets (washrooms), street lights, trash cans (litter bins) and post (mail) boxes. External signage is also a part of the street furniture. Public transportation intensifies within complex entities like cities, and people tend to travel more and more. All these developments contribute to the attention given to public outdoor signage. It is a sensible starting point to design the signage taking other street furniture into consideration.

4.7.5. BASIC ELEMENTS OF VISUAL SIGNAGE DESIGN

It is essential to any design process to start by reducing the complexity of the many relevant factors and data into a few basic principles that need to be addressed first. Afterwards, variations can be made to further develop all the applications needed in a project. It is crucial to stick to this order and avoid the common pitfall in all design work, which is to start too early with 'polishing the design details'.

The visual aspect of sign design has four basic elements:
—individual (dimensional) letters or illustrations
—text and illustration on panels
—the technology to update or retrieve information
—the frame or construction needed to install the sign in its chosen location.

4.7.5.1. Individual letters or illustrations

The most simple—and in fact one of the most beautiful ways—to put letters and illustrations onto a building is just to paint these on the wall. In this way, no additional elements that complicate or visually conflict with the surroundings are needed. No specific panel dimensions, no material thickness or surface characteristic, just the pure graphic form in its most basic expression. The art of direct painting on walls has almost totally disappeared (except for graffiti). Silk screening and vinyl cutting have replaced the original hand work. Both techniques come close to the painted quality.

Sign applications on the exterior of buildings require a less vulnerable technique, especially when put on rough surfaces. Ancient Egyptian temples and tombs still show us in a magnificent way how images and script can remain relatively untouched by natural elements even after thousands of years. The old Roman

Direct application of texts or illustrations on the building surface are visually the most pleasing way to integrate signage within the architecture. Six variations of these applications are shown: painted or silkscreened, vinyl-cut, carved or sandblasted, cut out of sheet material, box letters, and free-standing 'sculptured letters.

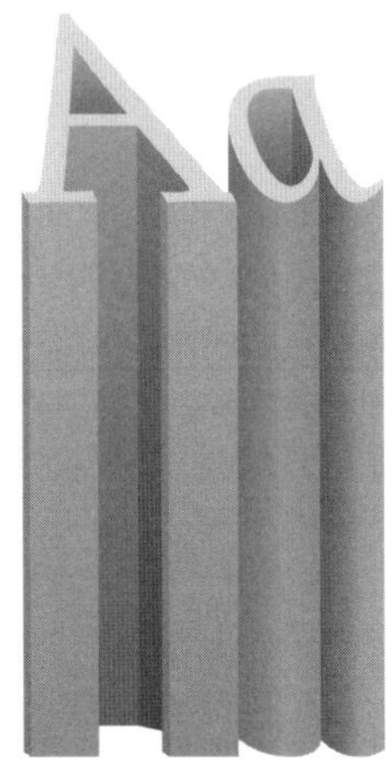

craftspeople followed in step by starting their work with painting letters on the wall then using a chisel to carve a more enduring representation. This technique is still practised. Some type designers think it is an essential part in the development of their skills. Eric Gill practised this craft all his life while designing many typefaces for print. Nowadays, automated routing machines can carve into any material to produce bas-relief letters and other graphic images.

In fact, any graphic file can now be reproduced in almost any material. Laser-, plasma- and waterjet-cutters can cut any shape out of practically any material. Some manufacturers specialise in combining (neon) light and loose lettering and have developed impressive collections of welded metal channel letters, still heavily depending on the skill of craftsmen.

Application of individual letters, logos or illustrations directly on buildings is often superior to the application of these elements on panels first. The best proof can easily be found in most shopping streets on the globe. Ugly and intrusive fluorescent light boxes dominate building facades. For this reason, German cities have altogether abandoned the use of light boxes for outdoor signage. An initiative that deserves imitation and should set an example for cities all over the world. Names of organisations near

Sign panels are archetypical for most signage. Six panel variations top to bottom, left to right: recessed into the wall, flush with the wall, on transparent material, cut out of sheet material, flat against the wall, and raised.

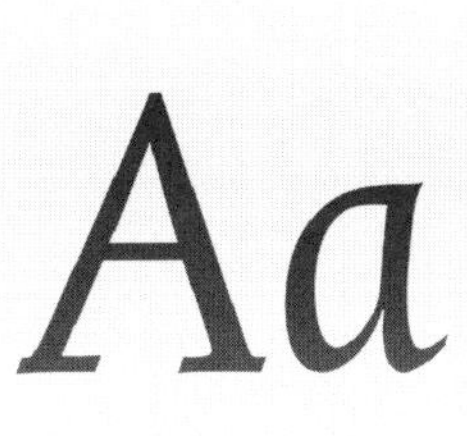

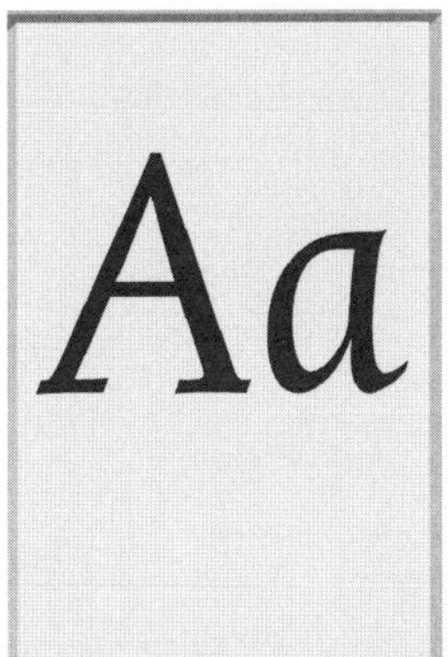

265
Accounting
ER Trump
TR Hoover

265
Accounting
ER Trump
TR Hoover

265
Accounting
ER Trump
TR Hoover

265
Accounting
ER Trump
TR Hoover

265
Accounting
ER Trump
TR Hoover

Painting on a wall or carving into it has been a means of human expression since prehistoric times. The Egyptians developed sophisticated combinations of low- and high-relief in various levels of depth. The Romans took the art of letter carving to the highest professional level and invented the delicate technique of fresco for wall paintings. Bas-relief (engraving) and paint (or thin adhesive foil) remain aesthetically the most pleasing techniques to put text (or graphics) on a wall. Because they are easier to produce, dimensional letters (high relief) are more often used for signage—although causing visual distortion.
The illustrations show from left to right: high relief (dimensional) text, painted, and two bas-relief examples in different depths.

A bas-relief door sign is, for the time being, only feasible for signs that are likely to be permanent.

entrances are best applied using individual elements directly attached to the wall, or integrated into the building elements.

Application of light projecting techniques by laser or other strong light sources directly onto a surface can dematerialise individual text or illustrations almost entirely, but requires quite specific environmental conditions in order to function effectively. Practically all signage projects include the application of individual letters and/or illustrations.

4.7.5.2. *Text and illustrations on panels*

The vast majority of all signs are sign panels, so a design vision must be developed about all aspects of sign panel application. Sign panels can be integrated wall or ceiling panel systems, can be made to contrast with their environment by varying the panel thickness, use of colour or material, or can be made to blend almost entirely into the existing space.
Panel dimensions are usually designed in one set of standard dimensions that can be related to other architectural elements.

4.7.5.3. *The technology to update or retrieve information*

The amount of different technologies required to update or retrieve signage information depends on the type of project and on its size. An initial decision on these matters has already been made in the phase of the design of the signage system. The list of sign types will have an indication, per sign type, of the technology to update the information. The visual design has to find a way to integrate all these different technologies, which may vary considerably.

4.7.5.4. *The frame or construction needed to keep the sign in its chosen location*

Careful positioning of each individual sign is a key factor for its functional quality. To meet this demand, signs can be mounted in every conceivable position: flat against or projecting from walls, or suspended from a ceiling, or freestanding on a floor or a desk top. A standard construction should be designed that makes all these types of fixings possible for sign panels of various sizes.

4.7.6. ELEMENTARY SET OF SIGN TYPES

By this phase in the design work, we have decided on (or at least have thought about and made sketches of) the very fundamental design elements. The next phase is the last preliminary before making the final design proposal. In the final phase, each individual sign type required in the project will have its own final design, based on a set of charts that outline all separate aspects of the design (for instance, material, colour, typography).

Before starting the final design work, it is useful to test design concepts developed according to an elementary set of sign types. Such a set is best composed with the types of signs that will be used most in the project and that cover the basic technologies needed. For an office building, the simplest set would include: a door (pictogram) sign, a door sign with easily updatable names, a directory and a wall-mounted directional sign. Further extensions may include: a meeting room sign, a projecting door sign, a suspended directional sign, and a free-standing sign for interior and exterior use. The work phase concludes with the selection of a final design concept. (See 'Elementary design steps'.)

4.7.7. DESIGNING A SIGNAGE PANEL SYSTEM

Ideally, the architectural design should leave generous empty space on all crucial locations for the signage designer to paint the signs by hand. This is an unrealistic concept these days. Yet, it is still a valuable concept for the architectural design to leave sufficient empty space at crucial locations. In today's reality, the major part of a signage job is to develop (or select) a coherent system—or a combination of systems—of signage panels. All so-called (modular) sign systems available on the market are in fact sign panel (or plaque) systems. Each system may vary in basic technology, for instance extruded or folded metal panels, or specially designed for indoor or outdoor use. They may also vary in the basic shape of the panels (like curved or flat). All are based on interchangeable parts of the individual sign. The basic variations of most of these sign systems include wall-mounted, suspended, projected and free-standing signs. Today, the possibility is also required to incorporate in the panel system in-house produced laser printed paper inserts. In the future, electronic screens may become standard extensions to all signage panel systems.

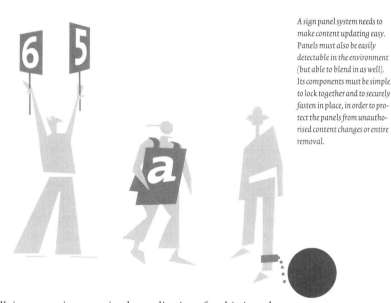

A sign panel system needs to make content updating easy. Panels must also be easily detectable in the environment (but able to blend in as well). Its components must be simple to lock together and to securely fasten in place, in order to protect the panels from unauthorised content changes or entire removal.

Not all signage projects require the application of sophisticated signage panel systems. A lot of projects will need more static and permanent signs. In these cases, the designer has few constraints in the design of the signage panels. In all other cases, a decision has to be made to either develop a panel system specifically for the project or to choose an existing system. Obviously, the first option is riskier and requires far more design and budget input. Another aspect to consider when deciding between the two options is the availability of system components after the initial installation is completed. Reorders for system components are likely to be easier for existing systems than for custom-made ones.

Any panel system must allow for the basic signage content. Left to right, top to bottom: marking destinations, showing directions and emergency escape routes, giving instructions, providing orientation in the environment, and accommodating a welcoming reception.

For designers brave enough to develop their own sophisticated signage panel system, here is a list of the standard requirements for such systems:

a. various text strip (slats) sizes to match various text heights
b. panel sizes must be adaptable
c. various colours must be applicable
d. interchangeability of system components is required
e. locking of components must be secure and concealed
f. panels must be capable of double-sided display
g. fixing options must be available for flat, projecting, suspending and free-standing positioning
h. panels must be vandal-proof, depending on type of use
i. possibility to produce in-house updates is required
j. application of dynamic messages (free/occupied) must be possible.

Elementary design steps

Signage design integrates a wide variety of design disciplines, like interior, product and graphic design. There are often very many different items to be designed. Under these circumstances, it is challenging to maintain one family look for every individual item. To reach this goal, the designer develops a kind of consistent 'visual grammar' for the project before starting to make detailed designs for each sign type. The visual grammar is a set of formal rules that govern all visual aspects. A good start to develop formal rules is to divide the (basic) design work into a few elementary steps, each concentrating on one aspect of the visual design. The steps may be followed in a linear order; however, in reality, design decisions will be taken going back and forth between these steps. Designing is a process of making constant (preliminary) decisions as well as reconsiderations when looking at the results. This process ends when a design result no longer needs to be reconsidered. Each elementary design step consists of making visual design proposals for a set of archetypical elements representing one specific design aspect (eg. graphics, elementary carriers, signage panel systems, and construction details).

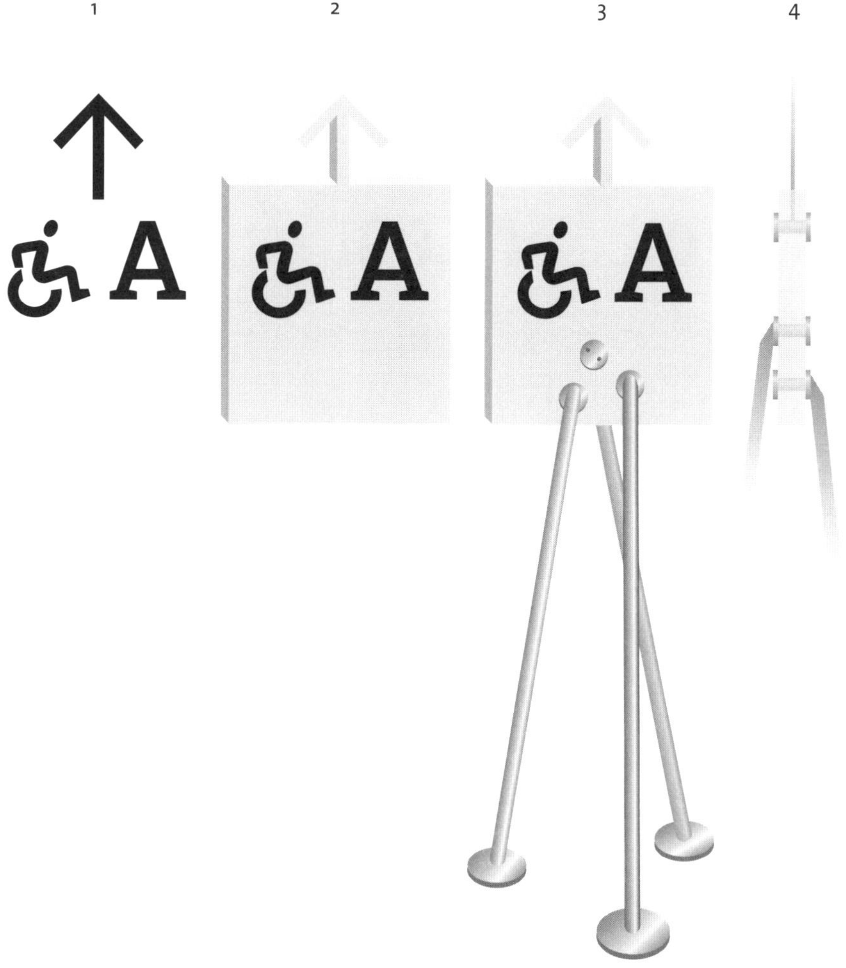

Consecutively focussing on one of the four elementary design aspects may help to create a coherent set of basic design elements. 1. The graphics, 2. Graphics and basic carriers, 3. Range of display panel types, 4. Basic construction details.

Sample sets showing the graphical part of the signage design.
The graphical part includes: a logo, typeface(s), pictograms, an arrow, maps, and the eventual addition of illustrative elements (shown in the lower examples).

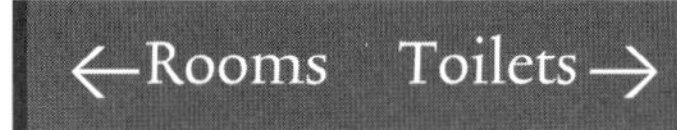

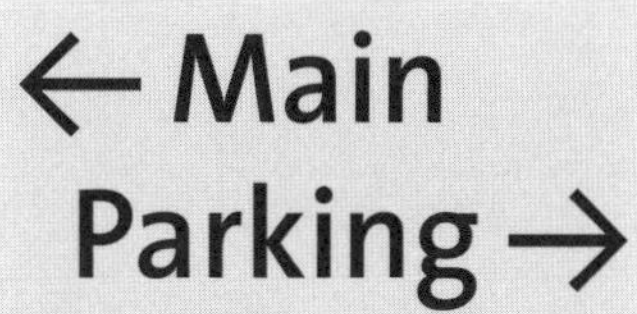

Sample sets showing the combination of graphics with their basic carriers.
Most graphical elements will first be put on their own carrier before application to the building site. Only a few sign types will be dimensional letters. A wide range of basically different production methods/carriers are almost standard today: dimensional or vinyl-cut letters, display screens, display panels and laserprint containers.

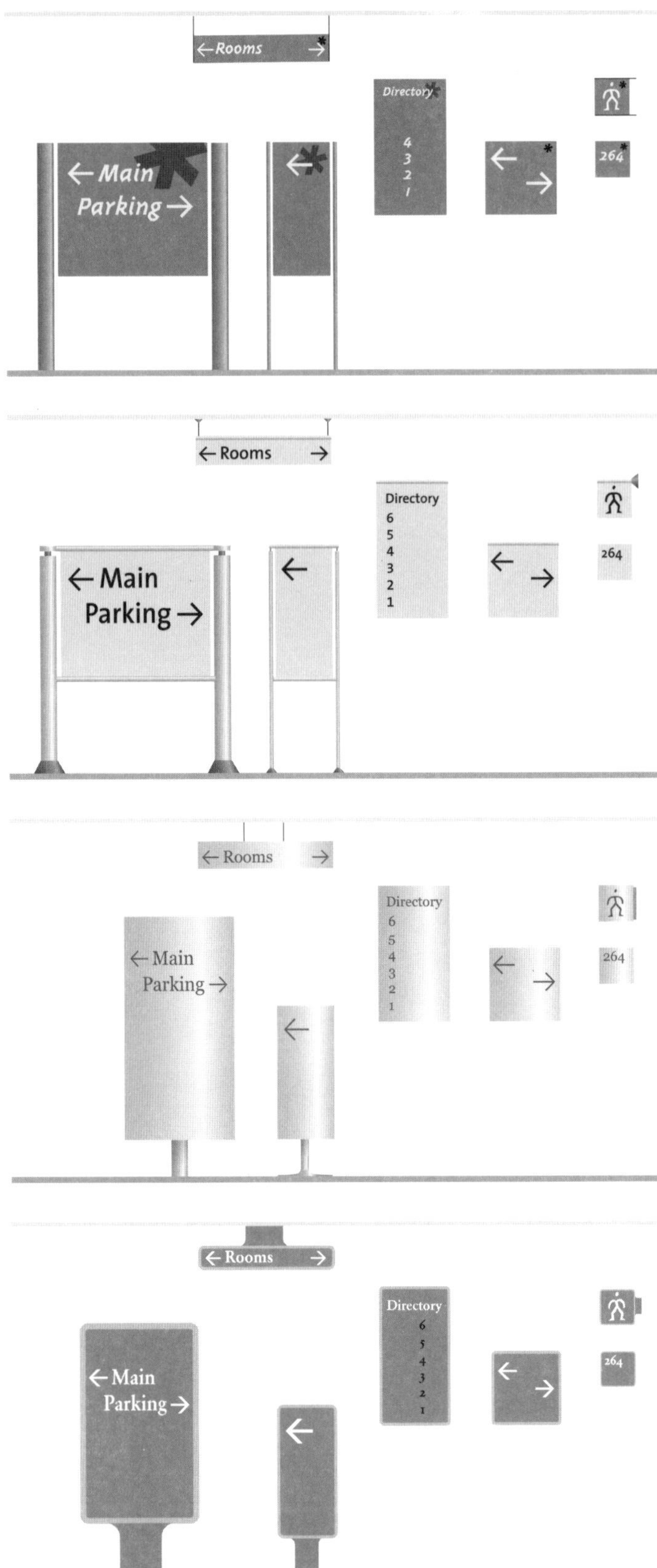

Examples of display panel system ranges.
A large variety of display panels are likely to be part of the signage design. These panels will need different types of support to mount them in different ways: free-standing (fixed as well as moveable), wall-mounted, projected and suspended. It is helpful to use a small range of archetypical sign types to test design ideas.

ROOMS
DIRECTORY
5
4
3
2
1
264
MAIN
PARKING

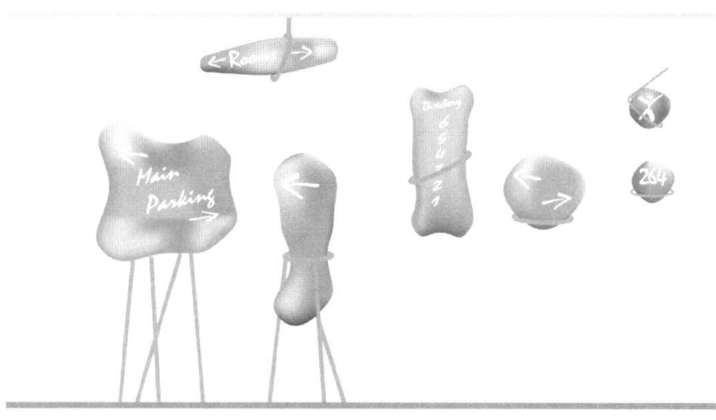
Main
Parking
264

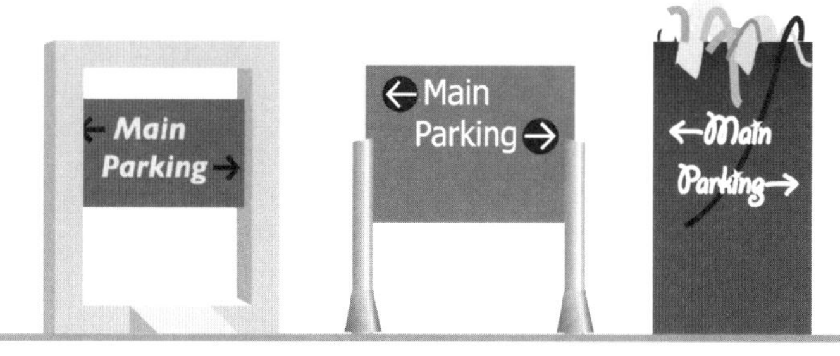
Main
Parking
Main
Parking
Main
Parking

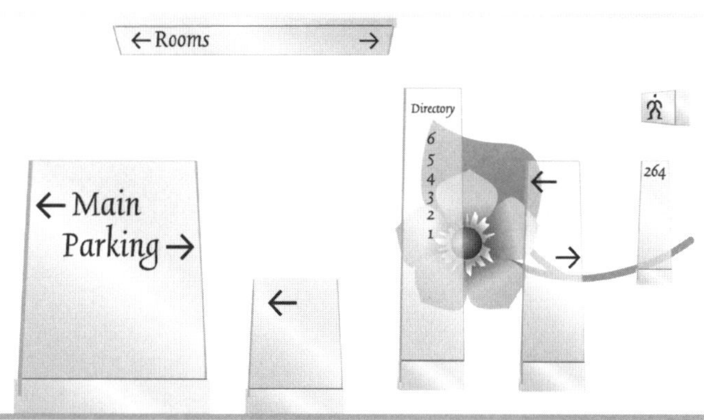
Rooms
Directory
6
5
4
3
2
1
264
Main
Parking

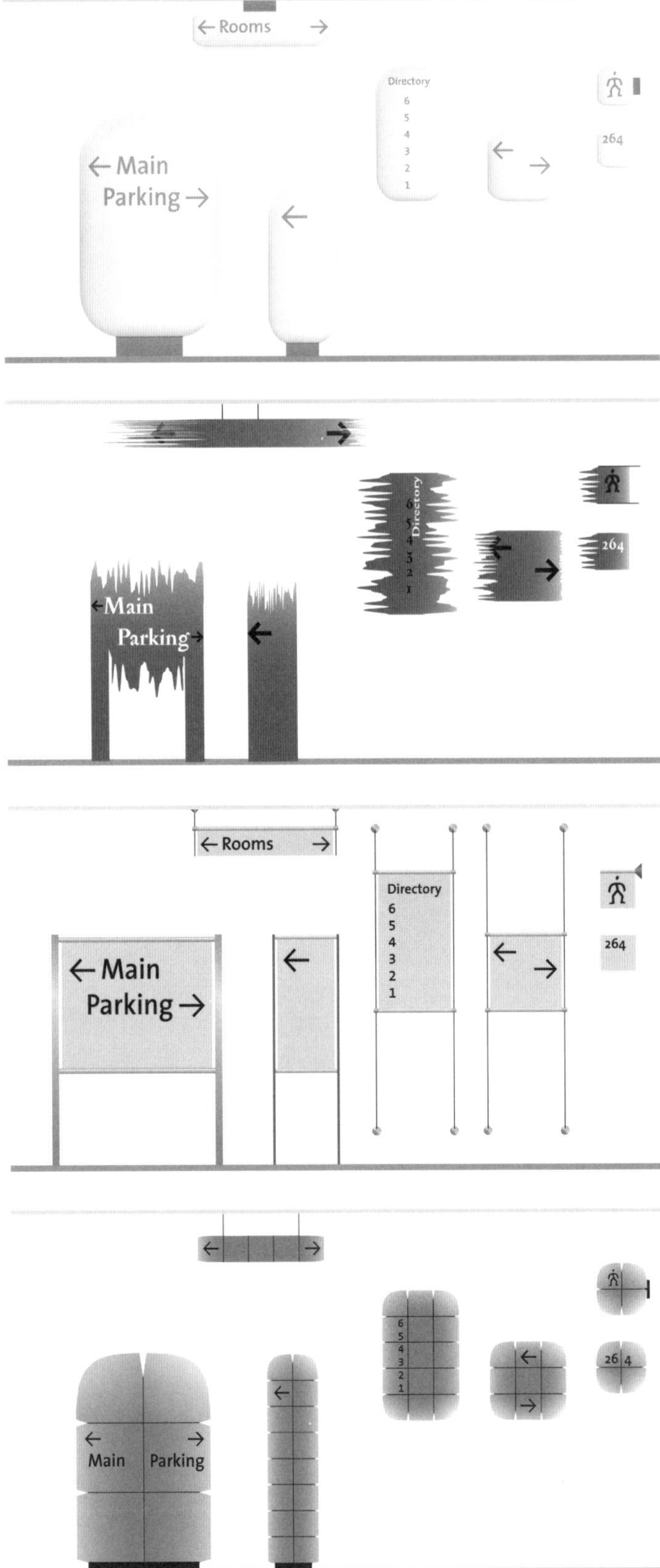

Rooms
Directory
6
5
4
3
2
1
264
Main
Parking
Main
Parking
Directory
6
5
4
3
2
1
264
Rooms
Directory
6
5
4
3
2
1
264
Main
Parking
6
5
4
3
2
1
26 4
Main
Parking

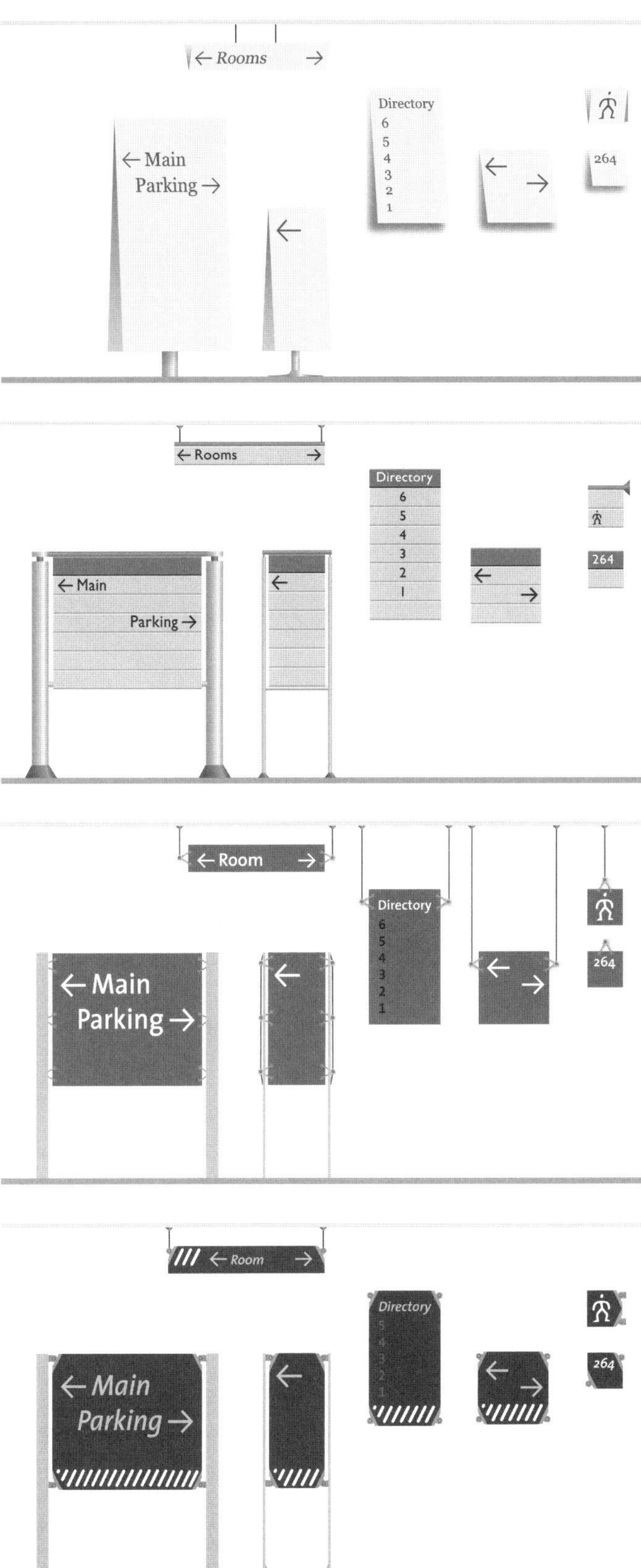
← Rooms →
← Main
Parking →
←
Directory
6
5
4
3
2
1
← →
264
← Rooms →
Directory
6
5
4
3
2
1
← Main
Parking →
←
← →
264
← Room →
Directory
6
5
4
3
2
1
← Main
Parking →
←
← →
264
← Room →
Directory
← Main
Parking →
←
← →
264

A sign type collection may turn out to be quite extensive. An overview of the sign type library developed for the signage of the city of Lyon (France, 1998 - 2001). Design by Intégral, Ruedi Baur and Associates.

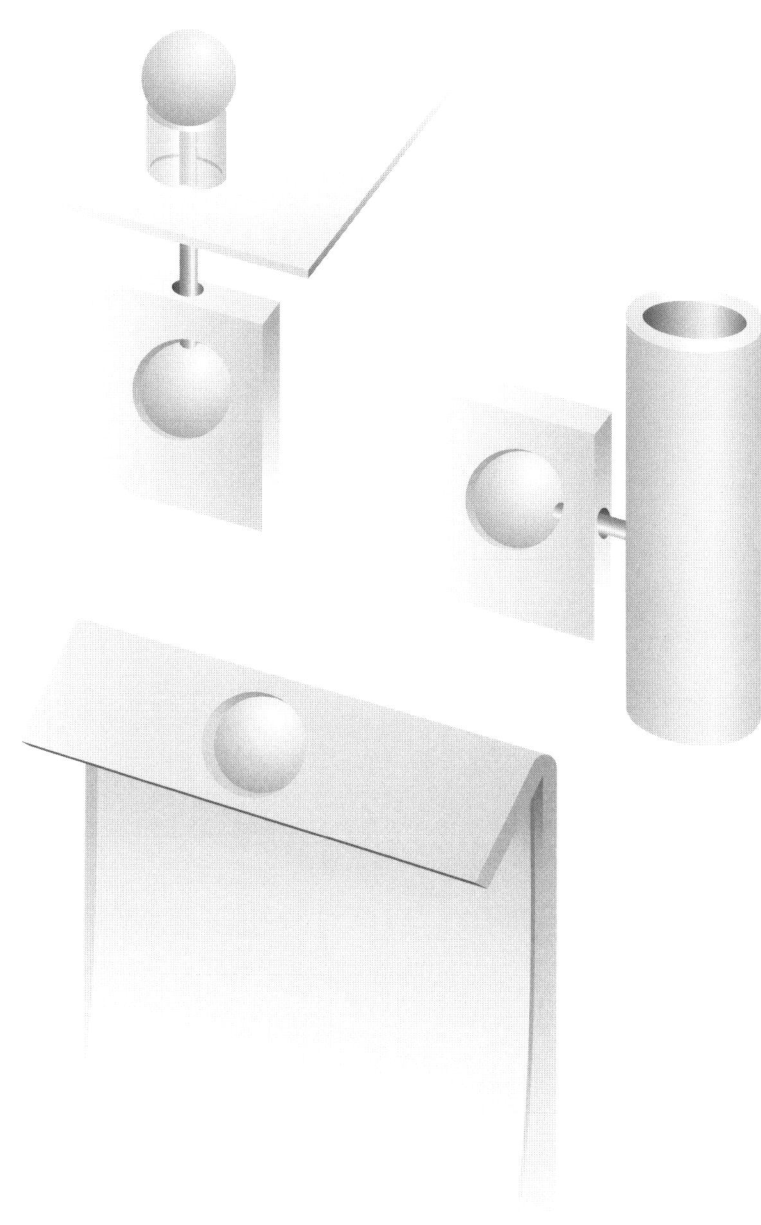

Sample sketches for basic construction details.
All three-dimensional objects need detailed construction drawings. Designing (or selecting) simple and consistent construction principles may economise production and enhance the family look of all the items used in the project.

The forces of nature

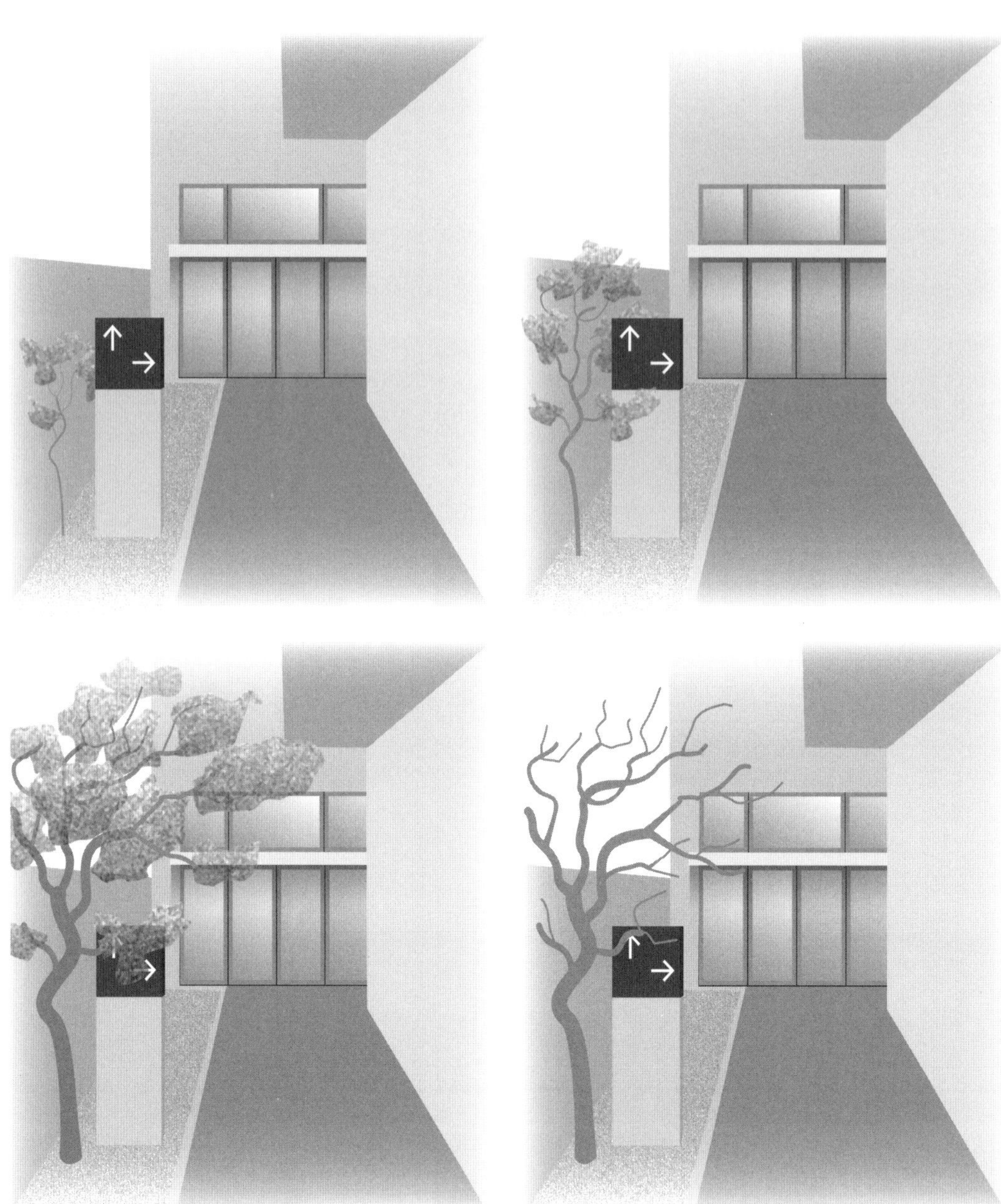

Signs want to draw maximum attention while employing minimum means. This results in a delicate balance that can easily be destroyed. Special attention is needed for signs placed in environments influenced by natural conditions. Natural environments change over the years, over the seasons and during the day. Consecutive seasons make plants change in shape and they may become visually dominating over the years. Natural light changes dramatically during the course of the day. Adding artificial light can make a real difference in some cases.

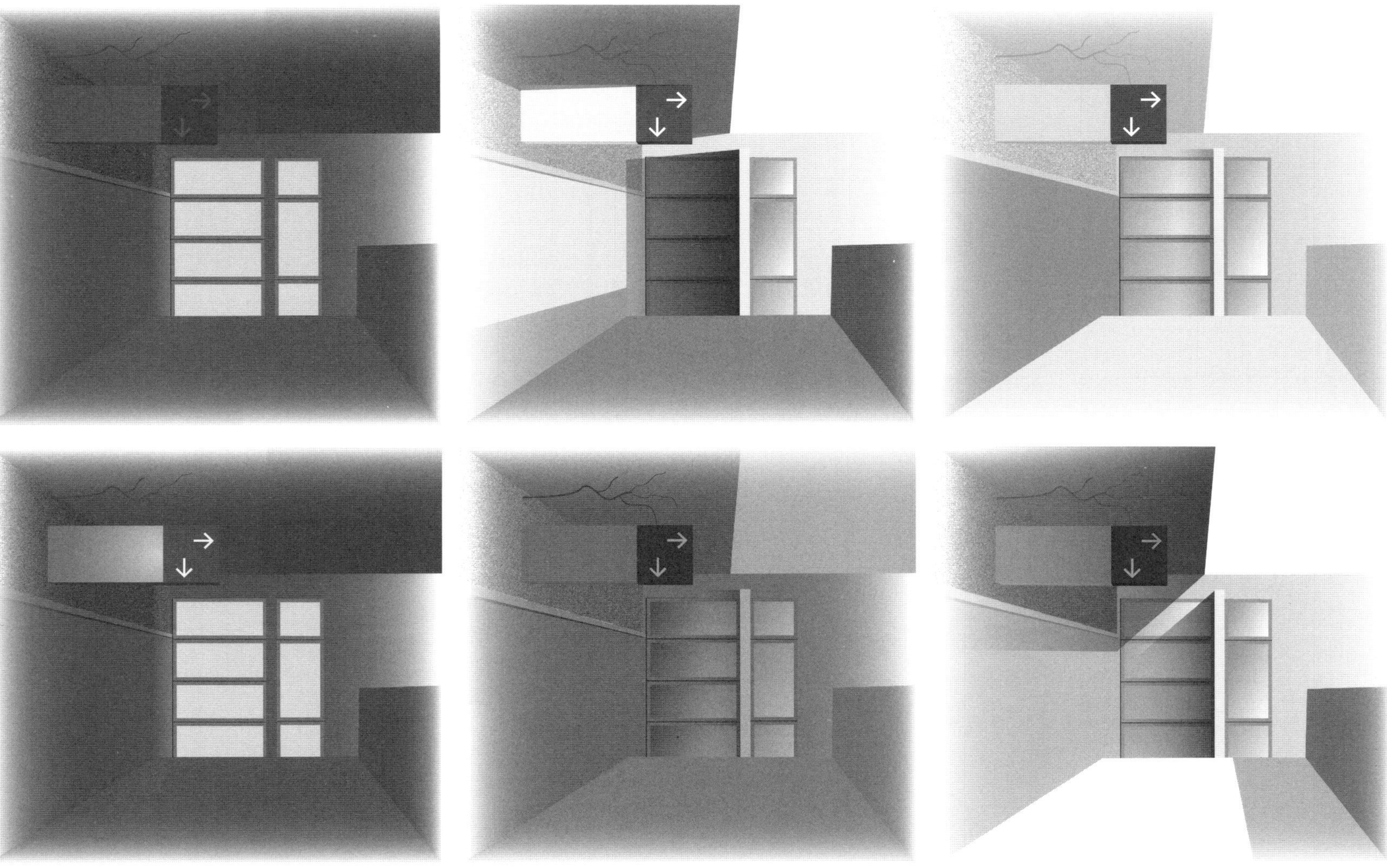

Size matters

Size is an important consideration in visual design. Size has a strong impact. Appreciation of size differs between cultures. The American adoration of size is without precedent. The Japanese, by contrast, appreciate minute detail and perfection in craftsmanship, rather than size. The recent general appreciation for larger sizes—against all environmental odds—is explained by the assumption that increased size gives the owner a higher sense of safety. Whatever the reason, size has always been related to expressing power, wealth and sexual appeal.

Size matters not only for functional reasons. Size is an effective way to express prestige, status, wealth, attractiveness. Size may generate strong feelings of lust, desire or envy (and also disgust).

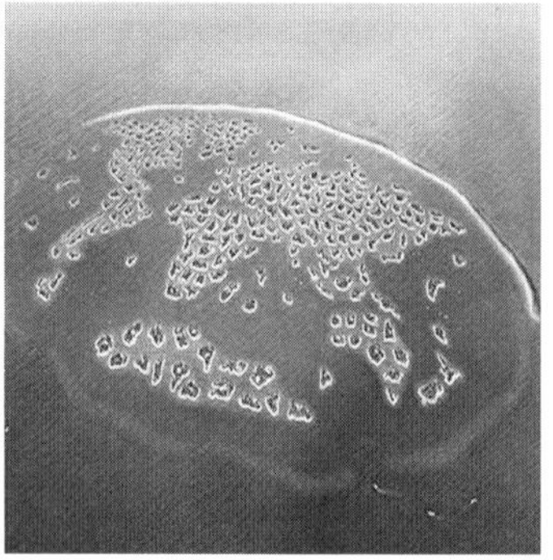

Size is no longer a constraint in construction. Artists use the natural environment for their creations. Real estate developers are now fusing the shape of a project with the shape of its brand. From left to right: Land art by the Finnish artist Hanna Vainio; two artificial island complexes in Dubai: the Palm Island and the World Islands projects. Recognising the shape of the logo in the projects themselves will only be possible when observed from a satellite (or from an airplane at cruising altitude).

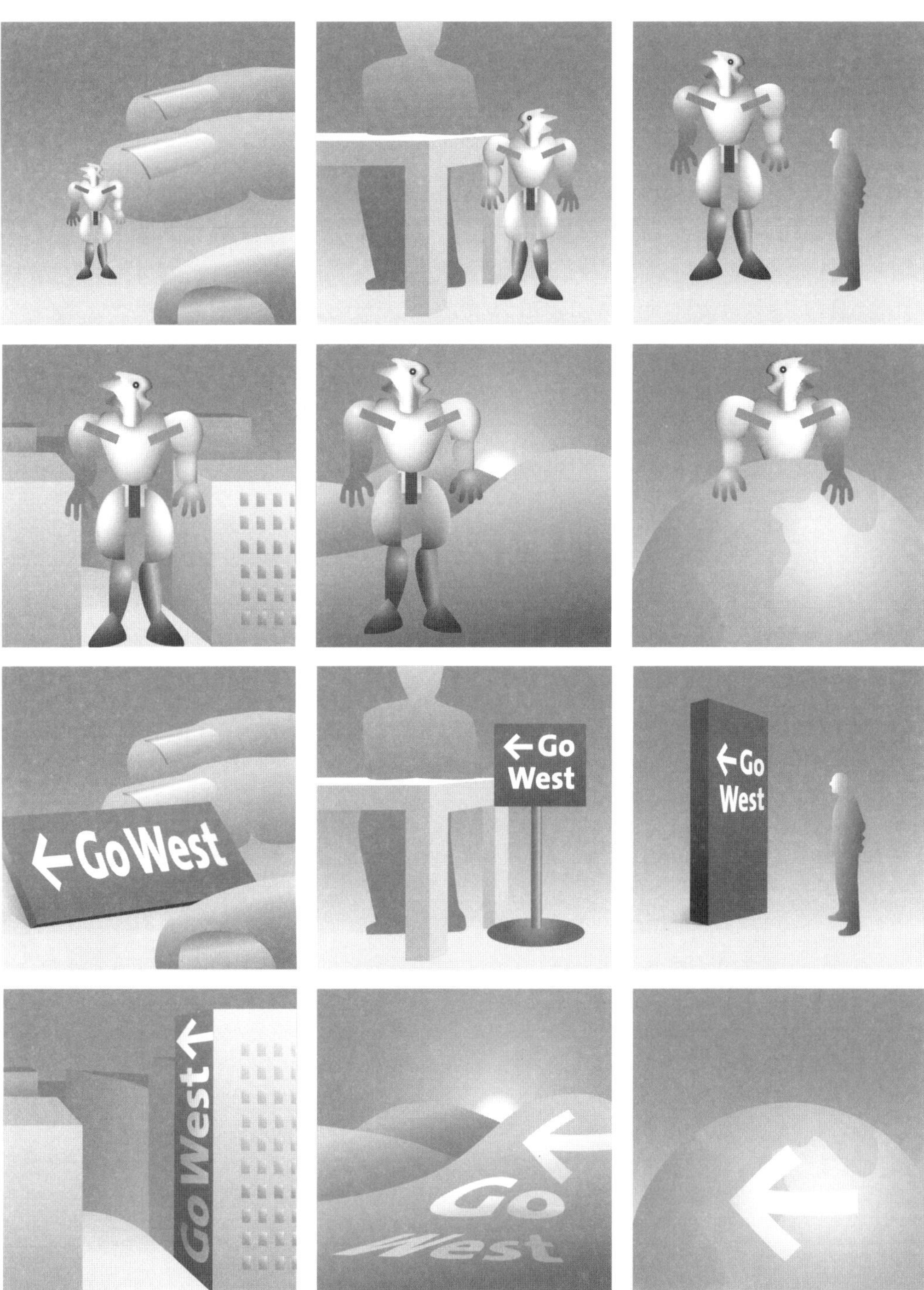

Size heavily influences the impact of an otherwise identical message or an identically shaped object.

The impression of the size of objects and images is relative to their surrounding environment. For instance, all objects look bigger when placed indoors as opposed to outdoors. The environment is not the only determinant for the perceived size; there are other factors, such as: (from top to bottom) environmental illumination, traffic density, combination of lighting and traffic, and type of materials used for making the object.

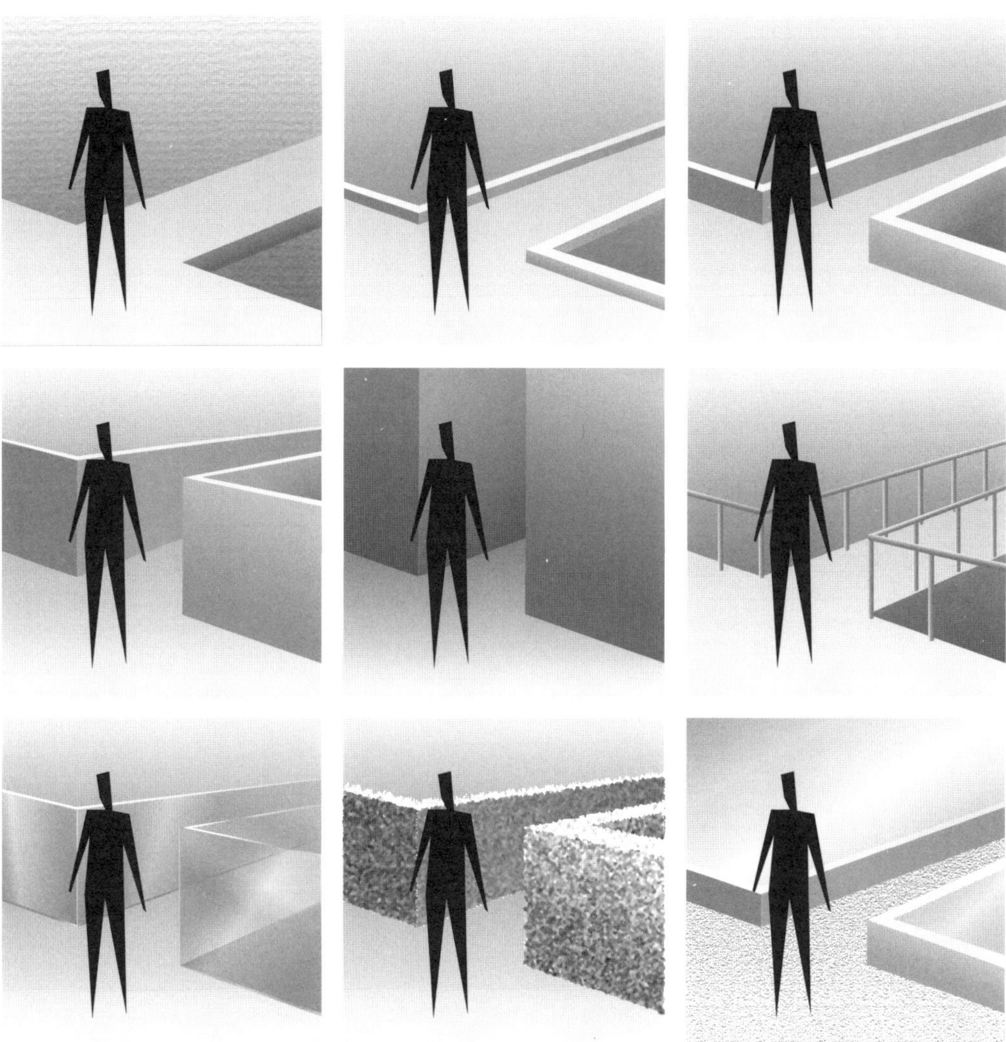

The functionality—and the emotional impression—of a path is heavily influenced by the way it is bordered. The illustrations show a variety of border heights and types of materials. While the dimensions of the path (the footprint) have been kept identical, the visual impression of each image is distinctly different.

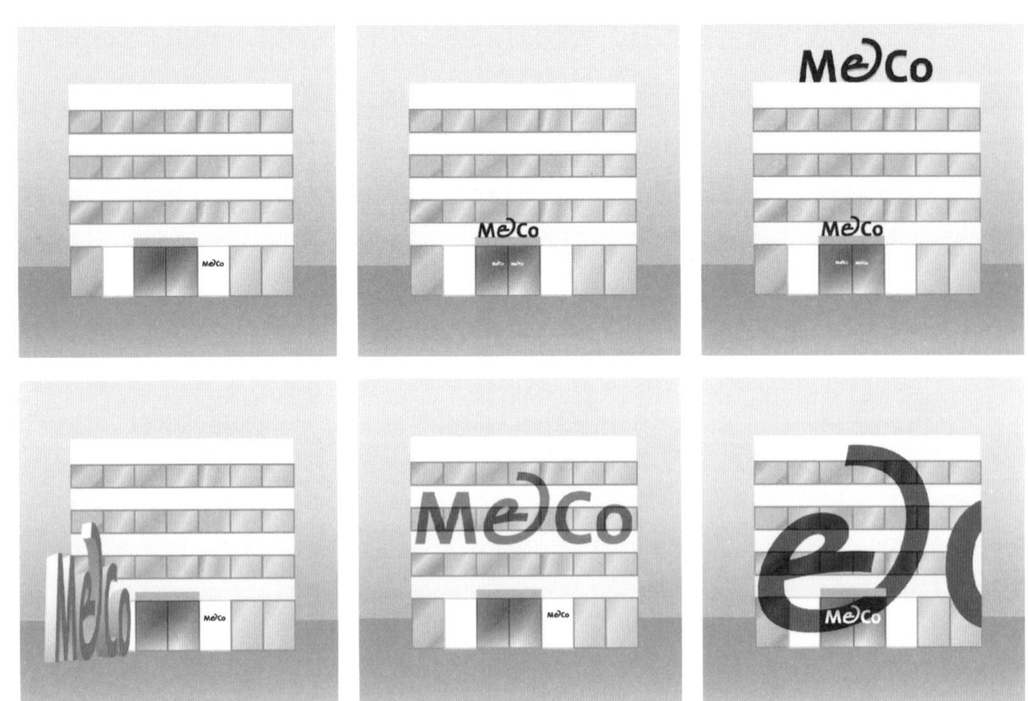

The combination of advanced print technology and sophisticated adhesive vinyl foil made 'super graphics' possible, in any size, applied on any surface, both inside as well as outside of buildings. These pictures show the wide variety of possible applications (not only using vinyl foil) from a small logo next to the main entrance to a situation where the graphics dominate the architectural design.

A cashier's desk can be transformed from the anonymous humble clerk with a simple desktop sign to a 'money-star' in a theatrical, TV-like, stage setting.

Door number identification shown in a sequence from a simple small label to a jumbo-jet sized numeral.

Floor number signs are favoured by most signage designers as a playground for typographic design.

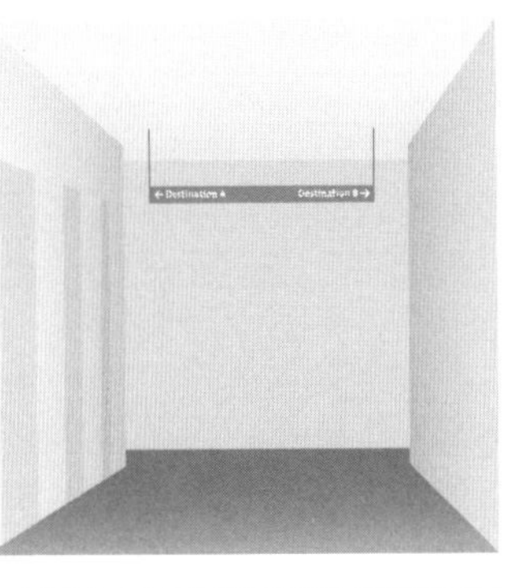
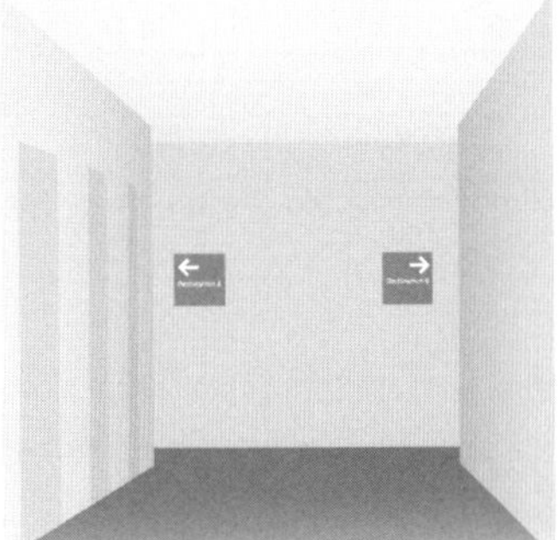
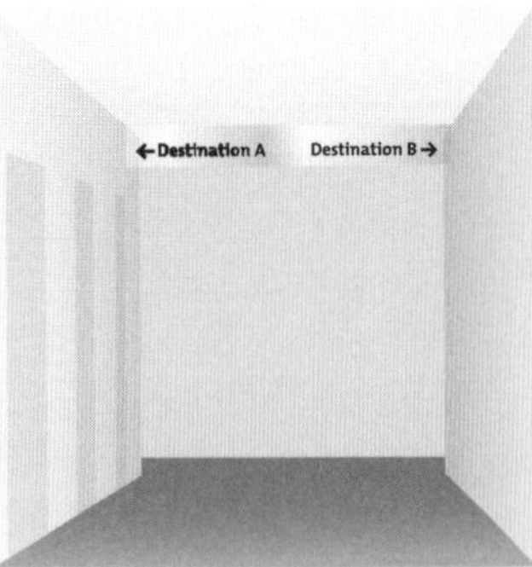

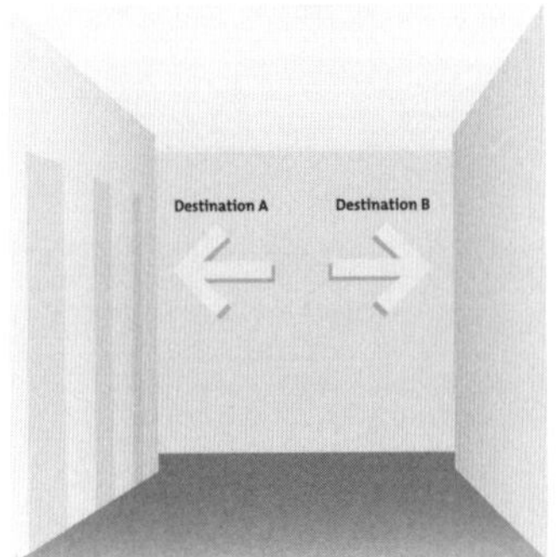

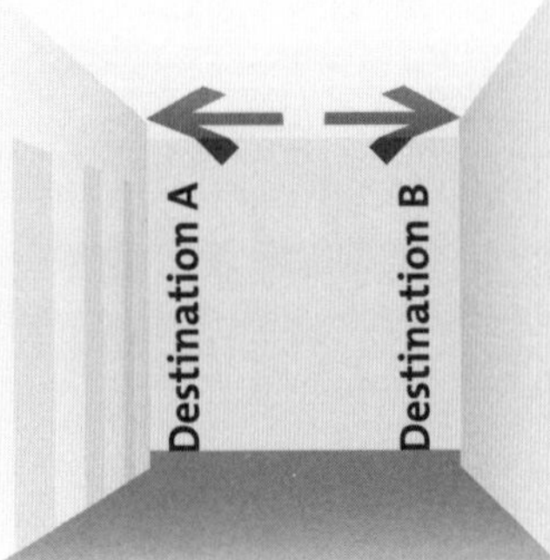

Architects are notorious for their aversion to signs. Directional signs, in particular, may interfere visually with the spatial design. It is often troublesome to match sign panels seamlessly with the architectural design. Therefore, using transparent panels or applying the graphics directly on the surface is favoured by architects. An alternative approach can change the signage from an unavoidable addition (or nuisance to some) into an essential part of the architectural design concept.

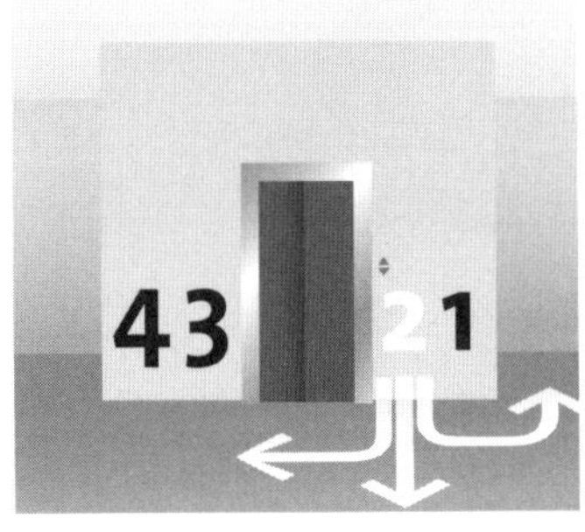

Elevators/lifts are essential transit corridors, which makes lift lobby signs particularly important. Also, in this situation, size and combination of functions can make a difference.

Signs are made in a wide variety of materials. Production costs of each individual design will vary immensely, while the basic communication value will remain almost identical. But the difference in construction will influence durability, and most important, the 'look and feel' of the sign.

Size and dimensions define our impression of a space, but the the type of illumination in that space has an even bigger influence on our perception. Light modifies all perceived sizes and dimensions. These illustrations show (from top to bottom and left to right) traditional fluorescent lighting, transparent parts in ceiling and floor, transparent walls, transparent doors, a complete one-sided glass wall and a one-sided open space.

The influence of technology

The influence of technological developments on design ideas can hardly be overstated. The general use of the computer, for instance, has changed design. Signage designers should also anticipate or even dream about possible applications of existing and future technologies. This sketchy overview may be of help in this process. The relevant technological developments can be roughly divided into four categories: first, the general miniaturisation of all equipment; second, the dramatic simplification and ease of navigation; third, the extensive possibilities of remote control; and finally, the changes in the way we communicate with machines and machines communicate with each other.

THE GREAT DISAPPEARING ACT

The most dramatic change in all technological development is the reduction in size of equipment. The essential functional parts of most devices are no longer visible to the human eye. The functional process is carried out on a microscopic or even molecular/atomic level. Traditional mechanical constructions can be reduced beyond visibility in nanotechnology.

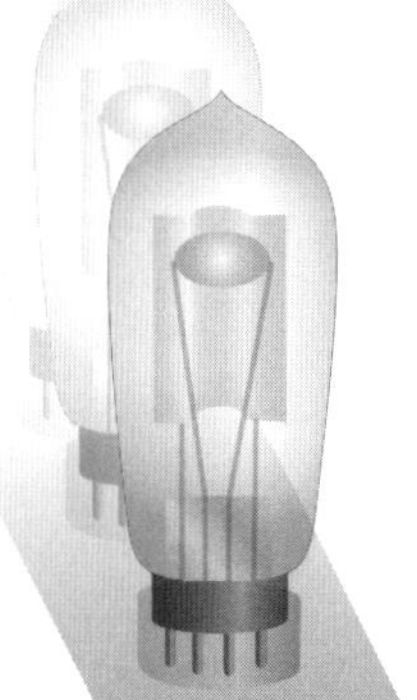
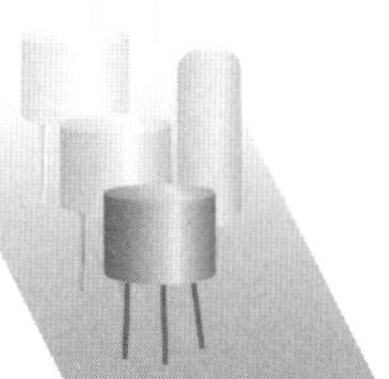

The advent of transistors (semiconductors) marked the beginning of the electronic/digital age. Transistors are the quintessential switches and amplifiers in all electric circuits. The first semiconductors were bulb-like glass vacuum tubes, soon replaced by small crystal-based transistors, and in turn followed by 'printed' integrated circuits comprising many transistors in a wired setting. We are now living in the age of ever smaller microprocessors called chips. The drop in size is following the still valid 'Moore's Law'. At the moment a pinhead can hold 1 million transistors and a chip more than 1 billion. Modern display technology is also only possible with the use of tiny transparent transistors. Not only the space but also the amount of electricity that computing needs has imploded.

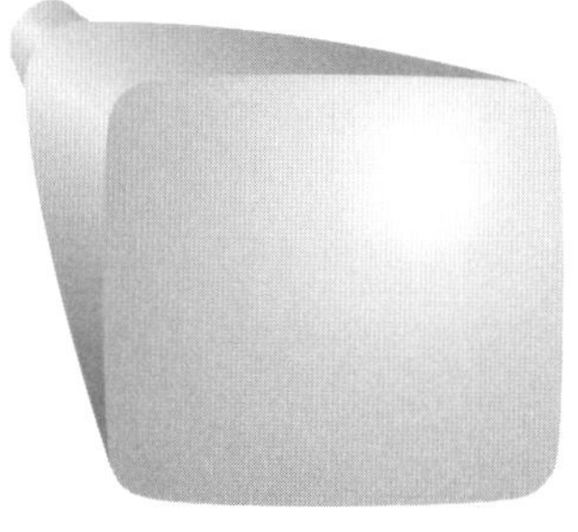

The first electronic displays were bulky glass vacuum tubes, now replaced by far more compact types in an endless range of sizes. Electronic displays can be fabricated almost paper-thin and consume very little power (e-paper).

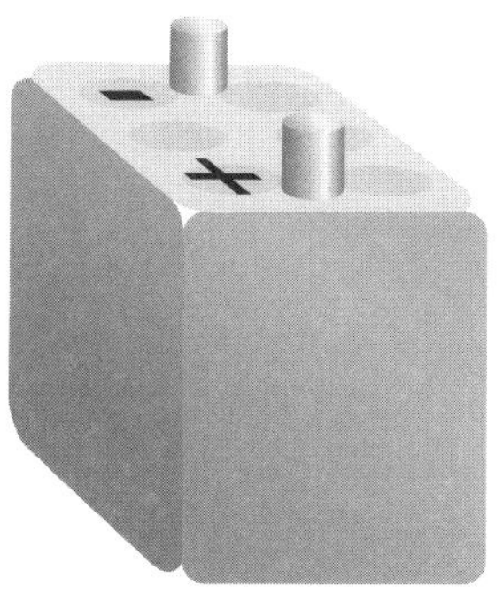
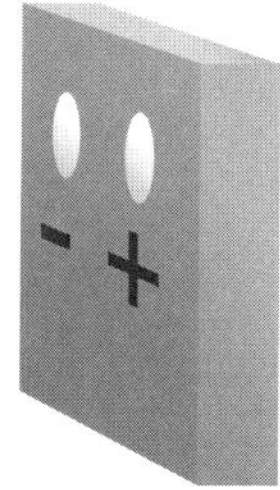

Storage of electricity has become more efficient and is delivered in smaller, longer-lasting containers.

Production of electricity used to require mechanical generators. More recently, fuel cells were developed that use chemical processes instead and may even replace the need for batteries. Solar cells only need (sun)light to function. The use of light as energy source (photovoltaic) is advancing impressively. Soon, energy sources will be printed, painted or woven into textiles.

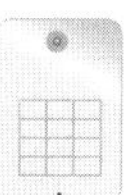

Speakers, microphones, antennae and cameras have become miniature devices—only expected to drop further in size. Mobile phones will combine more and more functions: voice, a plethora of other messaging or mailing functions, navigation, and facilitation of a growing variety of transactions.

ELECTRONIC NAVIGATION

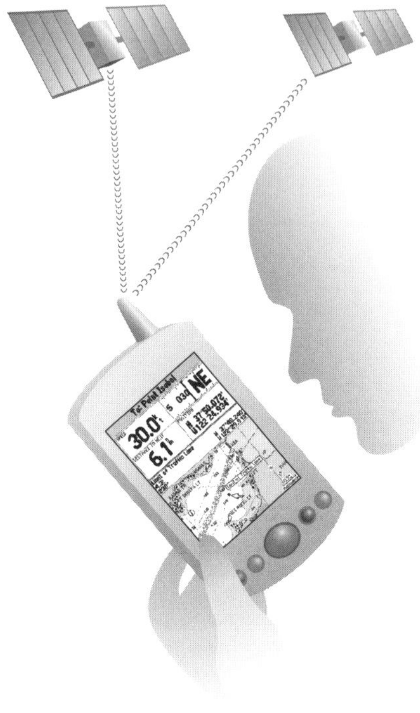

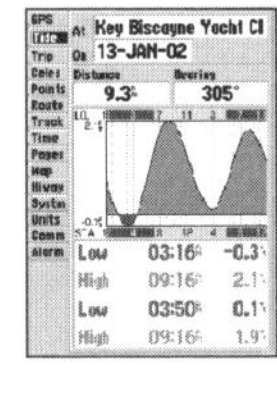

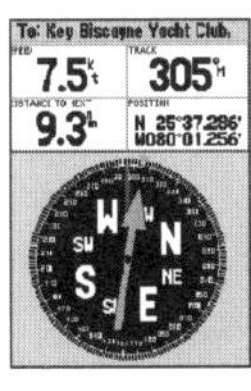

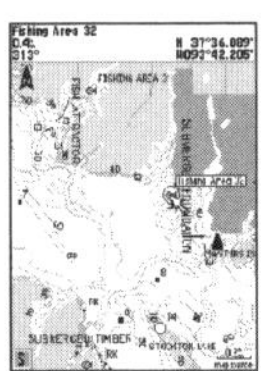

Maritime navigation used to be a complicated activity. Finding your exact location on the globe required the use of instruments like a sextant to 'shoot' the sun (or moon), and complicated calculations on a map to chart the journey. That process is history. The Global Positioning System [GPS] has made navigation extremely simple. Small navigation devices tell us exactly where we are, where we are heading, at what speed, and the expected arrival time. Additional screens may inform us about a large variety of other conditions along the way, for instance, where good fishing grounds are located, or the local weather forecast.

Navigation may be religiously important as well. Muslims are expected to pray facing in the direction of Mecca. Hotel rooms in Muslim countries have a simple paper sign on the wall that shows the proper direction.

GPS navigation is becoming part of everyday devices, like mobile phones. Navigational information can be stripped down to providing very simple instructions, like 'follow the arrow', without losing much of its core functionality. Future developments may incorporate GPS navigation in small personal gear.

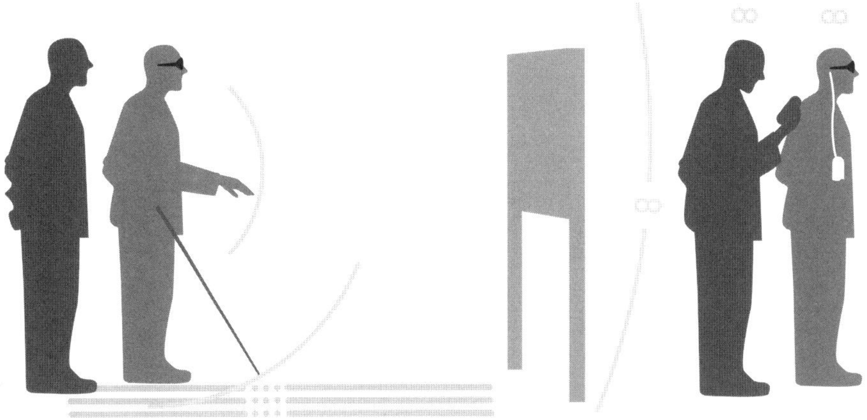

GPS navigation will change the need for signage in our environment. It may also reduce the differences between the visually fit and the visually impaired. Currently, the latter have a very limited browsing radius and also need the help of specific facilities to explore their environment. When both are using GPS, one reads while the other listens to the instructions.

Traffic signs of all sorts have used and are still using many ways of updating signs by various forms of (automated) remote control. Large traffic hubs use centralised cable networks to update the electronic signage.

Signs in buildings can also be updated from a distance. For conference centres or offices smaller cable network systems are on the market. Screen displays extend the ways information is provided.

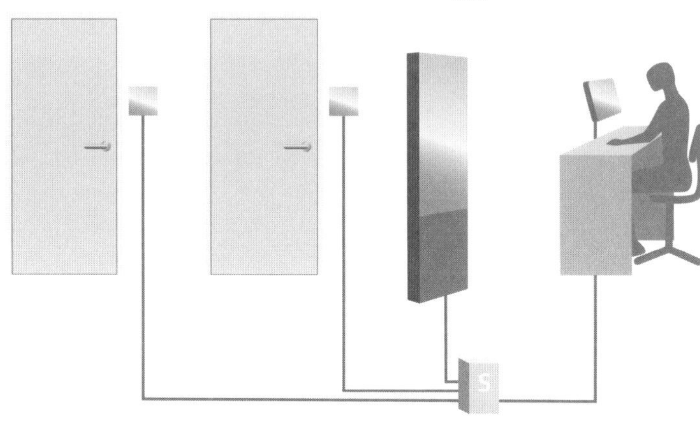

Networks can also be made wireless; the displays in the network will need a small receiver.

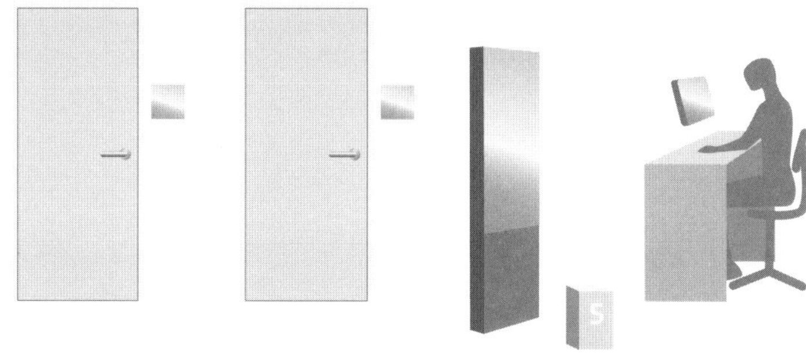

An alternative way of using a wireless network, is via the internet as a distribution channel and main server. In that case, signs can be updated from anywhere within reach of a WIFI *connection. Proprietary systems of remote control, used for a wide variety of applications, are capable of doing the same; but the use of the internet seems specifically appropriate for applications like signage. Moreover, more and more security systems make use of the internet.*

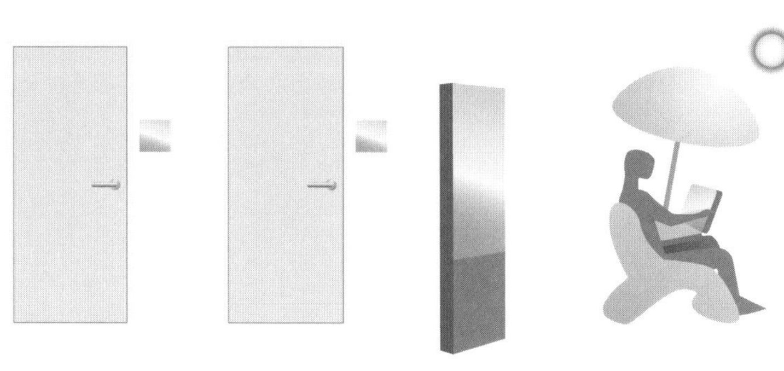

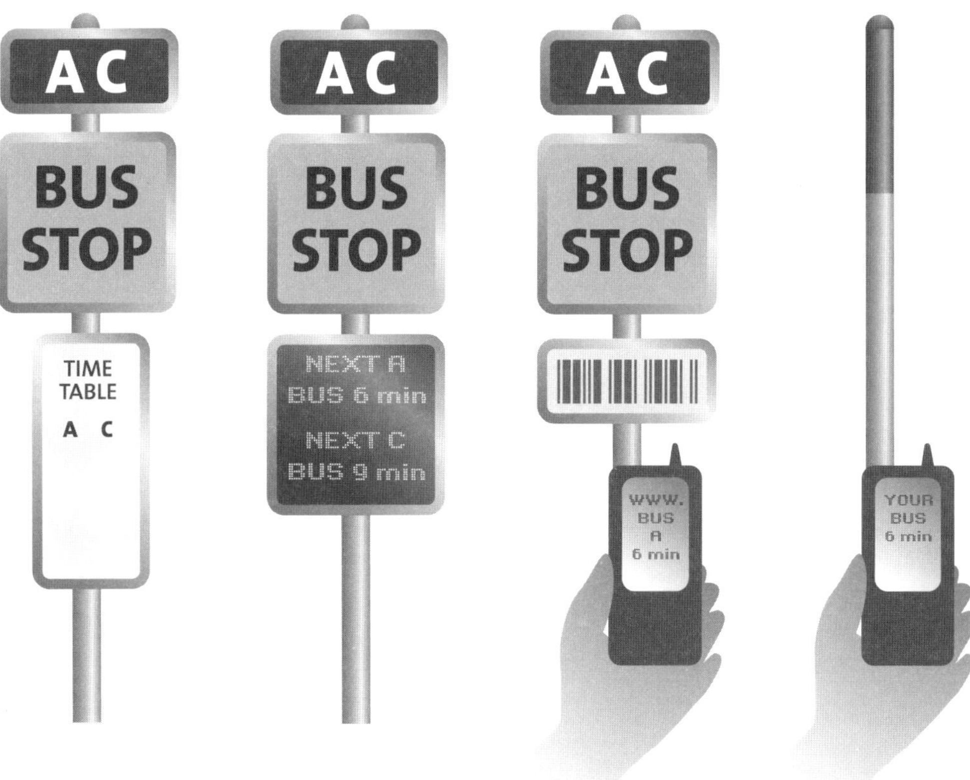

Printed timetables on bus stop poles are disappearing. Wired or wireless connected electronic screens are used for all types of public transit in city centres. There are many alternative ways to convey time tables. A zebra code could be scanned by a mobile phone (with a camera). The scan would automatically open an internet connection leading to a page with all relevant information for that bus stop. Ultimately, the whole method of retrieving information could be reversed. We ask our 'digital assistant' to broadcast our desired destination, the request will be processed by transit providers who will offer the most appropriate connection. Our mobile phone will subsequently start guiding us to the nearest bus stop.

Small patches with a printed barcode are already widely used in Japan to create direct links to internet sites by capturing the barcode image with the camera of a mobile phone. These codes are called QR (Quick Response) codes and can be found on a wide variety of products from movie posters to supermarket items to business cards. The internet links make all kinds of additional information available, like performance schedules in nearby theatres, or detailed fabrication and nutrition information. They also make it possibile to download information directly into one's own digital database.

Communication with machines became a necessity when machines started to take over human work. OCR *(Optical Character Reading) alphabets were designed to be readable by both humans and machines. Zebra coding deviated from that principle to allow for easier machine readability. The magnetic strip(e) was introduced to hold more information on a small size and a tiny chip can hold even more. All these technologies need a scanner to release (or update) source information. The latest development of the radio tag (*RFID *Tag, Radio Frequency Identification Tag) works without close range scanning and can be combined with reading and/or writing chips. Widespread use of radio tags is likely to reshape our environment once again.*

Optical
Charact
er Read
ing 123
4567890

Left to right, top to bottom: OCR *typeface, barcode, magnetic strip(e), chip card and radio tag. The sizes shown are no indication of the real sizes.*

We deal with a lot f different items to do transactions, get right-of-access, or to identify ourselves. Most of these items have themselves become outputs of automated machines and may also in turn be used as inputs for other machines. There must be room for a shortcut in this procedure where machine-produced paperwork is only needed to feed other machines. The mobile phone will play a growing role and will eliminate the need for most (or all?) of these printed items. To communicate with a machine-steered environment we are increasingly likely to get lost without the help of our mobile phone/personal digital assistant, which will not only translate all incoming information for us but will also gain the same authority as our passport does today. In fact, we all are likely to need our own 'mobile digital clone', or 'smart companion', to be able to communicate with our environment in the future.

Nobody and nothing will be an independent entity for much longer. The holistic world view will become a material reality. Everyone and everything will be connected to something or someone else in some way or other. We transmit and receive messages constantly—increasingly through a wireless connection. Objects do the same: they transmit information about their current condition or data about their origin. We can interact wirelessly with these objects: review information, store new information, give or receive instructions. Communication between objects has basically the same options.
The younger generation—especially young girls—seems to be in a constant dialogue with their mobile phones even when in company: talking, listening, sending and receiving text messages, playing music or games, looking at movies. Dialogues with objects or digital personalities will become a normal part of daily life, in addition to communication with fellow humans. Most of the exchange of information is still on a one-to-one basis; it can be called private since only a few participate in the communication process. This trend is changing now. Wireless telecommunication is starting to make use of the wide dissemination of public digital displays in practically any size. Software has been developed to send text messages or images directly from one's mobile phone to a public screen of projected images. This technology is called public texting or digital graffiti. From now on we will have the choice of communicating privately or publicly. Narrowcasting or micro-casting will become part of everyone's life.

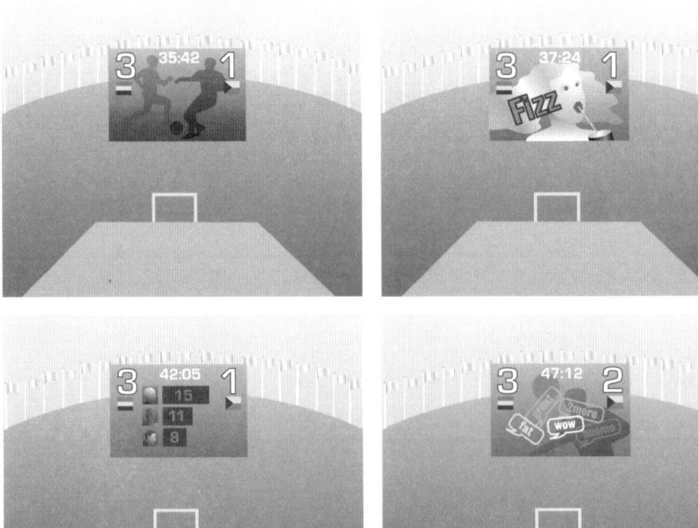

Sports stadiums are building increasingly large display screens. The screens may show a wide variety of different information, like close-ups of the game, advertisements, players' statistics and a potential for the audience to interact with the screen.

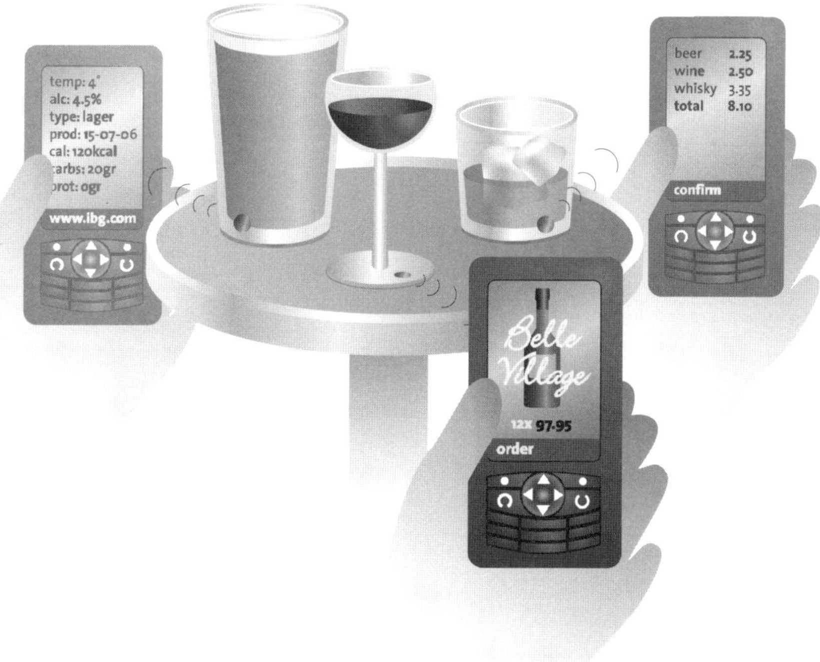

Radio tags on tableware in restaurants and pubs could change the way we order and pay for our consumption. All kinds of information can be stored on the radio tags and can be retrieved by a mobile. For instance, the ingredients and production specifications of the drinks ordered, or a link to the website of a producer may create the possibility of ordering bottles of the same product that will be sent directly to our homes. Payments for orders will be done through the mobile phone as well.

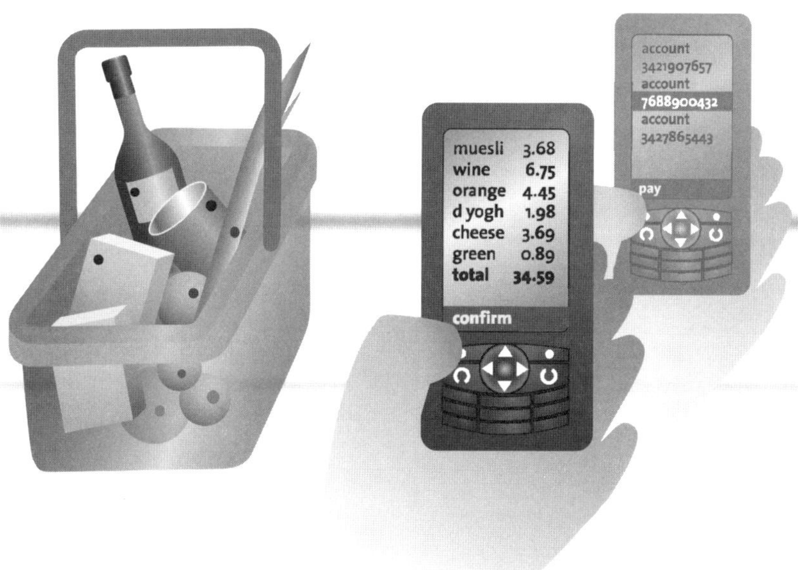

All supermarket goods will carry small radio tags that transmit information about each product. Paying for the merchandise will become a fast and simple procedure with no cashiers involved. All articles in the shopping basket will first pass a scanner that receives the information from the radio tags. The listing of all articles and the total amount due will be sent to the mobile of the purchaser, who has to confirm the planned purchase. Thereafter, the amount due will also be paid through the mobile. The second scan will clear and release the purchases.

Advanced display technology in combination with standard wireless connectivity will create very dynamic ways of branding and advertising. Pubs and restaurants, for example, will start to change advertisements according to the time of the day or the weather conditions: breakfast in the morning, ice-cream on a warm sunny day, and announcing 'happy hour' only during the actual time.

Customers with mobile phones will be able to interact directly in (projected) display images. This activity is called public texting, digital graffiti, or Wiffiti. For example, everybody can watch how customers play games together, talk to each other, or hold poetry competitions.

GLOBAL NETWORKS

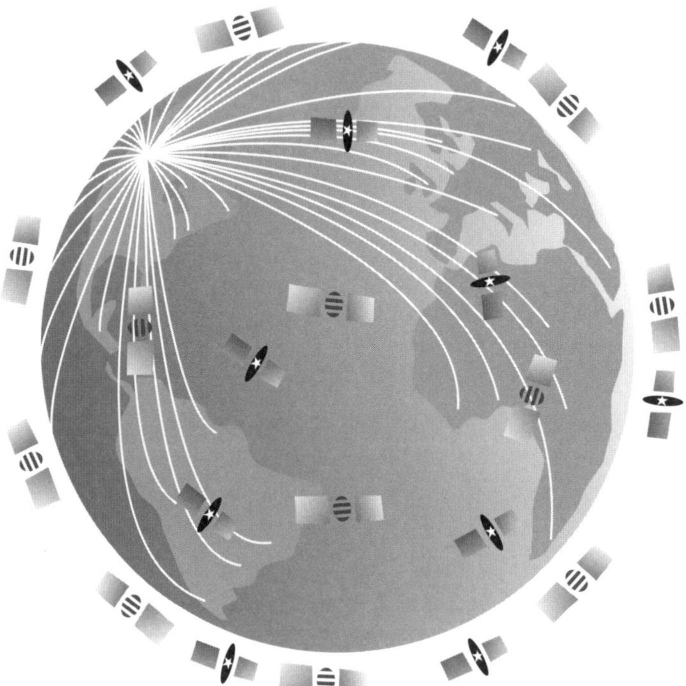

The digitised society has made global communication networks indispensable. Traditional cable communication networks remained practically unchanged until a digitised economy needed its own super highways to flow unrestricted. Huge amounts were invested to build both a global fibre optic cable-wired network as well as a wireless one using satellites. The US Department of Defense has played a pivotal role by investing billions of dollars in setting up these networks. The GPS (Global Positioning System) network is entirely an initiative of the US military and has made electronic navigation a possibility for all of us. Also the approximately 800 active satellites in orbit at the time of writing are 50% American and half of these are financed by the US government. Financial power is of the essence. The maintenance of the 27 satellites in the GPS system alone costs about 750 million dollars each year. Global communication networks have become political considerations. Europe has started to build its own GPS network, and other large governments will certainly follow.

Not only the networks themselves, but also the most popular software to use them has become a matter of large investments and near monopolised efforts. Again, and for a major part, all American initiatives. The American company Google develops search software and builds gigantic server networks, including hundreds of thousands of individual computers, which can put the entire worldwide internet content on their system to ease retrieval of data. Google has also started to digitise print libraries. The ultimate goal is to make as much data as possible available cheaper and faster than any of its rivals, giving a whole new meaning to the concept of public libraries.

The effects of these networks are startling. With only the help of handheld devices we may know our location within one metre accuracy wherever we are; we have access to all information on the web and can check or change the content of any device we have linked to the network.

4.8. Basic products, materials and techniques

After the design concept is developed and tested by application on the major sign types, further specification is needed for the production of the signs. The possibilities for the manufacture of signage design concepts are vast.

As previously mentioned, it is possible to make beautiful and functional signage by only using a brush and some paint (with of course, the right skill to use these simple instruments). Life can be pretty simple, but not in the signage industry of today. Signs are made of practically all kinds of material, and the different methods by which the letters or the illustrations can be produced is also overwhelming. Sign systems are available in endless varieties. Signage panels are made out of every conceivable material. It is almost impossible to give an overview of what is available on the market for signage production. Yet, some technologies and 'systems' have already been on the market for decades and are still used. Some are really ancient methods, like painted or chiselled typography. Below is an attempt to give an introduction to the signage 'Pandora's box'.

4.8.1. INTEGRATED SIGNAGE PANEL SYSTEMS

Most so-called sign systems are signage panel systems, mostly limited to interior use only. The systems available all meet—more or less—the list of requirements for signage panel systems, although not in all cases in a sophisticated manner. There are a number of technical varieties available.

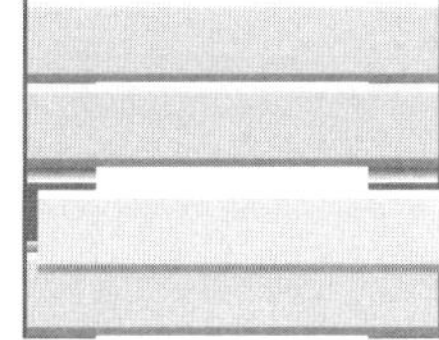

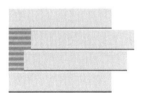

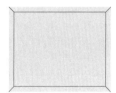

4.8.1.1. Aluminium extrusions

A lot of sign systems are based on aluminium extrusions, in combination with moulded plastic accessories and sheet materials. The way the extrusions are applied differs with each system.
—Components can be inserted and removed from the face of the panel (face-fitting). The aluminium profiles are snapped into a plastic holder.
—Components are slid in from the side (side-fitting). The aluminium profiles are made to slide into each other. A locking device will secure the profiles in a fixed position.
—The aluminium profiles are used to construct rectangular frames that can hold panels. These systems very much resemble picture frames.
—The aluminium profiles are used as stanchions with special components to hold panels. These systems are mostly used for outdoor signage.

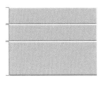

4.8.1.2. *Fabricated metal sheets*

Metal sheets can be fabricated in a wider variety of shapes than extrusions. Large curved surfaces are easier to produce in fabricated metal sheets. Signage panel systems made out of metal sheets are principally based on the same modular component structure as the systems made out of extrusions.

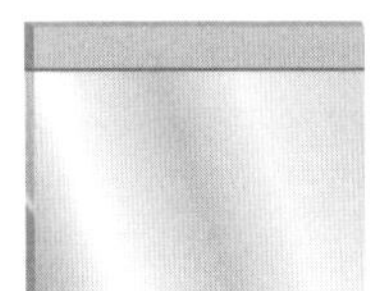

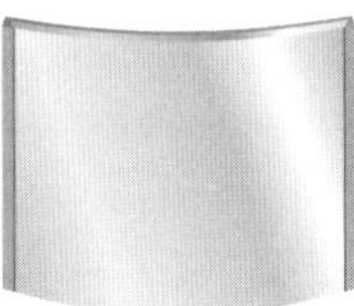

4.8.1.3. *Acrylic cassettes*

Laser printers have become widely available and can produce excellent graphic quality. Prints can be made on film or paper in any specified colour. Signage panels systems have been developed that use these prints as the sign content. The panels consist of container-like cassettes that can hold printed film or paper. The technical sophistication of individual systems varies considerably, some use injection-moulded components, while others are based on thermal folded flat acrylic sheets.

4.8.2. INDIVIDUAL SIGN TYPE PRODUCTS

There are a large number of products on the market that cover one or a small series of individual sign types. The number of different sign types required in large projects is vast. It is almost impossible to put all the variations needed into one integrated sign system. Besides, every project requires very specific sign types. Specialised products can cover these specific needs.

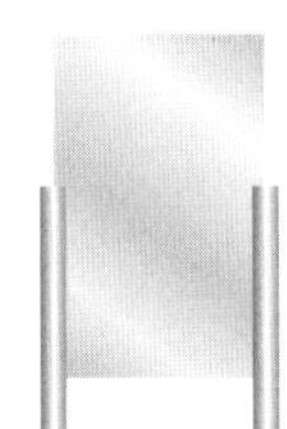

4.8.2.1. *Exterior signs*

Exterior architectural signs need far less variety in sign types than interior signs. These types of signs must be robust and vandal-proof. In some cases, direct illumination attached to the sign itself is required. Products in this category are a combination of extruded stanchions and/or frames that can hold metal or synthetic panel material.

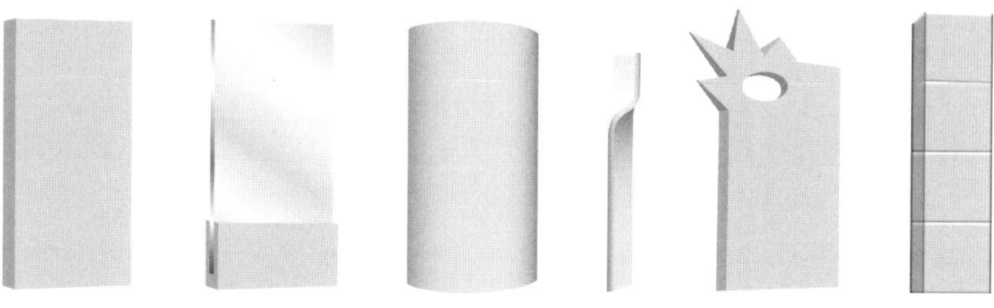

4.8.2.2. Monolithic signs

Free-standing signs without visible posts or stanchions are called monoliths. This sign type is usually large and is often used for free-standing directories. A number of products are designed to construct this type of sign.

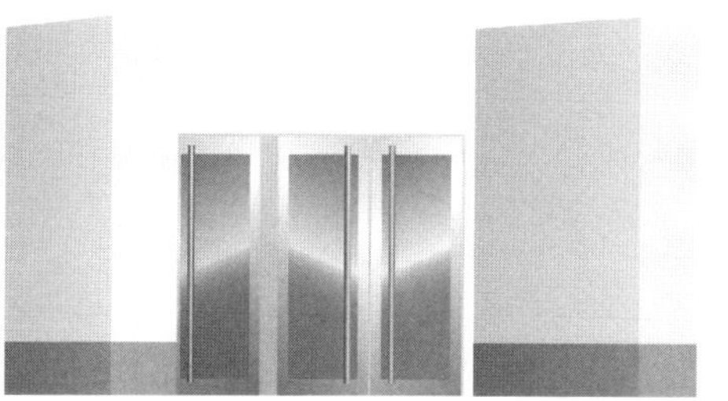

4.8.2.3. Flexible surface sign boxes

With the arrival of strong, durable and flexible surface material on the market, frame systems were developed to fix (with click rails) it in various shapes and keep it in place under tension. Sign boxes can be made in extremely large sizes. Some types of flexible material are translucent and allow internal illumination.

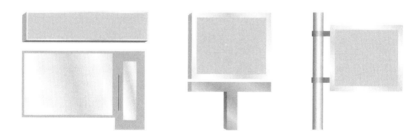

4.8.2.4. Traditional sign boxes

Traditional sign boxes are made of an extruded frame that can hold acrylic sheets. Many sign boxes have fluorescent light inside. Shopping streets all over the world are overcrowded with this type of sign, the vast majority being embarrassingly big and downright ugly.

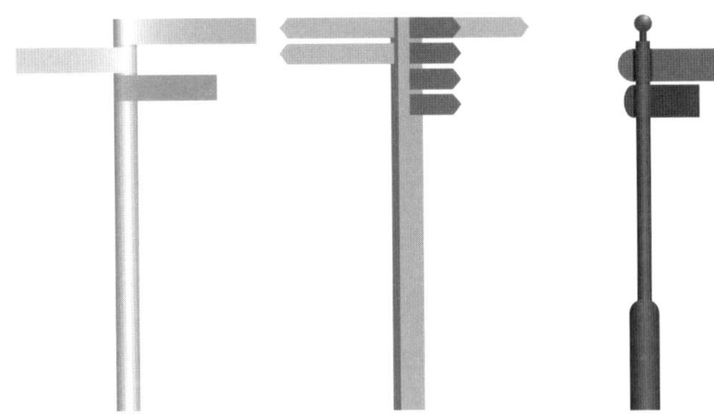

4.8.2.5. Finger post signs

The finger post is perhaps one of the most archetypal sign types. It consists of one post that can hold many individual signs, each directed physically towards the precise direction of the named destination. A few products are available for this type of sign.

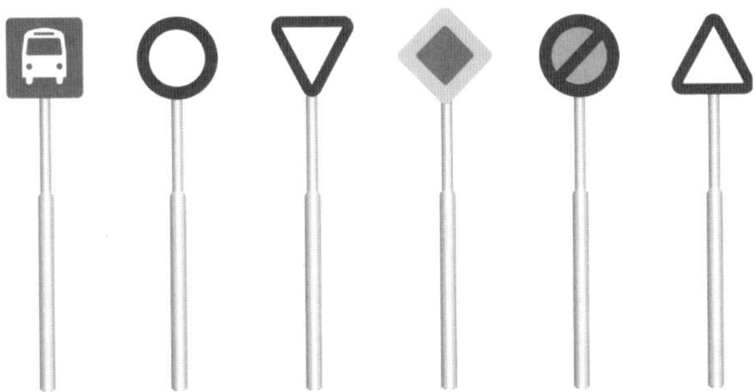

4.8.2.6. Traffic signs

Traffic signs are a completely separate category of signs. Architectural signage projects in some cases only use a few of this type of sign.

4.8.2.7. Mandatory signs

A few companies have specialised in providing series of mandatory signs by keeping a large number of this type of sign in stock. Mandatory signs for use in architectural signage differ from country to country, although there are efforts to create an international standard for this type of sign.

4.8.2.8. Emergency signs

Emergency signs are produced by companies that specialise in emergency signage. Big buildings may have quite complicated systems for safety and security. Fire and smoke detection can be integrated in emergency signage.

4.8.2.9. Flags and banners

New printing technology has made it possible to print on very large flexible surfaces. These printed surfaces can be durable and weather resistant. A number of products that are on the market consist of accessories for making banners of various sizes. Some companies have traditionally specialised in the production of flags and masts. The ranges provided by these companies are currently quite extensive.

4.8.2.10. Back-lit directories

A type of sign especially popular in big buildings in the US is a type of directory with illuminated text that can be updated by replacing individual text strips. The black strips have translucent lettering. These types of directories can be large and prestigious objects in entrance lobbies. A number of products have been developed with special technology for this type of directory.

4.8.2.11. Poster frames and display cabinets

All kinds of printed material, such as posters, notices, bulletins or individual messages, need to be displayed. A large number of products are available that cover these needs, ranging from simple picture frame products to complicated free-standing lockable cabinets that can be illuminated.

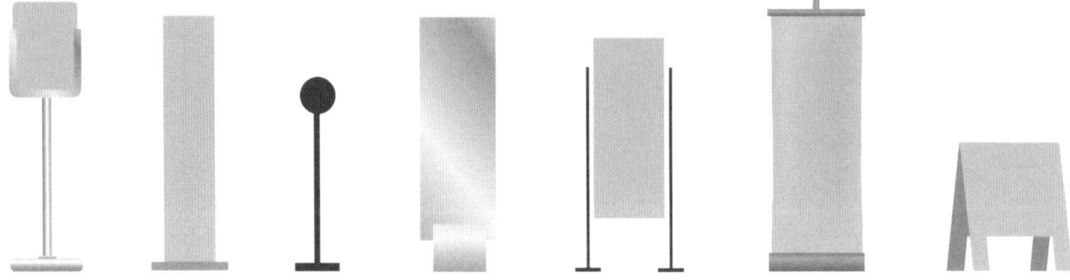

4.8.2.12. Free-standing signs

Simple free-standing signs, message holders or display devices used to be on average rather crudely constructed types of signs. A few products are now available offering more elegant solutions. 'Pop signs' with digital prints on vinyl foil or fabric are immensely popular.

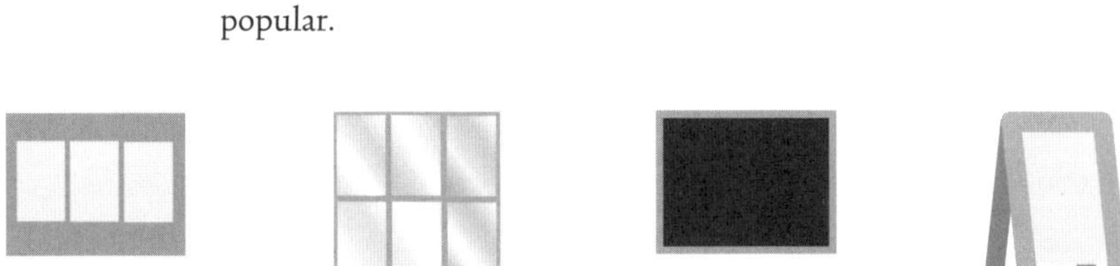

4.8.2.13. Bulletin boards and message holders

One of the simplest sign types are notice or bulletin boards. This sign type has a number of specialised products. Some companies, specialising in lecture room equipment, also offer similar products.

4.8.2.14. Loose letter systems

Sign systems based on the composition of loose letters on sign panels have lost their functional edge. Practically all text for signs is now produced on computers. A few products remain on the market that can be used for specific purposes, such as price indication signs.

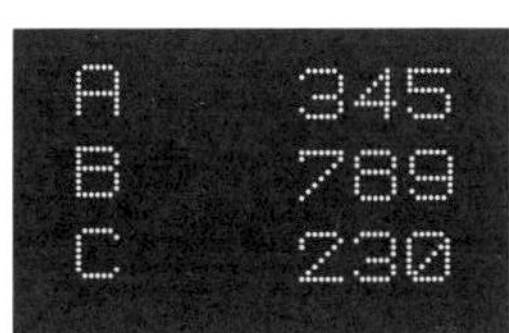

4.8.2.15. Electronic display systems

Public transportation facilities make more and more use of electronic display systems. These systems are often custom-made for the organisations that use them. A number of systems on the market are mostly used for small commercial display purposes. Electronic display systems may also play a role in architectural signage, for instance in waiting rooms.

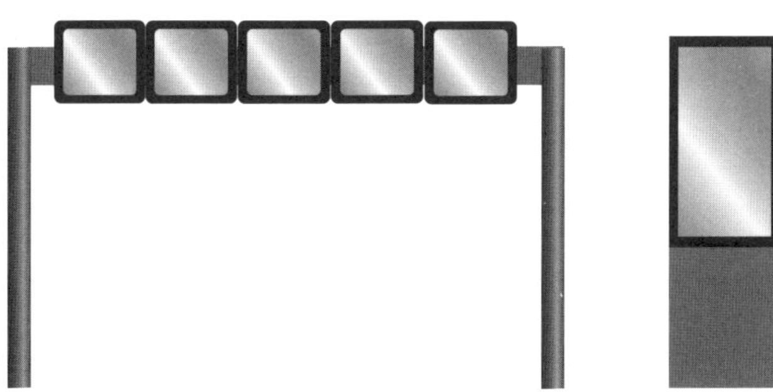

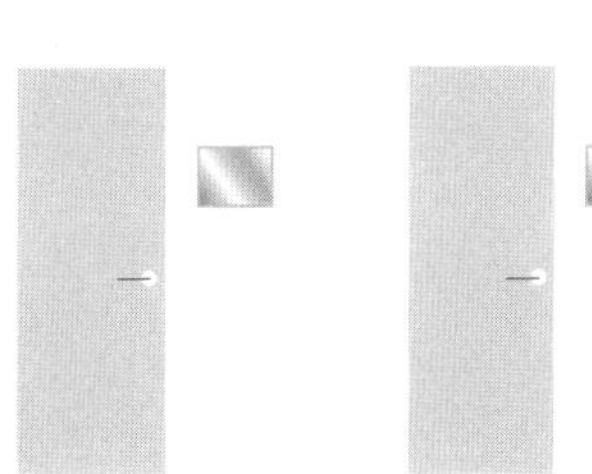

4.8.2.16. Screen network systems

Airports and other transit centres were the first facilities to use screen network systems to inform passengers about arrivals and departures. Smaller network systems are now on the market that may be used for meeting rooms or training centres in a building.

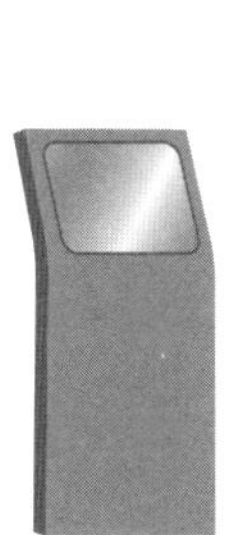

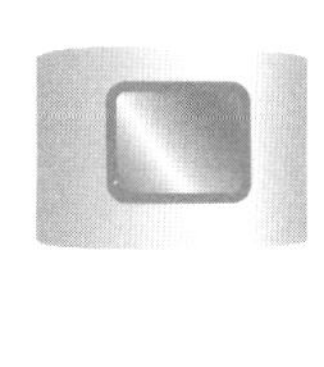

4.8.2.17. Interactive kiosks

Interactive screens are applied to all kinds of directories and for commercial purposes. Originally this type of sign was 'stand-alone'. More and more interactive screens are connected to a telecom network. This allows information to be directly retrieved from the internet. Public telephones are also acquiring more interactive facilities. The technology involving telecom networks and interactive screens is probably still in its infancy, though it has great potential.

The first group shows flexible materials, from left to right:
- (adhesive) foils in limitless varieties
- weather-resistant synthetic tissues
- paper-based material for indoor use.

The second group shows synthetic panels, from left to right:
- translucent panels
- mono-coloured or textured panels
- ultra-light foam plastics.

4.8.3. BASIC MATERIALS

Signs are made out of practically all kinds of material. A few panel materials are specially developed and fabricated for signage and display purposes. Basic materials, like stone, wood, glass and metal, are used for signage, but the most 'basic' materials these days are composites, alloys, granulates or laminates. Moreover, the amount of purely synthetic material is huge and growing every day. The overview given below is therefore very concise.

4.8.3.1. Flexible materials

A relatively recent development is the application of super graphics on flexible materials. Digital printing machines are now available that can print huge sizes. Outer walls of buildings under construction may use this technique to turn the whole building into one enormous advertising totem. There is practically no limitation on size or type of graphics to be used for some type of flexible materials. Some can be very strong and weather-resistant. Some types of material are translucent and can be applied in space frames or as banners.

There are basically three types of flexible material on the market:

—synthetic translucent materials.

—woven or knitted tissue mixed with various materials. The open structure of this material enhances its wind resistance.

—Paper-based materials for indoor applications.

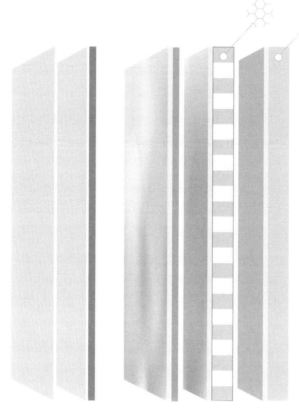

Laminates: sandwich panels combining different materials. From left to right:
- cellulose and synthetic resin
- aluminium with a synthetic core
- wood laminates
- honeycomb core
- foam synthetic core.

Granulates: panels made of composites of different materials. From left to right:
- stone with binding material
- wood and polyurethane
- endless other mixes.

4.8.3.2. Adhesive film (foils)

Adhesive film must be one of the most commonly applied materials in the sign-making industry. This type of film has in fact replaced the traditional paint. The number of different types of film available is huge. All conceivable applications seem to be covered by specific products. Here is a list of the main categories of these products:

—Permanent or temporary applications

The type of film available is categorised according to its type of application: indoor, outdoor, signs for temporary or permanent use. The required resistance of the material under various weather conditions is also an indication of the type of film to be used.

—Fleet marking

One of the most durable films for outdoor use is the type that is used for so-called 'fleet marking'. This type is applied to all kinds of commercial vehicles, such as airplanes, trains, buses and trucks.

—Translucent films

Translucent films are available in various grades of translucency. Fluorescent light boxes make use of this kind of film.

—Perforated films

Perforated films can be printed and applied on glass panels and will remain sufficiently transparent after application. This material can be applied inside windows of buildings for the creation of super graphics while leaving the transparency of the window from the inside intact.

—Floor- or wall-marking

Special film is developed for application to all sorts of walls or even on floors.

—Reflective material

Different types of light reflecting (or even light emitting) film are available. These films were originally specially developed for traffic and safety signs.

4.8.3.3. Synthetic panel material

Natural fossil oil gave rise to a gigantic industry of fuels and synthetic materials. The amount of different types of plastics available is huge. A limited number of these are used for signage panels. The overview below only highlights a few of the major types and applications.

—Acrylic panels

Acrylic panels are available in various degrees of transparency from crystal clear to completely non-translucent. A large collection of colours is available with a range of finishings, from matt, to satin, to glossy. A limited number of special surface structures are also a part of the often extended ranges. A limited number of big acrylic manufacturers dominate the market. Acrylic is most commonly used for internally illuminated signs.

—*Polycarbonate panels*
Polycarbonate panels have qualities comparable with acrylic panels, but are less brittle. In fact, this material is almost unbreakable. It is used in places where vandal-proof qualities or special security is an important requirement.

—*Thermo-forming or vacuum-forming*
Thermo-forming or vacuum-forming is a technique for producing curved (edged) panels or individual letters. Vacuum-forming is not purely an aesthetic enhancement; it also gives greater strength to the signage panel. Some types of plastic are specially designed for these applications.

—*Special light-diffusing plastics*
Traditional light boxes are relatively thick and need a lot of fluorescent light tubes inside to create an even and uniformly lit surface. Special synthetic material has been developed that provides more even light diffusion over the whole surface when only one side of the panel has a light fitting (fixture).

—*Polyurethane-based panels*
Polyurethane-based panels are made of a composite material of synthetic resin and cellulose. This type of material can be made very hard and is extremely durable. It is used for table tops and facade cladding. It is also applied to outdoor signage.
One-sided thin panels of this material are available in enormous varieties and are laminated on all kinds of materials. It is a popular finishing for interior products.

—*Sandwich panels*
Sandwich panels combine two types of material. Sandwiches with thin anodised aluminium sheets on the outside and a polyurethane core are particularly popular for signage.
Thick panels are produced using a 'honeycomb' structure of thin aluminium strip or paper on the inside and synthetic covers on the outside.

—*Foam plastic panels*
Foam plastic panels are relatively light and strong. Foaming is a technique where small pockets of air are integrated only in the core of the material. This type of material is specifically suitable for signage applications.

Plastic panels are not only used as support materials. Letters (or illustrations) can be cut out of panels and applied as loose elements as well. Casting or moulding plastic shapes is also a relatively easy manufacturing technique. Small loose letters may be cast and complete signs can also be made by moulding reinforced fibreglass.

4.8.3.4. *Metals*

All basic manufacturing methods, like casting, moulding, die-cutting and laminating metals, are used for signage. Metal panels are probably still the most commonly used basic material for signs — especially outdoor signs.
—Aluminium panels are popular products for signage purposes. Aluminium is light, strong, and only slightly corrosive under most circumstances.
—Stainless steel is far more expensive, but harder and considerably stronger than aluminium. It can be polished in various ways and is available in various quality grades up to practically non-corrosive for the most aggressive environments. Stainless steel is the 'premium' choice of material for signs.
—Bronze, copper and brass are applied in special cases where the specific traditional qualities of these metals are required.
—Galvanised steel is stronger and heavier than aluminium. The galvanising process—the application of a layer of zinc—prevents the natural rusting of steel for at least 7 to 20 years. There are various ways of applying the zinc layer. Thermal galvanising—a dip in melted zinc—is the most durable way.
—Acrylic and aluminium are often used in combination for illuminated signs. Letters are cut out of an aluminium panel and the acrylic panel placed behind gives colour to the cut-out text, seals off the panel surface and holds the loose elements of letters, like the inner shape of the letter 'O'. The most sophisticated 'cut-and-fill' method of application is to put acrylic letter shapes back into the cut out spaces of the aluminium panel. This way, the translucent illustration is completely flush with the surface of the sign.
—Fabricated sheet metal signs or channel letter signs are hollow, thin-walled three-dimensional signs. This construction method requires a lot of experience and skill. Each individual letter is constructed by welding or soldering separate pieces together. The most advanced craftspeople can combine polished metals and neon into very elaborate letter forms.

4.8.3.5. *Wood*

Wood is certainly one of the oldest signage materials. There is still a traditional craft of hand carving signs, especially popular in the USA and England (for certain types of signs). Wood has the advantage of requiring relatively simple fabrication methods. The application of wood can create a friendly and warm atmosphere. The disadvantage of wood is the maintenance required to prevent it from decaying.

In the building industry, wood has regained popularity over the use of aluminium and plastic frame profiles. Modern wood conservation methods have reduced the disadvantages of wood considerably. Expensive and very durable types of wood like teak or oak do not have any disadvantage compared to other durable materials. Environmental considerations, like global deforestation, might reduce its application.

4.8.3.6. Other materials

—Paper has always been used for signage, indoors as well as outdoors. Obviously, it is applied only for temporary usage. Laser printers have popularised the use of paper for indoor signage: in small sizes for door signs, or in larger sizes for paper banners in exhibitions or commercial displays. Synthetic paper—or film—is more durable than natural paper and can be printed basically in the same way as paper. It is also produced in a wide range of different degrees of translucency.
—Stone is without a doubt the oldest basic material for signs. While paper is the most ephemeral basic material, stone is the most durable. Some types of stone are far more durable than others; granite is the hardest, limestone and sandstone are the softest and marble and slate are somewhere in between. Composite—or aggregate—material is a mix of natural stone with different kinds of binding material. It is cheaper than stone, since it can be cast into tiled units. Stone comes in an endless variety of colours and markings. It can be finished in every conceivable way, from a smooth, mirror-like, polished surface to a rough 'jack-hammered' natural rock look. The companies with the most experience in the various methods of applying typography to stone are those of tombstone or monument makers. Water jet-cutters now make it possible to cut any shape out of the hardest stone.
—Ceramic, brick, and concrete building materials are all cast in some way or other. The mould can include text or graphics and become part of the signage. Tiles can also be painted or silk-screened before being glazed.
—Glass and mirrors can be stained, etched, sandblasted or painted to carry information.
—Fibre-optics are bundles of thin glass fibre rods (strands) that can transport light without losing much intensity. Changeable signs can be manufactured using this material.
—Magnetic tape is a thick rubberised film containing magnetic particles. It sticks to metal surfaces and is applied for changeable text strips or temporary signs.

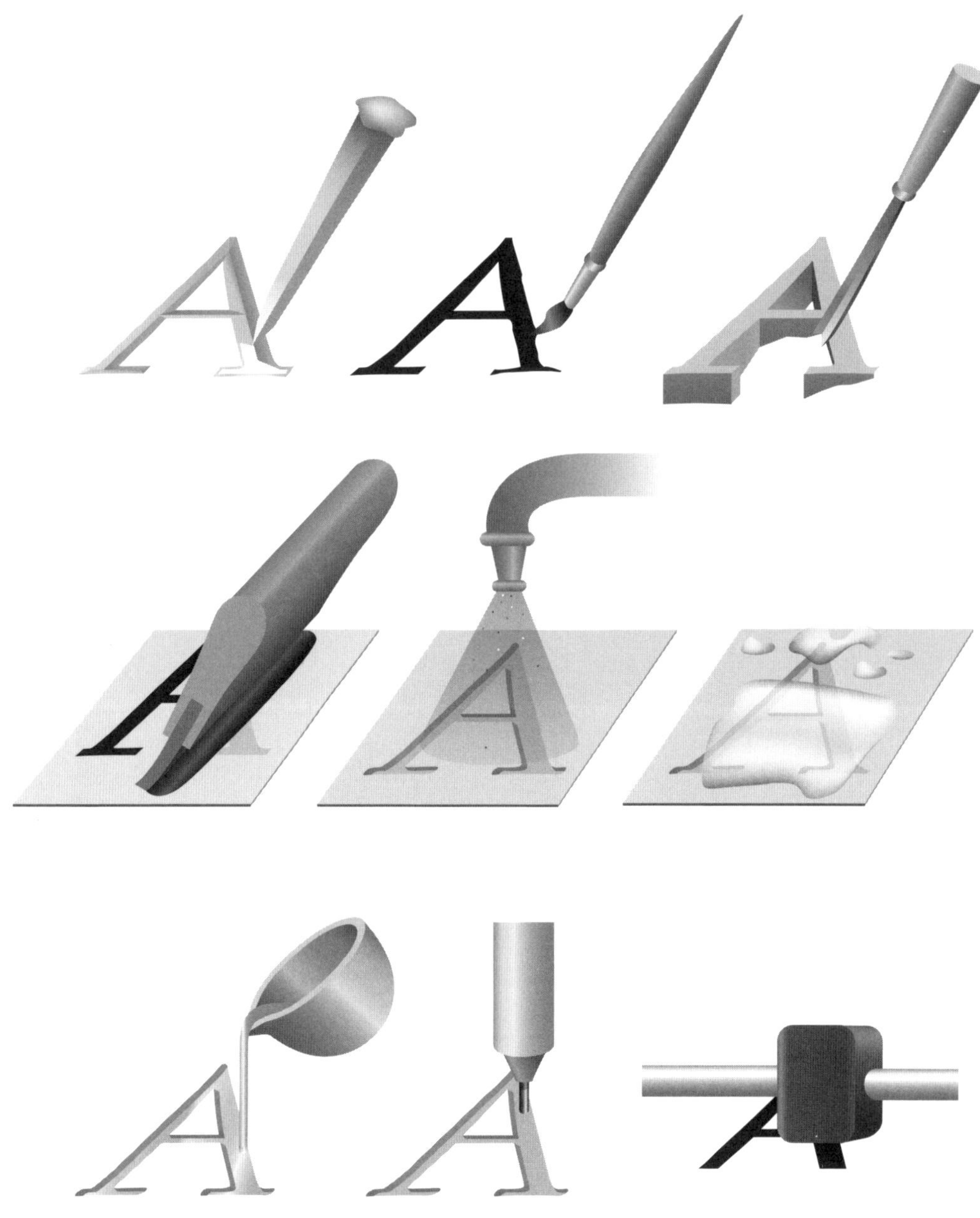

Imprint and shaping techniques

The top row shows examples of the large variety of manual production methods, like stone-carving, hand-painting and woodcarving.
The middle row shows examples of masking methods, like silk-screening, sandblasting and etching into surfaces.
The bottom row shows examples of a mix of different techniques, like using dies to produce moulded shapes, using a router or engraving machine to produce recessed letters that can be filled in later with paint, and the immensely popular technique of inkjet printing, which makes printing possible on almost any kind of material in almost any size.

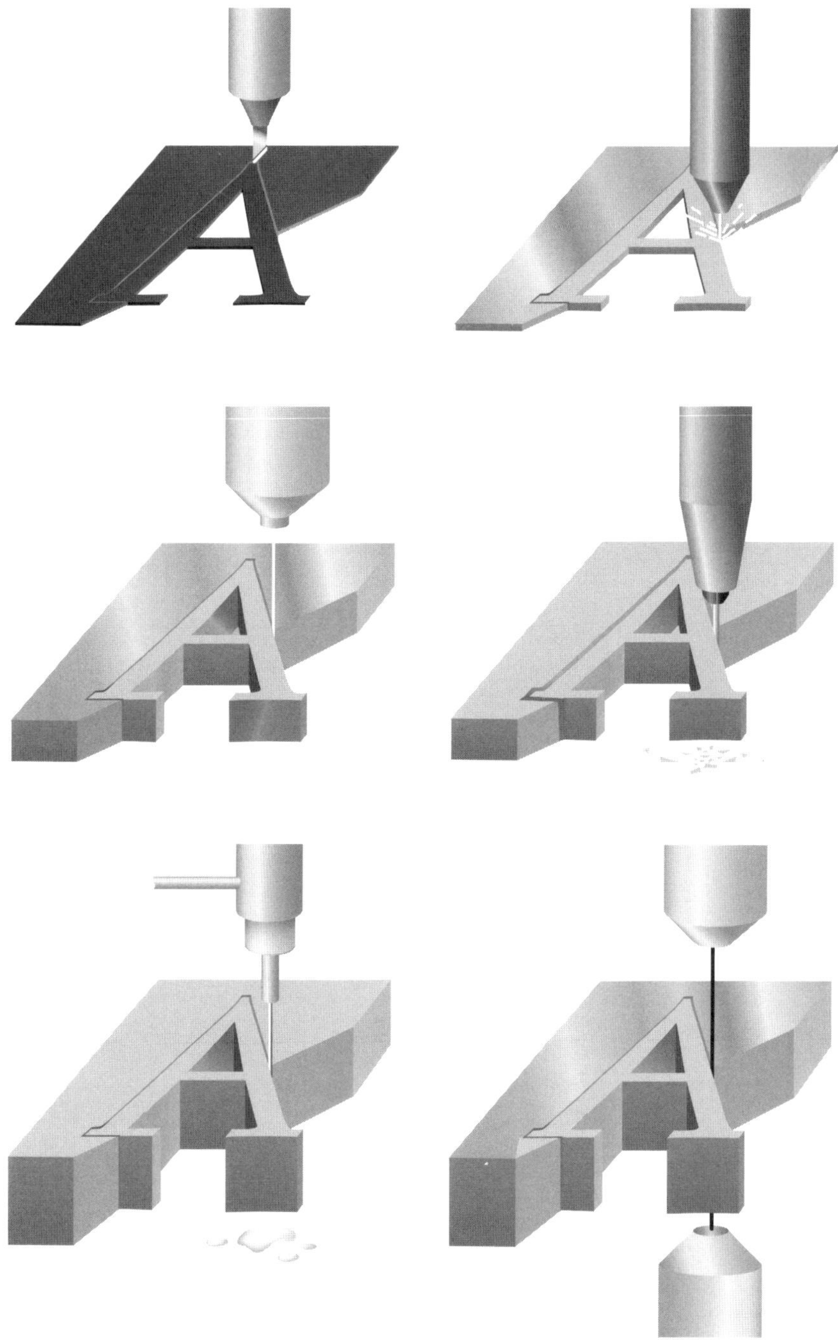

The types of fabrication machines illustrated on this page are all members of the large family of automated cutting machines. All use digital data to navigate the tools cutting through the material. Some machines are capable of using the same electronic data as used for graphics software.
The top row shows the popular vinyl-cutter and the laser-cutter.
The second row shows the plasma-cutter, capable of cutting through thick metal panels, and a traditional routing machine cutting wood, plastics and aluminium.
The bottom row shows a water jet-cutter, which uses a thin beam of water mixed with abrasive material released under very high pressure, and a thermal wire cutting machine, capable of cutting through thick materials.

4.8.4. IMPRINT AND SHAPING TECHNIQUES

Computer Aided Manufacturing (CAM) and digital imaging techniques have dramatically changed the traditional methods for producing text and other graphics. Typography and illustrations are now mainly both designed on a computer and produced —more or less—with digitised production machines. Some techniques can only be applied on specific surfaces or types of material, and effectively need a sign panel to carry the message, while other techniques can be applied directly onto a building or a facility's surface.

4.8.4.1. Manual production

—Hand-painting was the traditional skill of all sign-makers. They were calligraphers on a grand scale. This skill is now almost completely taken over by the application of vinyl-cut letters. Graffiti artists still practice this art unsolicited. The brush is replaced as a tool by the aerosol spray can.
—Stone-carving is still practised, although often replaced by more mechanical production methods. Hand-chiselled letters are still the best way of putting typography into stone.
—Wood-carving for signage purposes is also still practised. It is popular for some types of signs in the US and the UK.
—Hand-engraving in metal or glass is a rare practice for signage.
—Hand-sawing or cutting of letters or graphics has become an unusual production method.

4.8.4.2. Masking methods

—Stencils made from thin metal are still used to paint letters directly on surfaces. Typical applications are large packaging material, road markings, and codes on large objects.
—Silk-screening is still widely used for signage. It is one of the most elegant production methods.
—'Letter-transfer' was a production method where silk-screened letters were first put onto a special carrier sheet. A layer of adhesive material was later applied to the sheet on the printed side. The letters could then be rubbed off from the carrier sheet to stick on a panel surface. This method has virtually disappeared.
—Sand-blasting is the technique of blowing fine sand under high pressure onto a surface. A mask of rubberised material is used to cover the parts that should be left untreated. This method can be applied to stone, glass, or (hard) wood.

4.8.4.3. Using dies

To make a die for each individual letter is a complicated and expensive production method. It is not much used anymore.
—Die cutting is a method where cutting dies are used to cut individual letters out of thin material.
—Hot stamping is a technique used to impress a die in the shape of a letter form into a surface with (metal) foil in between.
—Moulds are used to produce individual plastic or metal letters. Moulds can be made relatively simply (pressing a master form

into special oily sand), or be fairly complicated and expensive to fabricate (injection moulds). The latter type of moulds can become part of precise and high-speed production machines.

4.8.4.4. *Other mechanical and chemical techniques*

—Engraving machines have played an essential role in letter production. In fact, engraving machines are routers using small diameter cutters that allow production of sharp corners. The first such machines were called 'pentographs'. A set of masters for each font was used to make type in different sizes. Today all engraving machines use digitised instruction. After engraving, the form can be filled in with ink or left blank.

—Etching is a method for taking material away from a surface by chemical reaction. Glass and metal surfaces can be treated this way. This technique is often combined with a photographic reproduction of an image. Light exposure of specially prepared surfaces can create a resistance to the etching liquid so that only the unexposed parts of the surface are etched out. Etching has become a rare technique for signage.

Laser technology has advanced tremendously in the past 20 years. Laser applications for shaping and imprint are numerous. Almost any material can be cut, shaped, engraved or marked, like cutting, shaping and engraving stainless-steel or stone, logos or date markings (tattoos) on food products, and decorations on leather, paper or textiles.

4.8.4.5. *Cutting machines*

Cutting material has become a digitised manufacturing process. Digital data are used to guide tools that cut automatically through the material. Digital data created by the designer can often be used directly for production; therefore most graphics software can be employed. The different types of machines available are used to cut different kinds of materials.

—Vinyl cutting machines use a small knife that cuts through thin vinyl tape. It is the 'Ford car' for all sign manufacturers.

—Automated routers are cutting machines based on traditional mechanical cutting. They are nowadays used mostly to make shapes out of wooden (or aluminium) panels.

—Laser cutting machines are optical 'thermo-cutters'. They cut plastics and metals with a thin beam of laser light. The thickness of the material to be cut is limited. Aluminium or copper cannot be used because the heat melts the material and transforms it into a mirror-like surface that reflects the laser beam and stops the process.

—Plasma cutting machines are also thermo-cutters, based on traditional welding technology. A thin beam of gas, of a very high temperature (in plasma state), cuts through all kinds of metal. Depending on the power of the machine, very thick material (up to 250 mm) can be cut using this method.

—Water jet (or abrasive) cutting machines use a very thin beam of water under extremely high pressure that may contain abrasive particles to enhance the power of the jet stream. It can cut through any material, even stone and glass of considerable thickness.

—Wire EDM (Electrical Discharge Machining) cutting machines use a brass wire under high electric current to cut through all conductive materials.

4.8.4.6. *Wide-format digital printing*

Digital Ink Jet printing technology makes it possible to print on a wide variety of materials in almost limitless sizes. The technology does not need pressure to print the image, like all traditional printing methods. Instead, small drops of ink are sprayed onto the surface by a small nozzle. This nozzle builds up the image in parallel horizontal movements over the surface. All types of graphics, including full colour photography, can be printed this way. These are ideal production machines for large sign types —super graphics—such as outdoor and indoor banners and murals.

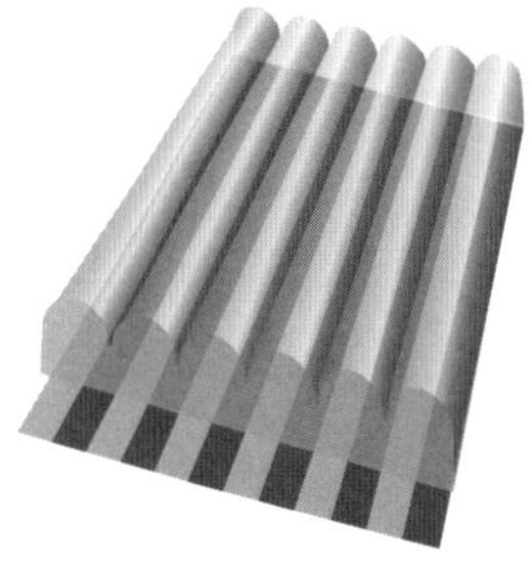

Lenticulars are a special type of laminated prints. The grooves in the surface function as lenses that focus your sight—when in motion—on alternating parts of the underlying print, thereby creating an animated or 3D image.

4.8.4.7. *Laminated prints*

—Paper prints can be laminated in transparent plastic sheets to create durable prints.
—Prints can also be part of polyurethane panels, thus creating extremely durable graphics.

4.8.5. ILLUMINATION AND SCREENS

Illuminated signage is almost a separate part of the signage industry. Digital screen technology is becoming slowly but surely more and more a part of signage projects. Although the two technologies have different backgrounds, they overlap nowadays in certain applications. Both technologies need the same source of energy: electricity.

Three basic traditional light sources: incandescent, fluorescent and neon.

4.8.5.1. *Incandescent light*

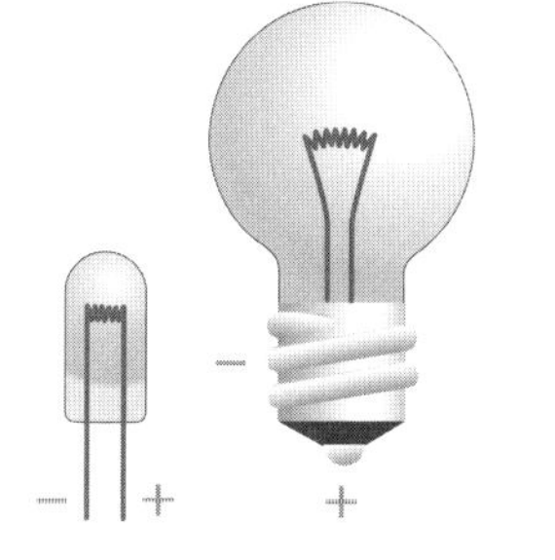

The traditional electric light bulb has a (tungsten) metal part that is heated up to white hot by an electric current. The bulb contains a gas that prevents the glowing part from burning away by oxidation. This type of light consumes a lot of energy and produces a lot of heat. It is not very much used for signage. Halogen spots or floodlights are used instead.

4.8.5.2. *Fluorescent light*

Fluorescent light tubes use far less energy and produce far less heat. It is the typical light source for most buildings. There is a huge variety of bulbs and tubes available on the market. The technical principle is based on an electric current that is sent through both ends of a tube filled with gas which emits ultra-violet radiation. A layer of fluorescent powder on the inside of the tube will glow because of the radiation, thus producing white light. Fluorescent tubes are the traditional light source for light boxes or floodlights.
Fluorescent lights are produced in many variations of 'white light colour' (light temperatures) and may change the colour of objects quite dramatically from their daylight appearance.

4.8.5.3. *Neon*

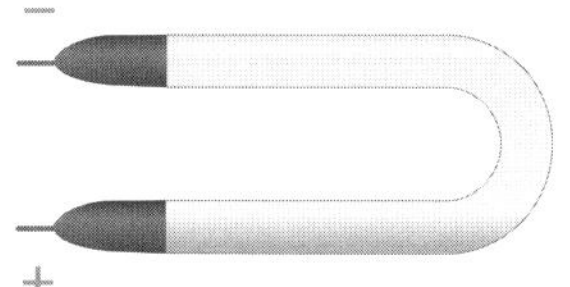

Neon is the name of an inert, colourless, gaseous element. It lights up when contained in a glass tube and exposed to an electric current. The principle is the same as that of fluorescent lights, only neon tubes can be manufactured and shaped per piece, whereas fluorescent light tubes are industrially produced at standardised lengths and in standard colours. Neon tubes can be made in practically any shape, length or colour, using various combinations of different type of gasses and fluorescent coatings inside the glass tube. The light can also be switched off and on instantaneously (unlike fluorescent tubes). These qualities create endless possibilities and variations for signage applications. Casinos in Las Vegas and brand signs in Tokyo have shown the most monumental examples of neon sign technology. Neon is often used in combination with fabricated channel letters.

4.8.5.4. LED

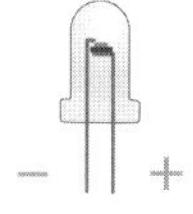

LEDs (Light Emitting Diodes) are semi-conductors. This type of semi-conductor lights up when an electric current is passed through the combination of two types of material. LEDs use little current and have a long life. Their first humble applications were the tiny red 'on' indicators for electrical appliances. Subsequently, new technological developments have created a far wider use for LEDs. Further developments may change their future application dramatically; they may take over the current position held by neon or fluorescent light sources. LEDs are already applied in various products such as traffic lights and huge animated murals.
—LEDs can be combined with integrated circuit boards, creating screens made with areas of LEDs that can be animated. Originally

used for small one-line boxes with red running text composed on a rather rough matrix, now LEDs are available in small matrix, and even four-colour applications.

4.8.5.5. Electroluminescent foils

Electroluminescent foils are light-emitting foils. Fluorescent material is sandwiched between two thin transparent electricity-conducting plastic layers. The fluorescent part emits light when a current is passed through it. The fluorescent part may be applied in any shape, so it is possible to produce transparent sheets where only certain parts will emit light.

Light quantity and temperature

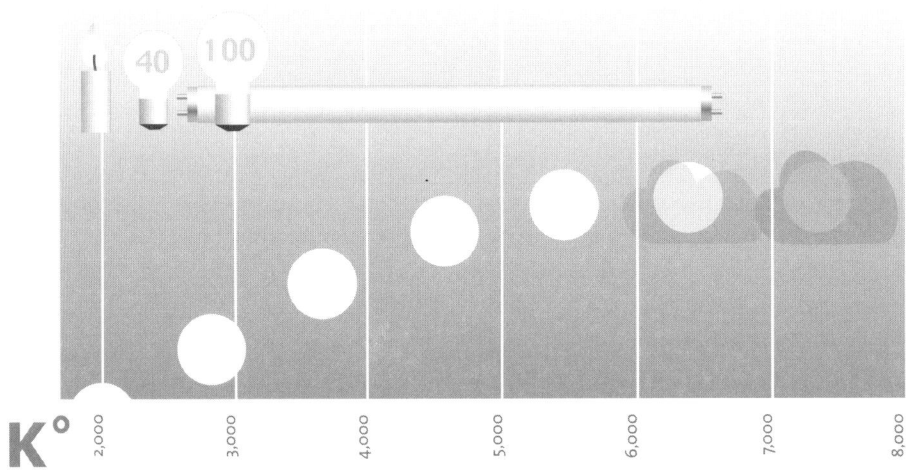

Light conditions have a strong emotional impact on the way we perceive our environment. This diagram shows the daily changes in natural light compared with artificial light sources. The light temperature is expressed in degrees (of) K(elvin). The function of a space should match the emotional impression of the light in that space. There are cultural differences; Asian countries prefer 'cooler' light. Light temperature (K) in combination with light intensity (Lux) and the amount of light sources used determine the atmosphere in a space. It has also a tremendous impact on the perceived size.

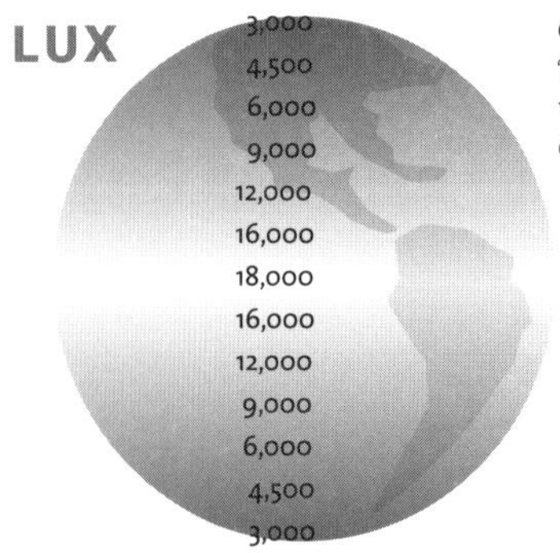

Outdoor illuminance levels related to latitude.
The lux figures represent a level exceeded 85% of the time between 9 am and 5 pm throughout the working year. The large global differences explain why people living closer to the equator prefer on average higher levels of artificial light.

LUX

0.001

0.1 – 1

400 – 1,000

1,000 – 5,000

5,000 – 10,000

10,000 – 100,000

The differences in natural light conditions. From left to right, top to bottom: starlight (eye sensitivity starts at 0.01 lux), moonlight (from 1 lux onwards we start to see colours), sunset, early morning, cloudy sky midday, clear sky midday. 10 lux equals 1 foot-candle (the light illuminance on an object 1 foot away from a burning candle)

LUX

10 – 40

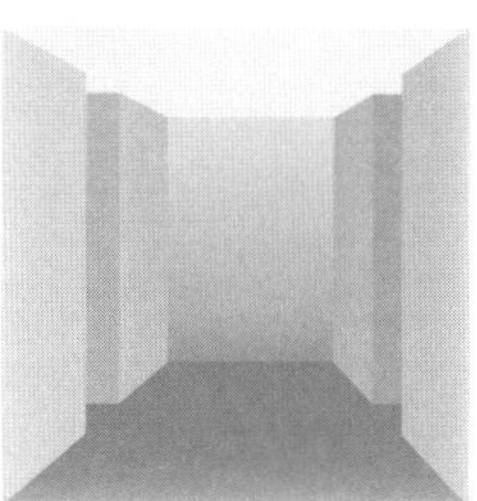

50 – 100

100 – 400

300 – 500

300 – 1,000

3,000 – 10,000

Average illuminance levels in relation to functional conditions. From left to right, top to bottom: parking areas and public spaces, access corridors, working spaces (depending on the type of work), computer desktop, reading and writing spaces, medical surgical rooms.

4.8.5.6. LEP

LEPS (Light Emitting Polymers) are the latest development in the production of very thin, low energy-consuming display technology. This technology is based on a further automation of the production of integrated circuit boards. Complicated minuscule structures of diodes and transistors are applied to flexible and transparent surfaces with ink jet printing technology. It may take some time to get used to the idea, but light bulbs can be 'printed' these days.

4.8.5.7. CRT

CRTs (Cathode Ray Tubes) is the name of our good old TV screen. The image is built up by a precise bombardment of electrons coming from an 'electron cannon' in the back of a vacuum glass tube and directed to the fluorescent layer in the front. The fluorescent layer lights up on the spot where it is hit by electrons. The technology is still around, creating clear, sharp and crisp images, but the screen tube is bulky and the imaging process is quite energy consuming.

4.7.5.8. LCD

LCD (Liquid Crystal Display) technology is already rather old, but is still under further development. Liquid crystals do not produce light; on the contrary, the only thing the (liquid) crystals are good at is being either transparent or cutting light off completely when an electric current is sent through them. Liquid crystal displays always need a light source, which may be ambient light falling on the display and reflected by a mirror behind, or one of the above mentioned light sources placed behind or on top of the display. The rather simple stroke shapes that form the different figures from zero to nine were the first applications on LCD displays. Now they are produced in very complicated 4-colour displays in combination with colour and polarisation filters. Most laptop computers carry LCD screens.
LCD technology will soon be 'printable', which may mean that the giant super graphics that are now printed on banners, or display boards, will become animated pictures in the future.

4.8.5.9. Plasma screens

The traditional TV screen first got a flat front and then became 'Digital and High Resolution'. Now it looks like the traditional screens will be replaced by plasma screens. Plasma screens can be really flat and can be far bigger in size, because the image is produced with a different technology. An electron beam is no longer needed to draw the images. The plasma screen holds a thin layer of gas between two glass panels. The gas lights up on the spots where the electric current is passed through. A complicated integrated circuit ensures that this happens in a very precise and organised way, resulting in crystal clear pictures with high resolution. Plasma screens are likely to replace the current CRT tubes used in signage projects.

Four major screen types

—Left: CRT *(Cathode Ray Tube) screen. Three beams of electrons hit and light up* RGB *coloured phosphor dots printed on the inside of a glass tube. A grille layer helps to focus the beams. The shapes and patterns of the phosphor elements may differ; for instance, like the line pattern in 'Trinitron' tubes.*

—Right: Plasma screen. A layer of rectangular-shaped, tiny hollow RGB *coated phosphor cells, filled with ionised gas (plasma), is placed between two layers of glass with a printed electronic circuit covering each individual cell. When a current is sent though a phosphor cell, the plasma will produce* UV *light which will light up the phosphor coating.*

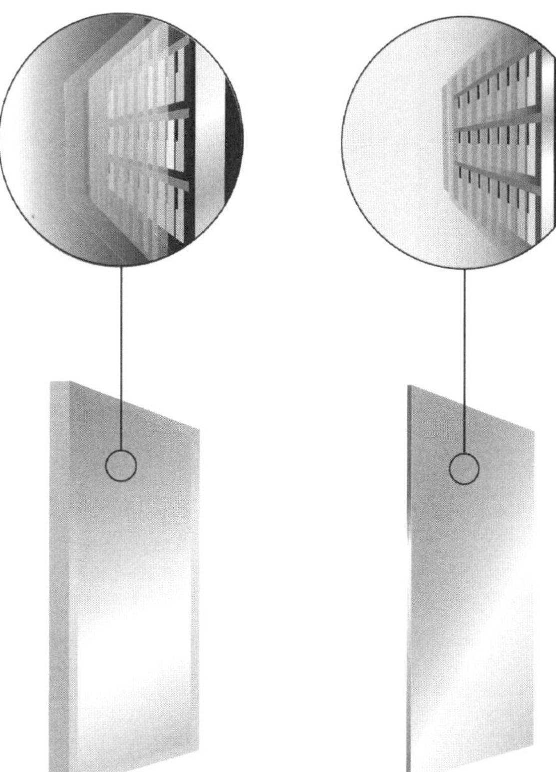

—Left: LCD *(Liquid Crystal Display) screen. A backlit panel sends light through a complicated sandwich of different (ultra-thin) layers: a polarising filter, a glass substrate carrier, a layer with a printed circuit of transparent transistors, a layer with liquid crystal cells, a layer with a transparent electrode circuit,* RGB *colour filter cells, a glass substrate, and finally a second polarising filter. Electric current sent through the individual liquid crystal cells will make them more or less transparent, thus influencing the amount of visible backlight per cell.*

—Right: LEP *(Light Emitting Polymer) screen. Different ultra-thin layers are inkjet printed on a thin transparent plastic carrier: a transparent transistor circuit layer, a layer with* RGB *light emitting cells, and a layer with a transparent electrode circuit.*

LCD	Resolutions
0.5"	600 × 800
3.9" 3.5" 2.5"	320 × 320 240 × 320 176 × 208 132 × 176 160 × 160 130 × 130

LCD	CRT	Resolutions
23"	23"	1280 × 1024 1600 × 1280
19"	19"	

LCD	CRT	Resolutions
21"	21"	640 × 480
19"	19"	800 × 600
17"	17"	1024 × 768
15"	15"	1152 × 864
14"	14"	1600 × 1200
12"	12"	
10.4"		

Resolutions

1280 × 768
1680 × 1050
1920 × 1200
2560 × 1600

LCD **Plasma**

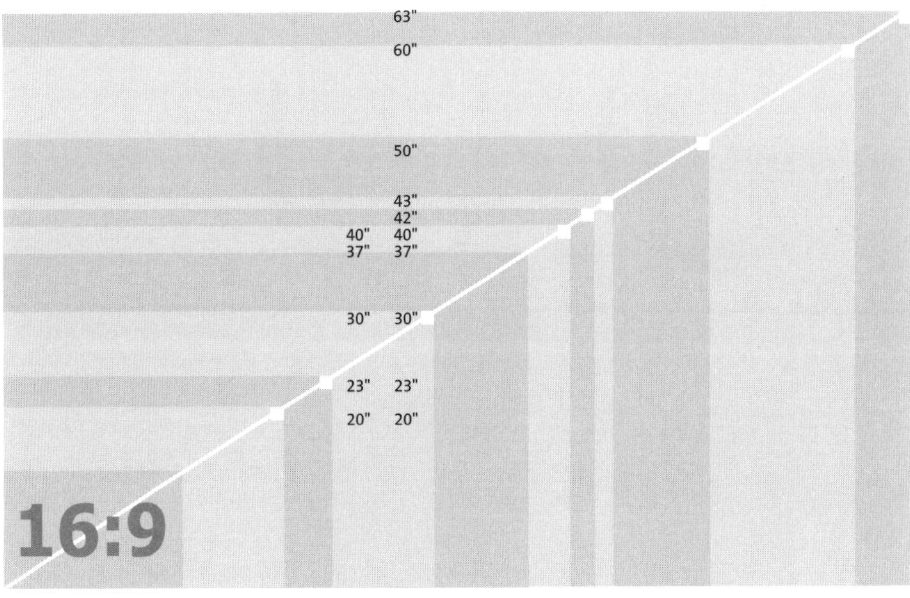

Display screens are produced in a large range of different sizes. The screen ratio is traditionally 4:3 or 4:5. For bigger screens the 'wide screen' ratio of 16:9 has become popular. Screen ratios for handhelds are different and do not to have a traditional range. The three screen technologies shown are: CRT, LCD *and Plasma. The top range are special* LCD *applications like camera viewers or displays used for rear projection screens. Energy consumption with a size range of the three display systems:* LCD *1"– 82" is low; Plasma 20"–71" is medium;* CRT *19"– 40" is high.*

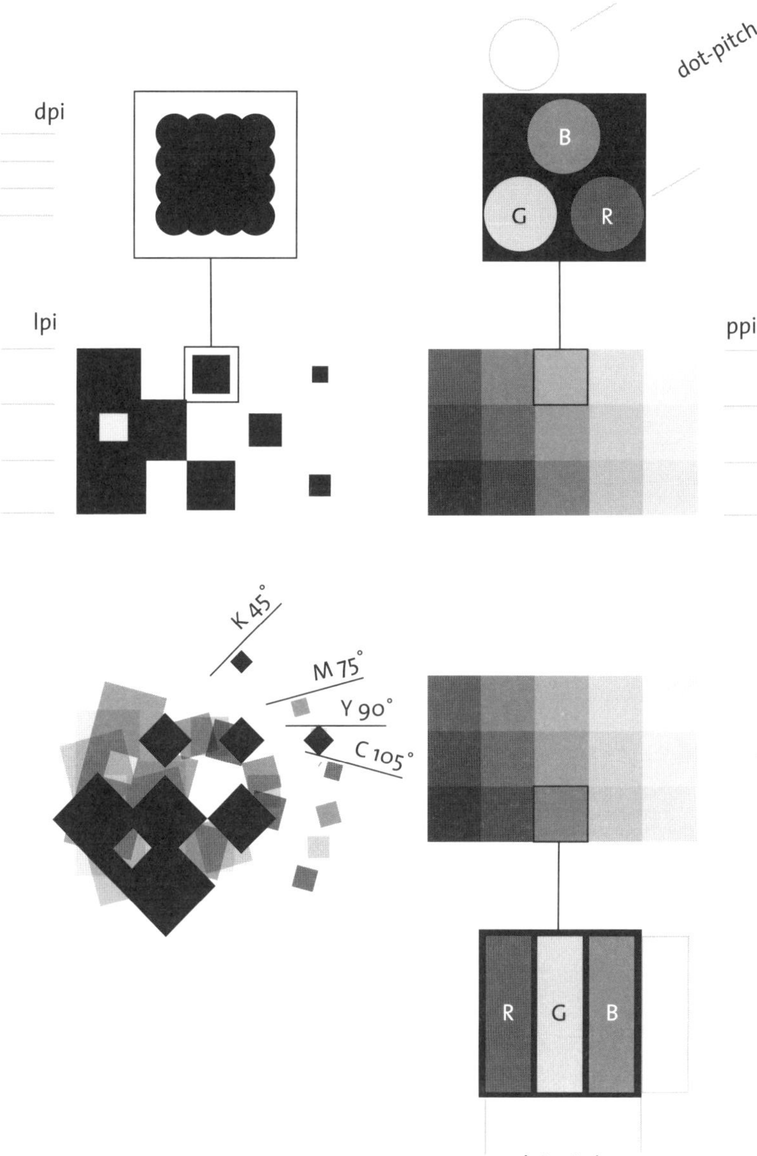

Imaging for print (left column) and for screen (right column).
Terminology to define image resolution may be confusing at times.
For print top to bottom: laser printers and image setters build all images with identical dots (resolutions 150 – 2400 dpi), halftone images make use of rasters to mimic grey values (resolution 25 – 200 lpi), full-colour images are made by printing rasters in 4 colours over each other under a different angle. Rasters can be used in various configurations.
For screen, top to bottom: screens use light cells (dots, lines or rectangles) to build up the image. Individual light cells can change their luminosity (resolution 0.07 – 1 mm dot pitch). Today practically all screens are full-colour screens, each screen pixel consists of three RGB dots. Screen (pixel) resolutions are on average around 72 dpi, but are smaller for handheld devices and very small for camera viewers or projectors.

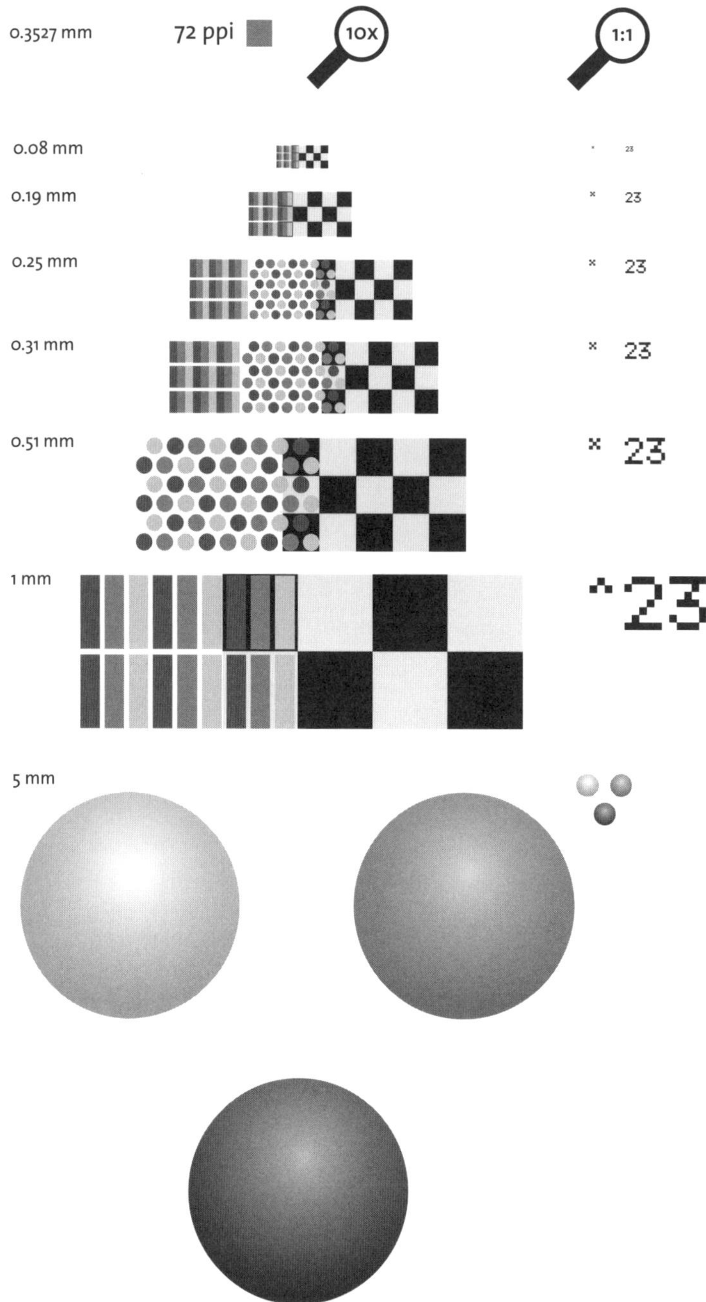

Screen resolution expressed in dot-pitch.
One image pixel contains at least 3 (RGB) dots. The dot-pitch is the distance between two neighbouring pixels of the same colour. The dot-pitch practically equals the minimum image pixel (maximum image resolution on a screen). Applications from top to bottom: 0.1 – 0.070 mm for LCD camera viewers and screen projectors; 0.19 – 0.25 mm for handheld LCD screens; 0.25 – 0.31 mm for computer screens and hi-res TV (LCD & CRT); 0.65 – 0.51 mm for traditional TV; around 1 mm for plasma screens; from 3 mm up for full colour (jumbo) LED screens.

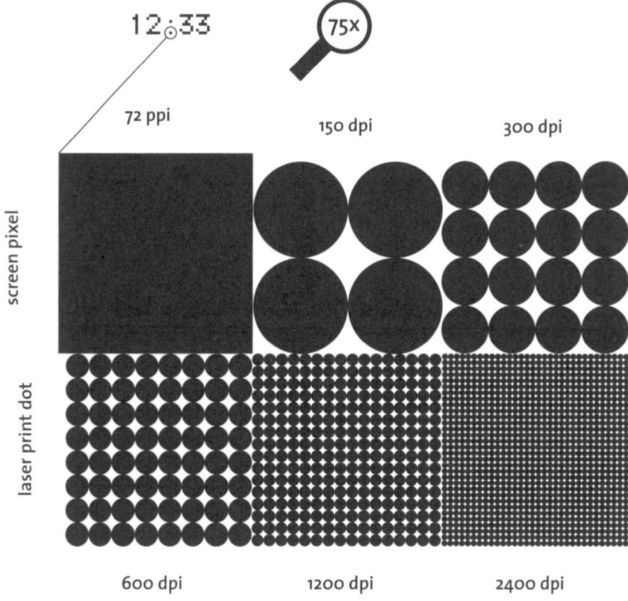

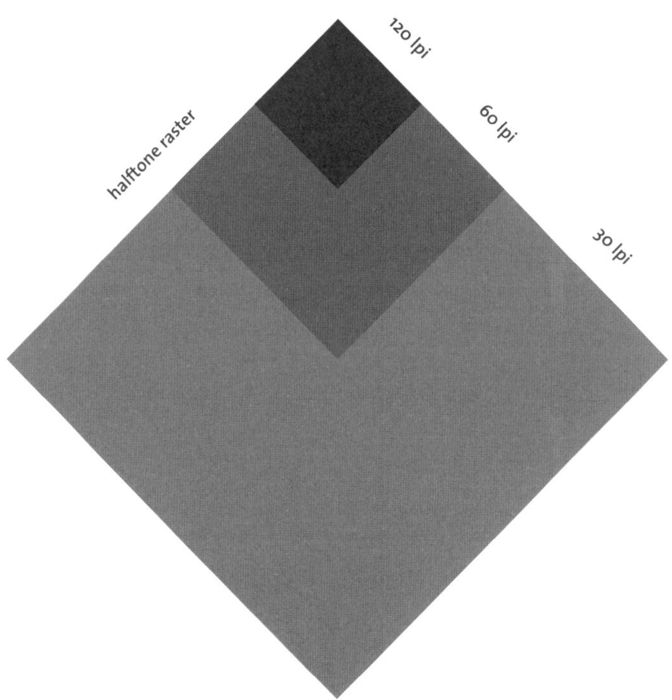

A comparison between the sizes of screen pixels, printer dots and halftone rasters.
The average computer screen has a resolution of 72 ppi (pixels per inch) and the average office printer has 300–600 dpi (dots per inch). Professional image setters may reach resolution levels where the human eye can no longer detect dots. Office printers are moving in the direction of professional image setters, resulting in better reproduction of halftone images. The halftone image is made with halftone rasters. The resolution of these rasters is expressed in lines (of raster elements) per inch.

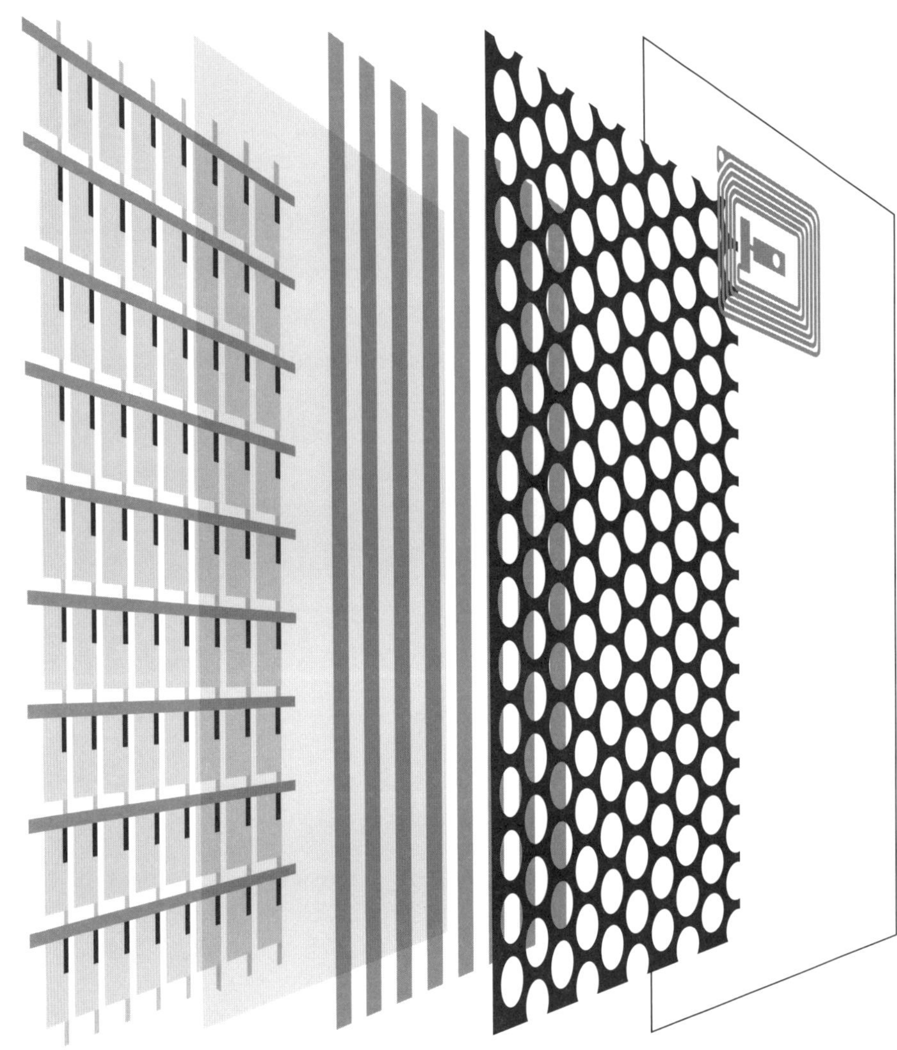

Future dynamic displays may be inkjet printed in any size on any kind of (flexible) material, comparable with the current 4-colour inkjet print technology. The sandwich of inkjet printed layers may include: a transparent transistor circuit layer, a light emitting polymer RGB cell layer, a transparent electrode circuit layer, a voltaic (solar cells) layer, and a receiver/sender/microprocessor layer.

4.8.6. FINISHES

The finish is the final surface treatment of a product. It determines the characteristics in the appearance of the 'skin'. In 3D modelling this last phase would be called 'texture mapping'. There are endless varieties in the way products can be finished. There are three main categories: mechanical treatment of the surface, like polishing; a chemical treatment, like anodising; or covering the surface with a layer, like coating. The reasons for doing a specific finish may differ; sometimes it is only done for aesthetic reasons, but often it is needed to stop or at least slow down the process of decay. Conservation and surface enhancement are the two important objectives of all finishes.

4.8.6.1. Natural oxidation

Some materials do not need a treatment for conservation. These materials may even get more beautiful after being unprotected and exposed to normal outdoor conditions. This applies to metals like bronze, zinc, copper, or special types of steel, like Corten steel. Some types of stone and wood, like teak, also age nicely. Even some plastics after many years of use get a special 'patina' that gives the material a special attractive quality. Just like humans, most materials turn greyish over time and lose their smooth surface.

There are—regrettably—also many fake treatments to make materials look old from the first day onwards. That type of treatment is a disgrace; we have to be patient and leave it to time to do its work properly. Fake aging is only of service to antique cheats and Hollywood producers.

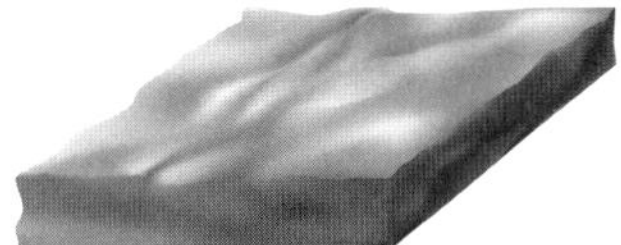

Surface treatments can change the visual impression of materials dramatically. The surface of stone, for instance, can be subjected to a wide variety of mechanical treatments that change its appearance.

4.8.6.2. Mechanical treatments

The surface of stone (or granulates) can be finished in various ways: rough like natural mountain rock, soft and matt like an egg shell, shiny like a mirror, and every variation in between.

The surface treatment can almost take away the natural characteristics of the material. The ancient Greek sculptors could make white marble look like white, featherweight woven gowns. Metals can be polished with special paste and cloth, or can be given a matt structure by sandblasting. Wood can also be polished, but is mostly sanded or planed.

4.8.6.3. Chemical treatments

Not all treatments under this heading are in the strict sense of the word 'chemical'.

—Galvanising is a treatment where iron is covered with a thin layer of zinc, either by chemical means, or by dipping the whole piece in molten zinc.

—Anodising is giving aluminium a thin layer of aluminium oxide. It can be done in different colours and may result in different surface structures. The treatment gives the material a nice even surface and hardens it at the same time.

—Chroming is a process where a thin layer of chrome is put over

the surface of a different metal. The same can be done with a variety of other metals, like brass or tin. There are various complicated techniques around to add thin layers of metal on practically any type of base material.
—Bleaching is a treatment for wood where the wood tone is made lighter.
—There are numerous other methods where chemicals are used to alter the surface structure or the colour of stone, wood or metal. The ones mentioned above are only the most commonly used treatments.

4.8.6.4. Coatings & ink

Painting, or enamelling with a brush or spraying equipment, no longer properly describes the various ways by which a coat is applied to a material. Coating is the word that is now used instead. The varieties of coatings, both in the basic material used and in the way the coat is put onto the surface, are endless. The type of material to be coated requires the use of specific base materials and specific ways or conditions to ensure maximal adherence.
—Vitreous enamelling is a method to make an extremely durable coat on iron panels. First a layer of coloured powder is put onto the surface, then the panel is heated in an oven until the powder melts onto the surface. The finished coating is as hard as glass. The surface of chinaware (porcelain) is treated in a comparable way, that is why this method is also called 'porcelain enamelled'.
—Powder coating is a comparable process with the above. Here a powder is sprayed onto a surface (also using the force of static electricity) and then heated.
—Two-component polyurethane painting is also quite durable. The coated surface will have the hardness and structure of hard plastic.
—The list of 'special effect' coatings is continually growing. Popular types of coatings may vary from season to season, according to fashion. Metal coatings are at the top of the list for constant development, led by the automotive industry, where the type of coating is an important marketing tool. To name a few types of special effect coatings: metallic and pearl paint let the colour of the paint change depending on the angle of light reflection. Fluorescent paint reflects more light than traditional paint does, hence this type of paint seems to 'glow'.
The finish of paint can be matt, satin (eggshell) or glossy. Today, the choice is extended with surfaces that may have various structures or may even be made to look like felted textile.
—The application of 'transfers' in combination with paint can create surfaces of almost any type of material on metal. For instance, the imitation of all kinds of wood and stone is quite sophisticated theses days. 'Surface mapping' is not limited anymore to 3D software applications; any background material can be given a surface to look like any other material, even like the surface of freshly fallen snow.

—Wood has its own list of varnishing methods and coatings. A lot of types are transparent to show the natural wood grain.

4.8.6.5. Vandal-resistant coatings

Signs placed in certain environments are attractive objects for graffiti or vandalism. Special anti-graffiti paints have been developed to make removal of graffiti easier. This is in most cases a crystal-clear two-component polyurethane coating that is put over the existing paint and lettering.

4.8.6.6. Fluorescent and phosphorescent paint and ink

Special types of paint and (silkscreen) ink have been developed that radiate or reflect visible light differently. There are two basic differences. Fluorescent pigments transform UV radiation into visible light, so these pigments seem to reflect more light. Phosphorescent pigments store (light) energy, and are capable of releasing visible light in the dark. This self-luminous effect will last only for minutes or hours at best. A mix with radio-active material will energise the phosphors continuously.
The lightfastness of fluorescent pigments is often short. White fluorescent paint is a favourite of some signage designers.

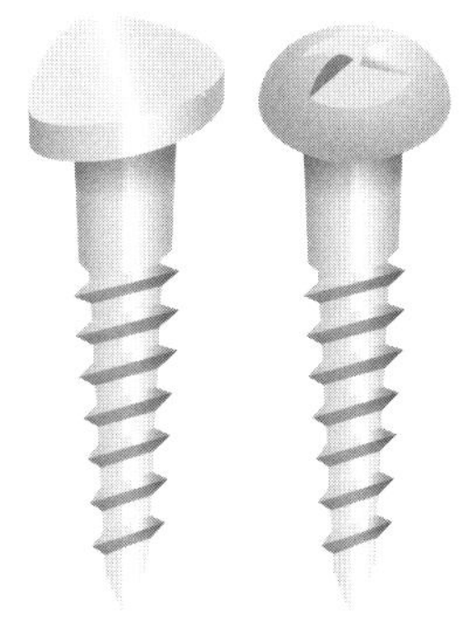

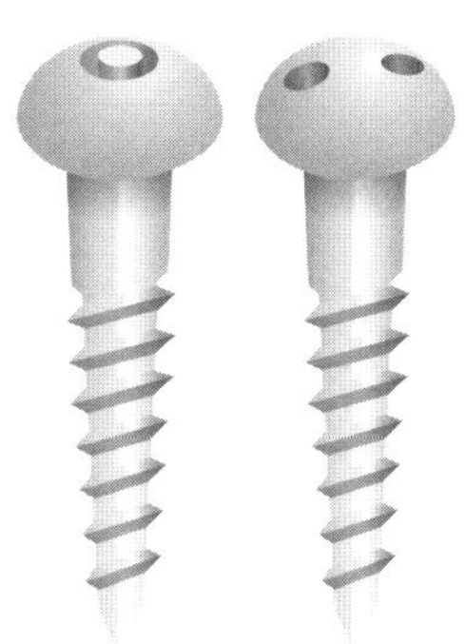

Vandal-proof fasteners make it difficult or practically impossible to remove signs after installation. Specially designed screw heads need proprietary fastening tools; others can only be turned in one direction (the fastening direction).

4.8.7. FIXING METHODS

The installation of signs on site is an important and distinct phase in a signage project. Most signs are not integrated into the building, but rather produced as separate items that need secure attachment to all kinds of different building materials. Various types of fasteners are generally used to complete the job. The preferred way for fixing is one that takes little time, and also one that keeps the fastening material as invisible as possible—'Blind fastening' or 'secret fixing' as it is sometimes called. This preference is understandable, as visible screws or nails do not generally create very sophisticated signs. Yet there is a point in making the method of fixing a clearly visible part of the design. High-tech architecture has demonstrated the beauty that clearly visible sophisticated constructions may have. The pursuit of clarity and openness in the use of contrasting materials and methods of assembly is still a valuable starting point in design.
In signage projects, there are a number of different categories of fastening materials.

4.8.7.1. Traditional fastening materials

This category covers all materials that establish a mechanical connection between the building and the sign, like screws, nails and various types of plugs. It is a very secure and reliable way of fastening, but makes installation time-consuming. It is recommended that only non-corrosive metals be used for this material and practically all fixing materials fall within this category.
Public areas and public transportation vehicles may suffer from the activities of signage collectors, people that steal signs as collector's items. As a remedy, there are screws with special heads on

the market that cannot be screwed in and out with regular screw drivers.

4.8.7.2. *Adhesive tapes*

The wide range of industrial adhesive (foam) tapes available is often used to fix small signs on flat surfaces, especially on surfaces like glass where traditional fasteners are useless. There are special tapes to use for specific materials. Adhesives can create excellent connections; however, as is the case with all non-mechanical fastening materials, meticulousness is the key to good results. Surfaces have to be very clean and the working surroundings dust-free and dry. A residue of some type of building material left on the surface, like silicon, can ruin a connection completely. Although some types of tape have a long life, most lose their capacities over time.

4.8.7.3. *Glues*

What is said for adhesive tapes can be said for glues. Glues have replaced traditional fasteners in many industries, even in the aviation industry where safety is a high priority. But conditions in factories can be controlled far better than on site. Sometimes a combination of adhesive tape and glue is used to make the connections. Two component glues can also produce very strong connections. An adhesive tape can be used to hold the sign in position until the glue hardens.

4.8.7.4. *Hook-and-loop fasteners*

This type of fastener is 'reclosable'; it consists of two combined elements that grip each other. It can be taken apart again using some force, and then put back together afterwards. The material is also called 'Velcro' after a brand name of this material. There are various types of hook-and-loop fasteners available; some are light and are also used in the garment industry, while some are made of strong solid plastic (dual lock).

4.8.7.5. *Magnetic tape*

Magnetic foil is a thick tape that sticks to metal surfaces. It is used for temporary signs, or signs that need frequent updating. The signs—when not covered with a transparent protective shield—are very easy to remove.

4.9. Typography & typefaces

Text is still by far the most important ingredient in signage. (That is to say, the most important remaining part after everything has been done to ensure that the need for signage is reduced to its bare minimum.) Maps, exploded or bird's-eye views may be of great help to better understand the environment. Pictograms and illustrations can make browsing for clues that help wayfinding or heeding mandatory information easier, and can also create a friendly atmosphere. Nevertheless, textual information remains the core of all wayfinding and instruction. This fact must have kept signage design for the most part an activity reserved for graphic designers. Not for all assignments, though. Signage design may be carried out by people with a wide variety of educational backgrounds and core skills. Many may not have a basic knowledge about typography. For this reason, there follows a brief overview of the fundamentals of type and typography relating to the specific aspects of type to be used for signage.

4.9.1. THE GENERAL ASPECTS

Language is the basis of human civilisation, first as verbal communion, later in handwritten form, and now mostly in typographical form. Textual information is currently transmitted and stored in startling amounts. Type refers to letters designed for reproduction with the help of machines. Typography means the way type is used to compose complete messages. Typography deals primarily with the visual aspects of text and not with its content. Nevertheless, content and visual representation can never be entirely separated because appearance is an integral part of a message. Typography has four major aspects: a psychological one that deals with style and identity; a physiological one that deals with visual perception; a practical one that deals with the functional aspects of type; and a technical one that deals with the production of type. These will be discussed in order, but first some attention must be given to a basic characteristic of all typography.

4.9.2. CREATING VISUAL ORDER

There is one fundamental characteristic of typography that is very specific to the field of visual design and that is its very strong relationship to our sense for visual harmony and order. In that respect, it is comparable with music. It is not the shape of the individual letter that counts when designing type, it's how all the letters work together in the composition of a complete text, just like individual tones must harmonise together in some way to make a piece of music, instead of just making noise (or atonal music). Musical harmony also appears to have quite a strict mathematical foundation. That is not as clear for typography, although a mathematical structure has obviously always been at its core.

The human eye/brain combination is capable of surveying extremely complex images in order to detect and isolate relevant detail. Our ability to both browse and effectively spot minute differences in details must have a profound genetic foundation. Maybe it goes back to our hunter's instincts. Hunters are capable of spotting tiny differences in the visual harmony of natural vegetation. This ability is quintessential for survival. Effectively dealing with a potential threat or hunting opportunity relies entirely on this browsing quality.

Our emotional response to colours is also often linked to natural phenomena, like a blue sky, a yellow sun or grey rocks. Our sense of visual order may be based on the natural order of all vegetation. The size of each plant and the amount of space it occupies among other plants is relative to its size. The outcome of the flora's struggle for survival is visual harmony. It is basically the same harmony that we seek in good typography.

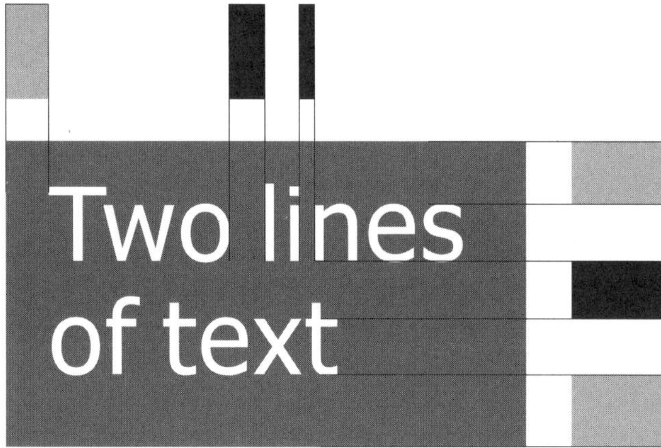

In typography, blank spaces follow a strict order of increasing sizes. Letter spaces are the smallest, followed by word spaces, leading (spaces between lines) and finally the layout margins.

4.9.2.1. Spacing

Creating visual order is the first and foremost quality in typographic design. A clear, sophisticated, refined and consistent visual order distinguishes the work of the professional from that of the amateur. Of course, there are many and varied ways to create visual order; size, stroke thickness and colour are all important means. Yet, there is one essential tool for all typography: blank space. Typography is a lot about the order that is achieved by a thoroughly controlled balancing act between the blank spaces and the spaces occupied by type or images on a given surface. The blank spaces are thus just as important as the images. The blank spaces in typography all have different names according to their function. The amount of blank space used follows a strict hierarchy to group the various typographical elements together visually. This means that the smallest amount of a generic blank space—the letter space—will set the tone for the rest of the blank spaces to be used.

Below is a list of the various types of blank spaces, arranged by increasing size.

spacing spacing spacing spacing
spacing spacing spacing spacing
spacing spacing spacing spacing

—Letter spacing concerns the blank space between individual letters. The generally accepted quality norm in typography is that all letters should have visually the same distance between each other. It is the first and foremost basic rule to creating order. Nevertheless, this rule is often heavily violated. Good letter spacing can be done by anybody as long as sufficient attention is given to it. One does not need professional training to produce proper letter spacing, as we are all capable of putting one object visually in the middle between two other objects. Well, that is all it takes. Slightly more difficult to create is neutrally spaced type. Neutral spacing is the creation of a balance between two types of blank spaces, the spaces needed to separate individual letters, and the blank space included within each letter. The trick to make this more easily visible is to reverse the normal image; the letter shapes are blank and all spaces are black. In neutrally spaced type, all black spaces will have to be equal.

Letter spacing is either narrow, neutral or wide (top to bottom). Neutral spacing attempts to create equal visual spaces between inner letter spaces and the surrounding space. Neutral spaced type is best for common reading text size, very small type needs wider spacing, and big type allows narrower spacing.

Letter spacing
Letter spacing
Letter spacing
Letter spacing

Type designers create not only specific individual letter shapes, but also determine the amount of letter and word spacing. Some typefaces are considerably more narrow spaced than others.

spa
pac
aci
cin
ing

Carrying out proper letter spacing does not take professional training. It can be done by anyone with normal eyesight when following this procedure: separate the first letter triplet from the word to be letter spaced and put the second letter visually in the middle of the other two, then keep on moving to the following triplets.

—Word spacing concerns the blank spaces between each word. This space should also preferably be constant throughout the text. An exception to this rule applies for a long text that is justified on both the right and left side, but this is not a favourable type of layout for most signage purposes.
Word spaces should be just wide enough to create a visual separation between words. A rule of thumb used to be a width between one third or one fourth of the type size.
—Leading concerns the blank spaces between the lines in a text. Typefaces with a relatively large x-height need more leading than typefaces with long descenders and ascenders. Long lines need more leading than short ones.
—Margins are the blank spaces between text and illustrations and the edges of the total surface. These spaces are the largest, together with the spaces used to separate parts of a text.
Our symphony of blank spaces is hereby completed.

When type was still tangible, graphic designers did not need to decide on most of the spacing possibilities mentioned above. The type designer had embedded most spacing (unchangeable) in the type itself. Today, we are able to alter and fine-tune these spaces ourselves, even up to a visually undetectable level of one hundredth of a millimeter. So, there cannot be any excuse for badly spaced typography. Regrettably, it remains one of the most eye-catching sins in type production.

4.9.2.2. Basic proportions

Another set of conventions in type design is a major contribution to the visual order. This concerns the basic proportions of letters. First, there are letter height conventions. All letters relate to 4 strictly defined heights:
—All letters and all other characters are placed on (or are related to) the baseline.
—The x-height is the height of most lower-case letters. Since lower case letters are by far the most used letters in text, their x-height is therefore the most important visual height in type, far more important than the type size. Type size is therefore a bad indication for the visual size of type, whereas an x-height indication is a better one.
—The cap-height is the fixed height of all capital (or upper-case) letters in one type size.
—The ascender height is the height of all lower-case letters with ascenders.
—The descender height is the height of all lower-case, or capital letters with descenders.

36pt 36pt
Hhjx Hhjx
26pt 36pt
Hhjx Hhjx

General type size is usually a bad indication of the visual size of a typeface. The x-height size is by contrast a far better indication. To equalise the visual size differences between typefaces, the type size may need to be adjusted.

Second, we have the letter width conventions. In this case, the order is less strict than in height, but a few widths are predominant in most typefaces. For instance, the widths of the letters 'o' and 'H' will set the tone for the the width of all the other letters in the whole typeface family. Letter width also has a technical aspect:

all individual characters must have one minimum unit width in common in order to make lines of the same length possible. Type production has always been very concerned with letter width. A typewriter was 'mono-spaced' because the sheet transportation was fixed at only one distance, so all letters had to have the same width. More sophisticated type production systems, for instance, were based on 18 or 54 unit systems. Today, the situation is somewhat split between two extremes. At one end, typography for screen display requires very limited differences in letter widths caused by the visual representation on a relatively coarse grid structure of individual screen pixels. At the other end, modern image setters produce images in a resolution that is far higher that the resolution capacity of the retina of our own eyes. Here, letter width has become totally irrelevant in technical terms. Yet, the traditional letter width conventions are still obeyed in most cases.

nhum ceopqgbd
nhum ceopqgbd
lijftsar kxyvwz
lijftsar kxyvwz

Type design for text typefaces generally follows strong conventions. This illustration shows a range of lowercase letters of two quite distinct typefaces. The identical rectangle placed behind each letter reveals the strong similarities in the proportions of the different characters.

Perhaps it is a coincidence that the traditional minimum typographic measurement of 1 point is about the same size as one pixel on a screen of 72 DPI (dots per inch). There is one important difference, though, between the two systems. In traditional movable type all widths and heights had to fall within a grid of one point, but this constraint was only valid for the containers of the type, not for the shapes of the letters themselves—that aspect was totally free. With representation on a 72 dpi screen, the grid influences the shape of letters as well. In fact, today's technological constraints are in some ways more limiting than throughout the whole history of moveable type.

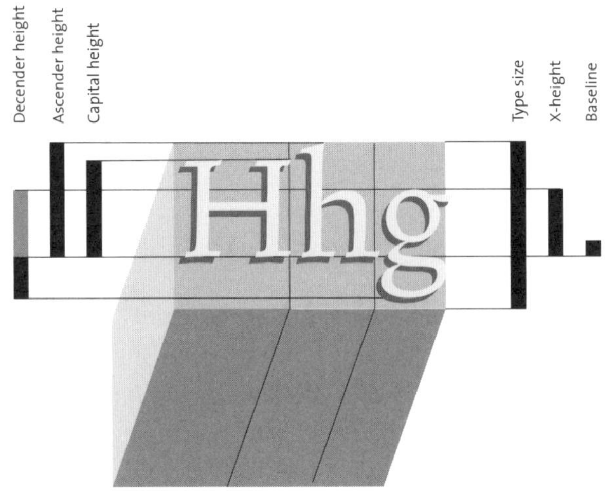

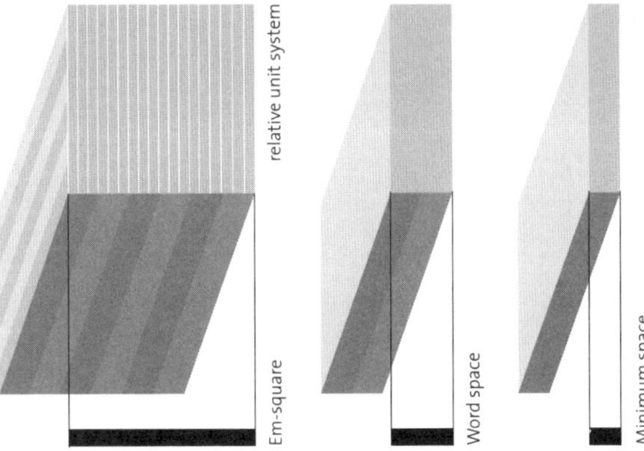

A lot of typographical expressions still refer to the period when typesetting was done with tangible objects. Many type designs are still based on unit systems that have become obsolete. A few traditions from the movable type period, like the traditional wordspace based on the em-square, seem to be forgotten.

For web pages the em-square is reintroduced as a benchmark for all typographic specifications, like word-, line- (leading), or even letter-spacing. The em-square can be divided in an endless range of fractions, percentages, or decimal notations.
There are 'Font-testers' available on the internet that allow practically any sensible or non-sensible way to specify type.

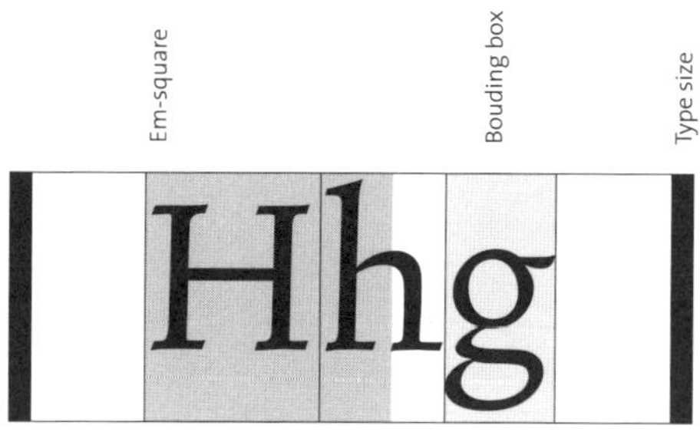

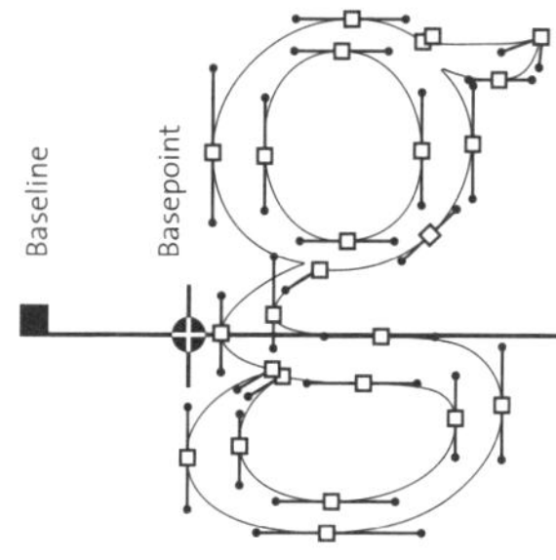

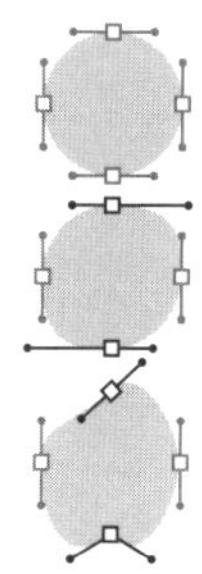

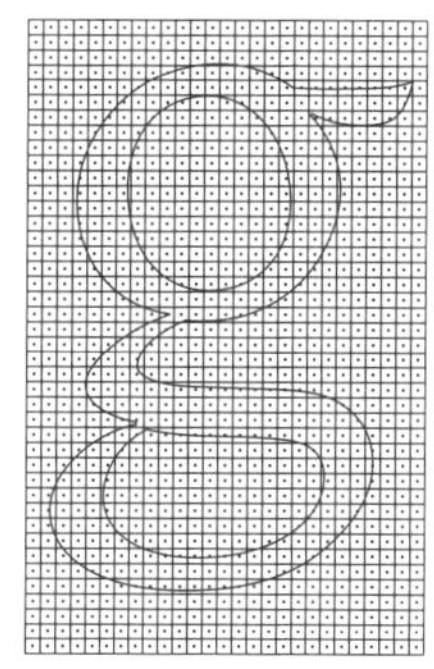

Digital type production has replaced the manipulation of tangible objects with high-speed calculations of mathematical formulas. What once were metal matrices are now collections of curves called splines that can be manipulated easily with just a keystroke. The output of digital data can be processed by various machines of reproduction. Electronic instructions can be added to a font in order to optimise its reproduction under different conditions.

4.9.3. TYPE IDENTITY AND STYLE

Each typeface has a 'personality' or a specific visual identity just like all products and all living (and non-living) things. The style differences between typefaces are huge and the number of different typefaces available are literally countless these days. Typeface selection is one of the major decisions in creating a certain style or atmosphere in typography. Like all other products of design, type follows the style preferences, fads and fashion of the day. That's why the pursuit of maintaining an image of being modern, or advanced, needs regular visual updating. The continual seasonal changes of style are no longer the exclusive domain of fashion design; all design has more or less followed suit.

4.9.3.1. Archetypical type styles

Typefaces are in some ways a clear exception to other products. Certain formal aspects of type have become rather strong archetypes that are still, for the most part, respected by type designers. The most important design conventions are the following:

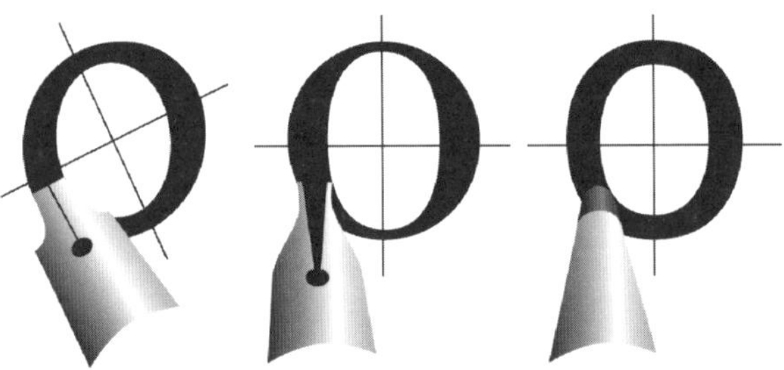

Three basic type styles can be related to different writing tools. The three styles may be called: Antiqua (Old Face), Modern Face, and Grotesk or Stroke Font. However, type style classification systems while widely available, are hardly ever uniform.

—Basic hand writing tools still count for three basic differences in type style. Before the invention of type, documents were copied by hand. The tools used were the reed and the quill pen; later we made use of the (metal) broad-nibbed pen. All these tools produce letter forms with a clear contrast between thin and thick strokes. Later still, engraving tools and flexible, pointy metal pens started influencing writing. The difference in stroke thicknesses were made by alternating the pressure on the pen. These two ways of making thin and thicker parts in letter strokes or 'letter contrast' are sometimes referred to as 'translation'—for the first method—and 'expansion', for the second.
Modern writing tools, like ballpoint pens, only produce lines of one thickness. Letters made with these tools have practically no contrast.

The Serif
The Sans-serif
The Mix

So-called serif and sans serif is an important style distinction. Today, the two can be found within one font family. A mix between the two is a relatively new addition to the font family.

—The distinction between serif and sans serif typefaces. Serifs are extensions in the corners at the end of letter strokes, presumably originating from the chiselled capital letters in Roman times. Sans serifs are a more modern invention that eliminates the serifs. Other names used to indicate the difference between the two are Old Style or Antiqua for serif typefaces and Gothic or Grotesque (Grotesk) for the sans serifs.
Not too long ago, hybrid versions between the serifs and sans serifs were developed. These typefaces no longer follow the

serif/sans serif style conventions. The amount of serifs appear in a reduced amount, resulting in a sort of mix between a serif and a sans serif typeface. Relatively recent is the development of designing a typeface family where there is a sans serif as well as a serif version (and even a 'mixed' one) within the same family.

The major style distinctions in all text type faces are the amount of letter contrast used in the type design, the type of serif employed (if any), the proportion of the letter 'o' and the size of the x-height in relation to the capital height.

The major style differences in text faces are the amount of letter contrast (the difference between the thin and the thick strokes), as well as the difference between the x-height and the H-height (or cap-height). The two samples (top row) show these distinct differences. In the bottom row, the x-height and H-height are made identical, which creates a visual similarity between the two typefaces.

4.9.3.2. Typeface style classification

When many variations are around, the need for some form of classification arises. Categorisation and classification are the traditional means to maintain some order in large collections. Regrettably, this often instigates senseless professional disputes. Nevertheless, such classification has to be generally accepted in order to function. Well, that is not really the case anymore in type design. No single classification system is generally accepted. One reason may be that the application of modern technology resulted in a true explosion of new typefaces, a lot of them being rather experimental or hybrid or 'sampled', and therefore, not easy to classify. There was for some time a generally accepted typeface classification set up by the ATypI (Association Typographique Internationale), an association of type designers. There was even a British Standard and a German DIN norm on this subject. Today, type classification is mostly in the hands of a few big font foundries/distributors, trying to create some order in their humongous collection of typefaces. Classifications have become a mix of marketing, functional, technological and historical descriptions of type aspects. In most cases, the classification is more comical than helpful. The classification offered seems to be an attempt to help selecting type only for those who have definitely lost their way in type territory. For these type of folk any aid will work, no matter how silly.

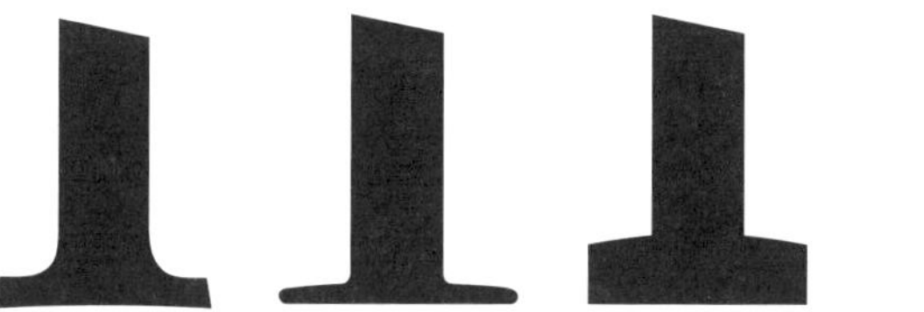

The distinct shape of the serif is an important element of the type style classification of serif fonts.

There are classification systems in use that are more serious. These classification systems arose when documents were no longer sent in a printed format, but directly in electronic format, stripped of all information about the visual representation of the document's content. This method marked the beginning of the Internet. The advantage of this method was that the files became small in size, so faster to transport, and the receiving party did not have to possess the same processing software and typeface licences as the sender to be able to 'open' and read the document. The software available at the receiver's end took over the visual representation part of the document's content. In order to recreate a typeface image that looked as close as possible to the one sent, a typeface at the receiver's end was selected on the basis of a standardised descriptive type classification system.

4.9.4. VISUAL PERCEPTION AND TYPE

The observations we make with our eyes do not match the measurements done with a ruler. We see things differently from what the ruler indicates. The way we experience alignment or size of objects is influenced by the shape of these objects. A ruler is certainly of help in creating typography, but the critical eye always has the last say in determining the final result. That is why we speak in typography about optical size, alignment, middle, and other typographic measurements.

For some reason, there is an unstoppable desire to contain the particularities of the human visual perception in strict mathematical formulae and rules. This development started in the Renaissance period when scholars were striving to uncover the mathematical and geometrical foundations of 'divine' (natural) proportions. Type designs made during that period also followed strict geometrical principles. Today, all type design is *de facto* based on mathematical formulae, but that is merely caused by modern production methods and is not the result of striving for 'divine' mathematics.
There is no mathematical foundation that can be applied to match the way our visual perception works. However, there are some empirical facts that are useful to know.

4.9.4.1. Perception of detail and rhythm

Our eyes are magnificent instruments. They do their work in almost any light conditions and have an impressive viewing range. At reading distance we can see minute details and spot very small differences. Too bad that our visual capabilities seem to be in a constant physiological decline, starting almost from the moment we are born. Ultimately, we all need the help of man-made lenses to compensate for this inevitable natural deterioration. In this respect, there is only one comforting fact in growing older; through experience, we have a better idea of what to expect when we use our eyes. That surely helps when 'reading' our environment effectively. Seeing is certainly not solely determined by the capabilities of the eyes, since ultimately it is our brain that determines the way we will make use of what we see.

4.9.4.2. Size and proportion

The shape of objects and the thickness of contours influences the perceived size of those objects.
—A square will look bigger than a triangle or a circle of the same size. That is why round letters like an 'O' or triangular shaped

Hhklxjg
exexex
HAOWJU

The specific shape of letters influences their perceived size. Type design compensates for this visual effect.

ones like an 'A', need to be a bit bigger than the 'H', for instance.
—Our alphabet has one-stroke letters like the 'l'. To emphasise their visual presence within a line of text, we make the ascender letters longer than the rest.
—A condensed (horizontally scaled) identical shape also looks slightly smaller in height.
—The weight of letters (the thickness of the letter strokes) influences the perceived height. Bold letters need to be slightly taller.

4.9.4.3. The optical middle

We perceive a horizontal middle when the lower part is a bit bigger than the upper part. This has consequences for typography and type design.
—Letters like HKBESX are not symmetrical: the lower part is always bigger than the upper part.
—Seemingly in contradiction with the rule, the ascenders are longer than the descenders. Or they may be the same length.

EKHXSB
EKHXSB

The optical middle is slightly higher than the mathematical one, here demonstrated by putting a letter series upside down under the original.

4.9.4.4. Character strokes

Characters are basically configurations of strokes. Traditionally, a number of 'optical corrections' are applied in some specific details of these configurations.
— Horizontal strokes will look thicker than vertical ones. So even the most geometrically shaped sans serif letters will be corrected in order to compensate for this effect.
—Stroke connections, like branches or crossings, always cause some visual clutter. The connections seem to be thicker at the connection points, like knots. To compensate for this effect, stroke connections are made thinner. Not only do our eyes create visual knots, printing ink tends to fill in between the connections, specially in smaller type sizes. Some typefaces are especially designed to compensate for this effect and catch the redundant ink in connection slits.
—The ends of strokes tend to visually round off a bit. Here as well,

Character strokes are visually corrected in a number of instances, as are stroke connections and stroke endings.

printing enhances this effect. To compensate for this optical illusion, the corners of the end strokes are made pointier.
—For that same reason, the flat parts of serifs are made a little bit curved. This makes the letters more elegant and less plump.

SS SS

an **an** an

Electronic letter manipulation may be handy, but only useful in very limited cases. It should not be used for creating italic or bold letters, for instance; that work should be left to type designers.

4.9.4.5. Electronic manipulation

Today, all typefaces are stored as electronic data. It is very easy to manipulate electronic data. All word processing and drawing software can, for instance, make existing type slanted or thicker 'on the fly'. These facilities cannot be considered proper typographical means. It is for the most part an improper use of technology, because the software is not sophisticated enough by far to create acceptable quality. Bold and Italic variations of a typeface must be created by design and not by electronic manipulation.

Of course, this is by no means an admonition not to use the abilities of the modern electronic media; it is meant to be an invitation to be very critical about the possibilities offered without losing a sharp eye for its potential. Changing the weight of characters to make visual appearance identical when used on both a light and a dark background is, for instance, something that can be done relatively easy by employing electronic means. This ability can be very handy in a signage design job.

Small text
Small text
Normal text
Normal text
Big text
Big text

Size influences the way we perceive text. Large letters can be more detailed, condensed, and have a tight letter spacing. By contrast, small letters need a larger x-height ratio, little detail and contrast, a bold stroke width and generous letter spacing.

4.9.4.6. Type size

The size of characters influences the way we perceive their shapes. During the first phases of the production of movable type, the moulds of each size of a typeface needed to be produced separately by hand. All moulds were adjusted slightly to accommodate the optical characteristics of the specific size produced. These methods of production have changed. Nowadays, often only one master is designed to produce all sizes, thus completely ignoring the way we perceive letter forms in relation to their size.
In principle, bigger letters can be more detailed and more elegant in shape than smaller ones. We gradually lose our sensitivity for detail and shape nuances when letters get smaller in size. To compensate for this effect, small letters have to be wider, have thicker strokes with less contrast, and need to be spaced wider.
Of course, it is important to realise that the size of a letter is strictly related to the reading distance. Regular typography made for print or screen will have a more or less fixed reading distance, but for signage purposes the situation is totally different. Reading distances may vary considerably. The principle remains the same, for the type size projected on our retina is the only thing that counts in the way we perceive shapes.

4.9.5. THE PRAGMATIC AND LINGUISTIC ASPECTS OF TYPE

Language has two strongly related outlets: a spoken version and a written one. Type and typography are the industrialised written version of language. Basically, typography consists of organised collections of sequences of individual graphic signs. Each sign has a specific function within each sequence. The kind of function may vary considerably; it may have a semantic or a syntactic purpose, but may also have a purely aesthetic one.

The difference between characters and glyphs: Characters are the individual graphic signs within a writing system. Glyphs are the various visual representations of a character. A glyph is by definition unique. A character is part of a generally accepted script convention.

A typeface has to carry at least one example (a master) of every individual graphic sign needed to do the job. The number of different graphic signs needed may be huge even for signage purposes. Some expressions are used in an attempt to classify the different types of graphic signs. 'Characters' and 'glyphs' are terms used to make a basic distinction between different kinds of signs. The glyphs stand for the full collection of all unique shapes in a typeface. One glyph may vary from another only in minor details, like having a thicker stroke, or being slightly slanted. The characters stand for all the different basic shapes, for instance, the different letters in an alphabet. Put in other words, glyphs refer to the specific shapes in a given typeface or font, and characters refer to the type of sign employed. Different typefaces may very well share the same collection of characters—standardised character sets exist for obvious reasons—but will never share the same glyphs. Glyphs are by definition unique shapes, belonging exclusively to a specific font family.

Another distinction used is between a 'typeface' and a 'font'. A typeface is the name given to a collection of visually closely related graphic signs. A font is the collection of formal data needed to effectively use and show or print each sign in the typeface. Today, typefaces may consist of very large collections of glyphs. A typeface may be split up into different font files. These large collections are called 'font families'.

Categories are hardly ever completely consistent, so the

distinction between the set of characters (or repertoire) and the glyphic variations of this set in the members of the font family is not clear cut, but it is a help to describe the large collection of graphic signs in a typeface.

4.9.5.1. *Character set or repertoire*

All human knowledge will result at some stage or other in the invention of a new graphic sign, used as a 'shortcut' to describe a new notion. Ever-growing knowledge means the universe of graphic signs is not a static one, but is expanding at an accelerating pace it seems, like our real universe. Graphic signs are called characters when used in fonts. Some characters are widely used, like the ones we use in common language, and some have a very specific and limited use.

To create some order, we speak of alphabetical and non-alphabetical characters. The first category of characters are also called letters.

—Our Latin alphabet consist of 26 letters. These come in two variations, a lower case version and a capital or upper case version. The names upper and lower case refer to the traditional location in the typesetter's cabinet where lead letters were stored. We only need both variations of the alphabet for syntactical reasons.

—Some of the 26 letters also have accented versions, mostly to accommodate the various languages that make use of the Latin script.

—Numerals are first in the category of non-alphabetical characters. The numerals we use have a non-Western origin. Our capital letters come from the Roman stone inscriptions; our lower case letters were developed to speed up handwriting and accommodate more efficient ways of communication when the French took over power from the Romans; our numerals come from the Arabic script. At the time of its development, the Arabs were scientifically ahead of Western civilisations.

Ten numerals are standard. Additional numerals can include fractioned numbers (originally used for interest rates) and superior or inferior numbers (for mathematical notations or reference marks). The latter are called superscript and subscript in the US.

—Punctuation marks help ease of reading when used in moderation. They eliminate ambiguity in text. Their use is slightly different depending on the language.

—Symbols are the ever-expanding collection of specific characters. They mark the development of our culture. Standard symbol sets may include everyday mathematical symbols, currency symbols, traditional typographical symbols (such as a paragraph symbol) or legal symbols (like the copyright or trademark symbol). Recently, the ancient '@' symbol has been given a new life as a universal symbol in all email addresses.

Character sets are more or less standardised. Originally, standards were made for the production of typewriters, but when documents started to be sent electronically, standardisation became a

The various categories in a (standard) character set for Latin script.

ABCDEFGHI
JKLMNOPQ
RSTUVWXYZ

Capital letters

abcdefghijkl
mnopqrstuv
wxyz

Lower case letters

éüçåêø

Language letter variations

1234567890

Numerals (tabular)

½ ¼ ¾ 12 12

Fractions, superior and inferior numerals

.,;:(-)?!'

Punctuation marks

+=%#@$&

Symbols

Standard character sets can be extended to create a font family. Font families tend to keep growing all the time.

ABCDEFGHI
JKLMNOPQR
STUVWXYZ

Small caps

1234567890
1234567890

Numerals (medieval and small tabular)

œßffifh

Ligatures

RNRtm

Swashes

Multi-script extensions

§♡

Dingbats, pictograms

abc abc **abc**
abc abc

Weight variation extensions

a a a

Proportion variation extensions

abcdefghijkl

Italic or oblique

abc abc

Style variation extensions

Alternate (unconventional) characters

must. The sender and the receiver both had to use the same electronic codes to represent identical characters. American companies and institutions are responsible for the development of these standards. Now there is an international standard of character codes that comprises 'all' world languages. It is called the Unicode. Still, business practices in the US have an enormous influence on the available standards, since American companies produce most hardware and software for the computers we all use.

4.9.5.2. Font family

Most (text) typefaces are issued with at least one font file containing a complete standard character set. Decorative or display typefaces, as well as 'titling' typefaces, may hold only a reduced number of characters. A lot of typefaces have more than one font file— in other words, have more members in their family. The extension of a font family may go in three directions. The first is the extension of adding more characters than a standard character set; this extension is often called an 'expert' set. The second is the addition of the traditional form variations in stroke weight and letter proportions. The third is a relatively new extension in the addition of style variations: serif, sans serif, and other.
An overview of the various extensions is given below.

—Traditional alternate character shape extension. There are two types of alternate character variations. First, small capital letters —Small Caps—are precisely what the name says they are: these capitals are smaller than capital letters and only slightly bigger than the x-height. They are used for abbreviations and in headings. Second, mediaeval (old style) numerals are designed to match more nicely with the lower case letters than the standard tabular or lining numerals, which are made to use in tables so that all numbers have a fixed height and width. Mediaeval numerals are the best choice for signage purposes. It is somewhat mysterious why tabular numerals are designed to be the same height as capital letters. There is hardly any functional need for this clumsy size, quite the contrary. Only recently have typefaces been designed with smaller—and far more functional—tabular numerals. At times, type design seems to hold to its traditions surprisingly long.
—Aesthetic enhancements/extensions also come in two variations. First, ligatures are characters that consist of two or three difficult letter combinations, like 'fi' for instance. These combinations are made into one shape to aesthetically enhance their visual representation.
Second, so-called 'swashes' are embellishments (curled extensions) on both capital and lower case letters. They may be used at the beginning and at the end of sentences.
—Multi-script extensions make typesetting in one type style possible for different scripts: for instance Japanese-Latin, or Arabic-Latin. This is an important feature for many signage jobs.

—Special symbol or 'dingbat' extensions will serve the need for specific symbols, or the desire to show more 'fun' within the same type style. Symbol and Dingbat fonts are also issued totally independently from any specific typeface.
—Weight variation extensions are the the traditional variations in stroke weight. There are three basic variations, a light, a medium (regular or book), and a bold version. Extended families may carry ultra light, semi-light, semi-bold, extra-bold, and ultra-bold (or black).
—Proportional variation extensions will go in two directions, a condensed and an extended variation. Four variations is the maximum in most cases: ultra-condensed, condensed, extended (wide) and ultra-extended (ultra-wide)
—Angle variation extensions. Normal 'straight' text is called Roman, the slightly slanted variation is called Italic or Oblique. The name Italic is the generic name and is also used for the oblique variation. However, there is a significant difference between a true Italic and an Oblique version. The oblique is a slightly slanted version of the Roman characters. The name Italic originates from an Italian calligraphic style; basically, a different style than the one we use for our lower case letters. This means that in addition to the slanted overall direction of all letters, some characters also have different 'skeleton' shapes, like for instance an '*a*' and an 'a'. Italics, in principle, are used for emphasising parts in a text, and do this job better than the oblique variations.
—Style variation extensions are a growing trend in type design. It is in principle an endless range. A number of typefaces are now available with serif, sans serif and semi serif or semi sans variations. Some have a 'monospaced' version (letter spacing like an old fashioned typewriter). Some have variations in a 'script' style, or even a 'blackletter' or some other style. Some typefaces come in all kinds of contour variations. Modern digital technology requires little investment to develop just another variation.
—Unconventional alternate characters. More and more typefaces are issued that include several unconventional alternate versions of a single character. There is no other need for these eccentric variations than the possibility to create a personalised version of an existing typeface. In fact, using particular letter shapes is characteristic of personal handwriting. Alternate characters bring this same quality into the realm of typography.

Making more variations available within one typeface tends to lead to exponential growth. A font family may easily become colossal in size. Some typefaces already deserve that name. It is questionable whether any useful purpose is served on occasions where growth seems to have got out of control. Mammoth fonts are likely to suffer from a sort of elephantiasis.

Digital production, combined with the need for personalised fonts, has led to font production whereby users can create their own font variation within the limits of two or three given

parameters. 'Multiple Master Fonts' is a font technology created by Adobe for this purpose. There are a limited number of typefaces around that make use of this technology which could be specifically useful for signage jobs.
Recently, more eccentric font developments allow personal variation using far more parameters, including 'mood' and 'stylistic' variations.

4.9.6. TYPE TECHNOLOGY

The technology to manufacture and to reproduce type has undergone dramatic changes in the past 25 years. Originally, type production—and the whole graphic industry—worked with tangible objects. A lot of typographic expressions still refer to that period. These expressions have become somewhat confusing in the current environment where all font production has become intangible. Not only fonts, but practically all manufacturing is computerised in some way or other, which means that input and processing is exclusively done in a digital format. For type reproduction this means the unavoidable involvement of machines that only 'eat bytes and excrete dots'. But the 'dot' reproduction on paper or on screen is far too limited to describe the current possibilities of type reproduction. As a matter of fact, the reproduction of type can be done (in principle) in any conceivable output. That fact is a bit overwhelming. However, we have to realise that we always had 'endless' possibilities with the help of others to translate and/or execute a message in whatever language, script, medium or material we wanted. The involvement of others is now less necessary. Increasingly, available software is doing all kinds of transformation or translation extremely fast and accurately. Today a text message can be electronically translated into many languages, (wirelessly) transmitted, made visible on screen or on paper, cut out of a plethora of materials from thin plastic foil to thick granite, made audible or tangible in any possible way. Effectively, means of transportation, translation, manipulation, and output will soon become practically limitless.

Digitisation of both our human communication and the instruction of machines has created a very fluid environment. Electronic data may be transported—and also altered—at the speed of light in vast quantities. Software applications create possibilities for manipulating data in order to overcome any constraint or to blend into any environment. But they also make it easy to create intentional obstacles and limitations, or even to corrupt data.
As with water, changes take effect very fast and may become a devastating force. Smooth applications are sometimes hindered by the commercial interests of individual companies. Business alliances between manufacturers change constantly and so do the possibilities of combining different software. This has led to a sort of general 'update terror' pushing users to a situation where hardware as well as software needs frequent replacement with newer versions to avoid incompatibility. The Digital Revolution

has unleashed almost limitless possibilities for communication and production, but effective applications may have a short life after initial installation. Many updates have questionable advantages other than the obvious commercial benefits for manufacturers. The average user effectively employs only a small fraction of all the possibilities offered.

The position of type designers and font foundries has changed completely with the arrival of the Digital Age. Type production used to be closely linked with fairly heavy investment in production machines and technology. That link has disappeared entirely, along with all non-digital technology for type production. A manufacturing tradition that served us for centuries has been erased in no more than two decades. Type design no longer needs a close connection with manufacturers. A lot of type designers issue their own designs these days, while others work for hardware or software developers, or for users who want their own specific typeface. Font design no longer requires investment in hardware to produce type. The type designer has all the design, production and distribution facilities needed in his own desktop computer. Investments are reduced to the labour input of the type designer. Type and fonts have become completely immaterial. Even the notion of 'original' and 'copy of the original' have disappeared. There is no longer an original model or drawing. Original design and copy are completely identical. What's more, by buying a font, in most cases, we have access to the most relevant data of the font. Fonts can easily be altered and distributed illegally. The contrast with the original situation that lasted for centuries could not be greater. Matrices of fonts used to be the core assets of some quite large businesses; now everyone who owns a computer possesses hundreds or even thousands of font 'matrices'.

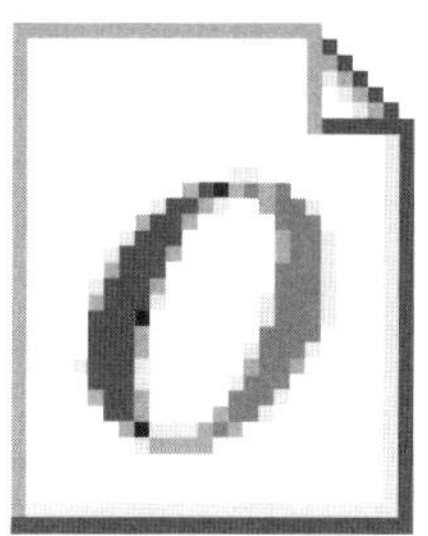

The most important font formats, from top to bottom. Postscript was the first, developed by Adobe. TrueType was the second, developed by Apple. The latest addition is called OpenType, developed by Adobe and Microsoft. OpenType is intended to be platform independent.

4.9.6.1. Font formats

Not all fonts can be used on all output devices. All font buyers wish this situation were different. Regrettably, there are a few obstacles between this wish and the reality of current business practice. It will be interesting to see how positions will change —or not—in the future.
There are different ways for the digital data of a font to be constructed and stored. Moreover, fonts always need a software application, such as word processing software, to manifest themselves effectively. In turn, application software needs hardware, such as a screen or a printer, to create visible results and thus become of any use to us. Manufacturers and software developers inevitably have to comply with mutual standards to make compatibility between applications that contain fonts possible. Mutual standards are pretty hard to establish, as most businesses prefer to follow a strategy of pursuing complete market dominance instead, resulting in commercial 'wars' of competing proprietary systems that have been raging since the beginning of the

digital revolution. The 'condition humaine' to overestimate the superiority of one's own ideas—especially with successful individuals—has advantages but often creates embarrassing limitations too.
The commercial battle is in itself nothing new. It has a very long history and is at the core of the currently prevailing liberal economic system, and supposedly responsible for much economic and technological progress. Commercial battles tend to be pretty short-sighted and rather unbalanced, to put it mildly. Some say it urgently needs adult guidance to serve our general well-being. Besides, we have reached the physical limits of economic competition. Competition—for the time being—is impossible beyond the boundaries of our planet, while globalisation implies the need for mutual standards that enable us to communicate with everyone on a global level. Business competition is unlikely to deliver those standards other than through (illegal) monopoly power. This leaves the initiative to international institutions or spontaneous 'freeware' initiatives. The latter being a totally new economic force underlining the different positions in the global digital era.

A font is a basic ingredient of visual communication. Originally, fonts were entirely proprietary to specific output devices. That is no longer the case, although fonts are not universally applicable (as they should be). There are three major 'standard font formats' around:
—Postscript is the name of the software Adobe released in 1984. Adobe is an American company that laid the foundation for the digitisation of the graphics industry. As a result of this, Adobe also became one of the most important font foundries.
—True Type is a competing font format later developed by Apple. It has a number of advantages over the Postscript format, including the ending of Apple's royalty payments to Adobe. Oddly enough, the True Type format became more important for Microsoft than for Apple itself.
—Open Type is the result of a collaboration between Microsoft and Adobe. It 'combines' the technologies of the two previous font formats. Open Type is also based on the Unicode standard for worldwide character encoding, which, in principle, makes it a font format with almost limitless possibilities for character output, including the application of different scripts within one font family. Open Type was introduced as an 'open format' to end all incompatibilities in font formats between different software platforms. Some skepticism about the final result of Open Type seems reasonable, taking into consideration the historical business practices of both companies that started Open Type.

4.9.6.2 Vector drawing formats

All shapes and drawings must be digitally stored in one of two types of format: as 'bitmaps' (little dots) or as 'vectors' (line drawings). Fonts originally contained both type of files, one for

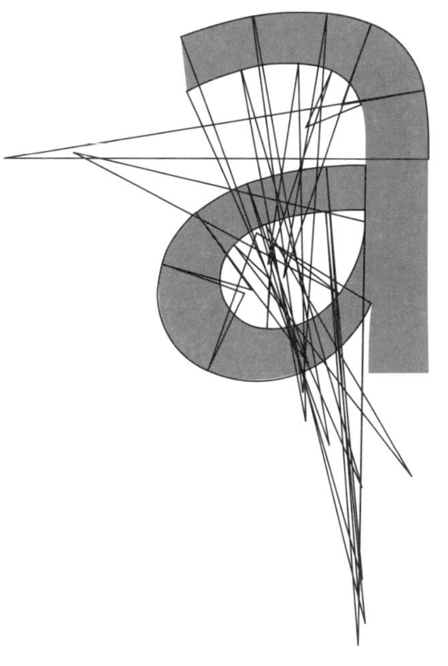

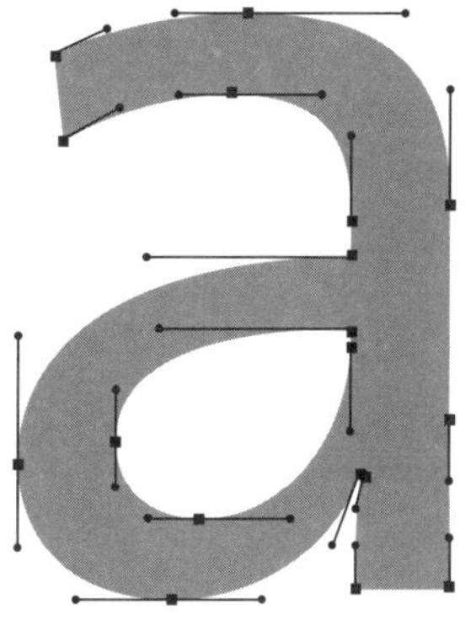

Engineers and graphic designers both make vector drawings. However, there is a difference between the types of vectors used. CAD-CAM drawings are still based on straight lines in combination with circle segments, whereas graphics software is based on 'splines' to define all curved lines. Sign manufacturers cannot always use spline vectors for their automated machines. The conversion from one format to the other may be problematic. Left above, CAD-CAM, right graphic splines.

reproduction on screen and one for the printer. That is no longer needed; the (vector) drawings of all characters may be used for both print and screen reproduction. Vector drawings are not used only for graphic purposes. Vectors can also be used for all kinds of cutting or routing machines. The sign-making industry thrives on this possibility. There is a fundamental difference, though, in the way traditional production machines for construction store drawing information. Traditionally, all engineering drawings are based on straight lines and (parts of) circles. All Computer Aided Design (or Manufacturing), in short CAD-CAM, is still based on this old principle. By contrast, all graphic software is based on another principle. The major difference between the two is the way curves are described. CAD software does this with the measures of circle radiuses, while graphic software is based on more complicated mathematical formulae for creating (describing) curves, called 'splines'.

There is software around that converts the two drawing formats into each other, but sometimes it still leads to unpleasant surprises, such as letter forms being redrawn or traced in an unprofessional or even sloppy manner. Signage designers now have unprecedented possibilities with their text files, but one shouldn't take proper execution for granted. Signage designers must remain very alert to this possibility.

4.9.6.3. Font hinting instructions

When text is reproduced on a screen or in print at a small size, so-called 'hinting instructions', which can be part of the font file, become important. The quality of these instructions will determine the quality of the reproduction of the letters. All glyph shapes will ultimately be reproduced, not in solid shapes, but in small dots, called pixels, when shown on a screen. The potential

problem arises when the vector drawings (called outlines) of the individual glyphs have to be translated into a pattern of small dots. When the grid pattern of the dots—called a raster—is very small and the letters rather large, the problem will not be visible, but in all other cases the quality will deteriorate and reading will become awkward. Screens have on average a far coarser grid than print, so text reproduction on screens is particularly sensitive to good hinting instructions.
The hinting instructions will influence the way the outlines 'fit' over the raster in order to optimise the rastered result. What it does is basically avoid irregularities in the reproduction, as these may occur for instance when a stem of a letter contains sometimes one and at other times two dots or pixels. The instructions will

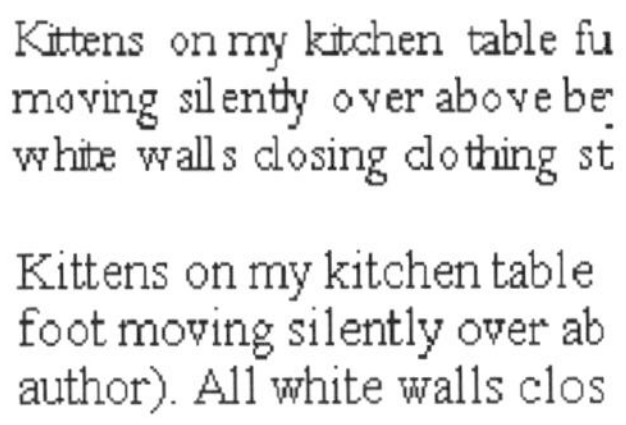

Kittens on my kitchen table fu
moving silently over above be
white walls closing clothing st

Kittens on my kitchen table
foot moving silently over ab
author). All white walls clos

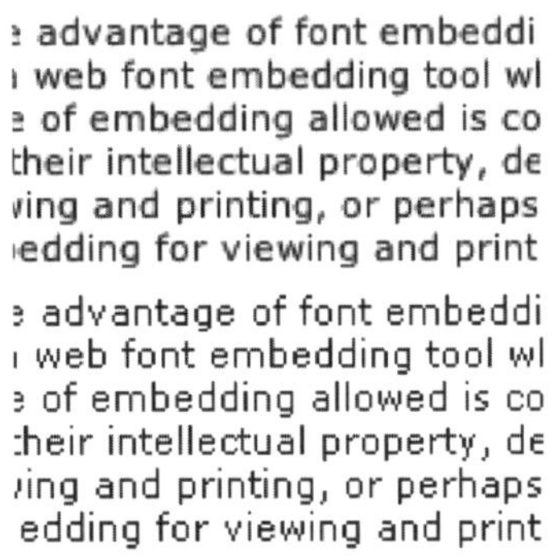

e advantage of font embeddi
web font embedding tool wl
e of embedding allowed is co
their intellectual property, de
ving and printing, or perhaps
bedding for viewing and print

e advantage of font embeddi
web font embedding tool wl
e of embedding allowed is co
their intellectual property, de
ving and printing, or perhaps
edding for viewing and print

Left:
A not 'hinted' font (top) and a hinted version where the outlines are optimised for the pixel grid. The crisp image is rare, since today practically all text on screens is anti-aliased.

Right:
Two identical text representations on a screen: the top version is anti-aliased, the bottom is not. There are a lot of different ways to 'smooth' letters, especially when reproduced on LCD screens. The most advanced methods use the RGB 'sub-pixels' to soften the jagged letter image.

ensure that the consistency of reproduction will be maintained in all cases. There are a number of ways of adding these instructions to a font file, relating to the way the 'rasteriser' works in the software that will be used.
When e-books came on the market, the interest in screen reproduction of text grew. Manufacturers promoted new software to improve screen representation, like 'Cleartype' (Microsoft) or 'Cooltype' (Monotype Imaging). These improvements were slight variations on traditional ways of dealing with 'jagged' images on a screen. To smooth the contours of the pixelised image, halftone (gray) pixels were used. This method is called anti-aliasing.
Surprisingly, font foundries hardly ever indicate the type of hinting instructions in their fonts, while in fact good hinting involves a considerable amount of work and may significantly improve reproduction quality. The other methods of anti-aliasing depend on the software used. Sometimes it will be possible to select one type of screen representation over another.

4.9.6.4. Working with type technology

Few professional activities have undergone such dramatic changes as the way we deal with type. A whole traditional profession of well-educated—and professionally often well organised—typesetters have practically disappeared, basically leaving the execution of their skills to the authors of the text themselves, or to graphic designers, or to anybody else more or less able to deal

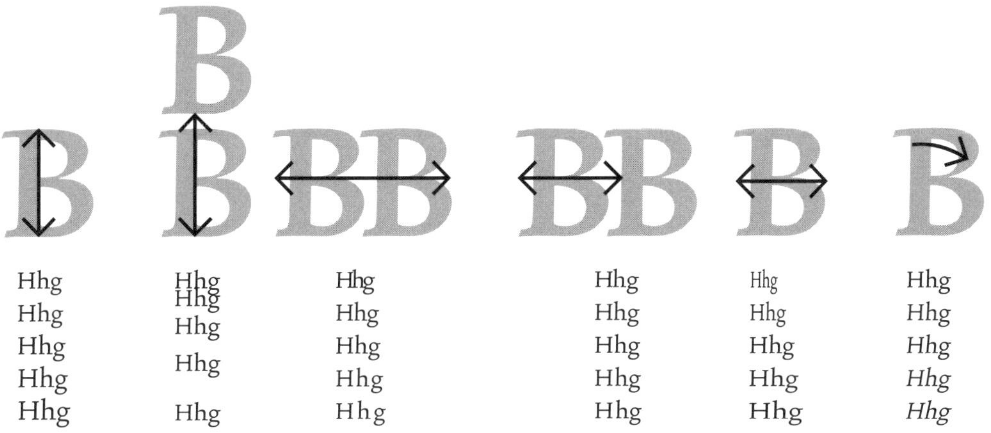

with computers. Everyone owning a computer can now do what these professionals used to do for us for centuries. In a technical sense, computer owners can do now far more than the traditional typesetters ever could. While sitting at our computer screen we can all manipulate type in practically every way we want far more easily and with far more possibilities than ever before. We can easily make alterations in, or additions to, the typeface we use. We can interfere in every way we wish with the designs offered to us. Unsolicited co-authorship lies within a mouse-click. There is no restriction whatsoever, except the ones we voluntarily impose upon ourselves (within the boundaries—of course—of the font license agreement and copyright law).
In this respect, it wouldn't hurt to realise that while the possibilities to create graphic images ourselves have exploded, the educated skill to use these possibilities sensibly has not grown at the same pace or manner. The major traditional skills needed to produce good type have remained in principle the same. The potential design power under our fingertips has grown immensely, yet training the eyes to create beauty takes just as much time and effort as it used to. About five years to learn and ten more to master.

An overview of the most elementary way by which we can specify type on our screens (and for print). The level of precision is one hundredth of either a millimetre or an inch. From left to right: type size, leading, overall letter spacing, individual letter spacing adjustments, letter width (not recommendable), slanting (not recommendable).

4.9.7. TYPE AND SIGNAGE

Producing good typography for signage is for the most part not very different than doing it for all other types of design. Signage has some specific aspects, though. Most typography is composed in a more or less compact format. Signage, by definition, is not. The individual items of a comprehensive signage system are spread over a large area. The user must be willing (and capable) to browse the environment to make proper use of the entire system. Signage is three-dimensional typography in the true sense of the word. Also the scope of the different types of users in signage projects is exceptionally large. Signage projects aim to reach by far the widest audience of any typography job, probably in most cases beyond realistic expectations.

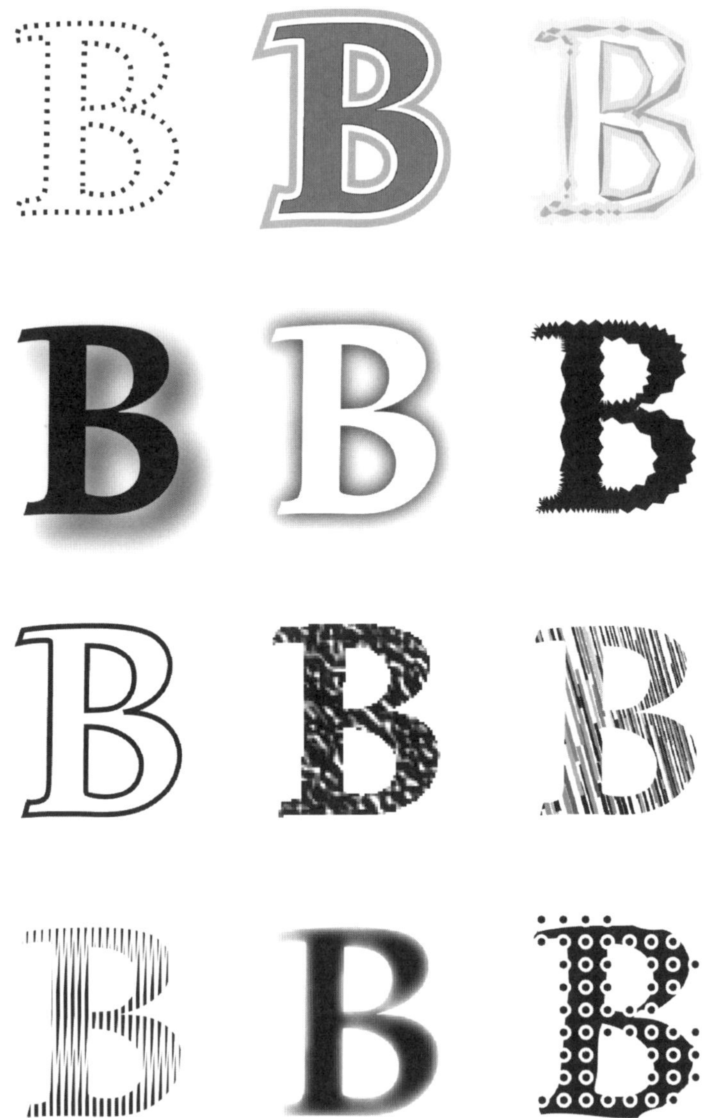

The graphical representation of a typeface has effectively become limitless. Earlier constraints have all disappeared.

Visualising 3D letter designs has become quite easy with our standard computer software tool box (of Pandora).

4.9.7.1. Legibility and readability

The obvious basic criteria for functional typography is that individual characters are legible and the composed text is readable. Readability is a slightly more complex process than legibility, because it is likely that most of us read, not by recognising strings of individual letters—which is the norm of legibility—but by recognising the image of complete words, parts of words, or even combinations of words.

A lot of research has been done to discover which typefaces are most legible and/or readable. The result of all this research has not contributed much to any deeper insight other than the confirmation of what was already known through well-trained typographers, nor did it have any considerable impact on the typographic profession. This is not very surprising since reading is a learned (nurtured) capability, thus based on what has been offered to us (for instance, by typographers). We are likely to read best what looks closest to what we have been taught, or we are accustomed to read. In short, we read best what we read most. Research will only confirm this empirical fact. We do not have any predispositioned qualities for reading or shape recognition. All our capabilities in this respect are the result of our habits.
A significant research result that may support this view has found that practically all white-skinned people have problems in recognising faces of other races. The opposite is just as true.
There are no human genetic qualities to be discovered that developed especially for reading or visual recognition. We have not been reading long enough for such a development to occur. Besides, it seems unlikely that individual reading capabilities will ever be part of preferable human reproduction qualities. This leaves our physical and individual visual capabilities to explore. The boundaries of our visual capabilities have been sufficiently known for a long time; they vary considerably per individual and change dramatically with age. Yet the desire for more research on readability seems unstoppable, despite the near certainty that such research is most likely a further waste of time and money.

In some cases, the quest for finding a scientific basis for ultimate readability leads to slightly annoying initiatives. Here are a few examples:
—Signage often has safety aspects. Clearly, typography should also serve safety requirements in the best possible way. However, this should be done without losing a proper perspective of its importance relative to the other factors involved. The contribution of typography in the rather complex conditions that determine optimal safe conditions is extremely small. Spatial, lighting, and interactive conditions, and content of signs, are far more important components, but far more complex to research. The fact that typeface legibility is a research pet should not result in an overestimation of the contribution of a specific typeface to safety. Consistent use of a once selected typeface, is obviously another

matter. Maintaining a certain level of consistency is one of the keys to enhanced safety. Most signage schemes still fail miserably in this respect.
—Many governmental or semi-governmental bodies issue recommendations or guidelines for signage, aiming for better readability or enhanced safety. A lot of these guidelines are far too specific and detailed, and are therefore more likely to obstruct finding the most appropriate solutions. Guidelines are often based on rigid design ideas (or even bad taste in the worst cases)

2 2 2 2

g g g G

rather than solid scientific evidence. The often recommended sans serif typefaces —contrary to the recommendations—are not more suitable for signage purposes than serif typefaces. This is a particularly persistent misconception.
The (subjective) influence of the researchers themselves on the (objective) outcome of the research results are well known. It is very likely that the somewhat odd letter shapes that we see on highway signs are the work of unskilled letter-tinkering engineers involved in research projects testing readability. The type designs seem to be based more on an engineer's sense of aesthetics than on solid visual perception evidence. Research results about readability have sometimes contradictory outcomes. Again, the personal visual preferences in the team of researchers seem to be an important factor in the findings.
—Typographical guidelines for signage also seem to be a regulator's favourite—at times with rather disturbing results. A European committee thought it wise to develop a European typeface, called 'Eurofont', to become mandatory for all European traffic signs. Beside being a perplexing misconception of the apparent priorities in European governance, developing mandatory European typefaces shows a failure to understand the importance of the European cultural heritage. The various visual

By far the highest budgets for typeface development are dedicated to signage for highways and roads. Multi-disciplinary teams are often involved in the process, in the past often without a type designer as a member of the team. The research results seem to express the aesthetic preferences of the engineers within the team. When (type) designers are involved, the research outcome is different.
From left to right: type developed for British roads in collaboration with designer Jock Kinneir (1963), type for US roads originally developed (1950) by Theodore Forbes for CalTrans, the 'Cleartype' font released in 2004 after years of development by a large team including type designers, and type for French roads that still expresses engineers' geometry.

cultures in Europe need preservation, if anything, and certainly not aesthetic normalisation. That would only lead to a dramatic loss. Moreover, traffic regulations still vary quite considerably within Europe. One member country, for instance, remains persistent in driving on the 'wrong side' of the road. More intense travel within Europe might become more comfortable and even safer by developing some form of standardisation in existing regulations, but it is hard to see what one uniform typeface could contribute where existing traffic regulations are still fundamentally different among the various EU countries. Typeface standardisation for European traffic signs is really a few bridges too far; in fact, it is a rather upsetting way of wasting taxpayer's money, even by governmental standards.

The sobering truth is that only a few pretty straightforward facts have some influence on the legibility or readability, of text on signs.
—Serifs help to guide the eyes along the individual lines of a text, so serif typefaces tend to do better for reading long texts than non-serifs.
—When the characters are very small, or observed from a long distance, details will diminish or disappear. Characters should be shaped as simply as possible under these circumstances, so sans serifs are likely to do better in these conditions than serifs. In this case, the psychological factor (habit) and the physiological one (eyesight quality) will balance each other out.
—Extreme conditions, like very small type or type seen from afar, also need slightly wider and even letter spacing. In general, it is likely that evenly balanced and neutrally spaced type reads best. Only under extreme conditions should type be set with wide letter and word spacing.

4.9.7.2. Special signage fonts

Some typefaces are specifically designed for signage projects. A few of these designs have even had some influence on typeface design in general. As said already, there is not a lot of difference in the way we read signs compared with all the other kinds of material we read. Yet, there are some specific constraints and it is useful to have some background knowledge about typefaces specifically designed for signage.

Let's start with an overview of the landmarks in the typefaces developed and/or used for signage projects.
—The typefaces used for signage design are often sans serif typefaces. However, there is no traditional link between the two. Unserifed letter forms have existed alongside the serifed ones throughout history. It is interesting to note that the first sans serif was cut in Paris in 1789. It was meant only to be used as embossed type for the blind to read with their fingers. The first sans-serif typeface for print was cut by William Caslon in 1812.
—Sans serifs became popular at the end of the nineteenth, and the

ABCDEFGHI
JKLMNOPQ
RSTUVWXYZ
abcdefghijkl
mnopqrstuv
wxyz
1234567890

1. *Akzidenz Grotesk*

ABCDEFGHI
JKLMNOPQ
RSTUVWXYZ
abcdefghijkl
mnopqrstuv
wxyz
1234567890

2. Franklin Gothic

ABCDEFGHI
JKLMNOPQ
RSTUVWXYZ
abcdefghijkl
mnopqrstuv
wxyz
1234567890

3. *Johnston*

ABCDEFGHI
JKLMNOPQ
RSTUVWXYZ
abcdefghijkl
mnopqrstuv
wxyz
1234567890

4. *Gill Sans*

ABCDEFGHI
JKLMNOPQ
RSTUVWXYZ
abcdefghijkl
mnopqrstuv
wxyz
1234567890

5. *Futura*

ABCDEFGHI
JKLMNOPQ
RSTUVWXYZ
abcdefghijkl
mnopqrstuv
wxyz
1234567890

6. *Helvetica*

Most of the examples of typefaces shown on these sample pages are not the original designs. The old ones had to be digitised to work on modern machines. Moreover, the original designs were made to be reproduced in book print. Popular typefaces will also be 'style updated' from time to time, in order to keep a modern image. Regrettably, over time the (re)designs often do not improve the original quality.

1. Akzidenz Grotesk, released in 1898 by Berthold in *Germany was extremely influential on signage design of large scale projects in the 1960s and 70s.*

2. Franklin Gothic, designed by Morris Fuller Benton and released in 1904 by ATF. It was *the American response to a strong European design dominance at the time.*

3. *The typeface for the London* Underground Railways, *designed by* Edward Johnston, *originally only for use in print, issued in 1916.*

4. Gill Sans, *designed by* Eric Gill *in 1927.* Eric Gill *was a student of* Edward Johnston *and the* Gill *became an immensely successful typeface.*

5. Futura *was designed by* Paul Renner *and issued in 1927.* Futura *is an authentic expression of the German* Bauhaus *design philosophy. It is still one of the most rigorously geometrical typefaces around.*

6. Helvetica *was originally issued under the name* 'Neue Haas Grotesk' *and released in 1957. The designer was* Max Miedingen. *The* Helvetica *is still one of the most widely sold typefaces and is often specified for signage projects.*

7. Univers was released at about the same time as the Helvetica in 1957. However, the design concept better anticipated the technological developments during that period. The designer is Adrian Frutiger.

8. Frutiger, by the same designer. This typefaces was designed for the new Paris Airport in 1975. It became a very popular typeface for print.

9. A typeface designed for the British Ministry of Transport in 1963 to be used for road signs. The designs were made by a team including two of the first specialised signage designers: Jock Kinneir and Margaret Calvert.

10. A sample of the large collection of 'Standard Alphabets for Traffic Control Devices' first published in 1945 by the US Bureau of Public Roads. This collection of typefaces is also called the Highway Gothic. Tobias Frère-Jones designed the Interstate based on these fonts. Cleartype is the font name of the latest development, scheduled to replace the original collection.

11. TheSans, designed in 1987 by Lucas de Groot as a spin-off of a commission by the Dutch Ministry of Transportation and Water management.

12. Scala, designed in 1988 by Martin Majoor for a Dutch Music Centre. In 1990 it was issued under its current font name.

ABCDEFGHI
JKLMNOPQ
RSTUVWXYZ
abcdefghijkl
mnopqrstuv
wxyz
1234567890

7. Univers

ABCDEFGHI
JKLMNOPQ
RSTUVWXYZ
abcdefghijkl
mnopqrstuv
wxyz
1234567890

8. Frutiger

ABCDEFGHI
JKLMNOPQ
RSTUVWXYZ
abcdefghijkl
mnopqrstuv
wxyz
1234567890

9. Transport

ABCDEFGHI
JKLMNOPQ
RSTUVWXYZ
abcdefghijkl
mnopqrstuv
wxyz
1234567890

10. Interstate

ABCDEFGHI
JKLMNOPQ
RSTUVWXYZ
abcdefghijkl
mnopqrstuv
wxyz
1234567890

11. TheSans

ABCDEFGHI
JKLMNOPQ
RSTUVWXYZ
abcdefghijkl
mnopqrstuv
wxyz
1234567890

12. Scala

ABCDEFGHI
JKLMNOPQ
RSTUVWXYZ
abcdefghijkl
mnopqrstuv
wxyz
1234567890

13. PMN Caecilia

ABCDEFGHI
JKLMNOPQ
RSTUVWXYZ
abcdefghijkl
mnopqrstuv
wxyz
1234567890

14. Triplex Serif

ABCDEFGHI
JKLMNOPQ
RSTUVWXYZ
abcdefghijkl
mnopqrstuv
wxyz
1234567890

15. Sun Antiqua

ABCDEFGHI
JKLMNOPQ
RSTUVWXYZ
abcdefghijkl
mnopqrstuv
wxyz
1234567890

16. Warnock Pro

ABCDEFGHI
JKLMNOPQ
RSTUVWXYZ
abcdefghijkl
mnopqrstuv
wxyz
1234567890

17. Mendoza

ABCDEFGHI
JKLMNOPQ
RSTUVWXYZ
abcdefghijkl
mnopqrstuv
wxyz
1234567890

18. Trinité

The range of typefaces suitable for signage projects is far wider than the traditional pick of bold sans serif fonts. In fact, all well-designed text typefaces may be applicable, but only the use of character sets with a low contrast (difference between the thick and thin strokes) are recommended.

13. PMN Caecilia, designed by Peter Matthias Noordzij.

14. Triplex Serif designed By Zuzana Licko in 1989.

15. Sun Antiqua, designed by Lucas de Groot, originally designed for Sun Microsystems in the US in 2001.

16. Warnock Pro (captions), designed by Robert Slimbach in 2000 for Adobe. The font is named after John Warnock, one of the founders of Adobe. This typeface is on the limit of a for signage acceptable letter contrast.

17. Mendoza, designed by José Almeida Mendoza in 1990.

18. Trinité, designed in 1982 by Bram de Does.

Typefaces used for signage do not necessarily have to be bold in weight. The 'book' weight may also lead to satisfactory results.

beginning of the twentieth century. The influential Akzidenz Grotesk was issued by the Berthold type foundry in Germany in 1898. The Franklin Gothic was designed in 1904 by Morris Fuller Benton and issued by ATF (the American Type Founders Company), an initiative to counter the huge European dominance in those days. Mr. Benton did that almost single-handedly. He designed 275 typefaces for his father, who ran the company.

—Edward Johnston was commissioned by the London Underground Railways to design a typeface to be used for promotional material and signage. The typeface was issued in 1916 and is still in use in an updated version called the New Johnston. The typeface design went contrary to the 'constructivist' and 'geometrical' style of that period. The immensely successful typeface Gill designed in 1927 by Eric Gill, was influenced by Johnston's Railway Type. Gill was a student of Johnston.

—The Futura is a very geometrical typeface designed by Paul Renner and issued in 1927. The design had considerable influence on the design of sans serif typefaces.

—The nineteen-fifties and early sixties marked the development

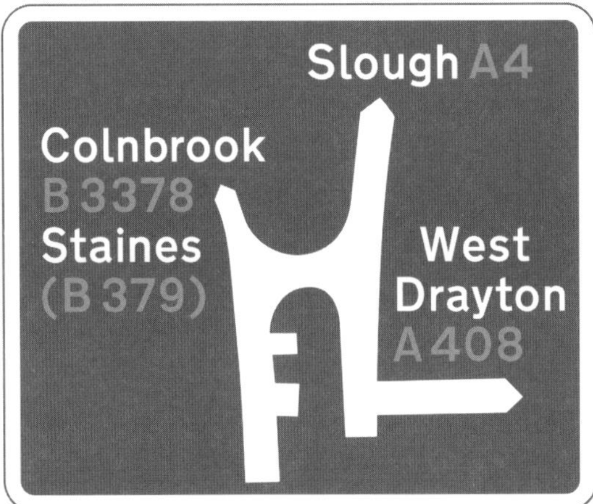

John Kinneir and Margaret Calvert were the designers in the team that designed the British road signs. The designs were first implemented in the sixties and are still in use. It remains an excellent example of accessible and clear information design, although some recent developments allow for too many codes and colours, which water down the original simplicity.

of the Neo-Gothics and Neo-Grotesks. The Helvetica, originally issued under the name 'Neue Haas Grotesk' (1957), designed by Max Miedingen, and the Univers (1957), by Adrian Frutiger, became blockbuster fonts. Helvetica became especially a 'darling' for signage design.

—Jock Kinneir and Margaret Calvert were commissioned by the British Ministry of Transport to design a new system of road signs. The first were installed in 1963. The designs became famous examples of how to make complex road structures easy to comprehend. Jock Kinneir also designed typefaces based on the Akzidenz Grotesk to be used on the signs. Jock Kinneir and his partners were most likely the first recognised signage designers. He was involved in many important signage projects, especially in the UK, such as the extensive identity project for British Rail, which had a profound impact on signage design. Jock Kinneir initially worked as an apprentice under Eric Gill.

—The sixties and seventies marked the start of many extensive visual identity programmes, often with related signage projects. Sans serif typefaces were almost without exception the first choice during that period. This type style fitted best in the prevailing spirit of large-scale 'efficient' design. The trendsetting signage for the New York subway system and Schiphol Airport in Amsterdam were both based on the Akzidenz Grotesk.
—Adrian Frutiger was commissioned to design a typeface for the new Parisian Airport called Roissy-Charles de Gaulle. The resulting typeface, bearing the name Frutiger, was released in 1975 and became an extremely popular typeface for print to this day.
—During the eighties and nineties type design became digital, and thus far cheaper to design and to distribute. The choice of typefaces for identity programs and signage projects also became far less rigid. There was an obvious reason behind this development; style varieties for conspicuous visual identities needed to be as wide as possible, with more and more organisations wanting to possess their own little niche in the ever-crowded world of visual identities. Type design started to boom and many typefaces were designed specifically for signage projects.
—At the time of writing, quite a number of specific signage fonts are available. The spectrum of different fonts is pretty wide. The fonts mentioned above were never designed for a digital format, but are now all comfortably and instantly downloadable from the Internet (after purchase). More recent fonts come in two categories: the typical highway/traffic type styles and type styles that may be used for print as well.
Some of these type families are positively obese; following the modern trend, they include endless variations in letter proportions, weights or collections of pictograms. To mention a few font names: Interstate, ClearViewOne, Vialog, FF Transit. Local transit networks also issue fonts, like Parisine and Metron.

In most signage projects a typeface has to be applied on both a light and a dark background. Our eyes perceive these two applications differently; light letters on a dark background always seem bigger than the inverse image. We compensate for this visual effect by making the light letters on a dark background slightly smaller and thinner. The top row below shows the differences that are not visible on the bottom row.

B B Like twins Like twins

B B Like twins Like twins

4.9.7.3. Inverse text imaging

Extensive signage projects often require dark text on a light background and the reverse. Creating an inverse image is only one simple mouse-click away these days. Too bad that our eyes do not

accept this breathtaking efficiency. To our eyes, light letters on a dark background look bigger and thicker than the reverse, so we have to make corrections if we want the two to be visually identical. Specific signage fonts offer negative and positive versions of one weight as part of the font family. However, it is not difficult to create these variations oneself. Drawing software allows the conversion of fonts to 'outlines'; these outlines can be given a contour in a line of any desired thickness. Adding (or subtracting) the contour to the original shape will provide the necessary variation. Purists may protest against this simple method, and they are right; real perfection needs a bit more refinement.
Perfectionists might also argue that signage projects need at least three or even four versions of type representation: positive and negative ones (often internally illuminated) a 'reflecting light' version for print, and one in coarse resolution for screen reproduction. Signage fonts attempt to provide optimal variations for these applications, often pushing the number of variations offered slightly too far.

Samples of a typeface with a high contrast (left) and one with a low contrast. Typefaces with a high contrast should be avoided for signage projects.

4.9.7.4. Letter contrast

As previously mentioned, there is not much difference between good typography for print or for signage. The obvious difference is of course that the average conditions under which one reads print are far more uniform than the conditions under which one reads messages on signs. Reading print is in mostly a predetermined action under pretty fixed circumstances (like the reading distance and a steady location). Reading signs is a different matter. First, relevant signs have to be 'found' by browsing the environment; then the (sign) reader is often moving while reading, and reading distances are not fixed but vary immensely and continually. All these conditions lead to a kind of typography for reading under extreme conditions, similar to reading text at small sizes. The most important implication is that typefaces with little contrast (the difference between the stroke widths) do better on average in signage projects.

4.9.7.5. Dual-language, multi-script and Braille

Signage projects attempt to service the widest possible audience. Multi-lingual signs are almost becoming a standard requirement. It is remarkable that even the US—a country that grew to become the most influential world power by offering its immigrants from all over the world strictly one currency, one language (and no free meals)—has recently adopted Spanish as a second official language. At the same time, the influence of the US as a predominant world power has made the English language the 'lingua franca' of our times. Perhaps never in history has one language had such a widespread dissemination. Public spaces, the world over, use English text more and more next to their own national language.

More than two languages may apply. The US also has one of the

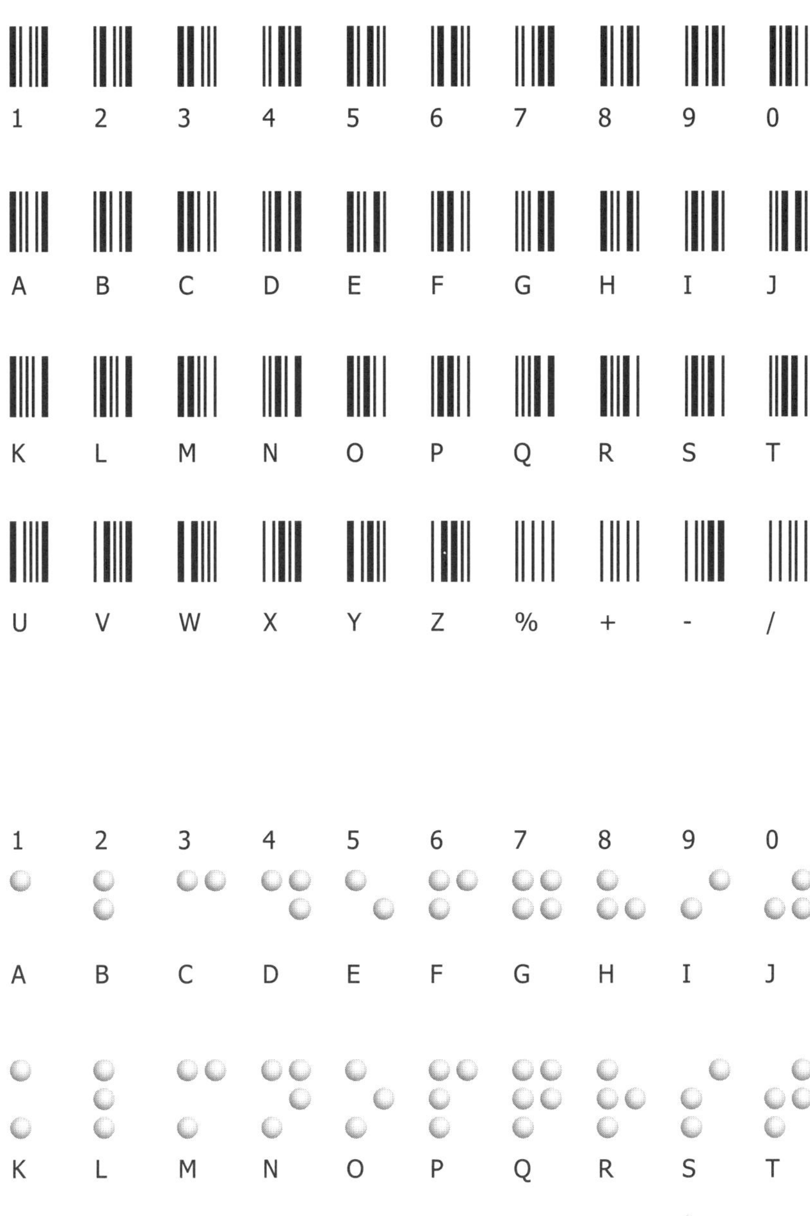

Signage projects are becoming increasingly multi-lingual. In addition, one or more writing systems are used to accommodate the visually impaired and to facilitate reading by electronic scanners. Top above, the Barcode alphabet, and below, the Braille alphabet.

strictest legislations in the world to accommodate its disabled citizens in certain aspects of their daily life. This means that Braille has to be used next to visibly readable text on some types of signs. This means that by now, we have already collected three variations of the same message—leaving the decision as to whether the Braille should also be in two languages to the future wisdom of the legislators. In signage, we also love to use pictograms—a fourth variation. It does get a bit crowded on some signs. From a typographic point of view, it is desirable that all the different variations have a shared characteristic in their visual presentation. Braille being the exception that is completely standardised and does not need to be visually prominent to be functional. Yet it also deserves a careful layout next to the other elements. A lot of fonts offer the possibility to produce text in most of the languages that make use of the Latin alphabet. Cyrillic and Greek are more and more offered as additional fonts within one family. Japan has its own multi-script fonts where the Roman and the Japanese scripts are combined within one typeface. All other scripts are falling behind in offering fonts that combine a Latin character variation, though there is a growing need for it.

Meanwhile, a sound and practical mind is welcome when trying to speak everybody's language on signs. Some say that language is the most democratic of all human endeavours. It is certainly a very malleable communication tool and in essence pretty local. (Even families create their own 'language'.) The 'universal' English language now has three official versions: British, American and International. The type of Spanish used in the US is sometimes called Spanglish. This version of Spanish adopts a lot of English (or half-English) words. Soon, Spanish speakers in Europe and Latin America will have no clue what 'Spanglish' is all about. Like Yiddish became a variation of Hebrew spoken by the Ashkenazi Jews living in Eastern Europe and is not understood by all Jews. A good feeling for consistency, in combination with a very practical mind, remains of supreme importance to avoid the common pitfalls in trying to address too many different audiences at the same time, resulting in nobody listening.

4.9.7.6. Extra characters; the arrow

A normal standardised font will have enough symbols and characters to carry out the average signage job. Numbers play an important role in signage, so the availability of a set of numbers that fit nicely in running text is important when selecting a font. Regrettably, most fonts only carry a set of tabular numbers in the size of capital letters. It is a quite peculiar and rather clumsy tradition in type design, since there is hardly any sensible use for these kinds of numbers with the exception of use in alphanumeral codes using capital letters. The situation can only be explained by the fact that type designers and typographers are often two distinct professions.

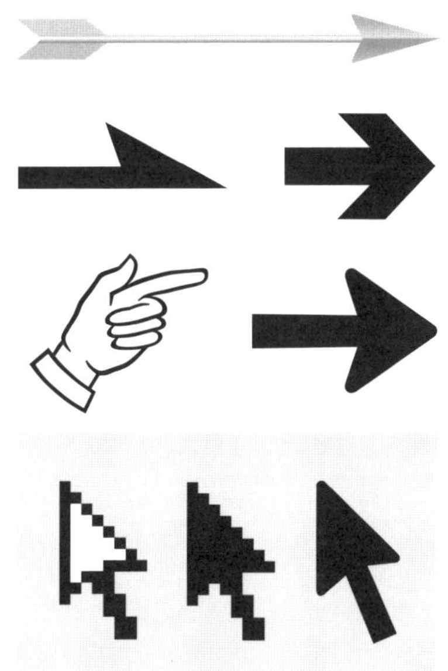

Arrows have a wide variety of uses. Some types of arrows are popular, but others have almost disappeared. Top the 'mother' weaponry version. Underneath, the Japanese arrow, which is no longer used, and the still popular British Rail arrow. Third row left, the traditional pointing finger and the arrow used for American road signs. The arrows we see most are the pointers on our computer screens, which are clearly inspired by the US road signs.

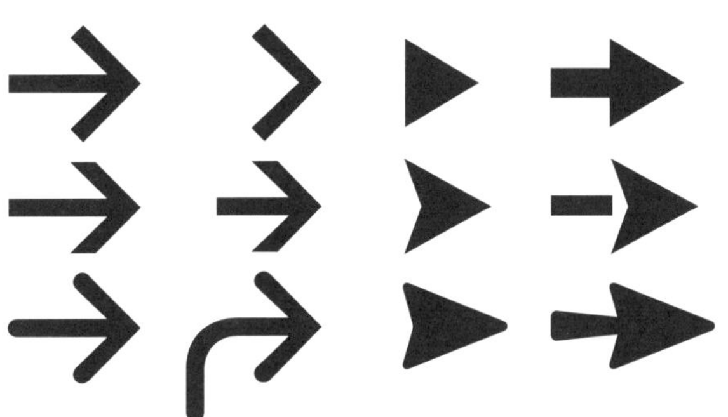

Four columns showing basic shape variations. First column, three basic detail variations; second, the shaft of the arrow can create endless permutations, sometimes providing extra routing information. Third column, three varieties of shaftless arrows, the last column in combination with possible shaft shapes.

One essential symbol is often absent from fonts that are not specially designed for signage purposes: the arrow. It is somewhat surprising that type designers do not offer the arrow as a standard addition to their fonts. Practically all corporate identity projects include signage as well. To have a font selected as a corporate style font is in the commercial interest of type designers, so it seems plausible to offer easy font application for signage as well. An entirely different view is to consider the arrow as a completely separate item with qualities of its own and not as part of the character set of a typeface. The arrow for British Rail has a recognisable and distinct character of its own. On average, it is advisable to make the arrow a 'family member' of the chosen typeface. How many positions, or variations, have to be available for the arrow? The absolute minimum amount is four: left, right, up and down, where 'straight ahead' and 'up' share the same arrow. This can become confusing in some instances. Adding diagonal arrows in all four directions is often helpful to point in a direction between 'straight' and 'turn'. Further additions may be useful, but can also be confusing. Generally accepted are arrow/pictograms for entrance and exit, but arrow variations for 'after-first-corner-left' or '-right' are exceptions and might therefore be misunderstood.

The standard set of arrows:
1. Take the left direction or go up on your left.
2. Straight on or go up.
3. Take the right direction or go up on your right.
4. Turn left.
5. Turn right.
6. Go down on your left.
7. Go down.
8. Go down on your right.

A possible addition to the standard set:
9. Entrance.
10. Turn back on your right.
11. Exit.
12. Turn back on your left.

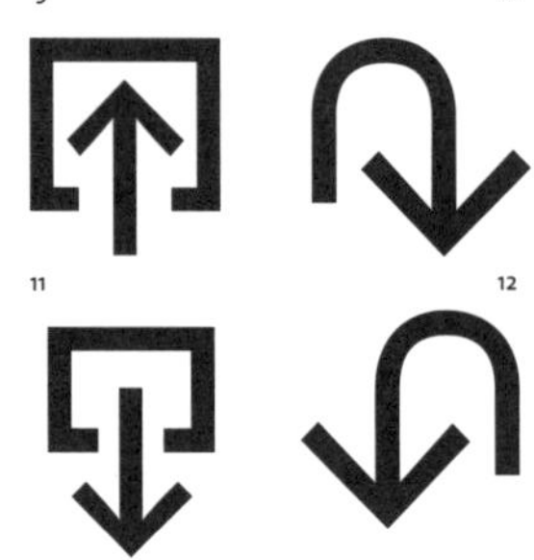

Arrows can be a totally integrated part of a typeface. In that case, the stem width of the letters and the shaft width of the arrow are identical or closely related. The size of the arrow will fit within the EM-square.

Ultimately, not only arrows could be fully integrated in the typeface, but also pictograms.

ABCDEF
abcdefg

The shape of the arrow is a favourite subject for slightly outlandish scrutiny by some signage professionals, but falls short of any convincing reason for these efforts. On the contrary, the arrow is most likely the only symbol in all signage projects that will be understood by everyone without exception. Even the Japanese stopped using their own type of arrow for signage purposes.

For the rest, signage jobs do not need extra symbols. That is to say, when we exclude all standardised and non-standardised pictograms and traffic symbols. Quite a collection altogether, deserving its own and next chapter.

4.9.7.7. Type size and reading distance

When used for print, type size is relevant for drawing initial attention and for leading the reader comfortably through the text. For signage, however, the reading distance may be a determining factor for the choice of type size. Some signs must be readable from a distance. The rule of thumb is that the x-height is related to a comfortable maximum reading distance of about 300 to 600 times its height. This rather big discrepancy in reading distance is due to the huge individual differences in our eyesight capabilities, even within the 'normal' range.

It is wise to be reminded that signs by definition do not necessarily require bigger type. People can be pretty comfortable reading bulletin boards while standing up, or even newspapers that are hung on the wall. Directories do not necessarily need big type. The size of a sign is often not determined by reading distance

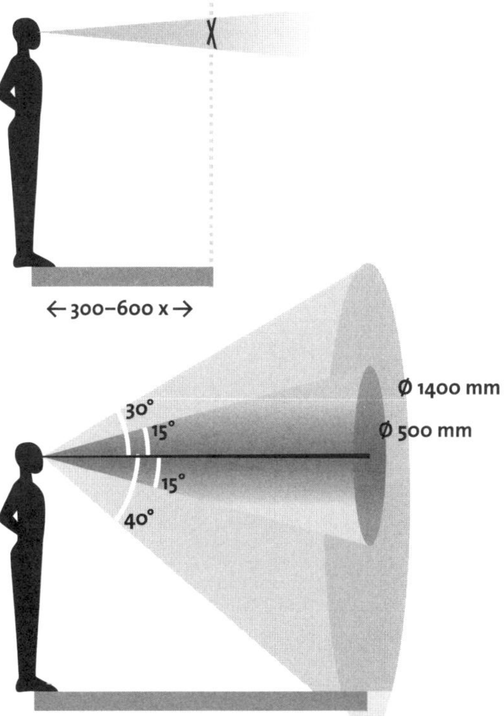

Maximum reading distance is between 300 and 600 times the x-height of a letter.

The central line of vision corresponds with the most sensitive part of the retina. This part is essential for reading. Around this part two other fields of vision can be defined, one that is important for browsing and one that corresponds with the periphery of the retina. This field is important for providing movement alerts in the environment. NB. Formal insight into the physical capabilities of human vision have limited value for creating effective communication, which depends on a large number of other factors within this framework.

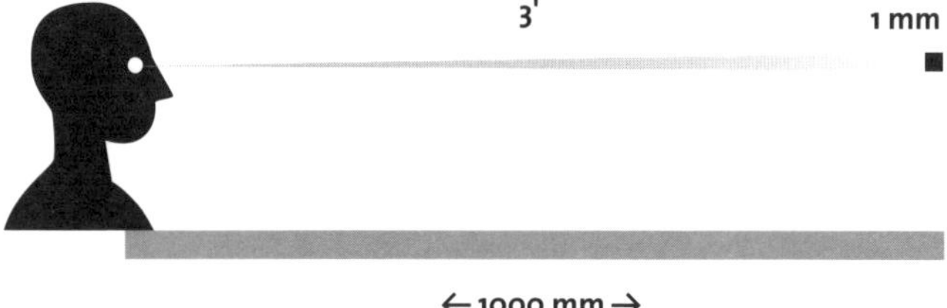

A minimum viewing angle of 3 minutes is often recommended for showing meaningful details in an image. A point of 1 mm square at a reading distance of 1 metre equals a 3-minute angle. Our maximum capacity to see separate dots is between 10 and 60 seconds of viewing angle.

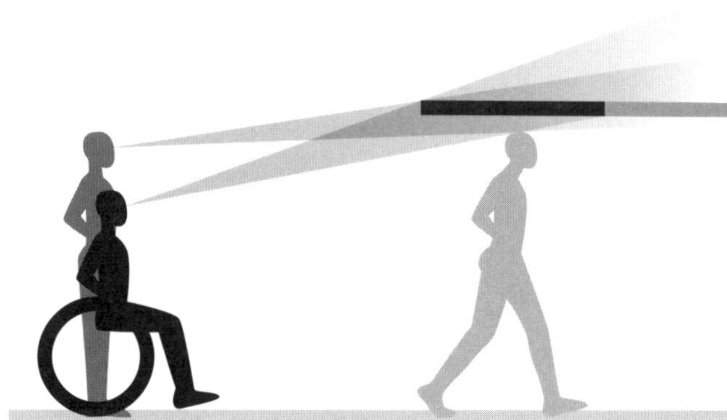

Wheelchair users have a reduced field of vision compared with other (adult) users.

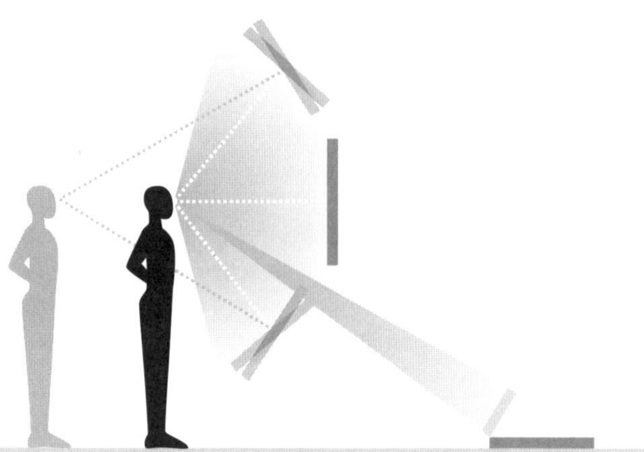

Most signs (in a building) will be read while standing up. The most convenient reading angle is in a plane perpendicular to our eyes. At close reading distance, sign panels may be positioned to meet this demand. At medium and long reading distance, panels can be vertical. Horizontally positioned signs only function at a very close reading range, such as a 'welcome' door mat. (Horizontal signs outdoors on the road are very simple and extremely elongated.)

requirements but by its capability to draw sufficient attention in its environment. In that sense, signs as well as traditional billboards follow basically the same rule.

Average x-height sizes for different reading distances:
5 –15 mm (3/16"- 5/8") for reading at arm's length distance, like door signs, wall directories, instructions.
15 - 45 mm (5/8"–2") for medium distance reading, like directional signs, or indoor destination signs.
40 - 120 mm (11/2"- 5") for long distance reading, like outdoor directional or destination signs.
The last category can include very wide signs; therefore the range of letter sizes may be extended. Big public areas like bus or train stations, or airports, require even bigger sizes. Highway signage is a category of its own.

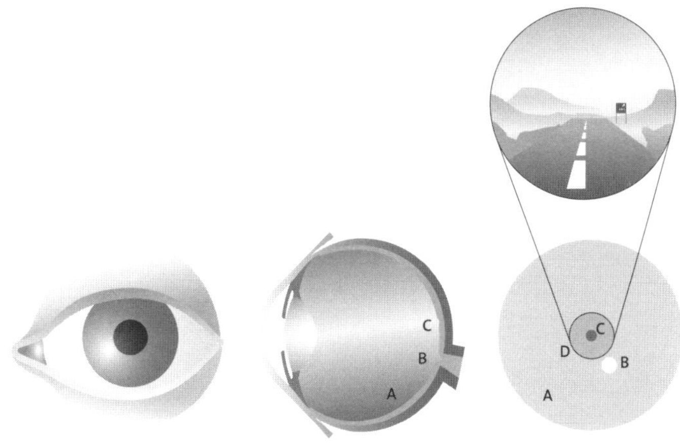

The human eye on a 1:1 scale. Left to right, front view, horizontal cross-section right eye, map of the light sensitive retina. The retina counts 130 million visual receptors, but the central part of the retina is by far the most important part for visual perception. The fovea (C) is only 1.5 mm in diameter and is essential for reading; around the fovea is the Ø 6 mm central retina (D), essential for browsing; the 'blind spot' (B) is not light sensitive; the rest of the retina (A).

Signage is typography in space. The variety of type sizes employed is huge.

a

a

4.9.7.8. Layout issues

Typography for signage must be a feat of austerity. Abundant typographic flavouring and spicing is likely to be overdone on signs. In most cases, we read signs in situations where the sign is covering only a fraction of our visual panorama. Effective communication requires absolute simplicity and concision in every possible way.

—The number of lines and words to appear on one sign must be reduced to the absolute minimum. A maximum of five items can be seen at one glance. Twelve words is already a lot (except in directories).

—The use of abbreviations is not recommended.

—Leading (line spacing) should be compact since lines are short in length. A line space of two-and-a-half times x-height is a rule of thumb. In exceptional cases it can be reduced to twice x-height.

—Word spacing should not be more than one third of the type size or even half the x-height.

—Only one typeface is allowed, preferably used in only one weight. Italics (not oblique Romans) are the best choice for emphasis in text.

—Capital letters (majuscules) are only used for the beginning of words, or for short headings. Languages differ in the use of majuscules. In German all nouns begin with a capital letter, English also has a tradition of using capital letters for names in general—as opposed to descriptions—every word consisting of a name starts with a capital letter, so these two languages have a tradition of using more capital letters at the beginning of words than other languages. Using capitals for the first letter of separate words does not make a text more readable. The ancient Romans used beautifully shaped majuscules exclusively to compose large messages on walls. Times have changed since then; it takes too long to read these typographic beauties and therefore this practice should be avoided.

—People's names, including gender, other title(s) and initials should not include the normal abbreviation points (full stops).

—Numerals used in text should be minuscule size, while numerals used in alphanumeric codes may be majuscule size.

—Simple left-aligned text is favourable. However, text aligned in the direction to be taken on directional signs may work best. Positioning of arrows should also follow this principle.

—Grouping destinations under one arrow often works better than giving each destination a separate arrow.

—Multi-lingual signs tend to be rather complex and are best avoided. If necessary, try to create a strict, consistent and simple order to separate one language from the other.

In principle, fonts that will do well as text fonts—particularly those that work well in small sizes—will do well for signage projects.

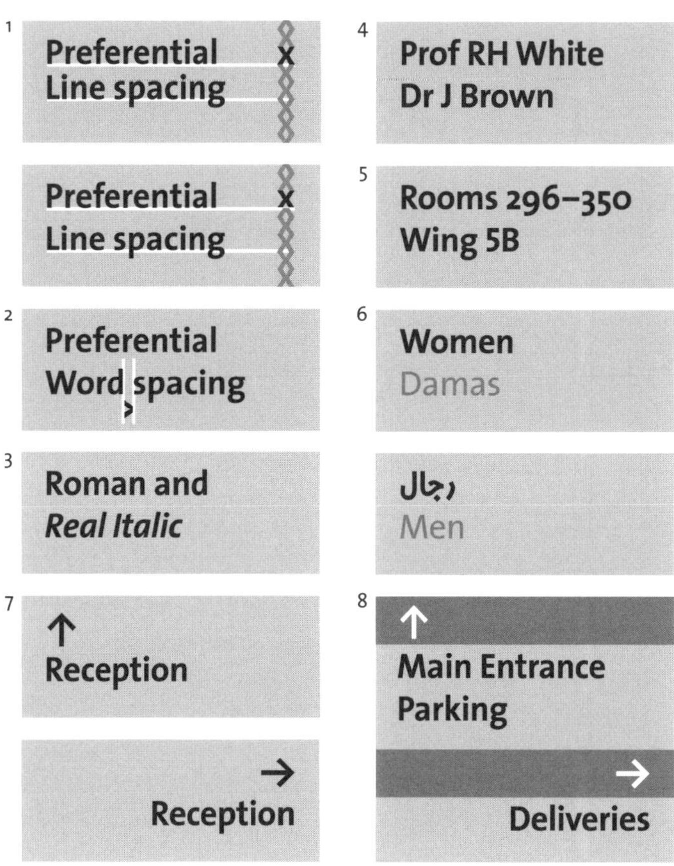

Layout preferences:
1. Line spacing (leading) should be 2.5 times the x-height, and in exceptional cases, 2 times.
2. Word spacing should be half the x-height.
3. Use real Italic letters, rather than oblique Romans
4. No points (full stops) are needed for personal names, abbreviations and titles.
5. Use only majuscule numerals for alphanumerical codes. In all other cases use mediaeval (old style) or small cap numerals.
6. Multi-lingual signs should have a very clear and consistent layout.
7. Left-aligned text is preferable, except on directional signs indicating a right turn.
8. Grouping different destinations under one arrow is preferable.

4.10. Pictograms & symbols

Nearly all signage projects will include non-textual signs. The use of pictographic signs has grown in the last decades; operating instructions put directly on devices or on screens have become for the most part pictographic. This is due to a wider international dissemination of products.
Pictographic signs may be called pictograms, pictographs, icons, graphic symbols or simply symbols. What unites these sorts of signs is that all are not a part of—or derived from—our alphabet. What separates them is the level of abstraction in the visual representation and/or the complexity of meaning. For instance, the text Men's Toilet may be represented by a simplified illustration of a man; a sign showing a simple red circle with a white stroke in the middle, means: 'no access allowed'. Textual information remains by far the most important ingredient on signs, but additional graphics play an important role as well. Traffic, safety, emergency and mandatory signs, for instance, often predominantly use pictograms or symbols.

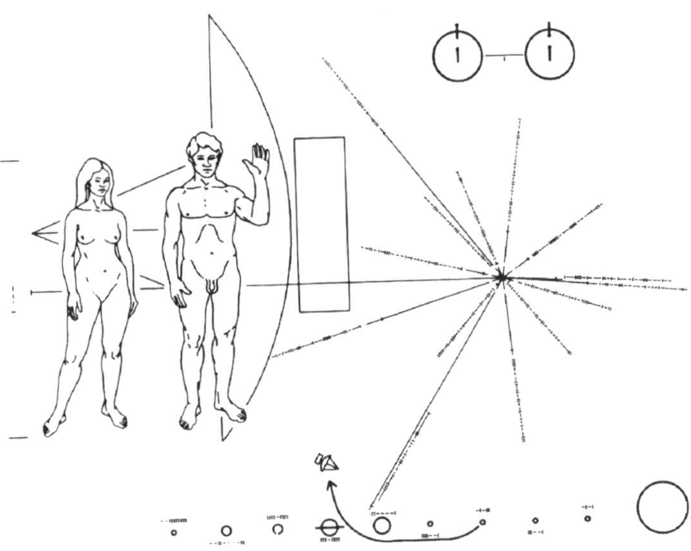

The ultimate goal of some types of visual representation is to find ways of expression that are expected to be universally understood. Astronomer Carl Sagan designed this illustration, which was sent into deep space by Pioneer 10 in 1972. The purpose of the plaque was to be a sort of address label in case the satellite came into the possession of another civilisation.

The advantage of pictograms and symbols over text is that they are concise and understood universally, crossing the barriers of individual languages or even literacy. Nobody would deny their claim of being concise—and therefore ideal for signage purposes. The claim of universal comprehension is another matter. In principle, one would assume that a (simple) illustration would make a straightforward reference clear to everyone. In reality, that is astonishingly untrue, even when rather simple pictograms are applied.

There is an ancient desire to have one universal language that is understood by everyone. The bible even gave this desire a moralistic aspect by introducing the story of the Tower of Babel, in which God punished humanity by giving each individual their own language and this became the root of all conflicts amongst mankind. Sharing one language is certainly not a guarantee for peaceful coexistence, but it is a rather efficient tool for communication. Throughout history, the affluent and well-educated from different societies have always found their common ground in speaking various languages; first it was Latin, then French, and now it's English. Societies have changed, international trade and mobility have increased, thus raising the need to reach much larger, and on average, less educated audiences. Pictograms and other graphic symbols were thought to fill that need. Perhaps they will eventually, but only through a normal learning process. Pictograms do not reveal their meaning spontaneously to everyone. More precisely, all mutual understanding is based on education.

Although the pictographic language we use for signage is extremely simple and far too crude to be compared with an average language, it shares the same limitations as all languages. First, understanding a vocabulary without having insight into the values and behaviour of the people that use that vocabulary is pretty useless. Objects might have different meanings in different societies. A dress or a skirt for instance, is woman's clothing for most westerners, but not for Scots, Arabs and certain Africans. Second, a vocabulary is never static. It changes with time because societies, habits, utensils, tools and preferences change. In addition, different languages also influence each other.

Language—also pictorial language—is nothing more than an expression of the ever-changing values and activities in societies. Everything will become outdated in time and very little in any vocabulary is part of a well-organised and logical structure, regardless of the many attempts of committees and regulators to keep some order.

In spite of some disadvantages, pictograms and symbols have kept their attraction and are still widely used. Some pictograms are officially standardised and some have the status of being legally enforceable instructions.

Examples of pictographic writing systems, from top to bottom, Egyptian hieroglyphs, Mayan glyphs. The Chinese characters became abstract over time and are the only ones of the three still in use.

4.10.1. HIGHLIGHTS OF THE MAJOR PICTOGRAM APPLICATIONS

Pictograms were not developed as toys for graphic designers. The first human writing systems were pictographic or ideographic, like the Egyptian hieroglyphs, the Mexican Mayan symbols and the Chinese characters. Of all these, only the Chinese survived, but only in an abstract form.

Scholars, professionals, craftsmen and tradesmen of every age have been restless creators of more or less abstract symbols as identifiers of their profession, or as expressions of their theories, or as branding of their goods or properties. Philosophers wish ultimately to reveal the complete secret of all existence, establishing a coherent 'theory of everything'. This all-embracing insight remains the ultimate human quest, yet modern science is split into endless specialisations. Universality is seen with more realistic eyes these days. That was not the case at the beginning of the last century when 'Esperanto' was created as a synthetic universal alphabetic language. Attempts were also made to create universal symbolic or pictographic languages.

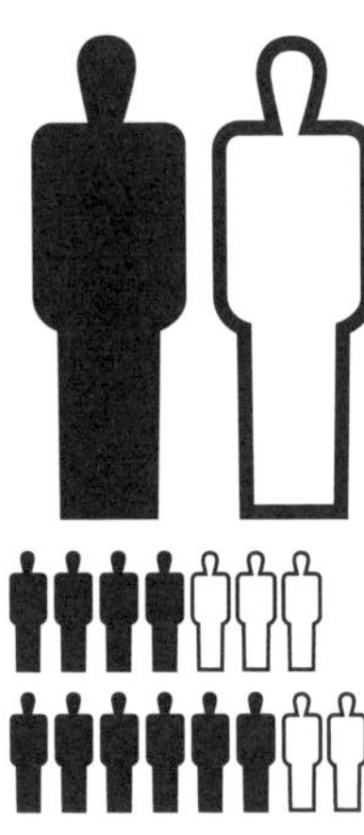

Otto Neurath is the father of ISOTYPE, the first modern pictographic system. It was mostly used to convey quantitative and statistical information.

4.10.1.1. Development of complex pictographic sign systems

Otto Neurath (1882 – 1945) is considered one of the founding fathers of the modern pictorial display of information. He was a sociologist and an economist. His career was heavily influenced by the Second World War. He started to make pictorial representations working in a housing planning department in Vienna. After the German invasion, he escaped Austria to find work in The Hague, in the Netherlands. After the German occupation of the Netherlands in 1940, he again fled, this time to Oxford in England. He founded in 1943 ISOTYPE (International System of Typographic Picture Education).
Gerd Arnzt was a Dutch graphic artist. He was head of the graphic studio under Otto Neurath and continued his work after Otto left. Gerd was in fact responsible for the design of the graphic signs. A student of Neurath, Rudolf Motley also dedicated his career to pictographic information and was the founder of Glyph Inc. Charles Bliss (1897 – 1985) is in many ways comparable with Otto Neurath. His background was in engineering and he started to elaborate on his ideas while working in a patent department in Vienna. His career was also heavily marked by the Second World War. A major difference between the two was that Bliss ended up in Australia, where nobody was very receptive to his ideas. He published 'International Semantography' in 1947 and a second edition 'Semantography (Blissymbolics)' in 1965. Blissymbolics have eventually found their major applications in certain health care facilities.

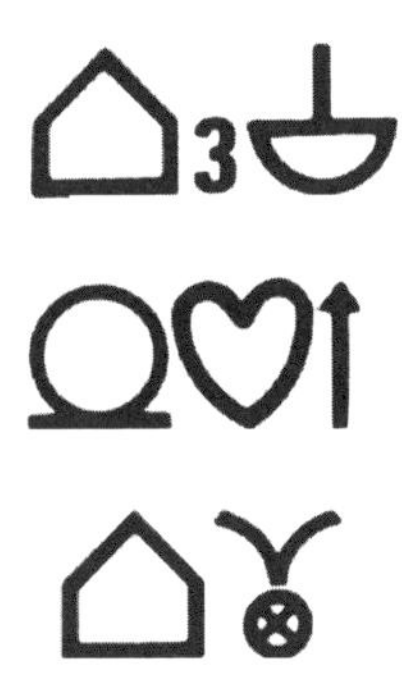

Charles Bliss spent most of his life developing a comprehensive pictographic language called 'Blissymbolics'.

4.10.1.2. Traffic and transportation hubs

With the arrival of the automobile a need for traffic signs arose. In 1909 in Paris at an International Convention of Circulation of Motor Vehicles, four traffic signs were proposed as warning for hazardous road conditions: a bump, a road crossing, a railroad crossing, and a curve. After the Second World War, the United Nations took over the role of standardising road signs, and the system has expanded a few times since. At the beginning of the seventies the American Department of Transport (DOT) asked the American Institute of Graphic Artists (AIGA) to develop a system of

In 1909, only four road signs were seen as enough to secure road safety. All four indicated hazardous road conditions: a bump, a railroad crossing, a sharp curve, and a road crossing.

pictograms, not to regulate traffic itself, but more to help organise traffic flow in and around bus stations, train stations, and airports. In 1974, 34 pictograms were published, and in 1979 sixteen more were added. Today, 50 copyright-free pictograms are freely downloadable from the internet.

The activities that started with traffic regulation eventually split into two different categories: traffic symbols and public information symbols often applied in public transit areas. The first category is heavily formalised and may be legally enforced, while the second is becoming more and more internationally standardised.

Overview of key international graphical symbols standards:
ISO 7000, Graphic symbols for use on equipment.
ISO 7001, Public information symbols.
ISO 7010, Graphical symbols—Safety signs in workplaces and public areas.
IEC 60417, Graphical symbols for use on equipment.
ISO 3864, Safety colours and safety signs.
ISO/IEC 80416, Basic principles for graphical symbols for use on equipment.
ISO 17724, Graphical symbols vocabulary.

4.10.1.3. Public Information Symbols

All symbols used in public spaces that do not have an enforceable legal status, like traffic or mandatory safety signs, are often called 'Public Information Symbols'. Organisations of graphic designers had a typical interest in the development of series of pictograms to be used in public spaces. In the early sixties, there was a widely shared desire to create international symbol systems. It was seen as a necessary mutual effort to create a universal visual language that could be understood by everyone on the planet.
The International Council of Graphic Design Associations, ICOGRADA, directly after its own establishment in 1963, created a Sign Symbol Commission headed by Peter Kneebone.
One of the initiatives of the committee was to instigate a competition for the design of 24 public information symbols, such as exit, telephone and toilet signs. They invited 650 Design Schools to take part in the competition. ICOGRADA released a few publications about the progress of this work, but never issued any generally accepted recommendations. However, there is still a working relationship between ICOGRADA and the ISO organisation that tries to establish an International Standardisation of Graphical Symbols.

4.10.1.4. National parks

Ever-growing national and international recreational travel activity increased the need for standardisation in wayfinding (navigational) systems and public information symbols, the latter not only to be used on signs but also on printed maps. Over the years large collections of pictograms have been developed by many national organisations involved in the management of national parks. These collections are often offered free of charge.

4.10.1.5. Zoos

Zoos are gratifying projects for pictogram design. Making tools to help people find the way to extensive collections of animals and plants creates an opportunity for designing youthful (the majority of the audience is very young) and playful signage. A remarkable signage project was designed in the early seventies for the National Zoological Park in Washington by the designers Lance Wyman and Bill Cannan. Pictograms for individual types of animals were developed along with the characteristic paw and claw tracks of the animals involved. Trails of tracks were used to mark the right path or directions. A more recent and high-profile project is the large series of pictograms developed by Michal Wein for the Zoo Decin in the Czech Republic.

4.10.1.6. Safety and security in public spaces and the workplace

Extensive legislation dealing with health and safety at work and in public places has resulted in the creation of large sets of pictograms, a collection that keeps on growing all the time. The use of these pictograms is mandatory; building owners and tenants have a legal obligation to use these pictograms with or without further textual instruction or explanation. By far the most used pictograms in and around buildings are mandatory signs. Every country has its own specific legislation and regulations. (Sometimes regulations may even differ between states or provinces within one country or even between cities.) Attempts are under way to establish international standards; the European Union is developing European Standards, for instance. A number of companies offer mandatory signs as so-called 'stock signs'. Regrettably, mandatory pictogram series suffer from the fact that they were created during different periods in time, which makes the complete set incoherent in visual style. Also the fact that these pictograms are often the result of 'designing by committee' contributes to the hotchpotch of different styles. There is much room for improvement in this much used category of pictograms, but only seldom do designers or stock sign manufacturers feel the need to remedy the inconsistency in visual design. The 2001 initiative of the HB Sign Company in London has been an admirable exception.

4.10.1.7. Olympic Games

The first sports pictograms for the Olympic Games were designed in 1948 for the Summer Games in London. The results were rather old-fashioned and looked like clumsily designed traditional crests. Modern design concepts arrived at the Summer Games of Tokyo in 1964. The pictogram series was developed by Masaru Katzumie in the role of art-director and Yoshiro Yamashita as graphic designer. The series was extended with the pictograms needed for the Winter Games in Sapporo 1972. The series were unmistakeably Japanese, built on millennia of Japanese crest design tradition.

The following series, made for the games in Mexico City 1968, looked quite different: simple, straightforward illustrations that tried to capture the Mexican visual culture. Later, the German designer Otl Aicher laid the foundation for a series of pictograms that emerged as a complete standardised visual language. All the design elements came under strict mathematical control. His designs were first used for the Munich Games 1972, later for Montreal 1976 and Calgary 1988. His work had a large impact on pictogram design. The extended series was later licensed to the Erco company in Germany and consists at the moment of hundreds of different pictograms. A visually related but less rigid and friendlier looking series of pictograms was developed for the Games in Moscow 1980. A Russian committee issued a design competition for art schools in Russia. The 27-year-old graduate Nikolai Belkov won the competition. To fill the need for service pictograms as well, 244 additional pictograms were designed by a large group of draughtsmen working in the Russian Graphic Design Training Centre under the guidance of Valerie Akopov.

A more Mediterranean view on pictogram design was shown in the series for the Summer Games in Barcelona 1992 and the Winter Games in Albertville. The grid, ruler and pencil were replaced by elegant strokes made with spontaneous swings of a brush, showing the European use of brushes, which is quite distinct from the way the Japanese or Chinese masters use these tools.

Designer Sarah Rosenbaum steered the approach to pictogram design in the opposite direction from the work of Otl Aicher. She created a strong visual image by taking local prehistoric rock carvings as a source of inspiration. The Modernist view on artistic progress was now definitively replaced by a technique of visual styling that allows for very effective identity building and branding. Her work concluded the previous era of—at times playful—functionalism. Entertainment, branding and merchandising became the new catchwords.

Today, environmental graphic design for the Olympic Games still plays an important role but it has become part of a very complicated project involving many disciplines working together in various specialised teams, all catering for what has become an immense international media event. Graphic design focusing on entertainment, new product introduction or opening events of all sorts, has become a professional specialisation in itself. Information design (and signage) are now only a small part of the overall design activity. Successful branding of the Games and keeping the entertainment level as high as possible during the event have become the major concerns of all the communication efforts. Information design elements like pictograms became part of the leading commercial goal and were transformed into lucrative candidates for merchandising of all sorts. Pictograms may even be registered as trademarks. Different series of pictograms are now designed to serve different target groups, related to age or special interest; each will be provided with their own signs, mascots or pins. People no longer take just a picture to take back home as souvenir; now they remember their experience by saying: 'Been there, bought the T-shirt'.

4.10.1.8. World Trade Fairs

For a long time World Trade Fairs served as windows to show the emerging world. The Eiffel Tower in Paris is the most striking remaining structure that was erected for the Paris Exhibition 1889. Pictograms and signage were always a regular part of these exhibitions but never received much attention with the exception of the design work done by Paul Arthur as art director of a team that developed a complete Standard Sign Manual for the Universal Exhibition in Montreal in 1976. It was the first time that a comprehensive manual for such a large event had been produced. Paul Arthur later wrote, with Romedi Passini, a general wayfinding guide for the Public Works Department in Canada.

4.10.1.9. Hospitals and health care facilities

Hospitals and other health care facilities have grown into a massive and complex industry that can occupy huge building complexes. Widespread global migration has created a very mixed clientele speaking various languages and also having different levels of literacy. Some patients cannot be addressed verbally. All these factors created a strong need for non-verbal communication systems.

There are a few pictographic sign systems that have been developed to replace verbal language in health care, not only for signage purposes, but also in order to communicate with patients —more specifically to aid diagnosis and therapy, medical instructions are given in a pictographic format. 'Blissymbolics' consists of 2000 signs that were first applied in the Ontario Crippled Children's Centre. Also in Australia, a system called COMPIC was developed by Lois Lanier. It consists of 1600 signs and aims to assist in communication with children who have physical and mental difficulties. Peter Houts developed a series of simple drawings that help to communicate with his predominantly AIDS and cancer patients. In cases where verbal communication is too limiting, he encourages every medical professional to use simple stick figures and doodles as diagnostic aids to deliver medical instructions.

Pictographic signs for signage purposes are also widely used in hospitals. There are attempts to standardise these pictograms. Most of the series produced are derived from the AIGA transportation pictograms, or the Olympic pictograms designed by Otl Eicher. The pictograms series made by the Dutch agency Tel Design are an exception. It is not an easy task to make simple visual representations of medical services, and that is an understatement. All kinds of psychological trauma or various medical conditions, as well as many modern techniques for diagnosis and therapy, cannot be visualised in an easy and comprehensible manner.

4.10.1.10. *Availability of pictogram series.*

The AIGA/DOT series of 50 pictograms is copyright-free and available on the Internet.
The Japan Sign Design Association has designed 150 pictograms copyright-free and downloadable from the Internet.
The International Standards Organisation (ISO) issues various standards on graphical symbols.
Most national standards organisations also issue series of safety and public information symbols.
The German company Erco has developed a large series of pictograms, based on the work of Otl Eicher. The German typeface Vialog includes an extensive set of pictograms.
A lot of governmental bodies involved in public transportation, national health care, tourism, public safety, safety at work and national parks issue their design manuals on the internet. These manuals sometimes include extended series of pictograms. Oddly enough, this attitude is in stark contrast to the attitude of the (public) bodies involved in establishing mandatory safety signs. These institutions do not make access to their publications particularly easy, let alone offer pictogram series for free. Quite the contrary. Standardised safety symbols can be purchased from Standard Institutes or specific publishers.
Health and safety 'picto fonts' issued by the companies Linotype and Adobe are of limited use.

4.10.2. TEST PROCEDURE FOR PICTOGRAMS

The ISO has devised a test method to check the effectiveness of proposals for pictograms (ISO 9186). The test consists of two separate parts: a comprehensibility judgment test and a comprehension test.
In the first test a group of people are shown alternative proposals for graphic symbols that try to convey one specific message. Each individual in the audience is then asked to give an estimate of the number of people they think would properly understand each alternative shown. Proposals can afterwards be rated according to scores. The second test is done in reverse, as a group of people is shown individual graphic symbols in a realistic setting and are individually asked to say what they think each symbol means. ISO has made ranking categories in relation to the proportion of correct answers. ISO recommends the score of 67% as the minimum for public release.

4.10.3. DESIGN ASPECTS

Designing a series of pictograms is rarely part of a signage design project, unless one is asked for instance to be involved in the signage of the Olympic Games. In most cases, an existing series of pictograms will be selected and applied in the project at hand. That procedure is not a necessity, though. There is an alternative option, which is to make a distinction between the safety and emergency pictograms and the pictograms generally used for common facilities, like toilets, cloakrooms, public phones, reception areas and cafeterias. The last category comprises a limited number of pictograms and a special design of these elements may make the design style of the whole project more poignant and coherent.

There are two fundamental and different ways to approach pictogram design within this context. One considers the pictograms a coherent but separate design style alongside the typography and another seeks complete integration with the typeface selected. The latter is in fact almost an extension of the typeface with pictographic signs. The advantage of the first approach is the freedom it offers the designer to be expressive in the design. The advantage of the second approach is that the pictograms can be more easily used on applications: in large sizes, like on signs next to doors, and in very small sizes on directories, (printed) maps and screen displays.

All design is influenced by the style in fashion at the time of its creation. A specific design style marks a period in time. That is also visible in the choice of pictogram style. The development of many pictograms was done during a time when all shapes were forced into pure geometric shapes, positioned on squarish grids. It was even assumed that this concept would enhance the ease of communication. A lot of the standardised series of pictograms carry the clear style preference for this concept. The logical part of our mind might agree with this vision, but the visual part of our brain does not. As raised in the chapter on typography, our eyes do not obey the measurements on a ruler. Visual order does not follow simple mathematical rules. Visual recognition of real objects is not best served by geometric simplification. The real task of designing a complete series of pictograms is often to preserve consistency in the overall visual representation. This seems to be very difficult. Most pictogram sets use 'stick figures' as sort of skeleton shapes, while the contours of objects are used both in solid shapes as well as in outline.

It is sensible to recommend always combining pictograms with a short text indicating their meaning. Even though this is redundant information, it combines the best of both worlds: easy detection and assured recognition. This principle implies a greater freedom in the creation of pictograms, especially the well-known ones that we find in every office building around the world. Here there is plenty of room for experimentation and variation, and the chance of misinterpretation becomes relatively small.

Overview of pictogram series

All pictograms are shown on a light background to make comparison easier.

Olympic Summer Games in Tokyo 1964 and Winter Games Sapporo 1972. Artistic director Masaru Katzumie, graphic designer Yoshiro Yamashita.

Olympic Summer Games Mexico City 1968. Artistic directors Manuel Villazón and Mathias Goerlitz, graphic designers Lance Wyman and Eduardo Terrazas.

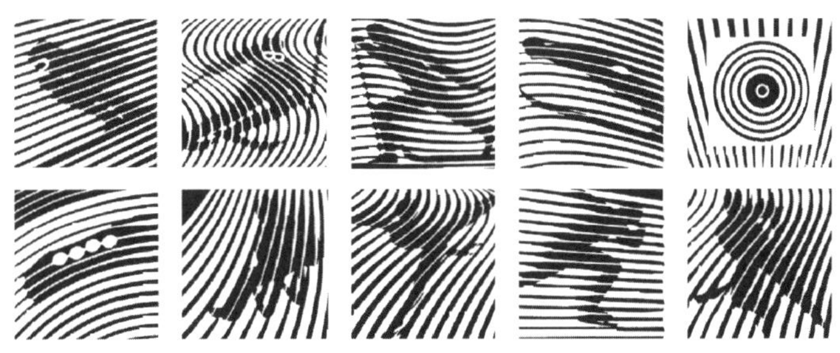

Olympic Winter Games Grenoble 1968, designer Roger Excoffon.

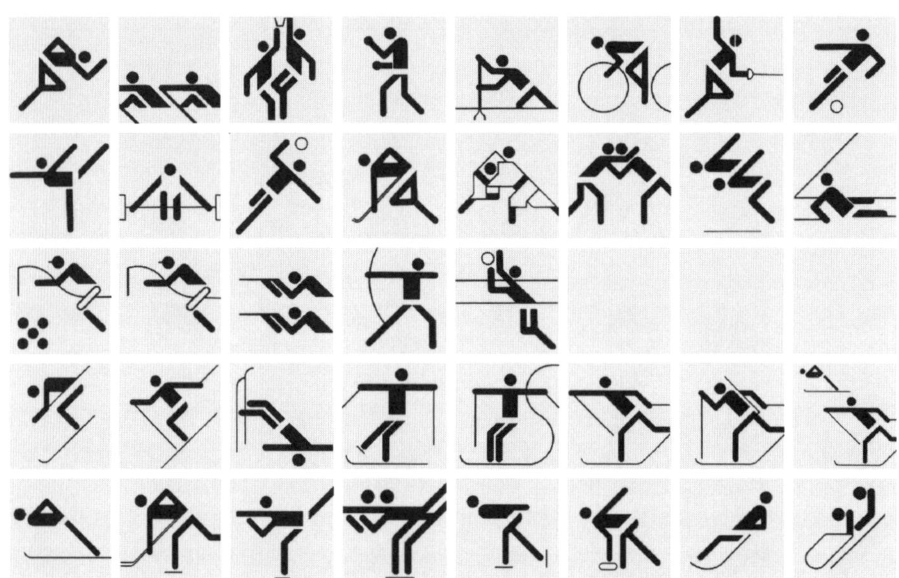

Olympic Summer Games Munich 1972, Montreal 1976 and Winter Games Calgary 1988. Designer Otl Aicher, adaptations for Montreal by Georges Huel and Pierre-Yves Pelletier.

Olympic Winter Games Innsbruck 1976, designer Alfred Kunzenmann.

Olympic Summer Games Moscow 1980, designer Nikolai Belkov.

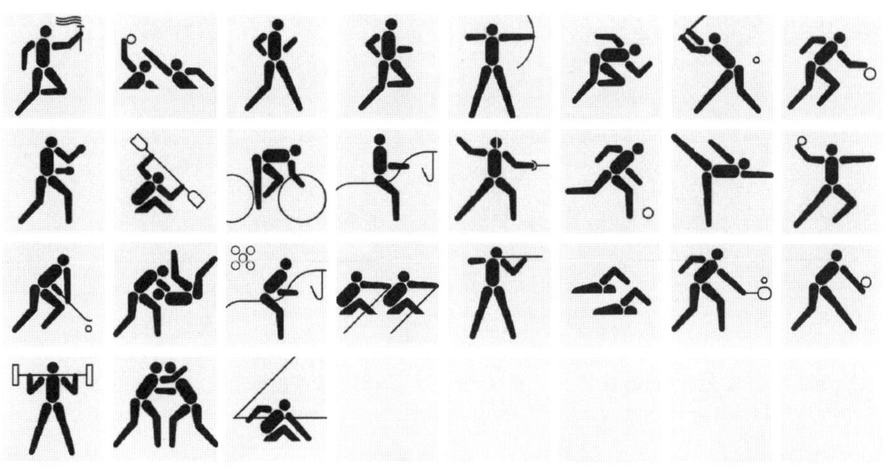

Olympic Summer Games Los Angeles 1984, designer Keith Bright and Associates.

Olympic Winter Games Sarajevo 1984, designer Radomir Vukovic.

Olympic Summer Games Seoul 1988, designers Cho Young-Jea, Hwang Bu-Yong and Kim Seung-Jin.

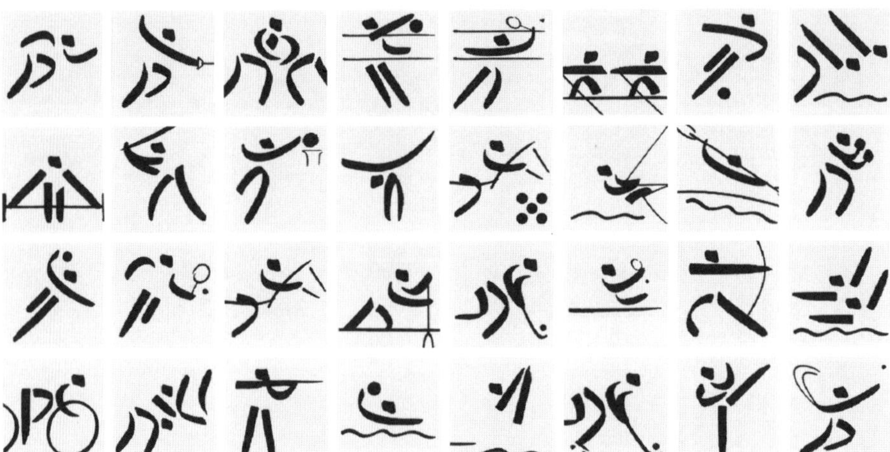

Olympic Summer Games Barcelona 1992, designer Josep Maria Trias.

Olympic Winter Games Albertville 1992, designer Alain Doré of the Agency Desgrippes in Paris.

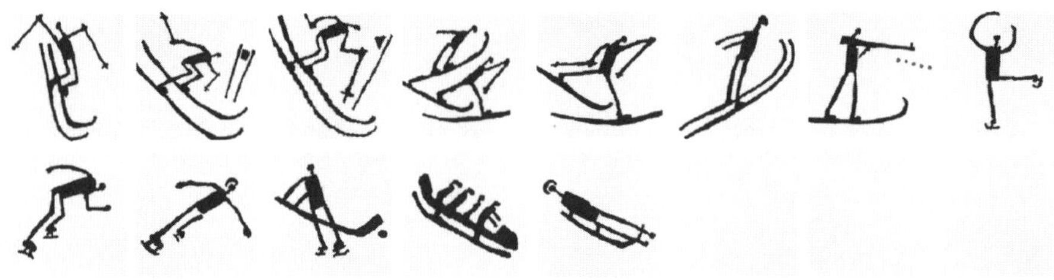

Olympic Winter Games Lillehammer 1994, designer Sarah Rosenbaum.

Olympic Summer Games Atlanta 1996, designers Malcolm Grear Designers.

Olympic Summer Games Sydney 2000, designer Paul Saunders Design.

Olympic Summer Games Athens 2004, design director Theodora Mantzaris.

Five different ways to illustrate a running athlete, revealing the changing style preferences over time.

Two quite different attempts to capture the grace of Olympic rhythmic gymnastics, left image by Paul Saunders, right by Malcolm Grear.

Expressing national identity by visual means is often the lead design motive when developing series of Olympic pictograms. For the 1972 Games in Sapporo, Yoshiro Yamashita simply built on a strong Japanese visual tradition. For the Lillehammer Games 1994, Sarah Rosenbaum claimed the Norwegian 'look and feel' by taking prehistoric rock carvings as a source of inspiration. Theodora Mantzaris used ancient Greek (pottery) paintings as a source for the 2004 Athens Games.

The Chinese, like the Japanese, have such a strong visual culture that the pictogram/logo for the Beijing Games of 2008 just follows centuries of visual tradition and is unmistakably Chinese.

Between 1974 and 1979, fifty pictograms were developed in a collaboration between the American Institute of Graphic Artists and the US Department of Transportation. The AIGA *Signs and Symbols Committee members included: Thomas Geismar, Seymour Chwast, Rudolf de Harak, John Lees and Massimo Vignelli.*

For the Universal Exhibition in Montreal 1967, designer Burt Kramer developed a series of animal pictograms to identify the different sections of two mammoth parking lots that accommodated 12,000 cars.

Designers Lance Wyman and Bill Cannan developed a series of pictograms in the early seventies for the National Zoological Park in Washington. Paw and claw tracks were used as trail markers to show direction.

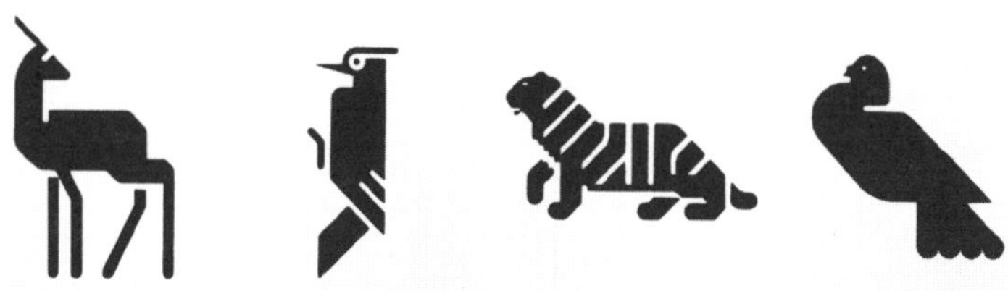

Examples of a series of pictograms designed in the mid-seventies by Gert-Jan Leuvelink (Tel Design) to distinguish dwelling areas in large extensions to the Dutch cities Maarssen and Maarssenbroek.

In 1994 designer Michal Wein started developing a large series of pictograms for the Zoo Decin in the Czech Republic. They are used for visual identity, information panels and signage.

Starting in 1972, Jean Widmer designed over the following seven years 550 pictograms to indicate all the highlights of an area, displayed on huge sign panels along the highways in France.

In 1980 Studio Dumbar designed an extensive pictogram series for the Westeinde Hospital in The Hague (only a part of the series is shown here). The series is offered copyright-free for non-commercial applications.

Examples of the symbols developed by ITT in Bombay, India.

Examples of the Hospital Symbol Graphics, Australian Standards AS 2786–1985.

In 2001 the HB *Sign Company in London took an excellent initiative by commissioning type designer Jeremy Tankard to redesign in one coherent visual style the complete set of pictograms to be found in most buildings. Mandatory signs are by far the largest part of this collection.*

So-called 'stick figures' play a major role in pictographic instructions. The design results tend to show physical anomalies. To overcome this problem the 'animated pictogram' may be used. This one was designed by Yukio Ota on software developed by Alan Kitching in 1983.

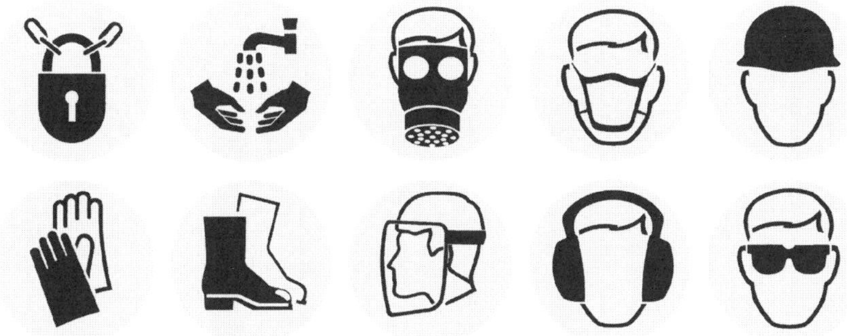

British Standards for mandatory safety symbols have had a strong influence internationally. However, the current standard collection has grown over the years into a hotchpotch of different visual styles and large differences in visual quality. The series shown here is an excellent part of the total set. It was developed in the sixties mainly to secure safety on construction sites.

The application of customised rasters binds the different styles of these pictograms together. Designed by the author in the mid-sixties for the Slotervaart Hospital in Amsterdam.

Many designers find inspiration in Japanese design. Traditional craft and design maintained strong and long-lasting ties in Japan. It resulted in an extremely rich and inspiring graphic culture that found ways to implement geometric abstractions in simplified illustrations, in a less rigid way than is often found in western culture.
Designs made by Yukio Ota, Yoshiro Yamashita and anonymous others.

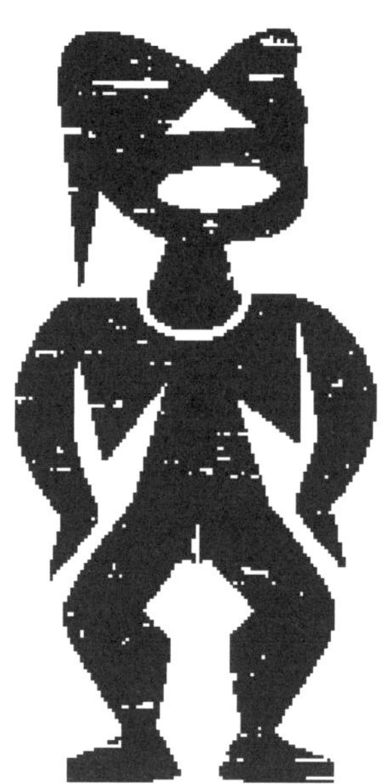

In the past, individual cultures maintained distinct visual styles. One style could remain constant and be further perfected over hundreds or even thousands of years. Today, we use (ancient) styles as sources of inspiration, or in order to create a graphic identity with a specific 'look & feel'.

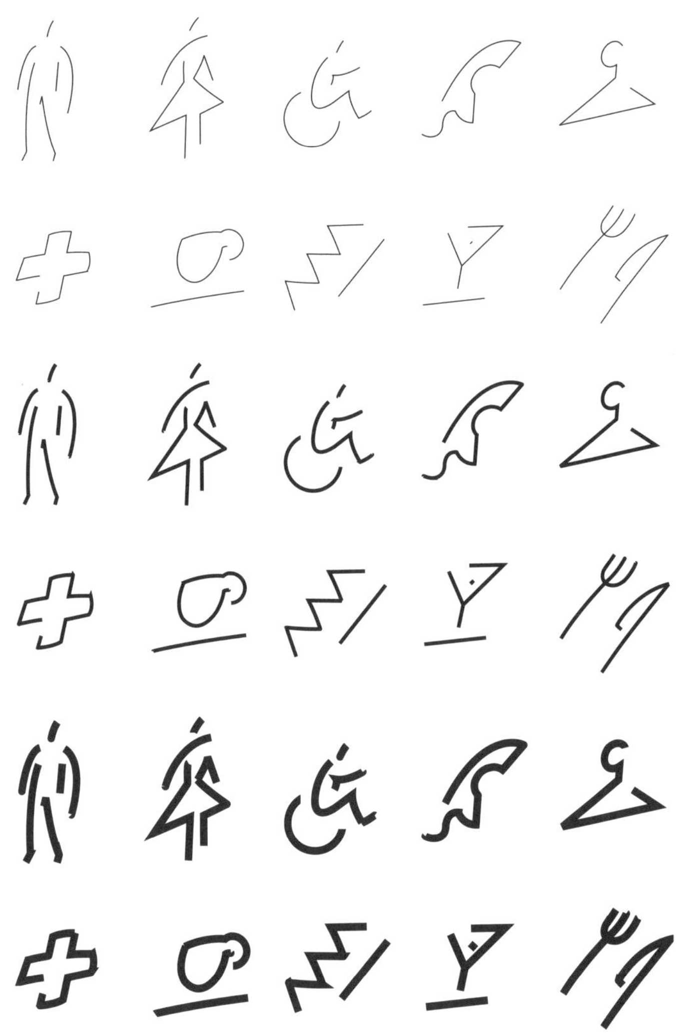

A series of pictograms designed to make complete stem width adaptation possible with the weight of the selected signage typeface. Designed by the author in 1990.

A series of pictograms with a Mediterranean flavour, including some mandatory symbols. Designed by the author in 1989.

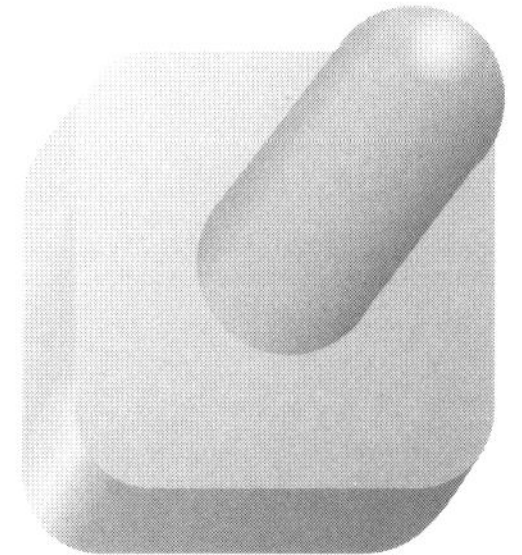

The 'wheelchair' and the 'running-man exit' pictograms are without a doubt the most familiar standardised pictograms. By contrast, the 'ladies & gentlemen' pictograms are certainly the most widely used but also come in a boundless variety of symbols & illustrations.
The Japanese designer Tokuzo Shigi came up with a very straightforward and elementary solution, made of wood.

Ladies X Gents Y Disabled O

LADIES GENTS DISABLED
X Y O

ladies gents disabled

ladies gents disabled

Ladies Gents Disabled

LADIES GENTS DISABLED

ladies gents disabled

ladies gents disabled

Ladies Gents Disabled

Ladies Gents Disabled

Ladies Gents Disabled

Ladies Gents Disabled

ladies gents disabled

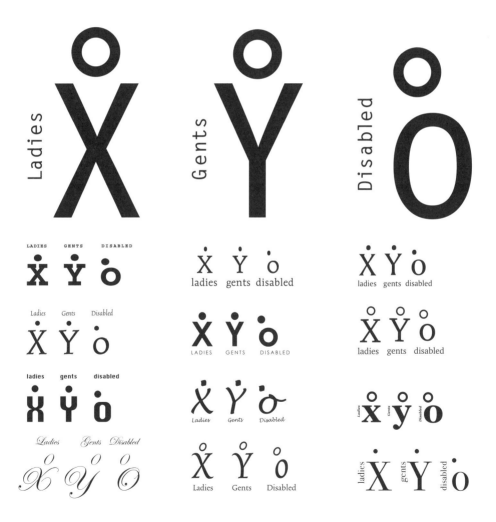

Pictograms can also be made with the typeface used for the signage project.
Design idea by Sarah Rosenbaum 2004.

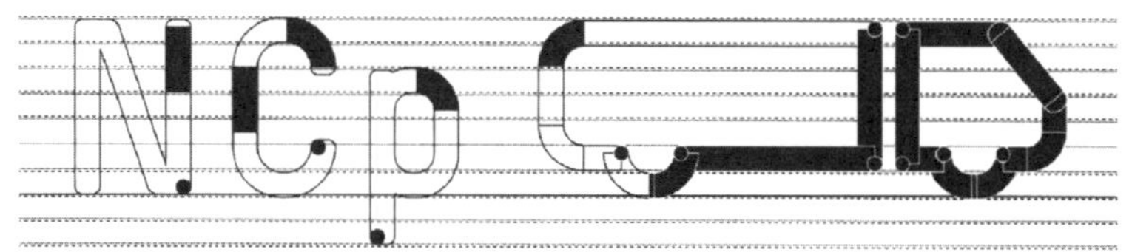

Simple Köln Bonn Symbols

Design firm 'Intégral' (Ruedi Baur and Associates) designed in 2002 the visual corporate identity for the airport of Köln Bonn in Germany. Typeface and pictograms are completely integrated in every design detail.

Examples of a pictogram series for the Air France timetables. Designers Adrian Frutiger and Bruno Pfaffi in the eighties.

Examples of pictograms for the Touring Club Italiano to be used in 10-point size for printed guides, as well as for street signs. Designed by Bob Noorda in the seventies.

A series of frequently applied pictograms that can be used on screens or in small print and can also be adjusted to the weight of the selected typeface. Designed by the author 1990.

The pictograms as well as the arrow can be custom-designed to become almost part of the typeface used for the signage project. Pictogram and arrow designed by the author.

Pictogram series may step out of their strict conventions and be used in a more illustrative way. Designed by the author in 1990.

4.11. Illustrations & maps

The arrow and the map must be the two items most closely associated with navigation. It could very well be that with the help of new electronic navigational devices, these two may play an increasingly important role in wayfinding. Mastering our environment started with making maps. It is almost as important as writing and calculating. There are many examples of exquisite cartography. It is a craft built on centuries of drawing experience. An extensive signage project cannot be achieved successfully without using a map of some sort. The different ways to design a map are almost limitless and inspiring examples abound. There are only a few design constraints. The most functional maps are the portable ones that can be consulted when required during the journey. The position of a static map always has to correspond to the viewpoint of the user. For the rest, there is a lot of design freedom. Of course, map design has to be appropriate to the project. The signage for an historic city centre, an exhibition ground, a zoo or a park, need something different than that for an office building, a museum or a hospital.
In some instances, maps are redundant as a signage tool and are only produced to make a flashy graphic at the entrance of a building. Maps do not have to be complicated to function properly. The museum that prints a simple map on its entry ticket does an excellent job of creating an extremely handy piece of paper.

The design of maps has not undergone major changes over time. Drawing software has made maps easier to produce, thus more widely available, and there is a general trend towards simplification. By contrast, very illustrative maps are also still produced. The only exception is the maps we use to show public transportation networks. In 1933 the London Underground released a new map showing its network, that set an example for every map created thereafter. Instead of giving priority to the exact geographic location of transportation stops, this map showed the various lines in a most simplified way, avoiding visual clutter and providing clear indications for transfer stops. Ironically, this groundbreaking step forward in map design was not done by a designer or cartographer, but by an electrical engineering draftsman, Harry Beck—at his own initiative and during his free time. His professional background was clearly visible in the design.
Trying to find your way around in the maze of an underground network is something different from finding your way around in a nature resort or an exhibition park. The first needs no other clues than the connection of lines and names of stations. Functional maps in this category can be very abstract. For the second, it can be very helpful if landmarks are indicated on the map. These types of maps may need more realistic reference points. The most realistic ones in this category are maps showing the area in 'bird's-eye view'.

Like all other graphic matter, maps can also be made into three-dimensional objects, which allows use of textured surfaces and raised letters or raised parts on the map. Certain parts, like waterways, can be cut out entirely, creating a bas-relief of the actual feature. Sometimes, complete maquettes are built for wayfinding purposes.

The most important requirement in all map design—especially for complex environments—is to emphasise the helpful references in the real environment and to ignore the confusing ones. Although this sounds simple, in fact it remains quite a labour-intensive job.

Maps placed in a fixed location have to match seamlessly with their environment. The compass directions in plane and on the map projection must be identical. This is the only way to avoid confusion. In this way all directions from the 'you-are-here' dot are obvious: left from the dot is to the left, right from the dot is to the right, above the dot is behind the map, under the dot is behind the viewer. This sound principle should never be violated.

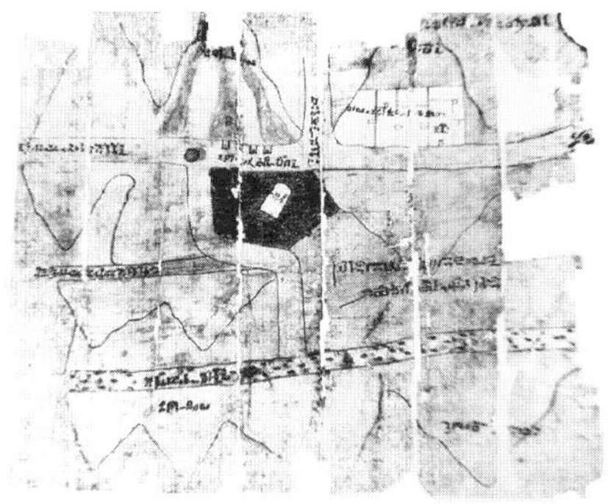

A papyrus map from around 1500 BC and a Palestinian mosaic map from 565 AD. Maps are part of the earliest signs of human civilisation. The oldest found is a map of a settlement painted on a rock wall.

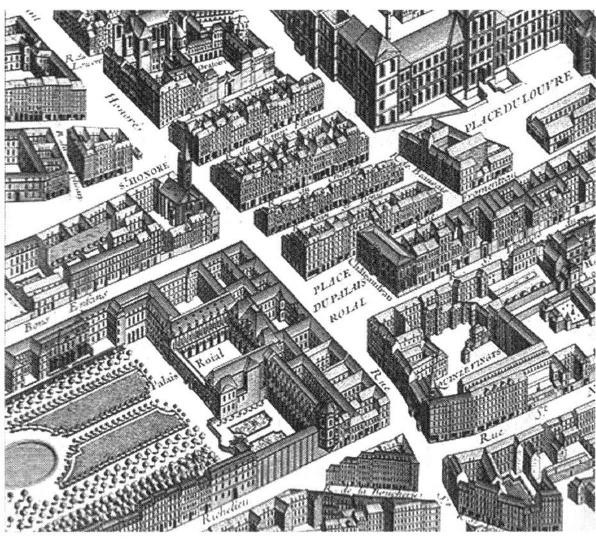

In 1739 Louis Bretez finished his series of copper plate engraved maps of Paris, showing the situation as it was 5 years earlier when he received the commission from Michel Etienne Turgot. The maps became famous as the 'Turgot Plan de Paris'.

The city maps of Hermann Bollmann and his staff are highly praised. Bollmann Bildkarten Verlag published bird's-eye view city maps for over 60 years, mostly of European cities. The illustration above shows a part of the New York Manhattan map. This map was hand-drawn in the 1960 s using about 67,000 photographs, of which 1700 were taken from the air.

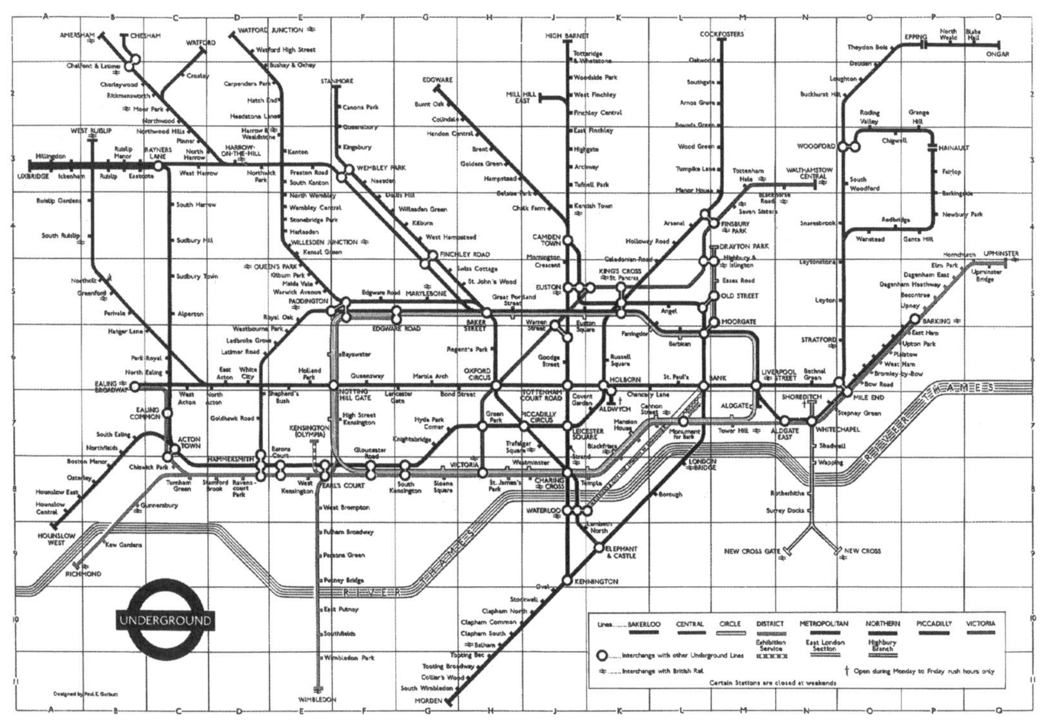

Transit maps give an overview of the stops and hubs of the individual lines in a public transit network. The foundation of the design for this kind of map was laid not by a designer or cartographer but by an electrical engineer called Harry Beck. He designed, on his own account and in his free time, the London Underground map around 1930. In his design he followed the way electric circuits were drafted. All maps since have basically followed his example.

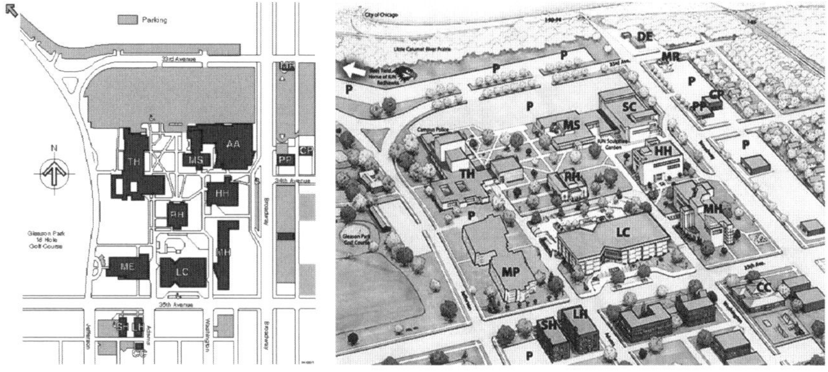

*Two different versions of the Indiana University Northwest campus site.
Left, the traditional map; right, the bird's eye view version.*

The campus map of the University of Salford. Most maps are produced digitally these days. Vector drawings make for relatively small file sizes, so can be issued through the internet where details can be enlarged without losing much quality.

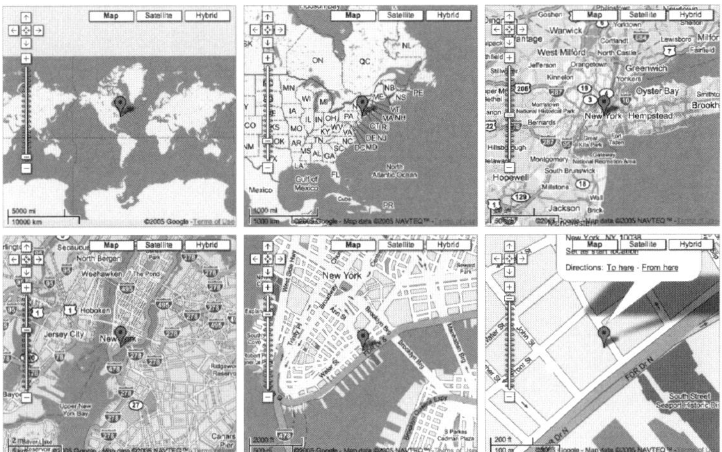

The American company Google offers a free service on their website where all addresses in North America can be found. It is possible to zoom in and out on a series of maps that could even be useful when coming from outer space. Soon the rest of the world may follow suit.

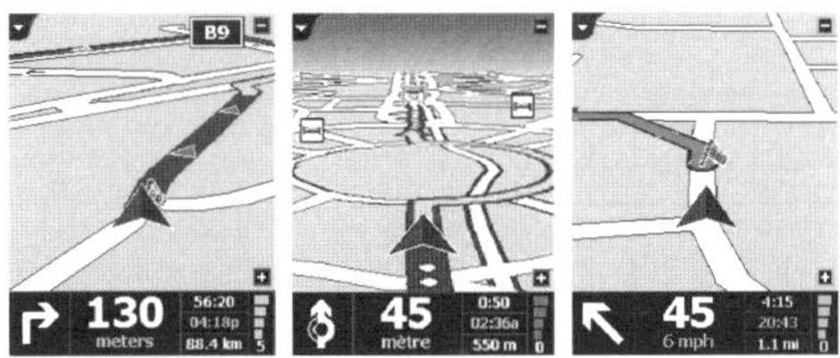

Screen shots from the TomTom navigation screen, a product of a Dutch company. Google (and other companies) have perfected the way to use interactive maps to help us find the way to our destinations. However, the future is most likely leaning towards navigation systems that reduce finding the way to simply following instructions. Screen images, if desired in combination with spoken text, will guide us step-by-step to our destinations.

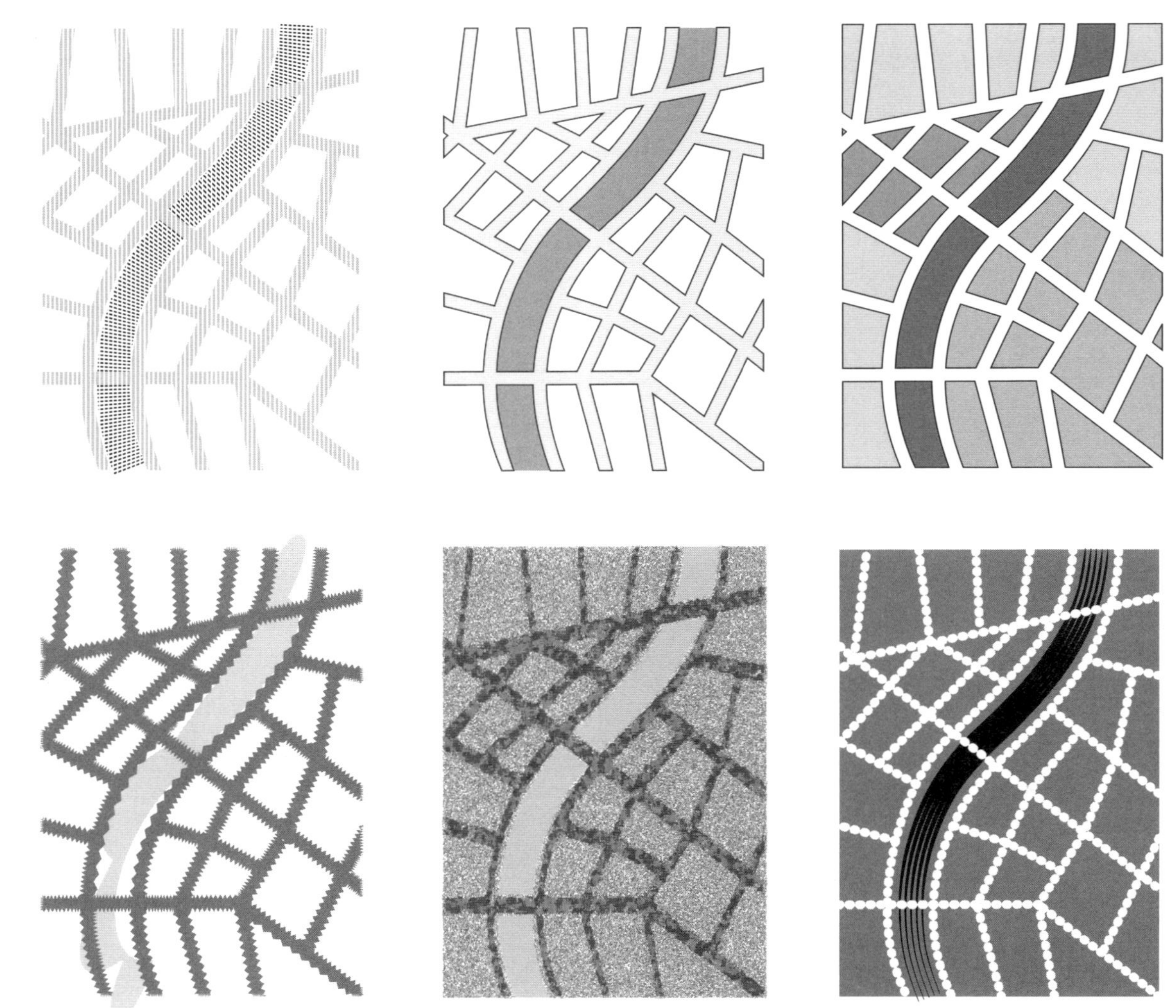

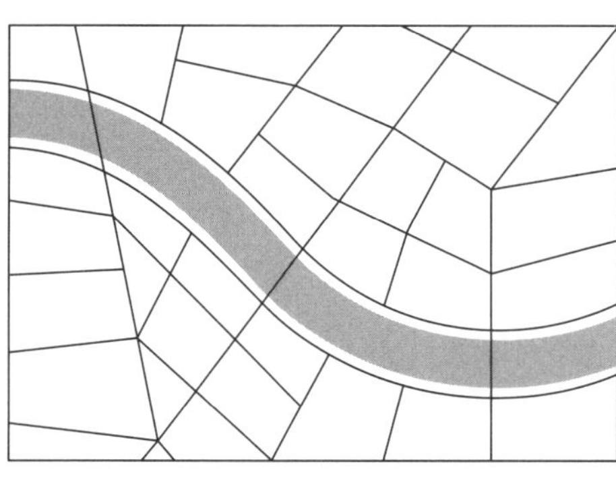
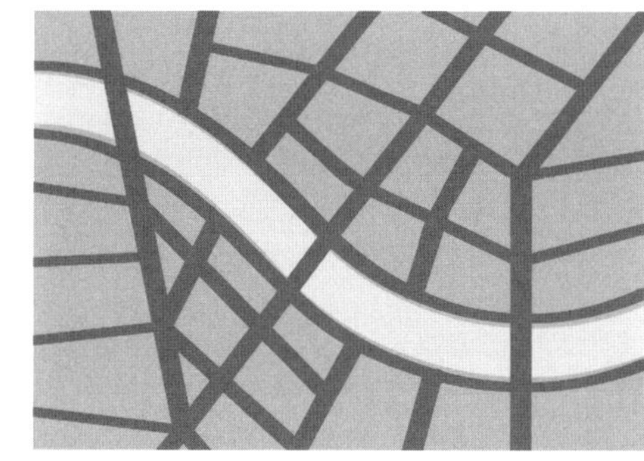
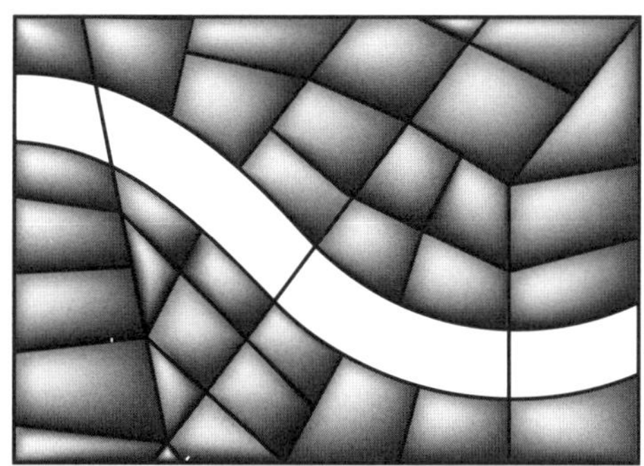

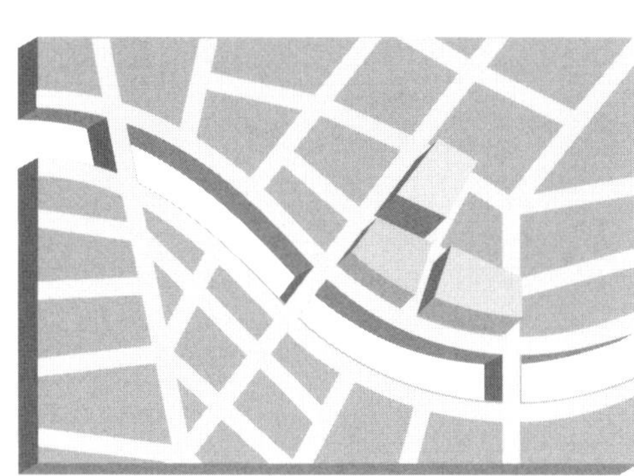
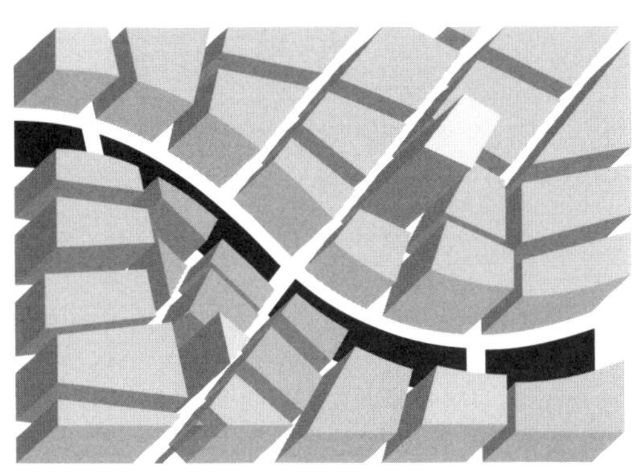

Graphic software makes endless variation possible in the visual representation of maps. Advanced material-cutting technology also makes three-dimensional maps a not-too-costly alternative. The tactile quality of this type of map may be useful for the visually impaired. The overall visual consistency of every item playing a part in the signage program should remain the ultimate benchmark when deciding which visual representation to select.

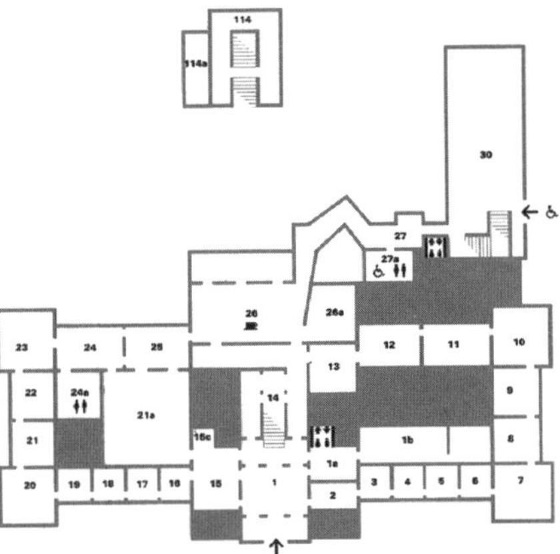

Bare-bones simple maps have the advantage that they can be printed in small sizes, on an entrance ticket, for example. A map that can be carried around is functionally superior to a mounted one. This map is for the 'Stedelijk Museum' in Amsterdam.

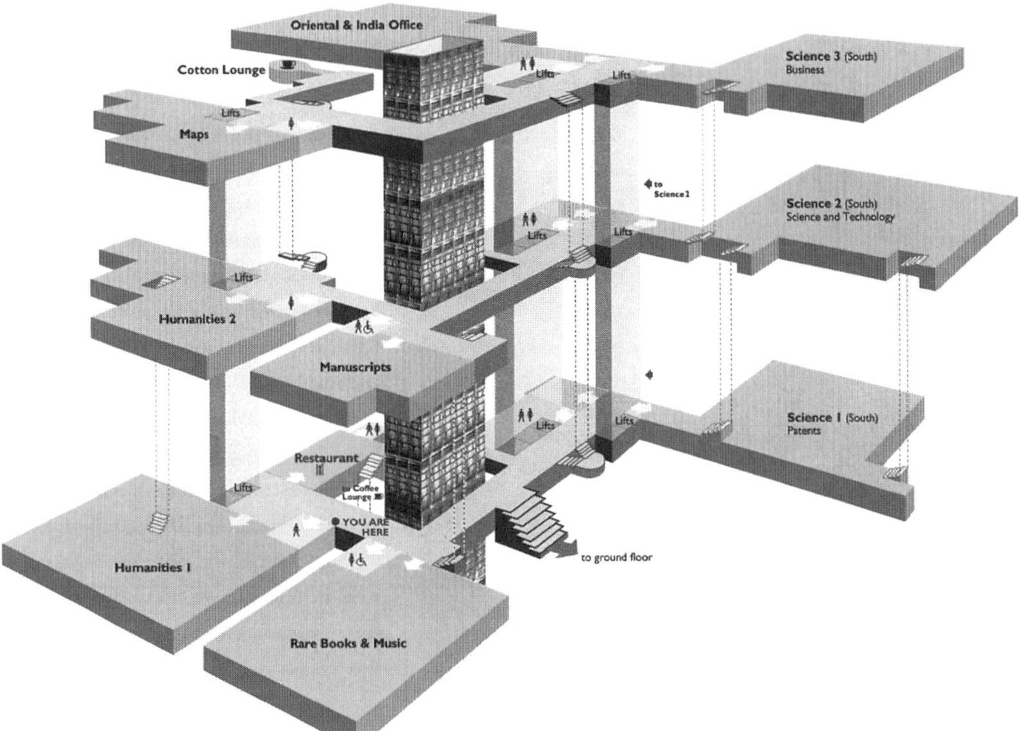

Occupants of large buildings usually love visually spectacular three-dimensional directories. In most cases they are more visually impressive than useful for wayfinding purposes. An exception is this visually stunning as well as informative building floor plan map for the British Library in London. Design Colette Miller, Information Design Unit, UK.

4.11.1. THE USE OF ILLUSTRATIONS

Illustrations may be used to support or replace names or alphanumeric coding. In general, images are remembered more easily than numbers. Unlike computers, the human brain seems to store and retrieve complex representative images better than simple abstract ones. Illustrations may be used, for instance, as identifiers for sections in parking areas or for sections or spaces in buildings. Clearly, the use of illustrations as opposed to codes will create a totally different atmosphere in any place. Also, the potential variety in the design of illustrations is immensely greater. Combinations of illustrations and numbers are also used; simple floor numbers are integrated or accompanied by illustrations to create a specific identity for each floor or a unique sense of place.

Illustrations may also replace pictograms, or even function as landmarks. Murals, also called 'super graphics', are easy to produce these days. Print technology is no longer constrained by size. Images produced on our computer screens can now be blown up to nearly unlimited proportions. Signage designers are now capable of almost recreating a building entirely by graphical means. Small signs can now be replaced by 'indications' covering a whole wall, the ceiling, or the floor. All these technological niceties are extremely powerful means that can easily get designers overexcited. One shouldn't get carried away entirely by the potential of these technologies, but instead should keep a keen eye on how the means employed fit together in a sensible way. A lot of signage projects suffer from an unbalanced approach, often overstressing the importance of the spectacular items within the signage system.

Technological developments have made production of large-scale illustrations relatively inexpensive. The next development will include large panels that can show animated images or the inexpensive production of three-dimensional items.
New developments in LED technology already allow the production of huge displays, carrying light sources with enough power to allow daytime use. Computer Aided Manufacturing technology applied to all kinds of cutting machines has made 3D objects easier to produce. These popular technologies are under ongoing development. Size and scale of reproduction will be less and less of a constraint. The boundaries between reproduction and reality will be further blurred.

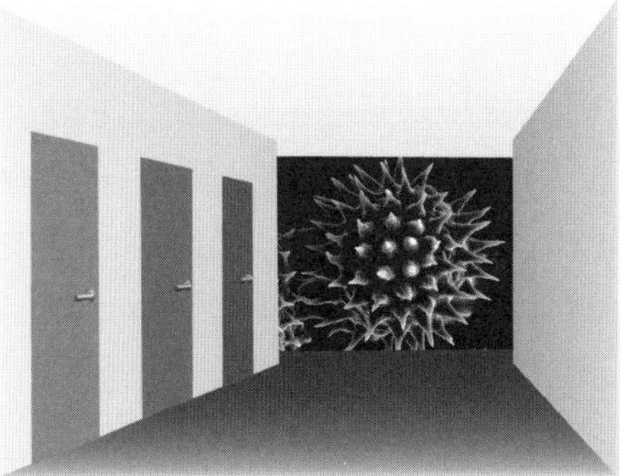

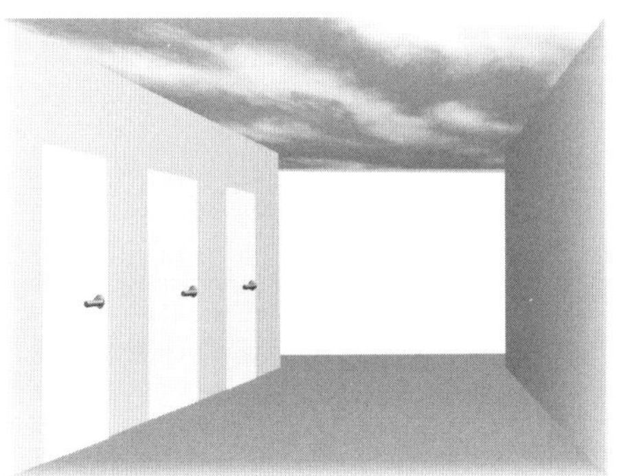

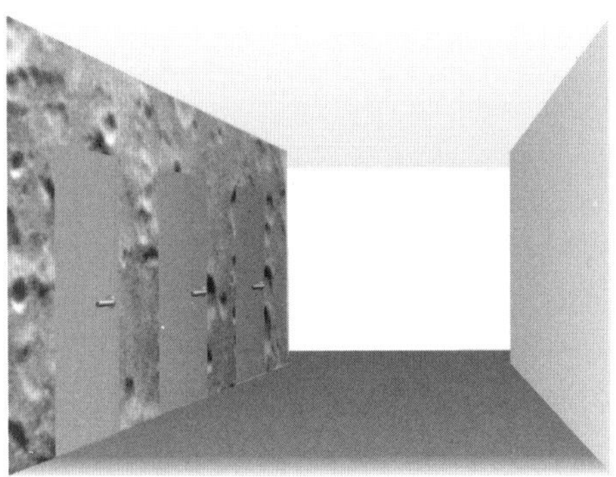

Illustrations can be applied at almost any scale onto a growing variety of base materials. Printed adhesive foils are available for a wide range of applications—even for on the floor. Current fabric and tapestry production allows short-run customised print versions. Computer manufacturing and advanced material-cutting technologies have made complex illustrative applications in traditional materials, like stone and tiles, a feasible design option.

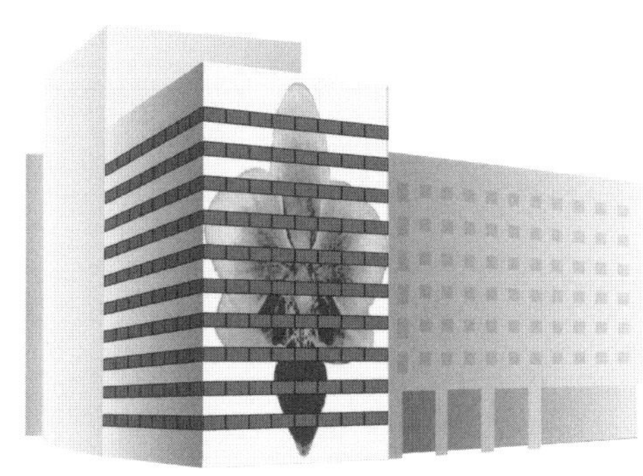

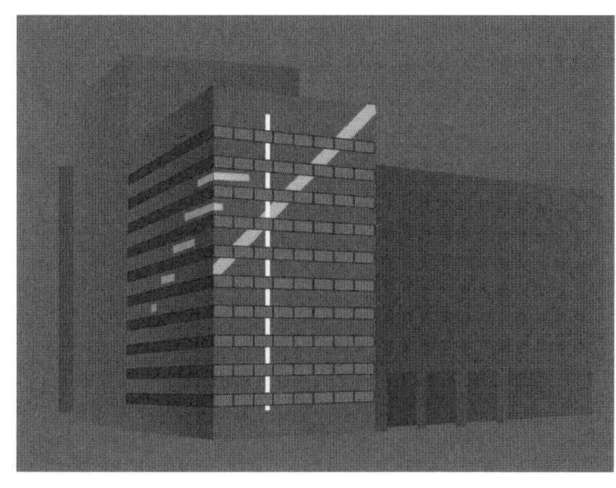

Large-scale print technology combined with translucent vinyl or fabric can create extremely powerful visual effects. LED *technology allows fabrication of huge animated displays, that are even visible under daylight conditions. Both technologies can turn buildings into spectacular landmarks.*

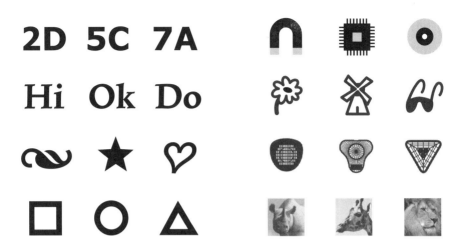

2D 5C 7A

Hi Ok Do

Illustrations have stronger empathetic qualities than names or alphanumerical codes, although the latter have the advantage of being able to be placed in a simple (alphabetic) order. The simplicity of visual representation is not relevant for recognition or ease of remembering.

Three-dimensional illustrative objects have a strong visual impact and can be employed effectively to emphasise key locations in a building or at a site.

Illustrative floor-level indicators for a parking garage in New York (1998, US). Each ascending floor shows Mother Earth seen from a greater distance. Designer Keith Godard.

Illustrative floor level indicators showing large swarms of small local animals and insects, like ladybirds, snails, butterflies, frogs, grasshoppers, bees and hummingbirds. Parking garage in Charlotte (2000, US). Designer Keith Godard.

Mosaic hats in the subway station at 23rd street in New York, now called the 'hat' station, (2003). Designer Keith Godard.

A collection of bouncing ball icons are used to identify departments in the Dutch Westeinde Hospital (1980). Designers, Studio Dumbar.

Left: illustrative additions to the directional signs for Disney World, Florida (1990, USA). Designers, Sussman Prejza studio. Right: photographic illustrations play an essential role in the signage for the city of Lyon (1998 – 2001, France). Designer, Intégral, Ruedi Baur Associates.

4.12. Systems of measurement; the grid

A system of measurement, or a grid, plays an important role in all design work. Architects are used to working with grid patterns, a system of fixed measurement that defines the exact positions and measurements of all the important structural parts of a building. Traditional building materials were confined to maximum dimensions, a limitation that created a sort of natural order in all building structures. Traditional crafts also worked with standard measurements for certain items, like a door, a corridor, or a ceiling height. Japanese architecture used to be one of the most traditional; all floor dimensions were based on the size of a tatami floor mat.

With the arrival of concrete as a building material, many of the traditional measurements no longer have a functional basis. Concrete allows great freedom in construction. Perhaps the new freedom was too unrestrained for some. One of the pioneers in concrete building design, architect Le Corbusier, developed a system of measurement that he applied in all his architecture. His system was based on the proportions of the human body, following classic predecessors. He called the system 'le Modulor'. Modular grid systems became fashionable in all types of design. Some of it was functional, but a lot was applied more as a styling instrument. The high-tech structures of the American architect Buckminster Fuller really needed a modular base. The Swiss graphic designer Müller-Brockmann was one of the first to demonstrate that typography based on a grid system created a pleasant visual order that could enhance readability and simplify production for print. But experiments in basing typefaces on a coarse and simple grid pattern were only sensible for creating display type. Letter shapes cannot be forced into a too simple structure without losing readability.

Not only designers were looking for a new order; so were lawmakers. A lot of legislation and regulation has been produced that set standard (or minimum/maximum) measurements for building facilities. The standardisation relates mostly to dwelling and working conditions, safety and accessibility of buildings to disabled visitors. Also the building industry itself, with the help of architects, has created standardisation in the built environment. Ultimately, all buildings are used by people, so a natural order of measurement has to be observed in relation to what we humans are capable of doing in the most comfortable way. Therefore, the average human proportions must be obeyed in some way or other.

For centuries, Japanese floor sizes were related to the (almost) standardised size (90 x 180 cm, 35.5" x 70") of the Tatami floor mat. Traditional Japanese architecture is based on a strict system of measurement.

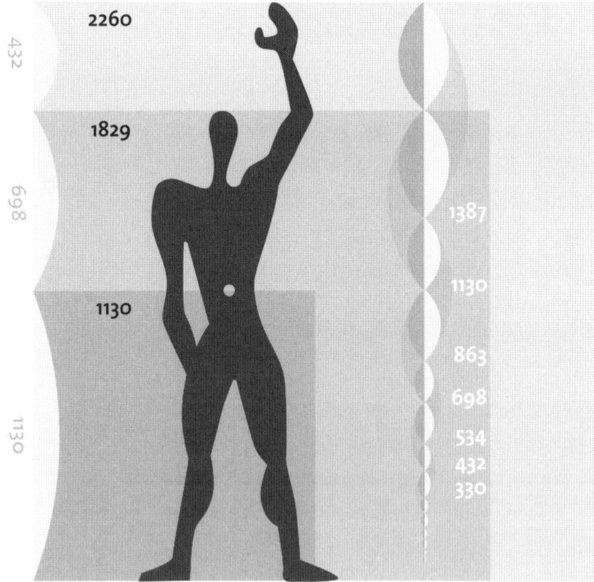

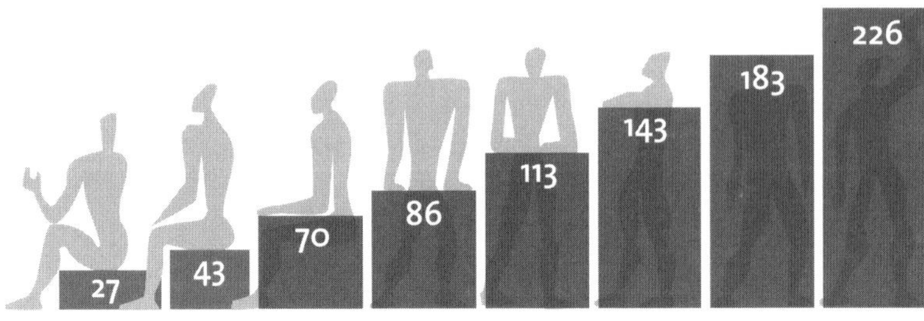

In 1947 the French/Swiss architect Le Corbusier presented a system of measurement based on the proportions of the human body, while at the same time integrating the Golden Section ratio, 1 : 1.618. He called his system 'Le Modulor'.

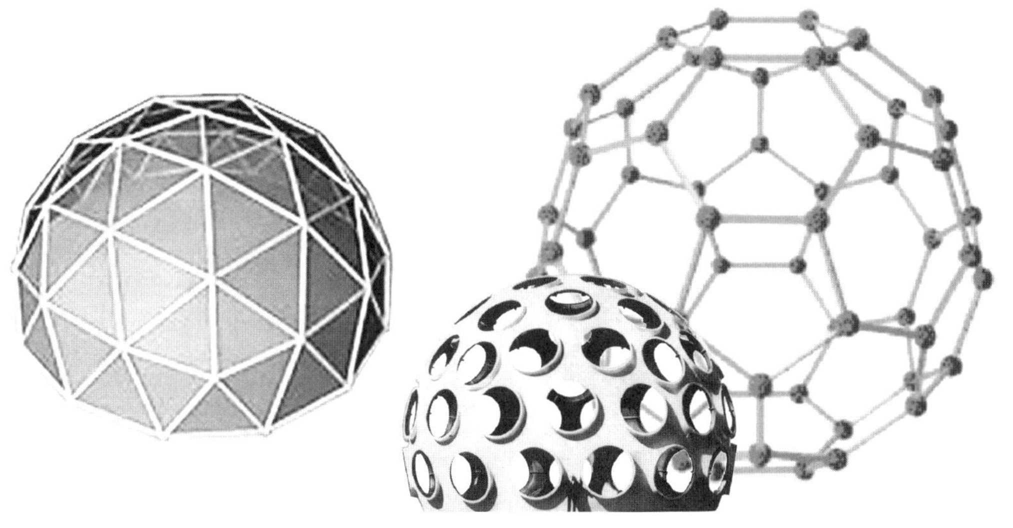

American inventor/architect Richard Buckminster Fuller, 1895 – 1983, spent his career designing constructions made with modular space frames. A very strong type of carbon molecules (and also a football) is constructed in the same way he often used for his own constructions. This molecule structure is called after him: 'Bucky Balls'.

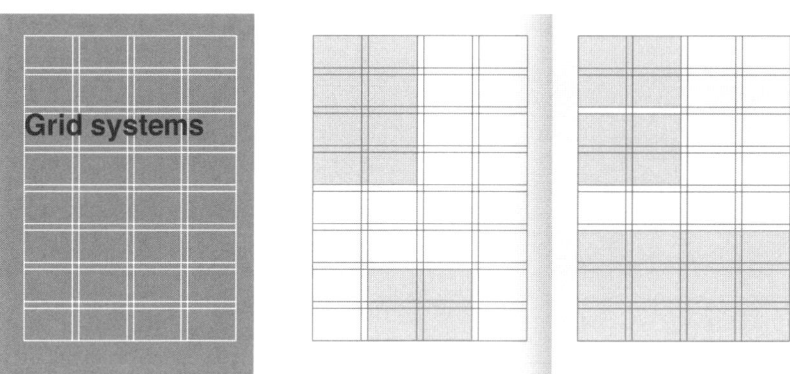

The Swiss designer Josef Müller-Brockmann, 1914 – 1996, was one of the first to develop extensive 'grid systems' for graphic design. His 1961 book 'Grid systems for Graphic Design' had a major impact on the profession.

Type design based on a simple grid will become less easy to read.

4.12.1. PANEL SIZE

It is not easy to avoid the use of sign panels in a signage project. In most cases, a series of different sized panels are needed. It is important to maintain as much as possible the same proportions within the series. All panels that share identical proportions will maintain a family look, even when their individual sizes are different. However, it may not be possible—or even desirable—to keep the same proportions for wall, suspending and free-standing signs. Nonetheless, maintaining proportions within each category is advisable. It does create visual order when panel sizes have a mathematical relationship of some sort with one another. It also helps to reduce the number of different sizes to an absolute minimum. Complexity adds to visual clutter, the major enemy of signage design. Moreover, reduced variety limits the number of sign types needed in the project and economises on production costs.

For some time, the square was the favourite proportion for sign panels. It was supposedly a 'neutral' proportion that would distance itself from any architectural surrounding and stand out visually in a humble and non-conflicting way. There is some wishful thinking in this theory, which became popular at the same time that square grid systems were admired. It is unlikely that there is anything like a neutral proportion that would suit all architectural styles. The only neutral aspect of a square might be that is does not have a 'direction'. It does not 'lie down', or 'stand up', so to speak; it is neither horizontal nor vertical.
A lot of light switches and other electrical gear is offered on square back plates, so there could be a simple proportional match with these devices. Yet, it will be wise to study the most eye-catching proportions the architect has devised for the building and assimilate these proportions. To assimilate does not necessarily mean to copy these proportions. Obviously, door dimensions and proportions deserve special attention as, do modular wall or work space systems.

4.12.2. PANEL PROPORTIONS

Throughout history, proportions have been a topic of interest for many scientists, artists and designers. During the Renaissance period geometry became of special interest to art and science. By exploring the geometric patterns and proportions found in nature, scholars hoped to establish 'divine' proportions conceived by the Ultimate Creator. The human body in particular has been studied intensively and inspired Vitruvius, Da Vinci and Dürer to propose 'fundamental' proportions.
The square, the circle, and most of all the Golden Section or Golden Mean were considered to create fundamentally sound proportions. Shapes made in the proportions of the Golden Mean seem to be experienced as harmonious by most and will be found in all human creations of all times. The square—and its multiples—is also often used as a 'modulus' for proportions.

For signage design, standardised paper sizes are obviously also important proportions since printed paper often plays an important role in certain sign types. The same can be said more and more for standardised screen display sizes. Screen displays are predominantly manufactured in inches; paper sizes have two main standardisations, the American 'legal/letter' size and the European 'A-series'.

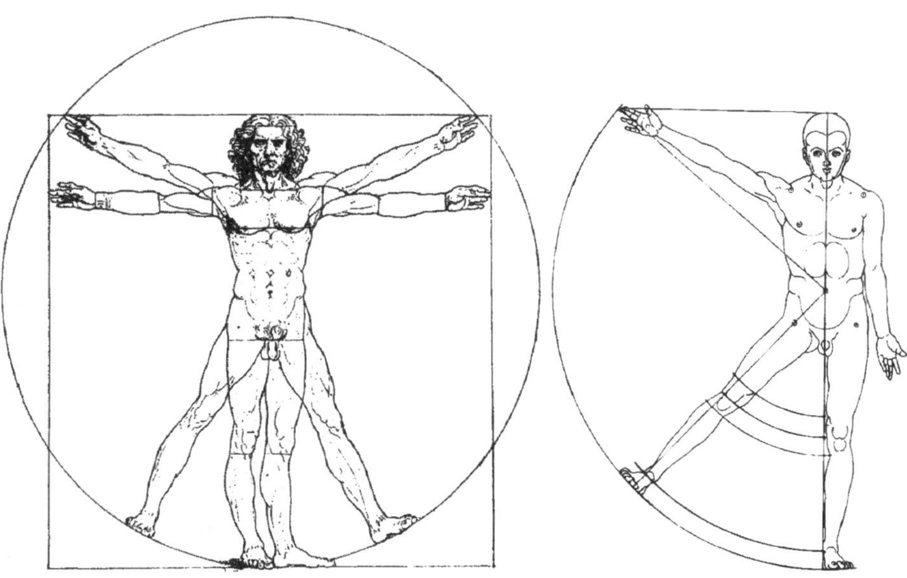

Geometry studies by Leonardo da Vinci, 1452 – 1519 (left) and Albrecht Dürer, 1471 – 1528 (right). Numerous artists and scientist have tried to reveal 'divine' geometry in nature.

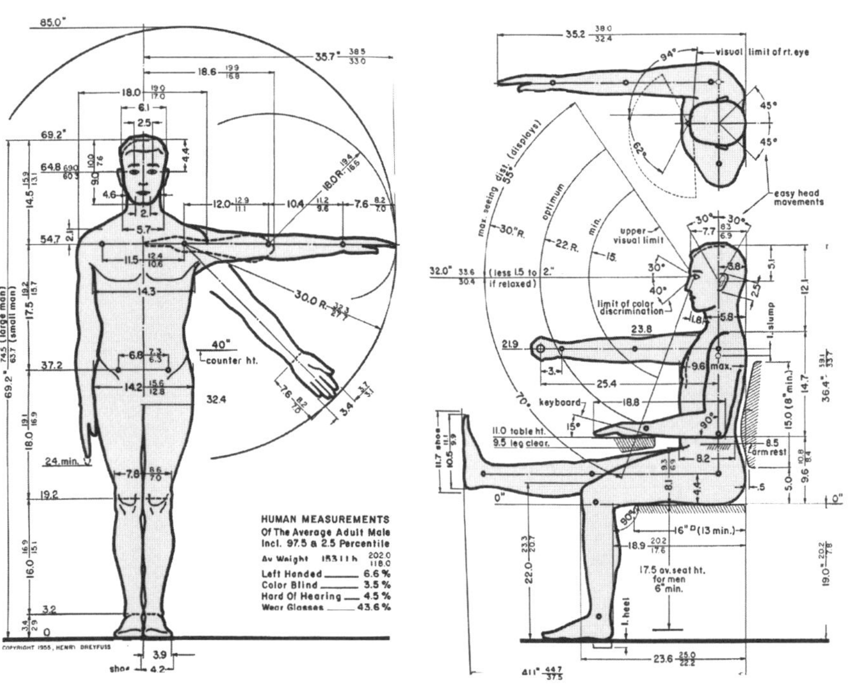

Industrial designer Henry Dreyfuss documented in the 1950 s the measurements of the average American male, female and child. These data were used in the product designs of the numerous commissions received by his company.

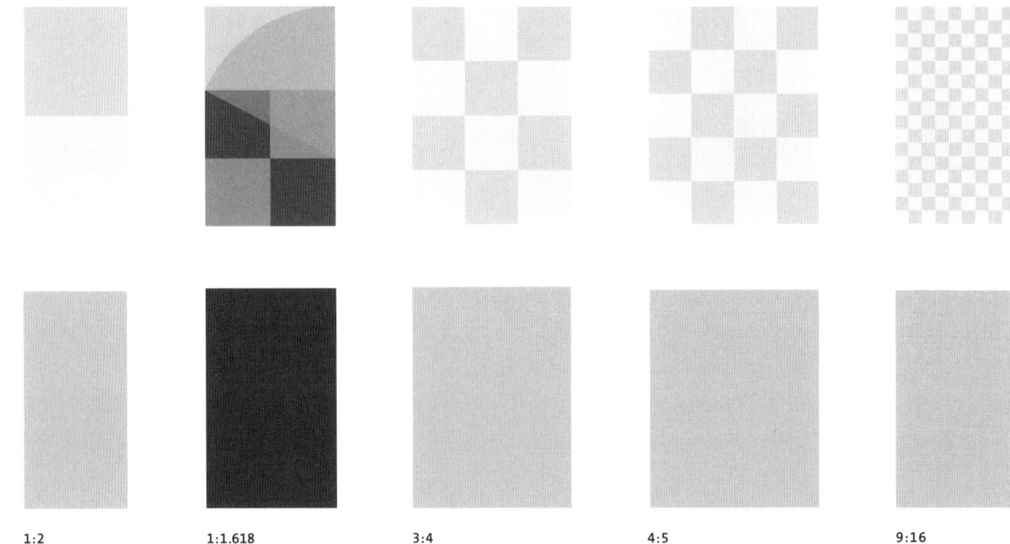

An overview of a number of traditional panel proportions, from left to right, the Tatami floor mat, the famous 'Golden Section', the two traditional proportions of photographic film and electronic displays, and the last is the most recent 'wide screen' addition.

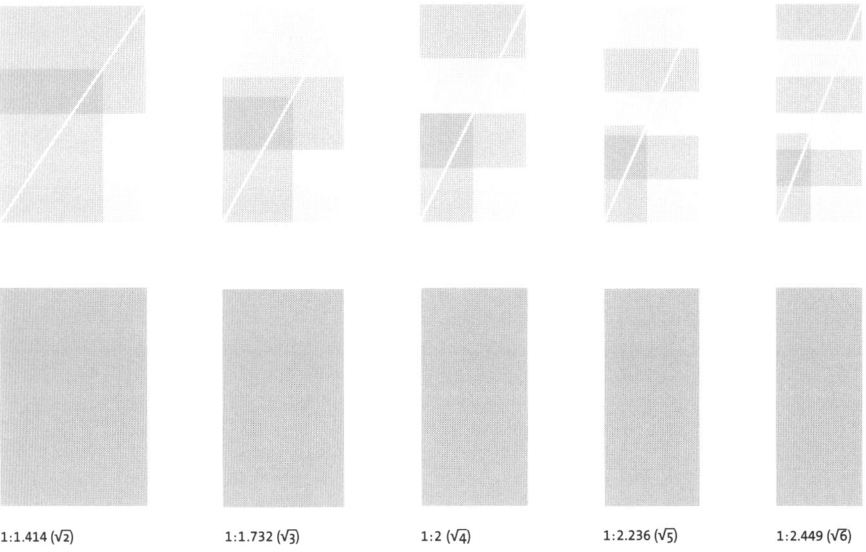

The series of proportions based on a ratio by which the length of one side is a root of the other. Shown above are roots 2 to 6. For root 2 half the size of the panel has the same proportions as the whole. The same applies for the other roots when the whole panel is divided by the number of the root. The European 'A' paper size series is based on the root 2 ratio.

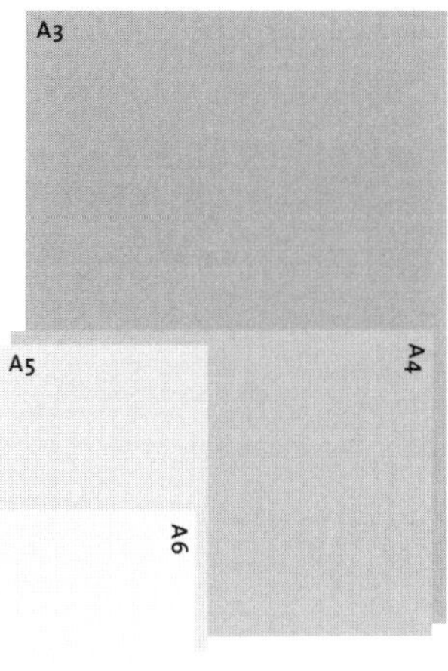

The international paper size standard that most countries follow is based on the European 'A' size series. The proportion is based on the root 2 figure, 1 : 1.414. Standard correspondence paper is A4 (210 x 297 mm). All consequent A-size numbers are either half or double this size. There is also a related 'B' and 'C' series of standard paper sizes that is based on a different base size. In the US, three standard sizes are mostly used, 'Letter' (8.5" x 11", 215.9 x 279.4 mm), 'Legal' (8.5" x 14", 215.9 x 355.6 mm) and 'Tabloid' (11" x 17") which is double the 'Letter' size.

Decimal

:1
:2
:3
:4
:6
:12

Duodecimal

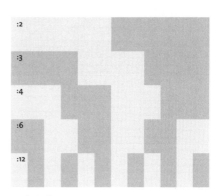

A duodecimal system, like the inch-based system, has the advantage of being easily divisible in more different ways than the metric (decimal) system. So, it will be sensible to mimic the advantageous properties of the duodecimal system when setting up a set of proportions in a metric system.

4.12.3. LAYOUT POSITIONING

The typography and the layout must be as consistent as possible throughout the whole project, whether it is put on panels first or applied directly onto walls. This includes not only the use of the selected typeface but also all other elements of the layout, such as letter size, letter spacing, leading and margins. All measurements will be related to the size of the panels. It will not be possible to create one layout that can be applied to every different sign type. The variety of messages required will be too diverse to fit into a single format. Nevertheless, the number of variations needs to be as small as possible and should at least remain consistent throughout the whole series of different sizes.
Modular sign panel systems must have identical layouts for all the different interchangeable elements of the system. This includes the layout of laser-printed paper inserts that may be part of the panel system.

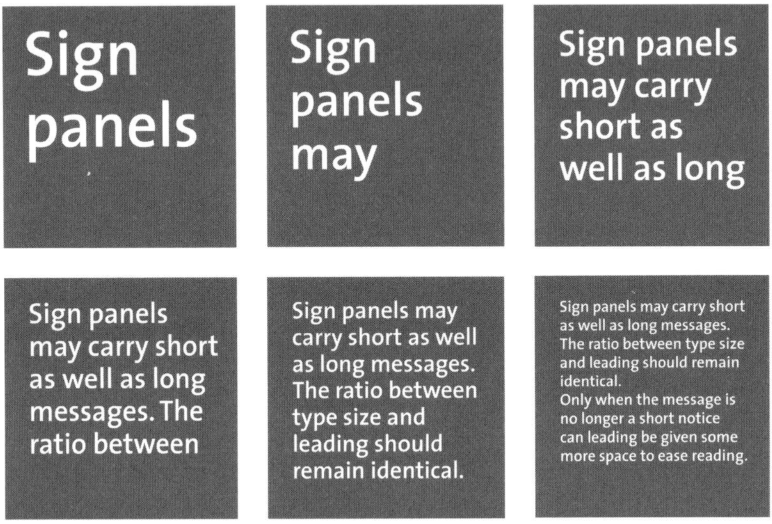

Text on signs needs to be concise; therefore, leading (line spacing) can be tight. All messages must keep identical leading in relation to type size. Long text may have more generous leading. Typographic style should be consistent, including representations on interactive media.

Interactive screens are becoming a regular part of signage projects. The typography on these devices should match the typography on all the other sign types. One would expect that it would be relatively easy for electronic devices to adopt a certain typographic style, but that does not appear to be true in all cases.

4.12.4. POSITIONING IN SPACE

Levelled floors and perpendicular walls are still the visual cornerstones of architecture. Some contemporary architects, like Frank Gehry or Zaha Hadid, try to break away from these traditions as much as possible, but they remain exceptions. Certainly the arrival of computers in architectural practices has made buildings more curved and skewed, but strict horizontal and vertical shapes dominate our built environment. The verticals are the rhythm of elements in plan, the horizontals are related to human measurements and are extremely important for our sense of order in space. The positions of the signage items will have to conform with this situation. Signage elements will be centred between or in alignment with existing architectural elements . Material thickness and the measurements of the architecture, in plan and in elevation, should be carefully considered and taken into account when positioning signs.

Careful consideration and foresight is important because the most intense confrontation between signage and architecture is the way the signs are positioned spatially. Finding harmony is difficult in situations where the signage was conceived as an afterthought. The margins for selecting different positioning options for the signs are very narrow, at the risk of losing essential functionality. Signs need easy detection and readability. This demand makes sign positioning extremely inflexible.

It is sad to observe that the very limited manoeuvring space for signs often leads to a clash with the architectural design. It is argued, time and again in this book, that architects should make signage an integral part of their master plan. If the signage is left as a part of the interior design to be added later, like the selection and layout of furniture, there will be a high chance of design collisions. It is almost beyond comprehension that what is considered landmark architecture, such as airports and train stations, fails pathetically in practically all cases on the level of the smooth integration of the signage within the architectural design. Contemporary buildings need to communicate efficiently with their users and visitors. Provision to make that possible is an essential function of the building, just as much as lighting or air conditioning.

As previously stated, the horizontal measurements within the built environment are related to those of an average human body. Door handles have standard mounting heights, just like railings, parapets and light switches. These standard heights are almost the same the world over. For signage, two mounting positions are ideal, one at our eye-level and another above our heads, just out of reach of our hands.

26A

57

2745

west

Nelson

7

28
B

6

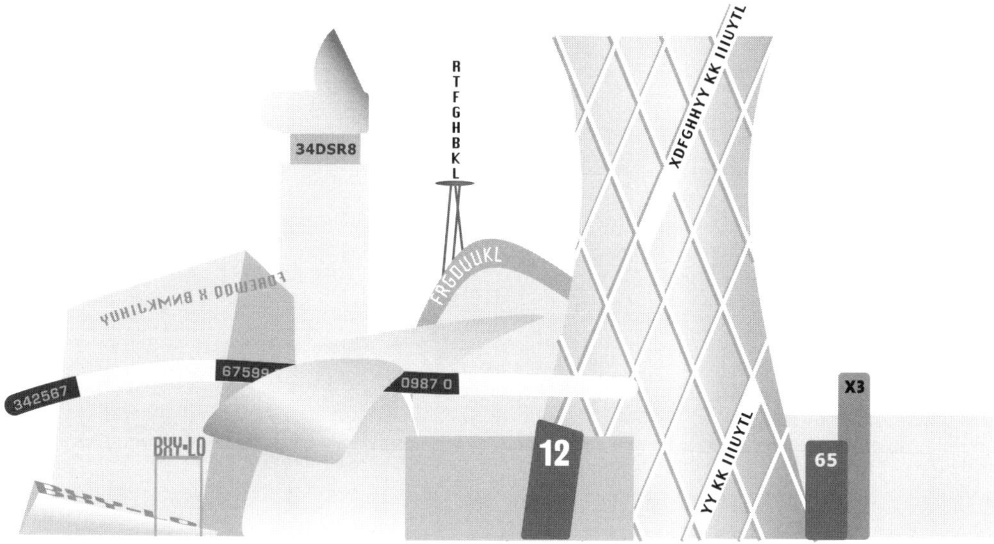

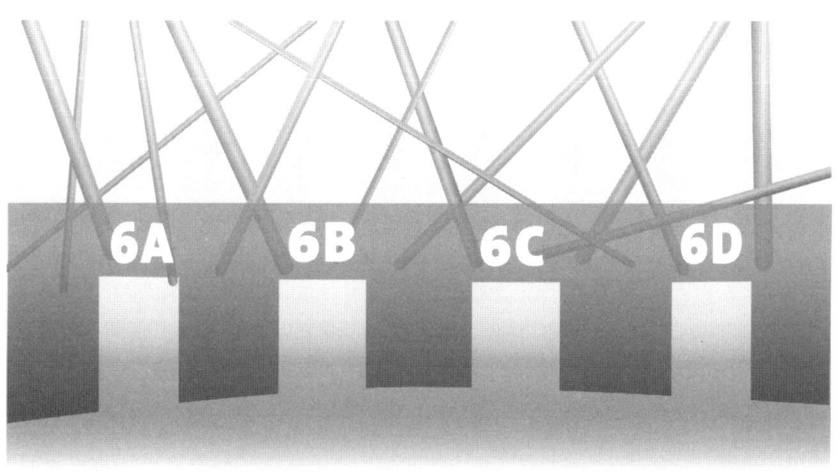

It is strongly recommended that some kind of provision for the signage be made during the architectural design phase. For signage intensive projects, like airports, transit hubs, leisure or shopping facilities, this is an essential requirement.

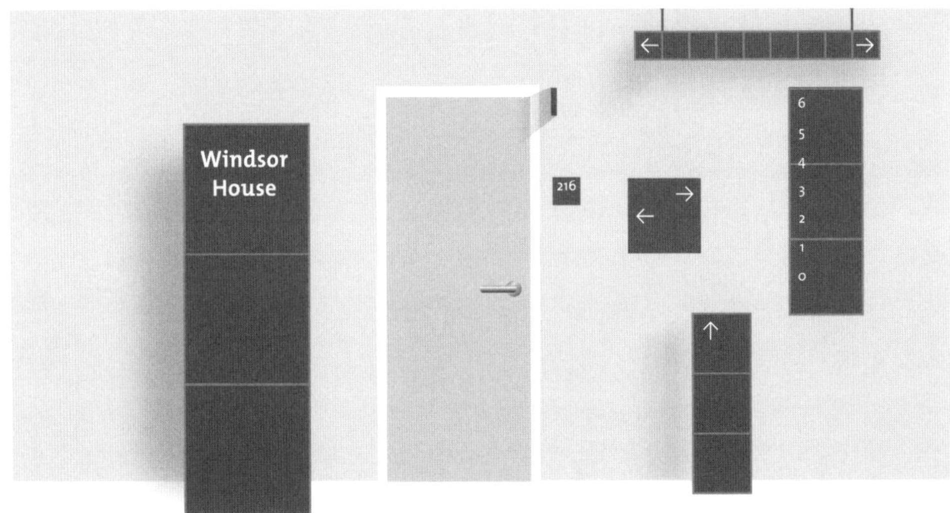

Keeping sign panel proportions identical helps to create a family look for all the different sign types used. Regrettably, maintaining one single proportion is often not possible or even desirable. Yet, basing panel sizes and graphic layout on a modular grid will create visual order and therefore ease of use (and production). A square module is often employed for this reason.

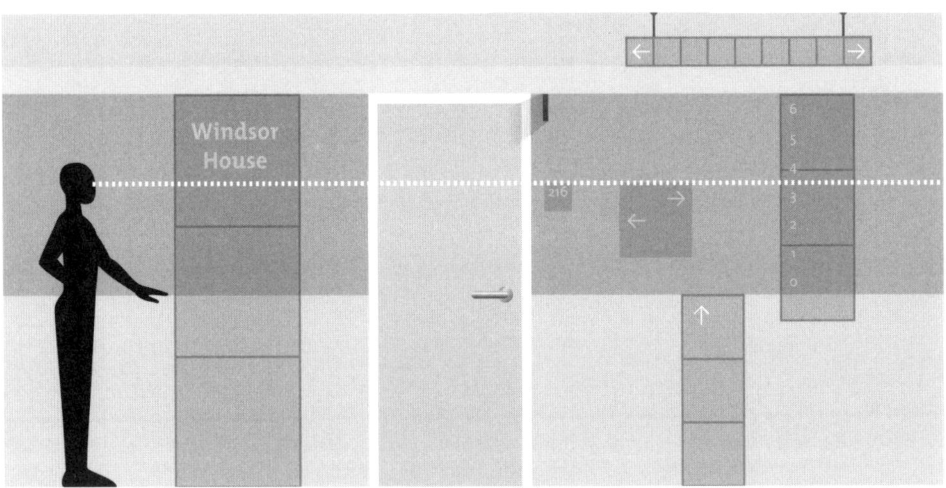

The positioning of signage items should take into account the measurements used in the architecture. Door (entrance) heights, ceiling heights and the heights of railings are important indicators. The average eye-level height is specifically important for positioning signs.

The 30 x 30 cm, 1' x 1' grid

One grid size is often used in signage projects. The 30 x 30 cm (1' x 1') grid is used for sign panel measurements as well as for mounting heights. The following pages show a wide spectrum of different signs applied in different environments: the airport, the highway, the city street and inside a building.

There are a few key standard heights relevant for signs.
1. Minimum parapet height 90 - 100 cm (3' – 3.5')
2. Eye-level height 150 - 165 cm (5' – 5.5')
3. Minimum clearance height for people 210 cm (7')
4. Minimum height (mandatory) traffic signs 210 cm (7')
5. Minimum clearance height (highway) traffic 520 cm (17')
(cm/foot measurements given are rounded off, 1 foot = 30.48 cm)

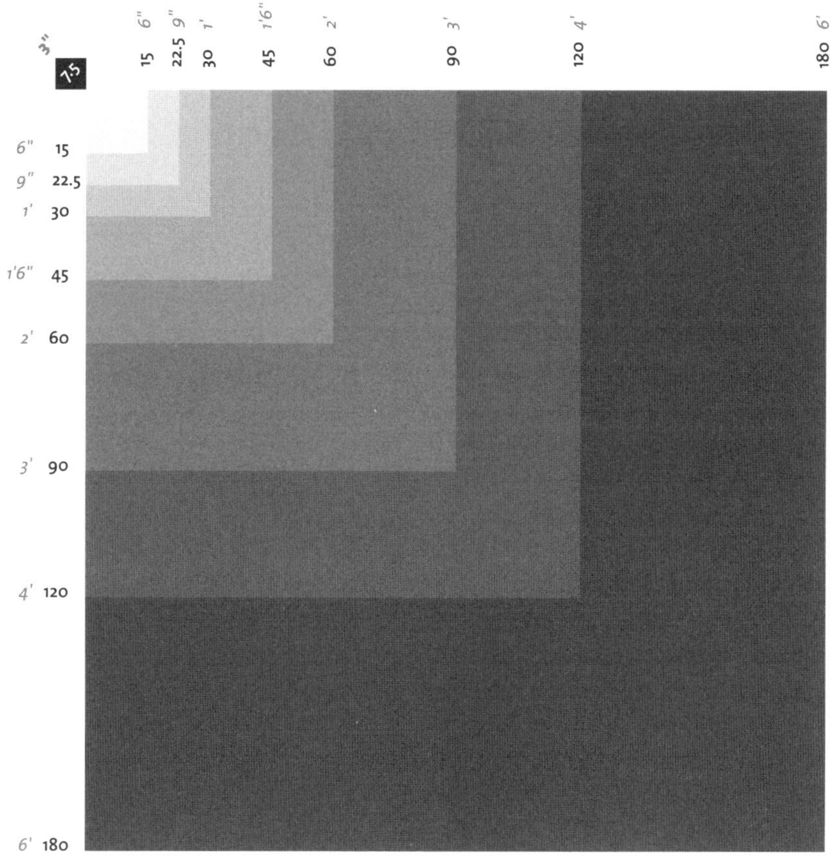

Sign panel systems offered on the market are not standardised in size. However, a range of measurements based on a module of 75 mm or 3 inches is often used. Door signs will be around 150 x 150 mm or 6 x 6 inches, wall direction panels around 300 x 300 mm (1' x 1'), small free-standing signs around 300 x 1200 mm (1' x 4'), directories around 300 x 600 mm (1' x 2'), suspending direction signs around 150 x 1200 mm (0.5' x 4'), monoliths around 600 x 1200 mm (2' x 6'). The widespread use of paper laserprinted inserts have introduced some exceptional sizes. Sizes of facilities used in North America tend to be bigger than elsewhere.

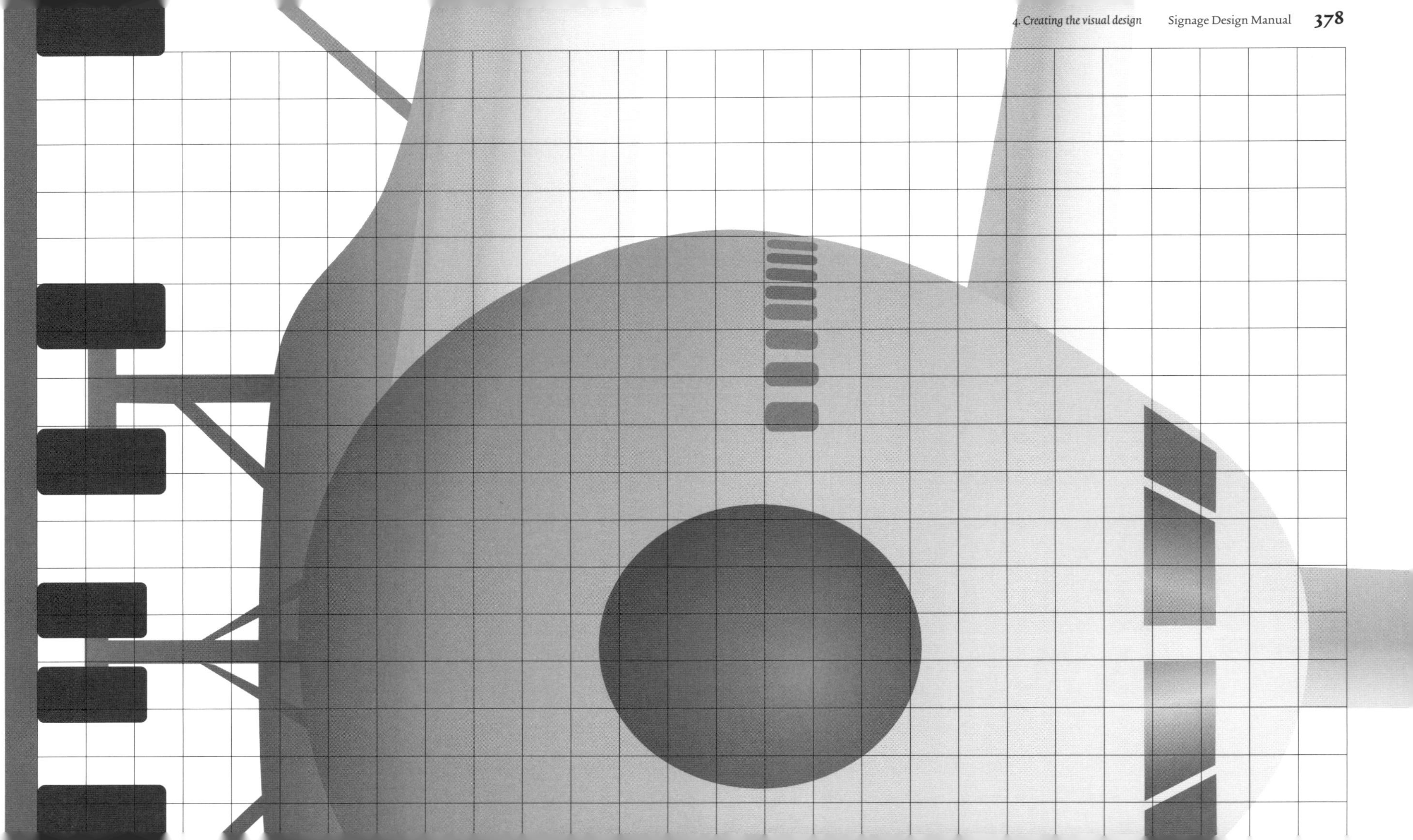

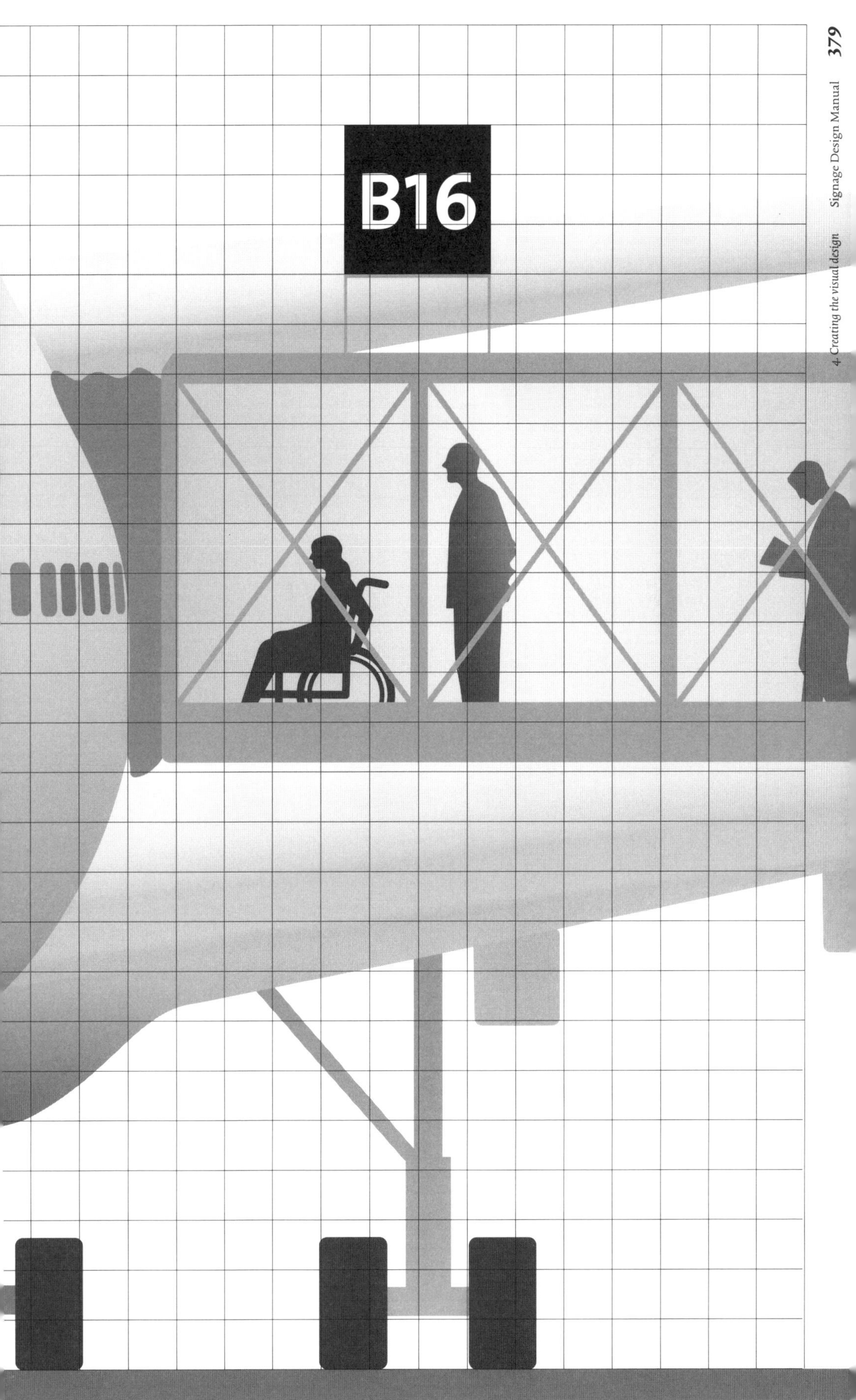

The 30 x 30 cm (1' x 1') grid in an airport.

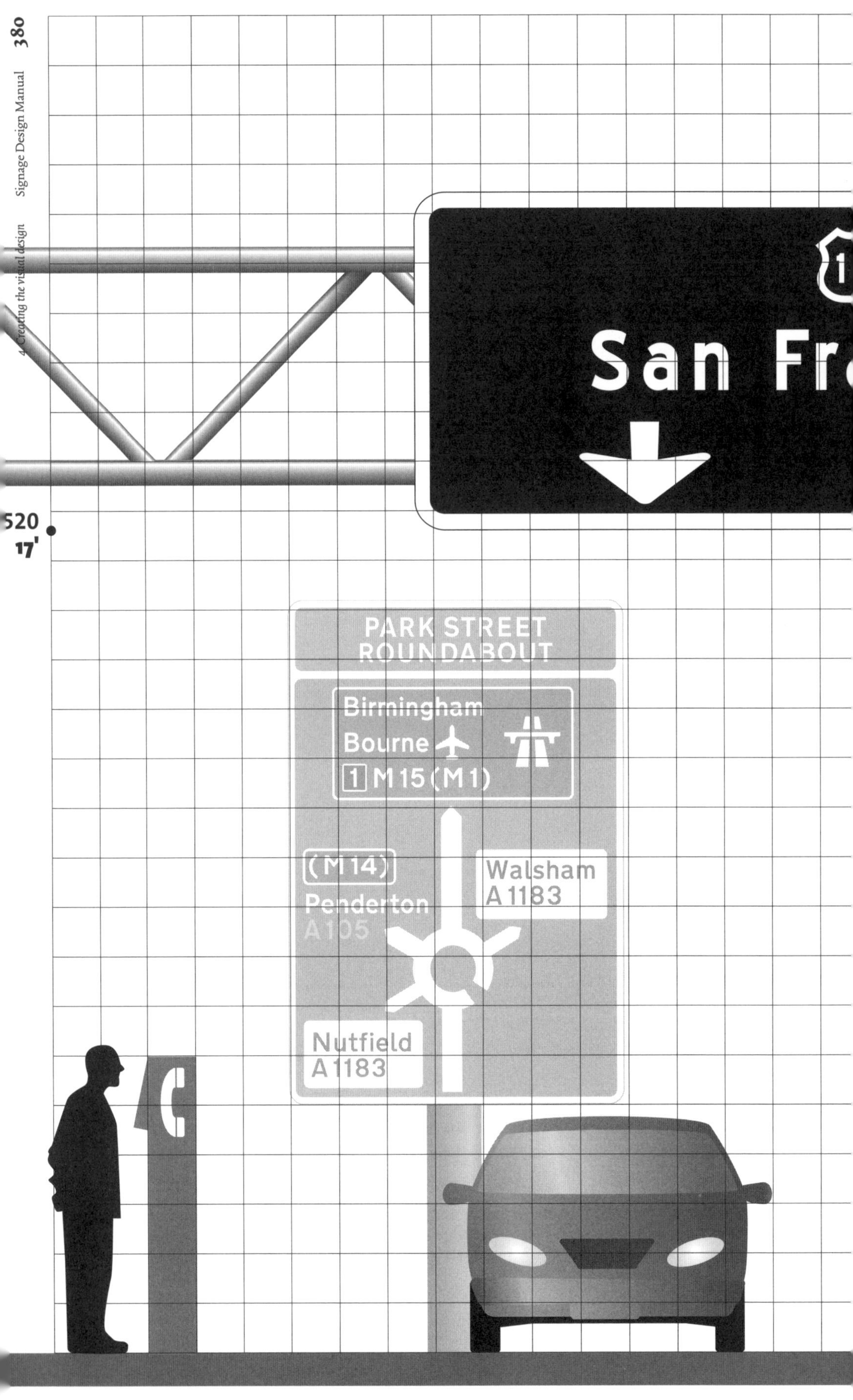
520
17'
San Fr
PARK STREET
ROUNDABOUT
Birmingham
Bourne
1 M15 (M1)
(M14)
Penderton
A105
Walsham
A1183
Nutfield
A1183

The 30 x 30 cm (1′ x 1′) grid on the highway, and the minimum traffic clearance.

270
9'
100
3.5'
Hotel
Bellevue

The 30 x 30 cm (1' x 1') grid in the city street.

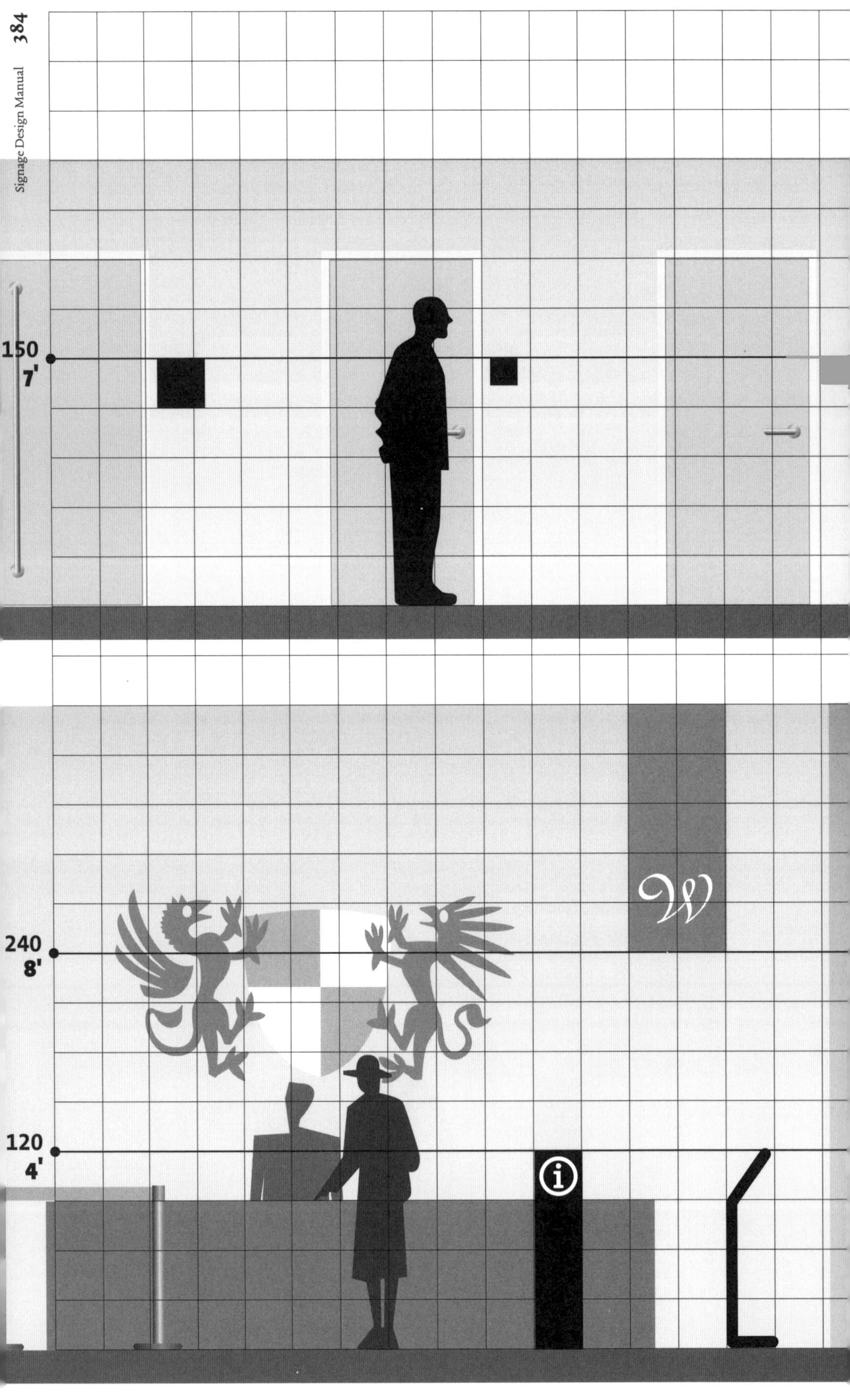
150
7'
240
8'
W
120
4'
i

The 30 x 30 cm (1' x 1') grid inside two floors of a building.

4.13. Colour

Colour is one of the most empathetic parts of a design; it matches music in inciting emotional response. Most of us have a love affair with one or a few colours. In some cases the relationship only lasts as long as fashion supports it; in other cases it's a lifelong bond. Colours may generate strong feelings. We have favourite ones, but also ones we hate. We give colours personal qualities like trustworthy, cheerful or reserved. A lot of cultural customs are linked to specific colours; like birth or marriage. Colour is an important element in national or religious symbols and corporate logos. The retail business teaches us that colour is commercially more important than shape. For example, the most beautifully made and fashionable garments seem impossible to sell when not available in the desired colours and at the right time.

Johannes Itten constructed a colour wheel of 12 colours that shows the basic colour groups: (1) The three primary colours: yellow, red and blue. (2) The three secondary colours by mixing the primary: green, orange and violet. (3) The six tertiary colours by mixing the two previous type of colours.

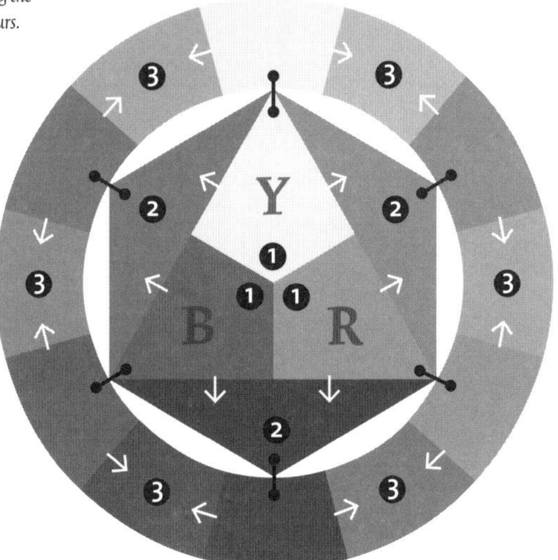

Johannes Itten also visualised his colour wheel as a twelve-pointed star, showing the construction of his primary, secondary and tertiary colours in a simple way.

With colours we express ourselves; the colours we wear are almost a part of our identity. Some colours indeed have the status of a strong convention, like dark blue or grey suits, or white wedding dresses. Different cultures have different colour conventions; black is the 'colour' for mourning in the West, but in the East it is white.

Signage also has a number of conventional colours. Traffic directional signs often use a white background with black text or a blue or green background with white lettering. The colour codes for traffic signs are for the most part a generally accepted convention. Yellow became popular as background colour for airport signage.

4.13.1. COLOUR THEORY

Light is a specific range of electromagnetic radiation frequencies that can be detected by our eyes. At the lower frequency end of our visual spectrum is the 'infrared' range that we can no longer see but may feel when radiation is strong enough; at the higher frequency end we enter the ultraviolet range, no longer visible for us, but potentially harmful starting with getting sunburn.

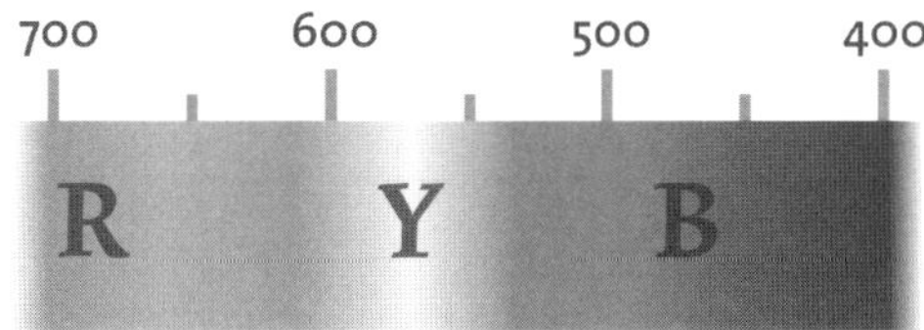

The visual spectrum is not a closed circle as the colour wheel suggests. It is a very small section of a band of electromagnetic waves that we can detect with our eyes.

The 'neutral' white daylight is not composed of one single wavelength. Daylight is a combination of all the colours of the visible spectrum. A rainbow shows us all the components separately. The colour of daylight is by no means constant; it changes during the course of the day and also depends on weather conditions, the season and the geographical location on the globe. There is very little that is absolute or stable in the colours we see and use. Colour impressions change dramatically when seen under different lighting conditions. Colour impressions are influenced heavily by surrounding colours. All paint, lamp and screen colours will change over time. Moreover, our individual sensitivity to colour varies. Humans are not a colour-calibrated species. Colours are notoriously hard to describe and to control other than by reference to their individual formal physical measurements. Yet, there are a few physical phenomena worth knowing about for signage designers which are best explained by putting the spectral colours not on a straight line of cumulative frequencies, but in a circle, creating a so-called colour wheel. The first colour wheel was created by Isaac Newton at the end of the seventeenth century. His research was the start of many subsequent colour theories. Over time, many different colour wheels were constructed. The one made by Johannes Itten, in 1921, is probably still the one most used today. Colour theory is still a work in progress, but a number of principles are generally accepted.

Colour can be described within three different parameters. The hue of a colour (h) indicates the exact position on the colour wheel. The brightness (b) indicates the level of addition of white or black. The saturation (s) indicates the intensity of the colour. At the lowest intensity all colours show only their grey values.

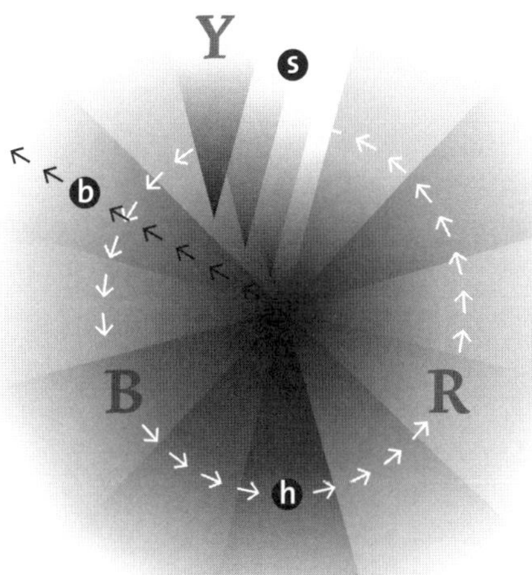

4.13.1.1. Physical aspects of colour

Colour is often described with reference to three different parameters:

—The hue, describes the colour in the spectral sense. It determines its specific position on the colour wheel, or its exact wavelength.

—The level of saturation, describes the 'pureness' of a colour on a scale between 100 to 0 percent.

—The brightness of a colour, describes the amount of added of pure white or black, ranging on a scale from pure white to total black.

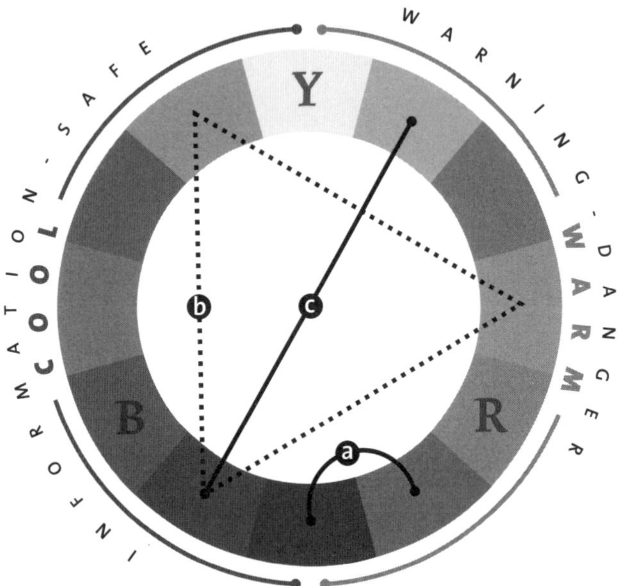

The colour wheel has a 'warm' half and a 'cool' half. For signage purposes, the yellows and the reds are used for warning and danger signs. The blues and greens are used for information signs and 'safe' indications. Theories about colour combinations are abundant; a few basics are:
(a) analogue colours are neighbouring colours and are always harmonious when used together.
(b) the three basic colours are positioned in a triangle; by turning the triangle, high-contrasting colour combinations will be found.
(c) Complementary colours are positioned directly opposite each other. These colours have the strongest contrast when used in combination.

4.13.1.2. Types of colour combinations

Certain colours and colour combinations have specific qualities:

—Primary colours are three specific colours in a triangular position to each other on the colour wheel. Primary colours are considered the three basic colours from which all other colours can be made. There are two types of primary colours depending on the way they are mixed. We can mix colours by using colour pigments to produce paint or ink and we can mix colours by using colour filters that colour the light. Colour printing is based on Yellow, Magenta and Cyan as basic colours (CMYK) and the image on our computer screen is based on Red, Green and Blue (RGB). The result of mixing basic colours in the two systems is dramatically different. Mixing 100% of the three basic colours for print should result in black. This is only true in theory and that's why a black ink (K) is added to make the process more stable. On our computer screens mixing 100% of the basic colours has the opposite effect, it produces white light. That's why the first method of colour mixing is called additive and the second subtractive.

When we do not refer to specific applications, we call our primary colours Yellow, Red and Blue.

—The triangle of three specific colours can be turned around into other positions on the colour wheel. By flipping the position of the primary colours we get three secondary colours: green, orange and violet.
—Johannes Itten turned the six-pointed star of primary and secondary colours one more time to create a twelve-pointed star. The additional range has no simple practical use and does not refer to specific colour names. The same can be said for specific colours that can be found by putting all kinds of other geometrical shapes over the colour wheel.
—The colour wheel can be divided vertically into two halves, a cool half and a warm half.
—Each pair of colours situated precisely opposite each other on the colour wheel are called complementary colours. These colours are each other's most contrasting colour, even up to a level that their edges may start to visually vibrate when put side by side. When we stare for some time at a field of a specific colour and then look at a white wall or sheet of paper we will see the phantom complementary colour of the colour we were staring at.
—Neighbouring colours on the colour wheel are called analogue colours; these have little contrast with their adjacent colours and are by definition harmonious when combined.

4.13.2. COLOUR HARMONY

Bookshelves can be filled with books written about colour harmony. Every culture, or even every country can be recognised by its preference for certain colour combinations. Northern countries use different colour combinations from southern countries. The Japanese have a different national colour palette from the Norwegians, the British or the Chinese. Often a comparison is made between harmony in music and that in colour. Johannes Itten was one of the many who constructed detailed theories about the relationship between colour and music. It remains a favourite subject for a final study project in art schools. Probably the most important link between the two is in their potential emotional impact—and maybe we are more sensitive to a musical dissonance than to a colour dissonance.
To support the required atmosphere, a nightclub or a carnival parade makes use of different colour combinations from those used in a courtroom or a mortuary. There are few rules to create harmonious colour combinations or an appropriate atmosphere of a space other than the rather obvious ones. There are no 'good' colours or 'bad' colours, as there are no good or bad measurements. It all depends on the right combination to create harmony and interesting environments.

Harmony, or a sense of order and a relaxing atmosphere, is best achieved by using analogue or ton-sur-ton colour combinations. Bright colours should play the soloist part in the colour orchestra and can only impress when given proper space to excel. Colour impression is strongly related to the size of the coloured surface.

A colour impression multiplies with the size of its application. Collections of colour samples are always shown in very small sizes and would need far less saturation to give a comparable impression when applied to a wall. Not taking this effect into account is the classic beginner's mistake when specifying colour for large surfaces. Graphic designers are used to small print sizes and minuscule type; colours used in interiors are a completely different matter.

4.13.3. COLOUR CONTRAST

Detectability of a sign in its environment, and legibility of type on a sign, are certainly served by keeping sufficient contrast with their respective backgrounds. The contrast can be achieved by using either (or both) contrasting colours or contrasting brightness (difference in grey tone values). As said already, smaller sizes require far stronger colours in order to be effective; that is why contrasts in typography are almost entirely based on distinction in shape (morphological discrimination) to create order and very little use of colour. Dark red is the only colour typographic purists will consider functional next to traditional black. The background is nearly always very light in colour. Using reverse text—white text out of a black background—is the ultimate way to draw the attention in traditional typography. The convention in signage is to use either a white background (with black text, as in print) or a dark-coloured or black background with white text. Sign panels coloured in the mid-grey tone value range may be risky to use. Yet, it is important to keep an open mind; tradition has its virtues and is certainly worth knowing, but nothing should be taken for granted. There is no best way to draw attention or make oneself understood. It all depends on the circumstances and the mix of means employed. Following rules slavishly may easily lead to mediocre results. It would be like actors speaking on stage with well-articulated clear voices in one tonal range; formally correct but hopelessly failing to draw the attention of the audience. Good actors sometimes whisper, murmur, shout and moan, because each variation works best to convey a specific message.

4.13.4. COLOUR CODING

Signage has a long tradition in using colour codes, mostly related to traffic, health, and safety at work or in public places. Red and green signs were probably first used by the railways for 'go' and 'stop' signs. The famous 'Red Flag Act' of 1865 required a person carrying a red flag to walk ahead of all engined vehicles in the UK. Traffic lights soon followed, introducing the yellow colour as a warning or alert sign in between the go and stop signs.
Since then, regulations on national and international levels have been regularly updated and extended with colour codes for traffic and safety. Most countries use a red band for prohibition signs, a yellow background for warning signs, a blue background for mandatory signs, a green background for safety signs and a red

background for fire-fighting equipment. Good practice recommends not to use these colours for other types of colour coding. That is not easy, to say the least, since primary and secondary colours have the clearest distinction. Traffic signs also make use of these colours for standard signs, with slight variations in different countries.

Clients and architects have a weak spot for proprietary colour coding, although its functionality is questionable. First, the number of colours that can be used is limited; three primary colours, red, blue and yellow; three secondary colours, green, orange and violet; three non-colours, black, white and grey; plus a number of arbitrary ones like brown, pink, beige, or purple. Colours used for coding must carry names with an indisputable reference like olive, mustard, navy, sky. Second, colour codes have to be learned and remembered. Third, the colours used may interfere with existing (legal) codes. Fourth, colours fade over time and will look different under different lighting conditions. Fifth, some people are colour-disabled. Sixth, colour coding may raise costs of the installation and maintenance of the signage.

The size of a coloured surface influences the intensity of the colour impression. A larger size needs less hue to give a comparable impression.

Colour coding will be most useful for path/track coding, inside, but mostly outside buildings. Footpaths have a long tradition of using colour codes. Another useful application for colour codes is to mark areas. Colours can be very helpful as transitional aides. In fact, this type of coding follows the old Anglo-Saxon tradition of painting a different colour in every room in the house to give it a different atmosphere.

4.13.5. COLOURFASTNESS

Some colours deteriorate faster than others, just like different kinds of basic materials. Some colour pigments are far more stable than others, especially when exposed to sunlight and/or put in aggressive or polluted environments. Discolouring can have many causes, like the primer used, the binder material, the colour pigment and the finish or sealing. Binders and seal varnishes tend to get browner and darker over time. Some pigments bleach, fade or are 'fugitive'. As a rule of thumb, bright pinkish, purplish, and greenish colours tend to be unstable. Fluorescent colours will lose their properties over time. There are international standards for testing colourfastness.

4.14. Interactive design

Industrial production methods have changed profoundly during the Digital Revolution. The way products are designed and manufactured has not only changed, but whole new fields of business have been added to existing ones while some traditional ones have disappeared entirely. Print has always been in some way or other the core medium for most graphic design, but that is no longer true. Production of print has become far easier, which has resulted in a dramatic growth of printed products, but this development has not prevented that more and more graphic design being made for on-screen presentation, exclusively or at least primarily.

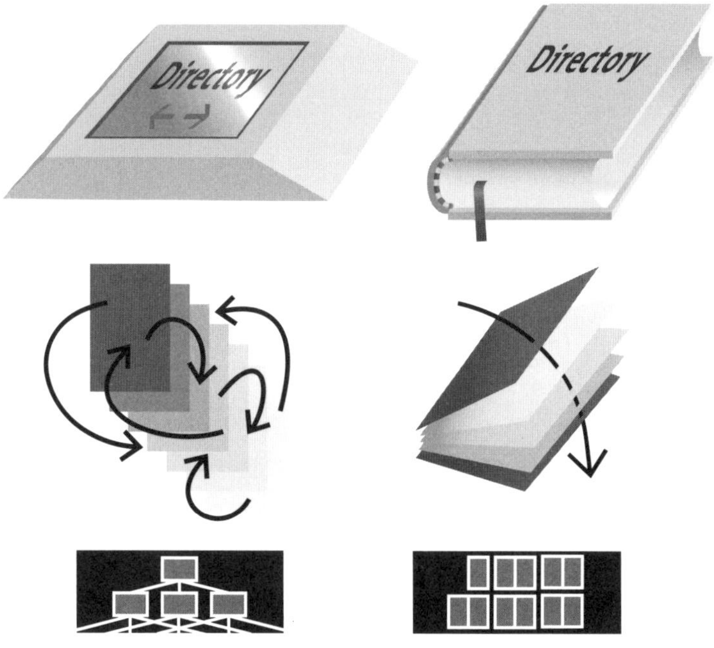

Interactive digital media (left) have a fundamentally different structure from the traditional printed media (right). The way we use the two is therefore rather different. Traditional media have a simple linear structure. Retrieving information from them is conventional and straightforward. Digital media, by contrast, need dedicated navigation tools to retrieve information. The quality of these tools determines the level of accessibility. The possibilities to create navigation tools are boundless and there is still little design convention, increasing the chances of the user getting lost.

On-screen graphic presentation largely follows the same design principles as graphics for print. However, there is a huge discrepancy in the possibilities that can be employed. The problem is that these possibilities are in fact boundless. First, all normal constraints for print production disappear completely, like limited use of colour, size of content or print run. All these traditional considerations have become irrelevant. Second, all types of media can be incorporated, like video, sound and animation. Third, the possibilities by which the user can customise the content have exploded. Printed material can basically be either read or ignored, it cannot be altered. With the arrival of the first media that needed electricity to function, like radio & TV, the user could change a few aspects of the visual (or auditory) presentation. Interactivity with media started here. The electronic media made profound user participation possible in the way content is consumed and presented. Of course, all these niceties come with a price. To use print, one needs only sufficient eyesight. To use storage devices like CD-ROMs or tapes, one also needs a player device, appropriate software, and an electricity source. To use media directly on line one needs much more: a phone connection, a service provider, appropriate hardware and a lot of just the right kind of software, which keeps on constantly changing. The possibilities of 'open connection' media are almost endless for both receiver and sender, but it requires constant reinvestment for continued use. Clearly, manufacturers do not particularly object to this situation.

Having the possibility to interact with content may create huge advantages, like always keeping information easily (or even automatically) up-to-date and tailoring the representation to the personal needs of each user. It is an ideal situation, not given for free though; we have to learn how to offer and how to use interactive media properly. Everyone knows how to use a brochure or a book, and the user has great freedom on how and when to use it. Watching TV or a movie is also a pretty simple and straightforward activity, but offers far less flexibility. Interactive media may combine the advantages of both previous media but also have the huge disadvantage that use is far from obvious. Everyone using interactive media gets regularly and hopelessly stuck at some stage or other. This is such a common experience that we have simply gotten used to it. The major cause of this problem is that interactive media tend to be amorphic in size and content. When using printed matter we know from the start whether we are dealing for instance with a simple handout or a dictionary. Quickly browsing the content of printed matter is very easy to do. On screen, clearly confined content no longer exists, (hyper)links can take you with just a mouse click literally anywhere at the speed of light. No more page numbers, linear storylines and (back)covers in the new media.

4.14.1. NAVIGATION & INFORMATION ARCHITECTURE

Many similarities exist between designing a signage project and designing multimedia applications. Both need a clear and simple system for navigation to guide the user through a site. Information architecture and websites are words coined with the arrival of interactive media, and they show a closer relation with a three-dimensional environment than with the traditional two dimensional graphic world. Failing to supply easy navigation in the new multimedia world will get users hopelessly lost. (Nobody gets lost in printed matter.) The internet boom has generated bookshelves full of information about how to design functional navigation systems or Graphic Users Interfaces (GUI), sometimes more universally referred to as human-computer interfaces. Yet, the development of navigational design conventions is still in its infancy. A lot of navigation is still directed more towards designers than users.

The history of 15 years of website navigation is illustrative of the developments. Websites were at first like electronic stacks of printed pages with an arrow or a simple link that would take you from one page to the next, or hyper-links that would take you instantly somewhere else inside or outside the website. Soon one had no idea anymore how the page on the screen was related to the whole site. One had to return to the home page to regain some overview. Later, most websites kept all their navigational instruments and directory always visible, a constant window showing the changing information, as if one was sitting in a car. Special site maps were added that provided an overview of how the site was constructed. Now, navigation tools and directories are starting to 'flow', become transparent and follow the cursor movements of the user. Some additional dynamic locational—where am I?—information would still be helpful, comparable with information given by conventional navigational instruments. One can still get lost easily while travelling on the super-fast electronic highways.

4.14.2. MULTIMEDIA HYPE

The relatively sudden availability of easily accessible and almost limitless resources at low cost—if any—created an uncontrolled hype in multimedia applications. A CD-ROM can contain the content of a complete encyclopedia at manufacturing costs lower than a package of chewing gum. Distribution costs have almost disappeared. On the web, we can consult traditional information resources like an encyclopedia for free. The general use of 'search engines' has changed our concept of retrieving and conveying information. A whole universe of potential new businesses came into perspective, with 'free' as the key buzzword. A lot of the applications put on the market turned out to be very short-lived. There appeared to be too little money in free supply. We still suffer from a general offer that is far too loaded with disorganised content and too many options. Most multimedia applications are still too complicated.

Automated Teller Machines (ATM) are one of the applications that became highly successful, as did various ticket dispensing machines, once we learned how to make these machines simple enough. These are very uncomplicated applications with bare-bones simple navigation facilities. The next step is that most of us will start to use self-check-in facilities at airports.

Multimedia kiosks have been on the market now for almost 20 years. The amount of different types of kiosk applications offered today is close to overwhelming, carrying names like Point Of Sales or Point Of Interest (POS/POI). Some kiosk applications allow for connectivity with almost any conceivable media: screen, print, speech, telephone and internet. Abundance does not seem to be the way to success; the simplest applications seem to be the lasting ones, whereas the complicated ones seem to cater to the never-ending snack-like appetite for gadgets—a sort of appetite that is by definition short-lived.

Interactive touch-screen kiosks are replacing traditional receptionists. In the future, a lovely virtual receptionist may return; first on the kiosk, then on your handheld device, and later as a life-size 3D projection.

4.14.3. SIGNAGE APPLICATIONS

Interactive multimedia applications for signage are concentrated around three different items: wayfinding information provided on a website, electronic directories and interactive touch-screen kiosks.

4.14.3.1. *Website map*

Most organisations will provide wayfinding information on their website through a map showing relevant highways and public transportation stops. Sometimes, such maps have animated features and/or can be downloaded as printable PDF files.
Some retail stores even go as far as putting a complete Virtual Reality (VR) replica of their own store on the web, which makes electronic visits a possibility, even though shoppers still seem to prefer the real world of bricks and mortar, smell and touch, over the limited look and feel delivered by mouse-browsing.

4.14.3.2. *Electronic directories*

Some buildings have enormous numbers of tenants. Scrollable electronic directories with alphabetic search facilities are a simple and straightforward solution to provide names with related room numbers. Sometimes, names of staff are added to this kind of directory. Easy updating is a must for these facilities.

4.14.3.3. *Touch-screen kiosks*

One of the first large-scale sophisticated kiosks for multimedia signage applications was for the Financial Centre in New York, designed in 1989 by Erwin Schlossberg. Various kiosks were spread over the site; each provided all kinds of information about the site and its tenants. A kiosk could could also produce print-outs with routing information. Shopping malls and museums were at first dedicated followers of this trend until it was discovered that printers will run out of paper or ink and may create quite a mess; in addition, a lot of the information is not easily accessible or is very little used. Continuous content management needs regular and skilled attention. All these considerations make sophisticated kiosk applications less popular for signage purposes.

The use of touch-screen kiosks has shifted more in the direction of entertainment and PR, at times, simply providing comparable information that is already available on websites. This type of kiosk is often placed in waiting rooms or reception areas, like an electronic version of the conventional literature display.

The amount of navigation tools can become daunting when information is provided through an internet site. Three types of user interfaces appear on screen: that of the system software, the browser software and the navigation tools of the site itself.

4.14.3.4. Future developments

Accessibility of the internet is spreading to various handheld devices, and cable connections are no longer necessary. Personal accessories like mobile phones, digital assistants and pocket computers are getting connected to the web. More and more website information can be consulted everywhere. A future general personal possession of mobile GPS (Global Positioning System) receivers could lead to a situation where an up-to-date building map could be instantly downloaded from the web and the GPS would automatically lead us all the way to our destination.

It is said that the Digital Revolution killed distance. Handheld wireless internet connections will eliminate the importance of locations. All resources of information will be accessible all the time and from practically any location. The same can be said for the reverse situation; information can be distributed from any location, all the time, to devices that are part of a wireless network. The content of signage screens in a network could be altered any time from any location.

4.14.4. PRODUCTION AND DESIGN

Multimedia design and production is almost totally a digital affair. One needs hardware to digitise information and hardware to make it audible and/or visible again, but all the rest is immaterial manipulation done by a plethora of different types of software. That fact does not necessarily make things easier. Multimedia productions tend to be complicated. The universal use of the internet has made the design and production of websites easier. So-called 'authoring software' facilitates production and design. Young graphic designers use multimedia software to single-handedly design uncomplicated websites, in most cases with the emphasis on the word 'uncomplicated'.

Touching 'hot spots' with the help of a touch-pad, a mouse or one's own finger is the way to navigate and extract electronically offered information. It is likely that for some applications human browsing will be replaced by automatic wireless exchange of electronic data between personalised radio tags and static sources.

More complicated productions may need a number of different professional skills; the 'content' part may need content developers, writers, photographers and illustrators; the 'technical part' may need technical designers and computer programmers; and the 'design' part may need, information architects, graphic designers and multimedia (interactive) designers. The maintenance of a website or kiosk also needs web(kiosk)masters and web editors.

Touch-screen kiosk design has lagged a bit behind the general trend in web design. In principle, there is little reason for this situation. A touch-screen is a screen with a special thermo-sensitive layer that replaces the mouse (or touch pad) for navigating by directly touching the screen with a fingertip. Kiosks may use the same HTML language that is used for all internet applications and can also use the same authoring software. The problem with the latter is that one needs to use fully equipped computers to make it all work. Access to the internet needs browser software that is related to the system software. It is somewhat far-fetched to use fully-fledged laptops inside kiosks; the result is that touch-screen kiosk software is in a somewhat backward niche compared with other mainstream software. It is complicated to change the typography and colours of standard kiosk interfaces to match the graphic design used in the rest of the signage. This situation will change in future; the internet will play a more central role.

Sound is slowly but surely becoming a more and more standard part of all multimedia applications. For signage purposes it has the huge advantage that spoken information could be of great help to the visually impaired. For the rest, sound can enhance (or change) the impression of visual matter dramatically, but sound can just as well be extremely silly and annoying.

Keeping information up to date is still a surprisingly weak part of multimedia design. Adding or changing information or pages in linear graphic products is extremely easy to do. The complicated spider webs of hyperlinks in multimedia productions makes updating and addition of information a difficult job. Clearly, this kind of content management is essential for the effectiveness of the whole application. In this case, it is also likely that easy-to-use content management software will become available.

Interactive media design is in one important aspect an historical landmark in the professional development of graphic design. The effectiveness of use of internet sites can be measured, and the behaviour of website visitors can be traced quite accurately. The feedback is extremely fast and can be customised to any specific need. This condition makes the effectiveness of information graphics easily measurable. Never before was feedback on the effectiveness of design work as accurate and fast.

4.14.5. TECHNICAL DESIGN ASPECTS

The most popular touch screens used to be the classic CRT screens, which are a bit clunky in weight and size, yet cheap (when not taking energy consumption into account) and long-lasting. LCD screens are in a strong runner-up position. These screens are lighter, far less clunky in size, use less energy, and have become considerably less expensive. The trend in the home TV display market is indicative for kiosk screens, which means that plasma touch screens will be the next wave. Energy-saving remains a serious issue with all electrical appliances. A lit-up but not used screen is an insult to any sensible strategy for energy consumption, but an unlit screen looks dead or out of order. This is the modern dilemma.

Most signage projects only employ one or a few screen display applications. It is not easy to fit just a few screens seamlessly into the design of the rest of the other sign panels. Yet it is sensible to try to integrate the interactive screens into the overall design. Measurement grids for sign panels should also be applied to the interactive facilities in the signage project.

5. Specifying and supervising manufacture and installation

To recapitulate the work phases so far: during the first work phase of designing the signage system, a comprehensive system is developed, mostly comprising a set of maps showing a limited number of sign types and a separate list of related messages for each sign employed. In the second phase, signs are assigned a specific visual appearance, based on one single inclusive design concept. In the last phase, the signs have to be manufactured and installed on site. This phase requires the creation of production specification documents and a structured selection of fabricators and production procedures. First, the procedure for choosing the manufacturer(s) has to be set out. Second, on the basis of the chosen procedure, bid documents must be prepared. Third, one or more manufacturer(s) must be commissioned. Fourth, further instruction and supervision of actual manufacturing and installation needs to be undertaken. In principle, this is all a rather well-known and straightforward process. The complication lies in the fact that even the best-structured processes will have various overlapping activities. One cannot separate each phase with a Chinese Wall. Moreover, procedures may vary according to type of client, type of job, type of commission, or even depending on local business practices.

5.1. Documentation and bidding

The first step is to establish a procedure for manufacturer selection. Most manufacturers related to the building industry try to get involved in potential projects as early as possible. They often contact designers to offer unsolicited services. It is considered to be of advantage to have some inside information about the project and the designers involved before the bidding process starts. There is also an advantage for designers to be in early contact with manufacturers. Through a manufacturer, a designer may get information about the latest product innovations, and most manufacturers are willing to give free technical advice. This is highly appreciated by many signage designers who do not have a background in engineering. There is nothing wrong with these kinds of early contacts, as long as no commitments are made at this stage.

5.1.1. Position of the signage designer

The level of involvement of the signage designer in the selection process depends heavily on the position of the designer. The signage job may be part of the general contractor's commission, or it may be a commission given by the future users of the building. The responsibilities for the signage designer will be different from one case to another. The signage design job may also be split into two separate ones; the design of the visual appearance of the signs on one hand, and all the rest of the work to be done on the other. In this respect, a contractor already working on the site may be asked to do this part, or alternatively, this part may be

assigned to a firm specialising in the implementation of the design work. In that case, the visual designer will hardly be involved in the selection process. In some cases, a procurement department will be heavily involved in the selection process and will take over a lot of the work.
The opposite extreme of this situation could be that the designer may act as contractor or fabricator of the designs as well. In that case, the complete signage budget will be in one pair of hands. Maybe, for very small projects, this can be an efficient business solution; in most cases, however, it is preferable that there be a clear distinction between the design responsibilities and the responsibilities for the realisation of the designs. A client is likely to get the best service when these responsibilities are separated.

5.1.2. TYPE OF CLIENT

Governmental clients and multi-national companies, in general, have standard procurement procedures that have to be followed. Trained and well-seasoned professionals employed in purchase or contract departments are likely to assist the signage designer in the selection process. For smaller organisations, the process may be far less formal. The signage designer has to see that all the common pitfalls in commercial transactions are avoided as much as possible.

5.1.3. TYPE OF BIDDING

In principle, there are three types of bidding procedures: one that will be publicly advertised and will therefore be open to everyone; one where a number of manufacturers will be invited to take part in a competitive bid; and one where all the conditions will be negotiated with one party alone. Variations on these three procedures may also occur; for instance, in cases where a pre-selection is done on global requirements then the precise conditions will be determined during later negotiations.

The most formal procedure is the public bid. This procedure requires the production of a complete contract package where virtually all conditions and production details have to be specified in advance. The selection procedure is often standardised or legally based. Most governmental bodies are required by law to issue public bids, sometimes even internationally, as is the case within the European Common Market. There is a real danger that these procedures will be quite counter-productive, in particular for signage jobs. Signage is involved with the production of many different items, yet most items are not very complicated to make. On average, there are a lot of items to specify, but very small budgets for architectural signage. Efficient production needs easy accessibility and direct communication between the parties involved. Too many formalities can easily frustrate the process. This is the reason why signage designers like to work with a limited number of specialised producers, because both parties are familiar with each other's standards of quality and design practices. The designer can concentrate on working on the design concept, leaving detailing and construction specification to a well-trusted party. Understandably, clients may be wary of this kind of close relationship, which may turn out to be uncompetitive in price. Again, one should be aware that signage budgets are relatively small and that the average costs for producing standard signage items are well-known. The potential dangers in forcing a collaboration between an under-bidding—but unfamiliar—manufacturer and a signage designer are not entirely hypothetical. Under these circumstances, both parties are likely to work under serious budget constraints, the space to manoeuvre becomes very limited, and as a result, the client might pay dearly with a considerable loss of quality in the final outcome of the signage project. 'Penny wise and pound foolish', should be a concern for any client dealing with a signage project.

The public bid and the invited bid have three stages. First, the issuing of a bid proposal accompanied with a letter that clearly indicates the bid period, the ultimate date to make remarks or queries by bidders, the project name and address, names and addresses of client and designer's representatives, date of final installation and a time schedule for a phased installation, and a payment schedule. Second, issuing a written notice or addendum may be necessary when bidders find errors, dubious parts, or inconsistencies in the documents received. All bidders must receive this additional information allowing sufficient time to make adjustments before the end of the bid period. Third, the announcement of the selected bidder.

The least formal way to select a manufacturer is to make a global selection first, solely on the basis of the specific requirements of the project at hand and the matching qualities of potential producers. This way of selection relies heavily on the reputation and portfolio of the producers. A possible disadvantage of this procedure is that price negotiation may be less easy because of the unavailability of competitive bids. By contrast, the advantage is that the designer may have less work to do since part of it may be shifted to the manufacturer, which can therefore result in considerably lower overall costs for the whole project.

Competitive bidding—especially when issued by governmental institutions—is a very formal procedure that assumes that the complete knowledge of manufacturing methods lies with the designer/specifier. There is no room for discussions with bidders to clarify design intent or to consider alternative fabrication techniques. By contrast, alternative commission procedures, like material and time arrangements, or a negotiated fee, create room for a potential fruitful interaction between fabricator and designer, assuming there is goodwill and skill input on both sides.

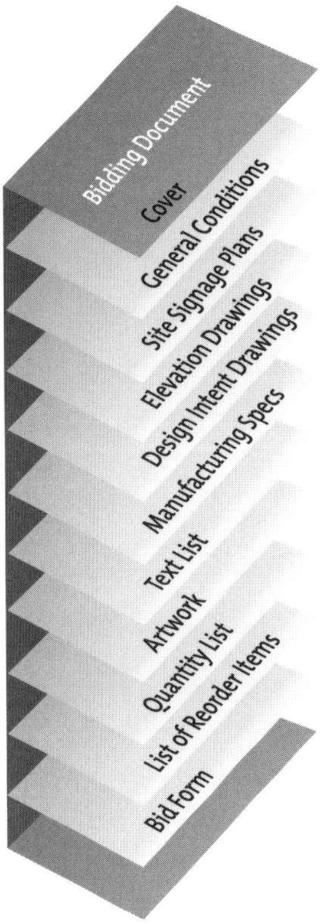

Bidding Document
Cover
General Conditions
Site Signage Plans
Elevation Drawings
Design Intent Drawings
Manufacturing Specs
Text List
Artwork
Quantity List
List of Reorder Items
Bid Form

5.1.4. STANDARD SET OF DOCUMENTS

Manufacturer's prices or bids will be based solely on the documents received. These documents must contain complete and unambiguous information about what has to be produced, for which location, how specific items have to be mounted on site and when the work has to be completed. All the conditional working procedures have to be specified as well. Comprehensive and unambiguous text is not easy to draft; it needs experience and training. Contractors typically try to interpret manufacturing specifications in a way that involves the lowest production costs. They do not necessarily look for a way to carry out the work that will produce the most lasting or best-looking result. Not so much out of bad intention, but because contractors have to compete in price against each other, so they tend to interpret specifications to their own advantage in order to win the contract. Designers have to specify in such a manner that quality loopholes are avoided as much as possible. Lawyers are not the only masters of interpretation; contractors may also turn out to be quite imaginative in this respect.

A listing and a content description of the various standard parts of a bid document is given below. This content may vary in accordance with the bidding procedure chosen.

5.1.4.1. Cover Sheet

The title on the cover sheet must indicate the activities to be undertaken, the name and address of the (building) site, the name of the client, the designer's representative and the date of issue.

5.1.4.2. General Conditions

The General Conditions are mostly general administrative conditions that do not relate to a specific job. These conditions may be very extensive, depending on the size of the job or the direct involvement of governmental bodies. Here is a listing of the major types of clauses:

—Bidder Qualification Guidelines.
These guidelines may describe the level of experience, commercial track record and type of specific professional skills required.

—Description of responsibilities of all parties involved.
These descriptions will apply to client, designer and contractor and/or sub-contractor alike.

—Cancellation clauses.
Cancellation clauses describe the conditions under which the contract may be cancelled.

—Copyright and authorship of the designer(s).
For example: All designs, specifications and drawings in this document are protected by copyright or any other intellectual property law. All designs were created to be used exclusively for the project described in this document. The contractor and eventual sub-contractors shall not disclose in any way the content of this document to anyone, except to the people directly involved in

carrying out the work, and then only to the extent that is relevant to carry out their job. All publications in any form need prior written permission from the authors.
The designers will grant the contractor (and eventual sub-contractors) the limited right to manufacture the designs shown in these documents solely for the purpose of completing the work described. The contractor (or sub-contractors) may not manufacture, reproduce or exhibit the designs without first obtaining the written approval of the designers. Modifications to the designs are not permitted without first obtaining the written approval of the designers.
—A listing of legal requirements.
Relevant national or international standards that need to be applied, along with all other relevant standards made by specific associations.
—Permits and code requirements.
Certain permits need to be obtained by the manufacturer in order to carry out the work. The type and quantity of permits needed depends heavily on specific local requirements.
—General conditions.
a. The contractor shall verify all dimensions and quantities given in this document and check all relevant measurements on site. The contractor shall be entirely responsible for the correct implementation of all items. The contractor will notify the designers immediately in all cases where inaccuracies or inconsistencies are found on the drawings and/or in the specifications, leaving the designer sufficient time to provide alternative design solutions.
b. The contractor shall be responsible for the quality of all materials and workmanship required to execute the work described in this document. This responsibility shall include all work done by sub-contractors.
c. Shop drawings of all sign types must be submitted for approval to the designers. Proceeding with production is only permitted after shop drawings have been signed off with final approval by the designer.
d. Final production will be preceded by the submission of samples, or prototypes of all materials, coatings and finishings to be used. Each approved sample will bear the signature of the designer before production starts. Along with the samples, the contractor will provide data of maximal variation tolerances for final production and reorders.
e. If the client or the designer has serious doubts about the quality of the work after completion and in consideration of the production specifications, the contractor shall provide an evaluation report made by an independent consultant at the contractor's expense.
f. To avoid problems caused by incomplete documents, it is advisable to indicate the number of pages in the document and to ask that the issuers be notified immediately when irregularities of any kind are discovered by the bidders.
—Guarantees to be provided by the manufacturer.

There may be different terms of guarantee for the different materials or techniques employed.
—Maintenance and reordering.
After installation of the signage, the system needs maintenance to keep it up to date. The contractor's part in this process needs to be specified.
—Engineering responsibilities assigned to the manufacturer.
—Outline of production specification/engineering assistance to be given by the manufacturer.
—Outline of assistance to be given by the manufacturer with installation specifications.
—Maintenance contract.
Some types of installation—like neon or security installations—are only sold in conjunction with a maintenance contract.

5.1.4.3. *Site Signage Plans*

Signage plans do not need to be very detailed for making price calculations. A global indication as to where each sign will be installed is sufficient. However, during the phase of supervising the installation, more detailed plans are required. Often, new drawings do not have to be produced; existing architectural drawings may also be used for this purpose.

5.1.4.4. *Elevation drawings*

Elevation drawings must be made to control precise installation. These drawings are less important for pricing, but indispensable for supervising the installation.

5.1.4.5. *Design Intent Drawings*

Each sign type will need a production specification that shows and describes its essential components: the production method of the message, the type of frame and/or panel that holds the message (if any), and the way the sign must be mounted in place.
Production work drawings have two major stages: first, the design intent drawings made by the designer, and second, the 'shop' drawings made by the manufacturer. The first type of drawings have to provide all the relevant information to make a price calculation: dimensions, the use of specific materials or production methods and the visual appearance are the most important aspects that must be clearly specified. Also specific functional aspects, like the method of message updating and maintenance procedures need to be clearly indicated.
Design intent drawings are usually made in a limited range of scales: 1:1, 1:5, 1:10, 1:20, 1:50 and 1:100.
All drawings must bear the name of the copyright owner, along with the copyright sign and the date of production. The drawings are part of a set of related documents: written manufacturing specifications, the messages list, the artwork and the quantity list. There must be clear cross-referencing between each item on the different documents.

5.1.4.6. Manufacturing specifications

Manufacturing specifications consist of two sections: a general section where general quality criteria for the use of materials, production methods or results are described, and a specific section that is an extension of the notes on the design intent drawings. On some occasions, there may be a somewhat odd limitation in specifying materials or products. Governmental bidding documents require that only generic materials, products and processes be specified. The idea behind this is to restrict any enterprise from monopolising the bidding process. In this case, the legislation that seeks to encourage open competition and the legislation that protects industrial property seem to collide. Open competition and industrial property protection are both believed to be the cornerstones of modern liberal societies. This political system has prevailed over alternatives because it delivers (at least for the time being) the best quality for the lowest price. But by not being able to specify specific brands, or protected products, governmental regulation may effectively benefit companies that do not invest in research, and may even be rejecting the advantage of specifying distinctive quality. In an attempt to match the unmatchable, specifications of protected products may be allowed, only when followed by the addition 'or a comparable product'. This is probably the best solution to serve open competition as well as to encourage further product development.

In the general section of the manufacturing specifications, quality criteria are formulated for the basic components of the work. Quality or Industry Standards are developed by Standards Institutes, governmental bodies and associations of industry groups. Most countries will have independent organisations where products and basic materials can be analysed and tested. These organisations can function as arbitrators in quality disputes and also often issue publications about various aspects of production technology.

The following is a concise overview of basic components that may be employed in signage projects.

Metal specifications

Metal is widely used for sign panels and frame constructions. Weight, strength, flatness and level of corrosive resistance (for exterior use) are important factors. Metal specifications may include:

—specific metal alloy
—corrosion resistance in specified environments
—type of surface treatment
—type of surface finishing.

Wood specifications

Soft natural materials like wood tend to be vulnerable. Wood discolours and changes shape over time. When used outdoors, wood may severely deteriorate over time. Modern technology has found many ways to counteract all kinds of disadvantages that the use of

wood may have. First grade plywood or MDF panels guarantee flatness. Several treatments can be specified, in some cases leaving little that is natural in the final product. Wood specifications may include:
—surface hardness
—type of glue used in laminates
—general quality indication.

Plastics & glass specifications

Plastics are used in all kinds of panel material, sometimes in a mix or a sandwich with natural materials. The different types of plastics or synthetic materials is practically endless and so are the specific qualities of each synthetic material. In signage projects, plastics (and glass) are often used for materials that need to be transparent. Specification may include:
—fire resistance
—hardness of surface
—fragility and shatterproof qualities.

Coating, enamelling or sealing specifications

Coating, enamelling or sealing specification may include:
—surface structure and level of gloss
—impact- and scratch-resistance
—thickness of layer tolerance
—homogeneity of surface (visibility of stripes or stains)
—limits in colour variations, namely for reorders
—level of colourfastness (stability)
—humidity resistance
—guarantees for life-span and endurance
—advised maintenance cycle.

Flatness of panel surfaces

The surfaces of sign panels must be homogeneous and smooth, but also flat. Metal panels especially that are not carefully produced do not meet this requirement. A production specification could be as follows: all panels must have faces of such flatness that when measured diagonally from corner to corner, the maximum deviation shall not exceed 4 mm (1/16").

Fasteners and fixing materials

The two most important conditions for fasteners are: first, that the material is totally non-corrosive, and second, that the fasteners are preferably applied in a concealed manner, and therefore not directly visible. Where fasteners are visible, the visible part must be the same colour as the surrounding surface.
In some instances 'vandal-proof' fixing is required, which means that special fasteners must be used that cannot be undone with traditional tools such as a regular screwdriver.

Colour specifications

There is a large variety of systems available that can be used to specify colour. Some large manufacturers have developed their own colour system. RAL (Reichs-Ausschuss für Lieferbedingungen) and PMS (Pantone Matching System) are both among the best known. Colours are notoriously difficult to specify. Moreover, colours are never stable; all will change over time and their visual impression depends largely on local lighting conditions and the size of the application. Specifying a colour by providing a colour sample is still an effective way to specify colour, quite impossible to standardise or to instruct by other means than providing the sample itself.

Finishing specifications

The finish of the surface may range from rough to flat and smooth to polished. The final surface treatment (or type of coating) determines the way the environmental light will be reflected on the surface. The sheen may range from being completely matt, like powder or velvet, to super-glossy, reflecting everything like a mirror. Mattish surfaces are often specified since these avoid glare under certain lighting conditions, although matt surfaces tend to deteriorate faster, particularly when used outdoors.
A completely new range of coatings and finishings has been created with nanotechnology. Extremely small (nano) particles fill up natural cavities in all kind of materials, changing their properties. Surfaces become self-cleaning, longer-lasting, vandal-, dirt- and corrosion-proof.There is unresolved environmental concern about employing this technology.

Application of text or images

There are limitless ways for producing text or images for signage. Vinyl-cut letters or images are one of the most popular methods of production. A lot of the specifications given for the coating of signs can also be specified for the application of text and images. In case the manufacturer has to produce type in-house, properly licensed typeface(s) must be available. Designers have to be cautious about how precisely the final letter forms will be produced. The digital outline data that designers are accustomed to are not necessarily applicable in signage production plants. Graphic software is basically different from construction software. This may result in the letters and images being retraced by craftspeople. In this process, undesired varieties of the selected typeface may occur. Therefore, it is advisable to specify maximum tolerances in type size, in stem thickness and in the maximum radiuses allowed for all sharp corners.
The different types of vinyls used for signage are extensive. First, there is the difference in whether the type of vinyl is printable or not. Second, there is the variation in thickness of the vinyl and its resistance under different conditions. Third, the durability of the vinyl is determined by the type of adhesive used.

5.1.4.7. Text list

The profession of typesetting has almost disappeared. Type is now produced by designers or by clients themselves, so the listing of messages may take the form of already produced type. The exact production procedure of type will depend largely on the size of the job and how type will be applied to the sign surface. For silkscreen production, for instance, it may be economical to screen identical text in one production run. This production method will influence the way the type will be produced. In any case, text lists must provide a clear overview of what, and how much, text has to be produced.

5.1.4.8. Artwork

Artwork is likely to be produced by the designer, nowadays practically all of it in the form of digital files. In all other cases, original artwork must be available for production.

5.1.4.9. Quantity lists

Each sign type has a design intent drawing. On each drawing an indication is also given of the number of items that have to be produced. A quantity list will provide a clear overview of all sign types and the quantities required for each.

5.1.4.10. List of reorder items

Reorders are essential for practically all signage projects. To control pricing and as preparation for a realistic maintenance budget for the signage, an overview must be made of all the items that are likely to be reordered.

5.1.4.11. Bid form

A fair comparison of bids to be received is an essential part of the selection process. To avoid comparing apples with oranges, it is advisable to develop a standard bid form. Through this form, all bidders will be forced to submit their offers in a way that makes comparison between them uncomplicated.

5.1.5. SELECTING A MANUFACTURER

After all bids are received, the designer(s) should review these bids first on the basis of errors and/or inconsistencies, and then make recommendations as to which bid deserves to be honoured with a commission. The bid with the lowest price is not necessarily the best offer. Prices offered may vary considerably. As a rule of thumb, prices that are 'too low' in comparison with the other bids, mean trouble in the execution. Either the bidder has made a mistake, or is hoping to turn a calculated loss into a profit during implementation. Whatever the reason, the inevitable consequence will be that money will become the prime issue during the execution. As a result, all real or perceived minor changes or additions to the original designs will be heavily discussed along the way. This will lead to extremely frustrating working conditions, which in turn is a guarantee for bad value for money. It is highly recommended that the final bidding price be considered as just one of the deciding factors of the bid, and not as the only one.

In the unhappy event that even the lowest bid exceeds the available signage budget, the designer will need to suggest price-lowering amendments, for instance in use of material or techniques. When even these do not produce enough cost reduction, there is no other solution than to reconsider the designs entirely. Going back to the computer-drawing-table during the process of selecting a manufacturer is far from an easy task.

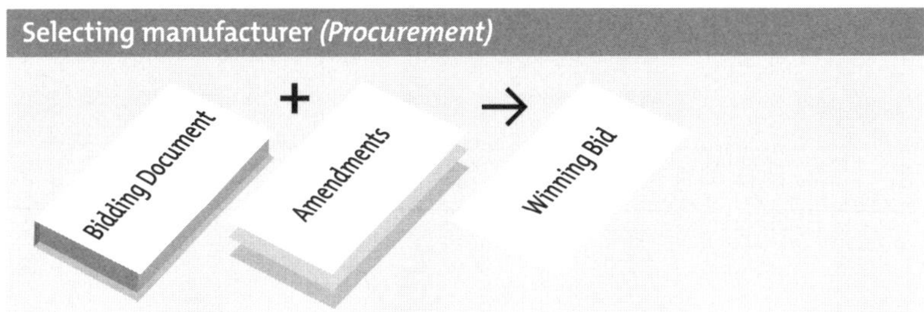

Costs and production specifications are not the only elements of the final manufacturer's contract. Liability insurances, bonding requirements and payment schedules will also have to be part of the agreement. The designer's opinion on these and other parts of the final contract is not important and can best be left to the client, or its purchase or procurement department.

5.2. Supervising manufacture

The intensity of the designer's involvement in the phase of supervising the manufacturing depends heavily on the level of detailed specifications in the bidding documents. Making only global specifications for the bidding phase may have the advantage of dividing the workload of the designer more equally over the various work stages, and may also leave more room for taking advantage of the specific qualities of the manufacturer selected. However, it will take more time (and will be more costly) to make final decisions at the supervising phase.

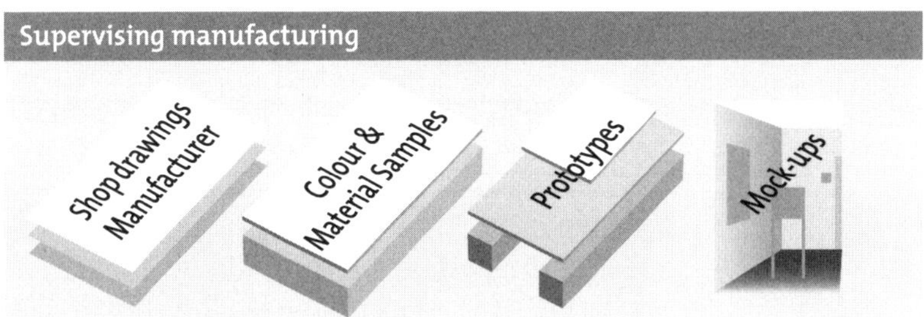

Supervising the manufacturing has three stages:
—detailed discussion about the bidding documents

—the release by the manufacturer of various submissions to be approved by the designer
—quality control at the manufacturer's plant.
If there is more than one (sub)contractor involved, it may result in following the same schedule for more parties simultaneously, plus the coordination between all the manufacturers involved.

5.2.1. DISCUSSION OF BIDDING DOCUMENTS

A good way to start working with the selected manufacturer(s) is by setting up a meeting and thoroughly discussing all the design intent drawings. People responsible for carrying out the work are not always completely involved during the phase of making price calculations. At this point, it is crucial to establish direct contact between designer and ultimate fabricator in order to avoid misunderstandings at the earliest possible stage, and in order to discuss the most suitable work stages.

5.2.2. TYPE OF SUBMISSIONS FOR PRODUCTION APPROVAL

The manufacturer's role is basically to transform the drawings showing the various designs into real-life functioning objects. To avoid, as much as possible, any friction in this transformation, small isolated real parts of the final products are separately produced for approval, together with drawings that provide information in detail about how all the items will actually be manufactured.

5.2.2.1. Shop drawings

The design intent drawings will be replaced completely by the so-called 'shop drawings'. These drawings will all be produced by the manufacturer. Shop drawings will show all the technical detail necessary for the craftspeople to carry out the work. The drawings will include full-scale construction details: information about material; mechanical, electrical, or electronic equipment; type of fasteners and so on. All structural parts on the drawings will be specified to meet all the relevant code requirements.

The manufacturer will be responsible for the structural qualities of the final results and must therefore also agree to the final construction. All shop drawings will be sent for approval to the designer, who will check the drawings according to the specifications of the original designs. Minor corrections should be directly marked on the shop drawings and sent back as soon as possible, bearing the designer's signature and the date it was checked. In the case of minor corrections, the words 'approved as noted' should be added. If the shop drawings need to be revised, first the manufacturer should be contacted to discuss the problem in person, and the drawing should be sent back, marked with a date and the words 'not approved, resubmit'. After the designer approves all the shop drawings, the design intent drawings have lost their initial importance; the shop drawings will supersede all previous drawings as reference when checking and approving the final results.

5.2.2.2. *Colour and material samples*

It is strongly recommended that samples be produced of all materials and finishings before final production starts. No description can fully replace the impression of real objects. Surface characteristics must be seen in their actual state to avoid undesired interpretations. Approved samples must be signed and dated on the sample itself by the designer and returned to the manufacturer. Sometimes two sets of samples are made, one for the designer to keep as personal reference.

5.2.2.3. *Prototypes*

A prototype is a fully functional, hand-made sample at full size of a sign type. The prototype is produced in entire conformity with the respective shop drawing. Obviously this is the ideal way to judge the final result. That is why submission of prototypes is often required for each sign type in the bidding documents. However, the need for prototype production depends on the quantity to be produced of a certain sign type. In cases where large quantities will be produced, prototyping is a must. The designer will be given a final chance to check the implications of the design very carefully and eventually make any final revisions. Not only will the designer be served in this procedure, but both client and manufacturer will also be given a full impression of the final result.
When individual hand or machine-cut letters are part of the project, one letter (or item) should be made in advance, including the device intended to mount it to its final location.

5.2.2.4. *Mock-ups on site*

Determining the precise size and position of signs is notoriously difficult. A mock-up of a sign or a series of signs placed at the final location is the ideal way to make decisions easier. In most cases there will be opportunities to produce mock-ups. The production of the signs will start when the site where the signs will be used is completed or approaching completion. A signage test can take place on a floor that is already completely finished. Simple mock-ups of sign designs can provide excellent insight into how the signs will be perceived. The small investment in simple cardboard models can prevent costly replacement afterwards.

5.2.3. QUALITY CONTROL AT THE WORKSHOP

Not all sign types have to be prototyped, some types are just too big or are one-offs. It is a good idea to organise one or more well-prepared meetings at the plant or the workshop during crucial production phases. The quality of the finish can be a point of special concern or disagreement. Careful finishing as well as making elegant or concealed assemblies of sign components is time-consuming. Cooperation between the designer and the fabricator can enhance quality. The designer has to make written minutes of these meetings immediately afterwards and send the minutes to all personnel involved.

5.3. Supervising installation

In the installation phase the signage project is approaching completion. There are a number of methods to specify the exact location of the signs to be installed.

5.3.1. ELEVATION DRAWINGS

Most signs will be fixed to walls. The architect does not usually make elevation drawings of all the walls in the building. The signage designer has to make simple elevation drawings indicating all the relevant measurements of all locations, like doors, elevators or staircases. Locations will often be similar, so a few standard drawings tend to cover all possibilities.

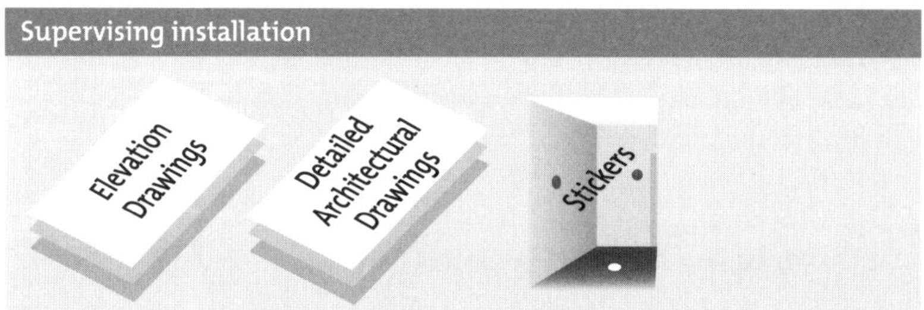

5.3.2. EXISTING ARCHITECTURAL DRAWINGS

When architectural drawings are available, new ones do not need to be produced. Sign locations can be marked very accurately in plan on these drawings. Most floors will have detailed architectural drawings; the ceilings are also often drawn in detail, showing the position of panels and light fittings (fixtures). These drawings may be very handy for the signage designer. However, stay very alert and critical when using these drawings, as architectural drawings might not match the reality of what is actually built!

5.3.3. STICKERS

Drawings may not cover every situation; building construction is not like industrial design, and a lot of irregularities may occur. It is highly recommended that the designer meets with the installer or sign manufacturer on site before installation starts. Walking around and inspecting the locations will prevent misinterpretations or undesired initiatives. Placing a simple sticker indicating the exact location is an extremely efficient specification tool. Do not forget to insist that all stickers be removed by the installers after installation inspection. Stickers tend to have irritatingly long lives.

5.3.4. SPECIAL FACILITIES

Certain signs may need special facilities to mount these signs at the desired locations. Heavy or large signs need special reinforcements to anchor them properly. Illuminated signs need proper connections to the electricity network and need to fit into the circuit system without disturbing it.

5.4. *Completion*

The formal final delivery of all the items in the signage contract is made upon completion. After all the signs have been installed at site, the designer has to make a completion report. The preparation for this report is best done by having a meeting with the manufacturer on site and inspecting all the signs in person together.
Afterwards, a written report is made and issued, listing each item with its specified defects. In the US this list is called a 'Punch List'. In England the activity is called 'snagging'. The manufacturer will be given a limited time to correct any defects. The following inspection after corrections have been carried out can be done by the designer alone. In most cases, this procedure will suffice; two or more completion inspection rounds are rarely needed to have all the signs meet the requirements of the contract.

5.4.1. INCOMPETENT CONTRACTORS

Regrettably, not all manufacturers will always make it to the completion phase. In extraordinary cases, the designer may unhappily discover that the contractor, or a sub-contractor is incompetent—or unable—to do the job properly. A bidding system that grants a commission to the lowest bidder without any consideration other than price may result in dealing with just such incompetent parties. Immediately it has become evident to the designer that the work is being carried out inadequately, the work to date should be reviewed with the client and a 'stop work' order should be issued. Sometimes, the problems can be solved by appointing another sub-contractor, but if all efforts to correct the problem fail, there is no other way forward than the cancellation of the contract with the original contractor and the search for another one to finish the work. These are difficult, time-consuming and costly situations, which fortunately are rare. However, all contracts must contain a cancellation clause to deal with this kind of eventuality.

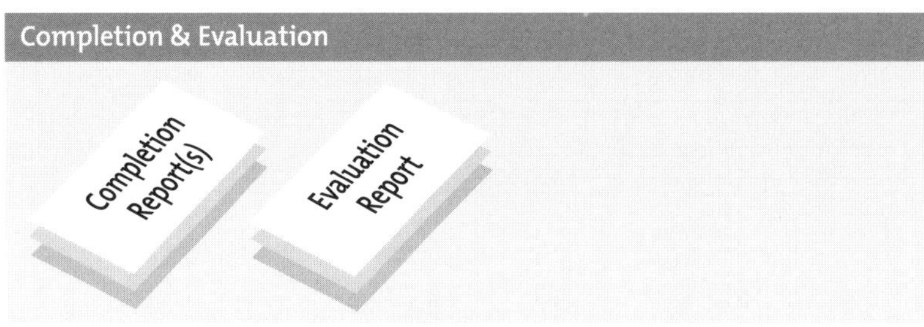

5.5. Evaluation

It is impossible to foresee completely how each sign will be perceived by visitors, employees or tenants. Every signage project reveals unexpected behaviour after it has been in use for a while. Human behaviour is not fully predictable. Therefore, it is recommendable to extend the commission of the signage designer with a feedback phase.

After three to six months of use, facility managers, receptionists and others in regular contact with users will have gathered interesting feedback on how the signage system is working in real life and what the major bottlenecks are in the wayfinding process. Not only will the signage be up for evaluation, in many cases the organisation itself will need to adapt to its new home. Changes arising out of this evaluation would be incorporated as well. After all the information is gathered, the designer has to design any necessary alterations or additions to the existing system.

Obviously, the evaluation of the signage has to be an ongoing procedure. The first evaluation may be an important one, but it had better not be the last. The signage must follow and reflect the organisation it is made for, in all its dynamics. If this crucial aspect of signage is denied, forgotten or missed, the whole system will soon become worse than obsolete. Worse, because it is better to provide no information whatsoever than to provide wrong data. Neglect of the signage will affect the image of the organisation. Never underestimate signage as a powerful public relations tool.

The continuous involvement of a signage designer is rarely advisable in the process of regular evaluations and updates. It is more important that the signage remains regularly on the maintenance agenda, just as the window cleaning and the elevator maintenance are, to name only two common and well-accepted activities in building maintenance.

6. Organising the maintenance

One of the common discrepancies in signage projects is the imbalance of attention given by the client to the need for ease of updating individual signs during the phase where competitive signage panel systems are judged and selected, as opposed to the attention given to organising this process properly after final installation. Updating may be easy to do, but signs do not update themselves automatically—although electronic signs may have that possibility when linked to other databases. In most cases, a simple procedure has to be set in place to organise the regular updating of signs.
Regrettably, most signage projects still deteriorate quickly after initial installation. To put it kindly, the attention given to organising the updating of a signage system is on average still far from satisfactory.

6.1. Signage Officer

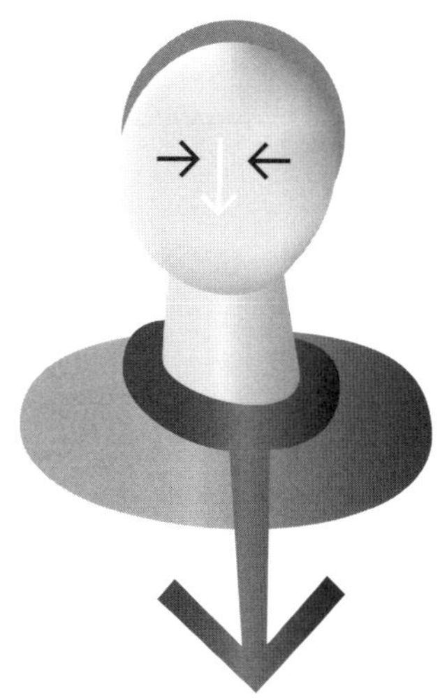

The Facilities Manager is responsible for the maintenance of facilities. This responsibility also includes, in most cases, the maintenance of the signage. Apparently, signage maintenance is difficult to control. Perhaps there are reasons why this is the case. A lot of the maintenance of a facility is carried out as daily routine (like room cleaning) or on a steady regular basis (like maintenance for safety or security systems or lifts). Signage falls uncomfortably between these two types of duties. Signage maintenance is also relatively easy to postpone. Everybody would notice a failure in the daily office cleaning. Equipment maintenance is partly regulated by law or may result in serious equipment failures, directly influencing the productivity of staff. The signage maintenance, however, has none of these immediate and urgent aspects, but it certainly deserves dedicated and close attention.

A solution may be to appoint a person who is uniquely responsible for the maintenance of the signage. Let's call this position the 'Signage Officer'. The position is unlikely to be a full-time job, but somebody can be given this (extra) title and additional job description. The work may be done by somebody like a secretary, a PR person, or a member of the facilities staff. The responsibility given to this person will require that all signs on the site provide correct information at all times and are also clean and in good condition. Even the last aspect is often embarrassingly overlooked. It happens too often that a building entrance has well maintained floors, walls and windows, but the entrance sign has not been touched in years. An incomprehensible omission in proper maintenance that involves hardly any extra work for the cleaning crew. Surprisingly, it fails to be noticed by anyone responsible passing it every day.

The Signage Officer establishes regular contact with the Personnel Department about changes in staff and with the

Facilities Department about internal relocations. Extensive building renovations or building extensions may involve participation with the building team. Clearly, the Signage Officer should be provided with sufficient technical data and specifications to do the job properly, and should establish a good working relationship with all external fabricators involved in the signage maintenance. For some types of buildings, updating signs may include instructing other staff members: for instance, patient names in hospitals may be updated by the medical staff themselves.

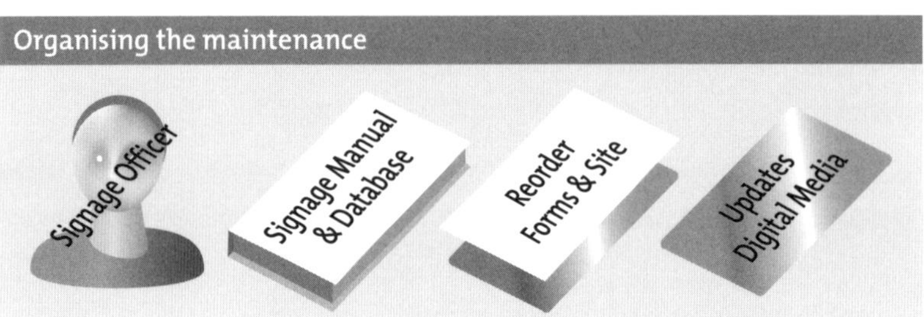

6.2. Signage Manual and database

After the completion of the signage project, most items installed will have related construction drawings and technical specifications (either as shop drawings or as design intent drawings). However, these drawings or specs are seldom entirely accurate. Moreover, the visual form in which these production specifications are available is not likely to be the most understandable, especially for somebody on the client's staff who is not involved daily in the designing or production of signage. Therefore, a concise and comprehensible signage manual has to be produced that describes all the sign types used at the site. This information is essential for everybody involved in updating the signage.

It is important that the Signage Manual covers not only the physical signs in the environment, but also the websites, touch-screen directories and screen networks that have become inseparable parts of the signage system. The design of the physical signs has to be consistent with the electronic signage.

6.2.1. SIGNAGE DATABASE

A sign database is part of any signage project over a certain size. Changes or extensions in the building or its tenants will require the updating of various types of signs. Databases with specific search facilities are almost indispensable for overseeing all the consequences of proposed changes.

6.3. Signage reorder forms

On average, signage manufacturers would rather not be bothered with reorders for projects they have installed themselves, unless the reorder quantity is substantial. They would rather hunt for 'new business'. This attitude is extremely unprofessional, because it deprives a client of an essential service and it does not express a comprehensive understanding of what signage is all about. Ultimately, this attitude gives the industry a bad name, which is very bad for business in general. However, the signage industry seems to find it difficult escape from this self-inflicted fate. Fortunately, not all signage manufacturers pursue this pointless strategy and many updates do not need the involvement of third parties anymore and can be done in-house these days. In-house laser printers can produce outstanding graphics that can be put onto a wide variety of different materials. But, as already said, signs do not get updated by clever little elves during the night while everybody is asleep. In reality, somebody has to organise the process and oversee its execution. Having in-house production facilities is by no means a guarantee that signs will be updated regularly.

Whether sign production is done in-house or by an external company, the ordering procedure needs to be as simple and as straightforward as possible. Designing a simple ordering procedure and a related form is a good way to run reorders smoothly.

6.4. Website reordering

Paper order forms sent by ordinary (snail) mail are rapidly becoming obsolete. More and more manufacturers connect with their clients through a website. All the relevant information for a client or a specific signage project will be accessible on a protected part of the website. In principle, this may be a very efficient way to organise updates. The time to transfer information is reduced to milliseconds, production specs can be updated very easily and all administration relating to transactions can be simplified.
In future, internet portals will provide services that help designers all the way through the different phases of a signage project, and updating after completion will be a seamless extension of these services. Domain names like 'My Signs' are already popping up.

6.5. Updating websites and touch screens

Electronic media are still in their infancy. One of the most fundamental advantages of these media is the efficiency of updating the information conveyed, but this is still often a painstaking process. All media used for signage purposes must have easy content management interfaces to do in-house updating in a fast and easy manner.

6.6. Updates for impaired users

Rapidly advancing technology and growing wealth have made modern societies extremely dynamic. It has become a tough task to design systems and procedures that keep even those for the non-impaired updated. Production methods for devices that can be used by impaired users are not as widely disseminated as more general production methods. This often results in this kind of updating falling behind. A more positive development may be that technological developments may make impaired users less dependent on custom-built devices.

6.7. Updating strategies

In most instances, we need signage to find the location of a person, an organisation, or the venue where an event is going to take place. There are a number of strategies or considerations involved in keeping the relevant signage up-to-date.

6.7.1. CENTRALISED OR DECENTRALISED IMPLEMENTATION

Responsibility for signage updates can be either the responsibility of a single unit or person, or a shared responsibility. The best option depends on the type and size of building. In cases where a lot of people move constantly to various locations, a decentralised process may be the most effective. Still, one person should have control over the whole process.

Computers connected to high-quality printers are now available in abundance in most buildings and an increasing number of sign types contain laser prints. The available computers are part of a network that provides internal communication and standardised procedures. Updating signage may be made a part of these standardised procedures. Office door signs, for instance, can be made available as printable templates to be updated by the inhabitants of a space themselves rather than by one specific working unit or person.

6.7.2. HOTELING OFFICES

New methods for organising office occupancy can reduce the need for signage updates dramatically. A growing number of offices are using the 'hoteling' method, which means that staff can book a room in their own office building when they need it. This method eliminates having their own office spaces and with it the name of a person on the door sign. As in a hotel, room numbers will be the key to wayfinding, and the need for updating door signs will be reduced dramatically. Also in this case, efficiency comes at a price; hotels will never be perceived as an extension of the home, whereas that may be so for a dedicated workspace. Most (Western) people want their name on their home door as on their workspace; nobody wants a name on their hotel room, quite the contrary.

The quest for efficient navigation techniques may lead to extremely unpleasant situations. Modern telecom technology is a good example where the quest for efficiency is sometimes at the expense of the user, often resulting in teeth-grinding lack of service. Nobody will cry over the reduced need for telephonists who only distribute incoming phone calls, but being sent instead into a labyrinth of senseless code pressing is nothing short of profoundly insulting. Navigation should never be solely technology-driven.

6.7.3. AUTONOMOUS OR LINKED TO EXISTING DATABASES

It seems that nobody is capable of doing any job properly anymore without the use of at least software for word-processing, spreadsheets and databases. Hardly any meeting or event is scheduled without employing appropriate software. Most future physical changes or events start their life in a computer. It seems practical to make use of this information to update signage as well.

A system consisting of computer network screens that makes use of events databases is already on the market. In this instance, the system of updating is completely automated. Complete automation is often feeble and not always a necessity, as data files can also be printed out and handed over to others to work with. It is well worth considering making existing computer output into handy tools for updating the signage system, thus avoiding the need to rely entirely on often delicate electronic networks.

Epilogue: Signage in the world to come

Developments in science and technology change the way we live, work and communicate. Future developments may make a lot of the methodology described in this book obsolete. It is conceivable that the need for having physical signs in the environment to instruct us or show us the right way to go will one day end. There may also be the start of a movement that wishes to eliminate, as much as possible, all signs of human interference in our environment. The value and respect for our natural environment must rise dramatically at some stage.

Developments in electronic identification, positioning and navigation systems may make traditional signage obsolete. Wayfinding for car users has already become a matter of typing in a destination, starting the car and following very simple spoken instructions that are also shown on a screen. What used to be a complicated task, involving careful route planning in advance, combined with extreme alertness and cleverness in signage interpretation during the journey, has become a piece of cake. What is already almost a standard equipment for cars will soon be usual for users of mobile phones or personal organisers, covering practically everyone in the West, and eventually the rest of the world.

The Global Positioning System (GPS) will become available to everyone, in combination with wireless devices of all sorts and electronic tracing with so-called radio tags will become so widely used that it will even replace the familiar barcodes on products.

Human civilisation started with the creation of tools that made the world more understandable, accessible and comfortable for people. We made aids that represented the real world in a form that made it easier for us to understand and use our natural environment. Maps and signs were part of a 'second reality' that we created in parallel with the real one. In making all-encompassing knowledge available in a digital format, we have adopted the building blocks of nature itself as part of our own tool box. Today, we can manipulate matter at the atomic and molecular level, and use electromagnetic waves travelling at the speed of light. Eventually, the additional human version of reality is going to merge with the real world in an inseparable way. We will no longer look around us to see what's happening, to memorise or to orient ourselves, we will rather use personalised electronic devices that will create possibilities and provide essential extra information to serve all our needs. In addition, any kind of human impairment will be resolved with this technology.

We will eventually add to our senses, which took millions of years to develop, an essential synthetic seventh sense—possibly the most powerful of all.

Appendix I: Diagram signage program summary

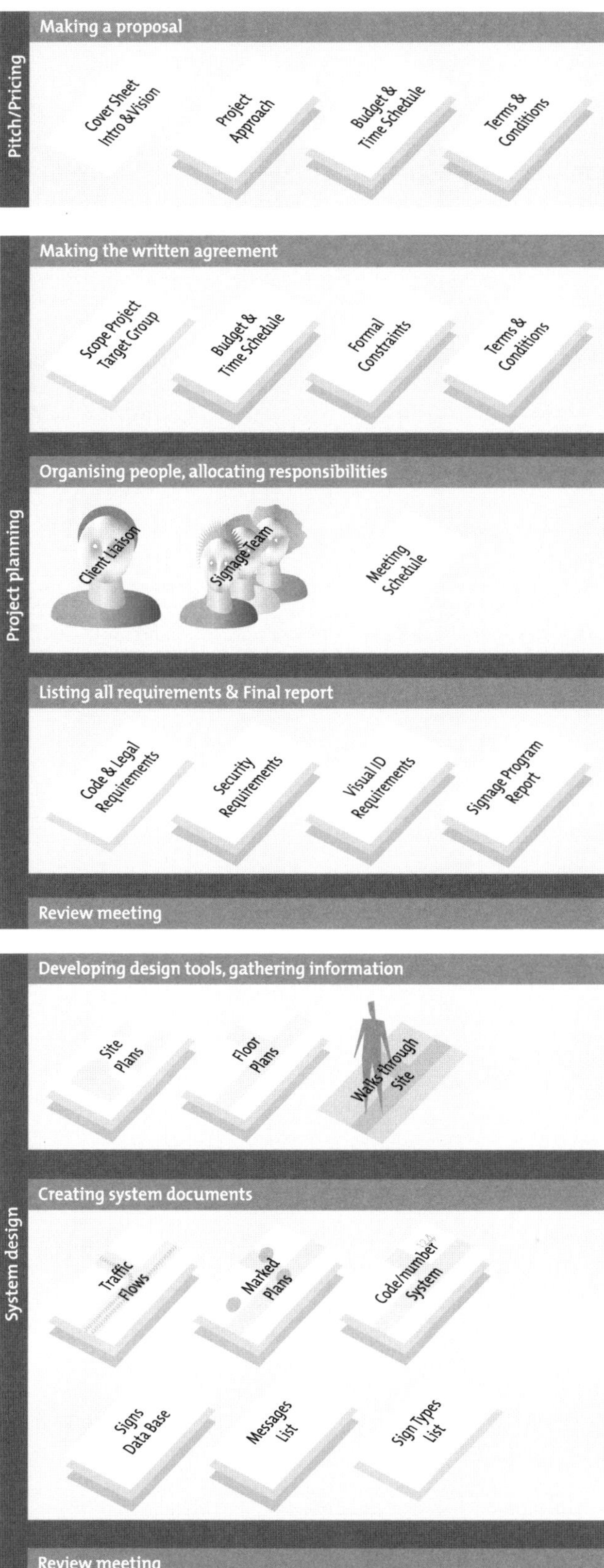

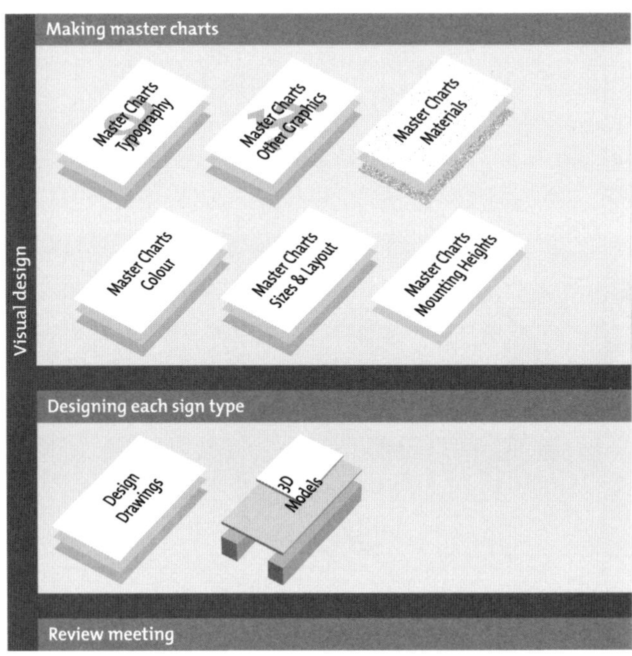
Visual design
Making master charts
Master Charts Typography
Master Charts Other Graphics
Master Charts Materials
Master Charts Colour
Master Charts Sizes & Layout
Master Charts Mounting Heights
Designing each sign type
Design Drawings
3D Models
Review meeting

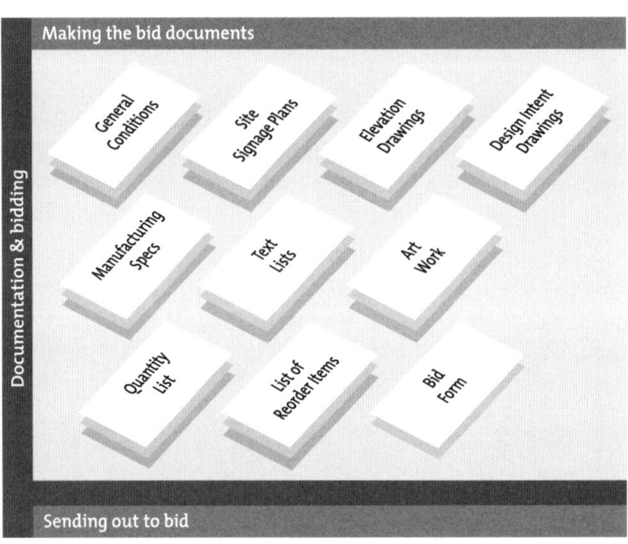
Documentation & bidding
Making the bid documents
General Conditions
Site Signage Plans
Elevation Drawings
Design Intent Drawings
Manufacturing Specs
Text Lists
Art Work
Quantity List
List of Reorder Items
Bid Form
Sending out to bid

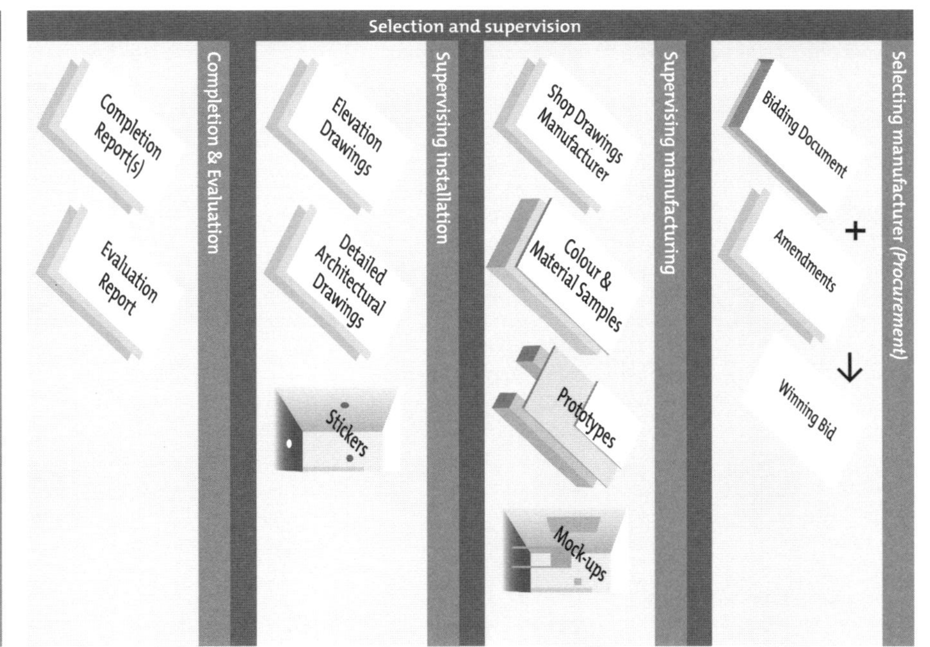
Selection and supervision
Selecting manufacturer (Procurement)
Bidding Document
+
Amendments
Winning Bid
Supervising manufacturing
Shop Drawings
Manufacturer
Colour &
Material Samples
Prototypes
Mock-ups
Supervising installation
Elevation
Drawings
Detailed
Architectural
Drawings
Stickers
Completion & Evaluation
Completion
Report(s)
Evaluation
Report

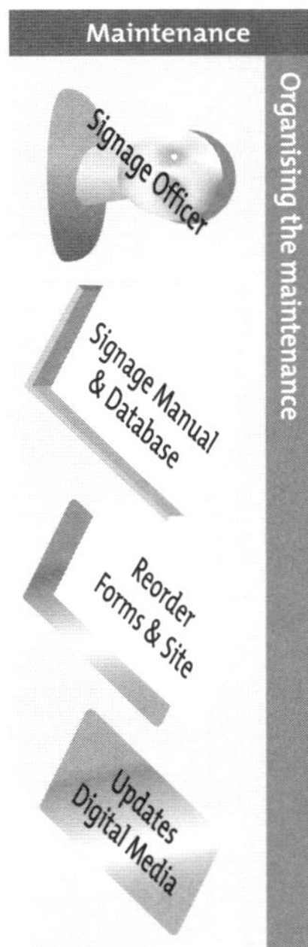
Maintenance
Organising the maintenance
Signage Officer
Signage Manual
& Database
Reorder
Forms & Site
Updates
Digital Media

Appendix II: ADA sign requirements

ADA STANDARDS FOR ACCESSIBLE DESIGN

The Americans with Disabilities Act (ADA) was signed into law in July 1990. The standards (or guidelines) supporting the law were first issued in July 1991 and have been updated since. The selections (4.1.1(16) and 4.30) given below are taken from the revised version as of July 1, 1994. The selections are not meant to be authoritative in any way; they intend to provide information about the parts most relevant for signage design. Further information can be obtained through the ADA section of the website of the US Ministry of Justice, at *http://www.usdoj.gov/crt/ada/adahom1.htm*. Also, the SEGD issues a popular White Paper about the ADA Guidelines.

* Text with an asterisk is taken from the relevant appendix which contains materials of an *advisory* nature and provides additional information that should help the reader to understand the minimum requirements of the guidelines or to design buildings or facilities for greater accessibility.

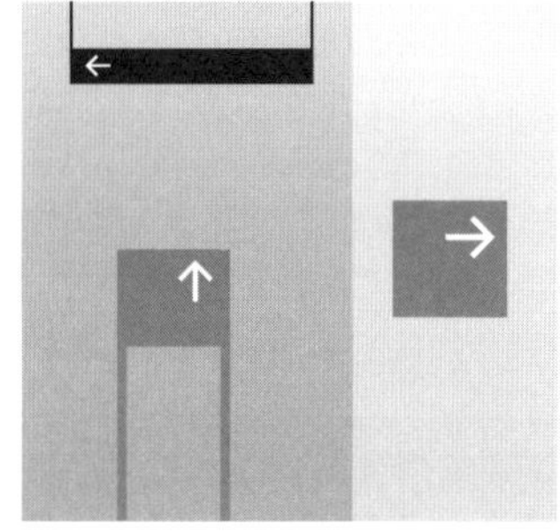

The ADA guidelines are limited to only two specific sign types. First, raised capital letters, numerals and Brailled characters are only required for (permanent) room designation signs. Second, the other relevant sign type comprises for the most part directional signs and even within this category ADA specifications are provided only for overhead signs.

4.1 Minimum Requirements
4.1.1 Application.*
(16) Building Signage:
(a) Signs which designate permanent rooms and spaces shall comply with 4.30.1, 4.30.4, 4.30.5 and 4.30.6.
(b) Other signs which provide direction to or information about functional spaces of the building shall comply with 4.30.1, 4.30.2, 4.30.3, and 4.30.5.
EXCEPTION: Building directories, menus, and all other signs which are temporary are not required to comply.

4.30 Signage.
4.30.1 General.*
Signage required to be accessible by 4.1 shall comply with the applicable provisions of 4.30.

*In building complexes where finding locations independently on a routine basis may be a necessity (for example, college campuses), tactile maps or pre-recorded instructions can be very helpful to visually impaired people. Several maps and auditory instructions have been developed and tested for specific applications. The type of map or instructions used must be based on the information to be communicated, which depends highly on the type of buildings or users. Landmarks that can easily be distinguished by visually impaired individuals are useful as orientation cues. Such cues include changes in illumination level, bright colors, unique patterns, wall murals, location of special equipment or other architectural features. Many people with disabilities have limitations in movement of their heads and reduced peripheral vision. Thus, signage positioned perpendicular to the path of travel is easiest for them to notice. People can generally distinguish signage within an angle of 30 degrees to either side of the centerlines of their faces without moving their heads.

The letter I, i is the narrowest one in the alphabet, the letter M,m is the widest. Meeting the required letter proportions—between 5:1 and 1:1—is only possible when using a monospaced (typewriter) typeface, see samples in first column. To widen the choice, the SEGD has suggested reading the instructions as 'average values' for a complete alphabet. The second column shows the range of stroke-widths within the given limitations. The requirements are excluded from the room designation signs.

4.30.2 Character Proportion.*

Letters and numbers on signs shall have a width-to-height ratio between 3:5 and 1:1 and a stroke-width-t o-height ratio between 1:5 and 1:10.

* The legibility of printed characters is a function of the viewing distance, character height, the ratio of the stroke width to the height of the character, the contrast of color between character and background, and print font. The size of characters must be based upon the intended viewing distance. A severely nearsighted person may have to be much closer to recognize a character of a given size than a person with normal visual acuity.

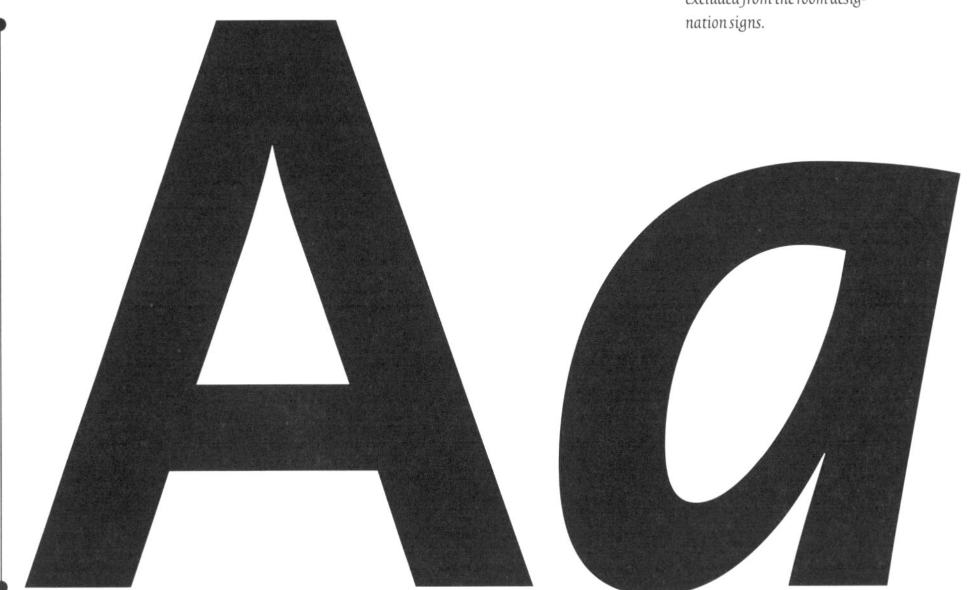

The minimum capital height—shown 1:1—for overhead directional signs is 3 inches. Normally, this letter height is used for reading distances between 75 and 150 feet. A 4-foot-wide sign panel will hold no more than about 16 characters and one arrow on one line.

4.30.3 Character Height.

Characters and numbers on signs shall be sized according to the viewing distance from which they are to be read. The minimum height is

measured using an upper case X. Lower case characters are permitted.
Height Above Finished Floor: Suspended or Projected Overhead in compliance with 4.4.2
Minimum Character Height: 3 in (75 mm) minimum.

4.4.2 Head Room. Walks, halls, corridors, passageways, aisles, or other circulation spaces shall have 80 in (2030 mm) minimum clear head room. If vertical clearance of an area adjoining an accessible route is reduced to less than 80 in (nominal dimension), a barrier to lind or visually-impaired persons shall be provided.

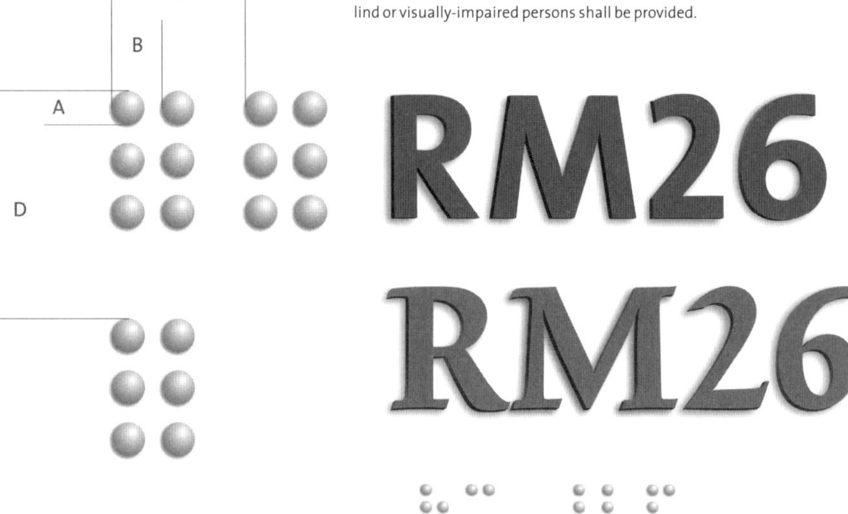

Above: the standard dimensions for literary Braille. A. dot diameter .059 inch (1.5 mm). B. dot spacing .090 inch (2.29 mm). C. cell character spacing .241 inch (6.12 mm) D. cell line spacing .393 inch (10 mm) Right: 1:1 samples of the minimum letter height of the raised characters in combination with the standard Braille size. The characters must be raised 1/32 inch (0.8 mm) from the surface.

4.30.4 Raised and Brailled Characters and Pictorial Symbol Signs (Pictograms).*

Letters and numerals shall be raised 1/32 in, upper case, sans serif or simple serif type and shall be accompanied with Grade 2 Braille. Raised characters shall be at least 5/8 in (16 mm) high, but no higher than 2 in (50 mm). Pictograms shall be accompanied by the equivalent verbal description placed directly below the pictogram. The border dimension of the pictogram shall be 6 in (152 mm) minimum in height.

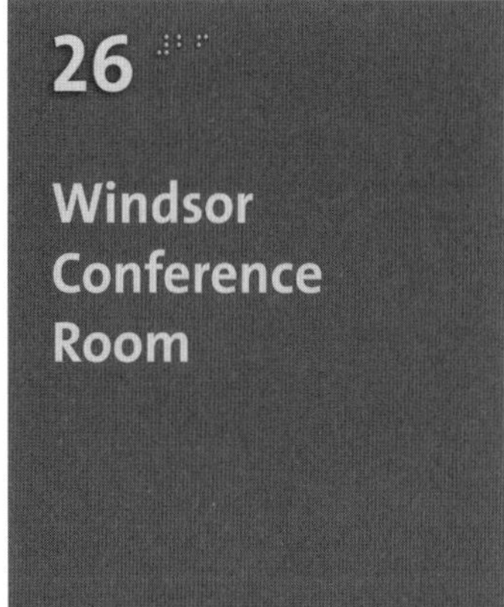

Applying an (alpha) numeral code on each room sign according to ADA standards will be sufficient in most cases. Pictograms can only be used starting from a minimum size and need verbal description about their meaning below.

* The standard dimensions for literary Braille are as follows: Dot diameter: .059 in, Inter-dot spacing .090 in, Horizontal separation between cells: .241 in, Vertical separation between cells: .395 in. Raised borders around signs containing raised characters may make them con-

fusing to read unless the border is set far away from the characters. Accessible signage with descriptive materials about public buildings, monuments, and objects of cultural interest may not provide sufficiently detailed and meaningful information. Interpretive guides, audio tape devices, or other methods may be more effective in presenting such information.

4.30.5 Finish and Contrast.*

The characters and background of signs shall be eggshell, matte, or other non-glare finish. Characters and symbols shall contrast with their background—either light characters on a dark background or dark characters on a light background.

*An eggshell finish (11 to 19 degree gloss on 60 degree glossimeter) is recommended. Research indicates that signs are more legible for persons with low vision when characters contrast with their background by at least 70 percent. Contrast in percent shall be determined by: Contrast = [(B1 - B2)/B1] x 100, where B1 = light reflectance value (lrv) of the lighter area and B2 = light reflectance value (lrv) of the darker area.
Note that in any application both white and black are never absolute; thus, B1 never equals 100 and B2 is always greater than 0. The greatest readability is usually achieved through the use of light-colored characters or symbols on a dark background.

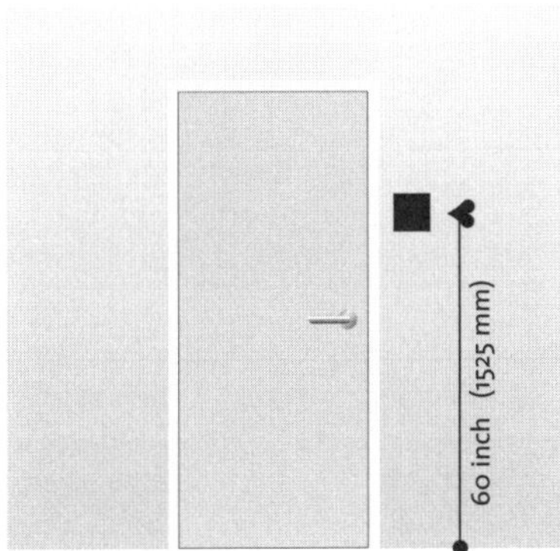

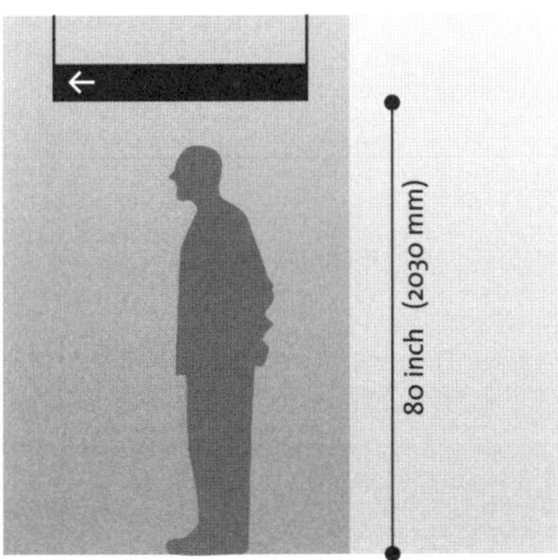

Room designation signs must be mounted with a fixed distance between the centre of the sign and the floor. Overhead signs must have a minimum clearance height.

4.30.6 Mounting Location and Height.

Where permanent identification is provided for rooms and spaces, signs shall be installed on the wall adjacent to the latch side of the door. Where there is no wall space to the latch side of the door, including at double leaf doors, signs shall be placed on the nearest adjacent wall. Mounting height shall be 60 in (1525 mm) above the finish floor to the centerline of the sign. Mounting location for such signage shall be so that a person may approach within 3 in (76 mm) of signage without encountering protruding objects or standing within the swing of a door.

4.30.7 Symbols of Accessibility.*

(1) Facilities and elements required to be identified as accessible by 4.1 shall use the international symbol of accessibility. The symbol shall be displayed as shown.
(2) Volume Control Telephones. Telephones required to have a volume control by 4.1.3(17)(b) shall be identified by a sign containing a depiction of a telephone handset with radiating sound waves.
(3) Text Telephones. Text telephones required by 4.1.3(17)(c) shall be identified by the international TDD symbol. In addition, if a facility has a

public text telephone, directional signage indicating the location of the nearest text telephone shall be placed adjacent to all banks of telephones which do not contain a text telephone. Such directional signage shall include the international TDD symbol. If a facility has no banks of telephones, the directional signage shall be provided at the entrance (e.g., in a building directory).
(4) Assistive Listening Systems. In assembly areas where permanently installed assistive listening systems are required by 4.1.3(19)(b) the availability of such systems shall be identified with signage that includes the international symbol of access for hearing loss.

Two rows of required symbols (pictograms), on top the 'International' range provided by the ADA guidelines, and below the SEGD recommendations (1992) for the design of these symbols.
Left to right: International Symbol for Accessibility, Symbol of Access for Hearing Loss, TDD Text Telephone Symbol, Volume Control Telephone Symbol.

* Paragraph 4 of this section requires signage indicating the availability of an assistive listening system. An appropriate message should be displayed with the international symbol of access for hearing loss since this symbol conveys general accessibility for people with hearing loss. Some suggestions are: 'Infrared Assistive Listening System available—Please ask', or 'Audio loop in use, turn T-switch for better hearing—or ask for help', or 'FM Assistive Listening System available—Please ask'.
The symbol may be used to notify persons of the availability of other auxiliary aids and services such as: real time captioning, captioned note taking, sign language interpreters, and oral interpreters.

4.30.8 Illumination Levels.*
(Reserved).

*Illumination levels on the sign surface shall be in the 100 to 300 lux range (10 to 30 footcandles) and shall be uniform over the sign surface. Signs shall be located such that the illumination level on the surface of the sign is not significantly exceeded by the ambient light or visible bright lighting source behind or in front of the sign.

NB. The ADA Accessibility Guidelines (ADAAG) are updated regularly. Many governmental bodies and private organisations are more or less involved in the ADA regulations. Endorsement of new guidelines is not done homogeneously by all parties involved. For instance, some—but not all—state governments have incorporated new ADA guidelines in their new building codes. Therefore it is advisable to enquire in advance about local conditions.

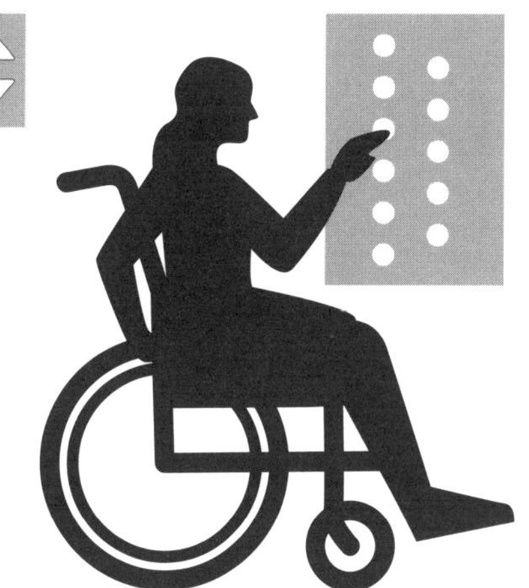

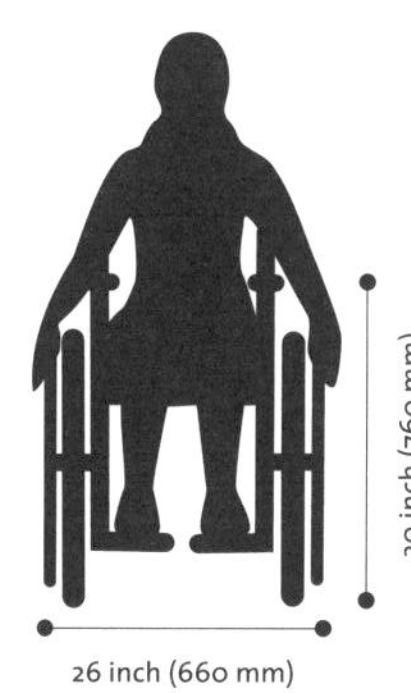

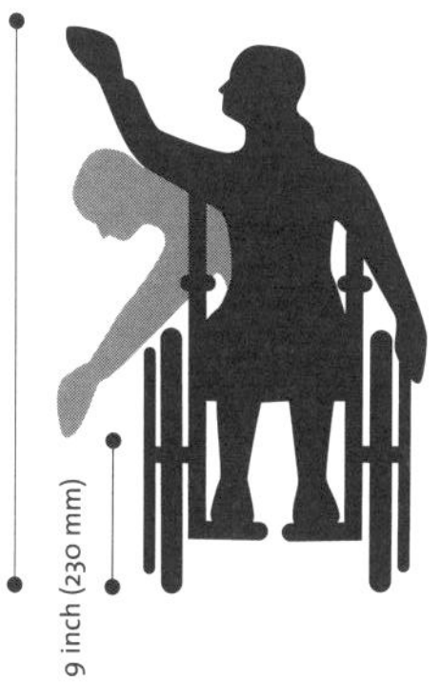

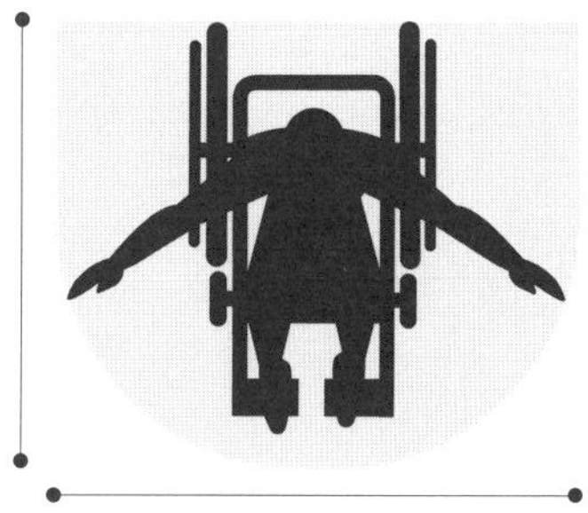

A representative overview of the ADA guidelines for wheelchair users. Numerals on elevator car control panels shall be a minimum of 5/8 inch (16 mm) high.

Selected Bibliography

A Sign Systems Manual, Crosby Fletcher Forbes, Studio Vista, UK 1970

Archigraphia, Walter Herdeg, The Graphis Press, Switzerland 1978

Architectural Signing and Graphics, John Follis and Dave Hammer, Whitney Library of Design, USA 1979

Design Protection, Dan Johnston, The Design Council, UK 1995

Design That Cares, Janet Carpman and Myron Grant, American Hospital Publishing, USA 1993

Designing for People, Henry Dreyfuss, Allworth Press, USA 1955

Environmental Graphics Sourcebook, Society of Environmental Graphic Designers SEGD, USA 1982

Geometry of Design, Kimberly Elam, Princeton Architectural Press, USA 2001

Handbook of Pictorial Symbols, Rudolf Modley, Dover Publications, 1976

Information Graphics, Peter Wildbur and Michael Burke, Thames & Hudson, UK 1998

Les Pictogrammes aux Jeux Olympiques, Message Olympique No 34, Switzerland 1992

Linksaf, rechtsaf, alsmaar rechtdoor..., Catalogue signage exhibition GVN, Netherlands 1976

Pictogram Design, Yukio Ota, Kashiwashobo Publishing, Japan 1993

Public Transportation Systems, CoCoMAS Committee, Sanno Institute, Japan 1976

Sign Design Guide, Peter Barker and June Fraser, JMU and Sign Design Society, UK [*no publication date*]

Signage, Charles McLendon and Mick Blackistone, McGraw-Hill, USA 1982

Signsystem design-manual, Kiyoshi Nishikawa, Gakugei Shuppan-sha, Japan 2002

Signwork, Bill Stewart, Granada Publishing, UK 1984

Symbol Signs for Public information, Taisei-Shuppan, Japan 2001

Wayfinding, Paul Arthur and Romedi Passini, McGraw-Hill, Canada 1992

Index

abbreviations 94, 320
acrylic and aluminium 258
acrylic cassettes 248
acrylic panels 256
acrylic sheets 248
ADA 44
  sign requirements 434
  signs 146
additive colour mixing 388
adhesive foil 211, 230
adhesive tapes 278
Adobe 296, 297, 298, 329
advertisements 96, 173, 175
aerosol spray 262
aesthetic design 26, 163
aesthetic qualities 157
A-frames 146
Aicher, Otl 327, 332
AIGA 98, 324, 328
AIGA/DOT *series of pictograms 329*
Air France 348
airport design 19, 61, 119
Akopov, Valerie 327
Akzidenz Grotesk 307, 310, 311
Albertville Winter Games 327, 334
aliasing 300
alphabetical characters 292
alphanumeric coding system 96
aluminium extrusions 247
aluminium panels 258
American Institute of Graphic Arts (AIGA) *98, 324, 328*
American Type Founders Company 310
Americans with Disabilities Act (ADA) 44
Amsterdam, city planning 60, 61, 64, 65
analogue colours 388, 389
analogue/ton-sur-ton combinations 389
ancient styles 345
angle variation extensions 295
anodising 275
Antiqua 286
Apple 297, 298
application of texts/illustrations 208
Arabic script 292
Arabic numerals 101
arbitrary colours 391
arches 66
archetypical type styles 286
archetypical visual impression of signs 190
architect 20, 28, 62
architect's disease 39
architectural design 62, 188, 197
architectural drawings 416
architectural elements, heights 192
architectural signage 19, 132, 140, 146
architecture, copyright 173, 175, 181
arenas 118
Arnzt, Gerd 324
arrow 216, 314, 315, 316, 320, 349
art and copy 96
Art Deco 198
Art Nouveau 198
art structures 65
Arthur, Paul 328
artificial speech 90
artwork 52, 412
ascender letters 282, 289
Association Typographique Internationale 287
ATF 310
Athens Summer Games 336
Atkins 200
Atlanta Summer Games 335
attribution mark 178
ATypI 287
audible information 37
automated cutting machines 261
automated routers 263
automated signs 75
Automated Teller Machines (ATM) 394
automatic sensors 103
awning 137, 146
axis road 65

back-lit directories 251
balloon sign 146
ball-points 286
banner 115, 138, 146, 251
Barcelona Summer Games 327, 334
barcode 95, 313
  alphabet 313
baseline 282
basic colours 388
basic design elements 191
basic elements of visual design 207
basic list of functions 115
basic materials 254
basic materials chart 51
basic shapes 197, 198
basic signage content 214
bas-relief 211
Bauhaus 307
Baur, Ruedi 348, 364
beauty contests 166
beauty/ugliness 156
Beck, Harry 351, 354
Beijing Games 337
Belkov, Nikolai 327, 332
belt road 65
belt signs 146
Berlage, Hendrik Petrus 202
Berne Convention of 1886 170
Berthold 307, 310
bidding
  bid form 412
  documents, discussion 414

process 52
type 404
billboards 136
bird's eye-view 105, 106, 351
bitmaps 298
blackboards 205
Blade Runner 61
bleaching 276
blind fastening 277
Bliss, Charles 324
Blissymbolics 328
Bluetooth 76
Bollmann Bildkarten Verlag 353
Bollmann, Hermann 353
border heights 229
Braille 88, 89, 90, 91, 312, 313, 314
brain mapping software 193
branches 79
branding 46, 67, 109, 175
brass 258
breaches of contract 184
Bretez, Louis 353
bric 259
bridges 65
brief 164, 167
Bright, Keith 333
brightness 387
British Library London, map 358
British Ministry of Transport 308, 310
British Rail arrow 315
broad-nibbed pen 286
bronze 258
Buckminster Fuller, Richard 365, 367
Bucky Balls 367
Buddhists 16
Buddhist temples 66
budget 47
building
basic heights 81
copyright 171, 181
building contractor 32
building directories 107, 146
building floors 385
building management 31
building types 57, 59, 117
bulletin board 109, 146, 252
bus terminals 119
Bu-Yong, Hwang 333

CAD-CAM drawings 199
Calgary Winter Games 327, 332
calligraphers 262
CalTrans 305
Calvert, Margaret 308, 310
CAM 262
Cannan, Bill 326, 339
canopy 137, 146
cap-height 282
capital letters 320
carriers 215
carving 211
cashier's desk 230
Caslon, William 306
Cathode Ray Tubes (CRT) 268, 269, 270
ceilings 204
panel systems 83
censorship 169
ceramic 259
chalkboard 146
chandelier sign 146
changeability of signs 69
channel letters 146, 258
character
characters/glyphs 291
height 435
proportion 435
set 292
shape extension 294
strokes 289
characteristic marks 92
charts 51, 191
check-list for sign type selection 116
chemical techniques 263, 275
chinaware 276
Chinese characters 73, 323
choreography, copyright 173
Christianity 16
chroming 275
cinemas 117
circulation pattern 65
citation of existing art 200
city street 383
civic sign 146
classification of sign types 133
Cleartype 300, 305, 308
ClearViewOne 311
client 27, 33, 404
cloakrooms 126
coatings 276
specifications 410
Coca-Cola 176
coding 95
code signs 146
coffee corners 126
cognitive impairment 37
colleges 118
colour 192, 214, 386
colour and light 82
colour blindness 37, 95
colour chart 51
colour coding 68, 82, 95, 104, 390
colour combinations 388
colour contrast 390
colour fastness 391
colour harmony 389
colour specifications 410
colour theory 386
colour wheel 388, 389
commercial right/moral right 178, 179
commercial signage 16, 19

communication 163
communication expert 31, 160
communication process 29
communication with machines 240
compass orientation 104
competition 166
unfair competition 176, 180
competitive bidding 405
COMPIC 328
completion 417
complex design projects 185
complexity 47
complimentary colours 388
compromise 186
computer screens 74
computer software, copyright 173
computer-aided design (CAD) 199
computer-aided manufacturing 262, 359
computer-aided systems 117
concrete 259
condensed shape 289
conditions 52
conductor 185
conference centres 117
confidentiality agreements 176, 183
consistency 68
console signs 146
construction 215, 223
construction sign 146
content changes 213
contrast 312
Cooltype 300
copper 258
copyright (author's right) 169, 172
copyright/copyleft 178
duration 177
fee collection 172
Corbusier, Le 365, 366
cornerstone 146
corporate identity 29, 46
Corten steel 275
costs, manufacturing and installation 48
counter sign 146
counterfeiting 180
couriers 41
cover sheet 406
creativity 186
crests 93
CRT 268, 269, 270
CRT screen 74
cut-and-fill letters 146
cutting machines 263388

Da Vinci, Leonardo 368, 369
database 58, 114
daylight 387
DDA 44
Department of Transportation (DOT) 98, 324
descender height 282
descender letters 289
Desgrippes 334
design
author's moral right 182
copyright 171, 181
commissions 184
competitions 166
concept 193
execution aids 58
fees 48
intent drawings 408
IP protection 174
objective 58
patent registration and protection (USA) 174
phase 51
proposals 164
rights 181, 182, 183
specifications 191
steps 215
team 185
designers and architects 20
designing 57, 159
desk sign 146
desktop sign 84
destination 113
clusters 67
identification 94
types 67
detail and rhythm 288
detectors 75
development of signage system 14, 193
diagram signage program summary 431
diagrams 191, 431
die cutting 262
dies 262
diffuse light 82
Digital Age 297
digital assistant 89, 200, 239
digital communication 86
digital data transmission 199
digital devices 145
digital graffiti 146, 150
digital information 89
digital ink 147
digital revolution 88, 296, 396
digital signage 147
digital type production 285
digital graffiti 242, 245
dimensional letters 140, 147, 211, 217
dingbat extensions 294
directional sign 147, 232
directories 106, 113, 147
directory of sign type names 132
disability 38, 44
Disability Discrimination Act (DDA) 44
disabled users 142, 147
Disney World 364
display cabinets 252
display panels 217, 218
display screens 217
display units 129

distribution nodes 66
divine proportions 288
documentation and bidding 52, 403
Does, Bram de 309
dominance of signage 16
Donaldson case 170
donor recognition 147
doors 97
  design 195
  fittings 204
  handles 81
  hanger 147
  number signs 194, 231
  sign 48, 202
Doré, Alain 334
DOT 98, 99
dot reproduction 296
double-sided display 214
drawings 93
  copyright 171
Dreyfuss, Henry 98, 369
droit moral 179
drop-off sign 147
dual lock 278
dual-language 312
Dubai 226
durability 233
Dürer, Albrecht 368, 369
Dutch Ministry of Transportation and Water Management 308
dynamic message 147, 214
dynamic signage 147

e-books 300
economic aspects of IP rights 179
EDM 263
Egyptians 16, 211
  architecture 198
  hieroglyphs 97, 323
  temples 208
Eicher, Otl 328, 329
Eiffel Tower 328
Einstein 174
electrical changeable sign pannels 72
Electrical Discharge Machining (EDM) 263
electrical engineer 31
electrical fittings 204
electricity, storage 235
electroluminescent foils 266
electronic cards 89
electronic deposit 184
electronic directories 106, 147, 395
electronic display systems 193, 234, 253
electronic letter manipulation 290
electronic navigation 236
electronic paper 72
electronic screens 213, 239
electronic systems 117
elevation drawings 408, 416
elevation placement chart 52
eloquence 200
email 97
elevators/lifts 123, 129, 232
  directory 107, 130, 147
embossed type 91, 306
emergencies 41, 42, 44, 93, 109, 129
  emergency exit signs 97, 98, 144, 204, 251
  emergency signs, legislation 32
emoticons 97
employees 184
em-square 284
enamelling specifications 410
engineers 19
English 323
engraving 211, 260, 263
entrance 80, 123, 124, 125, 203
entry sign 147
environment as context 62
environmental artist 30
environmental graphics 147
equipment 145
Erco 329
escalators 129, 131
escape routes map 147
Esperanto 324
etched plate 147
etching 260, 263
Eurofont 305
evaluation 52, 418
event signs 147
exchange of ideas 164
exchange of information 242
Excoffon, Roger 331
exhibit and display signs 147
exhibition of inventions (1873) 170
exhibition spaces 117, 126, 143
exit sign 147, 202
expansion 286
exploded view 105, 106
exterior signs 248
eye level 81, 376
eye-candy 200
eyesight, reduced 90

fabricated sheet metal signs 258
fabrication methods of signs 133
facade 203
face-fitting system 147
family look 215
family style 189
fashion styles 161
fasteners 410
fastening materials, traditional 277
ferry terminals 119
FF Transit 311
fibre-optics 259
field of vision 318
films, copyright 173
financial administrator 27
financial centre 396

finger-post 84, 147, 250
finishings 275
finish and contrast 437
specifications 411
fire brigade 32
fire equipment signs 129
fire evacuation map 147
fire exit 49, 129
fire fighting signs 98, 109
first-time users 39, 118
fixing 134
materials 410
methods 277
special facilities 417
flag 138, 147, 251
flat representation 105
fleet marking 147, 256
flexible materials 254
flip charts 205
floor directory 107, 148
floor level indicators 363
floor number 102, 130, 148, 231
floor/wall marking 156
fluorescent light 265
fluorescent pigments 277
fly-over 66
foam plastic panels 257
foam plastics 254
foil 254, 256
fonts 297, 298
families 291, 293, 294
formats 297
hinting 299, 300
font/typeface 291
testers 284
Forbes, Theodore 305
forgery 180
forks 79
form follows fun 155
form follows function 62, 155
form follows marketing appeal 62
fragrances, trademarks 175
frame holder 148
frame, construction 212
Franklin Gothic 307
free-standing sign 84, 252
French language 323
French roads 305
Frère-Jones, Tobias 308
Frutiger, Adrian 308, 310, 311, 348
fuel cells 235
full stops 321
Fuller Benton, Morris 307, 310
function/form 155s
functionalists 196
functionality 163, 279
functions of signs 111
Futura 307, 310

galvanising 275
garage 121
garbage in, garbage out 167
gates 66
gateway arch 148
Gehry, Frank 372
Geismar, Thomas 338
General Conditions 406
general information 109
Gill Sans 307, 310
Gill, Eric 209, 307, 310
give-and-take dynamics 165
glare 82
glass fibre 259
global networks 246
Global Positioning System (GPS) 75, 236, 237, 246, 396, 429
glues 277
glyph 299
Glyph Inc. 324
glyphs/characters 291
Godard, Keith 363, 364
Goerlitz, Mathias 331
Golden Mean 368
Golden Section 366, 368, 370
Google 355
governmental bodies 21
GPS 75, 236, 237, 246, 396, 429
graffiti 16, 139
granulates 255
graphic 215
graphic design 189
graphic designers 20, 57
graphic elements, chart 51
graphic signs 92
Graphic Users Interfaces (GUI) 97, 189, 199, 292
graphical elements 216, 217
graphical representation of typeface 302
graphical symbols 98
gray light directory 148
Grear, Malcolm 335, 336
Greek 314
sculptors 275
Grenoble Winter Games 331
grid 65, 100, 365
grid boards 69, 72
Grid Systems for Graphic Design 367
grid, 1' x 1' 377
grid-locator identification 148
Groot, Lucas de 309
Grotesk 286
ground signs 148
grouping of destinations 320, 321

Hadid, Zaha 372
halftone rasters 273
hand writing tools 286
handcrafted signs 139
hand-engraving 262
handicapped users 142
hand-painting 260

hand-sawing 262
Harak, Rudolf de 338
hat station 364
HB *Sign Company* 326, 342
health care facilities 118, 328
hearing impairment 37
heights, basic, in buildings 81
heights, standard 377
Helvetica 307, 310
heritage architect 30
hierarchical overview of signs 132
Highway Gothic 308
highway signs 135, 148, 305
Hirst, Damien 202
historic style developments 196
hook-and-loop fasteners 278
Hospital Symbol Graphics, Australian Standards 341
hospitals 118, 328
hot spots 397
hot stamping 262
hotel occupancy system 117
hotelling offices 40, 426
hotels 119
Houts, Peter 328
hue 387
Huel, Georges 332
human body 368
human eye 319
human interfaces 20
human platform 50
human-scaled environment 60
hybrid style combinations 200

ICOGRADA 325
icons 93, 97, 199
identification of the building 121
identification sign 113
identity 163
illiteracy 38
illiterate structures 199
illuminance levels 266, 267
illuminated items 48
illuminated letters 148
illuminated signs 204
illumination 115, 233
  levels 438
  screens 264
illustrations 68, 93, 96, 191, 216, 279, 351, 359, 360, 362
  copyright 182
  on panels 212
imaginary walk through a site 120
imaging
  for print 271
  for screen 271
I-mode 76, 77
impaired users 115, 125, 142
  updates for 426
implementation, centralised/decentralised 426
imprint and shaping techniques 260, 262
incandescent light 265
inclusive signage 142, 148
incompetence 417
independent designer 33
Indiana Northwest campus site, map 354
individual letters 208
individual sign type products 248
industrial design 20, 172
industrial production plants 145
Industrial Revolution 196
informal signs 139
information 113
  architecture 393
  desk 125
  in number 101
  methods 92
infra-red beams 89
in-house designer 33
ink 276
inkjet printed layers 274
inkjet printing 260, 264
innovation, level 47
Innsbruck Winter Games 332
inserts 71
inspection rounds 417
installation 416
instructions 107, 113, 129
instruments 145
Integral 348, 364
integrated design 202, 205
integrated signage panel system 247
integration of signs 203
integrity of personal creation 179
intellectual property (IP) 169, 172
  agreements 184
  clients 184
  deposit 184
  employees 184
  legal and moral aspects 177
  protection 182
  signage project 182
  violations 180, 183
intelligence of signs 70
interactive design 189, 392
interactive kiosks 193, 253
interactive screens 74
interchangeability of components 214
interior designer 29
internal communication 67
International Convention of Circulation of Motor Vehicles 324
International Council of Graphic Design Associations (IGOCRADA) 325
International Semantography 324
International Standardisation of Graphical Symbols 325
International Standards Organisation (ISO) 21, 98, 329
International System of Typographic Picture Education (ISOTYPE) 324
Internet 76, 175, 287, 393

intersections 79
Interstate 308, 311
intuitive wayfinding 63
invention 174
 exhibition (1873) 170
inverse text imaging 311
invisibility 234
invited bid 405
ISO 21, 98, 329
ISOTYPE 324
italics 295, 320, 321
ITT 341
Itten, Johannes 386, 387, 389

Japan 91, 239, 314
Japan Sign Design Association 329
Japanese architecture 366
Jewish language 314
Johnston, Edward 307, 310
Johnston's Railway Type 310
journalistic work, copyright 173

Katzumie, Masaru 326, 331
key facilities 92
key numbering 101
Kinneir, Jock 305, 308, 310
kiosk 148
Kitching, Alan 343
kitsch 159
Kneebone, Peter 325
Köln Bonn Airport 348
Kramer, Burt 338
Kunzenmann, Alfred 332

laboratories 117
labyrinth 64
ladies/gentlemen pictograms 347
laminated prints 264
laminates 255
landmarks 62, 64
landscape architect 30
Lanier, Lois 328
large format digital printing 148
large-scale print technology 361
Las Vegas 140, 265
laser beams 72
laser print cassette systems 71
laser print containers 217
laser printed paper 213
laser-cutting 261, 263
Latin 323
 alphabet 292, 314
 script 73, 293
layout 320
 copyright 182
 grid 115
 margins 280, 282
 positioning 372
LCD 268, 269, 270
LCD screens 74, 300, 398
leading 280, 282, 284, 301, 320, 372
lectern-shaped sign 148
lecture room equipment 205
LED 265
 display boards 73
Lees, John 338
legal requirements 32, 42
legibility 304
legislation 98, 314
 US 91
lenticulars 264
LEP 268, 269
letters 93
 board 148
 contrast 312
 cutting 148
 letter/number coding 5
 size 372
 spacing 280, 281, 284, 301, 372
 transfers 262
 width 282, 301
letters/building elements 199
Leuvelink, Gert-Jan 339
libraries 117, 126
library of sign types 59, 116, 132, 222
Licko, Zuzana 309
lift directory 147
lift lobbies 80, 232
lift signs 148
ligatures 294
light as natural path 90
light conditions 81, 95, 387
Light Emitting Diode (LED) 265
Light Emitting Polymers (LEP) 268, 269
light fitting systems 82, 204
light journals 73
light quantity 266
light signals 93
light switches 81
light-diffusing plastics 257
Lillehammer Winter Games 334, 337
line of vision 317
line spacing 321
line-tracking 103
linguistic aspects of type 290
Linotype 329
Liquid Crystal Display (LCD) 73, 268, 269, 270
Lisencing Act 169
list of sign types 58, 115
literature rack 148
lobby 125
location map 120
location of signs 78
location sign 113
locking of components 214
logo 28, 216
logotype or crest sign 148
London Summer Games 326
London Underground 351
 map 354

Railways 307, 310
look and feel 233, 345
looking with different eyes 165
loose letter systems 71, 252
Los Angeles Summer Games 333
Lyon 222

machine-cut letters 148
machines 145
Mackintosh, Charles Rennie 202
magnetic components 71
magnetic particles 73
magnetic tape 259, 278
maintenance 423
maintenance personnel 41
Majoor, Martin 308
majuscule numerals 321
management 26
management consultants 20
mandatory information 67, 108, 129
mandatory signs 44, 250, 343
Manhattan, city planning 60, 64, 65
Mantzaris, Theodora 337
manual 52
manual production 262
manufacturer 20, 32, 33
selection 52, 412
Manufacturing Specifications 409
map 28, 104, 216, 351
copyright 173
map/navigation 105
map/real situation 105
traffic flows 111
map designs, copyright 182
margin 372
marketing/communication 26
marks 93
marquee 137, 148
masking methods 262
master 290
master charts 192
materials 192
mathematical middle 289
matrices 297
Maya 16
symbols 323
maze 64
measurement systems 365
Mecca 236
mechanical alteration 71
mechanical techniques 263
mechanical treatments 275
medallion 149
mediaeval numerals 294, 321
meeting rooms 127, 128
Mendoza, Jose Almeida 309
mental map 63
message boards 137
message centre 149
message holders 252
metal matrices 285
metal pen 286
metal sheets 248
metal specifications 409
metals 258
Metron 311
Mexico City Olympic Games 327, 331
Mexico City, city planning 60
micro-casting 242
Microsoft 297, 298, 300
Miedingen, Max 307, 310
Miller, Colette 358
miniaturisation 234
mobile phone 77, 103, 235, 239, 242
mock-ups 415
Modern Face 286
Modernism 60, 327
modular components 71
modular sign system 149
Modulor 365, 366
mono-coloured/textured panels 254
monolith 84, 149, 249
Monotype Imaging 300
Montreal Olympic Games 327, 332
monument 149
'mood boards' 201
Moore's Law 234
Morse codes 93
Moscow Olympic Games 327
Moscow Summer Games 332
motels 119
Motley, Rudolf 324
moulds 262
mounting location and height 437
moveable sign 84
moving copy sign 149
Müller-Brockmann, Josef 365, 367
multi-lingual signs 320, 321
multimedia designer 189
multimedia hype 394
Multiple Master Font 295
multi-script 312
extensions 294
fonts 314
Munich Summer Games 327, 332
murals 136, 149, 359
copyright 182
museum 117, 200
music 91
compositions and recordings, copyright 173
Muslims 16, 236
muzak 91

names 320
nanotechnology 234
narrowcasting 242
National Parks 142, 325
national public monuments 117
natural conditions 224, 225

natural environment 226
natural light 82, 267
nature as model 63
negative version 312
Neo-Gothics 310
Neo-Grotesks 310
neon 265
neon signs 72, 149
network display systems 193
Neue Haas Grotesk 307, 310
Neurath, Otto 324
neutrally spacing 281
New Johnston 310
New York 140
Newton, Isaac 387
night-blindness 37
non-alphabetical characters 292
non-colours 391
non-competitive agreements 176, 183
non-disclosure agreements 176, 183
nonverbal wayfinding process 63
Noorda, Bob 348
Noordzij, Peter Matthias 309
notice signs 149
noticeboard 109, 149
notices 129
novels, copyright 173
novelty 163, 184
numbers, mystical properties 101
numerals 292, 320

oblique Romans 295, 320, 321
OCR 240
offices 127
  doors 128
  sign types 213
  spaces 101
Old Face 286
olfactory senses 91
Olympic Games 99, 326
Ontario Crippled Children Centre 328
open source movement 178
Open Type 297, 298
operating instructions 107
operation, maintenance and housekeeping 28
Optical Character Reading (OCR) 240
optical corrections 289
optical fibre display 73
optical size 288
optical/mathematical middle 289
orientation 112
  information 104
  signs 149
Ota, Yukio 343, 344
outdoor signs 143
outlines 300
overhead sign 149
overview of sign types 132
oxidation 275

painting 93, 211
  copyright 173
Palestinian mosaic map 352
panel proportions 368
panel size 192, 214, 368
  chart 52
panel surfaces 410
panel system 215
Pantone Matching System (PMS) 411
paper 259
paper-based material 254
paperflex 149
papyrus map 352
parapets 81
Paris 353
Paris Convention in 1880 170
Paris Exhibition 328
Paris, city planning 60, 65
Parisine 311
parking facilities 121, 122, 123, 136, 363
parks 65
passing off' 176
Passini, Romedi 328
patent 174
  Patent Letters 170
  protection 176
  registration 182
  right 172
pavement elements 206
pedestal sign 149
pedestrian signs 149
Pelletier, Pierre-Yves 332
pennant 149
pentographs 263
perception 165, 233
  visual 34
perforated films 256
permanent room designation signs 149
personal digital assistant 89, 200, 239
personal electronic travel guide 70
personal navigation 69, 75
personal wireless navigation 103
personalising 157
Pfaffi, Bruno 348
photographs 93
  copyright 173, 175
physical aspects of colours 388
physical changeability 71
physiologist 31
pictogram 38, 93, 96, 99, 191, 216, 279, 316, 322, 359, 436
  applications 323
  copyright 182
  series 331
  test procedure 329
Pioneer 322
pitching 168
pixels 299
placement of signs 78, 80
planning 50

plants 117
plaque 149
plasma cutting 261m 263
plasma displays 74
plasma screens 268, 269, 270
plastics and glass specifications 410
plays, copyright 173
PMN *Caecilia* 309
PMS 411
poems, copyright 173
POI/POS 394
point of interest marker 149
point of purchase signs 149
Point Of Interest/Point Of Sales (POI/POS) 394
polycarbonate panels 257
polyurethane painting 276
polyurethane-based panels 257
pop up signs 138, 149
pop signs 138
portable maps 105
portable signs 149
portal 79
position, of signage designer 403
positioning signs 58, 78, 192, 214
  in elevation 80
  in space 372
positive version 312
post and panel system 149
post/panel sign 84, 149
poster display 149
poster frames 252
post-modernism 155
Postscript 297, 298
powder coating 276
PR 109
Prejza, Sussman 364
preparation 164
primary colours 386, 391
primary signs 149
print technology 230
printer dots 273
'prior art' 184
problem solving 186
process control 145
product design 188
product name, trademark law 182
production and design 397
production approval 414
production instructions 115
production of type 279
professional field of signage 19
professional fields involved in design 187
professional organisations 21
project phases 50
project size 47
projecting sign 83
projection 72
projection equipment 205
proportional variation extensions 295
proportions 282
proportions of letters 287
prototypes 415
provision for signage 375
psychologist 31
public bid 404
Public Domain 169, 178, 207
public information symbols 325
public interest, intellectual property 177
public relations 28, 67
public texting 146, 150, 242, 245
public transportation stops 120
Public Works in Canada, guide 328
pubs 243, 244
Punch List 417
punctuation marks 292
pylon 150

quality control 415
quality judgement of design 163
quantity list sign types 52, 412
Quick Response (QR) codes 239
quill pen 286

radial roads 65
Radio Frequency Identification (RFID) Tag 240
radio tag technology 96, 243
railings 66, 81
railway stations 119
raised/Brailled characters 436
RAL 411
rasters 300, 343
readability 304
readerboard 150
reading angle 318
reading distance 317
reception 80
reception areas 141
  furniture 203
recreation buildings 118
Red Flag Act 390
reference points 63
reflective material 256
regulatory signs 150
Reichs-Ausschuss für Lieferbedingungen (RAL) 411
remote control 75, 234, 238
removal of signs 213
Renaissance 288
Renner, Paul 307, 310
reorders 214, 412
repetition 68
responsibility 26
restaurants 119, 243, 244
restrictive information signs 150
retail stores 188
retrieve information 212
reviewing meetings 164
RFID tag 240
RGB sub-pixels 300
right of distribution 169

right to copy principle 169
ring road 65
Roads 305
  British 310
  signs 135, 150
Roissy-Charles de Gaulle 311
roman 295
Romans 211
  architecture 198
  letters 208, 286
  majuscules 320
  numerals 101
  stone inscriptions 292
roof signs 150
room numbering 100, 127
Rosenbaum, Sarah 327, 334, 337, 347
Rosetta Stone 97
route guiding information 103
rules of thumb figures 47
running human being, Greek vase/EEC 97, 336
running text 73
Russian Graphic Design Training centre 327

safety and security 28, 41, 45, 108, 129, 326
safety symbols, standardised 329
Saga, Carl 322
samples 415
sampling 180
sand-blasting 260, 262
sandwich panels 257
sans serif faces 197, 286, 289, 294, 305, 306
Sapporo Winter Games 326
Sarajevo Winter Games 333
saturation 387
Saunders, Paul 335, 336
Scala 308
Scent of a Woman 92
Schiphol Airport 61, 311
Schlossberg, Erwin 396
schools 118
scientific research 19
scoreboard 150
screen 69
  pixels 273
  ratio 270
  resolution 272
screen network systems 74, 127, 205, 253
screen types 269
scriptural narratives 16
sculptures 93, 96
  copyright 173
sealing specifications 410
secondary colours 386, 391
secret fixing 277
section identification 127
security 108, 257
security requirements 28, 41, 45
SEGD 21
selection consultant/designer 33
selection designs 168
self-explanatory facilities 92
self-luminous 277
Semantography (Blissymbolics) 324
semiotics 92
sense of place 65
senses 86
sensors 75
Seoul Summer Games 333
serendipity 193
Serif 286, 294, 306
service rooms 101
set of documents, standard 406
set of elementary sign types 212, 213
set of plans 58
Seung-Jin, Kim 333
seventh sense 88, 89
shaftless arrow 315
shape/function 92
share alike mark 178
Shigi, Tokuzo 347
shop drawings 414
shopping malls 118
side-fitting system 150
sign administrator 150
sign bloc 79
sign boxes 249
sign content 133
sign mountings 83
sign panels 150, 209
sign positioning in space 134
Sign Symbol Commission 325
sign types 192
  elementary 212
  global positions 112
  library 222
  map 112
signage
  applications 395
  audit 59
  check-up 59
  collectors 277
  commission 57
  development 14
  fonts, special 306
  functions 67
  manual and database 424
  methodology 57, 58
  officer 150, 423
  plan 58, 110
  reorder forms 424
  technology 57, 58
signals 93
signing an agreement 184
silk-screening 260, 262
similarity to original 183, 184
simplification 234
site identification 150
site maps 394
Site Signage Plans 408
size and proportions 226, 288

size/environment 228
size/impact 227
skeleton structure 63
sketching phase 193
slanting 301
slat 150
Slimbach, Robert 309
small caps 294
Smitshuijzen, Edo 343, 346, 349, 350
snagging 417
snipe sign 150
so-authorship 301
social trade-off 177
Society for Environmental Graphic Designs (SEGD) 21
solar cells 235
sources of inspiration 193
Spanglish 314
spatial design 232
spatial structure 64
special effect coatings 276
specialised engineers 19
specifications 52
splines 285, 299
split-flap message boards 72
sports stadium 117
spotlight 82
squares 65
stainless steel 258
stair markings 150
staircases 131
stairways 123
Standard Alphabets for Traffic Control Devices 308
standard heights 192
standard set of arrows 316
Standard Sign Manual, Universal Exhibition Montreal 328
standardisation 98, 99
Standards Institutes 21
static/dynamic information 70
stating the message 58
Stationers Company 169
Statute of Anne 169, 177
stealing intangible property 179, 180
Stedelijk Museum Amsterdam, map 358
stencils 262
stick figures 330, 343
stickers 416
stock signs 326
stone 259
carving 150, 260, 262
masonry 150
stopping the work 417
streamlining 198
street furniture 205, 207
street number sign 124
street signs 136
Stroke Front 286
Studio Dumbar 341, 364
style 46, 163
identity 279
developments 198, 199
building 62
variation extensions 295
periods 159
styling agencies 162
subtractive colour mixing 388
subway stations 119
New York 311
Sun Antiqua 309
super graphics 144, 150, 230, 264, 359
supermarket goods 188, 243
supervision 52, 413
surface mapping 276
surplus information 68
suspended sign 83, 150
swashes 294
Sydney Summer Games 335
symbol extensions 294
Symbol Source Book 98
symbolic values 160, 161
symbols 93, 191, 202, 292, 322
symbols of accessibility 437
synthetic panels 154, 256
synthetic tissues 254
system design/visual design 187
system evaluation, criteria 68
system walls 204

tablet 150
tabular numerals 294
tack board 150
tactile information 37
tactile sense 91
tactile underfoot titles 91
Tankard, Jeremy 342
target audience 35, 57, 162
taste 91
technical design aspects 398
technical drawings, copyright 173, 182
technical engineering 26
technical rooms 128
technology, influence 234
TelDesign 328, 339
telecom systems 76, 205
telecommunication and computer technology 76
telephone boots 126
temperature 266
temporary signage 49
Terrazas, Eduardo 331
tertiary colours 386
testing design types 212
text files 52
text list 58, 412
text on panels 212
text strip sizes 214
text/images, application 411
theatres 117
theme/metaphor 200, 201

thermo-cutters 263
thermo-forming 257
TheSans 308
Thomas, Dylan 245
three-dimensional objects 359
  copyright 182
three-dimensional typography 301, 303
thumb figures 47
time schedule 49
time-limited design protection 181
timetables on bus stop poles 239
toilets 126
Tokyo 140, 265
  city planning 60
  Summer Games 331
TomTom navigation 355
touch screens 74, 202
  kiosks 395, 397
  updating 425
Touring Club Italiano 348
Tower of Babel 322
Trade Mark Right 170
trade secrets 176
  protection 182
trademark 175, 181
  protection/registration 175
traffic and transportation 19, 30
traffic flow charts 111
traffic flows 110
traffic lights 72
traffic signage 206
traffic signs 150, 250, 306, 324
traffic symbols 325
trail marking 142
transistors 234
transit centres 137
transit facilities 119
transit maps 354
transition points 65, 66
transitional sign 150
translation 286
translucent films 256
translucent panels
transmission, wireless 87
transmitter-card 103
travel speed and infrastructure 60, 61
travelling and sign positioning 78
trend followers 162
trend outcasts 162
trendsetters 162
trial and error 193
Trias, Josep Maria 334
Trinité 309
Triplex Serif 309
True Type 297, 298
Turgot, Michel Etienne 353
TV screens 74
typeface/font 216, 279, 291, 307
  chart 51
  design for text typefaces 283
  identity and style 286
  signage 301
  size 290, 301
  size and reading distance 317
  technology 296, 300
  territory 287
typeface style classification 287
  British Standard 287
  German DIN norm 287
types of screens 74
typography 279
  copyright 173, 175, 182
  specifications 191

UK
  design registration 174
  legislation 42
  wood-carving 258, 262
unconventional alternate characters 295
understanding signs 68
UNESCO 170
unfair competition 176
Unicode 294, 298
uniformity 64
unit system 100
Univers 308, 310
Universal Copyright Convention, Paris (1971) 170
universities 118
University of Salford, campus map 355
unregistered design rights 174
updating 213, 214
  update terror 296
  impaired users 426
  information 69
  signs 238
  strategies 426
  technology 212
  updatability 70
  websites and touch screens 425
  urban planning 60
USA
  Bureau of Public Roads 308
  Department of Defense 246
  design registration 174
  legislation 91
  wood-carving 258, 262
user norm 35
  experience designer 189
  interface 396
  physical condition 35
  profession, function, background 39

vacuum-forming 257
Vainio, Hanna 226
vandalism 118, 214, 248, 257, 277, 410
  vandal-proof fasteners 277
  vandal-proof qualities 115
  vandal-resistant coatings 277
vector drawing 298, 299

vehicle graphics 151
vehicle signs 151
vehicle-scaled environment 60
Velcro 278
Velde, Henri van der 202
Vialog 311, 329
video wall 151
viewing angle 318
Vignelli, Massimo 338
vignettes 93
Villazón, Manuel 331
vinyl graphics 151
vinyl-cutting 217, 261, 262, 263
violation of rights and trademarks 180, 181, 183
Virtual Reality (VR) 395
vision, cone 81
visitors 39
visual 3D letter designs 303
visual appearance 93
visual clues 63
visual coherence 192
visual communication 189
visual design 51, 115, 156
  vs. system design 187
visual grammar 215
visual hierarchy 64
visual identity 29, 157, 190
visual impairment 36
visual order 158, 279
visual perception 34, 279
visual perception and type 288
visual personality 157
visual security 158
visual sense 90
visual spectrum 387
visual style 50, 62, 200
vitreous enamelling 151, 276
Vitruvius 36
Vukovic, Radomir 333

wall-mounted sign 83
Warnock Pro 309
Washington, Zoo 339
washrooms 126
water-jet cutting 261, 263
waterways engineering 10
web designer 189
web pages 284
website
  map 395
  navigation 393
  reordering 425
  updating 425
weight of letters 289
weight variation extensions 295
Wein, Michael 326, 340
welcome 80, 109
welded metal channel letters 209
Westeinde Hospital The Hague 341, 364
wheel chair users 80, 318, 439
wide-format digital printing 264
Widmer, Jean 340
wiffiti 146, 150, 151, 245
Wi-fi 76, 238
window sign 151
WIPO 170, 174
wire EDM cutting 263
Wireless Personal Digital Assistants 88
wireless technology 76
wireless telecommunication 242, 244
wood 258
wood specifications 409
wood-carving 260, 262
word spacing 280, 281, 282, 284, 320, 321
work plan 50, 187
work safety 145
work strategy, list of sign types 116
work-station sign 84
World Intellectual Property Organisation (WIPO) 170
World Trade Fairs 328
World Trade Organisation (WTO) 170
Wright, Frank Lloyd 202
writers block 186
WTO 170
Wyman, Lance 326, 331, 339

x-height 282, 287

Yamashita, Yoshiro 331, 337
Yiddish 314
you-are-here sign 151, 352
Young-Jea, Cho 333

zebra code 95, 151, 239, 240
zoo 325
  Decin 326, 340